Mastering Linux Administration

Take your sysadmin skills to the next level by configuring
and maintaining Linux systems

Alexandru Calcatinge

Julian Balog

Mastering Linux Administration

Group Product Manager: Pavan Ramchandani

Publishing Product Manager: Prachi Sawant

Book Project Manager: Ashwini Gowda

Senior Editors: Shruti Menon and Adrija Mitra

Technical Editor: Irfa Ansari

Copy Editor: Safis Editing

Proofreader: Safis Editing

Indexer: Rekha Nair

Production Designer: Jyoti Kadam

Senior DevRel Marketing Coordinator: Marylou De Mello

First published: June 2021

Second edition: March 2024

Production reference: 1230224

Published by Packt Publishing Ltd.

Grosvenor House

11 St Paul's Square

Birmingham

B3 1RB, UK.

ISBN 978-1-83763-069-1

www.packtpub.com

This is to everyone who did not believe in me, and to everyone who believed in me.

To my mother and father, my twin sister, my beloved Uca, and my truthful friends.

In memory of my late grandfather, Miron, who would have loved to see this new book finished before he passed away.

Contributors

About the author

Alexandru Calcatinge is an open-minded architect with a background in computer science and mathematics. He is a senior university lecturer with a PhD in urban planning from Ion Mincu University of Architecture and Urban Planning and a postgraduate degree in DevOps from Caltech's Center for Technology and Management Education (CTME). He teaches students about architectural programming and development and open source technologies. He has authored five books on architecture and urban planning and numerous scientific articles on urban and rural development. Alex was certified as a Linux trainer in 2017. He loves the DevOps philosophy and the possibilities that cloud technologies bring for the future. He is also a certified programming analyst, computer network administrator, trainer, designer, and life coach.

I want to thank the people who have been close to me and supported me unconditionally, especially my parents, my twin sister, and my friends. I want to express my deepest gratitude to my one and only Uca for sticking by my side during a time of turmoil, and for her constant support and trust in me.

Julian Balog is a senior software engineer with more than 15 years of experience in the industry. Currently, his work primarily focuses on application delivery controllers, containerized workflows, networking, and security. With a never-ending passion for Linux and open-source technologies, Julian is always in pursuit of learning new things while solving problems and making things work through simple, efficient, and practical engineering. He lives with his wife, two children, and an Aussie-doodle in the greater Seattle area, Washington.

The authors would like to thank the wonderful editorial and production team at Packt for their professional leadership, dedication, and guidance throughout the writing of this book. We are indebted to them for many helpful suggestions and the comprehensive revision of the drafts. We are also grateful to the reviewers for their critical comments. We could not have hoped for a better team and support.

About the reviewers

Himanshu Sharma has nearly 18 years of experience in designing, architecting, and developing cloud and network software. He previously worked for some of the biggest companies such as Brocade and Juniper and start-ups such as Netskope. Currently, he is working with Netskope as a Principal Engineer, responsible for Netskope's security service offering. He designed, architected, and developed Netskope's advanced threat protection services from the ground up. He has a keen interest and experience in developing scalable cloud services with cutting-edge technologies. His favorite hobbies are skiing and playing video games.

I would like to thank my wife, Puja, who gave me all her support, and my two loving and beautiful daughters, Navya and Jaanvi.

Also, I want to thank my brother, Sudhanshu, for always having my back, and my parents for all their sacrifices to get me where I am today.

Dennis Salamanca is a passionate technology enthusiast with a solid track record of over 12 years in the IT industry. Throughout his career, he has had the privilege of working with renowned industry leaders such as Amazon, VMware, Microsoft, and Hewlett-Packard Enterprise. His dedication to continuous learning is reflected in an extensive collection of over 15 technical certifications spanning various domains including cloud, storage, Linux, Kubernetes, and virtualization. Notably, he is actively involved in the development team for Linux+ and Cloud+ certifications and proudly contributes as a member of the esteemed CompTIA Linux and Cloud Subject Matter Experts and Technical Advisory Committee.

I would like to acknowledge my wife and family for all their support over these years. Without their motivation and support, nothing would've been possible.

Table of Contents

5

Working with Processes, Daemons, and Signals   155

Part 2: Advanced Linux Administration

6

Working with Disks and Filesystems   187

7

Networking with Linux   215

8

Linux Shell Scripting   265

9

Securing Linux   323

Part 3: Server Administration

11

Working with Virtual Machines 417

12

Managing Containers with Docker   445

13

Configuring Linux Servers   471

Part 4: Cloud Administration

14

Short Introduction to Cloud Computing   501

15

Deploying to the Cloud with AWS and Azure   521

Preface

Mastering Linux Administration provides the ultimate coverage of modern server and cloud administration technologies.

Technology evolves at an unprecedented speed, and Linux and related technologies are at the forefront of innovation. This makes it really hard to keep up and learn new things. Present Linux administrators need to know about more than just Linux, thus containerization and cloud technologies are essential for the future DevOps expert.

Linux is the operating system that powers almost everything, from IoT to personal computers to servers, and is the foundation for all cloud technologies. It enables you to master the cloud through the power of the command line.

You will begin by learning about the command line, working with files, processes, users, packages, and filesystems, then you will begin administering network services and hardening security, and finally, you will learn about cloud computing, containers, and orchestration. You will learn how to work at the command line, learn about the most important Linux commands, and master users, processes, and services administration. You will also learn how to harden Linux security using iptables. At the end, you will work with containers, hypervisors, virtual machines, Ansible, and Kubernetes and learn how to deploy Linux on AWS and Azure. By the end of this book, you will have mastered Linux and you will be confident in working with Linux from bare metal to the cloud, in a pure DevOps fashion.

Who this book is for

This book is for Linux administrators who want to understand the fundamentals, as well as modern concepts of Linux system administration. Windows system administrators looking to extend their knowledge to the Linux OS will also benefit from this book.

What this book covers

Chapter 1, *Installing Linux*, shows you how to install Linux on physical hardware (bare-metal) and inside a virtual machine in Windows. As we are targeting future Linux system administrators, the command line will be used most of the time, with little reference to the GUI. The future Linux professional will learn how to install Linux and how the boot process works.

Chapter 2, The Linux Shell and Filesystem, teaches you how to use the command line and introduces you to the most widely used commands in Linux. You will learn about the structure of a basic command, how the Linux filesystem is organized, the structure of the Linux operating system, and the structure of a file. By the end of the chapter, you will also know how to use VI/VIM, one of the widely used command-line text editors in Linux.

Chapter 3, Linux Software Management, explains how to use specific software management commands, how software packages work depending on the distribution of choice, and how to build your own packages.

Chapter 4, Managing Users and Groups, shows you how to manage user accounts in Linux. This is one of the most important tasks a Linux system administrator should master. You will be introduced to the general concepts, the specific files for user administration, and how to manage accounts. By the end of the chapter, you will know how to work with permissions and how to change them, and you will understand the special permissions and attributes.

Chapter 5, Working with Processes, Daemons, and Signals, explores processes, signals, and services in Linux. You will learn how to manage them, how to use them, and what the differences are between them.

Chapter 6, Working with Disks and Filesystems, teaches you how to manage disks and filesystems, understand storage in Linux, use **Logical Volume Management (LVM)** systems, and how to mount and partition.

Chapter 7, Networking with Linux, discusses how networking works in Linux, including the key concepts and how to configure your network from the command line and GUI.

Chapter 8, Linux Shell Scripting, shows you how to create and use Bash shell scripts for task automation in Linux. This will prove an invaluable asset for any system administrator.

Chapter 9, Securing Linux, delves into advanced topics of Linux security. You will learn how to work with SELinux and AppArmor.

Chapter 10, Disaster Recovery, Diagnostics, and Troubleshooting, shows you how to do a system backup and restore in a disaster recovery scenario. Also, you will learn how to diagnose and troubleshoot a common array of problems.

Chapter 11, Working with Virtual Machines, describes how to set up and work with KVM virtual machines on Linux.

Chapter 12, Managing Containers with Docker, introduces containers and discusses how to use Docker-specific tools to deploy your applications.

Chapter 13, Configuring Linux Servers, shows you how to configure different types of Linux servers, from **Domain Name System (DNS)**, **Dynamic Host Configuration Protocol (DHCP)**, **Secure Shell (SSH)**, **Samba** file-sharing servers, and **Network File System (NFS)**. This is one of the core foundations for any good Linux system administrator.

Chapter 14, *Short Introduction to Computing*, covers the basics of cloud computing. You will be presented with core technologies such as **infrastructure-as-a-service (IaaS)**, **platform-as-a-service (PaaS)**, **containers-as-a-service (CaaS)**, **DevOps**, and cloud management tools.

Chapter 15, *Deploying to the Cloud with AWS and Azure*, explains how to deploy Linux to AWS and Azure.

Chapter 16, *Deploying Applications with Kubernetes*, teaches you how to use Kubernetes to monitor and secure your deployments and how to manage your containers and networks. You will learn what Kubernetes is and how to use its diverse community approaches.

Chapter 17, *Infrastructure and Automation with Ansible*, introduces Ansible, including how to configure it, and how to manage playbooks, modules, and servers. At the end of this chapter, you will be a master of automation.

To get the most out of this book

You will need Ubuntu Linux LTS or Debian Linux to perform the examples in this book. No prior knowledge of Linux is necessary.

If you are using the digital version of this book, we advise you to type the code yourself or access the code from the book's GitHub repository (a link is available in the next section). Doing so will help you avoid any potential errors related to the copying and pasting of code.

Download the example code files

You can download the example code files for this book from GitHub at `https://github.com/PacktPublishing/Mastering-Linux-Administration-Second-Edition`. If there's an update to the code, it will be updated in the GitHub repository.

We also have other code bundles from our rich catalog of books and videos available at `https://github.com/PacktPublishing/`. Check them out!

Conventions used

There are a number of text conventions used throughout this book.

`Code in text`: Indicates code words in text, database table names, folder names, filenames, file extensions, pathnames, dummy URLs, user input, and Twitter handles. Here is an example: "To check the contents of a binary `deb` package, you can use the `ar` command."

A block of code is set as follows:

```
spec:
    replicas: 1
```

Any command-line input or output is written as follows:

```
$ sudo zypper search nmap
```

When we wish to draw your attention to a particular part of a code block or command, the relevant lines or items are set in bold:

```
uid=1004(alex2) gid=1100(admin)
groups=1100(admin),1200(developers),1300(devops),1400(managers)
```

Bold: Indicates a new term, an important word, or words that you see onscreen. For instance, words in menus or dialog boxes appear in **bold**. Here is an example: "Navigate to **Virtual Machines**, select your instance, and click **Size** under **Availability + Scale**."

> **Tips or important notes**
> Appear like this.

Get in touch

Feedback from our readers is always welcome.

General feedback: If you have questions about any aspect of this book, email us at customercare@ packtpub.com and mention the book title in the subject of your message.

Errata: Although we have taken every care to ensure the accuracy of our content, mistakes do happen. If you have found a mistake in this book, we would be grateful if you would report this to us. Please visit www.packtpub.com/support/errata and fill in the form.

Piracy: If you come across any illegal copies of our works in any form on the internet, we would be grateful if you would provide us with the location address or website name. Please contact us at copyright@packt.com with a link to the material.

If you are interested in becoming an author: If there is a topic that you have expertise in and you are interested in either writing or contributing to a book, please visit authors.packtpub.com.

Share Your Thoughts

Once you've read *Mastering Linux Administration*, we'd love to hear your thoughts! Scan the QR code below to go straight to the Amazon review page for this book and share your feedback.

https://packt.link/r/1837630690

Your review is important to us and the tech community and will help us make sure we're delivering excellent quality content.

Download a free PDF copy of this book

Thanks for purchasing this book!

Do you like to read on the go but are unable to carry your print books everywhere?

Is your eBook purchase not compatible with the device of your choice?

Don't worry, now with every Packt book you get a DRM-free PDF version of that book at no cost.

Read anywhere, any place, on any device. Search, copy, and paste code from your favorite technical books directly into your application.

The perks don't stop there, you can get exclusive access to discounts, newsletters, and great free content in your inbox daily

Follow these simple steps to get the benefits:

1. Scan the QR code or visit the link below

https://packt.link/free-ebook/9781837630691

2. Submit your proof of purchase
3. That's it! We'll send your free PDF and other benefits to your email directly

Part 1:
Basic Linux Administration

In this first part, you will master the Linux command line and basic administrative tasks, such as managing users, packages, files, services, processes, signals, and disks.

This part has the following chapters:

- *Chapter 1, Installing Linux*
- *Chapter 2, The Linux Shell and Filesystem*
- *Chapter 3, Linux Software Management*
- *Chapter 4, Managing Users and Groups*
- *Chapter 5, Working with Processes, Daemons, and Signals*

1

Installing Linux

Recent years have been marked by a significant rise in the adoption of **Linux** as the operating system of choice for both server and desktop computing platforms. From enterprise-grade servers and large-scale cloud infrastructures to individual workstations and small-factor home appliances, Linux has become an ever-present platform for a wide range of applications.

The prevalence of Linux, perhaps now more than ever, brings into the spotlight much-needed administration skills for a growing community of system administrators and developers. In this book, we take a practical approach to Linux administration essentials, with the modern-day system administrator, DevOps team member, and developer in mind.

In this second edition, we will adopt a slightly different approach to installing Linux. As this is a book meant for more advanced readers, we will no longer discuss the basic aspects of installing the operating system in such detail as in the first edition. The information has been updated to the most relevant aspects available as of the beginning of 2023 with regard to operating system versioning.

In this first chapter, we'll guide you through the Linux installation process, either on physical hardware (bare metal) or using a **Virtual Machine (VM)**.

Here are the topics we cover in this chapter:

- Introducing the Linux operating system
- Installing Linux – the basics
- Enabling the Windows Subsystem for Linux
- Installing Linux – the advanced stages
- Linux distributions – a practical guide

Technical requirements

We will use the following platforms and technologies in this chapter:

- Linux distributions: Ubuntu
- VM hypervisors: Oracle VM VirtualBox, VMware Workstation Player, and Hyper-V
- VM host platforms: Windows 11 (equally applicable on macOS)

Introducing the Linux operating system

Linux is a relatively modern operating system created in 1991 by Linus Torvalds, a Finnish computer science student from Helsinki. Originally released as a free and open source platform prohibiting commercial redistribution, Linux eventually adopted the GNU **General Public Licensing (GPL)** model in 1992. This move played a significant role in its wide adoption by the developer community and commercial enterprises alike. It is important to note that the Free Software Foundation community distinctly refers to Linux operating systems (or distributions) as **GNU/Linux** to emphasize the importance of GNU for free software.

Initially made for Intel x86 processor-based computer architectures, Linux has since been ported to a wide variety of platforms, becoming one of the most popular operating systems currently in use. The genesis of Linux could be considered the origin of an open source alternative to its mighty predecessor, Unix. This system was a commercial-grade operating system developed at the AT&T Bell Labs research center by Ken Thompson and Dennis Ritchie in 1969.

Exploring Linux distributions

A Linux operating system is typically referred to as a **distribution**. A Linux distribution, or **distro**, is the installation bundle (usually an ISO image) of an operating system that has a collection of tools, libraries, and additional software packages installed on top of the Linux **kernel**. A kernel is the core interface between a computer's hardware and its processes, controlling the communication between the two and managing the underlying resources as efficiently as possible.

The software collection bundled with the Linux kernel typically consists of a bootloader, shell, package management system, graphical user interface, and various software utilities and applications.

The following diagram is a simplified illustration of a generic Linux distribution architecture:

	Daemons	Applications	Libraries	Shell
User Space	Shared Libraries			
	Kernel			
Kernel Space	Drivers			
	Hardware (CPU, RAM, I/O)			

Figure 1.1 – Simplified view of a generic Linux architecture

There are hundreds of Linux distributions currently available. Among the oldest and arguably most popular ones are **Debian**, **Fedora**, **openSUSE**, **Arch Linux**, and **Slackware**, with many other Linux distributions either based upon or derived from them. Some of these distros are divided into commercial and community-supported platforms.

> **Important note**
>
> As writing this second edition, CentOS became a rolling release and is the base from which future **Red Hat Enterprise Linux** (**RHEL**) versions are derived. Its place was taken by other free community distributions that use the RHEL binaries. Among those, **Rocky Linux** is a good example, and we will reference it throughout this book. One other community distribution based on RHEL is **AlmaLinux**.

One of the key differences among Linux distributions is the package management system they use and the related Linux package format. We'll get into more detail on this topic in *Chapter 3*. For now, the focus is on choosing the right Linux distribution based on our needs. But before being able to decide, you should first know a little about some of the most widely used distributions. Therefore, in the next section, we will briefly present to you some Linux distros.

Common Linux distributions

This section summarizes the most popular and common Linux distributions at the time of writing this edition, with emphasis on their package manager type. Most of these distros are free and open source platforms. Their commercial-grade variations, if any, are noted:

- **Fedora, CentOS Stream and RHEL**: CentOS and its derivatives use **Red Hat Package Manager** (**RPM**) as their package manager. **CentOS Stream**, now a rolling release distribution, is based on the open source Fedora project. It is suited to both servers and workstations. RHEL is a commercial-grade version derived from CentOS Stream, designed to be a stable platform with long-term support. The community distribution that uses RHEL binaries is Rocky Linux.

- **Debian**: The package manager for Debian and most of its derivatives is **Debian Package** (DPKG). Debian is releasing at a much slower pace than other Linux distributions, such as Linux Mint or Ubuntu, for example, but it's relatively more stable.

- **Ubuntu**: Ubuntu uses **Advanced Package Tool** (APT) and DKPG as package managers. Ubuntu is one of the most popular Linux distributions, releasing every 6 months, with more stable **Long Term Support** (LTS) releases every other year.

- **Linux Mint**: Linux Mint also uses APT as its package manager. Built on top of Ubuntu, Linux Mint is mostly suitable for desktop use, with a lower memory usage than Ubuntu (with the Cinnamon desktop environment, compared to Ubuntu's GNOME). There's also a version of Linux Mint built directly on top of Debian, called **Linux Mint Debian Edition** (LMDE).

- **openSUSE**: openSUSE uses **RPM**, **Yet another Setup Tool** (YaST), and **Zypper** as package managers. openSUSE has two versions available: one is called Tumbleweed and is a rolling release, a leading-edge Linux distribution; the other is Leap, a regular release version, which uses the same code base as SUSE Linux Enterprise. Both versions are suited to desktop and server environments. SUSE Linux Enterprise Server is a commercial-grade platform. openSUSE was regarded as one of the most user-friendly desktop Linux distributions before the days of Ubuntu.

> **Important note**
>
> In this book, our focus is mainly on the Linux distributions that are widely used in both community and commercial deployments, such as **Ubuntu**, **Fedora/Rocky Linux**, and **openSUSE**. Most of the examples in this book are equally appliable to any Linux distro. We will specify which one we use for given examples or scenarios.

Now that you know a fair amount of information about the most common Linux distros, in the next section we will give you some hints on how to choose a Linux distribution.

Choosing a Linux distribution

There are many aspects involved in selecting a Linux distribution, based on various functional requirements. A comprehensive analysis would be far beyond the scope of this chapter. However, considering a few essential points may help with making the right decision:

- **Platform**: The choice between a server, a desktop, or an embedded platform is probably one of the top decisions in selecting a Linux distribution. Linux server platforms and embedded systems are usually configured with the core operating system services and essential components required for specific applications (such as networking, HTTP, FTP, SSH, and email), mainly for performance and optimization considerations. On the other hand, Linux desktop workstations are loaded (or pre-loaded) with a relatively large number of software packages, including a graphical user interface for a more user-friendly experience. Some Linux distributions come with server and desktop flavors (such as **Ubuntu**, **Fedora**, and **openSUSE**), but most distros have a minimal operating system, with further configuration needed (such as **Rocky Linux**, and **Debian**). Usually, such distributions would be good candidates for Linux server platforms. There are also Linux distributions specifically designed for desktop use, such as **elementary OS**, **Pop!_OS**, or **Deepin**. For embedded systems, we have highly optimized Linux distros, such as **Raspbian** and **OpenWRT**, to accommodate small-form factor devices with limited hardware resources.

- **Infrastructure**: Today we see a vast array of application and server platform deployments spanning from hardware and local (on-premises) data centers to hypervisors, containers, and cloud infrastructures. Weighing a Linux distribution against any of these types of deployments should take into consideration the resources and costs involved. For example, a multi-CPU, large-memory, and generally high-footprint Linux instance may cost more to run in the cloud or a **Virtual Private Server** (**VPS**) hosting infrastructure. Lightweight Linux distributions take fewer resources and are easier to scale in environments with containerized workloads and services (for instance, with Kubernetes and Docker). Most Linux distributions now have their cloud images available for all major public cloud providers (for instance, Amazon AWS, Microsoft Azure, and Google Compute Engine). Docker container images for various Linux distributions are available for download on Docker Hub (`https://hub.docker.com`). Some Docker images are larger (heavier) than others. For example, the **Ubuntu Server** Docker image outweighs the **Alpine Linux** Docker image considerably, and this may tip the balance when choosing one distribution over the other. Also, to address the relatively new shift to containerized workflows and services, some Linux distributions offer a streamlined or more optimized version of their operating system to support the underlying application infrastructure. For example, Fedora features the **Fedora CoreOS** (for containerized workflows) and **Fedora IoT** (for Internet of Things ecosystems).

- **Performance**: Arguably, all Linux distributions can be tweaked to high-performance benchmarks in terms of CPU, GPU, memory, and storage. Performance should be considered very closely with the platform and the application of choice. An email backend won't perform very well on a Raspberry Pi, while a media streaming server would do just fine (with some external storage attached). The configuration effort for tuning the performance should also be taken into consideration. **Rocky Linux**, **Debian**, **openSUSE**, **Fedora** and **Ubuntu** all come with server and desktop versions reasonably optimized for their use. The server versions can be easily customized for a particular application or service, by only limiting the software packages to those that are essential for the application. To further boost performance, some would go to the extent of recompiling a lightweight Linux distro (for instance, **Gentoo**) to benefit from compiler-level optimizations in the kernel for specific subsystems (for instance, the networking stack or user permissions). As with any other criteria, choosing a Linux distribution based on some application or platform performance is a balancing act, and most of the time, common Linux distros will perform exceptionally well.

- **Security**: When considering security, we have to keep in mind that a system is only as secure as its weakest link. An insecure application or system component would put the entire system at risk. Therefore, the security of a Linux distribution should be scrutinized as it pertains to the related application and platform environment. We can talk about *desktop security* for a Linux distro serving as a desktop workstation, for example, with the user browsing the internet, downloading media, installing various software packages, and running different applications. The safe handling of all these operations (against malware, viruses, and intrusions) would make for a good indicator of how secure a system can be. There are Linux distros that are highly specialized in application security and isolation and are well suited for desktop use: **Qubes OS**, **Kali Linux**, **Whonix**, **Tails**, and **Parrot Security OS**. Some of these distributions have been developed for penetration testing and security research.

  On the other hand, we may consider the *server security* aspect of Linux server distributions. In this case, regular operating system updates with the latest repositories, packages, and components would go a long way to securing the system. Removing unused network-facing services and configuring stricter firewall rules are further steps for reducing the possible attack surface. Most Linux distributions are well equipped with the required tools and services to accommodate this reconfiguration. Opting for a distro with *frequent* and *stable* upgrades or release cycles is generally the first prerequisite for a secure platform (for instance, **Rocky Linux**, **RHEL**, **Ubuntu LTS**, or **SUSE Enterprise Linux**).

- **Reliability**: Linux distributions with aggressive release cycles and a relatively large amount of new code added in each release are usually less stable. For such distros, it's essential to choose a *stable* version. **Fedora**, for example, has rapid releases, being one of the fastest-progressing Linux platforms. Yet, we should not heed the myths claiming that Fedora or other similar fast-evolving Linux distros, such as openSUSE Tumbleweed, are less reliable. Don't forget, some of the most reliable Linux distributions out there, **RHEL** and **SUSE Linux Enterprise (SLE)**, are derived from Fedora and openSUSE, respectively.

There's no magic formula for deciding on a Linux distribution. In most cases, the choice of platform (be it server, desktop or IoT) combined with your own personal preferences is what determines the Linux distribution to go for. With production-grade environments, most of the previously enumerated criteria become critical, and the available options for our Linux platform of choice would be reduced to a few industry-proven solutions.

> **Important note**
>
> In this book, our focus is mainly on the Linux distributions that are widely used in both community and commercial deployments, such as **Ubuntu**, **Fedora/Rocky Linux**, and **openSUSE**. That said, most of the examples in this book are equally applicable to any Linux distro. We will specify which one we use for given examples or scenarios.

Now that you know a bit about what a Linux distribution is, along with the most commonly used ones and their use cases, in the following two sections we will present the basic and advanced aspects of Linux installation.

Installing Linux – the basics

This section serves as a quick guide for the basic installation of an arbitrary Linux distribution. For hands-on examples and specific guidelines, we use Ubuntu. We also take a brief look at different environments hosting a Linux installation. There is an emerging trend of hybrid cloud infrastructures, with a mix of on-premises data center and public cloud deployments, where a Linux host can either be a bare-metal system, a hypervisor, a VM, or a Docker container.

In most of these cases, the same principles apply when performing a Linux installation. For detail on Docker-containerized Linux deployments, see *Chapter 13*.

In the following sections, we will show you how to install Linux on bare metal and on a Windows 11 host using different VM hypervisors, and using WSL. Installing on a macOS host is basically the same as installing on Windows using a VM hypervisor, and we will not cover that.

How to install Linux on bare metal

This section describes the essential steps required for a Linux installation on **bare metal**. We use this term when referring to hardware such as laptops, desktops, workstations, and servers. In a nutshell, the main steps are downloading the ISO image, creating bootable media, trying out the live mode, and finally, doing the installation.

The steps used here are equally applicable to virtual machine installations, as you will see in the following sections.

Step 1 – Download

We start by downloading our Linux distribution of choice. Most distributions are typically available in ISO format on the distribution's website. For example, we can download Ubuntu Desktop at `https://ubuntu.com/download/desktop`.

Using the ISO image, in the next step we can create the bootable media required for the Linux installation. We can also use the ISO image to install Linux in a VM, as shown in the next section.

Step 2 – Create the bootable media

As we install Linux on a PC desktop or workstation (*bare-metal*) system, the bootable Linux media is generally a CD/DVD or a USB device. With a DVD-writable optical drive at hand, we can simply burn a DVD with our Linux distribution ISO. But because modern-day computers, especially laptops, rarely come equipped with a CD or a DVD unit of any kind, the more common choice for bootable media is a USB drive.

> **Important note**
>
> There's also a third possibility of using a **Preboot eXecution Environment** (**PXE**) boot server. PXE (pronounced *pixie*) is a client-server environment where a PXE-enabled client (PC/BIOS) loads and boots a software package over a local or wide area network from a PXE-enabled server. PXE eliminates the need for physical boot devices (CD/DVD, USB) and reduces the installation overhead, especially for a large number of clients and operating systems. Probing the depths of PXE internals is beyond the scope of this chapter, but we will give you a short introduction on how it works for Linux installations by the end of this chapter. A good starting point to learn more about PXE is `https://en.wikipedia.org/wiki/Preboot_Execution_Environment`.

A relatively straightforward way to produce a bootable USB drive with a Linux distribution of our choice is via using tools such a **UNetbootin** (`https://unetbootin.github.io`) or **Balena Etcher** (`https://www.balena.io/etcher`). Both UNetbootin and Etcher are cross-platform utilities, running on Windows, Linux, and macOS.

We will use Balena Etcher for this example of creating a bootable USB drive in Windows:

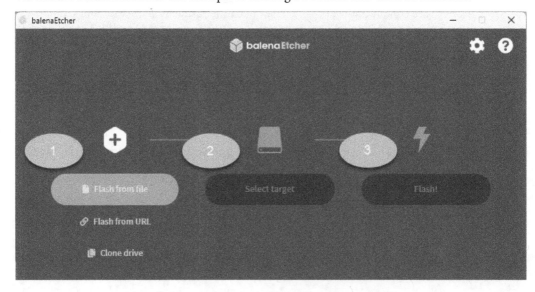

Figure 1.2 – Create a bootable USB drive with Balena Etcher

Here are the basic steps for creating a bootable USB drive with Ubuntu Desktop using Balena Etcher. We assume the Ubuntu Desktop ISO image has been downloaded and Etcher is installed (in our case on Windows 11):

1. Choose the ISO file with your Linux distribution of choice.
2. Select the USB target destination disk.
3. Flash the previously selected disk with the ISO of your choice.

The process should take a couple of minutes and the USB drive will be ready. Now, let's look at how we can take the bootable media for a spin.

Step 3 – Try it out in live mode

This step is optional.

Most Linux distributions have their ISO image available for download as *live* media. We say most because not all of them offer this option, at least not by default. Nevertheless, among those who do offer live media by default are **Ubuntu** and **Fedora**.

Once we have the bootable media created with our Linux distribution of choice, we can run a live environment of our Linux platform without actually installing it. In other words, we can evaluate and test the Linux distribution before deciding whether we want to install it or not. The live Linux operating system is loaded in the system memory (RAM) of our PC, without using any disk storage. We should make sure the PC has enough RAM to accommodate the minimum required memory of our Linux distribution.

When booting the PC from a bootable media, we need to make sure the boot order in the BIOS is set to read our drive with the highest priority. On a Mac, we need to press the *Option* key immediately after the reboot start-up chime and select our USB drive to boot from. When on a PC, make sure you access your BIOS interface and select the appropriate device for boot. Depending on your system, you will either have to press one of the *F2*, *F10*, *F12*, or *F1* keys after hitting *Enter*, or the *Delete* key, as a general rule. In some specific cases, there could be another *Function* key assigned for this. The keys that you need to press are usually specified at the bottom of the initial bootup screen.

Upon reboot, the first splash screen of our Linux distribution should give us the option of running in live mode, as seen in the following illustration for Ubuntu Desktop (**Try Ubuntu**):

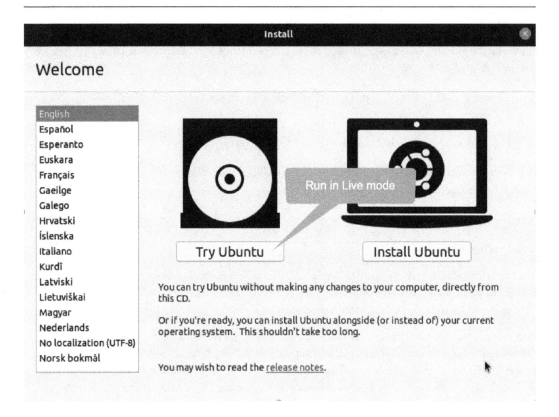

Figure 1.3 – Choosing live mode for Ubuntu Desktop

Next, let's take a look at the installation procedure of our Linux distro, using the bootable media.

Step 4 – Perform the installation

We start the installation of our Linux distribution by booting the PC from the bootable media created in *step 2*. To ensure the system can boot from our external device, we are sometimes required to change the boot order in the BIOS, especially if we boot from a USB drive. Do as specified in the previous paragraph to select the right boot drive.

In the following sections, we showcase the installation process of Ubuntu using its ISO images. We choose the Desktop and Server versions for Ubuntu and highlight the main differences between them. As a comparison, Rocky Linux and CentOS Stream come in a single flavor, in essence, a server platform with an optional graphical user interface. Similar to those, openSUSE offers one installation medium for both desktop and server installs. Fedora, on the other hand, has different installation mediums for desktop and server.

We will now walk you through the process of installing Linux inside a VM.

Linux in a VM

In each of the subsections in the *Installing Linux* section, we will also provide a brief guide on how to prepare a VM environment for the related Linux platform.

A VM is an isolated software abstraction of a physical machine. VMs are deployed on top of a **hypervisor**. A hypervisor provides the runtime provisioning and resource management of VMs. A couple of general-purpose hypervisors used are the following:

- **Oracle VM VirtualBox** (`https://www.virtualbox.org`)
- **VMware Workstation** (`https://www.vmware.com/products/workstation-pro.html`)
- **Hyper-V** (available only in Windows Pro, Enterprise, or Education)

The first two of these hypervisors are cross-platform virtualization applications and run on both Intel and AMD processor architectures on Windows, macOS, and Linux. The latter is only available on Windows Pro, versions 10 and 11.

> **Important note**
>
> At the time of writing this book, hypervisors for the Apple silicon Macs are provided only by VMware Player and Parallels. Oracle VirtualBox is still in preview for the **Advanced RISC Machines** (**ARM**) architecture. Both solutions from VMware and Parallels are paid-for software on macOS, so you will need to purchase them in order to use them.

The difference between installing Linux on a VM compared to a physical machine is minor. The notable distinction is related to the VM sizing and configuration steps, making sure the minimum system requirements of the Linux distribution are met. Thus, in the following sections we will install Ubuntu on VMware Workstation under Windows.

Please take into account that installing Linux on VMware Player under macOS is very similar, and we will not duplicate the process in this edition of the book. macOS functionality was discussed in the first edition of the book, but given the limited availability of hypervisors for the Apple silicon platform, we have decided to skip it in this edition. Regarding Linux availability on bare-metal Apple silicon Macs, you could visit Asahi Linux, a project that aims to bring a fully functional Linux distribution to Apple silicon computers. Asahi Linux is available at `https://asahilinux.org/`.

In the next section, we briefly illustrate the installation of Ubuntu Server LTS. If we plan to install Ubuntu in a VM, there are some preliminary steps required for provisioning the VM environment. Otherwise, we proceed directly to the *Installation* section.

VM provisioning using VMware Workstation

In the following steps, we will create a VM based on Ubuntu Server using VMware Workstation on Windows 11. At the time of writing, version 17 of the software is available for both free and commercial use.

1. The first step after initializing the hypervisor is to click on **Create a New Virtual Machine**. This will open a new window with the new virtual machine wizard, where you can select the ISO image for the Linux distribution you want to install.

2. Click **Browse** and then open the image from your hard drive or download destination.

3. Click **Next** and you will have to give a name to the new VM and choose a location on your disk for installation. We will leave the default destination as provided by the hypervisor and name the VM Ubuntu Server 22.04.1.

4. Click **Next**. In the following window that appears, you have to give the maximum disk size for the VM. By default, it is set to 20 GB as the recommended size for Ubuntu Server. We will leave it as is.

5. By clicking **Next** once more, a window with the VM settings is provided. By default, the hypervisor provides 2 CPU cores and 4 GB of RAM to the VM. You can click on the **Customize hardware** button to change the defaults, depending on your hardware availability. As a rule, we recommend having at least 16 GB of RAM on your system and an 8-core CPU to be able to create reasonable-sized VMs. When everything is set up as you want, click on the **Close** button on the lower right side of the window. You are now back to the main wizard window.

6. Click **Finish** to complete the setup and create and initialize the VM. In the following screenshot you can see the newly created VM, running inside VMware

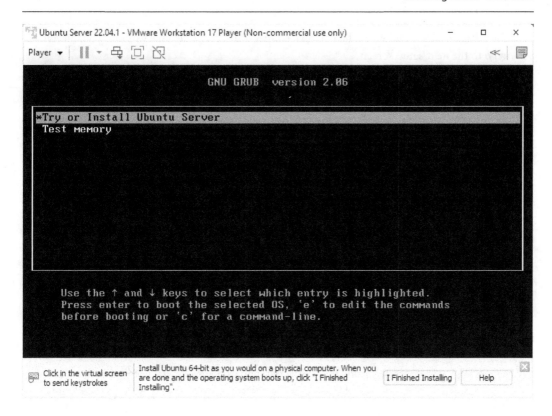

Figure 1.4 – Power-up and Linux installation on a new VM

Installation process

Here's the normal installation process for Ubuntu Server LTS, following the initial boot into setup mode:

1. The initial welcome screen prompts for the **language** of your choice. Select the one you prefer and press *Enter* on your keyboard.

2. You might be prompted to apply an *installer update* if available. You have the options to update the installer or continue without updating. We choose to update the installer if prompted.

3. If there is no update available, the next screen prompts you to select your **keyboard layout**. Select accordingly. In our case, it is English. Select **Done** and press *Enter*.

4. The next prompt asks you to choose the **base for the installation** from the following options: **Ubuntu Server** and **Ubuntu Server (minimized)**. You also have the option to search for **third-party drivers**. We choose **Ubuntu Server** and select the third-party driver option. You can make your way around the options on the screen using either *Tab* or the *Arrow* keys. To select an option, press the *Space* key. Select **Done** and press *Enter*.

5. The next screen will show you the **network connections**. If the defaults work for you, hit *Enter* to go to the next setup screen.

6. You will be asked about **proxy configuration**. If you don't require this, just hit *Enter* to go to the next screen.

7. You will now be asked to configure the default Ubuntu **mirror** for the repository archives. Edit this according to your location, or just leave the defaults provided by the installer. Press *Enter*.

8. The next screen prompts you to configure **storage** and **partitioning**. We will just use the entire 20 GB disk with the default settings, so select **Done** and press *Enter*.

9. A storage **configuration summary** is provided. If everything is according to your requirements, just hit *Enter*.

10. A **warning** will pop up, asking whether you are definitely happy with the settings and willing to continue with the installation. Hit *Enter*.

11. The next screen asks for your **profile information**, including your name, the server's name, the username, and password. Set those up and go to the next screen.

12. You will be asked to choose whether to **install an openSSH server** or not. Select the option to install openSSH. If you have any SSH key(s) you would like to import, you can provide them here. Once finished, go to the next screen.

13. You will be prompted to select and install **specific snap packages** for your new server installation. Depending on your requirements, you can install these now, or choose to manually install them later on. Among the provided packages are `docker`, `microk8s`, `powershell`, `nextcloud`, and `livepatch`. Select what you need to meet your requirements and continue to the next screen.

14. The **installation process** begins. This could take a couple of minutes. Be patient and wait for the reboot option to appear once the operating system is installed.

After you reboot, the login screen appears and you will be able to use your new Ubuntu Server VM from inside Windows 11 using VMware Workstation. We have now completed the Ubuntu Server installation.

Installing any other distribution is very similar to installing Ubuntu. When installing desktop variants, a graphical user interface will be available. In the preceding example, as we installed a server-specific operating system, the graphical user interface was missing, having just a minimal text-based interface.

We will not walk you through the installation process of any other distribution, but we will show you the Rocky Linux installation interface:

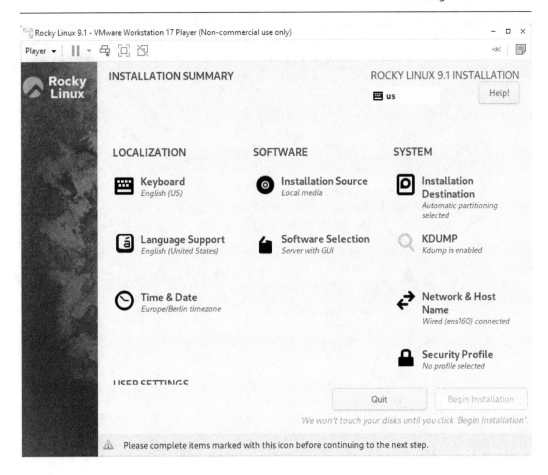

Figure 1.5 – The Rocky Linux installation GUI

So far, we have learned how to perform a basic installation of Linux. Along the way, we created a bootable USB flash drive for our installation media, most commonly used for Linux PC platform installations. We briefly covered VM-specific Linux environments using the VMware Workstation hypervisor for Windows 11.

In the following section, we'll learn how to install and run a Linux distribution on the Windows platform without the use of a standalone hypervisor by using the Windows Subsystem for Linux.

VM provisioning using Hyper-V

In the following steps, we will create a VM based on Ubuntu Server, using Microsoft's Hyper-V solution available on Windows 11 Pro.

The first step is to activate the Hyper-V hypervisor, as it is not activated by default. For this, we will need to go to **Windows Features** and select the **Hyper-V** checkbox, as shown in the following figure. After activation, a restart is required.

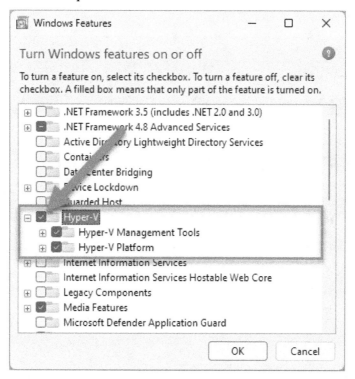

Figure 1.6 – Activating Hyper-V on Windows 11 Pro

To create a new VM, you will have to start **Hyper-V Manager**. The application has a three-pane interface. In the **Actions** pane on the right, you should see the **New** option. Click on it and select the **Virtual Machine…** option. This will open a new window where you can configure the new VM with the following steps:

1. Set the name and location; we will give it the name `Ubuntu` and leave the default location as is. Click **Next**.

2. Set the generation of the VM. You have two options, **Generation 1** and **Generation 2**. The second option will be suitable for UEFI-based BIOS and Network installation (PXE). We will select **Generation 1** and click **Next**.

3. Specify the amount of RAM. By default, this is set to 4 GB minimum, with the option of dynamic memory selected. We will leave the default as is. Click **Next**.

4. Configure networking by selecting the appropriate option from the dropdown. You have three options: **Not Connected**, **Default Switch**, **WSL**; we will select **Default Switch** and click **Next**.

5. Configure a virtual hard drive by setting the size and location. Click **Next**.

6. In the following window, you have the option to install an operating system now or at a later time. We will select the Ubuntu Desktop ISO image from our location of choice and click **Next**.

7. The following window shows the summary of the VM's configuration. You can change any of it by going back from here. Once done, click the **Finish** button and the VM will be created.

The following screenshot shows the new Ubuntu VM running inside Hyper-V:

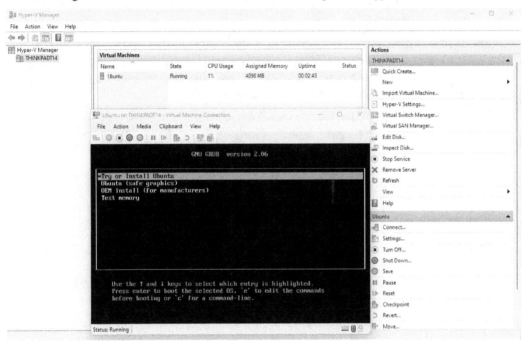

Figure 1.7 – New Ubuntu VM using Hyper-V

The installation process is similar to the one shown in the previous section, thus we will not reproduce it here again. In the next section, we will use another hypervisor, this time from Oracle.

VM provisioning using Oracle's VirtualBox

Oracle's **VirtualBox** is a free-to-use piece of software that is multi-platform, available on Windows, macOS and Linux. We will show you how to create a Linux VM from Windows 11. We assume that you have VirtualBox already installed. Once you start it, a user-friendly interface is available. The following steps are used to create a new VM. We will use Fedora Workstation for our example:

1. Click on the **New** icon to start the process of creating a new VM. This will open a new window where information about the VM's name and operating system type and ISO location need to be provided. This new window is in **Guided Mode** by default. You have the option on the lower right side of the window to choose the **Expert Mode**. This will give you more control over the creation process.

2. Provide all the needed information. In our case, we will use Fedora, so we will give it the name `Fedora`. Point to the ISO file's location and the type of the operating system will change automatically. If you are in **Expert Mode**, you will have some more auto-hidden sections for **Unattended Install**, **Hardware**, and **Hard Disk** options.

3. Because we are installing Fedora, the **Unattended Install** section is grayed out (see *Figure 1.11*). This option is supported by only a few operating systems (Ubuntu, RHEL, Oracle Linux, and Windows).

4. In the **Hardware** section, we will provide the amount of system memory and processors we want the new VM to have. Choose according to your hardware resources, but keep in mind that each operating system has specific system requirements. In our case, we will choose 4 GB of RAM and 2 vCPUs.

5. The **Hard Disk** section is where you choose the amount of disk space for the VM's hard disk. Again, choose according to your resources, but keep in mind that a minimal amount is required to meet specific system requirements. In our opinion, a minimum of 20 GB of hard disk space should be provided. Choose the location of the virtual hard drive and click **Finish**.

6. The VM will be created and the window will close, bringing you back to the initial VirtualBox window. Here, you will see all the relevant information about the VM. To power it on, just click on the **Start** button (the one with a big green right arrow).

7. A new window with the VM will appear.

The following screenshot shows the VM creation window inside VirtualBox:

Figure 1.8 – VirtualBox interface

As you can see, creating Linux VMs with all three major hypervisors available (from VMware, Oracle, and Microsoft) is very straightforward and relatively easy to do. No matter which solution you use, the process of installing Linux in a VM is the same.

Aside from VM provisioning, Microsoft Windows offers a relatively new way to run Linux, and this is by using the Windows Subsystem for Linux. We will show you how in the next section.

Enabling Windows Subsystem for Linux

Software developers and system administrators often face a tough decision in choosing the appropriate hardware and operating system platform for the specific requirements of their work or environment. In the past, Windows professionals frequently discovered that some standard development tools, frameworks, or server components were available on the Linux or macOS platforms while lacking native support on Windows. **Windows Subsystem for Linux (WSL)** attempts to close this gap.

WSL is a Windows platform feature that provides a native GNU/Linux runtime along with the Windows desktop environment available for both versions 10 and 11 of Windows. WSL enables the seamless deployment and integration of select Linux distributions on top of the Windows kernel, without the need for a dedicated hypervisor. With WSL enabled, you can easily install and run Linux as a native Windows application.

> **Important note**
>
> Without WSL, we could only deploy and run a Linux distribution on a Windows platform by using a standalone hypervisor, such as Hyper-V, Oracle VM VirtualBox, or VMware Workstation. WSL eliminates the need for a dedicated hypervisor. At the time of writing, WSL is a Windows kernel extension with a hypervisor embedded.

In this section, we provide the steps required to enable WSL and run an Ubuntu distribution on Windows. Since Windows 11 version 21H2 and Windows 10 versions 21H2 and 22H2, WSL is available by default from the Windows Store, so there is no need to use the command line to install and set it up. Go to the Microsoft Store and search for `WSL`. From the list shown, select the application shown in the following figure:

Figure 1.9 – WSL application from the Windows Store

After installing WSL, all you need to do is to install any Linux distributions available for it. If you attempt to open the freshly installed WSL application, you will get a terminal message saying that the WSL has no distribution installed. This means that you will need to install a distro by going back to Microsoft Store and searching for one. For example, if you search for `Linux` inside Microsoft Store, you will get results including SUSE Linux Enterprise Server, Oracle Linux, Kali Linux, Ubuntu LTS, Debian, and openSUSE Leap, among others.

> **Important note**
>
> Make sure you have Hyper-V enabled in Windows, as it is the service responsible for running WSL. To enable it, go to **Windows Features**, and select **Hyper-V** from the list, then click on **OK**. After installing the necessary components, a restart is required. Hyper-V is available by default on Windows 11 Pro, Enterprise and Education, but *NOT* on Home edition.

Now you can install a Linux distribution from Microsoft Store. We will try doing this with Ubuntu for our demonstration. After installation, you can open the application, create a user, and start using it inside the command line – it is that easy. To open the new Linux distribution, enter its name in the search bar, hit *Enter*, and a new terminal window with the Linux distribution is opened directly in Windows Terminal application, as shown in the following screenshot:

Figure 1.10 – Ubuntu inside a Windows Terminal window using WSL

Furthermore, you will have access to the distribution's filesystem directly from **File Explorer** inside Windows. The following screenshot shows the Ubuntu filesystem accessible from **File Explorer**:

Name	Date modified	Type	Size
boot	4/18/2022 1:28 PM	File folder	
dev	2/6/2023 11:41 AM	File folder	
etc	2/6/2023 11:41 AM	File folder	
home	2/5/2023 3:06 PM	File folder	
lost+found	2/5/2023 3:06 PM	File folder	
media	1/3/2023 11:40 PM	File folder	
mnt	2/6/2023 11:28 AM	File folder	
opt	1/3/2023 11:40 PM	File folder	
proc	2/6/2023 11:41 AM	File folder	
root	1/3/2023 11:41 PM	File folder	
run	2/6/2023 11:41 AM	File folder	
snap	1/3/2023 11:41 PM	File folder	
srv	1/3/2023 11:40 PM	File folder	
sys	2/6/2023 11:41 AM	File folder	
tmp	2/5/2023 3:06 PM	File folder	
usr	1/3/2023 11:40 PM	File folder	
var	1/3/2023 11:41 PM	File folder	
bin	1/3/2023 11:40 PM	File	1 KB

Home
Alexandru - Personal

Desktop
Downloads
Pictures
Documents
Music
Videos

This PC
Local Disk (D:)
PHD (E:)
Network
Linux
Ubuntu
Ubuntu-22.04

24 items

Figure 1.11 – The Ubuntu filesystem in the File Explorer in Windows 11

WSL enables a swift adoption of Linux for a growing number of Windows professionals. As shown in this section, WSL is relatively easy to configure, and with WSL, there's no need for a dedicated hypervisor to run a Linux instance.

By now, you have learned how to install Linux on a VM inside Windows using three different hypervisors, the VMware Workstation, Microsoft's own Hyper-V, and Oracle's VirtualBox. As we stated earlier, the installation process on macOS is very similar and there is no need for us to spend any more space covering it, as it would only duplicate the output. The interface of VMware Fusion on macOS is similar to the one used in Windows, with minor changes.

Installing on bare metal is similar; the only difference is that you require physical access to the destination machines. As stated at the beginning of this chapter, there is one more way to install Linux, and this is over the network. This is a more advanced task that requires more attention to detail along with basic networking knowledge. Also, understanding the Linux boot process is mandatory.

In the next section, we will provide some details about the network installation process.

Installing Linux – the advanced stages

In this section, we will cover the more advanced aspects of installing Linux. As we saw in the previous sections, installation on bare metal and VM requires direct access to the given machines. But what if we do not have access to the location? Or there are so many machines that need to be set up, that completing the task manually would be tedious at best, and infeasible at worst?

Installing Linux in an enterprise environment with tens or hundreds of machines in use can be done using an automated environment by booting through the network. As we stated earlier, a detailed overview of the network boot technique is out of the scope of this book; nevertheless, we will describe the process and show you the most important aspects of it, as none of the prominent books out there discuss this.

But first, to better understand how network booting works, let us take a short look at the Linux boot process.

The Linux boot process

How does Linux boot? We will give you a comprehensive view of the process without getting into too many details.

When you first start your Linux-powered computer or virtual machine, the **BIOS** (or boot firmware) starts loading and initiates a bootloader. The BIOS has a specific configuration and is loaded by the manufacturer onto a memory chip on the motherboard (in the case of physical computers, not VMs). The BIOS has information about the hardware and capabilities of controlling peripherals such as keyboards and monitors. It also has information about the operating system and the location of the bootloader. Some of this information is user controlled and can be changed according to the user's needs, such as the boot sequence for example, or password protection. The BIOS also has control over the **network interface controllers** (**NICs**) and all the external ports, including USB and display ports. But this is about all it can do, as it requires a bootloader to further initiate any operating system existing on the disk.

A newer version of the BIOS is the **Unified Extensible Firmware Interface** (**UEFI**). It has the same advantages as the older BIOS, but offers more interactive interfaces and better support for newer operating systems. The drawback, however, is the lack of software support from third-party vendors.

There is also **Secure Boot**, a feature introduced to offer an extra layer of security for the operating system and the software that runs. Some Linux distributions support it, but not all of them. Secure Boot uses a digital signature that proves the authenticity of the operating system. In order to support Secure Boot, the operating system developer must obtain a valid certificate for the software that can be verified on boot to prove that the system is valid and has not been tampered with.

Now that we know what the BIOS, UEFI and Secure Boot are, let us learn about the bootloader. Once **Power-On Self Test** (**POST**) is finished, the **bootloader** is accessed to load the operating system. POST is a series of tests that are conducted upon startup to ensure that the hardware is fully functional. What is a bootloader? It is the bridge between the hardware and the operating system. It is stored in the boot sector of the bootable storage. It can be either a partition or the very first block of the storage medium.

The bootloader used on Linux is the **Grand Unified Bootloader** (**GRUB**). It is responsible for loading the kernel of the operating system. The kernel is the central component of Linux, responsible for all the software components, drivers, services, and hardware integration. All of this forms what we call user space. It is the GRUB that has the capacity to support network booting.

The information provided in this section is sufficient to get a grasp of the Linux boot process. We will now detail the use of network boot to install Linux in the following section.

PXE network boot explained

Earlier in this chapter we mentioned the **PXE** (pronounced *pixie*) boot option. What exactly is PXE? It is a service that uses different networking protocols for booting over the network. It is based on different protocols and standards that were introduced forty years ago to define the much-needed network boot interoperability, also known as the **Network Bootstrap Program** (**NBP**).

The protocols that PXE is based on are **Trivial File Transfer Protocol** (**TFTP**), **Dynamic Host Configuration Protocol** (**DHCP**), and the UDP/IP stack using the **Hyper Text Transfer Protocol** (**HTTP**). These three are the base for PXE's application programming interface. Nowadays, most network cards available on the market already have the PXE firmware installed. This makes PXE the standard for network boot on many architectures. For more information on the latest PXE version 2.1, visit the following link: `https://web.archive.org/web/20110524083740/http://download.intel.com/design/archives/wfm/downloads/pxespec.pdf`.

For PXE to work, we need to have a PXE server on the network. This machine will provide the necessary bootable files in response to client requests on the network. For this, at least a DHCP and a TFTP server need to be installed on the PXE server. In addition, a **Network File System (NFS)** server must also be installed, as this protocol is required for network file sharing and is used in modern Linux operating systems.

But before we go into further detail, let us discuss how network boot works. PXE relies on a client/server environment where different machines are equipped with PXE-enabled NICs. The network configuration of the PXE environment was developed so that it does not interfere with the existing network configuration. As DHCP and TFTP are needed, the PXE environment makes sure that it does not interfere with the existing DHCP configuration of the non-PXE router from the local network. This is a well-thought-out design for corporate environments.

In a basic scenario, after all clients are set up for PXE boot (an option available from the BIOS on almost every computer), the NICs send DHCP requests over the network in order to find the local PXE server. In order to be able to correctly respond to those requests, PXE uses a sort of proxy DHCP that sends IP and mask information of the TFTP server back to the PXE-enabled clients. This way, it does not interfere with the local network's DHCP server.

Setting up a PXE server is beyond the scope of this chapter, but useful information about what this is and how it works is relevant and can be found at `https://ubuntu.com/server/docs/install/netboot-amd64` and `https://www.redhat.com/sysadmin/pxe-boot-uefi`. However, further details, such as how to practically set up a DHCP server, will be found in *Chapter 13*.

For a PXE server to work, there are some specific steps to take, depending on the installation root you follow. There are several options available, as you can use iPXE (an open source network boot firmware), `cloud-init` (specific to Ubuntu), or kickstart (for Fedora-based systems). Nonetheless, setting up DHCP, TFTP, and NFS servers is required, with the DNS server being optional (details on setting up these servers are available in *Chapter 13*).

As you'll see these details later, we will not include them here. This is the introductory chapter, intended to make you comfortable with different ways to install Linux, and we will slowly build upon this foundation throughout the book to get you ready for the more advanced stuff as you go through the chapters.

In the next section, we will give you some scenarios of using certain Linux flavors depending on specific needs. We will present to you what we consider to be the appropriate distributions and applications to use in different case studies. Please keep in mind that installing applications and working with package managers will be discussed in more detail in *Chapter 3*.

Linux distributions – a practical guide

The following use cases are inspired by real-world problems, taken mostly from the authors' own experience in the system administration and software engineering field. Each of these scenarios presents the challenge of choosing the right Linux distribution for the job.

Case study – development workstation

This case study is based on the following scenario made from the perspective of a software developer:

> *I'm a backend/frontend developer, writing mostly in Java, Node.js, Python, and Golang, and using mostly IntelliJ and VS Code as my primary IDE. My development environment makes heavy use of Docker containers (both building and deploying) and I occasionally use VMs (with VirtualBox) to deploy and test my code locally. I need a robust and versatile development platform.*

Let's look at the functional and system requirements before deciding which Linux distribution is fit for the job:

- **Functional requirements**: The requirements suggest a relatively powerful day-to-day development platform, either a PC/desktop or a laptop computer. The developer relies on local resources to deploy and test the code (for instance, Docker containers and VMs), perhaps frequently in an offline (airplane mode) environment if on the go.

- **System requirements**: The system will primarily be using the Linux desktop environment and window manager, with frequent context switching between the **Integrated Development Environment** (**IDE**) and Terminal windows. The required software packages for the IDE, Docker, hypervisor (VirtualBox), and tools should be readily available from open source or commercial vendors, ideally always being up to date and requiring minimal installation and customization effort.

Choosing the Linux distribution

The choice of Linux distribution here would be the **Ubuntu Desktop Long Term Support** (**LTS**) platform. Ubuntu LTS is relatively stable, runs on virtually any hardware platform, and is mostly up to date with hardware drivers. Software packages for the required applications and tools are generally available and stable, with frequent updates. Ubuntu LTS is an enterprise-grade, cost-effective, and secure operating system suitable for organizations and home users alike.

Besides Ubuntu, **Fedora** and **openSUSE** are equally suitable for a developer's workstation. Choosing between them depends on whether you need a **Debian-** or **Red Hat/SUSE**-based ecosystem, and whether you need more up-to-date packages or not.

Case study – secure web server

This case study is based on the following scenario made from the perspective of a DevOps engineer:

I'm looking for a robust platform running a secure, relatively lightweight, and enterprise-grade web server. This web server handles HTTP/SSL requests, offloading SSL before routing requests to other backend web servers, websites, and API endpoints. No load-balancing features are needed.

Let's look at the **functional requirements** in this case study. When it comes to open source, secure, and enterprise-grade web servers, the top choices are usually NGINX, Apache HTTP Server, Node.js, Apache Tomcat, and lighttpd. Without going into the details of selecting one web server over another, let's just assume we pick Apache HTTP Server. It has state-of-the-art SSL/TLS support, excellent performance, and is relatively easy to configure.

We can deploy this web server in VPS environments, in local (*on-premises*) data centers, or the public cloud. The deployment form factor is either a VM or a Docker container. We are looking for a relatively low-footprint, enterprise-grade Linux platform.

Choosing the Linux distribution

Our choice of Linux distribution is **Rocky Linux** or **AlmaLinux**. Most of the time, those two distributions are a perfect match for Apache HTTP Server. They are relatively lightweight, coming only with bare-bones server components and an operating system networking stack. Both Rocky and Alma are widely available as VPS deployment template from both private and public cloud vendors. Our Apache HTTP Server can run as a Docker container on top of Rocky Linux or AlmaLinux, as we may need to horizontally scale to multiple web server instances. More details on setting up a web server are provided in *Chapter 13*.

Use case – personal blog

This case study is based on the following scenario made from the perspective of a software engineer and blogger:

I want to create a software engineering blog. I'll be using the Ghost blogging platform, running on top of Node.js, with MySQL as the backend database. I'm looking for a hosted Virtual Private Server (VPS) solution by one of the major cloud providers. I'll be installing, maintaining, and managing the related platform myself. Which Linux distribution should I use?

Let's discuss the **functional requirements** for this use case. We are looking for a self-managed publicly hosted **Virtual Private Server** (**VPS**) solution. The related hosting cost is a sensitive matter. Also, the maintenance of the required software packages should be relatively easy. We foresee frequent updates, including the Linux platform itself.

Choosing the Linux distribution

Our picks for the Linux distribution in this scenario would be either **Debian Stable** or **Ubuntu Server LTS**. As previously highlighted, Ubuntu is a robust, secure, and enterprise-class Linux distribution. **Debian** is equally stable and offers good options for applications. The platform maintenance and administration efforts are not demanding. The required software packages – Node.js, Ghost, and MySQL – are easily available and are well maintained. Ubuntu Server has a relatively small footprint. We can run our required software stack for blogging easily within the Ubuntu system requirements so the hosting costs would be reasonable.

Use case – media server

This case study is based on the following scenario made from the perspective of a home theater aficionado:

> *I have a moderately large collection of movies (personal DVD/Blu-ray backups), videos, photos, and other media, stored on Network Attached Storage (NAS). The NAS has its own media server incorporated, but the streaming performance is rather poor. I'm using Plex as a media player system, with Plex Media Server as the backend. What Linux platform should I use?*

Based on this description, let's identify the **system requirements** for this use case. The critical system requirements of a media server are speed (for a high-quality and smooth streaming experience), security, and stability. The related software packages and streaming codecs are subject to frequent updates, so platform maintenance tasks and upgrades are quite frequent. The platform is hosted locally, on a PC desktop system, with plenty of memory and computing power in general. The media is being streamed from the NAS, over the in-house **Local Area Network (LAN)**, where the content is available via an NFS share.

Choosing the Linux distribution

Both **Debian** and **Ubuntu** would be excellent choices for a good media server platform. Debian's *stable* release is regarded as rock solid and very reliable by the Linux community, although it's somewhat outdated. Both feature advanced networking and security, but what may come as a decisive factor in choosing between the two is that Plex Media Server has an ARM-compatible package for Debian. The media server package for Ubuntu is only available for Intel/AMD platforms. If we owned a small-factor ARM-processor-based appliance, Debian would be the right choice. Otherwise, **Ubuntu LTS** would meet our needs here just as well.

Now that you know about different use cases, it is time to pick your Linux distribution and start playing with it. In this chapter, we provided you with a plethora of information that will prove invaluable as you start your journey with Linux.

Summary

In this chapter, we learned about Linux distributions, with a practical emphasis on choosing the right platform for our needs and performing the related installation procedures.

Throughout the chapter, the main emphasis was on the Ubuntu distribution. In the spirit of a practical approach, we covered VM environments running Linux. We also took a short route through the Windows realm, where we touched upon WSL, a modern-day abstraction of Linux as a native Windows application.

With the skills learned in this chapter, we hope you'll have a better understanding of how to choose different flavors of Linux distros based on your needs. You've learned how to install and configure Linux on a variety of platforms. You will use some of these skills throughout the rest of the book, but most importantly, you'll now be comfortable quickly deploying the Linux distribution of your choice and testing with it.

Starting with the next chapter, we'll take a closer look at the various Linux subsystems, components, services, and applications. *Chapter 2, The Linux Shell and Filesystem*, will familiarize you with the Linux filesystem internals and related tools.

Questions

Here are a few questions and thought experiments that you may ponder, some based on the skills you learned in this chapter, and others revealed in later parts of the book:

1. If we have a relatively large number of Linux VM instances or distros deployed and running at the same time, how could we make it easier to manage them?

    Hint: Use **Vagrant**, a tool for building and managing VM environments.

2. Can we run multiple Linux instances in WSL?

    Hint: We can.

Further reading

Here are a few Packt titles that can help you with the task of Linux installation:

- *Fundamentals of Linux*, by Oliver Pelz
- *Mastering Ubuntu Server – Fourth Edition*, by Jay LaCroix
- *Mastering Linux Administration – First Edition*, by Alexandru Calcatinge and Julian Balog

2

The Linux Shell and Filesystem

Understanding the **Linux filesystem**, **file management** fundamentals, and the basics of the **Linux shell** and **command-line interface** (**CLI**) is essential for a modern-day Linux professional.

In this chapter, you will learn how to use the Linux shell and some of the most common commands in Linux. You will learn about the structure of a basic Linux command and how the Linux filesystem is organized. We'll explore various commands for working with files and directories. Along the way, we'll introduce you to the most common command-line text editors. We hope that by the end of this chapter, you'll be comfortable using the Linux CLI and be ready for future, more advanced explorations. This chapter will set the foundation for using the Linux shell, and for more information about the shell, go to *Chapter 8, Linux Shell Scripting*.

We're going to cover the following main topics:

- Introducing the Linux shell
- The Linux filesystem
- Working with files and directories
- Using text editors to create and edit files

Technical requirements

This chapter requires a working installation of a standard Linux distribution, on either server, desktop, PC, or **Virtual Machine** (**VM**). Our examples and case studies use the Ubuntu and Fedora platforms, but the commands and examples explored are equally suitable for any other Linux distribution.

Introducing the Linux shell

Linux has its roots in the Unix operating system, and one of its main strengths is the command-line interface. In the old days, this was called *the shell*. In **UNIX**, the shell is invoked with the sh command. The shell is a program that has two streams: an *input stream* and an *output stream*. The input is a command given by the user, and the output is the result of that command, or an interpretation of it. In other words, the shell is the primary interface between the user and the machine.

The main shell in major Linux distributions is called **Bash**, which is an acronym for **Bourne Again Shell**, named after Steve Bourne, the original creator of the shell in UNIX. Alongside Bash, there are other shells available in Linux, such as **ksh**, **tcsh**, and **zsh**. In this chapter and throughout the book, we will cover the Bash shell, as it is the most widely used shell in modern Linux distributions.

> **Important note**
> Distributions such as Debian, Ubuntu, Fedora, CentOS Stream, RHEL, openSUSE, SLE, and Linux Mint, just to name a few, use the *Bash* shell by default. Other distributions, such as Kali Linux, have switched to *zsh* by default. Manjaro offers zsh on some editions. For those who use macOS, you should know that zsh has been the default shell for some years now. Nevertheless, you can install any shell you want on Linux and make it your default one. In general, shells are pretty similar, as they do the same thing, but they add different *extras* to usability and features. If you are interested in a specific shell, feel free to use it and test out the differences between others.

One shell can be assigned to each user. Users on the same system can use different shells. One way to check the default shell is by accessing the /etc/passwd file. More details about this file and user accounts will be discussed in *Chapter 4, Managing Users and Groups*. For now, it is important to know where to look for the default shell. In this file, the last characters from each line represent the user's default shell. The /etc/passwd file has the users listed on each line, with details about their **process identification number (PID)**, **group identification number (GID)**, username, home directory, and basic shell.

To see the default shell for each user, execute the following command by using your user's name (in our case, it is packt):

```
cat /etc/passwd | grep packt
```

The output should be a list of the contents of the /etc/passwd file. Depending on the number of users you have on your system, you will see all of them, each one on a separate line. An easier way to see the *current shell* is by running the following command:

```
echo $0
```

This shows what exactly is running your command, which in the case of the CLI is the shell. The `$0` part is a **bash special parameter** that refers to the currently running process. In the following screenshot you will see the output of the previous two commands we used to discover the shell and a comparison between the output of the `echo $0` command on Ubuntu and on Debian:

```
packt@neptune:~$ cat /etc/passwd | grep packt
packt:x:1000:1000:alexandru calcatinge:/home/packt:/bin/bash
packt@neptune:~$ echo $0
-bash
```

```
alexandru@debian:~$ echo $0
/bin/bash
alexandru@debian:~$
```

Figure 2.1 – Commands used to see the running shell

As you can see, running the `echo $0` command gives us different outputs but with the same message: the running shell is Bash. If you have other shells that you prefer, you can easily assign another shell to your user, if you already have it installed. However, if you know Bash, you will be comfortable with all the other available shells.

> **Important note**
> *The Linux shell is case-sensitive*. This means that everything you type inside the command line should respect this. For example, the `cat` command used earlier used lowercase. If you type `Cat` or `CAT`, the shell will not recognize it as being a command. The same rule applies to file paths. You will notice that default directories in your home directory use uppercase for the first letter, as in `~/Documents`, `~/Downloads`, and so on. Those names are different from `~/documents` or `~/downloads`.

In this chapter, you will learn how to use Linux commands and the shell in addition to learning about its filesystem. You will learn about software management in *Chapter 3*, thus showing you how to install another shell now would mean that we will get ahead of ourselves. We want you to slowly but steadily build your Linux knowledge, so we will show you in the next chapter how to install a new shell. For now, Bash is sufficient, and we will use it throughout the book.

If you want to see all the shells that are installed on your system, you can run the following command:

```
cat /etc/shells
```

In our case, the output with all the installed shells (by default) in Ubuntu Server 22.04.2 LTS is shown in the following image:

```
packt@neptune:~$ cat /etc/shells
# /etc/shells: valid login shells
/bin/sh
/bin/bash
/usr/bin/bash
/bin/rbash
/usr/bin/rbash
/usr/bin/sh
/bin/dash
/usr/bin/dash
/usr/bin/tmux
/usr/bin/screen
packt@neptune:~$ ▮
```

Figure 2.2 – The shells available by default in Ubuntu

This will show you all the shells installed. You can use any of those or can install new ones as we will show you in *Chapter 3*. Also, in *Chapter 4*, when we work with user accounts, you will get to learn how you can change a user's shell.

The following section will introduce you to shell connection types.

Establishing the shell connection

We can make two different types of connections to the shell: `tty` and `pts`. The name `tty` stands for **teletypewriter**, which was a type of terminal used at the beginning of computing. This connection is considered a native one, with ports that are direct connections to your computer. The link between the user and the computer is mainly found to be through a keyboard, which is considered to be a native terminal device.

The `pts` connection is generated by SSH or Telnet types of links. Its name stands for **pseudo terminal slave**, and it is an emulated connection made by a program, in most cases `ssh` or `xterm`. It is the slave of the **pseudo-terminal device**, which is represented as `pty`.

In the next section, we will further explore the connections to virtual terminals available in Linux.

Virtual consoles/terminals

The terminal was thought of as a device that manages the input strings (which are commands) between a process and other I/O devices such as a keyboard and a screen. There are also **pseudo terminals**, which are emulated terminals that behave the same way as a **classical terminal**. The difference is that it does not interact with devices directly, as it is all emulated by the Linux kernel, which transmits the I/O to a program called the shell.

Virtual consoles are accessible and run in the background, even though there is no open terminal. To access those virtual consoles, you can use the commands *Ctrl + Alt + F1*, *Ctrl + Alt + F2*, *Ctrl + Alt + F3*, *Ctrl + Alt + F4*, *Ctrl + Alt + F5*, and *Ctrl + Alt + F6*. These will open `tty1`, `tty2`, `tty3`, `tty4`, `tty5`, and `tty6`, respectively, on your computer.

We will explain this using an Ubuntu 22.04.2 LTS Server VM installation, but it is identical in Rocky Linux too. After starting the VM and being prompted to log in with your username and password, the first line on the screen will be something similar to the following output:

```
Ubuntu 22.04.2 LTS neptune tty1
```

If you press any of the preceding key combinations, you will see your terminal change from `tty1` to any of the other `tty` instances. For example, if you press *Ctrl + Alt + F6*, you will see this:

```
Ubuntu 22.04.2 LTS neptune tty6
```

As we were using the server edition of Ubuntu, we did not have the GUI installed. But if you were to use a desktop edition, you will be able to use *Ctrl + Alt + F7* to enter `X graphical` mode, for example. The `neptune` string is the name we gave to our virtual machine.

If you are not able to use the preceding keyboard combinations, there is a dedicated command for changing virtual terminals. The command is called `chvt` and has the syntax `chvt N`. Even though we have not discussed shell commands yet, we will show you an example of how to use them and other related commands. This action can only be performed by an administrator account or by using `sudo`. Briefly, `sudo` stands for *superuser do* and allows any user to run programs with administrative privileges or with the privileges of another user (more details about this in *Chapter 4, Managing Users and Groups*).

In the following example, we will use Ubuntu to show you how to change virtual terminals. First, we will see which virtual terminal we are currently using to change it to another one without using the *Ctrl + Alt + Fn* keys.

The `who` command will show you information about the users currently logged in to the computer. In our case, as we are connected through SSH to our virtual machine, it will show that the user `packt` is currently using pseudo-terminal zero (`pts/0`):

```
packt      pts/0          2023-02-28 10:45 (192.168.122.1)
```

If we were to run the same command in the console of the virtual machine directly, we would have the following output:

```
packt      pts/0          2023-02-28 10:45 (192.168.122.1)
packt      tty1           2023-02-28 10:50
```

It shows that the user is connected to both the virtual terminal 1 (`tty1`) and also through SSH from our host operating system to the virtual machine (`pts/0`).

Now, by using the chvt command, we will show you how to change to the sixth virtual terminal. After running sudo chvt 6, you will be prompted to provide your password and immediately be switched to virtual terminal number six. Running who once more will show you all logged-in users and the virtual terminals they use. In our case will be pts/0, tty2, and tty6. Please take into consideration that your output could be different, as in different virtual terminal numbers.

Now that we know what types of shell connections are established, let us learn about the shell's prompt in the next section.

The command-line prompt

The **command-line prompt** or **shell prompt** is the place where you type in the commands. Usually, the command prompt will show the username, hostname, present working directory, and a symbol that indicates the type of user running the shell.

Here is an example from the Ubuntu 22.04.2 LTS Server edition (similar to Debian):

```
packt@saturn:~$
```

Here is an example from the Fedora 37 server (similar to Rocky Linux, RHEL, or AlmaLinux):

```
[packt@localhost ~]$
```

Here is a short explanation of the prompt:

- packt is the name of the user currently logged in
- saturn and localhost are the hostnames
- ~ represents the home directory (it is called a tilde)
- $ shows that the user is a regular user (when you are logged in as an administrator, the sign changes into a hashtag, #)

Also, when using openSUSE, you will notice that the prompt is different than the ones in Ubuntu/ Debian and Fedora/RHEL. The following is an example of the prompt while running the Leap 15.4 server edition:

```
packt@localhost:~>
```

As you can see, there is no dollar sign ($) or hashtag (#), only a greater than sign (>). This might be confusing at first, but when you will use the root user, the sign will eventually change to the hashtag (#). The following is an example:

```
localhost:/home/packt #
```

Let's look at the shell command types next.

Shell command types

Shells work with **commands**, and there are two types that they use: internal ones and external ones. **Internal commands** are built inside the shell. **External commands** are installed separately. If you want to check the type of command you are using, there is the `type` command. For example, you can check what type of command `cd` (change directory) is:

```
packt@neptune:~$ type cd
cd is a shell builtin
```

The output shows that the `cd` command is an internal one, built inside the shell. If you are curious, you could find out the types of other commands that we will show you in the following sections by writing type in front of the command's name. Let us see some more examples in the following image:

```
packt@neptune:~$ type date
date is /usr/bin/date
packt@neptune:~$ type ls
ls is aliased to `ls --color=auto'
packt@neptune:~$ type man
man is /usr/bin/man
packt@neptune:~$ type grep
grep is aliased to `grep --color=auto'
packt@neptune:~$ type echo
echo is a shell builtin
packt@neptune:~$ type touch
touch is /usr/bin/touch
packt@neptune:~$ type pwd
pwd is a shell builtin
packt@neptune:~$ type elif
elif is a shell keyword
packt@neptune:~$
```

Figure 2.3 – Different types of commands in Linux

Now that you know some of the types of Linux commands, let us dissect the command's structure and learn about its components.

Explaining the command structure

We have already used some commands, but we did not explain the structure of a Linux command. We will do that now for you to be able to understand how to use commands. In a nutshell, Unix and Linux commands have the following form:

- The command's name
- The command's options
- The command's arguments

Inside the shell, you will have a general structure such as the following:

```
command [-option(s)] [argument(s)]
```

A suitable example would be the use of the `ls` command (`ls` comes from a *list*). This command is one of the most-used commands in Linux. It lists files and directories and can be used with both options and arguments.

We can use `ls` in its simplest form, without options or arguments. It lists the contents of your present working directory (pwd). In our case, it is the home directory, indicated by the ~ tilde character in the shell's prompt (see *Figure 2.10*).

The `ls` command with the `-l` option (lowercase L) uses a long listing format, giving you extra information about files and directories from your present working directory (pwd):

```
packt@saturn:~$ ls
Desktop  Documents  Downloads  Music  Pictures  Public  snap  Templates  Videos
packt@saturn:~$ ls -l
total 36
drwxr-xr-x 2 packt packt 4096 feb 28 12:32 Desktop
drwxr-xr-x 2 packt packt 4096 mar  1 21:05 Documents
drwxr-xr-x 2 packt packt 4096 feb 28 12:32 Downloads
drwxr-xr-x 2 packt packt 4096 feb 28 12:32 Music
drwxr-xr-x 2 packt packt 4096 feb 28 12:32 Pictures
drwxr-xr-x 2 packt packt 4096 feb 28 12:32 Public
drwx------ 3 packt packt 4096 feb 28 12:32 snap
drwxr-xr-x 2 packt packt 4096 feb 28 12:32 Templates
drwxr-xr-x 2 packt packt 4096 feb 28 12:32 Videos
packt@saturn:~$ ls -l ~/Documents
total 0
-rw-rw-r-- 1 packt packt 0 mar  1 21:04 file1
-rw-rw-r-- 1 packt packt 0 mar  1 21:04 file2
-rw-rw-r-- 1 packt packt 0 mar  1 21:04 file3
-rw-rw-r-- 1 packt packt 0 mar  1 21:05 report1
-rw-rw-r-- 1 packt packt 0 mar  1 21:05 report2
-rw-rw-r-- 1 packt packt 0 mar  1 21:05 report3
-rw-rw-r-- 1 packt packt 0 mar  1 21:05 report4
-rw-rw-r-- 1 packt packt 0 mar  1 21:05 report5
```

Figure 2.4 – Using the ls command with both options and attributes

In the preceding example, we used `ls  -l  ~/Documents/` to show the contents of the ~/Documents directory. Shown here is a way to use the command with both options and attributes, without changing our present working directory to ~/Documents.

In the following section, we will show you how to use the manual pages available by default in Linux.

Consulting the manual

Any Linux system administrator's best friend is the manual. Each command in Linux has a manual page that gives the user detailed information about its use, options, and attributes. If you know the command you want to learn more about, simply use the `man` command to explore. For the `ls` command, for example, you use `man ls`.

The manual organizes its command information into different sections, with each section being named by convention to be the same on all distributions. Briefly, those sections are `name`, `synopsis`, `configuration`, `description`, `options`, `exit status`, `return value`, `errors`, `environment`, `files`, `versions`, `conforming to`, `notes`, `bugs`, `example`, `authors`, `copyright`, and `see also`.

Similar to the manual pages, almost all commands in Linux have a `-help` option. You can use this for quick reference.

For more information about the `help` and `man` pages, you can check each command's help or manual page. Try the following commands:

```
$ man man
$ help help
```

When you use the manual, keep in mind that it is not a step-by-step how-to guide. It is technical documentation that might be confusing at first. Our advice is to use the `man` pages as much as you can. Before you search for anything on the internet, try to read the manual first. This will be a good exercise, and you will become proficient with Linux commands in no time.

Consider the manual your friend, similar to the textbooks you used in high school or college. It will give you first-hand information when you most need it. If you take into consideration situations where outside internet access is limited, with no access to search engines, the built-in manual will be your best companion. Learn to use its powers to your advantage.

In the following section, you will learn about the Linux filesystem.

The Linux filesystem

The **Linux filesystem** consists of a logical collection of files that are stored on a partition or a disk. Your hard drive can have one or many partitions. Those partitions usually contain only one filesystem, and they can extend to an entire disk. One filesystem could be the `/` (`root`) filesystem and another the `/home` filesystem. Or, there can be just one that contains all filesystems.

Generally, using one filesystem per partition is considered to be good practice by allowing for logical maintenance and management. As everything in Linux is a file, physical devices such as hard drives, DVD drives, USB devices, and floppy drives are treated as files too. In this section, you will learn about the directory structure, how to work with files, and some very useful editing techniques from the command line.

Directory structure

Linux uses a **hierarchical** filesystem structure. It is similar to an upside-down tree, with the root
(`/`) at the base of the filesystem. From that point, all the branches (directories) spread throughout
the filesystem.

The **Filesystem Hierarchy Standard** (**FHS**) defines the structure of Unix-like filesystems. However,
Linux filesystems also contain some directories that aren't yet defined by the standard.

Exploring the Linux filesystem from the command line

Feel free to explore the filesystem yourself by using the `tree` command. In Fedora Linux, it is already
installed, but if you use Ubuntu, you will have to install it by using the following command:

```
$ sudo apt install tree
```

Do not be afraid to explore the filesystem, because no harm will be done just by looking around. You
can use the `ls` command to list the contents of directories, but `tree` offers different graphics. The
following image shows you the differences between the outputs:

```
packt@neptune:~$ ls -la
total 36
drwxr-x--- 4 packt packt 4096 Feb 28 10:37 .
drwxr-xr-x 3 root  root  4096 Feb 27 08:58 ..
-rw------- 1 packt packt 1039 Mar  1 18:56 .bash_history
-rw-r--r-- 1 packt packt  220 Jan  6 2022 .bash_logout
-rw-r--r-- 1 packt packt 3771 Jan  6 2022 .bashrc
drwx------ 2 packt packt 4096 Feb 27 08:59 .cache
-rw------- 1 packt packt    0 Feb 27 10:52 .lesshst
-rw-r--r-- 1 packt packt  807 Jan  6 2022 .profile
drwx------ 2 packt packt 4096 Feb 27 08:58 .ssh
-rw-r--r-- 1 packt packt    0 Feb 27 08:59 .sudo_as_admin_successful
-rw-rw-r-- 1 packt packt   67 Feb 27 14:33 users
packt@neptune:~$ tree -a
.
├── .bash_history
├── .bash_logout
├── .bashrc
├── .cache
│   └── motd.legal-displayed
├── .lesshst
├── .profile
├── .ssh
│   └── authorized_keys
├── .sudo_as_admin_successful
└── users

2 directories, 9 files
packt@neptune:~$ ▮
```

Figure 2.5 – Comparing the output of ls -la commands and tree -a commands

The tree command has different options available, and you can learn about them by using the manual. Let us use the tree command by invoking the -L option, which tells the command how many levels down to go, and the last attribute states which directory to start with. In our example, the command will go down one level, starting from the root directory, represented by the forward slash as an argument (see *Figure 2.12*):

```
$ tree -L 1 /
```

Start exploring the directories from the structure by using the tree command, as shown here:

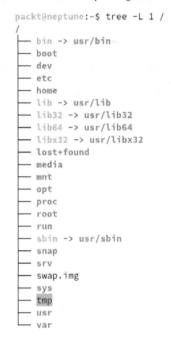

Figure 2.6 – The tree command with option and argument on Ubuntu

> **Important note**
> Remember that some of the directories you are about to open will contain a large number of files and/or other directories, which will clutter your terminal window.

The following are the directories that exist on almost all versions of Linux. Here's a quick overview of the Linux root filesystem:

- /: Root directory. The root for all other directories.
- /bin: Essential command binaries. The place where binary programs are stored.

- `/boot`: Static files of the boot loader. The place where the kernel, bootloader, and `initramfs` are stored.
- `/dev`: Device files. Nodes to the device equipment, a kernel device list.
- `/etc`: Host-specific system configuration. Essential config files for the system, boot time loading scripts, `crontab`, `fstab` device storage tables, `passwd` user accounts file.
- `/home`: user Home directory. The place where the user's files are stored.
- `/lib`: Essential shared libraries and kernel modules. Shared libraries are similar to **Dynamic Link Library** (**DLL**) files in Windows.
- `/media`: Mount point for removable media. For external devices and USB external media.
- `/mnt`: Mount point for mounting a filesystem temporarily. Used for legacy systems.
- `/opt`: Add-on application software packages. The place where *optional* software is installed.
- `/proc`: Virtual filesystem managed by the kernel. a special directory structure that contains files essential for the system.
- `/sbin`: Essential system binaries. Vital programs for the system's operation.
- `/srv`: Data for services provided by this system.
- `/tmp`: Temporary files.
- `/usr`: Secondary hierarchy. The largest directory in Linux that contains support files for regular system users:
  - `/usr/bin` – system-executable files
  - `/usr/lib` – shared libraries from `/usr/bin`
  - `/usr/local` – source compiled programs not included in the distribution
  - `/usr/sbin` – specific system administration programs
  - `/usr/share` – data shared by the programs in `/usr/bin` such as config files, icons, wallpapers or sound files
  - `/usr/share/doc` – documentation for the system-wide files
- `/var`: Variable data. Only data that is modifiable by the user is stored here, such as databases, printing spool files, user mail, and others; `/var/log` – contains log files that register system activity

Next, we're going to learn how to work with these files and directories.

Working with files and directories

Remember that everything in Linux is a file. A directory is a file too. As such, it is essential to know how to work with them. Working with files in Linux implies the use of several commands for basic file and directory operations, file viewing, file creation, file location, file properties, and linking. Some of the commands, which will not be covered here, have uses closely related to files. These will be covered in the following section.

Understanding file paths

Each file in the FHS has a *path*. The path is the file's location represented in an easily readable representation. In Linux, all the files are stored in the root directory by using the FHS as a standard to organize them. Relations between files and directories inside this system are expressed through the forward-slash character (/). Throughout computing history, this was used as a symbol that described addresses. Paths are, in fact, addresses for files.

There are two types of paths in Linux, relative ones and absolute ones. An **absolute path** always starts with the root directory and follows the branches of the system up to the desired file. A **relative path** always refers to the **present working directory** (**pwd**) and represents the relative path to it. Thus, a relative path is always a path that is relative to your present working directory.

For example, let us refer to an existing file from our home directory, a file called poem. Being inside the home directory, and our pwd command being the home directory for packt, the absolute path of the file called poem would be as follows:

```
/home/packt/poem
```

If we were to show the contents of that file using the cat command, for example, we would use the command with the absolute path:

```
cat /home/packt/poem
```

The relative path to the same file would be relative to pwd, so in our case, where we're already inside the home directory, using the cat command would be like this:

```
cat poem
```

The absolute path is useful to know about when you work with files. After some practice, you will come to learn the paths to the most-used files. For example, one file that you will need to learn the path for is the passwd file. It resides in the /etc directory. Thus, when you will refer to it, you will use its absolute path, /etc/passwd. Using a relative path to that file would imply that you are either inside its parent directory or somewhere close in the FHS.

Working with relative paths involves knowing two special characters used to work with the FHS. One special character is the dot (.), and it refers to the current directory. The other is two consecutive dots (. .) and refers to the parent directory of the current directory. When working with relative paths, make sure that you always check what directory you are in. Use the pwd command to show your present working directory.

A good example of working with relative paths is when you are already inside the parent directory and need to refer to it. If you need to see the accounts list from your system, which is stored inside the passwd file, you can refer to it by using a relative path. For this exercise, we are inside our home directory:

```
packt@neptune:~$ pwd
/home/packt
packt@neptune:~$ cat passwd
cat: passwd: No such file or directory
packt@neptune:~$ cat ../../etc/passwd
```

Figure 2.7 – Using the relative path of a file

Here, we first check our present working directory with the pwd command, and the output will be our home directory's path, /home/packt. Secondly, we try to show the contents of the passwd file using the cat command right from the home directory, but the output will be an error message saying that there is no such file or directory inside our home directory. We used the relative path, which is always relative to our present working directory, hence the error. Thirdly, we use the double-consecutive dots special characters to refer to the file with its relative path. In this case, the command is cat ../../etc/passwd.

> **Tip**
>
> Always use the *Tab* key on your keyboard for autocompletion and to check whether the path you typed is correct or not. In the preceding example, we typed ../../etc and pressed *Tab*, which autocompleted with a forward slash. Then, we typed the first two letters of the file we were looking for and pressed *Tab* again. This showed us a list of files inside the /etc directory that started with pa. Seeing that passwd was in there, we knew that the path was right, so we typed two more s characters and pressed *Tab* again. This completed the command for us and we pressed *Enter/Return* to execute the command.

The path in the final command is relative to our home directory and it translates as follows: *concatenate the file with the passwd name that is located in the /etc directory in the parent directory (first two dots) of the parent directory (second two dots) of our current directory (home)*. Therefore, the /etc/passwd absolute path is translated into a relative path to our home directory like this: ../../etc/passwd.

Next, we are going to learn about basic file operations in Linux.

Basic file operations

Daily, as a system administrator, you will manipulate files. This includes creating, copying, moving, listing, deleting, linking, and so on. The basic commands for these operations have already been discussed throughout this chapter, but now it is time to get into more detail about their use, options, and attributes. Some more advanced commands will be detailed in the following sections.

Creating files

There are situations when you will need to **create** new files. You have one option to create a new empty file with the `touch` command. When you use it, it will create a new file with you as the file owner and with a size of zero, because it is an empty file.

In the following example, we create a new file called `new-report` inside the `~/packt/` directory:

```
packt@neptune:~$ pwd
/home/packt
packt@neptune:~$ touch new-report
packt@neptune:~$ ls -l new-report
-rw-rw-r-- 1 packt packt 0 Mar  2 14:24 new-report
packt@neptune:~$ touch new-report
packt@neptune:~$ ls -l new-report
-rw-rw-r-- 1 packt packt 0 Mar  2 14:25 new-report
packt@neptune:~$ █
```

Figure 2.8 – Using the touch command to create and alter files

The `touch` command is also used to change the modification time of a file without changing the file itself. Notice the difference between the initial time when we first created the `new-report` file and the new time after using the `touch` command on it. You can also change the access time by using the `-a` option of the `touch` command. By default, the long listing of the `ls` command shows only the modification/creation time. If you want to see the access time, there is the `atime` parameter you can use with the `--time` option. See the example used in the following figure:

```
packt@neptune:~$ ls -l new-report
-rw-rw-r-- 1 packt packt 67 Mar  2 14:30 new-report
packt@neptune:~$ touch -a new-report
packt@neptune:~$ ls -l --time=atime new-report
-rw-rw-r-- 1 packt packt 67 Mar  2 14:31 new-report
packt@neptune:~$ █
```

Figure 2.9 – Using touch to alter the access time

The modification, creation, and access time stamps are very useful, especially when using commands such as `find`. They give you a more *granular* search pattern. We will get back to this command with more examples in future sections.

Files can also be created by using redirection and the `echo` command. `echo` is a command that prints the string given as a parameter to the standard output (the screen). The output of the `echo` command can be written directly to a file by using the output redirection:

```
packt@neptune:~$ echo this is a presentation
this is a presentation
packt@neptune:~$ echo this is also a presentation > art-file
packt@neptune:~$ cat art-file
this is also a presentation
packt@neptune:~$ echo this is a new presentation >> art-file
packt@neptune:~$ cat art-file
this is also a presentation
this is a new presentation
packt@neptune:~$
```

Figure 2.10 – Using echo with output redirection

In the preceding example, we redirected the text from the `echo` command to the presentation file. It did not exist at the beginning, so it was automatically created by the command. The first `echo` command added a line to the file by using the `>` operator. The second `echo` command appended a new line of text to the end of the file, by using the `>>` operator.

Listing files

We have already used some examples with the `ls` command before, so you are somewhat familiar with it. We covered the `-l` option as an example of the command's structure. Thus, we will not cover it any further here. We will explore new options for this essential and useful command:

- `ls -lh`: The `-l` option lists the files in an extended format, while the `-h` option shows the size of the file in a human-readable format, with the size in kilobytes or megabytes rather than bytes.

- `ls -la`: The `-a` option shows all the files, including hidden ones. Combined with the `-l` option, the output will be a list of all the files and their details.

- `ls -ltr`: The `-t` option sorts files by their modification time, showing the newest first. The `-r` option reverses the order of the sort.

- `ls - lS`: The `-S` option sorts the files by their size, with the largest file first.

- `ls -R`: The `-R` option shows the contents of the current or specified directory in recursive mode.

A method used frequently for listing files and directories is called **long listing**, and it uses the `ls -la` command. Let's look at it in detail here, even though we will discuss this thoroughly in *Chapter 4, Managing Users and Groups*.

One example of a long listing used on our home directory can be seen in *Figure 2.11*, when we compared the output of `ls -la` with the output of the `tree` command. The following code snippet is a short example:

```
total 48
drwxr-x--- 5 packt  packt 4096 Mar  2 14:44 .
drwxr-xr-x 3 root    root   4096 Feb 27 08:58 ..
-rw-rw-r-- 1 packt  packt    55 Mar  2 14:46 art-file
-rw------- 1 packt  packt 1039 Mar  1 18:56 .bash_history
```

In the output, the first row after the command shows the number of blocks inside the directory listed. After that, each line represents one file or subdirectory, with the following detailed information:

- The first character is the type of the file: d for the directory, : for the file, l for a link, c for the character device, and b for the block device
- The following nine characters represent the permissions (detailed in *Chapter 4, Managing Users and Groups*)
- The hard link for that file (see the *Working with links* subsection in this chapter)
- The owner's PID and GID (details in *Chapter 4, Managing Users and Groups*)
- The size of the file (the number depends on whether it is in human-readable format or not)
- The last modification time of the file
- The name of the file or directory

The first two lines are a reference to itself (the dot) and to the parent directory (the two dots from the second line).

The next section will teach you how to copy and move files.

Copying and moving files

To copy files in Linux, the `cp` command is used. The `mv` command moves files around the filesystem. This command is also used to rename files.

To copy a file, you can use the `cp` command in the simplest way:

```
cp source_file_path destination_file_path
```

Here, `source_file_path` is the name of the file to be copied, and `destination_file_path` is the name of the destination file. You can also copy multiple files inside a directory that already exists. If the destination directory does not exist, the shell will signal to you that the target is not a directory.

Now let's look at some variations of these commands:

- cp -a: The -a option copies an entire directory hierarchy in recursive mode by preserving all the attributes and links. In the following example, we copied the entire dir1 directory that we previously created inside our home directory, to a newly created directory called backup_dir1 by using the -a option:

```
packt@neptune:~$ ls
art-file  dir1  new-report  users
packt@neptune:~$ mkdir backup_dir1
packt@neptune:~$ ls
art-file  backup_dir1  dir1  new-report  users
packt@neptune:~$ cp -a dir1/ backup_dir1/
packt@neptune:~$ ls backup_dir1/
dir1
packt@neptune:~$ ▌
```

Figure 2.11 – Using the copy command with the -a option

- cp -r: This option is similar to -a, but it does not preserve attributes, only symbolic links.

- cp -p: The -p option retains the file's permissions and timestamps. Otherwise, just by using cp in its simplest form, copies of the files will be owned by your user with a timestamp of the time you did the copy operation.

- cp -R: The -R option allows you to copy a directory recursively. In the following example, we will use the ls command to show you the contents of the ~/packt/ directory, and then the cp -R command to copy the contents of the /files directory to the /new-files one. The /new-files directory did not exist. The cp -R command created it:

```
packt@neptune:~$ ls
art-file  backup_dir1  dir1  new-report  users
packt@neptune:~$ mkdir files
packt@neptune:~$ cd files/
packt@neptune:~/files$ touch files{1..6}
packt@neptune:~/files$ cd ..
packt@neptune:~$ ls
art-file  backup_dir1  dir1  files  new-report  users
packt@neptune:~$ cp -R files/ new-files
packt@neptune:~$ ls
art-file  backup_dir1  dir1  files  new-files  new-report  users
packt@neptune:~$ cd new-files/
packt@neptune:~/new-files$ ls
files1  files2  files3  files4  files5  files6
packt@neptune:~/new-files$ ▌
```

Figure 2.12 – Using the cp -R command

Moving files around is done with the mv command. It is either used to move files and directories from one destination to another or to rename a file. The following is an example in which we rename files1 into old-files1 using the mv command: mv files1 old-files1.

There are many other options that you could learn about just by visiting the manual pages. Feel free to explore them and use them in your daily tasks.

Working with links

Links are a compelling option in Linux. They can be used as a means of protection for the original files, or just as a tool to keep multiple copies of a file without having separate hard copies. Consider it as a tool to create alternative names for the same file.

The ln command can be used to do this and create two types of links:

- Symbolic links
- Hard links

Those two links are different types of files that point to the original file. A **symbolic link** is a physical file that points to the original file; they are linked and have the same content. Also, it can span different filesystems and physical media, meaning that it can link to original files that are on other drives or partitions with different types of filesystems. The command used is as follows:

```
ln -s [original_filename] [link_filename]
```

Here is an example in which we listed the contents of the ~/packt directory and then created a symbolic link to the new-report file using the ln -s command and then listed the contents again:

```
packt@neptune:~$ ls
art-file  backup_dir1  dir1  files  new-files  new-report  users
packt@neptune:~$ ln -s new-report new-report-link
packt@neptune:~$ ls -l
total 28
-rw-rw-r-- 1 packt packt   55 Mar  2 14:46 art-file
drwxrwxr-x 3 packt packt 4096 Mar  2 15:20 backup_dir1
drwxrwxr-x 2 packt packt 4096 Mar  2 15:19 dir1
drwxrwxr-x 2 packt packt 4096 Mar  2 16:04 files
drwxrwxr-x 2 packt packt 4096 Mar  2 16:04 new-files
-rw-rw-r-- 1 packt packt   67 Mar  2 14:30 new-report
lrwxrwxrwx 1 packt packt   10 Mar  2 16:10 new-report-link -> new-report
-rw-rw-r-- 1 packt packt   67 Feb 27 14:33 users
packt@neptune:~$
```

Figure 2.13 – Using symbolic links

You can see that the link created is named new-report-link and is visually represented with an -> arrow that shows the original file that it points to. You can also distinguish the difference in size between the two files, the link and the original one. The permissions are different too. This is a way to know that they are two *different* physical files. To double-check that they are different physical files, you can use the ls -i command to show the **inode** before every file. In the following example, you can see that new-report and new-report-link have different inodes:

```
packt@neptune:~$ ls -li
total 28
137603 -rw-rw-r-- 1 packt packt   55 Mar  2 14:46 art-file
137621 drwxrwxr-x 3 packt packt 4096 Mar  2 15:20 backup_dir1
137604 drwxrwxr-x 2 packt packt 4096 Mar  2 15:19 dir1
137631 drwxrwxr-x 2 packt packt 4096 Mar  2 16:04 files
137638 drwxrwxr-x 2 packt packt 4096 Mar  2 16:04 new-files
137599 -rw-rw-r-- 1 packt packt   67 Mar  2 14:30 new-report
137849 lrwxrwxrwx 1 packt packt   10 Mar  2 16:10 new-report-link -> new-report
131094 -rw-rw-r-- 1 packt packt   67 Feb 27 14:33 users
packt@neptune:~$
```

Figure 2.14 – Comparing the inodes for the symbolic link and original file

If you want to know where the link points to and you do not want to use ls -l, there is the readlink command. It is available in both Ubuntu and CentOS. The output of the command will simply be the name of the file that the symbolic link points to. It only works in the case of symbolic links:

```
packt@neptune:~$ readlink new-report-link
new-report
```

In the preceding example, you can see that the output shows that the new-report-link file is a symbolic link to the file named new-report.

In contrast, a **hard link** is a different virtual file that points to the original file. They are both physically the same. The command is simply ln without any options:

```
ln [original-file] [linked-file]
```

In the following example, we created a hard link for the new-report file, and we named it new-report-ln:

```
packt@neptune:~/links$ echo the first report > new-report
packt@neptune:~/links$ cat new-report
the first report
packt@neptune:~/links$ ln new-report new-report-ln
packt@neptune:~/links$ ls -l
total 8
-rw-rw-r-- 2 packt packt 17 Mar  2 16:23 new-report
-rw-rw-r-- 2 packt packt 17 Mar  2 16:23 new-report-ln
packt@neptune:~/links$ echo hard link report >> new-report-ln
packt@neptune:~/links$ cat new-report-ln
the first report
hard link report
packt@neptune:~/links$ cat new-report
the first report
hard link report
packt@neptune:~/links$ ls -li
total 8
138839 -rw-rw-r-- 2 packt packt 34 Mar  2 16:24 new-report
138839 -rw-rw-r-- 2 packt packt 34 Mar  2 16:24 new-report-ln
packt@neptune:~/links$
```

Figure 2.15 – Working with hard links

In the output, you will see that they have the same size and the same inode, and after altering the original file using `echo` and output redirection, the changes were available to both files. The two files have a different representation than symbolic links. They appear as two different files in your listing, with no visual aids to show which file is pointed to. Essentially, a hard link is linked to the inode of the original file. You can see it as a new name for a file, similar to but not identical to renaming it.

Deleting files

In Linux, you have the remove (`rm`) command for deleting files. In its simplest form, the `rm` command is used without an option. For more control over how you delete items, you could use the `-i`, `-f`, and `-r` options:

- `rm -i`: This option enables interactive mode by asking you for acceptance before deleting:

```
packt@neptune:~$ ls
art-file    dir1   links      new-report      users
backup_dir1  files  new-files  new-report-link
packt@neptune:~$ rm -i art-file
rm: remove regular file 'art-file'? y
packt@neptune:~$ ls
backup_dir1 dir1  files  links  new-files  new-report  new-report-link  users
packt@neptune:~$
```

Figure 2.16 – Removing a file interactively

In the preceding example, we deleted `art-file` by using the `-i` option. When asked to interact, you have two options. You can approve the action by typing `y` (yes), or `n` (no) to cancel the action.

- `rm -f`: The `-f` option deletes the file by force, without any interaction from the user:

```
packt@neptune:~$ ls
backup_dir1  dir1  files  links  new-files  new-report  new-report-link  users
packt@neptune:~$ rm -f new-report-link
packt@neptune:~$ ls
backup_dir1  dir1  files  links  new-files  new-report  users
packt@neptune:~$
```

Figure 2.17 – Force remove a file

We deleted the `new-report-link` file created earlier by using the `rm -f` command. It did not ask for our approval and deleted the file directly.

- `rm -r`: This option deletes the files in recursive mode, and it is used to delete multiple files and directories. For example, we will try to delete the `new-files` directory. When using the `rm` command in its simplest way, the output will show an error saying that it cannot delete a directory. But when used with the `-r` option, the directory is deleted right away:

```
packt@neptune:~$ ls
backup_dir1  dir1  files  links  new-files  new-report  users
packt@neptune:~$ rm new-files/
rm: cannot remove 'new-files/': Is a directory
packt@neptune:~$ rm -r new-files/
packt@neptune:~$ ls
backup_dir1  dir1  files  links  new-report  users
packt@neptune:~$
```

Figure 2.18 – Remove a directory recursively

> **Important note**
>
> We advise *extra caution* when using the `rm` command. The most destructive mode is to use `rm -rf`. This will delete files, directories, and anything without warning. Pay attention as there is no going back from this. Once used, the damage will be done.

Most of the time, removing files is a one-way street, with no turning back. This makes the process of deleting files a very important one, and a backup before a deletion could save you a lot of unnecessary stress.

Creating directories

In Linux, you can create a new directory with the mkdir command. In the following example, we will create a new directory called development:

```
mkdir development
```

If you want to create more directories and sub-directories at once, you will need to use the -p option (p from the parent), as shown in the following figure:

```
packt@neptune:~$ mkdir -p reports/month/day
packt@neptune:~$ tree reports/
reports/
└── month
    └── day

2 directories, 0 files
packt@neptune:~$ ▯
```

Figure 2.19 – Creating parent directories

Directories are files too in Linux, only that they have special attributes. They are essential to organizing your filesystem. For more options with this useful tool, feel free to visit the manual pages.

Deleting directories

The Linux command for removing directories is called rmdir. It is designed to default by deleting only empty directories. Let's see what happens if we try to delete a directory that is not empty:

```
packt@neptune:~$ rmdir reports/
rmdir: failed to remove 'reports/': Directory not empty
packt@neptune:~$ ▯
```

Figure 2.20 – Using the rmdir command

This is a precautionary measure from the shell, as deleting a directory that is not empty could have disastrous consequences, as we've seen when using the rm command. The rmdir command does not have a -i option such as rm. The only way to delete the directory using the rmdir command is to delete files inside it first manually. However, the rm -r command shown earlier is still useful and more versatile when deleting directories.

Now that you know how to work with directories in Linux, we will proceed to show you commands for file viewing.

Commands for file viewing

As everything in Linux is a file, being able to view and work with file contents is an essential asset for any system administrator. In this section, we will learn commands for file viewing, as almost all files contain text that, at some point, should be readable.

The cat command

This command was used in some of our previous examples in this chapter. It is short for *concatenate* and is used to print the contents of the file to the screen. We have used cat several times during this chapter, but here is yet another example. We have two existing files, one called new-report and the other called users. Let us show you how to use cat in the following image:

```
packt@neptune:~$ cat new-report
Lorem ipsum dolor sit amet, consectetur adipiscing elit, sed do eiusmod tempor i
ncididunt ut labore et dolore magna aliqua.
packt@neptune:~$ cat new-report users
Lorem ipsum dolor sit amet, consectetur adipiscing elit, sed do eiusmod tempor i
ncididunt ut labore et dolore magna aliqua.
packt      pts/0          2023-02-27 13:49 (192.168.124.1)
/home/packt
packt@neptune:~$
```

Figure 2.21 – Example of using the cat command

In this example, we first used the command to show the contents of only one file, the one called new-report. The second command was used to show the contents of two files at once, both new-report and users. The cat command is showing the contents of both on the screen. Both files are located in the same directory, which is also the user's working directory. If you would like to concatenate the contents of files that are not inside your present working directory, you would need to use their absolute path.

The cat command has several options available, which we will not cover here, as most of the time, its purest form will be the most used. For more details, see the manual pages.

The less command

There are times when a file has so much text that it will cover many screens, and it will be difficult to view on your terminal using just cat. This is where the less command is handy. It shows one screen at a time. How much a screen means, it all depends on the size of your terminal window. Let's take, for example, the /etc/passwd file. It could have multiple lines that you would not be able to fit in just one screen. You could use the following command:

```
$ less /etc/passwd
```

When you press *Enter*, the contents of the file will be shown on your screen. To navigate through it, you could use the following keys:

- Space bar: Move forward one screen
- *Enter*: Move forward one line
- *b*: Move backward one screen
- */*: Enter search mode; this searches forward in your file
- *?*: Search mode; this searches backward in your file
- *v*: Edit your file with the default editor
- *g*: Jump to the beginning of the file
- *Shift + g*: Jump to the end of the file
- *q*: Exit the output.

The `less` command has a multitude of options that could be used. We advise you to consult the manual pages to find out more information about this command.

The head command

This command is handy when you only want to print to the screen the beginning (the head) of a text file. By default, it will print only the first 10 lines of the file. You can use the same `/etc/passwd` file for the head exercise and execute the following command. Watch what happens. It prints the first 10 lines and then exits the command, taking you back to the shell prompt:

```
head /etc/passwd
```

One useful option of this command is to print more or less than 10 lines of the file. For this, you can use the `-n` argument or simply just – with the number of lines you want to print. For the `/etc/passwd` file, we will first use the head command without any options, and then we will use it with the number of lines argument, as shown in the following figure:

```
packt@neptune:~$ head /etc/passwd
root:x:0:0:root:/root:/bin/bash
daemon:x:1:1:daemon:/usr/sbin:/usr/sbin/nologin
bin:x:2:2:bin:/bin:/usr/sbin/nologin
sys:x:3:3:sys:/dev:/usr/sbin/nologin
sync:x:4:65534:sync:/bin:/bin/sync
games:x:5:60:games:/usr/games:/usr/sbin/nologin
man:x:6:12:man:/var/cache/man:/usr/sbin/nologin
lp:x:7:7:lp:/var/spool/lpd:/usr/sbin/nologin
mail:x:8:8:mail:/var/mail:/usr/sbin/nologin
news:x:9:9:news:/var/spool/news:/usr/sbin/nologin
packt@neptune:~$ head -n 3 /etc/passwd
root:x:0:0:root:/root:/bin/bash
daemon:x:1:1:daemon:/usr/sbin:/usr/sbin/nologin
bin:x:2:2:bin:/bin:/usr/sbin/nologin
packt@neptune:~$ head -3 /etc/passwd
root:x:0:0:root:/root:/bin/bash
daemon:x:1:1:daemon:/usr/sbin:/usr/sbin/nologin
bin:x:2:2:bin:/bin:/usr/sbin/nologin
packt@neptune:~$ ▊
```

Figure 2.22 – Using the head command

Many other options that this command provides can prove useful for your work as a system administrator, but we will not cover them here. Feel free to explore them yourself.

The tail command

The `tail` command is similar to the `head` command, only it prints the last 10 lines of a file, by default. You can use the same -n argument as for the head command, to see a specific number of lines from the end of a file. However, the `tail` command is commonly used for actively watching log files that are constantly changing. It can print the last lines of the file as other applications are writing to it. Take, for example, the following line:

```
tail -f /var/log/syslog
```

Using the -f option will make the command watch the /var/log/syslog file as it is being written. It will show you the contents of the file on the screen effectively. The -f option will cause the tail command to stop during a log rotation, and in this case, the -F option should be used instead. When using the -F option, the command will continue to show the output even during a log rotation. To exit that screen, you will need to press *Ctrl* + *C* to go back to the shell prompt. The following is an example of the output of the previous command:

```
packt@neptune:~$ tail -f /var/log/syslog
Mar  2 18:54:26 neptune systemd[1]: Starting Time & Date Service...
Mar  2 18:54:27 neptune dbus-daemon[643]: [system] Successfully activated servic
e 'org.freedesktop.timedate1'
Mar  2 18:54:27 neptune systemd[1]: Started Time & Date Service.
Mar  2 18:54:27 neptune snapd[653]: storehelpers.go:769: cannot refresh: snap ha
s no updates available: "core20", "lxd", "snapd"
Mar  2 18:54:27 neptune snapd[653]: autorefresh.go:551: auto-refresh: all snaps
are up-to-date
Mar  2 18:54:57 neptune systemd[1]: systemd-timedated.service: Deactivated succe
ssfully.
Mar  2 19:04:26 neptune systemd[1]: Starting Cleanup of Temporary Directories...
Mar  2 19:04:26 neptune systemd[1]: systemd-tmpfiles-clean.service: Deactivated
successfully.
Mar  2 19:04:26 neptune systemd[1]: Finished Cleanup of Temporary Directories.
Mar  2 19:17:01 neptune CRON[1081]: (root) CMD (   cd / && run-parts --report /e
tc/cron.hourly)
Mar  2 19:27:39 neptune systemd[1]: Started Session 4 of User packt.
Mar  2 19:27:47 neptune systemd[1]: Starting Update APT News...
Mar  2 19:27:47 neptune systemd[1]: Starting Update the local ESM caches...
Mar  2 19:27:48 neptune systemd[1]: esm-cache.service: Deactivated successfully.
Mar  2 19:27:48 neptune systemd[1]: Finished Update the local ESM caches.
Mar  2 19:27:48 neptune systemd[1]: apt-news.service: Deactivated successfully.
Mar  2 19:27:48 neptune systemd[1]: Finished Update APT News.
```

Figure 2.23 – The use of tail command for real-time log file observation

Next, let us learn how to view file properties in Linux.

Commands for file properties

There could be times when just viewing the contents of a file is not enough, and you need extra information about that file. There are other handy commands that you could use, and we describe them in the following sections.

The stat command

The stat command gives you more information than the ls command does. The example in the following figure shows a comparison between the ls and stat outputs for the same file:

```
packt@neptune:~$ ls
backup_dir1  development  dir1  files  links  new-report  reports  users
packt@neptune:~$ ls -l new-report
-rw-rw-r-- 1 packt packt 124 Mar  2 19:05 new-report
packt@neptune:~$ stat new-report
  File: new-report
  Size: 124           Blocks: 8          IO Block: 4096   regular file
Device: fd00h/64768d    Inode: 137599     Links: 1
Access: (0664/-rw-rw-r--)  Uid: ( 1000/   packt)   Gid: ( 1000/   packt)
Access: 2023-03-02 19:06:00.455577063 +0000
Modify: 2023-03-02 19:05:55.243562331 +0000
Change: 2023-03-02 19:05:55.243562331 +0000
 Birth: 2023-03-02 14:24:14.834170882 +0000
packt@neptune:~$ ▊
```

Figure 2.24 – Using the stat command

The `stat` command gives you more information about the name, size, number of blocks, type of file, inode, number of links, permissions, UID and GID, and `atime`, `mtime`, and `ctime`. To find out more information about it, please refer to the Linux manual pages.

The file command

This command simply reports on the type of file. Here is an example of a text file and a command file:

```
packt@neptune:~$ file new-report
new-report: ASCII text
packt@neptune:~$ file /usr/bin/wh
whatis            which             whiptail          whoami
whereis           which.debianutils who
packt@neptune:~$ file /usr/bin/who
/usr/bin/who: ELF 64-bit LSB pie executable, x86-64, version 1 (SYSV), dynamical
ly linked, interpreter /lib64/ld-linux-x86-64.so.2, BuildID[sha1]=98fb99c65957c7
4a5216e69b3dd5032df976a2dc, for GNU/Linux 3.2.0, stripped
packt@neptune:~$ file /usr/bin/which
/usr/bin/which: symbolic link to /etc/alternatives/which
packt@neptune:~$ file /usr/bin/whoami
/usr/bin/whoami: ELF 64-bit LSB pie executable, x86-64, version 1 (SYSV), dynami
cally linked, interpreter /lib64/ld-linux-x86-64.so.2, BuildID[sha1]=a18184f5d26
fce82fe5ccf842d3cf7b9c729030f, for GNU/Linux 3.2.0, stripped
packt@neptune:~$ █
```

Figure 2.25 – Using the file command

Linux does not rely on file extensions and types as some other operating systems do. In this respect, the `file` command determines the file type more by its contents than anything else.

Commands for configuring file ownership and permissions

In Linux, **file security** is set by ownership and permissions. **File ownership** is determined by the file's owner and the owner's group. Judging by the owner, a file may have one of three types of ownership assigned to it: *user*, *group*, and *other*. The user is, most of the time, the owner of a file. Whoever created the file is its owner. The owner can be changed using the `chown` command. When setting up group ownership, you determine the permissions for everyone in that group. This is set up using the `chgrp` command. When it comes to other users, the reference is to everyone else on that system, someone who did not create the file, so it is not the owner, and who does not belong to the owner's group. Other is also known as, or referred to as the world.

Besides setting user ownership, the system must know how to determine user behavior, and it does that through the use of **permissions**. We will do a quick review of a file's properties by using the `ls -l` command:

```
packt@neptune:~$ ls -l
total 32
drwxrwxr-x 3 packt packt 4096 Mar  2 15:20 backup_dir1
drwxrwxr-x 2 packt packt 4096 Mar  2 18:51 development
drwxrwxr-x 2 packt packt 4096 Mar  2 15:19 dir1
drwxrwxr-x 2 packt packt 4096 Mar  2 16:04 files
drwxrwxr-x 2 packt packt 4096 Mar  2 16:23 links
-rw-rw-r-- 1 packt packt  124 Mar  2 19:05 new-report
drwxrwxr-x 3 packt packt 4096 Mar  2 18:52 reports
-rw-rw-r-- 1 packt packt   67 Feb 27 14:33 users
```

Figure 2.26 – Long listing output

In the preceding examples, you see two different types of permissions for the files inside our home directory. Each line has 12 characters reserved for special attributes and permissions. Out of those 12, only 10 are used in the preceding examples. Nine of them represent the permissions, and the first one is the file type. There are three easy-to-remember abbreviations for permissions:

- r is for read permission
- w is for write permission
- x is for execute permission
- - is for no permission

The nine characters are divided into three regions, each consisting of three characters. The first three characters are reserved for user permissions, the following three characters are reserved for group permissions, and the last three characters represent other, or global permissions.

File types also have their codes, as follows:

- d: The letter d shows that it is a directory
- -: The hyphen shows that it is a file
- l: The letter l shows that it is a symbolic link
- p: The letter p shows that it is a named pipe; a special file that facilitates the communication between programs
- s: The letter s shows that it is a socket, similar to the pipe but with bi-directional and network communications
- b: The letter b shows that it is a block device; a file that corresponds to a hardware device
- c: The letter c shows that it is a character device; similar to a block device

The permission string is a 10-bit string. The first bit is reserved for the file type. The next nine bits determine the permissions by dividing them into 3-bit packets. Each packet is expressed by an **octal number** (because an octal number has three bytes). Thus, permissions are represented using a power of two:

- `read` is 2 ^ 2 (two to the power of two), which equals 4
- `write` is 2 ^ 1 (two to the power of one), which equals 2
- `execute` is 2 ^ 0 (two to the power of zero), which equals 1

In this respect, file permissions should be represented according to the following diagram:

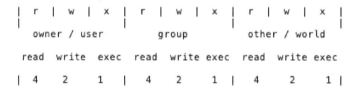

Figure 2.27 – File permissions explained

In the preceding diagram, you have the permissions shown as a string of nine characters, just like you would see them in the `ls -la` output. The row is divided into three different sections, one for owner/user, one for group, and one for other/world. These are shown in the first two rows. The other two rows show you the types of permissions (`read`, `write`, and `execute`) and the octal numbers in the following paragraph.

This is useful as it relates the octal representations to the character representations of permissions. Thus, if you were to translate a permission shown as `rwx r-x` into octal, based on the preceding diagram, you could easily say it is `755`. This is because, for the first group, the owner, you have all of them active (`rwx`), which translates into *4+2+1=7*. For the second group, you have only two permissions active, `r` and `x`, which translates into *4+1=5*. Finally, for the last group, you have also two permissions active, similar to the second group (`r` and `x`), which translates to *4+1=5*. Now you know that the permission in the octal is `755`.

As an exercise, you should try to translate into octal the following permissions:

- `rwx rwx`
- `rwx r-x`
- `rwx r-x - - -`
- `rwx - - - - - -`
- `rw- rw- rw-`
- `rw- rw- r - -`

- rw- rw- - - -
- rw- r- - r- -
- rw- r- - - - -
- rw- - - - - - -
- r - - - - - - - -

> **Important note**
>
> There are some other vital commands such as umask, chown, chmod, and chgrp, which are used to change or set the default creation mode, owner, mode (access permissions), and group, respectively. They will be briefly introduced here as they involve setting the file's properties, but for a more detailed description, please refer to *Chapter 4, Managing Users and Groups*.

Commands for file compression, uncompression, and archiving

In Linux, the standard tool for archiving is called tar, from tape archive. It was initially used in Unix to write files to external tape devices for archiving. Nowadays, in Linux, it is also used to write to a file in a compressed format. Other popular formats, apart from tar archives, are gzip and bzip for compressed archives, together with the popular zip from Windows. Now let's look at the tar command in detail.

The tar command for compressing and un-compressing

This command is used with options and does not offer compression by default. To use compression, we would need to use specific options. Here are some of the most useful arguments available for tar:

- tar -c: Creates an archive
- tar -r: Appends files to an already existing archive
- tar -u: Appends only changed files to an existing archive
- tar -A: Appends an archive to the end of another archive
- tar -t: Lists the contents of the archive
- tar -x: Extracts the archive contents
- tar -z: Uses gzip compression for the archive
- tar -j: Uses bzip2 compression for the archive
- tar -v: Uses verbose mode by printing extra information on the screen
- tar -p: Restores original permission and ownership for the extracted files
- tar -f: Specifies the name of the output file

There is a chance that in your daily tasks, you will have to use these arguments in combination with each other.

For example, to create an archive of the `files` directory, we used the `-cvf` arguments combined, as shown here:

```
packt@neptune:~$ ls
backup_dir1  development  dir1  files  links  new-report  reports  users
packt@neptune:~$ tar -cvf files-archive.tar files/
files/
files/files4
files/files1
files/files5
files/files6
files/files3
files/files2
packt@neptune:~$ ls
backup_dir1  dir1     files-archive.tar  new-report  users
development  files    links              reports
```

Figure 2.28 – Using the tar command

The archive created is not compressed. To use compression, we would need to add the `-z` or `-j` arguments. Next, we will use the `-z` option for the `gzip` compression algorithm. See the following example and compare the size of the two archive files. As a general rule, it is advised to use an extension for such files:

```
packt@neptune:~$ tar -czvf files-archive-gzipped.tar.gz files
files/
files/files4
files/files1
files/files5
files/files6
files/files3
files/files2
packt@neptune:~$ ls -l files-archive-gzipped.tar.gz files-archive.tar
-rw-rw-r-- 1 packt packt   189 Mar  2 20:08 files-archive-gzipped.tar.gz
-rw-rw-r-- 1 packt packt 10240 Mar  2 20:04 files-archive.tar
```

Figure 2.29 – Compressing a tar archive using gzip

To uncompress a tar archive, you can use the `-x` option (shown at the beginning of this subsection). For example, let us uncompress the `files-archive.tar` file that we created earlier in this subsection, and also add a target directory for the uncompressed files to be added to by using the `-C` option. The target directory needs to be created beforehand. To do this, we will use the following commands:

```
mkdir uncompressed-directory
tar -xvf files-archive.tar -C uncompressed-directory
```

This will extract the files from the archive and add them to the uncompressed-directory directory. To uncompress a `gzip`-compressed archive, for example, `files-archive-gzipped.tar.gz`, we will add the `-z` option to the ones already used in the previous command, as shown in the following snippet:

```
tar -xvzf files-archive-gzipped.tar.gz -C uncompressed-directory
```

There you go, now you know how to archive and unarchive files in Linux. There are other useful archiving tools in Linux, but `tar` is still the most commonly used one. Feel free to explore the others or other useful options for `tar`.

Commands for locating files

Locating files in Linux is an essential task for any system administrator. As Linux systems contain vast numbers of files, finding files might be an intimidating task. Nevertheless, you have handy tools at your disposal, and knowing how to use them will be one of your greatest assets. Among these commands, we will discuss `locate`, `which`, `whereis`, and `find` in the following sections.

The locate command

The `locate` command is not installed by default on Ubuntu. To install it, use the following command to create an index of all the file locations on your system:

```
sudo apt install mlocate
```

Thus, when you execute the command, it searches for your file inside the database. It uses the `updatedb` command as its partner.

Before starting to use the locate command, you should execute `updatedb` to update the location database. After you do that, you can start locating files. In the following example, we will locate any file that has `new-report` in its name:

```
packt@neptune:~$ locate new-report
/home/packt/new-report
/home/packt/links/new-report
/home/packt/links/new-report-ln
packt@neptune:~$ 
```

Figure 2.30 – Using the locate command

If we were to search for a file with a more generic name, such as `presentation`, the output would be too long and irrelevant. Here is an example where we used output redirection to a file and the `wc` (word count) command to show only the number of lines, words, and bytes of the file to the standard output:

```
packt@neptune:~$ locate presentation > /home/packt/locate-search && wc /home/pac
kt/locate-search
   8    8 663 /home/packt/locate-search
packt@neptune:~$ cat locate-search
/usr/share/mime/application/vnd.ms-powerpoint.presentation.macroenabled.12.xml
/usr/share/mime/application/vnd.oasis.opendocument.presentation-flat-xml.xml
/usr/share/mime/application/vnd.oasis.opendocument.presentation-template.xml
/usr/share/mime/application/vnd.oasis.opendocument.presentation.xml
/usr/share/mime/application/vnd.openxmlformats-officedocument.presentationml.pre
sentation.xml
/usr/share/mime/application/vnd.openxmlformats-officedocument.presentationml.sli
de.xml
/usr/share/mime/application/vnd.openxmlformats-officedocument.presentationml.sli
deshow.xml
/usr/share/mime/application/vnd.openxmlformats-officedocument.presentationml.tem
plate.xml
```

Figure 2.31 – Using the locate command with output redirection and the wc command

In the preceding output, the resulting file has eight lines. This means that there were eight files located that have the string presentation in their name. The exact number is used for the words inside the file, as there are no spaces between the paths, so every line is detected as a single word. Also, the resulting file has 663 bytes. Feel free to experiment with other strings. For more options for the locate command, please refer to the Linux manual pages.

The which command

This command locates an executable file (program or command) in the shell's search path. For example, to locate the ls command, type the following:

```
packt@neptune:~$ which ls
/usr/bin/ls
```

You see that the output is the path of the ls command: /usr/bin/ls.

Now try it with the cd command:

```
which cd
```

You will see that there is no output. This is because the cd command is built inside the shell and has no other location for the command to show.

The whereis command

This command finds *only* executable files, documentation files, and source code files. Therefore, it might not find what you want, so use it with caution:

```
packt@neptune:~$ whereis ls
ls: /usr/bin/ls /usr/share/man/man1/ls.1.gz
packt@neptune:~$ whereis cd
cd:
packt@neptune:~$ ▯
```

Figure 2.32 – Using the whereis command

Once again, the output for the cd command shows nothing relevant, as it is a built-in shell command. As for the ls command, the output shows the location of the command itself and the location of the manual pages.

The find command

This command is one of the most powerful commands in Linux. It can search for files in directories and subdirectories based on certain criteria. It has more than 50 options. Its main drawback is the syntax, as it is somehow different from other Linux commands. The best way to learn how the find command works is by example. This is why we will show you a large number of examples using this command, hoping that you will become proficient in using it. To see its powerful options, please refer to the manual pages.

The following is a series of exercises using the find command, that we thought would be useful for you to know. We will provide the commands to use, but we will not provide you with all the resulting outputs, as some can be fairly long.

- Find, inside the root directory, all the files that have the e100 string in the name and print them to the standard output:

```
sudo find / -name e100 -print
```

- Find, inside the root directory, all the files that have the file string in their name and are of type file, and print the results to the standard output:

```
sudo find / -name file -type f -print
```

- Find all the files that have the print string in their name, by looking only inside the /opt, /usr, and /var directories:

```
sudo find /opt /usr /var -name print -type f -print
```

- Find all the files in the root directory that have the .conf extension:

```
sudo find / type f -name "*.conf"
```

- Find all the files in the root directory that have the file string in their name and no extension:

```
sudo find / -type f -name "file*.*"
```

- Find, in the root directory, all the files with the following extensions: .c, .sh, and .py, and add the list to a file named findfile:

```
sudo find / -type f \( -name "*.c" -o -name "*.sh" -o -name
"*.py" \) > findfile
```

- Find, in the root directory, all the files with the .c extension, sort them, and add them to a file:

```
sudo find / -type f -name "*.c" -print | sort > findfile2
```

- Find all the files in the root directory, with the permission set to 0664:

```
sudo find / -type f -perm 0664
```

- Find all the files in the root directory that are read-only (have read-only permission) for their owner:

```
sudo find / -type f -perm /u=r
```

- Find all the files in the root directory that are executable:

```
sudo find / -type f -perm /a=x
```

- Find all the files inside the root directory that were modified two days ago:

```
sudo find / -type f -mtime 2
```

- Find all the files in the root directory that have been accessed in the last two days:

```
sudo find / -type f -atime 2
```

- Find all the files that have been modified in the last two to five days:

```
sudo find / -type f -mtime +2 -mtime -5
```

- Find all the files that have been modified in the last 10 minutes:

```
sudo find / -type f -mmin -10
```

- Find all the files that have been created in the last 10 minutes:

```
sudo find / -type f -cmin -10
```

- Find all the files that have been accessed in the last 10 minutes:

```
sudo find / -type f -amin -10
```

- Find all the files that are 5 MB in size:

```
sudo find / -type f -size 5M
```

- Find all the files that have a size between 5 and 10 MB:

  ```
  sudo find / -type f -size +5M -size -10M
  ```

- Find all the empty files and empty directories:

  ```
  sudo find / -type f -empty
  sudo find / -type d -empty
  ```

- Find all the largest files in the /etc directory and print to the standard output the first five. Please take into account that this command could be very resource heavy. Do not try to do this for your entire root directory, as you might run out of system memory:

  ```
  sudo find /etc -type f -exec ls -l {} \; | sort -n -r | head -5
  ```

- Find the smallest first five files in /etc directory:

  ```
  sudo find /etc -type f -exec ls -s {} \; | sort -n | head -5
  ```

Feel free to experiment with as many types of find options as you want. The command is very permissive and powerful. Use it with caution.

Commands for text manipulation

Text manipulation is probably the best asset of Linux. It gives you a plethora of tools to work with text at the command line. Some of the more important and widely used ones are grep, tee, and the more powerful ones such as sed and awk. However, we will come back to those commands in *Chapter 8*, when we will show you how to create and use scripts. In this section, we will only give you a hint on how to use them on the command line.

The grep command

This is one of the most powerful commands in Linux. It is also an extremely useful one. It has the power to search for strings inside text files. It has many powerful options too:

- grep -v: Show the lines that are not according to the search criteria
- grep -l: Show only the filenames that match the criteria
- grep -L: Show only the lines that do *not* comply with the criteria
- grep -c: A counter that shows the number of lines matching the criteria
- grep -n: Show the line number where the string was found
- grep -i: Searches are case insensitive
- grep -r: Search recursively inside a directory structure

- `grep -R`: Search recursively inside a directory structure *AND* follow all symbolic links
- `grep -E`: Use extended regular expressions
- `grep -F`: Use a strict list of strings instead of regular expressions

Here are some examples of how to use the `grep` command:

- Find out the last time the `sudo` command was used:

  ```
  sudo grep sudo /var/log/auth.log
  ```

- Search for the `packt` string inside text files from the `/etc` directory:

  ```
  grep -R packt /etc
  ```

- Show the exact line where the match was found:

  ```
  grep -Rn packt /etc
  ```

- If you don't want to see the filename of each file where the match was found, use the `-h` option. Then, `grep` will only show you the lines where the match was found:

  ```
  grep -Rh packt /etc
  ```

- To show only the name of the file where the match was found, use `-l`:

  ```
  grep -Rl packt /etc
  ```

Most likely, `grep` will be used in combination with shell pipes. Here are some examples:

- If you want to see only the directories from your current working directory, you could pipe the `ls` command output to `grep`. In the following example, we listed only the lines that start with the letter d, which represent directories:

  ```
  ls -la | grep '^d'
  ```

- If you want to display the model of your CPU, you could use the following command:

  ```
  cat /proc/cpuinfo | grep -i 'Model'
  ```

You will find `grep` to be one of your closest friends as a Linux system administrator, so don't be afraid to dig deeper into its options and hidden gems.

The tee command

This command is very similar to the `cat` command. Basically, it does the same thing, by copying the standard input to standard output with no alteration, but it also copies that into one or more files.

In the following example, we use the `wc` command to count the number of lines inside the `/etc/passwd/` file. We pipe the output to the `tee` command using the `-a` option (append if the file already exists), which writes it to a new file called `no-users` and prints it to the standard output at the same time. We then use the `cat` command to double-check the contents of the new file:

```
packt@neptune:~$ wc -l /etc/passwd | tee no-users
34 /etc/passwd
packt@neptune:~$ cat no-users
34 /etc/passwd
packt@neptune:~$
```

Figure 2.33 – Using the tee command

The `tee` command is more of an underdog of file-manipulating commands. While it is quite powerful, its use can easily be overlooked. Nevertheless, we encourage you to use its powers as often as you can.

In the following section, we will show you how to use text editors from the command line in Linux.

Using text editors to create and edit files

Linux has several command-line text editors that you can use. There are **nano**, **Emacs**, and **Vim**, among others. Those are the most used ones. There are also **Pico**, **JOE**, and **ed** as text editors that are less frequently used than the aforementioned ones. We will cover Vim, as there is a very good chance that you will find it on any Linux system that you work with. Nevertheless, the current trend is to replace Vim with nano as the default text editor. Ubuntu, for example, does not have Vim installed by default, but CentOS does. Fedora is currently looking to make nano the default text editor. Therefore, you might want to learn nano, but for legacy purposes, Vim is a very useful tool to know.

Using Vim to edit text files

Vim is the improved version of **vi**, the default text editor from Unix. It is a very powerful editing tool. This power comes with many options that can be used to ease your work, and this can be overwhelming. In this sub-section, we will introduce you to the basic commands of the text editor, just enough to help you be comfortable using it.

Vim is a mode-based editor, as its operation is organized around different modes. In a nutshell, those modes are as follows:

- `command` mode is the default mode, waiting for a command
- `insert` mode is the text insert mode
- `replace` mode is the text replace mode
- `search` mode is the special mode for searching a document

Let's see how we can switch between these modes.

Switching between modes

When you first open Vim, you will be introduced to an empty editor that only shows information about the version used and a few help commands. You are in command mode. This means that Vim is waiting for a command to operate.

To activate insert mode, press *I* on your keyboard. You will be able to start inserting text at the current position of your cursor. You can also press *A* (for append) to start editing to the right of your cursor's position. Both *I* and *A* will activate insert mode. To exit the current mode, press the *Esc* key. It will get you back to command mode.

If you open a file that already has text in it, while in command mode, you can navigate the file using your arrow keys. As Vim inherited the vi workflow, you can also use *H* (to move left), *J* (to move down), *K* (to move up), and *L* (to move right). Those are legacy keys from a time when terminal keyboards did not have separate arrow keys.

While still in command mode (the default mode), you can activate replace mode by pressing *R* on your keyboard. You can replace the character that is right at the position of your cursor.

While in command mode, search mode is activated by pressing the / key. Once in your mode, you can start typing a search string and then press *Enter*.

There is also last line mode, or ex command mode. This mode is activated by pressing :. This is an extended mode where commands such as w for saving the file, q for quitting, or wq for saving and quitting at the same time.

Basic Vim commands

Working with Vim implies that you are comfortable with using keyboard shortcuts for using basic commands. We will guide you to the Vim documentation page (https://vimdoc.sourceforge.net/) for all the commands available, and we will give you a quick glimpse of the most useful ones in the following image:

key	action	key	action
yy	copy a block of text	^	move the cursor to the beginning of the line
p	paste the copied block	$	move the cursor to the end of the line
u	undo the last operation	gg	move the cursor to the beginning of the document
x	delete next character to the right of the cursor	G	move the cursor to the end of the document
X	delete preceding character (relative to the cursor)	:n	move the cursor to line number "n"
dd	delete entire line on which the cursor is positioned	i	insert before the cursor's position
h	move the cursor left	I	insert at the beginning of the line
l	move the cursor right	a	append at the right of the cursor
k	move the cursor up	A	append at the end of the line
j	move the cursor down	o	insert at the beginning of next line
w	move the cursor right, to the beginning ot the next word	/	activate "search" mode and look for strings
b	move the cursor left, to the beginning of the previous word	?	search backward from the cursor's position
n	show the next position of the searched string		
N	show the previous position of the searched string		
:wq	save changes and exit Vim		
:q!	enforce exit without saving		
:w!	enforce save without exiting		
ZZ	save and quit the file		
:w file	save as a new file called "file"		

Figure 2.34 – Basic Vim commands

Vim can be quite intimidating for newcomers to Linux. There is no shame if you prefer other editors, as there are plenty to choose from. Now, we will show you a glimpse of nano.

The nano text editor

Vim is a powerful text editor and knowing how to use it is an important thing for any system administrator. Nevertheless, other text editors are equally powerful and even easier to use.

This is the case with **nano**, which is installed by default in Ubuntu and Rocky Linux and can be used right out of the box in both Linux distributions. The default editor is not set up in the `.bashrc` file by using the `$EDITOR` variable. However, in Ubuntu, you can check the default editor on your system by using the following command:

```
packt@neptune:~$ sudo update-alternatives --config editor
There are 4 choices for the alternative editor (providing /usr/bin/editor).

  Selection    Path                Priority   Status
------------------------------------------------------------
* 0            /bin/nano            40        auto mode
  1            /bin/ed             -100       manual mode
  2            /bin/nano            40        manual mode
  3            /usr/bin/vim.basic   30        manual mode
  4            /usr/bin/vim.tiny    15        manual mode

Press <enter> to keep the current choice[*], or type selection number: []
```

Figure 2.35 – Checking the default text editor on Ubuntu

You can invoke the nano editor by using the `nano` command on Ubuntu/Debian and Fedora/ Rocky Linux or openSUSE. When you type the command, the nano editor will open, with a very straightforward interface that can be easier to use than Vim or Emacs for example. Feel free to use your preferred text editor.

Summary

In this chapter, you learned how to work with the most commonly used commands in Linux. You now know how to manage (create, delete, copy, and move) files, how the filesystem is organized, how to work with directories, and how to view file contents. You now understand the shell and basic permissions. The skills you have learned will help you manage files in any Linux distribution and edit text files. You have learned how to work with Vim, one of the most widely used command-line text editors in Linux. Those skills will help you to learn how to use other text editors such as nano and Emacs. You will use these skills in almost every chapter of this book, as well as in your everyday job as a system administrator.

In the next chapter, you will learn how to manage packages, including how to install, remove, and query packages in both Debian and Red Hat-based distributions. This skill is important for any administrator and must be part of any basic training.

Questions

In our second chapter, we covered the Linux filesystem and the basic commands that will serve as the foundation for the entire book. Here are some questions for you to test your knowledge and for further practice:

1. What is the command that creates a compressed archive with all the files inside the /etc directory that use the .conf extension?

    Hint: Use the `tar` command just as shown in this chapter.

2. What is the command that lists the first five files inside /etc and sorts them by dimension in descending order?

    Hint: Use `find` combined with `sort` and `head`.

3. What command creates a hierarchical directory structure?

    Hint: Use `mkdir` just as shown in this chapter.

4. What is the command that searches for files with three different extensions inside the root?

    Hint: Use the `find` command.

5. Find out which commands inside Linux have the **Set owner User ID (SUID)** set up.

    Hint: Use the `find` command with the `-perm` parameter.

6. Which command is used to create a file with 1,000 lines of randomly generated words (one word per line)?

    Hint: Use the shuf command (not shown in this chapter).

7. Perform the same exercise as before, but this time generate a file with 1,000 randomly generated numbers.

    Hint: Use a for loop.

8. How do you find out when sudo was last used and which commands were executed by it?

    Hint: Use the grep command.

Further reading

For more information about what was covered in this chapter, please refer to the following Packt titles:

- *Fundamentals of Linux*, by *Oliver Pelz*
- *Mastering Ubuntu Server – Fourth Edition*, by *Jay LaCroix*

3

Linux Software Management

Software management is an important aspect of Linux system administration because, at some level, you will have to work with software packages as a system administrator. Knowing how to work with software packages is an asset that you will master after finishing this chapter.

In this chapter, you will learn how to use specific software management commands, as well as learn how software packages work, depending on your distribution of choice. You will learn about the latest **Snap** and **Flatpak** package types and how to use them on modern Linux distributions.

In this chapter, we're going to cover the following main topics:

- Linux software package types
- Managing software packages
- Installing new desktop environments in Linux

Technical requirements

No special technical requirements are needed for this chapter, just a working installation of Linux on your system. **Ubuntu**, **Fedora** (or **AlmaLinux**), or **openSUSE** are equally suitable for this chapter's exercises as we will cover all types of package managers.

Linux software package types

As you've already learned by now, a Linux distribution comes packed with a kernel and applications on top of it. Although plenty of applications are already installed by default, there will certainly be occasions when you will need to install some new ones or remove ones that you don't need.

In Linux, applications come bundled into **repositories**. A repository is a centrally managed location that consists of software packages maintained by developers. These could contain individual applications or operating system-related files. Each Linux distribution comes with several official repositories, but on top of those, you can add some new ones. The way to add them is specific to each distribution, and we will get into more details later in this chapter.

Linux has several types of packages available. Ubuntu uses `deb` packages, as it is based on Debian, while Fedora (or Rocky Linux and AlmaLinux) uses `rpm` packages, as it is based on RHEL. There is also openSUSE, which uses `rpm` packages too, but it was based on Slackware at its inception. Besides those, two new package types have been recently introduced – the snap packages developed by Canonical, the company behind Ubuntu, and the flatpak packages, developed by a large community of developers and organizations, including GNOME, Red Hat, and Endless.

The DEB and RPM package types

DEB and RPM are the oldest types of packages and are used by Ubuntu and Fedora, respectively. They are still widely used, even though the two new types mentioned earlier (snaps and flatpaks) are starting to gain ground on Linux on desktops.

Both package types are compliant with the **Linux Standard Base** (**LSB**) specifications. The last iteration of LSB is version 5.0, released in 2015. You can find more information about it at `https://refspecs.linuxfoundation.org/lsb.shtml#PACKAGEFMT`.

The DEB package's anatomy

DEB was introduced with the Debian distribution back in 1993 and has been in use ever since on every Debian and Ubuntu derivative. A `deb` package is a binary package. This means that it contains the files of the program itself, as well as its dependencies and meta-information files, all contained inside an archive.

To check the contents of a binary `deb` package, you can use the `ar` command. It is not installed by default in Ubuntu 22.04.2 LTS, so you will have to install it yourself using the following command:

```
$ sudo apt install binutils
```

There you go – you have installed a package in Ubuntu! Now, once `ar` has been installed, you can check the contents of any `deb` package. For this exercise, we've downloaded the `deb` package of a password manager called **1password** and checked its contents. To query the package, perform the following steps:

1. Use the `wget` command; the file will be downloaded inside your current working directory:

    ```
    wget https://downloads.1password.com/linux/debian/amd64/
    stable/1password-latest.deb
    ```

2. After that, use the `ar t 1password-latest.deb` command to view the contents of the binary package. The `t` option will display a table of contents for the archive:

```
packt@neptune:~$ ar t 1password-latest.deb
debian-binary
control.tar.gz
data.tar.xz
_gpgorigin
packt@neptune:~$ ▌
```

Figure 3.1 – Using the ar command to view the contents of a deb file

As you can see, the output listed four files, from which two are archives. You can also investigate the package with the `ar` command.

3. Use the `ar x 1password-latest.deb` command to extract the contents of the package to your present working directory:

```
$ ar x 1password-latest.deb
```

4. Use the `ls` command to list the contents of your directory. You will see that the four files have been extracted and are ready to inspect. The `debian-binary` file is a text file that contains the version of the package file format, which in our case is 2.0. You can concatenate the file to verify your package with the help of the following command:

```
$ cat debian-binary
```

5. The `control.tar.gz` archive contains meta-information packages and scripts to be run during the installation or before and after, depending on the case. The `data.tar.xz` archive contains the executable files and libraries of the program that are going to be extracted during the installation. You can check the contents with the following command:

```
$ tar tJf data.tar.xz | head
```

6. The last file is a gpg signature file.

> **Important note**
> A gpg file is a file that uses the GNU Privacy Guard encryption. It uses an encryption standard known as OpenGPG (defined by the RFC4880 standard). It is usually used to sign package files as it offers a safe way for developers to distribute software. For more information on this matter, you can read the official documentation at `https://www.openpgp.org/`.

The following screenshot shows the outputs of these commands:

```
packt@neptune:~$ ls
1password-latest.deb  development              _gpgorigin       package-list
backup_dir1           dir1                     links            poem
control.tar.gz        files                    locate-search    poem-spaces
data.tar.xz           files-archive-gzipped.tar.gz  new-report   reports
debian-binary         files-archive.tar        no-users         users
packt@neptune:~$ cat debian-binary
2.0
packt@neptune:~$ tar tJf data.tar.xz | head
./
./usr/
./usr/share/
./usr/share/doc/
./usr/share/doc/1password/
./usr/share/doc/1password/changelog.gz
./usr/share/icons/
./usr/share/icons/hicolor/
./usr/share/icons/hicolor/128x128/
./usr/share/icons/hicolor/128x128/apps/
```

Figure 3.2 – The contents of a deb package

Meta-information for each package is a collection of files that are essential for the programs to run. They contain information about certain package prerequisites and all their dependencies, conflicts, and suggestions. Feel free to explore everything that a package is made of using just the packaging-related commands.

Now that we know what a Debian-based package consists of, let's look at the components of a Red Hat package.

The RPM packages anatomy

The **Red Hat Package Manager** (**RPM**) packages were developed by Red Hat and are used in Fedora, CentOS, RHEL, AlmaLinux, Rocky Linux, SUSE, and openSUSE. RPM binary packages are similar to DEB binary packages in that they are also packaged as an archive.

Let's test the rpm package of 1password, just as we did with the deb package in the previous section:

1. Download the rpm package using the following command:

    ```
    # wget https://downloads.1password.com/linux/rpm/stable/
    x86_64/1password-latest.rpm
    ```

If you want to use the same `ar` command, you will see that in the case of `rpm`s, the archiving tool will not recognize the file format. Nevertheless, there are other more powerful tools to use.

2. We will use the `rpm` command, the designated low-level package manager for rpms. We will use the `-q` (query), `-p` (package name), and `-l` (list) options:

```
# rpm -qpl 1password-latest.rpm
```

The output, contrary to the `deb` package, will be a list of all the files related to the application, along with their installation locations for your system.

3. To see the meta-information for the package, run the `rpm` command with the `-q`, `-p`, and `-i` (install) options. The following is a short excerpt from the command's output:

```
[packt@fedora ~]$ rpm -qpi 1password-latest.rpm
warning: 1password-latest.rpm: Header V4 RSA/SHA512 Signature, key ID 2012ea22:
NOKEY
Name        : 1password
Version     : 8.10.0
Release     : 1
Architecture: x86_64
Install Date: (not installed)
Group       : default
Size        : 374273045
License     : LicenseRef-1Password-Proprietary
Signature   : RSA/SHA512, Tue 14 Feb 2023 12:59:08 AM EET, Key ID ac2d62742012ea
22
```

Figure 3.3 – Meta-information of the rpm package

The output will contain information about the application's name, version, release, architecture, installation date, group, size, license, signature, source RPM, build date and host, URL, relocation, and summary.

4. To see which other dependencies the package will require at installation, you can run the same `rpm` command with the `-q`, `-p`, and `--requires` options:

```
$ rpm -qp --requires 1password-latest.rpm
```

The output is shown in the following screenshot:

```
[packt@fedora ~]$ rpm -qp --requires 1password-latest.rpm
warning: 1password-latest.rpm: Header V4 RSA/SHA512 Signature, key ID 2012ea22:
NOKEY
/bin/sh
/bin/sh
libasound.so.2()(64bit)
libatk-1.0.so.0()(64bit)
libatk-bridge-2.0.so.0()(64bit)
libdrm.so.2()(64bit)
libgbm.so.1()(64bit)
libgdk_pixbuf-2.0.so.0()(64bit)
libgtk-3.so.0()(64bit)
libnss3.so()(64bit)
libuuid.so.1()(64bit)
libxshmfence.so.1()(64bit)
rpmlib(CompressedFileNames) <= 3.0.4-1
rpmlib(PayloadFilesHavePrefix) <= 4.0-1
rpmlib(PayloadIsXz) <= 5.2-1
udev
```

Figure 3.4 – Package requirements

You now know what Debian and Red Hat packages are and what they contain. DEB and RPM packages are not the only types available on Linux. They are perhaps the most widely used and known, but there are also other types, depending on the distribution you choose. Also, as we stated earlier, there are new packages available for cross-platform Linux use. Those newer packages are called flatpaks and snaps, and we will detail them in the following section.

The snap and flatpak package types

Snap and **Flatpak** are relatively new package types, and they are considered to be the future of apps on Linux. They both build and run applications in isolated containers for more security and portability. Both have been created to overcome the need for desktop applications' ease of installation and portability.

Even though major Linux distributions have large application repositories, distributing software for so many types of Linux distributions, each with its own kind of package types, can become a serious issue for **independent software vendors (ISVs)** or community maintainers. This is where both snaps and flatpaks come to the rescue, aiming to reduce the weight of distributing software.

Let's consider that we are ISVs, aiming to develop our product on Linux. Once a new version of our software is available, we need to create at least two types of packages to be directly downloaded from our website – a .deb package for Debian/Ubuntu/Mint and other derivatives, and a .rpm package for Fedora/RHEL/SUSE and other derivatives.

But if we want to overcome this and make our app available cross-distribution for most of the existing Linux distributions, we can distribute it as a flatpak or snap. The flatpak package would be available through **Flathub**, the centralized flatpak repository, and the snap package would be available through the Snap Store, the centralized snap repository. Either one is equally suitable for our aim to distribute the app for all major Linux distributions with minimal resource consumption and centralized effort.

> **Important note**
>
> Both package types are trying to overcome the overall fragmentation of the Linux ecosystem when it comes to packages. However, these two packages have different philosophies, even though they want to solve the same problem. Snaps emerged as a new type of package that would be available on the IoT and server versions of Canonical's Ubuntu, while flatpaks emerged from the need to have a coherent package type for desktop applications in Linux. Thus, flatpaks are not available on server or IoT versions of Linux, only for desktop editions. As both packages evolve, more and more distributions are starting to provide them by default, with flatpak being the winner in terms of the number of distributions that are offering it by default. On the other hand, snaps are mostly available by default on official Ubuntu versions, starting with version 23.04. Flatpaks are available by default in Fedora, openSUSE, Pop!_OS, Linux Mint, KDE neon, and other distributions.

The takeaway from this situation is that the effort to distribute software for Linux is higher than in the case of the same app packaged for Windows or macOS. Hopefully, in the future, there will be only one universal package for distributing software for Linux, and this will all be for the better for both users and developers alike.

The snap package's anatomy

The snap file is a **SquashFS** file. This means that it has its own filesystem encapsulated in an immutable container. It has a very restrictive environment, with specific rules for isolation and confinement. Every snap file has a meta-information directory that stores files that control its behavior.

Snaps, as opposed to flatpaks, are used not only for desktop applications but also for a wider range of server and embedded apps. This is because Snap has its origins in the Ubuntu **Snappy** for IoT and phones, the distribution that emerged as the beacon of convergence effort from Canonical, Ubuntu's developer.

The flatpak package's anatomy

Flatpak is based on a technology called **OSTree**. The technology was started by developers from GNOME and Red Hat, and it is now heavily used in Fedora Silverblue in the form of **rpm-ostree**. It is a new upgrade system for Linux that is meant to work alongside existing package management systems. It was inspired by Git since it operates similarly. Consider it as a version control system at the OS level. It uses a content-addressed object store, allows you to share branches, and offers transactional upgrades, as well as rollback and snapshot options, for the OS.

Currently, the project has changed its name to **libostree** for a smooth focus on projects that already use the technology. Among many projects that use it, we will bring just two into the discussion: flatpak and rpm-ostree. The rpm-ostree project is considered to be a next-generation hybrid package system for distributions such as Fedora and CentOS/RHEL. They are based on the Atomic project developed by Fedora and Red Hat teams, which brings immutable infrastructure for servers and desktops alike. The openSUSE developers had a similar technology developed called Snapper, which was an OS snapshot tool for its `btrfs` filesystems.

Flatpak uses libostree, which is similar to rpm-ostree, but it is solely used for desktop application containers, with no bootloader management. Flatpak uses sandboxing based on another project named **Bubblewrap**, which allows unprivileged users to access user namespaces and use container features.

Both snaps and flatpaks have full support for graphical installations but also have commands for easier installations and setup from the shell. In the following sections, we will focus solely on command operations for all package types.

Managing software packages

Each distribution has its own **package manager**. There are two types of package managers for each distribution – one for low-level and one for high-level package management. For an RPM-based distribution such as CentOS or Fedora, the low-level tool is the `rpm` command, while the high-level tools are the `yum` and `dnf` commands. For openSUSE, another major RPM-based distribution, the low-level tool is the same `rpm` command, but in terms of high-level tools, the `zypper` command is used. For DEB-based distributions, the low-level command is `dpkg` and the high-level command is `apt` (or the now deprecated `apt-get`).

What is the difference between low-level and high-level package managers in Linux? The low-level package managers are responsible for the backend of any package manipulation and are capable of unpacking packages, running scripts, and installing apps. The high-end managers are responsible for dependency resolution, installing and downloading packages (and groups of packages), and metadata searching.

Managing DEB packages

Usually, for any distribution, package management is handled by the administrator or by a user with root privileges (`sudo`). Package management implies any type of package manipulation, such as installation, search, download, and removal. For all these types of operations, there are specific Linux commands, and we will show you how to use them in the following sections.

The main repositories of Ubuntu and Debian

Ubuntu's official repositories consist of about 60,000 packages, which take the form of binary `.deb` packages or snap packages. The configuration of the system repositories is stored in one file, the `/etc/apt/sources.list` file. Ubuntu has four main repositories, also called package sources, and you will see them detailed inside the `sources.list` file. These repositories are as follows:

- `Main`: Contains free and open source software supported by Canonical
- `Universe`: Contains free and open source software supported by the community
- `Restricted`: Contains proprietary software
- `Multiverse`: Contains software restricted by copyright

All the repositories are enabled by default in the `sources.list` file. If you would like to disable some of them, feel free to edit the file accordingly.

In Debian, the repository information is stored in the same `/etc/apt/sources.list` file. The only difference is that it uses different names for the main package sources, as follows:

- `main`: Contains software that is compliant with Debian's free software guidelines
- `contrib`: Software that can, or not, be compliant with free software guidelines but is not part of the main distribution
- `non-free`: Software that is not open source and is not compliant with free software guidelines

Debian's and Ubuntu's source files are very similar as they have the same information structure inside. What is different is the parts that are specific to each distribution's package source.

Both are based on Debian's **advanced package tool** (**APT**), so we will detail it in the following section.

APT-related commands

Until four years ago, packages in any Debian-based distribution were implemented using the `apt-get` command. Since then, a new and improved command called `apt` (derived from the abbreviation **APT**) is used as the high-level package manager. The new command is more streamlined and better structured than `apt-get`, thus offering a more integrated experience.

Before doing any kind of work with the `apt` command, you should update the list of all available packages in your repositories. You can do this with the following command:

```
$ sudo apt update
```

The output of the preceding command will show you if any updates are available. The number of packages that require updates will be shown, together with a command that you could run if you want more details about them.

Before going any further, we encourage you to use the apt --help command as this will show you the most commonly used APT-related commands. The output is shown in the following screenshot:

```
Most used commands:
  list - list packages based on package names
  search - search in package descriptions
  show - show package details
  install - install packages
  reinstall - reinstall packages
  remove - remove packages
  autoremove - Remove automatically all unused packages
  update - update list of available packages
  upgrade - upgrade the system by installing/upgrading packages
  full-upgrade - upgrade the system by removing/installing/upgrading packages
  edit-sources - edit the source information file
  satisfy - satisfy dependency strings
```

Figure 3.5 – The most commonly used apt commands

Let's dive into some of these in more detail.

Installing and removing packages

Basic system administration tasks include installing and removing packages. In this section, we will show you how to install and remove packages using the apt command.

To install a new package, you can use the apt install command. We used this command at the beginning of this chapter when we talked about the DEB package's anatomy. Remember that we had to install the ar command as an alternative to inspect .deb packages. Back then, we used the following command:

```
$ sudo apt install binutils
```

This command installed several packages on the system and among them the one that we need to fulfill our action. The apt command automatically installs any requisite dependencies too.

To remove a package, you can use the apt remove or apt purge command. The first one removes the installed packages and all their dependencies installed by the apt install command. The latter will uninstall the packages, just like apt remove, but also deletes any configuration files created by the applications.

In the following example, we are removing the binutils applications we installed previously using the apt remove command:

```
$ sudo apt remove binutils
```

The output will show you a list of packages that are no longer needed and remove them from the system, asking for your confirmation to continue. This is a very good safety measure as it allows you to review the files that are going to be deleted. If you feel confident about the operation, you can add a -y parameter at the end of the command, which tells the shell that the answer to any question provided by the command will automatically be *Yes*.

However, using apt remove will not remove all the configuration files related to the removed application. To see which files are still on your system, you can use the find command. For example, to see the files related to the binutils package that were not removed, we can use the following command:

```
sudo find / -type d -name *binutils 2>/dev/null
```

The output will show the directories (hence the -type d option that was used with the command), where binutils-related files remain after the removal of the package.

Another tool that's used to remove packages and all the configuration files associated with them is apt purge. If you want to use the apt purge command instead of apt remove, you can use it as follows:

```
$ sudo apt purge binutils
```

The output is similar to the apt remove command, showing you which packages will be removed and how much space will be freed on the disk, and asking for your confirmation to continue the operation.

> **Important note**
> If you plan on using apt purge to remove the same package (in our case, binutils), you will have to install it again as it was removed using the apt remove command.

The apt remove command has a purge option too, which has the same outcome as the apt purge command. The syntax is as follows:

```
sudo apt remove --purge [packagename]
```

As stated earlier, when using the apt remove command, some configuration files are left behind in case the operation was an accident and the user wants to revert to the previous configuration. The files that are not deleted by the remove command are small user configuration files that can easily be restored. If the operation was not an accident and you still want to get rid of all the files, you can still use the apt purge command to do that by using the same name as those of the already removed packages.

Upgrading the system

Now and then, you will need to perform a system upgrade to ensure that you have all the latest security updates and patches installed. In Ubuntu and Debian, you will always use two different commands to accomplish this. One is `apt update`, which will update the repository list and makes sure it has all the information concerning the updates that are available for the system. The other command is `apt upgrade`, which upgrades the packages. You can use them both in the same command using metacharacters:

```
$ sudo apt update; sudo apt upgrade
```

The `update` command will sometimes show you which packages are no longer required, with a message similar to the following:

```
The following packages were automatically installed and are no longer
required:
  libfprint-2-tod1 libllvm9
Use 'sudo apt autoremove' to remove them.
```

You can use the `sudo apt autoremove` command to remove the unneeded packages after you perform the upgrade. The `autoremove` command's output will show you which packages will be removed and how much space will be freed on the disk and will ask for your approval to continue the operation.

Let's say that during our work with Ubuntu, a new distribution is released, and we would like to use that as it has newer packages of the software we use. Using the command line, we can make a full distribution upgrade. The command for this action is as follows:

```
$ sudo apt dist-upgrade
```

Similarly, we can also use the following command:

```
$ sudo apt full-upgrade
```

Upgrading to a newer distribution version should be a flawless process, but this is not always a guarantee. It all depends on your custom configurations. No matter the situation, we advise you to do a full system backup before upgrading to a new version.

Managing package information

Working with packages sometimes implies the use of information-gathering tools. Simply installing and removing packages is not enough. You will need to search for certain packages to show details about them, create lists based on specific criteria, and so on.

To search for a specific package, you can use the apt search command. It will list all the packages that have the searched string in their name, as well as others that use the string in various ways. For example, let's search for the nmap package:

```
$ sudo apt search nmap
```

The output will show a considerably long list of packages that use the nmap string in various ways. You will still have to scroll up and down the list to find the package you want. For better results, you can pipe the output to the grep command, but you will notice a warning, similar to the one shown in the following screenshot:

```
packt@neptune:~$ sudo apt search nmap | grep nmap
[sudo] password for packt:

WARNING: apt does not have a stable CLI interface. Use with caution in scripts.

  IPv4 address parser for the nmap format
libcoq-mathcomp-finmap/jammy 1.5.1-1 amd64
libnmap-parser-perl/jammy 1.37-1 all
  module to parse nmap scan results with perl
librust-cpp-synmap-dev/jammy 0.3.0-1 amd64
  Library for doing location lookup based on free openwlanmap.org data
  Library for doing location lookup based on free openwlanmap.org data
nmap/jammy-updates 7.91+dfsg1+really7.80+dfsg1-2ubuntu0.1 amd64
nmap-common/jammy-updates 7.91+dfsg1+really7.80+dfsg1-2ubuntu0.1 all
  Architecture independent files for nmap
nmapsi4/jammy 0.5~alpha2-3 amd64
  graphical interface to nmap, the network scanner
python-libnmap-doc/jammy 0.7.2-1 all
python3-libnmap/jammy 0.7.2-1 all
python3-nmap/jammy 0.6.1-1.1 all
```

Figure 3.6 – Output of the apt search command

Following the warning, the output shows a short list of packages that contain the nmap string, and among them is the actual package we are looking for, as highlighted in *Figure 3.5*.

To overcome that warning, you can use a legacy command called apt-cache search. By running it, you will get a list of packages as output, but it won't be as detailed as the output of the apt search command:

```
packt@neptune:~$ sudo apt-cache search nmap | grep nmap
golang-github-malfunkt-iprange-dev - IPv4 address parser for the nmap format
libcoq-mathcomp-finmap - finite sets and maps extension for Mathematical Compone
nts
libnmap-parser-perl - module to parse nmap scan results with perl
librust-cpp-synmap-dev - Sourcemap and full crate parsing support for `cpp_syn`
- Rust source code
libwlocate-dev - Library for doing location lookup based on free openwlanmap.org
 data
libwlocate0 - Library for doing location lookup based on free openwlanmap.org da
ta
nmap - The Network Mapper
nmap-common - Architecture independent files for nmap
nmapsi4 - graphical interface to nmap, the network scanner
```

Figure 3.7 – The output of the apt-cache command

Now that we know that the nmap package exists in Ubuntu repositories, we can investigate it further by showing more details using the apt show command:

```
$ apt show nmap
```

The output will show a detailed description, including the package's name, version, priority, origin and section, maintainer, size, dependencies, suggested extra packages, download size, APT sources, and description.

apt also has a useful list command, which can list packages based on certain criteria. For example, if we use the apt list command alone, it will list all the packages available. But if we use different options, the output will be personalized.

To show the installed packages, we can use the -- installed option:

```
$ sudo apt list --installed
```

To list all the packages, use the following command:

```
$ sudo apt list
```

For comparative reasons, we will redirect each output to a different file, and then compare the two files. This is an easier task to do to see the differences between the two outputs since the lists are reasonably large. We will now run the specific commands, as follows:

```
$ sudo apt list --installed > list-installed
$ sudo apt list > list
```

You can compare the two resulting files by using the ls -la command and observe the difference in size. You will see that the list file will be significantly larger than the list-installed file.

There are other ways in which to compare the two outputs, and we would like to let you discover them by yourself, as an exercise for this sub-section. Feel free to use any other APT-related commands you would like, and practice with them enough to get familiar with their use. APT is a powerful tool, and every system administrator needs to know how to use it to sustain a usable and well-maintained Linux system. Usability is closely related to the apps that are used and their system-wide optimization.

Managing RPM packages

RPM packages are the equivalent packages for Linux distributions such as Fedora, AlmaLinux, Rocky Linux, RHEL, and openSUSE/SLES. They have dedicated high-level tools, including dnf, yum, and zypper. The low-level tool is the rpm command.

In RHEL, the default package manager is **Yellow Dog Updater, Modified (YUM)** and it is based on **Dandified YUM (DNF)**, the default package manager in Fedora. If you use both Fedora and RHEL, for ease of use, you can use only one of those as they are the same command. For consistency, we will use YUM for all the examples in this chapter.

YUM is the default high-level manager. It can install, remove, update, and package queries, as well as resolve dependencies. YUM can manage packages installed from repositories or local .rpm packages.

The main repositories in Fedora/RHEL-based distributions

Repositories are all managed from the /etc/yum.repos.d/ directory, with configuration available inside the /etc/yum.conf file. If you do a listing for the repos directory, the output will be similar to the following screenshot:

```
[packt@venus ~]$ ls -l /etc/yum.repos.d/
total 44
-rw-r--r--. 1 root root 1019 Nov 15 09:42 almalinux-appstream.repo
-rw-r--r--. 1 root root  983 Nov 15 09:42 almalinux-baseos.repo
-rw-r--r--. 1 root root  947 Nov 15 09:42 almalinux-crb.repo
-rw-r--r--. 1 root root  983 Nov 15 09:42 almalinux-extras.repo
-rw-r--r--. 1 root root 1103 Nov 15 09:42 almalinux-highavailability.repo
-rw-r--r--. 1 root root  947 Nov 15 09:42 almalinux-nfv.repo
-rw-r--r--. 1 root root  959 Nov 15 09:42 almalinux-plus.repo
-rw-r--r--. 1 root root 1103 Nov 15 09:42 almalinux-resilientstorage.repo
-rw-r--r--. 1 root root  935 Nov 15 09:42 almalinux-rt.repo
-rw-r--r--. 1 root root  995 Nov 15 09:42 almalinux-saphana.repo
-rw-r--r--. 1 root root  947 Nov 15 09:42 almalinux-sap.repo
[packt@venus ~]$
```

Figure 3.8 – RHEL derivative repositories

All these files listed contain vital information about the repository, such as its name, mirror list, the gpg key's location, and enabled status. All the ones listed are official repositories.

YUM-related commands

YUM has many commands and options, but the most commonly used ones are related to package installation, removal, search, information query, system update, and repository listing.

Installing and removing packages

To install a package from a repository in AlmaLinux/Rocky Linux (or Fedora), simply run the `yum install` command. In the following example, we will install the GIMP application from the command line:

```
$ sudo yum install gimp
```

If you already have a package downloaded and would like to install it, you can use the `yum localinstall` command. Here, we have downloaded the 1password `.rpm` package:

```
wget https://downloads.1password.com/linux/rpm/stable/
x86_64/1password-latest.rpm
```

Then, we installed it with the following command:

```
sudo yum localinstall 1password-latest.rpm
```

The `localinstall` command automatically resolves the dependencies needed and shows the source (repository) for each of them.

This is a very powerful command that makes using the `rpm` command itself almost redundant in some cases. The main difference between the `yum install` and `yum localinstall` commands is that the latter is capable of solving dependencies for locally downloaded packages. While the former looks for packages inside the active repositories, the latter looks for packages to install in the current working directory.

To remove a package from the system, use the `yum remove` command. We will remove the newly installed 1password package:

```
sudo yum remove 1password.x86_64
```

You will be asked if you want to remove all the packages that the application installed. Choose accordingly and proceed.

> **Important note**
> The default action for pressing the *Enter* or *Return* key while inside a command dialogue in Fedora or RHEL derivatives is *N* (for no, or negative), while in Ubuntu, the default action is set to *Y* (for yes). This is a precautionary safety measure, which requires your extra attention and intervention.

The output, very similar to the output of the installation command, will show you which packages and dependencies will be removed if you proceed with the command.

As you can see, all the dependencies installed with the package using the `yum localinstall` command will be removed using the `yum remove` command. If you're asked to proceed, type `y` and continue with the operation.

Updating the system

To upgrade a Fedora/RHEL-based system, we can use the `yum upgrade` command. There is also a `yum update` command, which has the same effect by updating the installed packages:

```
$ sudo yum upgrade
```

You can use the `-y` option to automatically respond to the command's questions.

There is also an `upgrade-minimal` command, which installs only the newest security updates for packages.

Managing package information

Managing files with `yum` is very similar to managing files with `apt`. There are plenty of commands to use, and we will detail some of them – the ones we consider to be the most commonly used. To find out more about those commands and their use, run `yum --help`.

To see an overview of the `yum` command history and which package was managed, use the following command:

```
$ sudo yum history
```

This will give you an output that shows every `yum` command that was run, how many packages were altered, and the time and date when the actions were executed, as in the following example:

```
[packt@venus ~]$ sudo yum history
ID     | Command line              | Date and time    | Action(s)  | Altered
-------------------------------------------------------------------------------
     4 | remove 1password.x86_64   | 2023-03-05 10:32 | Removed    |   118 EE
     3 | localinstall 1password-la | 2023-03-05 10:31 | Install    |   118 EE
     2 | update -y                 | 2023-03-03 21:53 | I, U       |   106  <
     1 |                           | 2023-03-03 21:38 | Install    |   604 >E
[packt@venus ~]$
```

Figure 3.9 – Using the yum history command

To show details about a certain package, we have the `yum info` command. We will query the `nmap` package, similar to what we did in Ubuntu. In CentOS, the command will be as follows:

```
Available Packages
Name         : nmap
Epoch        : 3
Version      : 7.91
Release      : 10.el9
Architecture : x86_64
Size         : 5.4 M
Source       : nmap-7.91-10.el9.src.rpm
Repository   : appstream
Summary      : Network exploration tool and security scanner
URL          : http://nmap.org/
License      : Nmap
Description  : Nmap is a utility for network exploration or security auditing.
             : It supports ping scanning (determine which hosts are up), many
             : port scanning techniques (determine what services the hosts are
             : offering), and TCP/IP fingerprinting (remote host operating
             : system identification). Nmap also offers flexible target and port
```

Figure 3.10 – Using the yum info command

The output will show you the name, version, release, source, repository, and description, very similar to what we saw with the `.deb` packages.

To list all the installed packages or all the packages for that matter, we can use the `yum list` command:

```
# yum list
```

To see only the installed packages, run the following command:

```
# yum list installed
```

If we redirect the output of each command to specific files and then compare the two files, we will see the differences between them, similar to what we did in Ubuntu. The output shows the name of the packages, followed by the version and release number, and the repository from which it was installed. Here is a short excerpt:

```
xml-common.noarch        0.6.3-58.el9            @AppStream
xz.x86_64                5.2.5-8.el9_0           @anaconda
xz-libs.x86_64           5.2.5-8.el9_0           @anaconda
yajl.x86_64              2.1.0-21.el9_0          @AppStream
yum.noarch               4.12.0-4.el9.alma       @anaconda
zip.x86_64               3.0-33.el9              @anaconda
zlib.x86_64              1.2.11-35.el9_1         @baseos
```

Figure 3.11 – Excerpt of the yum list installed command

As we have covered the most commonly used commands for both DEB and RPM files, we did not cover a specific package manager for openSUSE and SUSE SLE called **Zypper**. We will quickly show you some commands to get you acquainted with Zypper and let you give openSUSE a try next.

Working with Zypper

In the case of openSUSE, **Zypper** is the package manager, similar to APT and DNF from Debian/Ubuntu and Fedora/RHEL. The following sections cover some useful commands.

Installing and removing packages

Similar to using APT and DNF, the Zypper package manager in openSUSE is used to install and remove packages using almost the same syntax. For example, we will install nmap using the zypper command. But first, let's search for the name in the respective repositories to see if it exists. We will use the following command:

```
sudo zypper search nmap
```

The output of this command is a list of packages containing the nmap string in their name, together with the type and a summary:

```
packt@localhost:~> sudo zypper search nmap
[sudo] password for root:
Loading repository data...
Reading installed packages...

S | Name                             | Summary                          | Type
--+---------------------------------+---------------------------------+--------
  | nmap                             | Network exploration tool and->  | package
  | nmap-parse-output                | A tool for analyzing Nmap sc->  | package
  | nmap-parse-output-bash-completion | Bash Completion for nmap-par-> | package
  | nmapsi4                          | A Graphical Front-End for Nmap  | package
  | python3-chainmap                 | Backport/clone of ChainMap f->  | package
  | python3-dragonmapper             | Identification and conversio->  | package
packt@localhost:~> ▯
```

Figure 3.12 – Using the zypper search command in openSUSE

You will notice S in the first column of the list. It consists of the status of the package, and the output will be different if the package was already installed.

From the search output, we can see that the name of the package for the Nmap application is nmap (it could have been a different name, hence why we used the search command in the first place), so we will proceed and install it on our system. We will use the zypper install command to do so.

> **Important note**
>
> In openSUSE, you can use short versions of the command. For example, instead of using `zypper install`, you can use `zypper in`, followed by the name of the package you want to install. The same goes for `zypper update`, which can be used as `zypper up`, and also for `dist-upgrade`, where you can use `dup`. Alternatively, you can use the `zypper remove` command as `zypper rm`. Check the manual pages for more information.

So, here is the command to install the nmap package:

```
sudo zypper install nmap
```

Alternatively, you can use the following command:

```
sudo zypper in nmap
```

You can see the output in the following screenshot:

```
packt@localhost:~> sudo zypper in nmap
Loading repository data...
Reading installed packages...
Resolving package dependencies...

The following 3 NEW packages are going to be installed:
  libpcap1 libssh2-1 nmap

3 new packages to install.
Overall download size: 5.6 MiB. Already cached: 0 B. After the operation,
additional 24.4 MiB will be used.
Continue? [y/n/v/...? shows all options] (y):
```

Figure 3.13 – Using the zypper in command

The output shows which packages will be installed. What is important to notice here is that Zypper is automatically dealing with dependencies, just like other package managers. Besides nmap, there are two more library packages ready to be installed. Type y to continue the installation and the packages will be installed.

Now, let's use the `zypper search nmap` command one more time to see how the list has changed when it comes to showing the package information about nmap:

```
S  | Name                             | Summary                        | Type
---+----------------------------------+--------------------------------+--------
i+ | nmap                             | Network exploration tool an-> | package
   | nmap-parse-output                | A tool for analyzing Nmap s-> | package
   | nmap-parse-output-bash-completion | Bash Completion for nmap-pa-> | package
   | nmapsi4                          | A Graphical Front-End for N-> | package
   | python3-chainmap                 | Backport/clone of ChainMap -> | package
   | python3-dragonmapper             | Identification and conversi-> | package
```

Figure 3.14 – Checking the status of nmap with zypper search

In the output, you will see that the first column of the list has `i+` in front of the `nmap` package we just installed. This means that the package and its dependencies are already installed. So, if you are searching for some package and it is already installed, you will know this by checking the first column of the list, which is the status column.

Now, let's remove the same package we already installed. We will use the following command:

```
sudo zypper remove nmap
```

Alternatively, we can use the following command:

```
sudo zypper rm nmap
```

The output is shown in the following screenshot:

```
packt@localhost:~> sudo zypper rm nmap
Reading installed packages...
Resolving package dependencies...

The following package is going to be REMOVED:
  nmap

1 package to remove.
After the operation, 23.8 MiB will be freed.
Continue? [y/n/v/...? shows all options] (y): 
```

Figure 3.15 – Using the zypper remove command

The output of this command shows which packages are going to be removed. As you can see, only the `nmap` package will be removed; the other dependencies installed that were alongside won't be removed. To remove them together with the package, use the `--clean-deps` argument when using the command. Details are shown in the following screenshot:

```
packt@localhost:~> sudo zypper rm --clean-deps nmap
Reading installed packages...
Resolving package dependencies...

The following 3 packages are going to be REMOVED:
  libpcap1 libssh2-1 nmap

3 packages to remove.
After the operation, 24.4 MiB will be freed.
Continue? [y/n/v/...? shows all options] (y): █
```

Figure 3.16 – Removing dependencies

Now that you've learned how to use `zypper` to install and remove packages in openSUSE, let's learn how to use it to update or upgrade the entire system.

Upgrading and updating the system

Before updating a system, you might want to see which updates are available. For this, you can use the following command:

```
zypper list-updates
```

The output of this command will show all the updates available on your system. To install the updates, use the following command:

```
sudo zypper update
```

An alternative is the following command:

```
sudo zypper up
```

If you use these commands with no parameters, as we just showed, all the available updates will be installed. You can also update individual packages by including the package name as a parameter for the `update` command.

Some more useful commands in openSUSE are used for adding and managing locks to a package if we don't want it to be updated or removed. Let's learn how to do this using the same nmap package. If you removed it as we did in the previous section, please install it again. We will add a lock, check for that lock, and then remove the lock for the package.

To add a lock to a package, use the `add-lock` or `zypper al` command. To see the locked packages on your system, you can use the `zypper ll` command (list locks); to remove a lock from a package, you can use the `zypper rl` command (remove locks):

```
packt@localhost:~> sudo zypper al nmap
Specified lock has been successfully added.
packt@localhost:~> sudo zypper ll

# | Name | Type    | Repository | Comment
--+------+---------+------------+--------
1 | nmap | package | (any)      |

packt@localhost:~> sudo zypper rl nmap
1 lock has been successfully removed.
```

Figure 3.17 – Adding and removing locks to and from packages with Zypper

Now, let's lock the nmap package again and try to remove it. You will see that the package will not be removed. First, you will be asked what to do to remove it. Details are shown in the following figure:

```
packt@localhost:~> sudo zypper al nmap
packt@localhost:~> sudo zypper remove nmap
Reading installed packages...
Resolving package dependencies...

Problem: conflicting requests
 Solution 1: remove lock to allow removal of nmap-7.92-150400.1.8.x86_64
 Solution 2: do not ask to delete all solvables providing nmap.x86_64 = 7.92-150
400.1.8

Choose from above solutions by number or cancel [1/2/c/d/?] (c): █
```

Figure 3.18 – Trying to remove a locked package

Updating is straightforward, and you also learned how to use the lock option in Zypper to protect different packages. Now that you know how to update your openSUSE system, we'll learn how we can find information about certain packages in the following section.

Managing package information

As shown when using the APT and DNF package managers in Ubuntu and Fedora, we can use Zypper in openSUSE to obtain information about packages. Let's use the same nmap package as in the previous section and obtain more information about it. To do this, we will use the zypper info command:

```
sudo zypper info nmap
```

As shown in *Figure 3.19*, the information provided is similar to that in Ubuntu and RHEL-based distributions. As we uninstalled the nmap package, the information shown in the output will state that the package is not installed. There is also a longer description for the package, which we did not include in the following screenshot:

```
-----------------------------
Repository      : Main Repository
Name            : nmap
Version         : 7.92-150400.1.8
Arch            : x86_64
Vendor          : SUSE LLC <https://www.suse.com/>
Installed Size  : 23.8 MiB
Installed       : No
Status          : not installed
Source package  : nmap-7.92-150400.1.8.src
Upstream URL    : https://nmap.org/
Summary         : Network exploration tool and security scanner
Description     :
```

Figure 3.19 – Using the zypper info command

Now, let's learn how to manage flatpaks and snaps on a Linux machine.

Using the snap and flatpak packages

Snaps and flatpaks are relatively new package types that are used in various Linux distributions. In this section, we will show you how to manage those types of packages. For snaps, we will use Ubuntu as our test distribution, while for flatpaks, we will use Fedora, even though, with a little bit of work, both package types can work on either distribution.

Managing snap packages on Ubuntu

Snap is installed by default in Ubuntu 22.04.2 LTS. Therefore, you don't have to do anything to install it. Simply start searching for the package you want and install it on your system. We will use the Slack application to show you how to work with snaps.

Searching for snaps

Slack is available in the Snap Store, so you can install it. To make sure, you can search for it using the snap find command, as in the following example:

```
$ snap find "slack"
```

In the command's output, you will see many more packages that contain the slack string or are related to the Slack application, but only the first on the list is the one we are looking for.

> **Important note**
> In any Linux distribution, two apps originating from different packages and installed with different package managers can coexist. For example, Slack can be installed using the `deb` file provided by the website, as well as the one installed from the Snap Store.

If the output says that the package is available, we can proceed and install it on our system.

Installing a snap package

To install the `snap` package for Slack, we can use the `snap install` command:

```
packt@neptune:~$ sudo snap install slack
[sudo] password for packt:
slack 4.29.149 from Slack installed
packt@neptune:~$
```

Figure 3.20 – Installing the Slack snap package

Next, let's see how we can find out more about the `snap` package we just installed.

Snap package information

If you want to find out more about the package, you can use the `snap info` command:

```
$ snap info slack
```

The output will show you relevant information about the package, including its name, summary, publisher, description, and ID. The last piece of information that's displayed will be about the available **channels**, which are as follows in the case of our Slack package:

```
commands:
  - slack
snap-id:      JUJH91Ved74jd4ZgJCpzMBtYbPOzTlsD
tracking:     latest/stable
refresh-date: today at 08:46 UTC
channels:
  latest/stable:      4.29.149 2022-11-28 (68) 121MB -
  latest/candidate:   ↑
  latest/beta:        ↑
  latest/edge:        ↑
  insider/stable:     -
  insider/candidate:  -
  insider/beta:       -
  insider/edge:       4.25.1   2022-04-01 (61) 108MB -
installed:            4.29.149          (68) 121MB -
```

Figure 3.21 – Snap channels shown for the Slack app

Each channel contains information about a specific version and it is important to know which one to choose. By default, the stable channel will be chosen by the `install` command, but if you would like a different version, you could use the `--channel` option during installation. In the preceding example, we used the default option.

Displaying installed snap packages

If you want to see a list of the installed snaps on your system, you can use the `snap list` command. Even though we only installed Slack on the system, in the output, you will see that many more apps have been installed. Some, such as `core` and `snapd`, are installed by default from the distribution's installation and are required by the system:

```
packt@neptune:~$ snap list
Name                Version        Rev    Tracking        Publisher   Notes
bare                1.0            5      latest/stable   canonical   base
core18              20230207       2697   latest/stable   canonical   base
core20              20230126       1822   latest/stable   canonical   base
gnome-3-34-1804     0+git.3556cb3  77     latest/stable   canonical   -
gtk-common-themes   0.1-81-g442e511 1535  latest/stable   canonical   -
lxd                 5.0.2-838e1b2  24322  5.0/stable/…    canonical   -
slack               4.29.149       68     latest/stable   slack       -
snapd               2.58.2         18357  latest/stable   canonical   snapd
```

Figure 3.22 – Output of the snap list command

Now, we'll learn how to update a snap package.

Updating a snap package

Snaps are automatically updated. Therefore, you won't have to do anything yourself. The least you can do is check whether an update is available and speed up its installation using the `snap refresh` command, as follows:

```
$ sudo snap refresh slack
```

Following an update, if you want to go back to a previously used version of the app, you can use the `snap revert` command, as in the following example:

```
$ sudo snap revert slack
```

In the next section, we'll learn how to enable and disable snap packages.

Enabling or disabling snap packages

If we decide to not use an application temporarily, we can disable that app using the `snap disable` command. If we decide to reuse the app, we can enable it again using the `snap enable` command:

```
packt@neptune:~$ snap disable slack
error: access denied (try with sudo)
packt@neptune:~$ sudo snap disable slack
slack disabled
packt@neptune:~$ sudo snap enable slack
slack enabled
packt@neptune:~$ ▌
```

Figure 3.23 – Enabling and disabling a snap app

Remember to use sudo to enable and disable a snap application. If disabling is not what you are looking for, you can completely remove the snap.

Removing a snap package

When removing a snap application, the associated configuration files, users, and data are also removed. You can use the snap remove command to do this, as in the following example:

```
$ sudo snap remove slack
```

After removal, an application's internal user, configuration, and system data are saved and retained for 31 days. These files are called snapshots, they are archived and saved under /var/lib/snapd/ snapshots, and they contain the following types of files: a .json file containing a description of the snapshot, a .tgz file containing system data, and specific .tgz files that contain each system's user details. A short listing of the aforementioned directory will show the automatically created snapshot for Slack:

```
packt@neptune:~$ sudo snap remove slack
slack removed
packt@neptune:~$ sudo ls /var/lib/snapd/snapshots/
1_slack_4.29.149_68.zip
packt@neptune:~$ ▌
```

Figure 3.24 – Showing the existing snapshots after removal

If you don't want the snapshots to be created, you can use the --purge option for the snap remove command. For applications that use a large amount of data, those snapshots could have a significant size and impact the available disk space. To see the snapshots saved on your system, use the snap saved command:

```
packt@neptune:~$ sudo snap saved
Set   Snap    Age      Version    Rev   Size     Notes
1     slack   3m40s    4.29.149   68      673B   auto
packt@neptune:~$
```

Figure 3.25 – Showing the saved snapshots

The output shows that in the list, in our case, just one app has been removed, with the first column indicating the ID of the snapshot (set). If you would like to delete a snapshot, you can do so by using the snap forget command. In our case, to delete the Slack application's snapshot, we can use the following command:

```
packt@neptune:~$ sudo snap saved
Set  Snap   Age     Version    Rev  Size    Notes
1    slack  3m40s   4.29.149   68       673B  auto
packt@neptune:~$ sudo snap forget 1
Snapshot #1 forgotten.
packt@neptune:~$ sudo snap saved
No snapshots found.
packt@neptune:~$
```

Figure 3.26 – Using the snap forget command to delete a snapshot

To verify that the snapshot was removed, we used the snap saved command again, as shown in the preceding figure.

Snaps are versatile packages and easy to use. This package type is the choice of Ubuntu developers, but they are not commonly used on other distributions. If you would like to install snaps on distributions other than Ubuntu, follow the instructions at https://snapcraft.io/docs/installing-snapd and test its full capabilities.

Now, we will test the other new kid on the block: flatpaks. Our test distribution will be Fedora, but keep in mind that flatpaks are also supported by Ubuntu-based distributions such as Linux Mint and elementary OS, and Debian-based distributions such as PureOS and Endless OS. A list of all the supported Linux distributions can be found at flatpak.org.

Managing flatpak packages on Fedora Linux

As flatpaks are available only as desktop applications, we will use Fedora Linux Workstation as our use case. In this scenario, you could use RHEL/AlmaLinux/Rocky Linux on a server, but Fedora for your workstation.

Similar to snaps, flatpaks are isolated applications that run inside sandboxes. Each flatpak contains the needed runtimes and libraries for the application. Flatpaks offer full support for graphical user interface management tools, together with a full set of commands that can be used from the **command-line interface (CLI)**. The main command is flatpak, which has several other built-in commands to use for package management. To see all of them, use the following command:

```
$ flatpak --help
```

In the following sections, we will detail some of the widely used commands for flatpak package management. But before that, let's say a few words about how flatpak apps are named and how they will appear on the command line so that there will be no confusion in this regard.

Each app has an identifier in a form similar to `com.company.App`. Each part of this is meant to easily identify an app and its developer. The final part identifies the application's name since the preceding one identifies the entity that developed the app. This is an easy way for developers to publish and deliver multiple apps.

Adding flatpak repositories

Repositories must be set up if you wish to install applications. Flatpaks call repositories **remotes**, so this will be the term by which we will refer to them.

On our Fedora 37 machine, flatpak is already installed, but we will need to add the `flathub` repository. We will add it with the `flatpak remote-add` command, as shown in the following example:

```
$ sudo flatpak remote-add --if-not-exists flathub https://dl.flathub.
org/repo/flathub.flatpakrepo
```

Here, we used the `--if-not-exists` argument, which stops the command if the repository already exists, without showing any error. Once the repository has been added, we can start installing packages from it, but not before a mandatory system restart.

In Fedora 37 and previous versions, not all the apps from the Flathub repository are available by default, but starting with version 38, developers are aiming to provide all the apps from Flathub out of the box by default. Let's learn how to install an application from Flathub on our Fedora Workstation.

Installing a flatpak application

To install a package, we need to know its name. We can go to `https://flathub.org/home` and search for apps there. We will search for a piece of software called **Open Broadcaster Software (OBS)** studio on the website and follow the instructions provided. We can either click on the **Install** button in the top right-hand corner or use the commands from the lower half of the web page. We will use the following command:

```
$ sudo flatpak install flathub com.obsproject.Studio
```

On recent versions of flatpak (since version 1.2), installation can be performed with a much simpler command. In this case, you only need the name of the app, as follows:

```
$ sudo flatpak install slack
```

The result is the same as using the first `install` command shown previously.

Managing flatpak applications

After installing an application, you can run it using the command line with the following command:

```
$ flatpak run com.obsproject.Studio
```

If you want to update all the applications and runtimes, you can use this command:

```
$ sudo flatpak update
```

To remove a flatpak package, simply run the `flatpak uninstall` command:

```
$ sudo flatpak uninstall com.obsproject.Studio
```

To list all the flatpak applications and runtimes installed, you can use the `flatpak list` command:

```
[packt@fedora ~]$ flatpak list
Name              Application ID                   Version Branch      Installation
OBS Studio        com.obsproject.Studio            29.0.2  stable      system
Mesa              …desktop.Platform.GL.default 22.3.5  22.08       system
Mesa (Extra)      …desktop.Platform.GL.default 22.3.5  22.08-extra system
Adwaita theme     org.kde.KStyle.Adwaita                   6.4         system
KDE Application… org.kde.Platform                          6.4         system
[packt@fedora ~]$
```

Figure 3.27 – The flatpak list command's output

To see only the installed applications, you can use the `--app` argument:

```
$ flatpak list --app
```

The commands shown here are the most commonly used for flatpak package management. Needless to say, there are many other commands that we will not cover here, but you are free to look them up and test them on your system. For a quick overview of the basic flatpak commands, you can refer to the following link: `https://docs.flatpak.org/en/latest/flatpak-command-reference.html`.

Flatpaks are versatile and can provide access to newer app versions. Let's say you want to use a solid base operating system, but the downside of that is that you will get old versions of base applications by default. Using flatpaks can overcome this and give you access to newer app versions. Feel free to browse the apps available on Flathub and test the ones you find interesting and useful.

You now know how to install new applications on your operating system, using either the command line or the graphical user interface. Apart from that, you can also install new desktop environments. We will show you how in the following section.

Installing new desktop environments in Linux

We will continue to use Fedora as an example, but the commands shown here can also be used for any RHEL-based distribution, such as AlmaLinux or Rocky Linux.

By default, Fedora Workstation uses GNOME as the desktop environment, but what if you would like to use another one, such as KDE? Before showing you how, we would like to give you some information about the graphical desktop environments available for Linux.

Linux is all about choice, and this can't be more true when it comes to **desktop environments** (DEs). There are dozens of DEs available, such as GNOME, KDE, Xfce, LXDE, LXQT, Pantheon, and others. The most widely used DEs on Linux are GNOME, KDE, and Xfce, and the first two have the largest communities. If you want to use the very best and latest of GNOME, for example, you can try distributions such as Fedora, openSUSE Tumbleweed with GNOME, or Arch Linux (or Manjaro). If you want to use the best of KDE, you can try KDE neon, openSUSE Tumbleweed with KDE, or Arch Linux with KDE (or Manjaro). For Xfce, you can try MX Linux (based on Debian), which defaults to Xfce, or openSUSE with Xfce. As a rule, the most widely used Linux distributions offer variants, also called *flavors* (in the case of Ubuntu) or *spins* (in the case of Fedora) with different desktop environments available. The RHEL and SUSE commercial versions come with GNOME only by default. For more information about the DEs described here, refer to the following websites:

- For KDE, visit www.kde.org

- For GNOME, visit www.gnome.org

- For Xfce, visit www.xfce.org

Now, let's learn how to install a different DE on our default Fedora Workstation.

Installing KDE Plasma on Fedora Linux

In Fedora and derivative distributions (and also in openSUSE), there are application groups available that ease the process of installing larger apps and their dependencies. And this becomes extremely useful when you're planning to install many apps as part of a larger *group*, just like a DE is.

To install a group, you can use the dnf install command and appeal the group using @ and the name of the group. Alternatively, you can use the dnf groupinstall command while using the name of the group within quotes.

To check the groups that are available from the Fedora repositories, you can use the following command:

```
$ dnf group list --all | grep "KDE"
```

The output will be a list of groups from Fedora repos, and somewhere in there, the **KDE Plasma Workspaces** will be available. To install it, you can use the following command:

```
$ sudo dnf groupinstall "KDE Plasma Workspaces"
```

Alternatively, you can use the following command:

```
$ sudo dnf install @kde-desktop-environment
```

This command will install the new KDE Plasma environment, as shown in the following figure:

```
[packt@fedora ~]$ sudo dnf group list --all | grep "KDE"
[sudo] password for packt:
    KDE Plasma Workspaces
[packt@fedora ~]$ sudo dnf groupinstall "KDE Plasma Workspaces"
```

Figure 3.28 – Installing the KDE Plasma DE

The installation might take a while, depending on your internet connection. To start using KDE Plasma as your DE, you will need to log out of the active session. On the login screen, select your user, and then, in the bottom-right corner, click on the wheel icon and select **Plasma** when the option becomes available. You will have two options, one for **Wayland** and the other for the **X11** display manager:

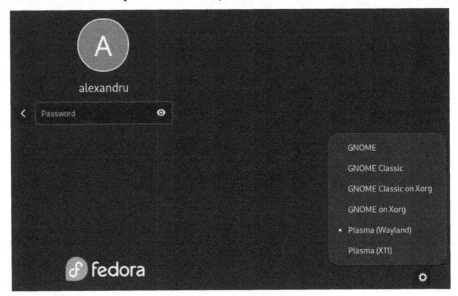

Figure 3.29 – Selecting Plasma (Wayland) on the login screen

Wayland is the newer option and might not have full support in KDE compared to the support it has in GNOME. Choose according to your preference.

Now, you can log into KDE Plasma on Fedora Workstation. The following screenshot shows the **Info Center** application inside KDE Plasma, with details about the installed version and hardware:

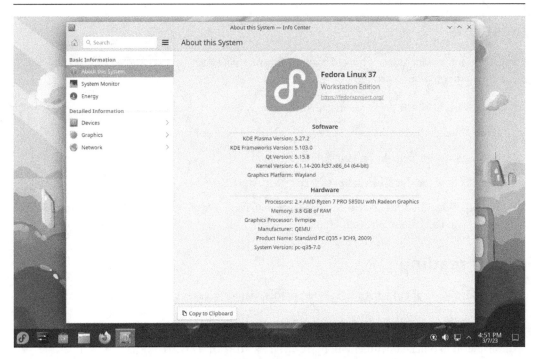

Figure 3.30 – Info Center in KDE Plasma on Fedora 37

With that, you have learned about working with packages in Linux, and even installing a new DE. This is sufficient for you to start fiddling around with your new OS. You can install new applications, configure them, and make your distribution the way you want it to be.

Summary

In this chapter, you learned how to work with packages in Ubuntu, Fedora/AlmaLinux, and openSUSE, and the skills you've learned will help you to manage packages in any Linux distribution. You learned how to work with both .deb and .rpm packages, and also the newer ones, such as flatpaks and snaps. You will use the skills you've learned here in every chapter of this book, as well as in your day-to-day job as a systems administrator – or even in your free time, enjoying your Linux operating system.

In the next chapter, we will show you how to manage user accounts and permissions, where you will be introduced to general concepts and specific tools.

Questions

Now that you have a clear idea of how to manage software packages, here are some exercises that will contribute further to your learning:

1. Make a list of all the packages installed on your system.

   Hint: Consider using the `apt list --installed` command.

2. Add support for flatpaks on your Ubuntu system.

   Hint: Follow the documentation at `flatpak.org`.

3. Test other distributions and use their package managers. We recommend that you try openSUSE and, if you feel confident, Arch Linux.

Further reading

For more information about what was covered in this chapter, please refer to the following resources:

- *Mastering Linux Administration – First Edition*, Alexandru Calcatinge, Julian Balog
- Snapcraft.io official documentation: `https://snapcraft.io/docs`
- Flatpak documentation: `https://docs.flatpak.org/en/latest/`
- openSUSE official documentation: `https://doc.opensuse.org/`

4

Managing Users and Groups

Linux is a multiuser, multitasking operating system, which means multiple users can access the operating system at the same time while sharing platform resources, with the kernel performing tasks for each user concurrently and independently. Linux provides the required isolation and security mechanisms to avoid multiple users accessing or deleting each other's files.

When multiple users are accessing the system, permissions come into play. We'll learn how **permissions** work in Linux, with their essential read, write, and execution tenets. We'll introduce you to the concept of a *superuser* (root) account, with complete access to the operating system resources.

Along the way, we'll take a hands-on approach to the topics learned, further deepening the assimilation of key concepts through practical examples. This chapter covers the following topics:

- Managing users
- Managing groups
- Managing permissions

We hope that by the end of the chapter, you will be comfortable with the command-line utilities for creating, modifying, and deleting users and groups, while proficiently handling file and directory permissions.

Let's take a quick look at the technical requirements for this chapter.

Technical requirements

You need a working Linux distribution installed on either a **virtual machine** (**VM**) or a desktop platform. In case you don't have one already, *Chapter 1, Installing Linux*, will drive you through the related process. In this chapter, we'll be using Ubuntu or Fedora, but most of the commands and examples used would pertain to any other Linux platform.

Managing users

In this context, a **user** is anyone using a computer or a system resource. In its simplest form, a Linux *user* or *user account* is identified by a name and a **unique identifier**, known as a **UID**.

From a purely technical point of view, in Linux, we have the following types of users:

- **Normal (or regular) users**: General-purpose, everyday user accounts, mostly suited for personal use and for common application and file management tasks, with limited access to system-wide resources. A regular user account usually has a *login* shell and a *home* directory.

- **System users**: These are similar to regular user accounts, except they may lack a login shell or a home directory. System accounts are usually assigned to background application services, mostly for security reasons and to limit the attack surface associated with the related resources—for example, a web server daemon handling public requests should run as a system account, ideally without login or root privileges. Consequently, possible vulnerabilities exposed through the web server would remain strictly isolated to the limited action realm of the associated system account.

- **Superusers**: These are privileged user accounts, with full access to system resources, including the permission to create, modify, and delete user accounts. The root user is an example of a superuser.

In Linux, only the root user or users with sudo privileges (**sudoers**) can create, modify, or delete user accounts.

Understanding sudo

The root user is the default superuser account in Linux, and it has the ability to do anything on a system. Ideally, acting as root on a system should generally be avoided due to safety and security reasons. With sudo, Linux provides a mechanism for *promoting* a regular user account to superuser privileges, using an additional layer of security. This way, a sudo user is generally used instead of root.

sudo is a command-line utility that allows a permitted user to execute commands with the security privileges of a superuser or another user (depending on the local system's security policy). sudo originally stood for *superuser do* due to its initial implementation of acting exclusively as the superuser, but has since been expanded to support not only the superuser but also other (restricted) user impersonations. Thus, it is also referred to as *substitute user do*. Yet, more often than not, it is perceived as *superuser do* due to its frequent use in Linux administrative tasks.

Most of the command-line tools for managing users in Linux require sudo privileges unless the related tasks are carried out by the root user. If we want to avoid using the root context, we can't genuinely proceed with the rest of this chapter—and create a user in particular—before we have a user account with superuser privileges. So, let's take this chicken-and-egg scenario out of the way first.

Most Linux distributions create an additional user account with superuser privileges, besides `root`, during installation. The reason, as noted before, is to provide an extra layer of security and safety for elevated operations. The simplest way to check whether a user account has `sudo` privileges is to run the following command in a terminal, while logged in with the related user account:

```
sudo -v
```

According to the `sudo` manual (`man sudo`), the `-v` option causes `sudo` to update the user's cached credentials and authenticate the user if the cached credentials expired.

If the user (for example, `julian`) doesn't have superuser privileges on the local machine (for example, `neptune`), the preceding command yields the following (or a similar) error:

```
Sorry, user julian may not run sudo on neptune.
```

In recent Linux distributions, the execution of a `sudo` command usually grants elevated permissions for a limited time. Ubuntu, for example, has a 15-minute `sudo` elevation span, after which time a `sudo` user would need to authenticate again. Subsequent invocations of `sudo` may not prompt for a password if done within the `sudo` cache credential timeout.

If we don't have a default superuser account, we can always use the root context to create new users (see the next chapter) and elevate them to **sudoer** privileges. We'll learn more about this in the *Creating a superuser* section, later in this chapter.

Now, let's have a look at how to create, modify, and delete users.

Creating, modifying, and deleting users

In this section, we explore a few command-line tools and some common tasks for managing users. The example commands and procedures are shown for Ubuntu and Fedora, but the same principles apply to any other Linux distribution. Some user management **command-line interface** (**CLI**) tools may differ or may not be available on specific Linux platforms (for example, `useradd` is not available on Alpine Linux, and `adduser` should be used instead). Please check the documentation of the Linux distribution of your choice for the equivalent commands.

Creating users

To create users, we can use either the `useradd` or the `adduser` command, although on some Linux distributions (for example, Debian or Ubuntu), the recommended way is to use the `adduser` command in favor of the low-level `useradd` utility. We'll cover both in this section.

`adduser` is a Perl script using `useradd`—basically, a shim of the `useradd` command—with a user-friendly guided configuration. Both command-line tools are installed by default in Ubuntu and Fedora. Let's take a brief look at each of these commands.

Creating users with useradd

The syntax for the useradd command is shown here:

```
useradd [OPTIONS] USER
```

In its simplest invocation, the following command creates a user account (julian):

```
sudo useradd julian
```

The user information is stored in a /etc/passwd file. Here's the related user data for julian:

```
sudo cat /etc/passwd | grep julian
```

In our case, this is the output:

```
packt@neptune:~$ sudo useradd julian
packt@neptune:~$ sudo cat /etc/passwd | grep julian
julian:x:1001:1001::/home/julian:/bin/sh
packt@neptune:~$ ▌
```

Figure 4.1 – The user record created with useradd

Let's analyze the related user record. Each entry is delimited by a colon (:) and is listed here:

- julian: Username
- x: Encrypted password (password hash is stored in /etc/shadow)
- 1001: The UID
- 1001: The user **group ID (GID)**
- : : The **General Electric Comprehensive Operating Supervisor (GECOS)** field—for example, display name (in our case, empty), explained later in this section
- /home/julian: User home folder
- /bin/sh: Default login shell for the user

> **Important note**
>
> The GECOS field is a string of comma-delimited attributes, reflecting general information about the user account (for example, real name, company, and phone number). In Linux, the GECOS field is the fifth field in a user record. See more information at https://en.wikipedia. org/wiki/Gecos_field.

We can also use the `getent` command to retrieve the preceding user information, as follows:

```
getent passwd julian
```

To view the UID (`uid`), GID (`gid`), and group membership associated with a user, we can use the `id` command, as follows:

```
id julian
```

This command gives us the following output:

```
packt@neptune:~$ sudo useradd julian
packt@neptune:~$ sudo cat /etc/passwd | grep julian
julian:x:1001:1001::/home/julian:/bin/sh
packt@neptune:~$ getent passwd julian
julian:x:1001:1001::/home/julian:/bin/sh
packt@neptune:~$ id julian
uid=1001(julian) gid=1001(julian) groups=1001(julian)
packt@neptune:~$
```

Figure 4.2 – The UID information

With the simple invocation of `useradd`, the command creates the user (`julian`) with some immediate default values (as enumerated), while other user-related data is empty—for example, we have no full name or password specified for the user yet. Also, while the home directory has a default value (for example, `/home/julian`), the actual filesystem folder will not be created unless the `useradd` command is invoked with the `-m` or the `--create-home` option, as follows:

```
sudo useradd -m julian
```

Without a home directory, regular users would not have the ability to save their files in a private location on the system. On the other hand, some system accounts may not need a home directory since they don't have a login shell. For example, a database server (for example, PostgreSQL) may run with a non-root system account (for example, `postgres`) that only needs access to database resources in specific locations (for example, `/var/lib/pgsql`), controlled via other permission mechanisms (for example, **Security-Enhanced Linux (SELinux)**).

For our regular user, if we also wanted to specify a full name (display name), the command would change to this:

```
sudo useradd -m -c "Julian" julian
```

The `-c`, `--comment` option parameter of `useradd` expects a *comment*, also known as the GECOS field (the fifth field in our user record), with multiple comma-separated values. In our case, we specify the full name (for example, `Julian`). For more information, check out the `useradd` manual (`man useradd`) or `useradd --help`.

The user still won't have a password yet, and consequently, there would be no way for them to log in (for example, via a **graphical user interface (GUI)** or **Secure Shell (SSH)**). To create a password for julian, we invoke the passwd command, like this:

```
sudo passwd julian
```

You can see the following output:

```
packt@neptune:~$ sudo passwd julian
New password:
Retype new password:
passwd: password updated successfully
packt@neptune:~$
```

Figure 4.3 – Creating or changing the user password

The passwd command will prompt for the new user's password. With the password set, there will be a new entry added to the /etc/shadow file. This file stores the secure password hashes (not the passwords!) for each user. Only superusers can access the content of this file. Here's the command to retrieve the related information for the user julian:

```
sudo getent shadow julian
```

You can also use the following command:

```
sudo cat /etc/shadow | grep julian
```

The output of both commands is shown in the following screenshot:

```
packt@neptune:~$ sudo getent shadow julian
julian:$y$j9T$mI5gG19NBCTDj1B2PVAr8/$/sK8PINvEm1KLYk1QnElw/05s4tJd.WtOUVOZpmaJLB
:19424:0:99999:7:::
packt@neptune:~$ sudo cat /etc/shadow | grep julian
julian:$y$j9T$mI5gG19NBCTDj1B2PVAr8/$/sK8PINvEm1KLYk1QnElw/05s4tJd.WtOUVOZpmaJLB
:19424:0:99999:7:::
packt@neptune:~$
```

Figure 4.4 – Information about the user from the shadow file

Once the password has been set, in normal circumstances, the user can log in to the system (via SSH or GUI). If the Linux distribution has a GUI, the new user will show up on the login screen.

As noted, with the useradd command, we have low-level granular control over how we create user accounts, but sometimes we may prefer a more user-friendly approach. Enter the adduser command.

Creating users with adduser

The `adduser` command is a Perl wrapper for `useradd`. The syntax for this command is shown here:

```
adduser [OPTIONS] USER
```

`sudo` may prompt for the superuser password. `adduser` will prompt for the new user's password and other user-related information (as shown in *Figure 4.5*).

Let's create a new user account (`alex`) with `adduser`, as follows:

```
sudo adduser alex
```

The preceding command yields the following output:

```
packt@neptune:~$ sudo adduser alex
Adding user `alex' ...
Adding new group `alex' (1002) ...
Adding new user `alex' (1002) with group `alex' ...
Creating home directory `/home/alex' ...
Copying files from `/etc/skel' ...
New password:
Retype new password:
passwd: password updated successfully
Changing the user information for alex
Enter the new value, or press ENTER for the default
        Full Name []:
        Room Number []:
        Work Phone []:
        Home Phone []:
        Other []:
Is the information correct? [Y/n]
```

Figure 4.5 – The adduser command

In Fedora, the preceding invocation of the `adduser` command will simply run without prompting the user for a password or any other information.

We can see the related user entry in `/etc/passwd` with `getent`, as follows:

```
getent passwd alex
```

The following is the output:

```
packt@neptune:~$ getent passwd alex
alex:x:1002:1002:,,,:/home/alex:/bin/bash
packt@neptune:~$
```

Figure 4.6 – Viewing user information with getent

In the preceding examples, we created a regular user account. Administrators or superusers can also elevate the privileges of a regular user to a superuser. Let's see how in the following section.

Creating a superuser

When a regular user is given the power to run `sudo`, they become a superuser. Let's assume we have a regular user created via any of the examples shown in the *Creating users* section.

Promoting the user to a superuser (or *sudoer*) requires a `sudo` group membership. In Linux, the `sudo` group is a reserved system group for users with elevated or `root` privileges. To make the user `julian` a sudoer, we simply need to add the user to the `sudo` group, like this (in Ubuntu):

```
sudo usermod -aG sudo julian
```

The `-aG` options of `usermod` instruct the command to append (`-a`, `--append`) the user to the specified group (`-G`, `--group`)—in our case, `sudo`.

To verify our user is now a sudoer, first make sure the related user information reflects the `sudo` membership by running the following command:

```
id julian
```

This gives us the following output:

```
packt@neptune:~$ sudo usermod -aG sudo julian
packt@neptune:~$ id julian
uid=1001(julian) gid=1001(julian) groups=1001(julian),27(sudo)
packt@neptune:~$
```

Figure 4.7 – Looking for the sudo membership of a user

The output shows that the `sudo` group membership (GID) in the `groups` tag is `27 (sudo)`.

To verify the `sudo` access for the user `julian`, run the following command:

```
su - julian
```

The preceding command prompts for the password of the user `julian`. A successful login would usually validate the superuser context. Alternatively, the user (`julian`) can run the `sudo -v` command in their terminal session to validate the `sudo` privileges. For more information on superuser privileges, see the *Understanding sudo* section earlier in the chapter.

With multiple users created, a system administrator may want to view or list all the users in the system. In the next section, we provide a few ways to accomplish this task.

Viewing users

There are a few ways for a superuser to view all users configured in the system. As previously noted, the user information is stored in the /etc/passwd and /etc/shadow files. Besides simply viewing these files, we can parse them and extract only the usernames with the following command:

```
cat /etc/passwd | cut -d: -f1 | less
```

Alternatively, we can parse the /etc/shadow file, like this:

```
sudo cat /etc/shadow | cut -d: -f1 | less
```

In the preceding commands, we read the content from the related files (with cat). Next, we piped the result to a delimiter-based parsing (with cut, on the : delimiter) and picked the first field (-f1). Finally, we chose a paginated display of the results, using the less command (to exit the command's output, press Q).

Note the use of sudo for the shadow file since access is limited to superusers only, due to the sensitive nature of the password hash data. Alternatively, we can use the getent command to retrieve the user information.

The following command lists all the users configured in the system:

```
getent passwd
```

The preceding command reads the /etc/passwd file. Alternatively, we can retrieve the same information from /etc/shadow, as follows:

```
sudo getent shadow
```

For both commands, we can further pipe the getent output to | cut -d: -f1 to list only the usernames, like this:

```
sudo getent shadow | cut -d: -f1 | less | column
```

The output will be similar to this:

```
packt@neptune:~$ cat /etc/passwd | cut -d: -f1 | less
packt@neptune:~$ sudo cat /etc/shadow | cut -d: -f1 | less
packt@neptune:~$ sudo getent shadow | cut -d: -f1 | less | column
root                    www-data                sshd
daemon                  backup                  syslog
bin                     list                    uuidd
sys                     irc                     tcpdump
sync                    gnats                   tss
games                   nobody                  landscape
man                     _apt                    usbmux
lp                      systemd-network         packt
mail                    systemd-resolve         lxd
news                    messagebus              fwupd-refresh
uucp                    systemd-timesync        julian
proxy                   pollinate               alex
packt@neptune:~$
```

Figure 4.8 – Viewing usernames

With new users created, administrators or superusers may want to change certain user-related information, such as password, password expiration, full name, or login shell. Next, we take a look at some of the most common ways to accomplish this task.

Modifying users

A superuser can run the usermod command to modify user settings, with the following syntax:

```
usermod [OPTIONS] USER
```

The examples in this section apply to a user we previously created (julian) with the simplest invocation of the useradd command. As noted in the previous section, the related user record in /etc/passwd has no full name for the user, and the user has no password either.

Let's change the following settings for our user (julian):

- **Full name**: To Julian (initially empty)
- **Home folder**: Move to /local/julian (from default /home/julian)
- **Login shell**: /bin/bash (from default /bin/sh)

The command-line utility for changing all the preceding information is shown here:

```
sudo usermod -c "Julian" -d /local/julian -m -s /bin/bash julian
```

Here are the command options, briefly explained:

- `-c, --comment "Julian"`: The full username
- `-d, --home local/julian`: The user's new home directory
- `-m, --move`: Move the content of the current home directory to the new location
- `-s, --shell /bin/sh`: The user login shell

The related change, retrieved with the `getent` command, is shown here:

```
getent passwd julian
```

We get the following output:

```
packt@neptune:~$ sudo usermod -c "Julian" -d /local/julian -m -s /bin/bash julia
n
packt@neptune:~$ getent passwd julian
julian:x:1001:1001:Julian:/local/julian:/bin/bash
packt@neptune:~$
```

Figure 4.9 – The user changes reflected with getent

Here are a few more examples of changing user settings with the `usermod` command-line utility.

Changing the username

The `-l, --login` option parameter of `usermod` specifies a new login username. The following command changes the username from `julian` to `balog` (that is, first name to last name), as illustrated here:

```
sudo usermod -l "balog" julian
```

In a production environment, we may have to add to the preceding command, as we may also want to change the display name and the home directory of the user (for consistency reasons). In a previous example in the *Creating users with useradd* section, we showcased the `-d, --home` and `-m, --move` option parameters, which would accommodate such changes.

Locking or unlocking a user

A superuser or administrator may choose to temporarily or permanently lock a specific user with the `-L, --lock` option parameter of `usermod`, as follows:

```
sudo usermod -L julian
```

As a result of the preceding command, the login attempt for the user `julian` would be denied. Should the user try to SSH into the Linux machine, they would get a **Permission denied, please try again** error message. Also, the related username will be removed from the login screen if the Linux platform has a GUI.

To unlock the user, we invoke the `-U`, `--unlock` option parameter, as follows:

```
sudo usermod -U julian
```

The preceding command restores system access for the user.

For more information on the `usermod` utility, please check out the related documentation (`man usermod`) or the command-line help (`usermod --help`).

Although the recommended way of modifying user settings is via the `usermod` command-line utility, some users may find it easier to manually edit the `/etc/passwd` file. The following section shows you how.

Modifying users via /etc/passwd

A superuser can also manually edit the `/etc/passwd` file to modify user data by updating the relevant line. Although the editing can be done with a text editor of your choice (for example, `nano`), we recommend the use of the `vipw` command-line utility for a safer approach. `vipw` enables the required locks to prevent possible data corruption—for example, in case a superuser performs a change at the same time regular users change their password.

The following command initiates the editing of the `/etc/passwd` file by also prompting for the preferred text editor (for example, `nano` or `vim`):

```
sudo vipw
```

For example, we can change the settings for user `julian` by editing the following line:

```
julian:x:1001:1001:Julian,,,:/home/julian:/bin/bash
```

The meaning of the colon (`:`)-separated fields was previously described in the *Creating users with useradd* section. Each of these fields can be manually altered in the `/etc/passwd` file, resulting in changes equivalent to the corresponding `usermod` invocation.

For more information on the `vipw` command-line utility, you can refer to the related system manual (`man vipw`).

Another relatively common administrative task for a user account is to change a password or set up a password expiration. Although `usermod` can change a user password via the `-p` or `--password` option, it requires an encrypted hash string (and not a cleartext password). Generating an encrypted password hash would be an extra step. An easier way is to use the `passwd` utility to change the password.

A superuser (administrator) can change the password of a user (for example, the user julian) with the following command:

```
sudo passwd julian
```

The output will ask for the new password for the respective user. To change the expiration time of a password (the password age), the chage command is used. For example, to set a 30-day password age for the user julian, we will use the following command:

```
sudo chage -M 30 julian
```

This will force the user julian to change their password every month. The password time availability is defined system-wide by the password policy. It is found inside the /etc/login.defs file, inside the **Password aging controls** section. If you change these entries, the password policy will be set for every user. Another common practice is to force the user to change the password at the first login. You can enforce this by using the following command (we will use julian as our example again):

```
sudo chage -d 0 julian
```

This command will force the user julian to enter their own password the first time they log in to the system.

Sometimes, administrators are required to remove specific users from the system. The next section shows a couple of ways of accomplishing this task.

Deleting users

The most common way to remove users from the system is to use the userdel command-line tool. The general syntax of the userdel command is shown here:

```
userdel [OPTIONS] USER
```

For example, to remove the user julian, a superuser would run the following command:

```
sudo userdel -f -r julian
```

Here are the command options used:

- -f, --force: Removes all files in the user's home directory, even if not owned by the user
- -r, --remove: Removes the user's home directory and mail spool

The userdel command removes the related user data from the system, including the user's home directory (when invoked with the -f or --force option) and the related entries in the /etc/passwd and /etc/shadow files.

There is also an alternative way, which could be handy in some odd cleanup scenarios. The next section shows how.

Deleting users via /etc/passwd and /etc/shadow

A superuser can edit the `/etc/passwd` and `/etc/shadow` files and manually remove the corresponding lines for the user (for example, `julian`). Please note that both files have to be edited for consistency and complete removal of the related user account.

Edit the `/etc/passwd` file using the `vipw` command-line utility, as follows:

```
sudo vipw
```

Remove the following line (for the user `julian`):

```
julian:x:1001:1001:Julian,,,:/home/julian:/bin/bash
```

Next, edit the `/etc/shadow` file using the `-s` or `--shadow` option with `vipw`, as follows:

```
sudo vipw -s
```

Remove the following line (for the user `julian`):

```
julian:$6$xDdd7Eay/RKYjeTm$Sf.../:18519:0:99999:7:::
```

After editing the preceding files, a superuser may also need to remove the deleted user's home directory, as follows:

```
sudo rm -rf /home/julian
```

For more information on the `userdel` utility, please check out the related documentation (`man userdel`) or the command-line help (`userdel --help`).

The user management concepts and commands learned so far apply exclusively to individual users in the system. When multiple users in the system have a common access level or permission attribute, they are collectively referred to as a group. Groups can be regarded as standalone organizational units we can create, modify, or delete. We can also define and alter user memberships associated with groups. The next section focuses on group management internals.

Managing groups

Linux uses groups to organize users. Simply put, a group is a collection of users sharing a common attribute. Examples of such groups could be *employees*, *developers*, *managers*, and so on. In Linux, a group is uniquely identified by a GID. Users within the same group share the same GID.

From a user's perspective, there are two types of groups, outlined here:

- **Primary group**: The user's initial (default) login group
- **Supplementary groups**: A list of groups the user is also a member of; also known as **secondary groups**

Every Linux user is a member of a primary group. A user can belong to multiple supplementary groups or no supplementary groups at all. In other words, there is one mandatory primary group associated with each Linux user, and a user can have multiple or no supplementary group memberships.

From a practical point of view, we can look at groups as a permissive context of collaboration for a select number of users. Imagine a *developers* group having access to developer-specific resources. Each user in this group has access to these resources. Users outside the *developers* group may not have access unless they authenticate with a group password if the group has one.

In the following section, we provide detailed examples of how to manage groups and set up group memberships for users. Most related commands require *superuser* or `sudo` privileges.

Creating, modifying, and deleting groups

While our primary focus remains on group administrative tasks, some related operations still involve user-related commands. Command-line utilities such as `groupadd`, `groupmod`, and `groupdel` are targeted strictly at creating, modifying, and deleting groups, respectively. On the other hand, the `useradd` and `usermod` commands carry group-specific options when associating users with groups. We'll also introduce you to `gpasswd`, a command-line tool specializing in group administration, combining user- and group-related operations.

With this aspect in mind, let's take a look at how to create, modify, and delete groups and how to manipulate group memberships for users.

Creating groups

To create a new group, a superuser invokes the `groupadd` command-line utility. Here's the basic syntax of the related command:

```
groupadd [OPTIONS] GROUP
```

Let's create a new group (`developers`), with default settings, as follows:

```
sudo groupadd developers
```

The group information is stored in the `/etc/group` file. Here's the related data for the developers group:

```
cat /etc/group | grep developers
```

The command yields the following output:

```
packt@neptune:~$ sudo groupadd developers
[sudo] password for packt:
packt@neptune:~$ cat /etc/group | grep developers
developers:x:1003:
packt@neptune:~$ ▌
```

Figure 4.10 – The group with default attributes

Let's analyze the related group record. Each entry is delimited by a colon (:) and is listed here:

- developers: Group name
- x: Encrypted password (password hash is stored in /etc/gshadow)
- 1003: GID

We can also use the getent command to retrieve the preceding group information, as follows:

```
getent group developers
```

A superuser may choose to create a group with a specific GID, using the -g, --gid option parameter with groupadd. For example, the following command creates the developers group (if it doesn't exist) with a GID of 1200:

```
sudo groupadd -g 1200 developers
```

For more information on the groupadd command-line utility, please refer to the related documentation (man groupadd).

Group-related data is stored in the /etc/group and /etc/gshadow files. The /etc/group file contains generic group membership information, while the /etc/gshadow file stores the encrypted password hashes for each group. Let's take a brief look at group passwords.

Understanding group passwords

By default, a group doesn't have a password when created with the simplest invocation of the groupadd command (for example, groupadd developers). Although groupadd supports an encrypted password (via the -p, --password option parameter), this would require an extra step to generate a secure password hash. There's a better and simpler way to create a group password: by using the gpasswd command-line utility.

> **Important note**
> gpasswd is a command-line tool that helps with everyday group administration tasks.

The following command creates a password for the `developers` group:

```
sudo gpasswd developers
```

We get prompted to enter and re-enter a password, as illustrated here:

```
packt@neptune:~$ sudo gpasswd developers
Changing the password for group developers
New Password:
Re-enter new password:
```

Figure 4.11 – Creating a password for the developers group

The purpose of a group password is to protect access to group resources. A group password is inherently insecure when shared among group members, yet a Linux administrator may choose to keep the group password private while group members collaborate unhindered within the group's security context.

Here's a quick explanation of how it works. When a member of a specific group (for example, `developers`) logs in to that group (using the `newgrp` command), the user is not prompted for the group password. When users who don't belong to the group attempt to log in, they will be prompted for the group password.

In general, a group can have administrators, members, and a password. Members of a group who are the group's administrators may use `gpasswd` without being prompted for a password, as long as they're logged in to the group. Also, group administrators don't need superuser privileges to perform group administrative tasks for a group they are the administrator of.

We'll take a closer look at `gpasswd` in the next sections, where we further focus on group management tasks, as well as adding users to a group and removing users from a group. But for now, let's keep our attention strictly at the group level and see how we can modify a user group.

Modifying groups

The most common way to modify the definition of a group is via the `groupmod` command-line utility. Here's the basic syntax for the command:

```
groupmod [OPTIONS] GROUP
```

The most common operations when changing a group's definition are related to the GID, group name, and group password. Let's take a look at each of these changes. We assume our previously created group is named `developers`, with a GID of `1003`.

To change the GID to `1200`, a superuser invokes the `groupmod` command with the `-g`, `--gid` option parameter, as follows:

```
sudo groupmod -g 1200 developers
```

To change the group name from `developers` to `devops`, we invoke the `-n,  --new-name` option, like this:

```
sudo groupmod -n devops developers
```

We can verify the preceding changes for the `devops` group with the following command:

```
getent group devops
```

The command yields the following output:

```
packt@neptune:~$ getent group developers
developers:x:1003:
packt@neptune:~$ sudo groupmod -g 1200 developers
packt@neptune:~$ getent group developers
developers:x:1200:
packt@neptune:~$ sudo groupmod -n devops developers
packt@neptune:~$ getent group devops
devops:x:1200:
```

Figure 4.12 – Verifying the group changes

To change the group password for `devops`, the simplest way is to use `gpasswd`, as follows:

```
sudo gpasswd devops
```

We are prompted to enter and re-enter a password.

To remove the group password for `devops`, we invoke the `gpasswd` command with the `-r, --remove-password` option, as follows:

```
sudo gpasswd -r devops
```

As the command has no visible outcome or message, we will be prompted back to the shell:

```
packt@neptune:~$ sudo gpasswd devops
Changing the password for group devops
New Password:
Re-enter new password:
packt@neptune:~$ sudo gpasswd -r devops
packt@neptune:~$ []
```

Figure 4.13 – Setting a new group password and removing a group password

For more information on `groupmod` and `gpasswd`, refer to the system manuals of these utilities (`man groupmod` and `man gpasswd`), or simply invoke the `-h,  --help` option for each.

Next, we look at how to delete groups.

Deleting groups

To delete groups, we use the `groupdel` command-line utility. The related syntax is shown here:

```
groupdel [OPTIONS] GROUP
```

By default, Linux enforces referential integrity between a primary group and the users associated with that primary group. We cannot delete a group that has been assigned as a primary group for some users before deleting the users of that primary group. In other words, by default, Linux doesn't want to leave the users with dangling primary GIDs.

For example, when we first added the user `julian`, they were assigned automatically to the `julian` primary group. We then added the user to the `sudoers` group.

Let's attempt to add the user `julian` to the `devops` group. A superuser may run the `usermod` command with the `-g`, `--gid` option parameter to *change* the primary group of a user. The command should be invoked for each user. Here's an example of removing the user `julian` from the `julian` primary group. First, let's get the current data for the user, as follows:

```
id julian
```

This is the output:

```
packt@neptune:~$ id julian
uid=1003(julian) gid=1003(julian) groups=1003(julian),27(sudo)
```

Figure 4.14 – Retrieving the current primary group for the user

Now, let us add the user `julian` to the `devops` group. The `-g`, `--gid` option parameter of the `usermod` command accepts both a *GID* and a group *name*. The specified group name must already be present in the system; otherwise, the command will fail. If we want to change the primary group (for example, to `devops`), we simply specify the group name in the `-g`, `--gid` option parameter, as follows:

```
sudo usermod -g devops julian
```

The output is shown in the following screenshot:

```
packt@neptune:~$ id julian
uid=1003(julian) gid=1003(julian) groups=1003(julian),27(sudo)
packt@neptune:~$ sudo usermod -g devops julian
packt@neptune:~$ id julian
uid=1003(julian) gid=1200(devops) groups=1200(devops),27(sudo)
packt@neptune:~$ 
```

Figure 4.15 – Changing the primary group of the user

The result is that the user julian is now part of the devops group.

Now, let us attempt to delete the devops group, which is the primary group for the user julian. Attempting to delete the devops group results in an error, as can be seen in *Figure 4.16* (the first command used). Therefore, we cannot delete a group that is not empty.

A superuser may choose to *force* the deletion of a primary group, invoking groupdel with the -f, --force option, but this would be ill advised. This is because the command would result in users with orphaned primary GIDs and a possible security hole in the system. The maintenance and removal of such users would also become problematic.

In order to be able to delete the devops group, we need to assign another group to the user julian. What we can do is assign it to the initial primary group called julian, and then attempt to delete the devops group, now that it is empty. First, let us assign the user julian to the julian group with the following command:

```
sudo usermod -g julian julian
```

At this point, it's safe to delete the group (devops), as follows:

```
sudo groupdel devops
```

The outcome from the preceding commands is this:

```
packt@neptune:~$ groupdel devops
groupdel: cannot remove the primary group of user 'julian'
packt@neptune:~$ sudo usermod -g julian julian
[sudo] password for packt:
packt@neptune:~$ id julian
uid=1003(julian) gid=1003(julian) groups=1003(julian),27(sudo)
packt@neptune:~$ sudo groupdel devops
packt@neptune:~$ getent group devops
packt@neptune:~$ 
```

Figure 4.16 – Successful attempt to delete the group

For more information on the groupdel command-line utility, check out the related system manual (man groupdel), or simply invoke groupdel --help.

Modifying groups via /etc/group

An administrator can also manually edit the /etc/group file to modify group data by updating the related line. Although the editing can be done with a text editor of your choice (for example, nano), we recommend the use of the vigr command-line utility for a safer approach. vigr is similar to vipr (for modifying /etc/passwd) and sets safety locks to prevent possible data corruption during concurrent changes of group data.

The following command opens the `/etc/group` file for editing by also prompting for the preferred text editor (for example, `nano` or `vim`):

```
sudo vigr
```

For example, we can change the settings for the `developers` group by editing the following line:

```
developers:x:1200:julian,alex
```

When deleting groups using the `vigr` command, we're also prompted to remove the corresponding entry in the group shadow file (`/etc/gshadow`). The related command invokes the `-s` or `--shadow` option, as illustrated here:

```
sudo vigr -s
```

For more information on the `vigr` utility, please refer to the related system manual (`man vigr`).

As with most Linux tasks, all the preceding tasks could have been accomplished in different ways. The commands chosen are the most common ones, but there might be cases when a different approach may prove more appropriate.

In the next section, we'll take a glance at how to add users to primary and secondary groups and how to remove users from these groups.

Managing users in groups

So far, we've only created groups that have no users associated. There is not much use for empty user groups, so let's add some users to them.

Adding users to a group

Before we start adding users to a group, let's create a few groups. In the following example, we create the groups by also specifying their GID (via the `-g,  --gid` option parameter of the `groupadd` command):

```
sudo groupadd -g 1100 admin
sudo groupadd -g 1200 developers
sudo groupadd -g 1300 devops
```

We can check the last groups created by using the following command:

```
cat /etc/group | tail -n 5
```

It will show us the last five lines of the `/etc/group` file. We can see the last five groups created.

Next, we create a couple of new users (alex2 and julian2 as we already have users alex and julian) and add them to some of the groups we just created. We'll have the admin group set as the *primary group* for both users, while the developers and devops groups are defined as *secondary* (or *supplementary*) *groups*. The code can be seen here:

```
sudo useradd -g admin -G developers,devops alex2
sudo useradd -g admin -G developers,devops julian2
```

The -g, --gid option parameter of the useradd command specifies the (unique) primary group (admin). The -G, --groups option parameter provides a comma-separated list (without intervening spaces) of the secondary group names (developers,devops).

We can verify the group memberships for both users with the following commands:

```
id alex2
id julian2
```

The output is shown in the following screenshot:

```
packt@neptune:~$ cat /etc/group | tail -n 5
alex:x:1002:
julian:x:1003:
admin:x:1100:
developers:x:1200:
devops:x:1300:
packt@neptune:~$ sudo useradd -g admin -G developers,devops alex2
packt@neptune:~$ sudo useradd -g admin -G developers,devops julian2
packt@neptune:~$ id alex2
uid=1004(alex2) gid=1100(admin) groups=1100(admin),1200(developers),1300(devops)
packt@neptune:~$ id julian2
uid=1005(julian2) gid=1100(admin) groups=1100(admin),1200(developers),1300(devop
s)
packt@neptune:~$ 
```

Figure 4.17 – Assigning groups to new users

As we can see, the gid attribute shows the primary group membership: gid=1100(admin). The groups attribute shows the supplementary (secondary) groups: groups=1100(admin),1200(developers),1300(devops).

With users scattered across multiple groups, an administrator is sometimes confronted with the task of moving users between groups. The following section shows how to do this.

Moving and removing users across groups

Building upon the previous example, let's assume the administrator wants to move (or add) the user alex2 to a new secondary group called managers. Please note that, according to our previous examples, the user alex2 has admin as the primary group and developers/devops as secondary groups (see the output of the id alex2 command in *Figure 4.18*).

Let's create a managers group first, with GID 1400. The code can be seen here:

```
sudo groupadd -g 1400 managers
```

Next, add our existing user, alex2, to the managers group. We use the usermod command with the -G, --groups option parameter to specify the secondary groups the user is associated with.

The simplest way to *append* a secondary group to a user is by invocation of the -a, --append option of the usermod command, as illustrated here:

```
sudo usermod -a -G managers alex2
```

The preceding command would preserve the existing secondary groups for the user alex2 while adding the new managers group. Alternatively, we could run the following command:

```
sudo usermod -G developers,devops,managers alex2
```

In the preceding command, we specified multiple groups (with no intervening whitespace!).

> **Important note**
> We preserved the existing secondary groups (developers/devops) and *appended* to the comma-separated list the managers additional secondary group. If we only had the managers group specified, the user alex2 would have been *removed* from the developers and devops secondary groups.

To verify whether the user alex2 is now part of the managers group, run the following command:

```
id alex2
```

This is the output of the command:

```
uid=1004(alex2) gid=1100(admin)
groups=1100(admin),1200(developers),1300(devops),1400(managers)
```

As we can see, the groups attribute (highlighted) includes the related entry for the managers group: 1400(managers).

Similarly, if we wanted to *remove* the user alex2 from the developers and devops secondary groups, to only be associated with the managers secondary group, we would run the following command:

```
sudo usermod -G managers alex2
```

This is the output:

```
packt@neptune:~$ sudo groupadd -g 1400 managers
packt@neptune:~$ sudo usermod -a -G managers alex2
packt@neptune:~$ id alex2
uid=1004(alex2) gid=1100(admin) groups=1100(admin),1200(developers),1300(devops)
,1400(managers)
packt@neptune:~$ sudo usermod -G managers alex2
packt@neptune:~$ id alex2
uid=1004(alex2) gid=1100(admin) groups=1100(admin),1400(managers)
packt@neptune:~$ ▌
```

Figure 4.18 – Verifying the secondary groups for the user

The groups tag now shows the primary group admin (by default) and the managers secondary group.

The command to remove the user alex2 from all secondary groups is shown here:

```
sudo usermod -G '' alex2
```

The usermod command has an empty string (' ') as the -G, --groups option parameter, to ensure no secondary groups are associated with the user. We can verify that the user alex2 has no more secondary group memberships with the following command:

```
id alex
```

This is the output:

```
packt@neptune:~$ id alex2
uid=1004(alex2) gid=1100(admin) groups=1100(admin),1400(managers)
packt@neptune:~$ sudo usermod -G '' alex2
packt@neptune:~$ id alex2
uid=1004(alex2) gid=1100(admin) groups=1100(admin)
packt@neptune:~$
```

Figure 4.19 – Verifying the user has no secondary groups

As we can see, the groups tag only contains the 1100(admin) primary GID, which by default is always shown for a user.

If an administrator chooses to remove the user `alex2` from a primary group or assign them to a different primary group, they must run the `usermod` command with the `-g`, `--gid` option parameter and specify the primary group name. A primary group is always mandatory for a user, and it must exist.

For example, to move the user `alex2` to the `managers` primary group, the administrator would run the following command:

```
sudo usermod -g managers alex2
```

The related user data can be obtained using the following command:

```
id alex2
```

The command yields the following output:

```
packt@neptune:~$ id alex2
uid=1004(alex2) gid=1100(admin) groups=1100(admin)
packt@neptune:~$ sudo usermod -g managers alex2
packt@neptune:~$ id alex2
uid=1004(alex2) gid=1400(managers) groups=1400(managers)
packt@neptune:~$ 
```

Figure 4.20 – Verifying the user has been assigned to the new primary group

The `gid` attribute of the user record in *Figure 4.21* reflects the new primary group: `gid=1400(managers)`.

If the administrator chooses to configure the user `alex2` without a specific primary group, they must first create an exclusive *group* (named `alex2`, for convenience), and have the GID matching the UID of the user `alex2` (`1004`), as follows:

```
sudo groupadd -g 1004 alex2
```

And now, we can remove the user `alex2` from the current primary group (`managers`) by specifying the exclusive primary group we just created (`alex2`), like this:

```
sudo usermod -g alex2 alex2
```

The related user record becomes this:

```
id alex2
```

This is the output:

```
packt@neptune:~$ id alex2
uid=1004(alex2) gid=1400(managers) groups=1400(managers)
packt@neptune:~$ sudo groupadd -g 1004 alex2
groupadd: group 'alex2' already exists
packt@neptune:~$ getent group | tail -n 2
managers:x:1400:
alex2:x:1004:
packt@neptune:~$ sudo usermod -g alex2 alex2
packt@neptune:~$ id alex2
uid=1004(alex2) gid=1004(alex2) groups=1004(alex2)
packt@neptune:~$ 
```

Figure 4.21 – Verifying the user has been removed from primary groups

The `gid` attribute of the user record reflects the exclusive primary group (matching the user): `gid=1004(alex2)`. Our user doesn't belong to any other primary groups anymore.

Adding, moving, and removing users across groups may become increasingly daunting tasks for a Linux administrator. Knowing at any time which users belong to which groups is valuable information, both for reporting purposes and user automation workflows. The following section provides a few commands for viewing user and group data.

Viewing users and groups

In this section, we will provide some potentially useful commands for retrieving group and group membership information. Before we get into any commands, we should keep in mind that group information is stored in the `/etc/group` and `/etc/gshadow` files. Among the two, the former has the information we're most interested in.

We can parse the `/etc/group` file to retrieve all groups, as follows:

```
cat /etc/group | cut -d: -f1 | column | less
```

The command yields the following output:

```
root            dip                 input
daemon          www-data            sgx
bin             backup              kvm
sys             operator            render
adm             list                lxd
tty             irc                 _ssh
disk            src                 crontab
lp              gnats               syslog
mail            shadow              uuidd
news            utmp                tcpdump
uucp            video               tss
man             sasl                landscape
proxy           plugdev             packt
kmem            staff               fwupd-refresh
dialout         games               plocate
fax             users               alex
voice           nogroup             julian
cdrom           systemd-journal     admin
floppy          systemd-network     developers
tape            systemd-resolve     devops
sudo            messagebus          managers
audio           systemd-timesync    alex2
```

Figure 4.22 – Retrieving all group names

A similar command would use getent, which we can use like this:

```
getent group | cut -d: -f1 | column | less
```

The output of the preceding command is identical to the output shown in *Figure 4.22*. We can retrieve the information of an individual group (for example, developers) with the following command:

```
getent group developers
```

This is the output:

```
packt@neptune:~$ cat /etc/group | cut -d: -f1 | column | less
packt@neptune:~$ getent group | cut -d: -f1 | column | less
packt@neptune:~$ getent group developers
developers:x:1200:julian2
packt@neptune:~$ █
```

Figure 4.23 – Retrieving information for a single group

The output of the preceding command also reveals the members of the developers group (julian2).

To list all groups a specific user is a member of, we can use the groups command. For example, the following command lists all groups the user alex is a member of:

```
groups alex
```

This is the command output:

```
packt@neptune:~$ groups alex
alex : alex devops managers
packt@neptune:~$ 
```

Figure 4.24 – Retrieving group membership information of a user

The output of the previous command shows the groups for the user alex, starting with the primary group (alex).

A user can retrieve their own group membership using the groups command-line utility without specifying a group name. The following command is executed in a terminal session of the user packt, who is also an administrator (superuser):

```
groups
```

The command yields this output:

```
packt@neptune:~$ groups
packt adm cdrom sudo dip plugdev lxd
packt@neptune:~$
```

Figure 4.25 – The current user's groups

There are many other ways and commands to retrieve user- and group-related information. We hope that the preceding examples provide a basic idea about where and how to look for some of this information.

Next, let's look at how a user can switch or log in to specific groups.

Group login sessions

When a user logs in to the system, the group membership context is automatically set to the user's primary group. Once the user is logged in, any user-initiated task (such as creating a file or running a program) is associated with the user's primary group membership permissions. A user may also choose to access resources in other groups where they are also a member (that is, supplementary or secondary groups). To switch the group context or log in with a new group membership, a user invokes the newgrp command-line utility.

The basic syntax for the `newgrp` command is this:

```
newgrp GROUP
```

In the following example, we assume a user (`julian`) is a member of multiple groups—`admin` as the primary group, and `developers/devops` as secondary groups:

```
id julian
```

This is the output:

```
packt@neptune:~$ id julian
uid=1003(julian) gid=1100(admin) groups=1100(admin),1200(developers),1300(devops)
packt@neptune:~$
```

Figure 4.26 – A user with multiple group memberships

Let's impersonate the user `julian` for a while. We are currently logged in as the user `packt`. To change to the user `julian`, we will use the following command:

```
su julian
```

Remember that the user `julian` needs to have their password set in order to authenticate.

When logged in as `julian`, the default login session has the following user and group context:

```
whoami
```

In our case, this is the output:

```
packt@neptune:~$ whoami
packt
packt@neptune:~$ su julian
Password:
$ whoami
julian
$
```

Figure 4.27 – Getting the current user

The `whoami` command provides the current UID (see more details on the command with `man whoami` or `whoami --help`), as follows:

```
groups
```

This is the output:

```
$ whoami
julian
$ groups
admin developers devops
$
```

Figure 4.28 – Getting the current user's groups

The groups command displays all groups that the current user is a member of (see more details on the command with man groups or groups --help).

The user can also view their IDs (user and GIDs) by invoking the id command, as follows:

```
id
```

This is the output:

```
$ groups
admin developers devops
$ id
uid=1003(julian) gid=1100(admin) groups=1100(admin),1200(developers),1300(devops)
$ ▮
```

Figure 4.29 – Viewing the current user and GID information

There are various invocations of the id command that provide information on the current user and group session. The following command (with the -g, --group option) retrieves the ID of the current group session for the user:

```
id -g
1100
```

In our case, the preceding command shows 1100—the GID corresponding to the user's primary group, which is admin (see the gid attribute in *Figure 4.30*). Upon login, the default group session is always the primary group corresponding to the user. If the user were to create a file, for example, the file permission attributes would reflect the primary group's ID. We'll look at the file permissions in more detail in the *Managing permissions* section.

Now, let's switch the group session for the current user to developers, as follows:

```
newgrp developers
```

The current group session yields this:

```
id -g
1200
```

The GID corresponds to the `developers` secondary GID, as displayed by the `groups` attribute in *Figure 4.30*: `1200 (developers)`. If the user created any files now, the related file permission attributes would have the `developers` GID:

```
$ id
uid=1003(julian) gid=1100(admin) groups=1100(admin),1200(developers),1300(devops)
$ id -g
1100
$ newgrp developers
$ id -g
1200
$ id
uid=1003(julian) gid=1200(developers) groups=1200(developers),1100(admin),1300(de
vops)
$ 
```

Figure 4.30 – Switching the group session

If the user attempts to log in to a group they are not a member of (for example, `managers`), the `newgrp` command prompts for the `managers` group's password:

```
newgrp managers
```

If our user had the `managers` group password, or if they were a superuser, the group login attempt would succeed. Otherwise, the user would be denied access to the `managers` group's resources.

We conclude here our topic of managing users and groups. The examples of the related administrative tasks used throughout this section are certainly all-encompassing. In many of these cases, there are multiple ways to achieve the same result, using different commands or approaches.

By now, you should be relatively proficient in managing users and groups, and comfortable using the various command-line utilities for operating the related changes. Users and groups are managed in a relational fashion, where users belong to a group or groups are associated with users. We also learned that creating and managing users and groups requires superuser privileges. In Linux, user data is stored in the `/etc/passwd` and `/etc/shadow` files, while group information is found in `/etc/group` and `/etc/gshadow`. Besides using the dedicated command-line utilities, users and groups can also be altered by manually editing these files.

Next, we'll turn to the security and isolation context of the multiuser group environment. In Linux, the related functionality is accomplished by a system-level access layer that controls the read, write, and execute permissions of files and directories, by specific users and groups.

The following section explores the management and administrative tasks related to these permissions.

Managing permissions

A key tenet of Linux is the ability to allow multiple users to access the system while performing independent tasks simultaneously. The smooth operation of this multiuser, multitasking environment is controlled via **permissions**. The Linux kernel provides a robust framework for the underlying security and isolation model. At the user level, dedicated tools and command-line utilities help Linux users and system administrators with related permission management tasks.

For some Linux users, especially beginners, Linux permissions may appear confusing at times. This section attempts to demystify some of the key concepts about file and directory permissions in Linux. You will learn about the basic permission *rights* of accessing files and directories—the *read*, *write*, and *execution* permissions. We explore some of the essential administrative tasks for viewing and changing permissions, using system-level command-line utilities.

Most of the topics discussed in this section should be regarded closely with users and groups. The related idioms can be as simple as *a user can read or update a file*, *a group has access to these files and directories*, or *a user can execute this program*.

Let's start with the basics, introducing file and directory permissions.

File and directory permissions

In Linux, permissions can be regarded as the *rights* or *privileges* to act upon a file or a directory. The basic rights, or *permission attributes*, are outlined here:

- **Read**: A *read* permission of a file allows users to view the content of the file. On a directory, the read permission allows users to list the content of the directory.

- **Write**: A *write* permission of a file allows users to modify the content of the file. For a directory, the write permission allows users to modify the content of the directory by adding, deleting, or renaming files.

- **Execute**: An *execute* or *executable* permission of a file allows users to run the related script, application, or service appointed by the file. For a directory, the execute permission allows users to enter the directory and make it the current working directory (using the cd command).

First, let's take a look at how to reveal the permissions for files and directories.

Viewing permissions

The most common way to view the permissions of a file or directory is by using the ls command-line utility. The basic syntax of this command is this:

```
ls [OPTIONS] FILE|DIRECTORY
```

Here is an example use of the `ls` command to view the permissions of the `/etc/passwd` file:

```
ls -l /etc/passwd
```

The command yields the following output:

```
-rw-r--r-- 1 root root 2010 Mar  9 08:57 /etc/passwd
```

The `-l` option of the `ls` command provides a detailed output by using the *long listing format*, according to the `ls` documentation (`man ls`).

Let's analyze the output, as follows:

```
-rw-r--r-- 1 root root 2010 Mar  9 08:57 /etc/passwd
```

We have nine segments, separated by single whitespace characters (delimiters). These are outlined here:

- `-rw-r--r--`: The file access permissions
- `1`: The number of hard links
- `root`: The *user* who is the owner of the file
- `root`: The *group* that is the owner of the file
- `2010`: The size of the file
- `Mar`: The month the file was created
- `9`: The day of the month the file was created
- `08:57`: The time of day the file was created
- `/etc/passwd`: The filename

Let's examine the file access permissions field (`-rw-r--r--`). File access permissions are defined as a 10-character field, grouped as follows:

- The first character (attribute) is reserved for the file type (see the *File types* section).
- The next 9 characters represent a 9-bit field, defining the effective permissions as 3 sequences of 3 attributes (bits) each: *user owner* permissions, *group owner* permissions, and *all other users'* permissions (see the *Permission attributes* section).

Let's take a look at the file type attributes.

File type attributes

The file type attributes are listed here:

- d: Directory

- -: Regular file

- l: Symbolic link

- p: Named pipe—a special file that facilitates communication between programs

- s: Socket—similar to a pipe but with bidirectional network communications

- b: Block device—a file that corresponds to a hardware device

- c: Character device—similar to a block device

Let's have a closer look at the permission attributes.

Permission attributes

As previously noted, the access permissions are represented by a 9-bit field, a group of 3 sequences, each with 3 bits, defined as follows:

- **Bits 1-3**: *User* owner permissions

- **Bits 4-6**: *Group* owner permissions

- **Bits 7-9**: *All* other users' (or *world*) permissions

Each permission attribute is a bit flag in the binary representation of the related 3-bit sequence. They can be represented either as a character or as an equivalent numerical value, also known as the *octal* value, depending on the range of the bit they represent.

Here are the permission attributes with their respective octal values:

- r: *Read* permission; $2 \wedge 2 = 4$ (bit 2 set)

- w: *Write* permission: $2 \wedge 1 = 2$ (bit 1 set)

- x: *Execute* permission: $2 \wedge 0 = 1$ (bit 0 set)

- -: *No* permission: 0 (no bits set)

The resulting corroborated number is also known as the *octal value* of the file permissions (see the *File permission examples* section). Here's an illustration of the file permission attributes:

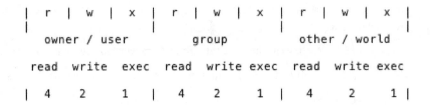

Figure 4.31 – The file permission attributes

Next, let's consider some examples.

File permission examples

Now, let's go back and evaluate the file access permissions for /etc/passwd: -rw-r--r--, as follows:

- -: The first character (byte) denotes the file type (a regular file, in our case)
- rw-: The next three-character sequence indicates the user owner permissions; (in our case, read (r); write (w); octal value = 4 (r) + 2 (w) = 6 (rw))
- r--: The next 3-byte sequence defines the group owner permissions (in our case, read (r); octal value = 4 (r))
- r--: The last three characters denote the permissions for all other users in the system (in our case, read (r); octal value = 4 (r))

According to the preceding information, the resulting octal value of the /etc/passwd file access permissions is 644. Alternatively, we can query the octal value with the stat command, as follows:

```
stat --format '%a' /etc/passwd
```

The command yields the following output:

```
644
```

The stat command displays the file or filesystem status. The --format option parameter specifies the access rights in octal format ('%a') for the output.

Here are a few examples of access permissions, with their corresponding octal values and descriptions. The three-character sequences are intentionally delimited with whitespace for clarity. The leading file type has been omitted:

- rwx (777): Read, write, and execute for all users including owner, group, and world
- rwx r-x (755): Read and execute for all users; the file owner has write permissions

- `rwx r-x ---` (750): Read and execute for owner and group; the owner has write permissions while others have no access

- `rwx --- ---` (700): Read, write, and execute for owner; everyone else has no permissions

- `rw- rw- rw-` (666): Read and write for all users; there are no execute permissions

- `rw- rw- r--` (664): Read and write for owner and group; read for others

- `rw- rw- ---` (660): Read and write for owner and group; others have no permissions

- `rw- r-- r--` (644): Read and write for owner; read for group and others

- `rw- r-- ---` (640): Read and write for owner; read for group; no permissions for others

- `rw- --- ---` (600): Read and write for owner; no permissions for group and others

- `r-- --- ---` (400): Read for owner; no permissions for others

Read, write, and execute are the most common types of file access permissions. So far, we have mostly focused on permission types and their representation. In the next section, we will explore a few command-line tools used for altering permissions.

Changing permissions

Modifying file and directory access permissions is a common Linux administrative task. In this section, we will learn about a few command-line utilities that are handy when it comes to changing permissions and ownership of files and directories. These tools are installed with any modern-day Linux distribution, and their use is similar across most Linux platforms.

Using chmod

The `chmod` command is short for *change mode*, and it's used to set access permissions on files and directories. The `chmod` command can be used by both the current user (owner) and a superuser.

Changing permissions can be done in two different modes: **relative** and **absolute**. Let's take a look at each of them.

Using chmod in relative mode

Changing permissions in **relative** mode is probably the easiest of the two. It is important to remember the following:

- *To whom* we change permissions: u = user (owner), g = group, o = others

- *How* we change permissions: + = add, - = remove, = = exactly as is

- *Which* permission we change: r = read, w = write, x = execute

Let's explore a few examples of using `chmod` in relative mode.

In our first example, we want to add write (w) permissions for all *other* (o) users (*world*), to myfile, as follows:

```
chmod o+w myfile
```

The related command-line output is shown here:

```
packt@neptune:~$ touch myfile
packt@neptune:~$ ls -l myfile
-rw-rw-r-- 1 packt packt 0 Mar  9 17:12 myfile
packt@neptune:~$ chmod o+w myfile
packt@neptune:~$ ls -l myfile
-rw-rw-rw- 1 packt packt 0 Mar  9 17:12 myfile
packt@neptune:~$
```

Figure 4.32 – Setting write permissions to all other users

In the next example, we remove the read (r) and write (w) permissions for the current user owner (u) of myfile, as follows:

```
chmod u-rw myfile
```

The command-line output is shown here:

```
packt@neptune:~$ ls -l myfile
-rw-rw-rw- 1 packt packt 0 Mar  9 17:12 myfile
packt@neptune:~$ chmod u-rw myfile
packt@neptune:~$ ls -l myfile
----rw-rw- 1 packt packt 0 Mar  9 17:12 myfile
packt@neptune:~$
```

Figure 4.33 – Removing read-write permissions for owner

We did not use sudo in either of the preceding examples since we carried out the operations as the current owner of the file (packt).

In the following example, we assume that myfile has read, write, and execute permissions for everyone. Then, we carry out the following changes:

- Remove the read (r) permission for the owner (u)

- Remove the write (w) permission for the owner (u) and group (g)

- Remove the read (r), write (w), and execute (x) permissions for everyone else (o)

This is illustrated in the following code snippet:

```
chmod u-r,ug-w,o-rwx myfile
```

The command-line output is shown here:

```
packt@neptune:~$ chmod u+rwx,ug+rwx,o+rwx myfile
packt@neptune:~$ ls -l myfile
-rwxrwxrwx 1 packt packt 0 Mar  9 17:12 myfile
packt@neptune:~$ chmod u-r,ug-w,o-rwx myfile
packt@neptune:~$ ls -l myfile
---xr-x--- 1 packt packt 0 Mar  9 17:12 myfile
packt@neptune:~$ █
```

Figure 4.34 – A relatively complex invocation of chmod in relative mode

Next, let's look at a second way of changing permissions: using the chmod command-line utility in absolute mode, by specifying the octal number corresponding to the access permissions.

Using chmod in absolute mode

The **absolute** mode invocation of chmod changes all permission attributes at once, using an *octal* number. The *absolute* designation of this method is due to changing permissions without any reference to existing ones, by simply assigning the octal value corresponding to the access permissions.

Here's a quick list of the octal values corresponding to effective permissions:

- 7 rwx: Read, write, and execute
- 6 rw-: Read and write
- 5 r-w: Read and execute
- 4 r--: Read
- 3 -wx: Write and execute
- 2 -w-: Write
- 1 --x: Execute
- 0 ---: No permissions

In the following example, we change the permissions of myfile to read (r), write (w), and execute (x) for everybody:

```
chmod 777 myfile
```

The related change is illustrated by the following command-line output:

```
packt@neptune:~$ chmod 777 myfile
packt@neptune:~$ ls -l myfile
-rwxrwxrwx 1 packt packt 0 Mar  9 17:12 myfile
packt@neptune:~$
```

Figure 4.35 – The chmod invocation in absolute mode

For more information about the chmod command, please refer to the related documentation (man chmod).

Let's now look at our next command-line utility, specializing in file and directory ownership changes.

Using chown

The chown command (short for *change owner*) is used to set the ownership of files and directories. Typically, the chmod command can only be run with *superuser* privileges (that is, by a *sudoer*). Regular users can only change the *group* ownership of their files, and only when they are a member of the target group.

The syntax of the chown command is shown here:

```
chown [OPTIONS] [OWNER][:[GROUP]] FILE
```

Usually, we invoke the chown command with both user *and* group ownerships—for example, like this:

```
sudo chown julian:developers myfile
```

The related command-line output is shown here:

```
packt@neptune:~$ sudo chown julian:developers myfile
[sudo] password for packt:
packt@neptune:~$ ls -l myfile
-rwxrwxrwx 1 julian developers 0 Mar  9 17:12 myfile
packt@neptune:~$
```

Figure 4.36 – A simple invocation of the chown command

One of the most common uses of chown is for *recursive mode* invocation, with the -R, --recursive option. The following example changes the ownership permissions of all files in mydir (directory), initially owned by root, to julian:

```
sudo chown -R julian:julian mydir/
```

The related changes are shown in the following command-line output:

```
drwxrwxr-x 2 packt packt 4096 Mar  9 17:37 subdir

mydir/subdir:
total 0
-rw-rw-r-- 1 packt packt 0 Mar  9 17:37 file1
-rw-rw-r-- 1 packt packt 0 Mar  9 17:37 file2
-rw-rw-r-- 1 packt packt 0 Mar  9 17:37 file3
packt@neptune:~$ sudo chown -R julian:julian mydir/
packt@neptune:~$ ls -lR mydir/
mydir/:
total 4
-rw-rw-r-- 1 julian julian    0 Mar  9 17:35 file1
-rw-rw-r-- 1 julian julian    0 Mar  9 17:35 file2
-rw-rw-r-- 1 julian julian    0 Mar  9 17:35 file3
drwxrwxr-x 2 julian julian 4096 Mar  9 17:37 subdir

mydir/subdir:
total 0
-rw-rw-r-- 1 julian julian 0 Mar  9 17:37 file1
-rw-rw-r-- 1 julian julian 0 Mar  9 17:37 file2
-rw-rw-r-- 1 julian julian 0 Mar  9 17:37 file3
```

Figure 4.37 – Invoking ls and chown in recursive mode

For more information about the chown command, please refer to the related documentation (man chown).

Next, let's briefly look at a similar command-line utility that specializes exclusively in group ownership changes.

Using chgrp

The chgrp command (short for *change group*) is used to change the *group* ownership for files and directories. In Linux, files and directories typically belong to a user (owner) or a group. We can set user ownership by using the chown command-line utility, while group ownership can be set with chgrp.

The syntax for chgrp is shown here:

```
chgrp [OPTIONS] GROUP FILE
```

The following example changes the group ownership of myfile to the developers group:

```
sudo chgrp developers myfile
```

The changes are shown in the following output:

```
packt@neptune:~$ sudo chgrp developers myfile
packt@neptune:~$ ls -l myfile
-rwxrwxrwx 1 julian developers 0 Mar  9 17:12 myfile
packt@neptune:~$ ▮
```

Figure 4.38 - Using chgrp to change group ownership

The preceding command has been invoked with superuser privileges (sudo) since the current user (packt) is not an admin for the developers group.

For more information about the chgrp utility, please refer to the tool's command-line help (chgrp --help).

Using umask

The umask command is used to view or set the default *file mode mask* in the system. The file mode represents the default permissions for any new files and directories created by a user. For example, the default file mode masks in Ubuntu are given here:

- 0002 for a regular user
- 0022 for the root user

As a general rule in Linux, the *default permissions* for new files and directories are calculated with the following formulas:

- 0666 – umask: For a new file created by a regular user
- 0777 – umask: For a new directory created by a regular user

According to the preceding formula, on Ubuntu, we have the following default permissions:

- File (regular user): 0666 – 0002 = 0664
- File (root): 0666 – 0022 = 0644
- Directory (regular user): 0777 – 0002 = 0775
- Directory (root): 0777 – 0022 = 0755

In the following examples, run on Ubuntu, we create a file (myfile) and a directory (mydir), using the terminal session of a regular user (packt). Then, we query the stat command for each and verify that the default permissions match the values enumerated previously for regular users (file: 664, directory: 775).

Let's start with the default file permissions first, as follows:

```
touch myfile2
stat --format '%a' myfile2
```

The related output is shown here:

```
664
```

Next, let's verify the default directory permissions, as follows:

```
mkdir mydir2
stat --format '%a' mydir2
```

The related output is shown here:

```
775
```

Here's a list with the typical umask values for files and directories on Linux systems:

umask value	Files		Directories	
0000	666	rw-rw-rw-	777	rwxrwxrwx
0002	664	rw-rw-r--	775	rwxrwxr-x
0022	644	rw-r--r--	755	rwxr-xr-x
0027	640	rw-r-----	750	rwxr-x---
0077	600	rw-------	700	rwx------
0277	400	r--------	500	r-x------

Figure 4.39 – Typical umask values on Linux

For more information about the umask utility, please refer to the tool's command-line help (umask --help).

File and directory permissions are critical for a secure environment. Users and processes should operate exclusively within the isolation and security constraints controlled by permissions, to avoid inadvertent or deliberate interference with the use and ownership of system resources. There are cases, particularly in user impersonation situations, when the access rights may involve some special permission attributes. Let's have a look at them.

Special permissions

In Linux, the ownership of files and directories is usually determined by the UID and GID of the user—or group—who created them. The same principle applies to applications and processes—they are owned by the users who launch them. The special permissions are meant to change this default behavior when needed.

Here are the special permission flags, with their respective octal values:

- `setuid`: $2 \wedge 2 = 4$ (bit 2 set)
- `setgid`: $2 \wedge 1 = 2$ (bit 1 set)
- `sticky`: $2 \wedge 0 = 1$ (bit 0 set)

When any of these special bits are set, the overall octal number of the access permissions will have an extra digit, with the leading (high-order) digit corresponding to the special permission's octal value.

Let's look at these special permission flags, with examples for each.

The setuid permission

With the `setuid` bit set, when an executable file is launched, it will run with the privileges of the file owner instead of the user who launched it. For example, if the executable is owned by `root` and launched by a *regular* user, it will run with `root` privileges. The `setuid` permission could pose a potential security risk when used inadequately, or when vulnerabilities of the underlying process could be exploited.

In the file access permission field, the `setuid` bit could have either of the following representations:

- `s` *replacing* the corresponding executable bit (`x`) (when the executable bit is present)
- `S` (the capital letter) for a non-executable file

The `setuid` permission can be set via the following `chmod` command (for example, for the `myscript.sh` executable file):

```
chmod u+s myscript.sh
```

The resulting file permissions are shown here (including the octal value): `-rwsrwxr-x` (`4775`).

Here is the related command-line output:

```
packt@neptune:~$ touch myscript.sh
packt@neptune:~$ chmod +x myscript.sh
packt@neptune:~$ ls -l myscript.sh
-rwxrwxr-x 1 packt packt 0 Mar  9 17:02 myscript.sh
packt@neptune:~$ chmod u+s myscript.sh
packt@neptune:~$ ls -l myscript.sh
-rwsrwxr-x 1 packt packt 0 Mar  9 17:02 myscript.sh
packt@neptune:~$ stat --format '%a' myscript.sh
4775
packt@neptune:~$
```

Figure 4.40 – The setuid permission

In the preceding screenshot, you can see the difference in permissions. Before applying the `chmod` command, the permissions are `-rwxrwxr-x`, and after applying the `setuid` permission with the `chmod` command, an s (referring to `setuid`) is included in the user's permission, `-rwsrwxr-x`. For more information on `setuid`, please visit `https://docs.oracle.com/cd/E19683-01/816-4883/secfile-69/index.html` or refer to the `chmod` command-line utility documentation (`man chmod`).

The setgid permission

While `setuid` controls user impersonation privileges, `setgid` has a similar effect on group impersonation permissions.

When an executable file has the `setgid` bit set, it runs using the permissions of the group that owns the file, rather than the group of the user who initiated it. In other words, the GID of the process is the same as the GID of the file.

When used on a directory, the `setgid` bit changes the default ownership behavior so that files created within the directory will have group ownership of the parent directory instead of the group associated with the user who created them. This behavior could be adequate in file-sharing situations when files can be changed by all users associated with the parent directory's owner group.

The `setgid` permission can be set via the following `chmod` command (for example, for the `myscript.sh` executable file, the original file, before applying `setuid` to it):

```
chmod g+s myscript.shw
```

The resulting file permissions are shown here (including the octal value): `-rwxrwsr-x` (`2775`).

The command-line output is shown here:

```
packt@neptune:~$ chmod g+s myscript.sh
packt@neptune:~$ ls -l myscript.sh
-rwxrwsr-x 1 packt packt 0 Mar  9 17:07 myscript.sh
packt@neptune:~$ stat --format '%a' myscript.sh
2775
packt@neptune:~$
```

Figure 4.41 – The setgid permission

For more information on `setgid`, please visit `https://en.wikipedia.org/wiki/Setuid` or refer to the `chmod` command-line utility documentation (`man chmod`).

The sticky permission

The `sticky` bit has no effect on files. For a directory with the `sticky` permission, only the user owner or group owner of the directory can delete or rename files within the directory. Users or groups with write access to the directory, by way of user or group ownership, cannot delete or modify files in the directory. The `sticky` permission is useful when a directory is owned by a privileged group whose members share write access to files in that directory.

The `sticky` permission can be set via the following `chmod` command (for example, for the `mydir` directory):

```
chmod +t mydir
```

The resulting directory permissions are shown here (including the octal value): `drwxrwxr-t (1775)`.

The command-line output is shown here:

```
packt@neptune:~$ mkdir mydir
packt@neptune:~$ chmod +t mydir
packt@neptune:~$ ls -ld mydir
drwxrwxr-t 2 packt packt 4096 Mar  9 17:10 mydir
packt@neptune:~$ stat --format '%a' mydir
1775
packt@neptune:~$
```

Figure 4.42 – The sticky permission

For more information on `sticky`, please visit `https://en.wikipedia.org/wiki/Setuid` or refer to the `chmod` command-line utility documentation (`man chmod`).

Interpreting permissions can be a daunting task. This section aimed to demystify some of the related intricacies, and we hope that you will feel more comfortable handling file and directory permissions in everyday Linux administration tasks.

Summary

In this chapter, we explored some of the essential concepts related to managing users and groups in Linux. We learned about file and directory permissions and the different access levels of a multiuser environment. For each main topic, we focused on basic administrative tasks, providing various practical examples and using typical command-line tools for everyday user access and permission management operations.

Managing users and groups, and the related filesystem permissions that come into play, is an indispensable skill of a Linux administrator. The knowledge gained in this chapter will, we hope, put you on track to becoming a proficient superuser.

In the following chapter, we continue our journey of mastering Linux internals by exploring processes, daemons, and **inter-process communication** (**IPC**) mechanisms. An important aspect to keep in mind is that processes and daemons are also *owned* by users or groups. The skills learned in this chapter will help us navigate the related territory when we look at *who runs what* at any given time in the system.

Questions

Here are a few thoughts and questions that sum up the main ideas covered in this chapter:

1. What is a superuser?

   Hint: Try `sudo`

2. Think of a command-line utility for creating users. Can you think of another one?

   Hint: Think about `adduser` and `useradd`

3. What is the octal value of the `-rw-rw-r—` access permission?

   Hint: Remember what the values of `r`, `w`, and `x` are: 4, 2, and 1

4. What is the difference between a primary group and a secondary (supplementary) group?

5. How do you change the ownership of a user's home directory?

6. Can you remove a user from the system without deleting their home directory? How?

Further reading

Here are a few Packt titles that can help you with the task of user management:

- *Mastering Ubuntu Server – Fourth Edition, Jay LaCroix*
- *Red Hat Enterprise Linux 9 Administration – Second Edition, Pablo Iranzo Gómez, Pedro Ibáñez Requena, Miguel Pérez Colino, and Scott McCarty*

5

Working with Processes, Daemons, and Signals

Linux is a multitasking operating system. Multiple programs or tasks can run in parallel, each with its own identity, scheduling, memory space, permissions, and system resources. **Processes** encapsulate the execution context of any such program. Understanding how processes work and communicate with each other is an important skill for any seasoned Linux system administrator and developer to have.

This chapter explores the basic concepts behind Linux processes. We'll look at different types of processes, such as **foreground** and **background** processes, with special emphasis being placed on **daemons** as a particular type of background process. We'll closely study the anatomy of a process and various inter-process communication mechanisms in Linux – **signals** in particular. Along the way, we'll learn about some of the essential command-line utilities for managing processes and daemons and working with signals. We will also introduce you to **scripts** for the first time in this book, which are described in detail later in *Chapter 8, Linux Shell Scripting*. If you feel like you need more information when dealing with the scripts in this chapter, take a look at *Chapter 8* in advance.

In this chapter, we will cover the following topics:

- Introducing processes
- Working with processes
- Working with daemons
- Exploring inter-process communication

> **Important note**
>
> As we navigate through the content, we will occasionally reference signals *before* their formal introduction in the second half of this chapter. In Linux, signals are almost exclusively used in association with processes, hence our approach of becoming familiar with processes first. Yet, leaving the signals out from some of the process' internals would do a disservice to understanding how processes work. Where signals are mentioned, we'll point to the related section for further reference. We hope that this approach provides you with a better grasp of the overall picture and the inner workings of processes and daemons.

Now, before we start, let's look at the essential requisites for our study.

Technical requirements

Practice makes perfect. Running the commands and examples in this chapter by hand would go a long way toward you learning about processes. As with any chapter in this book, we recommend that you have a working Linux distribution installed on a VM or PC desktop platform. We'll be using Ubuntu or Fedora, but most of the commands and examples would be similar on any other Linux platform.

Introducing processes

A **process** represents the running instance of a program. In general, a program is a combination of instructions and data, compiled as an executable unit. When a program runs, a process is created. In other words, a process is simply a program in action. Processes execute specific tasks, and sometimes, they are also referred to as **jobs** (or **tasks**).

There are many ways to create or start a process. In Linux, every command starts a process. A command could be a user-initiated task in a Terminal session, a script, or a program (executable) that's invoked manually or automatically.

Usually, the way a process is created and interacts with the system (or user) determines its process type. Let's take a closer look at the different types of processes in Linux.

Understanding process types

At a high level, there are two major types of processes in Linux:

- **Foreground** (*interactive*)
- **Background** (*non-interactive* or *automated*)

Interactive processes assume some kind of user interaction during the lifetime of the process. Non-interactive processes are unattended, which means that they are either automatically started (for example, on system boot) or are scheduled to run at a particular time and date via job schedulers (for example, using the at and cron command-line utilities).

Our approach to exploring process types mainly pivots around the preceding classification. There are various other views or taxonomies surrounding process definitions, but they could ultimately be reduced to either foreground or background processes.

For example, batch processes and daemons are essentially background processes. Batch processes are automated in the sense that they are not user-generated but invoked by a scheduled task instead. Daemons are background processes that are usually started during system boot and run indefinitely.

There's also the concept of parent and child processes. A parent process may create other subordinate child processes.

We'll elaborate on these types (and beyond) in the following sections. Let's start with the pivotal ones – foreground and background processes.

Foreground processes

Foreground processes, also known as **interactive processes**, are started and controlled through a Terminal session. Foreground processes are usually initiated by a user via an interactive command-line interface. A foreground process may output results to the console (`stdout` or `stderr`) or accept user input. The lifetime of a foreground process is tightly coupled to the Terminal session (parent process). If the user who launched the foreground process exits the Terminal while the process is still running, the process will be abruptly terminated (via a `SIGHUP` signal sent by the parent process; see *Signals* in the *Exploring inter-process communication* section for more details).

A simple example of a foreground process is invoking the system reference manual (`man`) for an arbitrary Linux command (for example, `ps`):

```
man ps
```

The `ps` command displays information about active processes. You will learn more about process management tools and command-line utilities in the *Working with processes* section.

Once a foreground process has been initiated, the user prompt is captured and controlled by the spawned process interface. The user can no longer interact with the initial command prompt until the interactive process relinquishes control to the Terminal session.

Let's look at another example of a foreground process, this time invoking a long-lived task. The following command (one-liner) runs an infinite loop while displaying an arbitrary message every few seconds:

```
while true; do echo "Wait..."; sleep 5; done
```

So long as the command runs without being interrupted, the user won't have an interactive prompt in the Terminal. Using *Ctrl + C* would stop (interrupt) the execution of the related foreground process and yield a responsive command prompt:

```
packt@neptune:~$ while true; do echo "Wait..."; sleep 5; done
Wait...
Wait...
Wait...
^C
packt@neptune:~$
```

Figure 5.1 – A long-lived foreground process

> **Important note**
>
> When you press *Ctrl + C* while a foreground process is running, a SIGINT signal is sent to the running process by the current (parent) Terminal session, and the foreground process is interrupted. For more information, see the *Signals* section.

If we want to maintain an interactive command prompt in the Terminal session while running a specific command or script, we should use a background process.

Background processes

Background processes – also referred to as **non-interactive** or **automatic processes** – run independently of a Terminal session, without expecting any user interaction. A user may invoke multiple background processes within the same Terminal session without waiting on any of them to complete or exit.

Background processes are usually long-lived tasks that don't require direct user supervision. The related process may still display its output in the Terminal console, but such background tasks typically write their results to different files instead (such as log files).

The simplest invocation of a background process appends an ampersand (&) to the end of the related command. Building on our previous example (in the *Foreground processes* section), the following command creates a background process that runs an infinite loop, echoing an arbitrary message every few seconds:

```
while true; do echo "Wait..."; sleep 10; done &
```

Note the ampersand (&) at the end of the command. By default, a background process would still direct the output (stdout and stderr) to the console when invoked with the ampersand (&), as shown previously. However, the Terminal session remains interactive. In the following figure, we are using the echo command while the previous process is still running:

```
packt@neptune:~$ while true; do echo "Wait..."; sleep 10; done &
[1] 983
packt@neptune:~$ Wait...
echo "Interactive Wait...
prompt"
Interactive prompt
packt@neptune:~$ Wait...
kill -9 983
packt@neptune:~$
```

Figure 5.2 – Running a background process

As shown in the preceding screenshot, the background process is given a **process ID (PID)** of 983. While the process is running, we can still control the Terminal session and run a different command, like so:

```
echo "Interactive prompt..."
```

Eventually, we can force the process to terminate with the `kill` command:

```
kill -9 983
```

The preceding command *kills* our background process (with PID 983). The corresponding signal that's sent by the parent Terminal session to terminate this process is `SIGKILL` (see the *Signals* section for more information) through the -9 argument in our command.

Both foreground and background processes are typically under the direct control of a user. In other words, these processes are created or started manually as a result of a command or script invocation. There are some exceptions to this rule, particularly when it comes to batch processes, which are launched automatically via scheduled jobs.

There's also a select category of background processes that are automatically started during system boot and terminated at shutdown without user supervision. These background processes are also known as daemons.

Introducing daemons

A **Daemon** is a particular type of background process that is usually started upon system boot and run indefinitely or until terminated (for example, during system shutdown). A daemon doesn't have a user-controlled Terminal, even though it is associated with a system account (`root` or other) and runs with the related privileges.

Daemons usually serve client requests or communicate with other foreground or background processes. Here are some common examples of daemons, all of which are generally available on most Linux platforms:

- `systemd`: The parent of all processes (formerly known as `init`)
- `crond`: A job scheduler that runs tasks in the background
- `ftpd`: An FTP server that handles client FTP requests
- `httpd`: A web server (Apache) that handles client HTTP requests
- `sshd`: A Secure Shell server that handles SSH client requests

Typically, system daemons in Linux are named with d at the end, denoting a daemon process. Daemons are controlled by shell scripts usually stored in the `/etc/init.d/` or `/lib/systemd/` system directory, depending on the Linux platform. Ubuntu, for example, stores daemon script files in `/etc/init.d/`, while Fedora stores them in `/lib/systemd/`. The location of these daemon files depends on the platform implementation of `init`, a system-wide service manager for all Linux processes.

The Linux init-style startup process generally invokes these shell scripts at system boot. But the same scripts can also be invoked via service control commands, usually run by privileged system users, to manage the lifetime of specific daemons. In other words, a privileged user or system administrator can *stop* or *start* a particular daemon through the command-line interface. Such commands would immediately return the user's control to the Terminal while performing the related action in the background.

Let's take a closer look at the `init` process.

The init process

Throughout this chapter, we'll refer to `init` as the *generic* system initialization engine and service manager on Linux platforms. Over the years, Linux distributions have evolved and gone through various `init` system implementations, such as `SysV`, `upstart`, `OpenRC`, `systemd`, and `runit`. There's an ongoing debate in the Linux community about the supremacy or advantages of one over the other. For now, we will simply regard `init` as a system process, and we will briefly look at its relationship with other processes.

`init` (or `systemd`, and others) is essentially a system daemon, and it's among the first process to start when Linux boots up. The related daemon process continues to run in the background until the system is shut down. `init` is the root (parent) process of all other processes in Linux, in the overall process hierarchy tree. In other words, it is a direct or indirect ancestor of all the processes in the system.

In Linux, the `pstree` command displays the whole process tree, and it shows the `init` process at its root – in our case, `systemd` (on Ubuntu or Fedora).

The output of the preceding command can be seen in the following screenshot:

```
packt@neptune:~$ pstree
systemd─┬─ModemManager───2*[{ModemManager}]
        ├─agetty
        ├─cron
        ├─dbus-daemon
        ├─multipathd───6*[{multipathd}]
        ├─networkd-dispat
        ├─polkitd───2*[{polkitd}]
        ├─rsyslogd───3*[{rsyslogd}]
        ├─snapd───7*[{snapd}]
        ├─sshd───sshd───sshd───bash───pstree
        ├─systemd───(sd-pam)
        ├─systemd-journal
        ├─systemd-logind
        ├─systemd-network
        ├─systemd-resolve
        ├─systemd-timesyn───{systemd-timesyn}
        ├─systemd-udevd
        ├─udisksd───4*[{udisksd}]
        └─unattended-upgr───{unattended-upgr}
```

Figure 5.3 – init (systemd), the parent of all processes

The `pstree` command's output illustrates a hierarchy tree representation of the processes, where some appear as parent processes while others appear as child processes. Let's look at the parent and child process types and some of the dynamics between them.

Parent and child processes

A **parent process** creates other subordinate processes, also known as **child processes**. Child processes belong to the parent process that spawned them and usually terminate when the parent process exits (stops execution). A child process may continue to run beyond the parent process's lifetime if it's been instructed to ignore the SIGHUP signal that's invoked by the parent process upon termination (for example, via the nohup command). See the *Signals* section for more information.

In Linux, all processes except the init process (with its variations) are children of a specific process. Terminating a child process won't stop the related parent process from running. A good practice for terminating a parent process when the child is done processing is to exit from the parent process itself after the child process completes.

There are cases when processes run unattended, based on a specific schedule. Running a process without user interaction is known as batch processing. We'll look at batch processes next.

Batch processes

A **batch process** is typically a script or a command that's been scheduled to run at a specific date and time, usually in a periodic fashion. In other words, batch processing is a background process that's spawned by a **job scheduler**. In most common cases, batch processes are resource-intensive tasks that are usually scheduled to run during less busy hours to avoid system overload. On Linux, the most commonly used tools for job scheduling are `at` and `cron`. While `cron` is better suited to scheduled task management complexities, `at` is a more lightweight utility, better suited for one-off jobs. A detailed study of these commands is beyond the scope of this chapter. You may refer to the related system reference manuals for more information (`man at` and `man cron`).

We'll conclude our study of process types with orphan and zombie processes.

Orphan and zombie processes

When a child process is terminated, the related parent process is notified with a `SIGCHILD` signal. The parent can go on running other tasks or may choose to spawn another child process. However, there may be instances when the parent process is terminated before a related child process completes execution (or exits). In this case, the child process becomes an **orphan process**. In Linux, the `init` process – the parent of all processes – automatically becomes the new parent of the orphan process.

Zombie processes (also known as **defunct processes**) are references to processes that have completed execution (and exited) but are still lingering in the system process table (according to the `ps` command).

The main difference between the zombie and orphan processes is that a zombie process is dead (terminated), while an orphan process is still running.

As we differentiate between various process types and their behavior, a significant part of the related information is reflected in the composition or data structure of the process itself. In the next section, we'll take a closer look at the makeup of a process, which is mostly echoed through the `ps` command-line utility – an ordinary yet very useful process explorer on Linux systems.

The anatomy of a process

In this section, we will explore some of the common attributes of a Linux process through the lens of the `ps` and `top` command-line utilities. We hope that taking a practical approach based on these tools will help you gain a better understanding of process internals, at least from a Linux administrator's perspective. Let's start by taking a brief look at these commands. The `ps` command displays a current snapshot of the system processes. This command has the following syntax:

```
ps [OPTIONS]
```

The following command displays the processes owned by the current Terminal session:

```
ps
```

The output of the preceding command can be seen in the following screenshot:

```
packt@neptune:~$ ps
      PID TTY          TIME CMD
      968 pts/0    00:00:00 bash
     1008 pts/0    00:00:00 ps
packt@neptune:~$
```

Figure 5.4 – Displaying processes owned by the current shell

Let's look at each field in the top (header) row of the output and explain their meaning in the context of our relevant process – that is, the bash Terminal session:

- PID: Each process in Linux has a PID value automatically assigned by the kernel when the process is created. The PID value is a positive integer and is always guaranteed to be unique.

  In our case, the relevant process is bash (the current shell), with a PID of 171233.

- TTY: **TTY** is short for **teletype**, more popularly known as a controlling Terminal or device for interacting with a system. In the context of a Linux process, the TTY attribute denotes the type of Terminal the process interacts with. In our example, the bash process representing the Terminal session has pts/0 as its TTY type. **PTS** or pts stands for **pseudo terminal slave** and indicates the input type – a Terminal console – controlling the process. /0 indicates the ordinal sequence of the related Terminal session. For example, an additional SSH session would have pts/1, and so on.

- TIME: The TIME field represents the cumulative CPU utilization (or time) spent by the process (in [DD-]hh:mm:ss format). Why is it zero (00:00:00) for the bash process in our example? We may have run multiple commands in our Terminal session, yet the CPU utilization could still be zero. That's because the CPU utilization measures (and accumulates) the time spent for each command, and not the parent Terminal session overall. If the commands complete within a fraction of a second, they will not amount to a significant CPU utilization being shown in the TIME field.

- CMD: The CMD field stands for command and indicates the name or full path of the command (including the arguments) that created the process. For well-known system commands (for example, bash), CMD displays the command's name, including its arguments.

The process attributes we've explored thus far represent a relatively simple view of Linux processes. There are situations when we may need more information. For example, the following command provides additional details about the processes running in the current Terminal session:

```
ps -l
```

The `-l` option parameter invokes the so-called *long format* for the `ps` output:

```
packt@neptune:~$ ps -l
F S   UID      PID    PPID  C PRI  NI ADDR SZ WCHAN  TTY            TIME CMD
0 S  1000      968     967  0  80   0  -  2216 do_wai pts/0      00:00:00 bash
0 R  1000     1058     968  0  80   0  -  2517 -      pts/0      00:00:00 ps
```

Figure 5.5 – A more detailed view of processes

Here are just a few of the more relevant output fields of the `ps` command:

- `F`: Process flags (for example, `0` – none, `1` – forked, and `4` – superuser privileges)
- `S`: Process status code (for example, `R` – running, `S` – interruptible sleep, and so on)
- `UID`: The username or owner of the process (the user ID)
- `PID`: The process ID
- `PPID`: The process ID of the parent process
- `PRI`: The priority of the process (a higher number means lower priority)
- `SZ`: The virtual memory usage

There are many more such attributes and exploring them all is beyond the scope of this book. For additional information, refer to the `ps` system reference manual (`man ps`).

The `ps` command examples we've used so far have only displayed the processes that are owned by the current Terminal session. This approach, we thought, would add less complexity to analyzing process attributes.

Besides `ps`, another command that's used is `top`, and it provides a live (real-time) view of all the running processes in a system. Its syntax is as follows:

```
top [OPTIONS]
```

Many of the process output fields displayed by the `ps` command are also reflected in the `top` command, albeit some of them with slightly different notations. Let's look at the `top` command and the meaning of the output fields that are displayed. The following command displays a real-time view of running processes:

```
top
```

The output of the preceding command can be seen in the following screenshot:

```
top - 12:02:40 up 32 min,  1 user,  load average: 0.00, 0.00, 0.00
Tasks: 113 total,   1 running, 112 sleeping,   0 stopped,   0 zombie
%Cpu(s):   0.0 us,   6.2 sy,   0.0 ni, 93.8 id,   0.0 wa,   0.0 hi,   0.0 si,   0.0 st
MiB Mem :   1976.0 total,   1424.6 free,   222.1 used,   329.3 buff/cache
MiB Swap:   1840.0 total,   1840.0 free,     0.0 used.   1604.8 avail Mem

  PID USER      PR  NI    VIRT    RES    SHR S  %CPU  %MEM     TIME+ COMMAND
    1 root      20   0  166492  11736   8288 S   0.0   0.6   0:02.13 systemd
    2 root      20   0       0      0      0 S   0.0   0.0   0:00.00 kthreadd
    3 root       0 -20       0      0      0 I   0.0   0.0   0:00.00 rcu_gp
    4 root       0 -20       0      0      0 I   0.0   0.0   0:00.00 rcu_par+
    5 root       0 -20       0      0      0 I   0.0   0.0   0:00.00 slub_fl+
    6 root       0 -20       0      0      0 I   0.0   0.0   0:00.00 netns
```

Figure 5.6 – A real-time view of the current processes

Here are some of the output fields, briefly explained:

- USER: The username or owner of the process
- PR: The priority of the process (a lower number means higher priority)
- NI: The nice value of the process (a sort of dynamic/adaptive priority)
- VIRT: The virtual memory size (in KB) – the total memory used by the process
- RES: The resident memory size (in KB) – the physical (non-swapped) memory used by the process
- SHR: The shared memory size (in KB) – a subset of the process memory shared with other processes
- S: The process' status (for example, R – running, S – interruptible sleep, I – idle, and so on)
- %CPU: CPU usage (percentage)
- %MEM: RES memory usage (percentage)
- COMMAND: Command name or command line

Each of these fields (and many more) are explained in detail in the top system reference manual (man top).

Every day, Linux administration tasks frequently use process-related queries based on the preceding presented fields. The *Working with processes* section will explore some of the more common usages of the ps and top commands, and beyond.

An essential aspect of a process's lifetime is the **status** (or **state**) of the process at any given time and the transition between these states. Both the ps and top commands provide information about the status of the process via the S field. Let's take a closer look at these states.

Process states

During its lifetime, a process may change states according to circumstances. According to the S (status) field of the ps and top commands, a Linux process can have any of the following states:

- D: Uninterruptible sleep
- I: Idle
- R: Running
- S: Sleeping (interruptible sleep)
- T: Stopped by a job control signal
- t: Stopped by the debugger during a trace
- Z: Zombie

At a high level, any of these states can be identified with the following process states:

- **Running**: The process is currently running (the R state) or is an idle process (the I state). In Linux, an idle process is a specific task that's assigned to every processor (CPU) in the system and is scheduled to run only when there's no other process running on the related CPU. The time that's spent on idle tasks accounts for the idle time that's reported by the top command.

- **Waiting**: The process is waiting for a specific event or resource. There are two types of waiting states: interruptible sleep (the S state) and uninterruptible sleep (the D state). Interruptible sleep can be disturbed by specific process signals, yielding further process execution. On the other hand, uninterruptible sleep is a state where the process is blocked in a system call (possibly waiting on some hardware conditions), and it cannot be interrupted.

- **Stopped**: The process has stopped executing, usually due to a specific signal – a job control signal (the T state) or a debugging signal (the t state).

- **Zombie**: The process is defunct or dead (the Z state) – it's terminated without being reaped by its parent. A zombie process is essentially a dead reference for an already terminated process in the system's process table. This will be discussed in more detail in the *Orphan and zombie processes* section.

To conclude our analysis of process states, let's look at the lifetime of a Linux process. Usually, a process starts with a running state (R) and terminates once its parent has reaped it from the zombie state (Z). The following diagram provides an abbreviated view of the process states and the possible transitions between them:

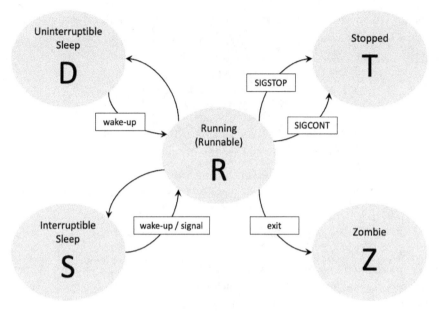

Figure 5.7 – The lifetime of a Linux process

Now that we've introduced processes and provided you with a preliminary idea of their type and structure, we're ready to interact with them. In the following sections, we will explore some standard command-line utilities for working with processes and daemons. Most of these tools operate with input and output data, which we covered in the *Anatomy of a process* section. We'll look at working with processes next.

Working with processes

This section serves as a practical guide to managing processes via resourceful command-line utilities that are used in everyday Linux administration tasks. Some of these tools were mentioned in previous sections (for example, ps and top) when we covered specific process internals. Here, we will summon most of the knowledge we've gathered so far and take it for a real-world spin by covering some hands-on examples.

Let's start with the ps command – the Linux process explorer.

Using the ps command

We described the ps command and its syntax in the *Anatomy of a process* section. The following command displays a selection of the current processes running in the system:

```
ps -e | head
```

The -e option (or -A) selects *all* the processes in the system. The head pipe invocation displays only the first few lines (10 by default):

```
packt@neptune:~$ ps -e | head
    PID TTY          TIME CMD
      1 ?        00:00:02 systemd
      2 ?        00:00:00 kthreadd
      3 ?        00:00:00 rcu_gp
      4 ?        00:00:00 rcu_par_gp
      5 ?        00:00:00 slub_flushwq
      6 ?        00:00:00 netns
      7 ?        00:00:01 kworker/0:0-events
      8 ?        00:00:00 kworker/0:0H-events_highpri
     10 ?        00:00:00 mm_percpu_wq
```

Figure 5.8 – Displaying the first few processes

The preceding information may not always be particularly useful. Perhaps we'd like to know more about each process, beyond just the PID or CMD fields in the ps command's output. (We described some of these process attributes in the *Anatomy of a process* section).

The following command lists the processes owned by the current user more elaborately:

```
ps -fU $(whoami)
```

The -f option specifies the full-format listing, which displays more detailed information for each process. The -U $(whoami) option parameter specifies the current user (packt) as the real user (owner) of the processes we'd like to retrieve. In other words, we want to list all the processes we own:

```
packt@neptune:~$ ps -fU $(whoami)
UID          PID    PPID  C STIME TTY          TIME CMD
packt        864       1  0 11:30 ?        00:00:00 /lib/systemd/systemd --user
packt        865     864  0 11:30 ?        00:00:00 (sd-pam)
packt        967     861  0 11:30 ?        00:00:00 sshd: packt@pts/0
packt        968     967  0 11:30 pts/0    00:00:00 -bash
packt       1079     968  0 12:31 pts/0    00:00:00 ps -fU packt
packt@neptune:~$ 
```

Figure 5.9 – Displaying the processes owned by the current user

There are situations when we may look for a specific process, either for monitoring purposes or to act upon them. Let's take a previous example, where we showcased a long-lived process and wrapped the related command into a simple script. The command is a simple while loop that runs indefinitely:

```
while true; do x=1; done
```

Using an editor of our preference (for example, nano), we can create a script file (for example, test.sh) with the following content:

```
packt@neptune:~$ nano test.sh
packt@neptune:~$ cat test.sh
#!/bin/bash
while true; do x=1; done
```

Figure 5.10 – A simple test script running indefinitely

We can make the test script executable and run it as a background process:

```
chmod +x test.sh
./test.sh &
```

Note the ampersand (&) at the end of the command, which invokes the background process:

```
packt@neptune:~$ chmod +x test.sh
packt@neptune:~$ ./test.sh &
[1] 1094
```

Figure 5.11 – Running a script as a background process

The background process running our script has a process ID (PID) of 1094. Suppose we want to find our process by its name (test.sh). For this, we can use the ps command with a grep pipe:

```
ps -ef | grep test.sh
```

The output of the preceding command can be seen in the following screenshot:

```
packt@neptune:~$ ps -ef | grep test.sh
packt      1094     968 99 12:41 pts/0     00:02:28 /bin/bash ./test.sh
packt      1097     968  0 12:44 pts/0     00:00:00 grep --color=auto test.sh
```

Figure 5.12 – Finding a process by name using the ps command

The preceding output shows that our process has a PID value of 1094 and a CMD value of /bin/bash ./test.sh. The CMD field contains the full command invocation of our script, including the command-line parameters.

We should note that the first line of the test.sh script contains #!/bin/bash, which prompts the OS to invoke bash for the script's execution. This line is also known as the **shebang** line, and it has to be the first line in a bash script. To make more sense of the CMD field, the command in our case is /bin/bash (according to the shebang invocation), and the related command-line parameter is the test.sh script. In other words, bash executes the test.sh script.

The output of the preceding `ps` command also includes our `ps | grep` command's invocation, which is somewhat irrelevant. A refined version of the same command is as follows:

```
ps -ef | grep test.sh | grep -v grep
```

The output of the preceding command can be seen in the following screenshot:

```
packt@neptune:~$ ps -ef | grep test.sh | grep -v grep
packt        1094      968 99 12:41 pts/0    00:04:57 /bin/bash ./test.sh
```

Figure 5.13 – Finding a process by name using the ps command (refined)

The `grep -v grep` pipe filters out the unwanted `grep` invocation from the `ps` command's results.

If we want to find a process based on a process ID (PID), we can invoke the `ps` command with the `-p|--pid` option parameter. For example, the following command displays detailed information about our process with PID set to `1094` (running the `test.sh` script):

```
packt@neptune:~$ ps -fp 1094
UID          PID    PPID  C STIME TTY          TIME CMD
packt        1094      968 99 12:41 pts/0    00:06:50 /bin/bash ./test.sh
```

Figure 5.14 – Finding a process by PID using the ps command

The `-f` option displays the detailed (*long-format*) process information.

There are numerous other use cases for the `ps` command, and exploring them all is well beyond the scope of this book. The invocations we've enumerated here should provide a basic exploratory guideline for you. For more information, please refer to the `ps` system reference manual (`man ps`).

Using the pstree command

`pstree` shows the running processes in a hierarchical, tree-like view. In some respects, `pstree` acts as a visualizer of the `ps` command. The root of the `pstree` command's output is either the `init` process or the process with the `PID` value specified in the command. The syntax of the `pstree` command is as follows:

```
pstree [OPTIONS] [PID] [USER]
```

The following command displays the process tree of our current Terminal session:

```
pstree $(echo $$)
```

The output of the preceding command can be seen in the following screenshot:

```
packt@neptune:~$ pstree $(echo $$)
bash──┬──pstree
      └──test.sh
```

Figure 5.15 – The process tree of the current Terminal session

In the preceding command, `echo $$` provides the `PID` value of the current Terminal session. `$$` is a Bash built-in variable that contains the `PID` value of the shell that is running. The `PID` value is wrapped as the argument for the `pstree` command. To show the related PIDs, we can invoke the `pstree` command with the `-p|--show-pids` option:

```
pstree -p $(echo $$)
```

The output of the preceding command can be seen in the following screenshot:

```
packt@neptune:~$ pstree -p $(echo $$)
bash(968)──┬──pstree(1117)
           └──test.sh(1094)
```

Figure 5.16 – The process tree (along with its PIDs) of the current Terminal session

The following command shows the processes owned by the current user:

```
pstree $(whoami)
```

The output of the preceding command can be seen in the following screenshot:

```
packt@neptune:~$ pstree $(whoami)
sshd────bash──┬──pstree
              └──test.sh
```

Figure 5.17 – The process tree owned by the current user

For more information about the `pstree` command, please refer to the related system reference manual (`man pstree`).

Using the top command

When it comes to monitoring processes in real time, the `top` utility is among the most common tool to be used by Linux administrators. The related command-line syntax is as follows:

```
top [OPTIONS]
```

The following command displays all the processes currently running in the system, along with real-time updates (on memory, CPU usage, and so on):

```
top
```

Pressing *Q* will exit the `top` command. By default, the `top` command sorts the output by CPU usage (shown in the `%CPU` field/column).

We can also choose to sort the output of the `top` command by a different field. While `top` is running, press *Shift + F* (F) to invoke interactive mode.

Using the arrow keys, we can select the desired field to sort by (for example, %MEM), then press *S* to set the new field, followed by *Q* to exit interactive mode. The alternative to interactive mode sorting is invoking the `-o` option parameter of the `top` command, which specifies the sorting field.

For example, the following command lists the top 10 processes, sorted by CPU usage:

```
top -b -o %CPU | head -n 17
```

Similarly, the following command lists the top 10 processes, sorted by CPU and memory usage:

```
top -b -o +%MEM | head -n 17
```

The `-b` option parameter specifies the batch mode operation (instead of the default interactive mode). The `-o +%MEM` option parameter indicates the additional (+) sorting field (%MEM) in tandem with the default %CPU field. The `head -n 17` pipe selects the first 17 lines of the output, accounting for the seven-line header of the `top` command:

```
packt@neptune:~$ top -b -o +%MEM | head -n 17
top - 12:59:24 up  1:29,  1 user,  load average: 1.00, 0.99, 0.71
Tasks: 115 total,   2 running, 113 sleeping,   0 stopped,   0 zombie
%Cpu(s):100.0 us,   0.0 sy,   0.0 ni,  0.0 id,   0.0 wa,   0.0 hi,  0.0 si,  0.0 st
MiB Mem :   1976.0 total,   1417.6 free,    211.7 used,    346.6 buff/cache
MiB Swap:   1840.0 total,   1840.0 free,      0.0 used.   1612.4 avail Mem

    PID USER      PR  NI    VIRT    RES    SHR S  %CPU  %MEM     TIME+ COMMAND
   1013 root      20   0  500400  64388  22584 S   0.0   3.2   0:00.74 fwupd
    665 root      20   0  727508  40732  20716 S   0.0   2.0   0:01.18 snapd
    421 root      rt   0  289312  27360   9072 S   0.0   1.4   0:00.49 multipa+
    720 root      20   0  109748  21292  13136 S   0.0   1.1   0:00.05 unatten+
    661 root      20   0   32652  18932  10284 S   0.0   0.9   0:00.04 network+
    381 root      19  -1   47856  15664  14572 S   0.0   0.8   0:00.12 systemd+
    669 root      20   0  392564  12880  10792 S   0.0   0.6   0:00.06 udisksd
    641 systemd+  20   0   25260  12452   8516 S   0.0   0.6   0:00.04 systemd+
    705 root      20  ·0  317948  11964  10060 S   0.0   0.6   0:00.03 ModemMa+
      1 root      20   0  166492  11736   8288 S   0.0   0.6   0:02.16 systemd
```

Figure 5.18 – The top 10 processes sorted by CPU and memory usage

The following command lists the top five processes by CPU usage, owned by the current user (`packt`):

```
top -u $(whoami) -b -o %CPU | head -n 12
```

The `-u $(whoami)` option parameter specifies the current user for the `top` command.

With the `top` command, we can also monitor specific processes using the `-p PID` option parameter. For example, the following command monitors our test process (with PID `243436`):

```
top -p 1094
```

The output of the preceding command can be seen in the following screenshot:

```
top - 13:02:58 up  1:32,  1 user,  load average: 1.00, 1.00, 0.78
Tasks:   1 total,   1 running,   0 sleeping,   0 stopped,   0 zombie
%Cpu(s):100.0 us,   0.0 sy,   0.0 ni,   0.0 id,   0.0 wa,   0.0 hi,   0.0 si,   0.0 st
MiB Mem :   1976.0 total,   1417.6 free,    211.7 used,    346.7 buff/cache
MiB Swap:   1840.0 total,   1840.0 free,      0.0 used.   1612.4 avail Mem

    PID USER       PR  NI    VIRT    RES    SHR S  %CPU  %MEM     TIME+ COMMAND
   1094 packt      20   0    7368   1468   1312 R  99.3   0.1  21:13.64 test.sh
```

Figure 5.19 – Monitoring a specific PID with the top command

We may choose to *kill* the process by pressing *K* while using the `top` command. We'll get prompted for this by the PID of the process we want to terminate:

```
top - 13:04:37 up  1:34,  1 user,  load average: 1.00, 1.00, 0.81
Tasks:   1 total,   1 running,   0 sleeping,   0 stopped,   0 zombie
%Cpu(s):100.0 us,   0.0 sy,   0.0 ni,   0.0 id,   0.0 wa,   0.0 hi,   0.0 si,   0.0 st
MiB Mem :   1976.0 total,   1417.6 free,    211.7 used,    346.7 buff/cache
MiB Swap:   1840.0 total,   1840.0 free,      0.0 used.   1612.4 avail Mem
PID to signal/kill [default pid = 1094]
    PID USER       PR  NI    VIRT    RES    SHR S  %CPU  %MEM     TIME+ COMMAND
   1094 packt      20   0    7368   1468   1312 R  99.9   0.1  22:52.66 test.sh
```

Figure 5.20 – Killing a process with the top command

The `top` utility can be used in many creative ways. We hope that the examples we've provided in this section have inspired you to explore further use cases based on specific needs. For more information, please refer to the system reference manual for the `top` command (`man top`).

Using the kill and killall commands

We use the `kill` command to terminate processes. The command's syntax is as follows:

```
kill [OPTIONS] [ -s SIGNAL | -SIGNAL ] PID [...]
```

The `kill` command sends a *signal* to a process, attempting to stop its execution. When no signal is specified, `SIGTERM` (`15`) is sent. A signal can either be specified by the signal's name without the `SIG` prefix (for example, `KILL` for `SIGKILL`) or by value (for example, `9` for `SIGKILL`).

The `kill -l` and `kill -L` commands provide a full list of signals that can be used in Linux:

```
packt@neptune:~$ kill -1
 1) SIGHUP        2) SIGINT       3) SIGQUIT      4) SIGILL       5) SIGTRAP
 6) SIGABRT       7) SIGBUS       8) SIGFPE       9) SIGKILL     10) SIGUSR1
11) SIGSEGV      12) SIGUSR2     13) SIGPIPE     14) SIGALRM     15) SIGTERM
16) SIGSTKFLT    17) SIGCHLD     18) SIGCONT     19) SIGSTOP     20) SIGTSTP
21) SIGTTIN      22) SIGTTOU     23) SIGURG      24) SIGXCPU     25) SIGXFSZ
26) SIGVTALRM    27) SIGPROF     28) SIGWINCH    29) SIGIO       30) SIGPWR
31) SIGSYS       34) SIGRTMIN    35) SIGRTMIN+1  36) SIGRTMIN+2  37) SIGRTMIN+3
38) SIGRTMIN+4   39) SIGRTMIN+5  40) SIGRTMIN+6  41) SIGRTMIN+7  42) SIGRTMIN+8
43) SIGRTMIN+9   44) SIGRTMIN+10 45) SIGRTMIN+11 46) SIGRTMIN+12 47) SIGRTMIN+13
48) SIGRTMIN+14  49) SIGRTMIN+15 50) SIGRTMAX-14 51) SIGRTMAX-13 52) SIGRTMAX-12
53) SIGRTMAX-11  54) SIGRTMAX-10 55) SIGRTMAX-9  56) SIGRTMAX-8  57) SIGRTMAX-7
58) SIGRTMAX-6   59) SIGRTMAX-5  60) SIGRTMAX-4  61) SIGRTMAX-3  62) SIGRTMAX-2
63) SIGRTMAX-1   64) SIGRTMAX
```

Figure 5.21 – The Linux signals

Each signal has a numeric value, as shown in the preceding output. For example, `SIGKILL` equals `9`. The following command will kill our test process (with PID `243436`):

```
kill -9 1094
```

The following command will also do the same as the preceding command:

```
kill -KILL 1094
```

In some scenarios, we may want to kill multiple processes in one go. The `killall` command comes to the rescue here. The syntax for the `killall` command is as follows:

```
killall [OPTIONS] [ -s SIGNAL | -SIGNAL ] NAME...
```

`killall` sends a signal to all the processes running any of the commands specified. When no signal is specified, `SIGTERM` (`15`) is sent. A signal can either be specified by the signal name without the `SIG` prefix (for example, `TERM` for `SIGTERM`) or by value (for example, `15` for `SIGTERM`).

For example, the following command terminates all the processes running the `test.sh` script:

```
killall -e -TERM test.sh
```

The output of the preceding command can be seen in the following screenshot:

```
packt@neptune:~$ killall -e -TERM test.sh
packt@neptune:~$ ps
    PID TTY          TIME CMD
    968 pts/0    00:00:00 bash
   1173 pts/0    00:00:00 ps
[1]+  Terminated              ./test.sh
```

Figure 5.22 – Terminating multiple processes with killall

Killing a process will usually remove the related reference from the system process table. The terminated process won't show up anymore in the output of ps, top, or similar commands.

For more information about the kill and killall commands, please refer to the related system reference manuals (man kill and man killall).

Using the pgrep and pkill commands

pgrep and pkill are pattern-based lookup commands for exploring and terminating running processes. They have the following syntax:

```
pgrep [OPTIONS] PATTERN
pkill [OPTIONS] PATTERN
```

pgrep iterates through the current processes and lists the PIDs that match the selection pattern or criteria. Similarly, pkill terminates the processes that match the selection criteria.

The following command looks for our test process (test.sh) and displays the PID value if the related process is found. Start the process again before using the following command as we killed it in the previous section. This will lead to a different PID value:

```
pgrep -f test.sh
```

The output of the preceding command can be seen in the following screenshot:

```
packt@neptune:~$ ./test.sh &
[1] 1178
packt@neptune:~$ pgrep -f test.sh
1178
```

Figure 5.23 – Looking for a PID based on name using pgrep

The -f | --full option enforces a full name match of the process we're looking for. We may use pgrep in tandem with the ps command to get more detailed information about the process, like so:

```
pgrep -f test.sh | xargs ps -fp
```

The output of the preceding command can be seen in the following screenshot:

```
packt@neptune:~$ pgrep -f test.sh | xargs ps -fp
UID          PID    PPID  C STIME TTY          TIME CMD
packt       1178     968 99 13:15 pts/0     00:02:07 /bin/bash ./test.sh
```

Figure 5.24 – Chaining pgrep and ps for more information

In the preceding one-liner, we piped the output of the pgrep command (with PID 243436) to the ps command, which has been invoked with the -f (long-format) and -p|--pid options. The -p option parameter gets the piped PID value.

The xargs command takes the input from the pgrep command and converts it into an argument for the ps command. Thus, when piping from pgrep to ps, the output of the first command was automatically converted as the argument for the second command. By default, xargs reads the standard input.

To terminate our test.sh process, we simply invoke the pkill command, as follows:

```
pkill -f test.sh
```

The preceding command will *silently* kill the related process, based on the full name lookup enforced by the -f|--full option. To get some feedback from the action of the pkill command, we need to invoke the -e|--echo option, like so:

```
pkill -ef test.sh
```

The output of the preceding command can be seen in the following screenshot:

```
packt@neptune:~$ pkill -ef test.sh
test.sh killed (pid 1178)
[1]+  Terminated              ./test.sh
```

Figure 5.25 – Killing a process by name using pkill

For more information, please refer to the pgrep and pkill system reference manuals (man pgrep and man pkill).

This section covered some command-line utilities that are frequently used in everyday Linux administration tasks involving processes. Keep in mind that in Linux, most of the time, there are many ways to accomplish a specific task. We hope that the examples in this section will help you come up with creative methods and techniques for working with processes.

Next, we'll look at some common ways of interacting with daemons.

Working with daemons

As noted in the introductory sections, daemons are a special breed of background process. Consequently, the vast majority of methods and techniques for working with processes also apply to daemons. However, there are specific commands that strictly operate on daemons when it comes to managing (or controlling) the lifetime of the related processes.

As noted in the *Introducing daemons* section, daemon processes are controlled by shell scripts, usually stored in the /etc/init.d/ or /lib/systemd/ system directories, depending on the Linux platform. On legacy Linux systems (for example, RHEL 6) and Ubuntu (even in the latest distros), the daemon script files are stored in /etc/init.d/. On RHEL 7/Ubuntu 18.04 and newer platforms, they are typically stored in /lib/systemd/. Feel free to do a listing of those two directories to see the contents.

The location of the daemon files and the daemon command-line utilities largely depends on the init initialization system and service manager. In *The init process* section, we briefly mentioned a variety of init systems across Linux distributions. To illustrate the use of daemon control commands, we will explore the init system called systemd, which is extensively used across various Linux platforms.

Working with systemd daemons

The init system's essential requirement is to initialize and orchestrate the launch and startup dependencies of various processes when the Linux kernel is booted. These processes are also known as **userland** or **user processes**. The init engine also controls the services and daemons while the system is running.

Over the last few years, most Linux platforms have transitioned to systemd as their default init engine. Due to its extensive adoption, being familiar with systemd and its related command-line tools is of paramount importance. With that in mind, this section's primary focus is on systemctl – the central command-line utility for managing systemd daemons.

The syntax of the systemctl command is as follows:

```
systemctl [OPTIONS] [COMMAND] [UNITS...]
```

The actions that are invoked by the systemctl command are directed at units, which are system resources that are managed by systemd. Several unit types are defined in systemd (for example, service, mount, socket, and so on). Each of these units has a corresponding file. These file types are inferred from the suffix of the related filename; for example, httpd.service is the service unit file of the Apache web service (daemon). For a comprehensive list of systemd units and detailed descriptions of them, please refer to the systemd.unit system reference manual (man systemd.unit).

The following command enables a daemon (for example, httpd, the web server) to start at boot:

```
sudo systemctl enable httpd
```

Typically, invoking systemctl commands requires superuser privileges. We should note that systemctl does not require the .service suffix when we're targeting service units. The following invocation is also acceptable:

```
sudo systemctl enable httpd.service
```

The command to disable the httpd service from starting at boot is as follows:

```
sudo systemctl disable httpd
```

To query the status of the httpd service, we can run the following command:

```
sudo systemctl status httpd
```

Alternatively, we can check the status of the httpd service with the following command:

```
sudo systemctl is-active httpd
```

The following commands stop or start the httpd service:

```
sudo systemctl stop httpd
sudo systemctl start httpd
```

For more information on systemctl, please refer to the related system reference manual (man systemctl). For more information about systemd internals, please refer to the corresponding reference manual (man systemd).

Working with processes and daemons is a constant theme of everyday Linux administration tasks. Mastering the related command-line utilities is an essential skill for any seasoned user. Yet, a running process or daemon should also be considered in relationships with other processes or daemons running either locally or on remote systems. The way processes communicate with each other could be a slight mystery to some. We will address this in the next section, in which we will explain how inter-process communication works.

Explaining inter-process communication

Inter-process communication (**IPC**) is a way of interacting between processes using a shared mechanism or interface. In this section, we will take a short theoretical approach to exploring various communication mechanisms between processes. For more details on this matter and some of the mechanisms used, head to *Chapter 8, Linux Shell Scripting*.

Linux processes can typically share data and synchronize their actions via the following interfaces:

- **Shared storage (files)**: In its simplest form, the shared storage of an IPC mechanism can be a simple file that's been saved to disk. The producer then writes to a file while the consumer reads from the same file. In this simple use case, the obvious challenge is the integrity of the read/write operations due to possible race conditions between the underlying operations. To avoid race conditions, the file must be locked during write operations to prevent overlapping I/O with another read or write action. To keep things simple, we're not going to resolve this problem in our naive examples, but we thought it's worth calling it out.

- **Shared memory**: Processes in Linux typically have separate address spaces. A process can only access data in the memory of another process if the two share a common memory segment where such data would be stored. Linux provides at least a couple of **application programming interfaces (APIs)** to programmatically define and control shared memory between processes: a legacy System V API and the more recent POSIX API, for example. Both these APIs are written in C, though the implementation of the producer and consumer mockups is beyond the scope of this book. However, we can closely match the shared memory approach by using the /dev/shm temporary file storage system, which uses the system's RAM as its backing store (that is, RAM disk).

  With /dev/shm being used as shared memory, we can reuse our producer-consumer model from the example in the previous point on *Shared storage*, where we simply point the storage file to /dev/shm/storage.

  The shared memory and shared storage IPC models may not perform well with large amounts of data, especially massive data streams. The alternative would be to use IPC channels, which can be enabled through the pipe, message queue, or socket communication layers.

- **Named and unnamed pipes**: **Unnamed** or **anonymous pipes**, also known as **regular pipes**, feed the output of a process to the input of another one. Using our producer-consumer model, the simplest way to illustrate an unnamed pipe as an IPC mechanism between the two processes would be to do the following:

```
producer.sh | consumer.sh
```

  The key element of the preceding code is the pipe (|) symbol. The left-hand side of the pipe produces an output that's fed directly to the right-hand side of the pipe for consumption.

  Named pipes, also known as **First-In, First-Outs (FIFOs)**, are similar to traditional (unnamed) pipes but substantially different in terms of their semantics. An unnamed pipe only persists for as long as the related process is running. However, a named pipe has backing storage and will last as long as the system is up, regardless of the running status of the processes attached to the related IPC channel. Typically, a named pipe acts as a file, and it can be deleted when it's no longer being used.

- **Message queues**: A message queue is an asynchronous communication mechanism that's typically used in a distributed system architecture. Messages are written and stored in a queue until they are processed and eventually deleted. A message is written (published) by a producer and is processed only once, typically by a single consumer. At a very high level, a message has a sequence, a payload, and a type. Message queues can regulate the retrieval (order) of messages (for example, based on priority or type):

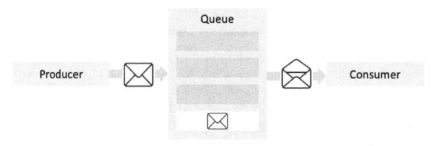

Figure 5.26 – Message queue (simplified view)

A detailed analysis of message queues or a mock implementation thereof is far from trivial, and it's beyond this chapter's scope. There are numerous open source message queue implementations available for most Linux platforms (RabbitMQ, ActiveMQ, ZeroMQ, MQTT, and so on).

IPC mechanisms based on message queues and pipes are unidirectional. One process writes the data; another one reads it. There are bidirectional implementations of named pipes, but the complexities involved would negatively impact the underlying communication layer. For bidirectional communication, you can think of using socket-based IPC channels (detailed in *Chapter 8, Linux Shell Scripting*).

- **Sockets**: There are two types of IPC socket-based facilities:

  - **IPC sockets**: Also known as Unix domain sockets, IPC sockets use a local file as a socket address and enable bidirectional communication between processes on the same host.

  - **Network sockets**: **Transport Control Protocol** (TCP) and **User Datagram Protocol** (**UDP**) sockets. They extend the IPC data connectivity layer beyond the local machine via TCP/UDP networking.

Apart from the obvious implementation differences, the IPC socket's and network socket's data communication channels behave the same.

Both sockets are configured as streams, support bidirectional communication, and emulate a client/server pattern. The socket's communication channel is active until it's closed on either end, thereby breaking the IPC connection.

- **Signals**: In Linux, a signal is a one-way asynchronous notification mechanism that's used in response to a specific condition. A signal can act in any of the following directions:

  - From the Linux kernel to an arbitrary process

  - From process to process

  - From a process to itself

  We mentioned at the beginning of this section that signals are yet another IPC mechanism. Indeed, they are a somewhat limited form of IPC in the sense that through signals, processes can coordinate synchronization with each other. But signals don't carry any data payloads. They simply notify processes about events, and processes may choose to take specific actions in response to these events.

In the next section, we will detail working with signals in Linux.

Working with signals

Signals typically alert a Linux process about a specific event, such as a segmentation fault (`SIGSEGV`) that's raised by the kernel or execution being interrupted (`SIGINT`) by the user pressing *Ctrl + C*. In Linux, processes are controlled via signals. The Linux kernel defines a few dozen signals. Each signal has a corresponding non-zero positive integer value.

The following command lists all the signals that have been registered in a Linux system:

```
kill -l
```

The output of the preceding command can be seen back in *Figure 5.21*. From the output, `SIGHUP`, for example, has a signal value of `1`, and it's invoked by a Terminal session to all its child processes when it exits. `SIGKILL` has a signal value of `9` and is most commonly used for terminating processes. Processes can typically control how signals are handled, except for `SIGKILL` (9) and `SIGSTOP` (19), which always end or stop a process, respectively.

Processes handle signals in either of the following fashions:

- Perform the default action implied by the signal; for example, stop, terminate, core-dump a process, or do nothing.

- Perform a custom action (except for `SIGKILL` and `SIGSTOP`). In this case, the process catches the signal and handles it in a specific way.

When a program implements a custom handler for a signal, it usually defines a signal handler function that alters the execution of the process, as follows:

- When the signal is received, the process' execution is interrupted at the current instruction

- The process' execution immediately jumps to the signal-handler function

- The signal handler function runs
- When the signal handler function exits, the process resumes execution, starting from the previously interrupted instruction

Here's some brief terminology related to signals:

- A signal is raised by the process that generates it
- A signal is caught by the process that handles it
- A signal is ignored if the process has a corresponding **no-operation** or **no-op** (**NOOP**) handler
- A signal is handled if the process implements a specific action when the signal is caught

Out of all the signals, SIGKILL and SIGSTOP are the only ones that cannot be caught or ignored.

Let's explore a few use cases for handling signals:

- When the kernel raises a SIGKILL, SIGFPE (floating-point exception), SIGSEGV (segmentation fault), SIGTERM, or similar signals, typically, the process that receives the signal immediately terminates execution and may generate a core dump – the image of the process that's used for debugging purposes.
- When a user types *Ctrl + C* – otherwise known as an **interrupt character** (**INTR**) – while a foreground process is running, a SIGINT signal is sent to the process. The process will terminate unless the underlying program implements a special handler for SIGINT.
- Using the kill command, we can send a signal to any process based on its PID. The following command sends a SIGHUP signal to a Terminal session with a PID of 3741:

```
kill -HUP 3741
```

In the preceding command, we can either specify the signal value (for example, 1 for SIGHUP) or just the signal name without the SIG prefix (for example, HUP for SIGHUP).

With killall, we can signal that multiple processes are running a specific command (for example, test.sh). The following command terminates all processes running the test.sh script and outputs the result to the console (via the -e option):

```
killall -e -TERM test.sh
```

The output of this command can be seen in *Figure 5.22*.

Linux processes and signals are a vast domain. The information we've provided here is far from a comprehensive guide on the topic. We hope that this short spin and hands-on approach to presenting some common use cases has inspired you to take on and possibly master more challenging issues.

Summary

A detailed study of Linux processes and daemons could be a major undertaking. Where worthy volumes on the topic have admirably succeeded, a relatively brief chapter may pale in comparison. Yet in this chapter, we tried to put on a real-world, down-to-earth, practical coat on everything we've considered to make up for our possible shortcomings in the abstract or scholarly realm.

At this point, we hope you are comfortable working with processes and daemons. The skills you've gathered so far should include a relatively good grasp of process types and internals, with a reasonable understanding of process attributes and states. Special attention has been paid to inter-process communication mechanisms, and signals in particular. For each of these topics, we will take a more detailed approach in *Chapter 8*. For now, we consider the information we've provided to be sufficient for understanding how inter-process communication works.

The next chapter will take our journey further into working with Linux disks and filesystems. We'll explore the Linux storage, disk partitioning, and **Logical Volume Management** (**LVM**) concepts. Rest assured that everything we've learned so far will be immediately put to good use in the chapters that follow.

Questions

If you managed to skim through some parts of this chapter, you might want to recap a few essential details about Linux processes and daemons:

1. Think of a few process types. How would they compare to each other?

2. Think of the anatomy of a process. Can you come up with a few essential process attributes (or fields in the `ps` command-line output) that you may look for when inspecting processes?

    Hint: What would be relevant for you, except CPU, RAM, or disk usage, for example?

3. Can you think of a few process states and some of the dynamics or possible transitions between them?

4. If you are looking for a process that takes up most of the CPU on your system, how would you proceed?

5. Can you write a simple script and make it a long-lived background process?

    Hint: Take a peek at *Chapter 8*, where we will teach you how to create and use shell scripts.

6. Enumerate at least four process signals that you can think of. When or how would those signals be invoked?

    Hint: Use the `kill -l` command. For more information, read the manual.

7. Think of a couple of IPC mechanisms. Try to come up with some pros and cons for them.

    Hint: The information in *Chapter 8* could help you.

Further reading

For more information about what was covered in this chapter, you can refer to the following Packt titles:

- *Linux Administration Best Practices*, by Scott Alan Miller
- *Linux Service Management Made Easy with systemd*, by Donald A. Tevault

Part 2:
Advanced Linux
Administration

In this second part, you will learn about advanced Linux system administration tasks, including working with disks and configuring networking, hardening Linux security, and system-specific troubleshooting and diagnostics.

This part has the following chapters:

- *Chapter 6, Working with Disks and Filesystems*
- *Chapter 7, Networking with Linux*
- *Chapter 8, Linux Shell Scripting*
- *Chapter 9, Securing Linux*
- *Chapter 10, Disaster Recovery, Diagnostics, and Troubleshooting*

6

Working with Disks and Filesystems

In this chapter, you will learn how to manage disks and filesystems, how to use the **Logical Volume Management** (**LVM**) system, and how to mount and partition the hard drive, as well as gain an understanding of storage in Linux. You will also learn how to partition and format a disk, as well as how to create logical volumes, and you will gain a deeper understanding of filesystem types. In this chapter, we're going to cover the following main topics:

- Understanding devices in Linux
- Understanding filesystem types in Linux
- Understanding disks and partitions
- Introducing LVM in Linux

Technical requirements

A basic knowledge of disks, partitions, and filesystems is preferred. No other special technical requirements are needed, just a working installation of Linux on your system. We will mainly use Ubuntu or Debian for this chapter's exercises. All the commands used in this chapter can be replicated on any Linux distribution, even if you don't use Debian or Ubuntu.

Understanding devices in Linux

As already stated on several occasions in this book, everything in Linux is a file. This also includes devices. **Device files** are special files in Unix and Linux operating systems. Those special files are interfaces to device drivers, and they are present in the filesystem as a regular file.

With no further ado, let's see how Linux abstraction layers work. This will give you an overview of how hardware and software are related and interconnected.

Linux abstraction layers

Now is as good a time as any to discuss Linux system abstraction layers and how devices fit into the overall picture. Any computer is generally organized into two layers (or levels) – the hardware and the software levels:

- **Hardware level**: This level contains the hardware components of your machine, such as the memory (RAM), **central processing unit** (**CPU**), and devices, including disks, network interfaces, ports, and controllers.

- **Software level**: For all these hardware components to work, the operating system (Linux, in our case) uses **abstraction layers**. Those layers exist in the **kernel**, which is the main software component of Linux. Without diving into more information, it is sufficient for you to know that Linux has these layers that are responsible for accessing low-level resources and providing the specific drivers for different hardware components. When the computer is booted up, the Linux kernel is loaded from the disk into the system's memory (RAM). Thus, inside the memory, there will be two separate regions, called **kernel space** and **user space**, and this would be the **software level**:

  - The kernel is the beating heart of the Linux operating system. The kernel resides inside the memory (RAM) and manages all the hardware components. It is the *interface* between the software and hardware on your Linux system.

  - The user space level is the level where user processes are executed. As presented in *Chapter 5, Working with Processes, Daemons, and Signals*, a process is a running instance of a program.

Where are devices in this grand scheme of things? Devices are managed by the *kernel*. To sum up, the kernel is in charge of managing processes, system calls, memory, and devices. When dealing with devices, the kernel manages **device drivers**, which are the interface between hardware components and software. All devices are accessible only in kernel mode, for a more secure and streamlined operation.

How does all this work? Well, the memory, known as RAM, consists of cells that are used to store information temporarily. Those cells are accessed by different programs that are executed and function as an intermediary between the CPU and the storage. The speeds of accessing memory are very high to secure a seamless process of execution. The management of user processes inside the user space is the kernel's job. The kernel makes sure that none of the processes will interfere with each other. The kernel space is usually accessed only by the kernel, but there are times when user processes need to access this space. This is done through **system calls**. A system call is the way a user process requests a kernel service through an active process inside the kernel space, for anything such as **input/output** (**I/O**) requests to internal or external devices. All those requests transfer data to and from the CPU, through RAM, to get the job done.

In the following section, we will introduce you to the naming convention in Linux and how device files are managed.

Device files and naming conventions

After seeing how the abstraction layers work, you may be wondering how Linux manages devices. Well, it does that with the help of **userspace /dev (udev)**, which is a device manager for the kernel. It works with **device nodes**, which are special files (also called **device files**) that are used as an interface to the driver.

Device files in Linux

udev runs as a daemon that listens to the user space calls that the kernel is sending, so it is aware of what kinds of devices are used and how they are used. The daemon is called udevd and its configurations are currently available under /etc/udev/udev.conf. You can concatenate the /etc/udev/udev.conf file to see its contents by running the following command:

```
cat /etc/udev/udev.conf
```

Each Linux distribution has a default set of rules that governs udevd. Those rules are normally stored under the /etc/udev/rules.d/ directory, as shown in the following screenshot:

```
packt@neptune:~$ ls -l /etc/udev/rules.d/
total 68
-rw-r--r-- 1 root root 63312 Aug  9  2022 70-snap.snapd.rules
-rw-r--r-- 1 root root   148 Feb 27 08:50 ubuntu--vg-ubuntu--lv.rules
```

Figure 6.1 – udevd rules location

> **Note**
>
> The kernel sends calls for events using the **Netlink** socket. The netlink socket is an interface for inter-process communication that's used for both userspace and kernel space processes alike.

The /dev directory is the interface between user processes and devices managed by the kernel. If you were to use the ls -la /dev command, you would see a lot of files inside, each with different names. If you were to do a long listing, you would see different file types. Some of the files will start with the letters *b* and *c*, but the letters *p* and *s* may also be present, depending on your system. Files starting with those letters are device files. The ones starting with *b* are **block devices**, and those starting with the letter *c* are **character devices**, as shown in the following screenshot:

```
packt@neptune:~$ ls -la /dev
total 4
drwxr-xr-x 20 root root      4080 Mar 16 07:09 .
drwxr-xr-x 19 root root      4096 Feb 27 08:54 ..
crw-r--r--  1 root root    10, 235 Mar 16 07:09 autofs
drwxr-xr-x  2 root root       360 Mar 16 07:09 block
crw-rw----  1 root disk    10, 234 Mar 16 07:09 btrfs-control
drwxr-xr-x  3 root root        60 Mar 16 07:09 bus
drwxr-xr-x  2 root root      3500 Mar 16 07:09 char
crw--w----  1 root tty      5,   1 Mar 16 07:09 console
lrwxrwxrwx  1 root root        11 Mar 16 07:09 core -> /proc/kcore
drwxr-xr-x  3 root root        60 Mar 16 07:09 cpu
crw-------  1 root root    10, 124 Mar 16 07:09 cpu_dma_latency
crw-------  1 root root    10, 203 Mar 16 07:09 cuse
drwxr-xr-x  7 root root       140 Mar 16 07:09 disk
brw-rw----  1 root disk    253,   0 Mar 16 07:09 dm-0
drwxr-xr-x  2 root root        60 Mar 16 07:09 dma_heap
drwxr-xr-x  3 root root        80 Mar 16 07:09 dri
crw-------  1 root root    10, 126 Mar 16 07:09 ecryptfs
crw-rw----  1 root video   29,   0 Mar 16 07:09 fb0
lrwxrwxrwx  1 root root        13 Mar 16 07:09 fd -> /proc/self/fd
```

Figure 6.2 – Device files inside the /dev directory

Let's see how disk devices are presented inside the /dev directory. But first, we've provided a few words about our working setup in the following note.

> **Important note**
>
> For most of the exercises in this book, we will be using virtual machines with planet names as hostnames, running different Linux-based operating systems. For example, neptune is running on Ubuntu 22.04.2 LTS Server, so when you see the neptune hostname on the shell's prompt, you will know we are on an Ubuntu-based system. We also have jupiter, running on the openSUSE 15.4 Leap server, saturn running on Fedora 37 Workstation, venus running on AlmaLinux, and mars running on a Debian 11.6 server. Inside a virtual machine, device drivers are presented with different names than on bare-metal systems. We will provide details when we discuss device naming conventions in the following section. For some examples, though, which are marked accordingly, we will also use our primary workstation, which is running on Debian 12 GNU/Linux.

As shown in *Figure 6.3*, the disk device, sda, is represented as a block device. Block devices have a fixed size that can easily be indexed. Character devices, on the other hand, can be accessed using data streams, as they don't have a size like block devices. For example, printers are represented as character devices. In the following screenshot, sg0 is an SCSI generic device, and not assigned to any disks in our case. We used our primary workstation running on Debian GNU/Linux and the device presented as sda is an external USB device:

```
brw-rw----  1 root    disk    8,    0 Mar 16 09:40 sda
brw-rw----  1 root    disk    8,    1 Mar 16 09:40 sda1
crw-rw----  1 root    disk   21,    0 Mar 16 09:38 sg0
```

Figure 6.3 – Disk drives inside the /dev directory

In comparison, when listing devices from our neptune virtual machine, we will have the output presented in the following screenshot:

```
brw-rw---- 1 root disk  252,  0 Mar 16 07:09 vda
brw-rw---- 1 root disk  252,  1 Mar 16 07:09 vda1
brw-rw---- 1 root disk  252,  2 Mar 16 07:09 vda2
brw-rw---- 1 root disk  252,  3 Mar 16 07:09 vda3
```

Figure 6.4 – Virtual devices inside a virtual machine

Device blocks presented with vdaX are virtual devices inside the virtual machine. You will learn more about virtual machines in *Chapter 11, Working with Virtual Machines*.

But for now, let's find out more about device naming conventions in Linux.

Understanding device naming conventions

Linux uses a device naming convention that makes device management easier and more consistent throughout the Linux ecosystem. udev uses several specific naming schemes that, by default, assign fixed names to devices. Those names are standardized for device categories. For example, when naming network devices, the kernel uses information compiled from sources such as firmware, topology, and location. On a Red Hat-based system, five schemes are used for naming a network interface, and we encourage you to look at these on the Red Hat customer portal official documentation website: https://access.redhat.com/documentation/en-us/red_hat_enterprise_linux/9.

On a Debian-based system, the naming convention is similar in that it's based on hardware buses' names for predictability. This is similar to all modern Linux-based operating systems.

You could also check what udev rules are active on your system. On Debian and Red Hat-based distributions, they are stored in the /lib/udev/rules.d/ directory.

When it comes to hard drives or external drives, the conventions are more streamlined. Here are some examples:

- **For classic IDE drivers used for ATA drives**: hda (the master device), hdb (the slave device on the first channel), hdc (the master device on the second channel), and hdd (the slave device on the second channel)

- **For NVMe drivers**: nvme0 (the first device controller – character device), nvme0n1 (first namespace – block device), and nvme0n1p1 (first namespace, first partition – block device)

- **For MMC drivers**: mmcblk (for SD cards using eMMC chips), mmcblk0 (first device), and mmcblk0p1 (first device, first partition)
- **For SCSI drivers used for modern SATA or USB**: sd (for mass storage devices), sda (for the first registered device), sdb (for the second registered device), sdc (for the third registered device), and so on, and sg (for generic SCSI layers – character device)

The devices that we are most interested in regarding this chapter are the mass storage devices. Those devices are usually **hard disk drives (HDDs)** or **solid-state drives (SSDs)**, which are used inside your computer to store data. These drives are most likely divided into partitions with a specific structure provided by the filesystem. We talked a little bit about filesystems earlier in this book in *Chapter 2, The Linux Shell and Filesystem*, when we referred to the Linux directory structure, but now, it is time to get into more details about filesystem types in Linux.

Understanding filesystem types in Linux

When talking about physical media, such as hard drives or external drives, we are *not* referring to the directory structure. Here, we are talking about the structures that are created on the physical drive when formatting and/or partitioning it. These structures, depending on their type, are known as filesystems, and they determine how the files are managed when stored on the drive.

There are several types of filesystems, some being native to the Linux ecosystem, while others are not, such as specific Windows or macOS filesystems. In this section, we will describe only the Linux-native filesystems.

The most widely used filesystems in Linux are the **extended filesystems**, known as Ext, Ext2, Ext3, and Ext4, the XFS filesystem, ZFS, and btrfs (short for **B-tree filesystem**). Each of these have their strengths and weaknesses, but they are all able to do the job they were designed for. The extended filesystems are the ones that were most widely used in Linux, and they have proven trustworthy all this time. Ext4, the latest iteration, is similar to Ext3, but better, with improved support for larger files, fragmentation, and performance. The Ext3 filesystem uses 32-bit addressing, while Ext4 uses 48-bit addressing, thus supporting files up to 16 TB in size. It also offers support for unlimited subdirectories as Ext3 only supports 32k subdirectories. Also, support for extended timestamps was added in Ext4, offering two more bits for up to the year 2446 AD, and online defragmentation at the kernel level.

Nonetheless, Ext4 is not a truly next-gen filesystem; rather, it is an improved, trustworthy, robust, and stable *workhorse* that failed the data protection and integrity test. Its journaling system is not suitable for detecting and repairing data corruption and degradation. That is why other filesystems, such as XFS and ZFS, started to resurface by being used in Red Hat Enterprise Linux, starting from version 7 (XFS) and in Ubuntu since version 16.04 (ZFS).

The case of `btrfs` is somewhat controversial. It is considered a modern filesystem, but it is still used as a single-disk filesystem and not used in multiple disk volume managers due to several performance issues compared to other filesystems. It is used in SUSE Linux Enterprise and openSUSE, is no longer supported by Red Hat, and has been voted as the future default filesystem in Fedora, starting with version 33.

Here are some more details on the major filesystem features:

- **Ext4**: The `Ext4` filesystem was designed for Linux right from the outset. Even though it is slowly being replaced with other filesystems, this one still has powerful features. It offers block size selection, with values between 512 and 4,096 bytes. There is also a feature called inode reservation, which saves a couple of inodes when you create a directory, for improved performance when creating new files.

  The layout is simple, written in **little-endian** order (for more details on this, visit `https://www.section.io/engineering-education/what-is-little-endian-and-big-endian/`), with block groups containing inode data for lower access times. Each file has data blocks pre-allocated for reduced fragmentation. There are also many enhancements that `Ext4` takes advantage of. Among them, we will bring the following into the discussion: a maximum filesystem size of 1 **exabyte** (**EB**), the ability to use multi-block allocation, splitting large files into the largest possible sizes for better performance, application of the allocate-on-flush technique for better performance, the use of the handy `fsck` command for speedy filesystem checks, the use of checksums for journaling and better reliability, and the use of improved timestamps.

- **ZFS**: This filesystem was created at Sun Microsystems and combines a file system and a logical volume manager into one solution. It was announced in 2004, with development starting in 2001, and was first integrated into the Solaris operating system, then used (not the default though) by Debian, FreeBSD, and others. ZFS is a highly scalable 128-bit system that offers simple administration, data integrity, scalability, and performance. Development of this filesystem is done through the **OpenZFS** open source project. ZFS offers a complex structure by using a copy-on-write mechanism, different from traditional filesystems. For more detailed information about ZFS, we recommend the following link: `https://openzfs.github.io/openzfs-docs/Getting%20Started/index.html`.

- **XFS**: Enterprise Linux is starting to change by moving away from `Ext4` to other competent filesystem types. Among those is `XFS`. This filesystem was first created by Silicon Graphics, Inc and used in the IRIX operating system. Its most important key design element is performance as it is capable of dealing with large datasets. Furthermore, it is designed to handle parallel I/O tasks with a guaranteed high I/O rate. The filesystem supports up to 16 EB with support for individual files up to 8 EB. XFS has a feature to journal quota information, together with online maintenance tasks such as defragmenting, enlarging, and restoring. There are also specific tools for backup and restore, including `xfsdump` and `xfsrestore`.

- **btrfs**: The B-tree filesystem (`btrfs`) is still under development, but it addresses issues associated with existing filesystems, including the lack of snapshots, pooling, checksums, and multi-device spanning. These are features that are required in an enterprise Linux environment. The ability to take snapshots of the filesystem and maintain its internal framework for managing new partitions makes `btrfs` a viable newcomer in terms of the critical enterprise ecosystem.

There are other filesystems that we did not discuss here, including **ReiserFS** and **GlusterFS**, **Network File System (NFS)**, **Samba CIFS File System (SMB)**, **ISO9660** for CD-ROMs and Joliet extensions, and non-native Linux ones, including **FAT**, **NTFS**, **exFAT**, and **APFS**, or **MacOS Extended**, among others. If you want to learn about these in more detail, feel free to investigate further; a good starting point is Wikipedia: `https://en.wikipedia.org/wiki/File_system`. To check the list of supported filesystems on your Linux distribution, run the `cat /proc/filesystems` command.

Linux implements a special software system that is designed to run specific functions of the filesystems. It is known as the **virtual file system** and acts as a bridge between the kernel and the filesystem types and hardware. Therefore, when an application wants to open a file, the action is delivered through the Virtual File System as an abstraction layer:

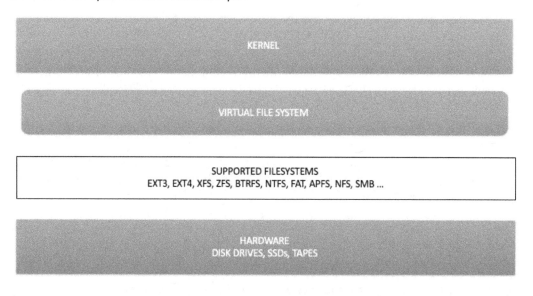

Figure 6.5 – The Linux Virtual File System abstraction layer

Basic filesystem functions include provisioning namespaces, metadata structures as a logical foundation for hierarchical directory structures, disk block usage, file size and access information, and high-level data for logical volumes and partitions. There is also an **application programming interface (API)** available for every filesystem. Thus, developers can access system function calls for filesystem object manipulation with specific algorithms for creating, moving, and deleting files, or for indexing, searching, and finding files. Furthermore, every modern filesystem provides a special access rights scheme that's used to determine the rules governing a user's access to files.

At this point, we have already covered the principal Linux filesystems, including EXT4, btrfs, and XFS. In the next section, we will teach you the basics of disks and partition management in Linux.

Understanding disks and partitions

Understanding disks and partitions is a key asset for any system administrator. Formatting and partitioning disks is critical, starting with system installation. Knowing the type of hardware available on your system is important, and it is therefore imperative to know how to work with it. One of these is the disk; let's look at this in further detail.

Common disk types

A **disk** is a hardware component that stores your data. It comes in various types and uses different interfaces. The main disk types are the well-known **spinning HDD**, the SSD, and the **non-volatile memory express** (**NVMe**). SSDs and NVMes use RAM-like technologies, with better energy consumption and higher transfer rates than original spinning hard drives. The following interfaces are used:

- **Integrated Drive Electronics** (**IDE**): This is an old standard that's used on consumer hardware with small transfer rates. It's now deprecated.

- **Serial Advanced Technology Attachment** (**SATA**): This replaced IDEs and has transfer rates of up to 16 GB/s.

- **Small Computer Systems Interface** (**SCSI**): This is used mostly in enterprise servers with RAID configurations with sophisticated hardware components.

- **Serial Attached SCSI** (**SAS**): This is a point-to-point serial protocol interface with transfer rates similar to SATA. It is mostly used in enterprise environments for their reliability.

- **Universal Serial Bus** (**USB**): This is used for external hard drives and memory drives.

Each disk has a specific geometry that consists of heads, cylinders, tracks, and sectors. On a Linux system, to see the information regarding a disk's geometry, you can use the fdisk -l command.

On our primary workstation, we have a single SSD running Debian 12 GNU/Linux and a USB device inserted in one of the ports. We will run the following command to obtain information about the drives on our machine:

```
sudo fdisk -l
```

The following screenshot shows excerpts of the `fdisk` command's output for both drives:

```
alexandru@debian:~$ sudo fdisk -l
Disk /dev/nvme0n1: 953.87 GiB, 1024209543168 bytes, 2000409264 sectors
Disk model: Lexar SSD NM620 1TB
Units: sectors of 1 * 512 = 512 bytes
Sector size (logical/physical): 512 bytes / 512 bytes
I/O size (minimum/optimal): 512 bytes / 512 bytes
Disklabel type: gpt
Disk identifier: A6049E7C-127A-40D3-9D3F-F5CF9D463B88

Device          Start       End    Sectors  Size Type
/dev/nvme0n1p1   2048   1050623    1048576  512M EFI System
/dev/nvme0n1p2 1050624   2050047    999424  488M Linux filesystem
/dev/nvme0n1p3 2050048 2000408575 1998358528 952.9G Linux filesystem

Disk /dev/sda: 7.5 GiB, 8053063680 bytes, 15728640 sectors
Disk model: Flash Disk
Units: sectors of 1 * 512 = 512 bytes
Sector size (logical/physical): 512 bytes / 512 bytes
I/O size (minimum/optimal): 512 bytes / 512 bytes
Disklabel type: dos
Disk identifier: 0x24248bcf

Device     Boot Start       End  Sectors  Size Id Type
/dev/sda1        2048 15728639 15726592  7.5G 83 Linux
```

Figure 6.6 – The output of the fdisk -l command showing disk information

The output of the `fdisk` utility may look intimidating at first, but rest assured that we will explain it to you so that it will look friendlier from now on. By using the `fdisk` utility without a specific partition as an argument, all the partition information available inside `/proc/partitions` will be shown. In the example shown in the preceding screenshot, you have details on two disks that are available on our system: a 1 TB Lexar NM620 SSD and an 8 GB USB flash drive attached. Let's explain how the 1 TB drive is shown:

- First, you have `Disk model` with the name of the drive, `Units` as sectors, each of which has a size of 512 bytes, `Disklabel type` as GPT, and `Disk identifier`, which is unique for each drive.

- Next is a table of the partitions available on the disk. This table has six columns (sometimes seven columns, as in the case of the USB flash drive, shown on the lower side of the screenshot). The first column has the `Device` header and shows the partition naming scheme. The second and third columns (in our example) show the starting and ending sectors. The fourth column shows the total number of sectors on the partition. The fifth column shows the size of the partition in human-readable format and the last column shows the type of the filesystem.

Knowing basic information about disk devices on your system is merely the starting point for working with disks and partitions on Linux. Disks are just a big chunk of metal if we don't format and partition them so that the system can use them. This is why, in the next section, we will teach you what partitions are.

Partitioning disks

Commonly, disks use **partitions**. To understand partitions, knowing a disk's geometry is essential. This legacy knowledge base is useful even when dealing with SSDs. Partitions are contiguous sets of sectors and/or cylinders, and they can be of several types: **primary**, **extended**, and **logical** partitions. A maximum number of 15 partitions can exist on a disk. The first four will be either primary or extended, and the remaining are logical partitions. Furthermore, there can only be a single extended partition, but they can be divided into several logical partitions until the maximum number is reached.

Partition types

There are two major partition types – the **Master Boot Record** (**MBR**) and the **GUID Partition Table** (**GPT**). MBR was intensively used up to around 2010. Its limitations include the maximum number of primary partitions (four) and the maximum size of a partition (2 TB). MBR uses hexadecimal codes for different types of partitions, such as 0x0c for FAT, 0x07 for NTFS, 0x83 for a Linux filesystem type, and 0x82 for swap. GPT became a part of the **Unified Extensible Firmware Interface** (**UEFI**) standard as a solution to some issues with MBR, including partition limitations, addressing methods, using only one copy of the partition table, and so on. It supports up to 128 partitions and disk sizes of up to 75.6 **Zettabytes** (**ZB**).

The partition table

The **partition table** of a disk is stored inside the disk's MBR. MBR is the first 512 bytes of a drive. Out of these, the partition table is 64 bytes and is stored after the first 446 bytes of records. At the end of MBR, there are 2 bytes known as the end of sector marker. The first 446 bytes are reserved for code that usually belongs to a bootloader program. In the case of Linux, the bootloader is called **GRand Unified Bootloader** (**GRUB**).

When you boot up a Linux system, the bootloader looks for the active partition. There can only be one active partition on a single disk. When the active partition is located, the bootloader loads items. The partition table has 4 entries, each of which is 16 bytes in size, with each belonging to a possible primary partition on the system. Furthermore, each entry contains information regarding the beginning address of cylinder/head/sectors, the partition type code, the end address of cylinder/head/sectors, the starting sector, and the number of sectors inside one partition.

Naming partitions

The kernel interacts with the disk at a low level. This is done through device nodes that are stored inside the /dev directory. Device nodes use a simple naming convention that tells you which disk is the one that requires your attention. Looking at the contents of the /dev directory, you can see all the available disk nodes, also referred to as disk drives, in *Figure 6.2* and *Figure 6.3* earlier in this section. A short explanation is always useful, so disks and partitions are recognized as follows:

- The first hard drive is always /dev/sda (for an SCSI or SATA device)

- The second hard drive is /dev/sdb, the third is /dev/sdc, and so on

- The first partition of the first disk is /dev/sda1

- The first partition of the second disk is /dev/sdb1

- The second partition of the second disk is /dev/sdb2, and so on

We specified that this is true in the case of an SCSI and SATA, and we need to explain this in a little more detail. The kernel gives the letter designation, such as *a*, *b*, and *c*, based on the ID number of the SCSI device, and not based on the position of the hardware bus.

Partition attributes

To learn about your partition's attributes, you can use the lsblk command. We will run it on our Debian system, as shown in the following screenshot:

```
alexandru@debian:~$ lsblk
NAME            MAJ:MIN RM    SIZE RO TYPE  MOUNTPOINTS
sda                 8:0  1    7.5G  0 disk
└─sda1              8:1  1    7.5G  0 part  /media/alexandru/9d7587da-3e17-464c-b01d-
d044b82f3736
nvme0n1           259:0  0  953.9G  0 disk
├─nvme0n1p1 259:1       0    512M  0 part  /boot/efi
├─nvme0n1p2 259:2       0    488M  0 part  /boot
└─nvme0n1p3 259:3       0  952.9G  0 part
  └─nvme0n1p3_crypt
                  254:0  0  952.9G  0 crypt
    ├─debian--vg-root
                  254:1  0  951.9G  0 lvm   /
    └─debian--vg-swap_1
                  254:2  0    976M  0 lvm   [SWAP]
```

Figure 6.7 – The output of lsblk

The `lsblk` command shows the device's name (the node's name from `sysfs` and the `udev` database), the major and minor device number, the removable state of the device (`0` for a non-removable device and `1` for a removable device), the size in human-readable format, the read-only state (again, using `0` for the ones that are not read-only and `1` for the read-only ones), the type of device, and the device's mount point (where available).

Now that we know more about the drive, let's learn how to alter a disk's partition table.

Partition table editors

In Linux, there are several tools we can use when managing partition tables. Among the most commonly used ones are the following:

- `fdisk`: A command-line partition editor, perhaps the most widely used one
- `Sfdisk`: A non-interactive partition editor, used mostly in scripting
- `parted`: The GNU (the recursive acronym for GNU is *GNU's Not Unix*) partition manipulation software
- `gparted`: The graphical interface for `parted`

Of these, we will only detail how to use `fdisk` as this is the most widely used command-line partition editor in Linux. It is found in both Ubuntu/Debian and RHEL/Fedora or openSUSE and many other distributions too.

But before we use `fdisk`, we would like to see the partitions that the operating system knows about. If you are not sure about the operations you just completed, you can always visualize the contents of the `/proc/partitions` file with the `cat` command:

```
alexandru@debian:~$ cat /proc/partitions
major minor  #blocks   name

  259        0 1000204632 nvme0n1
  259        1     524288 nvme0n1p1
  259        2     499712 nvme0n1p2
  259        3  999179264 nvme0n1p3
  254        0  999162880 dm-0
  254        1  998162432 dm-1
  254        2     999424 dm-2
    8        0    7864320 sda
    8        1    7863296 sda1
```

Figure 6.8 – Listing the /proc/partitions file

To use fdisk, you must be the root user. We advise you to use caution when using fdisk as it can damage your existing partitions and disks. fdisk can be used on a particular disk as follows:

```
alexandru@debian:~$ sudo fdisk /dev/sda

Welcome to fdisk (util-linux 2.38.1).
Changes will remain in memory only, until you decide to write them.
Be careful before using the write command.


Command (m for help): █
```

Figure 6.9 – Using fdisk for the first time

You will notice that when using fdisk for the first time, you are warned that changes will be done to the disk only when you decide to write them to it. You will also be prompted to introduce a command, and you will be shown the m option for help. We advise you to always use the help menu, even if you already know the most used commands.

When you type m, you will be shown the entire list of commands available for fdisk. You will see options to manage partitions, create new boot records, save changes, and others. Partition table editors are important tools for managing disks in Linux. Their use is incomplete if you do not know how to format a partition. In the next section, we will show you how to partition a disk drive.

Creating and formatting partitions

We will use the fdisk utility to create a new partition table on a USB memory stick plugged into our primary workstation running Debian GNU/Linux. We will create an MBR partition table using the following command:

```
sudo fdisk /dev/sda
```

We will use the o option to create an empty MBR partition table and then the w option to save the changes to disk. The output of the command is shown in the following screenshot:

```
alexandru@debian:~$ sudo fdisk /dev/sda

Welcome to fdisk (util-linux 2.38.1).
Changes will remain in memory only, until you decide to write them.
Be careful before using the write command.


Command (m for help): o
Created a new DOS (MBR) disklabel with disk identifier 0xc1fa6ca8.

Command (m for help): w
The partition table has been altered.
Calling ioctl() to re-read partition table.
Syncing disks.
```

Figure 6.10 – Creating a new MBR partition table with fdisk

With that, the partition table has been created, but there is no partition defined on the disk. While still inside the fdisk command-line interface, you can use the v option to verify the newly created partition table and the I option to see information about existing partitions. You will see some output saying that no partitions have been defined yet. So, it is time to set up a new partition.

To create a new partition, we will use the following series of options:

- The n option to start the creation processes
- The p option when asked to create either a primary (p) or extended (e) partition type
- Enter the partition number (use the default of 1)
- Enter the first sector (use the default of 2048)
- Enter the last sector – if you want a specific size for the partition, you can use size values in KB, MB, GB, and so on, or sector values (the default is the maximum size of the disk)
- If asked to remove any signatures, type Y to remove them
- w to write changes to disk

The output of the previous series of actions is shown in the following screenshot:

```
Command (m for help): n
Partition type
   p   primary (0 primary, 0 extended, 4 free)
   e   extended (container for logical partitions)
Select (default p): p
Partition number (1-4, default 1): 1
First sector (2048-15728639, default 2048):
Last sector, +/-sectors or +/-size{K,M,G,T,P} (2048-15728639, default 15728639):


Created a new partition 1 of type 'Linux' and of size 7.5 GiB.
Partition #1 contains a ext4 signature.

Do you want to remove the signature? [Y]es/[N]o: Y

The signature will be removed by a write command.

Command (m for help): w
The partition table has been altered.
Calling ioctl() to re-read partition table.
Syncing disks.
```

Figure 6.11 – Creating a new partition with fdisk

With that, the partition has been created, but it hasn't been formatted. Before we learn how to format partitions, let's learn how to back up a partition table.

There are situations when you will need to back up and restore your **partition tables**. As partitioning could go sideways sometimes, a good backup strategy could help you. To do this, you can use the dd utility. The command to use is as follows:

```
sudo dd if=/dev/sda of=mbr-backup bs=512 count=1
```

This program is very useful and powerful as it can clone disks or wipe data. Here is an example showing the output of the command:

```
alexandru@debian:~$ pwd
/home/alexandru
alexandru@debian:~$ sudo dd if=/dev/sda
sda    sda1
alexandru@debian:~$ sudo dd if=/dev/sda of=mbr-backup bs=512 count=1
1+0 records in
1+0 records out
512 bytes copied, 0.00138593 s, 369 kB/s
alexandru@debian:~$ ls
Desktop     Downloads    Music      Public      Videos
Documents   mbr-backup   Pictures   Templates
alexandru@debian:~$
```

Figure 6.12 – Backing up MBR with the dd command

The dd command has a clear syntax. By default, it uses the standard input and standard output, but you can change those by specifying new input files with the if option, and output files with the of option. We specified the input file as the device file for the disk we wanted to back up and gave a name for the backup output file. We also specified the block size using the bs option, and the count option to specify the number of blocks to read.

To restore the bootloader, we can use the dd command, as follows:

```
sudo dd if=~/mbr-backup of=/dev/sda bs=512 count=1
```

Now that you have learned how to use dd to back up a partition table, let's format the partition we created earlier. The most commonly used program for formatting a filesystem on a partition is mkfs. Formatting a partition is also known as *making* a filesystem, hence the name of the utility. It has specific tools for different filesystems, all using the same frontend utility. The following is a list of all filesystems supported by mkfs:

```
alexandru@debian:~$ ls -lh /sbin/mkfs*
-rwxr-xr-x 1 root root   15K Feb 13 10:48 /sbin/mkfs
-rwxr-xr-x 1 root root   35K Feb 13 10:48 /sbin/mkfs.bfs
-rwxr-xr-x 1 root root   43K Feb 13 10:48 /sbin/mkfs.cramfs
-rwxr-xr-x 1 root root   51K Oct 28 15:48 /sbin/mkfs.exfat
lrwxrwxrwx 1 root root    6 Feb  2 07:38 /sbin/mkfs.ext2 -> mke2fs
lrwxrwxrwx 1 root root    6 Feb  2 07:38 /sbin/mkfs.ext3 -> mke2fs
lrwxrwxrwx 1 root root    6 Feb  2 07:38 /sbin/mkfs.ext4 -> mke2fs
-rwxr-xr-x 1 root root   63K Feb  8 2021 /sbin/mkfs.fat
-rwxr-xr-x 1 root root  111K Feb 13 10:48 /sbin/mkfs.minix
lrwxrwxrwx 1 root root    8 Feb  8 2021 /sbin/mkfs.msdos -> mkfs.fat
lrwxrwxrwx 1 root root    6 Oct 31 16:14 /sbin/mkfs.ntfs -> mkntfs
lrwxrwxrwx 1 root root    8 Feb  8 2021 /sbin/mkfs.vfat -> mkfs.fat
```

Figure 6.13 – Details regarding the mkfs utility

To format the target disk as having the Ext4 filesystem, we will use the mkfs utility. The commands to execute are shown here:

1. First, we will run the fdisk utility to make sure that we select the largest disk correctly. Run the following command:

    ```
    sudo fdisk -l
    ```

2. Then, check the output with extreme caution and select the correct disk name.

3. Now that we know which disk to work with, we will use `mkfs` to format it as an `Ext4` filesystem. The output is shown here:

```
alexandru@debian:~$ sudo mkfs.ext4 /dev/sda
mke2fs 1.46.6 (1-Feb-2023)
Found a dos partition table in /dev/sda
Proceed anyway? (y,N) y
Creating filesystem with 1966080 4k blocks and 491520 inodes
Filesystem UUID: 9dfc7fe4-e4d4-4223-92d6-94dd7e8e6e69
Superblock backups stored on blocks:
    32768, 98304, 163840, 229376, 294912, 819200, 884736, 1605632

Allocating group tables: done
Writing inode tables: done
Creating journal (16384 blocks): done
Writing superblocks and filesystem accounting information: done
```

Figure 6.14 – Formatting an Ext4 partition using mkfs

When using `mkfs`, there are several options available. To create an `Ext4` type partition, you can either use the command shown in *Figure 6.14* or you can use the `-t` option followed by the filesystem type. You can also use the `-v` option for a more verbose output, and the `-c` option for bad sector scanning while creating the filesystem. You can also use the `-L` option if you want to add a label for the partition right from the command. The following is an example of creating an `Ext4` filesystem partition with the name `newpartition`:

```
sudo mkfs -t ext4 -v -c -L newpartition /dev/sda
```

Once a partition is formatted, it's advised that you check it for errors. Similar to `mkfs`, there is a tool called `fsck`. This is a utility that sometimes runs automatically following an abnormal shutdown or on set intervals. It has specific programs for the most commonly used filesystems, just like `mkfs`. The following is the output of running `fsck` on one of our partitions. After running, it will show whether there are any problems. In the following screenshot, the output shows that checking the partition resulted in no errors:

```
alexandru@debian:~$ sudo fsck -t ext4 /dev/sda
fsck from util-linux 2.38.1
e2fsck 1.46.6 (1-Feb-2023)
/dev/sda: clean, 11/491520 files, 55879/1966080 blocks
```

Figure 6.15 – Using fsck to check a partition

After partitions are created, they need to be mounted; otherwise, they cannot be used.

> **Important note**
>
> **Mounting** is an important action in Linux, and any other operating system for that matter. By mounting, you give the operating system access to the disk resource in such a way that it looks like it is using a local disk. On Linux, the external disk that is mounted is linked to a mount point, which is a directory on the local filesystem. Mount points are essential to POSIX-compatible operating systems, such as Linux. Mounting a disk makes it accessible to the entire operating system through mount points. For more information on mounting, visit `https://docs.oracle.com/cd/E19455-01/805-7228/6j6q7ueup/index.html`.

Each partition will be mounted inside the existing filesystem structure. Mounting is allowed at any point in the tree structure. Each filesystem is mounted under certain directories, created inside the directory structure. We will explore mounting and unmounting partitions in the next section.

Mounting and unmounting partitions

The **mounting** utility in Linux is simply called `mount`, and the **unmounting** utility is called `umount`. To see whether a certain partition is mounted, you can simply type `mount` and see the output, which will be of a significant size. You can use `grep` to filter it:

```
mount | grep /dev/sda
```

We are looking for `/dev/sda` in the output, but it is not shown. This means that the drive is not mounted.

To mount it, we need to make a new directory. For simplicity, we will show all the steps required until you mount and use the partition:

1. Create a new directory to mount the partition. In our case, we created a new directory called USB inside the `/home/alexandru` directory:

    ```
    mkdir USB
    ```

2. Mount the partition using the following command:

    ```
    sudo mount /dev/sda /home/alexandru/USB
    ```

3. Start using the new partition from the new location. As an example, we will copy the `mbr-backup` file we created a few steps back to the newly mounted USB memory stick using the following command:

    ```
    sudo cp mbr-backup USB/
    ```

The following is the output for all the commands from the preceding list:

```
alexandru@debian:~$ pwd
/home/alexandru
alexandru@debian:~$ mkdir USB
alexandru@debian:~$ sudo mount /dev/sda /home/alexandru/USB
alexandru@debian:~$
alexandru@debian:~$ sudo cp mbr-backup USB/
alexandru@debian:~$ ls -l USB/
total 4
-rw-r--r-- 1 root root 512 Mar 16 15:44 mbr-backup
alexandru@debian:~$ █
```

Figure 6.16 – Mounting an external memory stick

The mount command needs to be used with superuser permission. If you try to mount an external USB device without sudo, you will get the following message:

```
alexandru@debian:~$ mount /dev/sda /home/alexandru/USB
mount: /home/alexandru/USB: must be superuser to use mount.
       dmesg(1) may have more information after failed mount system call.
```

Figure 6.17 – Error for not using sudo with mount

The mount utility has many options available. Use the help menu to see everything that it has under the hood. Now that the partition has been mounted, you can start using it. If you want to unmount it, you can use the umount utility. You can use it as follows:

```
sudo umount /dev/sda
```

When unmounting a filesystem, you may receive errors if that partition is still in use. Being in use means that certain programs from that filesystem are still running in memory, using files from that partition. Therefore, you first have to close all running applications, and if other processes are using that filesystem, you will have to kill them, too. Sometimes, the reason a filesystem is busy is not clear at first, and to know which files are open and running, you can use the lsof command:

```
sudo lsof | grep /dev/sda
```

Mounting a filesystem only makes it available until the system is shut down or rebooted. If you want the changes to be persistent, you will have to edit the /etc/fstab file accordingly. First, open the file with your favorite text editor:

```
sudo nano /etc/fstab
```

Add a new line similar to the one that follows:

```
/dev/sda /mnt/sdb ext4 defaults 0 0
```

The /etc/fstab file is a configuration file for the filesystem table. It consists of a set of rules needed to control how the filesystems are used. This simplifies the need to manually mount and unmount each disk when used, by drastically reducing possible errors. The table has a six-column structure, with each column designated with a specific parameter. There is only one correct order for the parameters to work:

- **Device name**: Either by using UUID or the mounted device name

- **Mount point**: The directory where the device is, or will be, mounted

- **Filesystem type**: The filesystem type used

- **Options**: The options shown, with multiple ones separated by commas

- **Backup operation**: This is the first digit from the last two digits in the file; 0 = no backup, 1 = dump utility backup

- **Filesystem check order**: This is the last digit inside the file; 0 = no fsck filesystem check, with 1 for the root filesystem, and 2 for other partitions

By updating the /etc/fstab file, the mounting is permanent and is not affected by any shutdown or system reboot. Usually, the /etc/fstab file only stores information about the internal hard drive partitions and filesystems. The external hard drives or USB drives are automatically mounted under /media by the kernel's **hardware abstraction layer** (**HAL**).

By now, you should be comfortable with managing partitions in Linux, but there is still one type of partition we have not discussed: the **swap partition**. In the next section, we will introduce you to how swap works on Linux.

Swap partition

Linux uses a robust swap implementation. The virtual memory uses hard drive space when physical memory is full through swap. This additional space is made available either for the programs that do not use all the memory they are given, or when memory pressure is high. Swapping is usually done using one or more dedicated partitions as Linux permits multiple swap areas. The recommended swap size is at least the total RAM on the system. To check the actual swap used on the system, you can concatenate the /proc/swaps file or use the free command to see swap utilization, as shown in the following screenshot:

```
alexandru@debian:~$ cat /proc/swaps
Filename                Type        Size        Used        Priority
/dev/dm-2                           partition   999420                  300     -2
alexandru@debian:~$ free
               total       used       free      shared  buff/cache   available
Mem:        48124468    7763840   15675640       69204    25344948    40360628
Swap:         999420        300     999120
```

Figure 6.18 – Checking the currently used swap

If swap is not set up on your system, you can format a partition as swap and activate it. The commands to do that are as follows:

```
mkswap /dev/sda1
swapon /dev/sda1
```

The operating system is caching file contents inside the memory to prevent the use of swap as much as possible. This happens because memory is working at much higher speeds compared to hard drives or hard disk drives. Only when available memory is limited will swap be used. However, the memory that the kernel uses is never swapped; only the memory that the user space is using gets to be swapped. This assures data integrity for the kernel. Refer to the utilities we applied in *Chapter 5* to show memory usage in Linux.

Filesystems and partitions are the bare bones of any disk management task, but there are still several hiccups that an administrator needs to overcome, and this can be solved by using logical volumes. This is why, in the next section, we will introduce you to LVM.

Introducing LVM in Linux

Some of you may have already heard of **LVM**. For those who do not know what it is, we will explain it briefly in this section. Imagine a situation where your disks run out of space. You can always move it to a larger disk and then replace the smaller one, but this implies system restarts and unwanted downtimes. As a solution, you can consider LVM, which offers more flexibility and efficiency. By using LVM, you can add more physical disks to your existing volume groups while they're still in use. This still offers the possibility to move data to a new hard drive but with no downtime – everything is done while filesystems are online.

The utilities used in Linux for LVM management are called `pvcreate`, `vgcreate`, `vgdisplay`, `lvcreate`, `lvextend`, and `lvdisplay`. Let's learn how to use them.

As we don't have a system with LVM set up just yet, we will show you the steps that are necessary to create new LVM volumes by using another system with two internal drives: one with the operating system installed on it, and a second, internal one that's available. We'll be using Debian GNU/Linux, but the commands are the same for any other Linux-based operating system.

Follow these steps to create an LVM volume:

1. Use the `fdisk` command to verify the names of the available disks (you can also use `lsblk` for this step):

    ```
    sudo fdisk -l
    ```

    In our case, the second drive is /dev/sda.

2. Create the LVM physical volume with the pvcreate command:

```
sudo pvcreate /dev/sda
```

Using this command might not work from the beginning and give an error message regarding the status of the drive where you want to create a physical volume. It happened to us with one of the drives; here, we had to wipe the filesystem information from the drive using the wipefs utility. The output is shown in the following screenshot:

```
alexandru@debian:~$ sudo pvcreate /dev/sda
  Cannot use /dev/sda: device is partitioned
alexandru@debian:~$ wipefs --all /dev/sda
bash: wipefs: command not found
alexandru@debian:~$ sudo wipefs --all /dev/sda
/dev/sda: 8 bytes were erased at offset 0x00000200 (gpt): 45 46 49 20 50 41 52 5
4
/dev/sda: 8 bytes were erased at offset 0x1bf2975e00 (gpt): 45 46 49 20 50 41 52
54
/dev/sda: 2 bytes were erased at offset 0x000001fe (PMBR): 55 aa
/dev/sda: calling ioctl to re-read partition table: Success
alexandru@debian:~$ sudo pvcreate /dev/sda
  Physical volume "/dev/sda" successfully created.
```

Figure 6.19 – Using pvcreate to create an LVM physical volume

3. Create a new volume group to add the new physical volume to using the vgcreate command:

```
sudo vgcreate newvolume /dev/sda
```

4. You can see the new volume group by running the vgdisplay command:

```
alexandru@debian:~$ sudo vgcreate newvolume /dev/sda
  Volume group "newvolume" successfully created
alexandru@debian:~$ sudo vgdisplay newvolume
\\   --- Volume group ---
  VG Name               newvolume
  System ID
  Format                lvm2
```

Figure 6.20 – Creating and viewing details of the new volume

5. Now, let's create a logical volume using some of the space available from the volume group, using lvcreate. Use the -n option to add a name for the logical volume and -L to set the size in a human-readable manner (we created a 5 GB logical volume named projects):

```
alexandru@debian:~$ sudo lvcreate -n projects -L 5G newvolume
WARNING: ext4 signature detected on /dev/newvolume/projects at offset 1080. Wipe
  it? [y/n]: y
  Wiping ext4 signature on /dev/newvolume/projects.
  Logical volume "projects" created.
```

Figure 6.21 – Creating a logical volume using lvcreate

6. Check whether the logical volume exists:

```
sudo ls /dev/mapper/newvolume-projects
```

7. The newly created device can only be used if it's formatted using a known filesystem and mounted afterward, in the same way as a regular partition. First, let's format the new volume:

```
alexandru@debian:~$ sudo ls /dev/mapper/newvolume-projects
/dev/mapper/newvolume-projects
alexandru@debian:~$ sudo mkfs -t ext4 /dev/mapper/newvolume-projects
mke2fs 1.46.6 (1-Feb-2023)
Discarding device blocks: done
Creating filesystem with 1310720 4k blocks and 327680 inodes
Filesystem UUID: 1af332be-46a6-41f9-b343-271078ee6503
Superblock backups stored on blocks:
        32768, 98304, 163840, 229376, 294912, 819200, 884736

Allocating group tables: done
Writing inode tables: done
Creating journal (16384 blocks): done
Writing superblocks and filesystem accounting information: done
```

Figure 6.22 – Formatting the new logical volume as an Ext4 filesystem

8. Now, it's time to mount the logical volume. First, create a new directory and mount the logical volume there. Then, check its size using the df command:

```
alexandru@debian:~$ pwd
/home/alexandru
alexandru@debian:~$ mkdir LVM
alexandru@debian:~$ sudo mount /dev/mapper/newvolume-projects /home/alexandru/LVM
alexandru@debian:~$ df -h /home/alexandru/LVM/
Filesystem                      Size  Used Avail Use% Mounted on
/dev/mapper/newvolume-projects  4.9G   24K  4.6G   1% /home/alexandru/LVM
```

Figure 6.23 – Mounting the logical volume

9. All changes implemented hitherto are not permanent. To make them permanent, you will have to edit the /etc/fstab file by adding the following within the file:

```
/dev/mapper/newvolume-projects /home/alexandru/LVM ext4 defaults
1 2
```

10. You can now check the space available on your logical volume and grow it if you want. Use the vgdisplay command to see the following details:

```
sudo vgdisplay newvolume
```

11. You can now expand the logical volume by using the `lvextend` command. We will extend the initial size by 5 GB, for a total of 10 GB. The following is an example:

```
alexandru@debian:~$ sudo lvextend -L +5G /dev/mapper/newvolume-projects
  Size of logical volume newvolume/projects changed from 5.00 GiB (1280 extents) t
o 10.00 GiB (2560 extents).
  Logical volume newvolume/projects successfully resized.
```

Figure 6.24 – Extending the logical volume using lvextend

12. Now, resize the filesystem so that it fits the new size of the logical volume using `resize2fs` and check for the size with `df`:

```
alexandru@debian:~$ sudo resize2fs -p /dev/mapper/newvolume-projects
resize2fs 1.46.6 (1-Feb-2023)
Filesystem at /dev/mapper/newvolume-projects is mounted on /home/alexandru/LVM; on
-line resizing required
old_desc_blocks = 1, new_desc_blocks = 2
The filesystem on /dev/mapper/newvolume-projects is now 2621440 (4k) blocks long.
```

Figure 6.25 – Resizing the logical volume with resize2fs and checking for the size with df

LVM is an advanced topic that will prove essential for any Linux system administrator to have. The brief hands-on examples we provided in this section only show the basic operations that you need to work with LVM. Feel free to dig deeper into this topic if you need to.

In the following section, we will discuss several more advanced LVM topics, including how to take full filesystem snapshots.

LVM snapshots

What is an LVM snapshot? It is a frozen instance of an LVM logical volume. More specifically, it uses a **copy-on-write** technology. This technology monitors each block of the existing volume, and when blocks change, due to new writings, that block's value is copied to the snapshot volume.

The snapshots are created constantly and instantly and persist until they are deleted. This way, you can create backups from any snapshot. As snapshots are constantly changing due to the copy-on-write technology, initial thoughts on the size of the snapshot should be given when creating one. Take into consideration, if possible, how much data is going to change during the existence of the snapshot. Once the snapshot is full, it will be automatically disabled.

Creating a new snapshot

To create a new snapshot, you can use the `lvcreate` command, with the `-s` option. You can also specify the size with the `-L` option and add a name for the snapshot with the `-n` option, as follows:

```
alexandru@debian:~$ sudo lvcreate -s -L 5G -n linux-snapshot-01 /dev/mapper/newvol
ume-projects
[sudo] password for alexandru:
  Logical volume "linux-snapshot-01" created.
```

Figure 6.26 – Creating an LVM snapshot with the lvcreate command

In the preceding command, we set a size of 5 GB and used the name `linux-snapshot-01`. The last part of the command contains the destination of the volume for which we created the snapshot. To list the new snapshot, use the `lvs` command:

```
alexandru@debian:~$ sudo lvs
  LV                VG        Attr       LSize  Pool Origin   Data% Meta% Move Log Cpy%Sync Convert
  linux-snapshot-01 newvolume swi-a-s---  5.00g      projects 0.01
  projects          newvolume owi-aos--- 10.00g
```

Figure 6.27 – Listing the available volume and the newly created snapshot

For more information on the logical volumes, run the `lvdisplay` command. The output will show information about all the volumes, and among them, you will see the snapshot we just created.

When we created the snapshot, we gave it a size of 5 GB. Now, we would like to extend it to the size of the source, which was 10 GB. We will do this with the `lvextend` command:

```
alexandru@debian:~$ sudo lvextend -L +5G /dev/mapper/newvolume-linux--snapshot--01
  Size of logical volume newvolume/linux-snapshot-01 changed from 5.00 GiB (1280 extents)
  to 10.00 GiB (2560 extents).
  Logical volume newvolume/linux-snapshot-01 successfully resized.
```

Figure 6.28 – Extending the snapshot from 5 to 10 GB

As shown in the preceding screenshot, the name that the snapshot volume is using is different from the one we used. Even though we used the name `linux-snapshot-01` for the snapshot volume, if we do a listing of the `/dev/mapper/` directory, we will see that the name uses two more dashes instead. This is a convention that's used to represent logical volume files.

Now that you know how to create snapshots, let's learn how to restore a snapshot.

Restoring a snapshot

To restore a snapshot, first, you would need to unmount the filesystem. To unmount, we will use the `umount` command:

```
sudo umount /home/alexandru/LVM
```

Then, we can proceed to restore the snapshot with the `lvconvert` command. After the snapshot is merged into the source, we can check this by using the `lvs` command. The output of the two commands is shown in the following screenshot:

```
alexandru@debian:~$ sudo umount /home/alexandru/LVM
[sudo] password for alexandru:
alexandru@debian:~$ sudo lvconvert --merge /dev/mapper/newvolume-linux--snapshot--01
  Merging of volume newvolume/linux-snapshot-01 started.
  newvolume/projects: Merged: 100.00%
alexandru@debian:~$
alexandru@debian:~$ sudo lvs
  LV        VG        Attr       LSize  Pool Origin Data%  Meta%  Move Log Cpy%Sync Convert
  projects newvolume -wi-a----- 10.00g
```

Figure 6.29 – Restoring and checking the snapshot

Following the merge, the snapshot is automatically removed.

We have now covered all the basics of LVM in Linux. LVM is more complicated than normal disk partitioning. It might be intimidating to many, but it can show its strengths when needed. Nevertheless, it also comes with several drawbacks – for example, it can add unwanted complexity in a disaster recovery scenario or when a hardware failure occurs. But all this aside, it is still worth learning about.

Summary

Managing filesystems and disks is an important task for any Linux system administrator. Understanding how devices are managed in Linux, and how to format and partition disks, is essential. Furthermore, it is important to learn about LVM as it offers a flexible way to manage partitions.

Mastering those skills will give you a strong foundation for any basic administration task. In the following chapter, we will introduce you to the vast domain of **networking** in Linux.

Questions

If you managed to skim through some parts of this chapter, you might want to recap a few essential details about Linux filesystem and disk management:

1. Think of another tool to use for working with disks and install it.

   Hint: Try installing `parted` and use it from the command line. You can also use GParted from the GUI.

2. Experiment with using Disks (in GNOME) and KDE Partition Manager (in KDE) and use the command-line interface side by side.

   Hint: Keep both applications open and use the command-line utilities side by side. Try to format and mount a disk from the command line while keeping the GUI apps open.

3. Format new partitions using different filesystems.

   Hint: Use `btrfs` instead of `ext4`.

4. Explore your filesystem and disks.

   Hint: Use tools such as `lsblk`, `df`, and `fdisk`.

Further reading

For more information about what was covered in this chapter, please refer to the following Packt titles:

- *Linux Administration Best Practices*, by Scott Alan Miller
- *Mastering Ubuntu Server – Fourth Edition*, by Jay LaCroix

7

Networking with Linux

Linux networking is a vast domain. The last few decades have seen countless volumes and references written about Linux network administration internals. Sometimes, the mere assimilation of essential concepts can be overwhelming for both novice and advanced users. This chapter provides a relatively concise overview of Linux networking, focusing on network communication layers, sockets and ports, network services and protocols, and network security.

We hope that the content presented in this chapter is both a comfortable introduction to basic Linux networking principles for a novice user and a good refresher for an advanced Linux administrator.

In this chapter, we'll cover the following topics:

- Exploring basic networking – focusing on computer networks, networking models, protocols, network addresses, and ports. We'll also cover some practical aspects of configuring Linux network settings using the command-line Terminal.

- Working with network services – introducing common networking servers that run on Linux.

- Understanding network security.

Technical requirements

Throughout this chapter, we'll be using the Linux command line to some extent. A working Linux distribution, installed on either a **virtual machine** (**VM**) or a desktop platform, is highly recommended. If you don't have one already, go back to *Chapter 1*, *Installing Linux*, which will guide you through the installation process. Most of the commands and examples illustrated in this chapter use Ubuntu and Fedora, but the same would apply to any other Linux platform.

Exploring basic networking

Today, it's almost inconceivable to imagine a computer not connected to some sort of network or the internet. Our ever-increasing online presence, cloud computing, mobile communications, and **Internet of Things (IoT)** would not be possible without the highly distributed, high-speed, and scalable networks serving the underlying data traffic; yet the basic networking principles behind the driving force of the modern-day internet are decades old. Networking and communication paradigms will continue to evolve, but some of the original primitives and concepts will still have a long-lasting effect in shaping the building blocks of future communications.

This section will introduce you to a few of these networking essentials and, hopefully, spark your curiosity for further exploration. Let's start with computer networks.

Computer networks

A **computer network** is a group of two or more computers (or nodes) connected via a physical medium (cable, wireless, optical) and communicating with each other using a standard set of agreed-upon communication protocols. At a very high level, a **network communication infrastructure** includes computers, devices, switches, routers, Ethernet or optical cables, wireless environments, and all sorts of network equipment.

Beyond the *physical* connectivity and arrangement, networks are also defined by a *logical* layout via network topologies, tiers, and the related data flow. An example of a logical networking hierarchy is the three-tiered layering of the **demilitarized zone (DMZ)**, *firewall*, and *internal* networks. The DMZ is an organization's outward-facing network, with an extra security layer against the public internet. A firewall controls the network traffic between the DMZ and the internal network.

Network devices are identified by the following aspects:

- **Network addresses**: These assist with locating nodes on the network using **communication protocols**, such as the **Internet Protocol (IP)** (see more on IP in the *TCP/IP protocols* section, later in this chapter)

- **Hostnames**: These are user-friendly labels associated with devices that are easier to remember than network addresses

A common classification criterion looks at the *scale* and *expansion* of computer networks. Let's introduce you to **local area networks (LANs)** and **wide area networks (WANs)**:

- **LANs**: A LAN represents a group of devices connected and located in a single physical location, such as a private residence, school, or office. A LAN can be of any size, ranging from a home network with only a few devices to large-scale enterprise networks with thousands of users and computers.

Regardless of the network's size, a LAN's essential characteristic is that it connects devices in a single, limited area. Examples of LANs include the home network of a single-family residence or your local coffee shop's free wireless service.

For more information about LANs, you can refer to `https://www.cisco.com/c/en/us/products/switches/what-is-a-lan-local-area-network.html`.

When a computer network spans multiple regions or multiple interconnected LANs, WANs come into play.

- **WANs:** A WAN is usually a network of networks, with multiple or distributed LANs communicating with each other. In this sense, we regard the internet as the world's largest WAN. An example of a WAN is the computer network of a multinational company's geographically distributed offices worldwide. Some WANs are built by service providers, to be leased to various businesses and institutions around the world.

  WANs have several variations, depending on their type, range, and use. Typical examples of WANs include **personal area networks (PANs)**, **metropolitan area networks (MANs)**, and **cloud** or **internet area networks (IANs)**.

  For more information about WANs, you can refer to `https://www.cisco.com/c/en/us/products/switches/what-is-a-wan-wide-area-network.html`.

We think that an adequate introduction to basic networking principles should always include a brief presentation of the theoretical model governing network communications in general. We'll look at this next.

The OSI model

The **Open Systems Interconnection (OSI)** model is a theoretical representation of a multilayer communication mechanism between computer systems interacting over a network. The OSI model was introduced in 1983 by the **International Organization for Standardization (ISO)** to provide a standard for different computer systems to communicate with each other.

We can regard the OSI model as a universal framework for network communications. As the following figure shows, the OSI model defines a stack of seven layers, directing the communication flow:

Application Layer	7		User interaction and high-level APIs
Presentation Layer	6	data	Data translation into a usable format (e.g. encrypt/decrypt, encode/decode, compress/deflate)
Session Layer	5		Communication sessions (connections, sockets, ports)
Transport Layer	4	segments, datagrams	Reliable data segments using transmission control protocols (e.g. TCP, UDP)
Network Layer	3	packets	Data packets with addressing, routing and traffic control information (i.e. data path)
Data Link Layer	2	frames	Formatting the data as reliable data frames
Physical Layer	1	bits	Transmission/reception of raw bit streams over a physical medium

Figure 7.1 – The OSI model

In the layered view shown in the preceding figure, the communication flow moves from top to bottom (on the transmitting end) or bottom to top (on the receiving end). Before we look at each layer in more detail, let's briefly explain how the OSI model and data encapsulation and decapsulation work.

Data encapsulation and decapsulation in the OSI model

When using the network to transfer data from one computer to another, some specific rules are followed. Inside the OSI model, the network data flows in two different ways. One way is down, from Layer 7 to Layer 1, and this is known as **data encapsulation**. The other way, up from Layer 1 to Layer 7, is known as **data decapsulation**. Data encapsulation represents the process of sending data from one computer to another, while data decapsulation represents the process of receiving data. Let's look at these in greater detail:

- **Encapsulation**: When sending data, data from one computer is converted to be sent through the network, and it receives extra information as it is being sent though all the layers of the stack. The application layer (Layer 7) is the place where the user directly interacts with the application. Then, data is sent through the presentation (Layer 6) and session (Layer 5) layers, where data is transformed into a usable format. In the transport layer (Layer 4), data is broken into smaller chunks (segments) and receives a new TCP header. Inside the network layer (Layer 3), the data is called a packet, receives an IP header, and is sent to the data link layer (Layer 2), where it is called a frame and contains both TCP and IP headers. At Layer 2, each frame receives information about the hardware addresses of the source and destination (**media access control (MAC)** addresses) and information about the protocols to be used in the network layer (created by the **logical link control (LLC)** data communication protocol). At this point, a new field is added, called **Frame Check Sequence (FCS)**, which is used for checking errors. Then, the frames are passed through the physical layer (Layer 1).

- **Decapsulation**: When data is received, the process is identical, but in reverse order. This starts from the physical layer (Layer 1), where the first synchronization happens, after which the frame is sent through the data link layer (Layer 2), where an error check is done, by verifying the FCS field. This process is called a **Cyclic Redundancy Check (CRC)**. The data, which is now a packet, is sent through all the other layers. Here, the headers that were added during the encapsulation process are stripped off until they reach the upper layers and become ready to be used on the target computer. A graphic explanation is provided in the following figure:

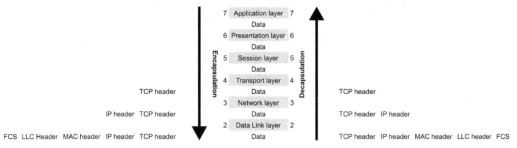

Figure 7.2 – Encapsulation and decapsulation in the OSI model

Let's look at each of these layers in detail and describe their functionality in shaping network communication.

The physical layer

The **physical layer** (or *Layer 1*) consists of the networking equipment or infrastructure connecting the devices and serving the communication, such as cables, wireless or optical environments, connectors, and switches. This layer handles the conversion between raw bit streams and the communication medium (which includes electrical, radio, or optical signals) while regulating the corresponding bit-rate control.

Examples of protocols operating at the physical layer include Ethernet, **Universal Serial Bus (USB)**, and **Digital Subscriber Line (DSL)**.

The data link layer

The **data link layer** (or *Layer 2*) establishes a reliable data flow between two directly connected devices on a network, either as adjacent nodes in a WAN or as devices within a LAN. One of the data link layer's responsibilities is flow control, adapting to the physical layer's communication speed. On the receiving device, the data link layer corrects communication errors that originated in the physical layer. The data link layer consists of the following subsystems:

- **Media access control** (**MAC**): This subsystem uses MAC addresses to identify and connect devices on the network. It also controls the device access permissions to transmit and receive data on the network.

- **Logical link control** (**LLC**): This subsystem identifies and encapsulates network layer protocols and performs error checking and frame synchronization while transmitting or receiving data.

The protocol data units controlled by the data link layer are also known as **frames**. A frame is a data transmission unit that acts as a container for a single network packet. Network packets are processed at the next OSI level (*network layer*). When multiple devices access the same physical layer simultaneously, frame collisions may occur. Data link layer protocols can detect and recover from such collisions and further reduce or prevent their occurrence.

There are also Ethernet frames, for example, which are encapsulated data that is defined for MAC implementations. The original IEEE 802.3 Ethernet format, the 802.3 **SubNetwork Access Protocol** (**SNAP**), and the Ethernet II (extended) frame formats are also available.

One more example of the data link protocol is the **Point-to-Point Protocol** (**PPP**), a binary networking protocol that's used in high-speed broadband communication networks.

The network layer

The **network layer** (or *Layer 3*) discovers the optimal communication path (or route) between devices on a network. This layer uses a routing mechanism based on the IP addresses of the devices involved in the data exchange to move data packets from source to destination.

On the transmitting end, the network layer disassembles the data segments that originated in the *transport layer* into network packets. On the receiving end, the data frames are reassembled from the layer below (*data link layer*) into packets.

A protocol that operates at the network layer is the **Internet Control Message Protocol** (**ICMP**). ICMP is used by network devices to diagnose network communication issues. ICMP reports an error when a requested endpoint is not available by sending messages such as *destination network unreachable*, *timer expired*, *source route failed*, and others.

The transport layer

The **transport layer** (or *Layer 4*) operates with **data segments** or **datagrams**. This layer is mainly responsible for transferring data from a source to a destination and guaranteeing a specific **quality of service** (**QoS**). On the transmitting end, data that originated from the layer above (*session layer*) is disassembled into segments. On the receiving end, the transport layer reassembles the data packets received from the layer below (*network layer*) into segments.

The transport layer maintains the reliability of the data transfer through flow-control and error-control functions. The flow-control function adjusts the data transfer rate between endpoints with different connection speeds, to avoid a sender overwhelming the receiver. When the data received is incorrect, the error-control function may request the retransmission of data.

Examples of transport layer protocols include the **Transmission Control Protocol** (**TCP**) and the **User Datagram Protocol** (**UDP**).

The session layer

The **session layer** (or *Layer 5*) controls the lifetime of the connection channels (or sessions) between devices communicating on a network. At this layer, sessions or network connections are usually defined by network addresses, sockets, and ports. We'll explain each of these concepts in the *Sockets and ports* and *IP addresses* sections. The session layer is responsible for the integrity of the data transfer within a communication channel or session. For example, if a session is interrupted, the data transfer resumes from a previous checkpoint.

Some typical session layer protocols are the **Remote Procedure Call** (**RPC**) protocol, which is used by interprocess communications, and **Network Basic Input/Output System** (**NetBIOS**), which is a file-sharing and name-resolution protocol.

The presentation layer

The **presentation layer** (or *Layer 6*) acts as a data translation tier between the *application layer* above and the *session layer* below. On the transmitting end, this layer formats the data into a system-independent representation before sending it across the network. On the receiving end, the presentation layer transforms the data into an application-friendly format. Examples of such transformations are encryption and decryption, compression and decompression, encoding and decoding, and serialization and deserialization.

Usually, there is no substantial distinction between the presentation and application layers, mainly due to the relatively tight coupling of the various data formats with the applications consuming them. Standard data representation formats include the **American Standard Code for Information Interchange** (**ASCII**), **Extensible Markup Language** (**XML**), **JavaScript Object Notation** (**JSON**), **Joint Photographic Experts Group** (**JPEG**), ZIP, and others.

The application layer

The **application layer** (or *Layer 7*) is the closest to the end user in the OSI model. This layer collects or provides the input or output of application data in some meaningful way. This layer does not contain or run the applications themselves. Instead, it acts as an abstraction between applications, implementing a communication component and the underlying network. Typical examples of applications that interact with the application layer are web browsers and email clients.

A few examples of Layer 7 protocols are the DNS protocol, the **HyperText Transfer Protocol** (HTTP), the **File Transfer Protocol** (FTP), and email messaging protocols, such as the **Post Office Protocol** (POP), **Internet Message Access Protocol** (IMAP), and **Simple Mail Transfer Protocol** (SMTP).

Before wrapping up, we should note that the OSI model is a generic representation of networking communication layers and provides the theoretical guidelines for how network communication works. A similar – but more practical – illustration of the networking stack is the TCP/IP model. Both these models are useful when it comes to network design, implementation, troubleshooting, and diagnostics. The OSI model gives network operators a good understanding of the full networking stack, from the physical medium to the application layer, and each level has **Protocol Data Units** (**PDUs**) and communication internals. However, the TCP/IP model is somewhat simplified, with a few of the OSI model layers collapsed into one, and it takes a rather protocol-centric approach to network communications. We'll explore this in more detail in the next section.

The TCP/IP network stack model

The **TCP/IP model** is a four-layer interpretation of the OSI networking stack, where some of the equivalent OSI layers appear consolidated, as shown in the following figure:

	OSI Model	TCP/IP Model	TCP/IP Protocols
7	Application Layer	Application Layer	DNS, HTTP, FTP, SMTP, SNMP, Telnet, ...
6	Presentation Layer		
5	Session Layer		
4	Transport Layer	Transport Layer	TCP, UDP, ...
3	Network Layer	Internet Layer	IP, ARP, ICMP, IGMP, ...
2	Data Link Layer	Network Interface Layer	Ethernet, Token Ring, Frame Relay, ATM, ...
1	Physical Layer		

Figure 7.3 – The OSI and TCP/IP models

Chronologically, the TCP/IP model is older than the OSI model. It was first suggested by the US **Department of Defense** (**DoD**) as part of an internetwork project developed by the **Defense Advanced Research Projects Agency** (**DARPA**). This project eventually became the modern-day internet.

The TCP/IP model layers encapsulate similar functions to their counterpart OSI layers. Here's a summary of each layer in the TCP/IP model.

The network interface layer

The **network interface layer** is responsible for data delivery over a physical medium (such as wire, wireless, or optical). Networking protocols operating at this layer include Ethernet, Token Ring, and Frame Relay. This layer maps to the composition of the *physical and data link layers* in the OSI model.

The internet layer

The **internet layer** provides *connectionless* data delivery between nodes on a network. Connectionless protocols describe a network communication pattern where a sender transmits data to a receiver without a prior arrangement between the two. This layer is responsible for disassembling data into network packets at the transmitting end and reassembling them on the receiving end. The internet layer uses routing functions to identify the optimal path between the network nodes. This layer maps to the *network layer* in the OSI model.

The transport layer

The **transport layer** (also known as the **transmission layer** or the **host-to-host layer**) is responsible for maintaining the communication sessions between connected network nodes. The transport layer implements error-detection and correction mechanisms for reliable data delivery between endpoints. This layer maps to the *transport layer* in the OSI model.

The application layer

The **application layer** provides the data communication abstraction between software applications and the underlying network. This layer maps to the composition of the *session, presentation, and application layers* in the OSI model.

As discussed earlier in this chapter, the TCP/IP model is a protocol-centric representation of the networking stack. This model served as the foundation of the internet by gradually defining and developing networking protocols required for internet communications. These protocols are collectively referred to as the *IP suite*. The following section describes some of the most common networking protocols.

TCP/IP protocols

In this section, we'll describe some widely used networking protocols. The reference provided here should not be regarded as an all-encompassing guide. There are a vast number of TCP/IP protocols, and a comprehensive study is beyond the scope of this chapter. Nevertheless, there are a handful of protocols worth exploring, frequently at work in everyday network communication and administration workflows.

The following list briefly describes each TCP/IP protocol and its related **Request for Comments (RFC)** identifier. The RFC represents the detailed technical documentation – of a protocol, in our case – that's usually authored by the **Internet Engineering Task Force (IETF)**. For more information about RFC, please refer to `https://www.ietf.org/standards/rfcs/`. Here are the most widely used protocols:

- **IP**: IP (*RFC 791*) identifies network nodes based on fixed-length addresses, also known as IP addresses. IP addresses will be described in more detail in the next section. The IP protocol uses datagrams as the data transmission unit and provides fragmentation and reassembly capabilities of large datagrams to accommodate small-packet networks (and avoid transmission delays). The IP protocol also provides routing functions to find the optimal data path between network nodes. IP operates at the network layer (*Layer 3*) in the OSI model.

- **ARP**: The **Address Resolution Protocol (ARP)** (*RFC 826*) is used by the IP protocol to map IP network addresses (specifically, **IP version 4 or IPv4**) to device MAC addresses used by a data link protocol. ARP operates at the data link layer (*Layer 2*) in the OSI model.

- **NDP**: The **Neighbor Discovery Protocol (NDP)** (*RFC 4861*) is like the ARP protocol, and it also controls **IP version 6 (IPv6)** address mapping. NDP operates within the data link layer (*Layer 2*) in the OSI model.

- **ICMP**: ICMP (*RFC 792*) is a supporting protocol for checking transmission issues. When a device or node is not reachable within a given timeout, ICMP reports an error. ICMP operates at the network layer (*Layer 3*) in the OSI model.

- **TCP**: TCP (*RFC 793*) is a connection-oriented, highly reliable communication protocol. TCP requires a logical connection (such as a *handshake*) between the nodes before initiating the data exchange. TCP operates at the transport layer (*Layer 4*) in the OSI model.

- **UDP**: UDP (*RFC 768*) is a connectionless communication protocol. UDP has no handshake mechanism (compared to TCP). Consequently, with UDP, there's no guarantee of data delivery. It is also known as a *best-effort protocol*. UDP uses datagrams as the data transmission unit, and it's suitable for network communications where error checking is not critical. UDP operates at the transport layer (*Layer 4*) in the OSI model.

- **Dynamic Host Configuration Protocol (DHCP)**: The DHCP (*RFC 2131*) provides a framework for requesting and passing host configuration information required by devices on a TCP/IP network. DHCP enables the automatic (dynamic) allocation of reusable IP addresses and other configuration options. DHCP is considered an application layer (*Layer 7*) protocol in the OSI model, but the initial DHCP discovery mechanism operates at the data link layer (*Layer 2*).

- **Domain Name System** (**DNS**): The DNS (*RFC 2929*) is a protocol that acts as a network address book, where nodes in the network are identified by human-readable names instead of IP addresses. According to the IP protocol, each device on a network is identified by a unique IP address. When a network connection specifies the remote device's hostname (or domain name) before the connection is established, DNS translates the domain name (such as `dns.google.com`) into an IP address (such as `8.8.8.8`). The DNS protocol operates at the application layer (*Layer 7*) in the OSI model.

- **HTTP**: HTTP (*RFC 2616*) is the vehicular language of the internet. HTTP is a stateless application-level protocol based on the request and response between a client application (for example, a browser) and a server endpoint (for example, a web server). HTTP supports a wide variety of data formats, ranging from text to images and video streams. HTTP operates at the application layer (*Layer 7*) in the OSI model.

- **FTP**: FTP (*RFC 959*) is a standard protocol for transferring files requested by an FTP client from an FTP server. FTP operates at the application layer (*Layer 7*) in the OSI model.

- **TELNET**: The **Terminal Network protocol** (**TELNET**) (*RFC 854*) is an application-layer protocol that provides a bidirectional text-oriented network communication between a client and a server machine, using a virtual terminal connection. TELNET operates at the application layer (*Layer 7*) in the OSI model.

- **SSH**: **Secure Shell** (**SSH**) (*RFC 4253*) is a secure application-layer protocol that encapsulates strong encryption and cryptographic host authentication. SSH uses a virtual terminal connection between a client and a server machine. SSH operates at the application layer (*Layer 7*) in the OSI model.

- **SMTP**: SMTP (*RFC 5321*) is an application-layer protocol for sending and receiving emails between an email client (for example, Outlook) and an email server (such as Exchange Server). SMTP supports strong encryption and host authentication. SMTP acts at the application layer (*Layer 7*) in the OSI model.

- **SNMP**: The **Simple Network Management Protocol** (**SNMP**) (*RFC 1157*) is used for remote device management and monitoring. SNMP operates at the application layer (*Layer 7*) in the OSI model.

- **NTP**: The **Network Time Protocol** (**NTP**) (*RFC 5905*) is an internet protocol that's used for synchronizing the system clock of multiple machines across a network. NTP operates at the application layer (*Layer 7*) in the OSI model.

Most of the internet protocols enumerated previously use the IP protocol to identify devices participating in the communication. Devices on a network are uniquely identified by an IP address. Let's examine these network addresses more closely.

IP addresses

An **IP address** is a fixed-length **unique identifier** (**UID**) of a device in a network. Devices locate and communicate with each other based on IP addresses. The concept of an IP address is very similar to a postal address of a residence, whereby mail or a package would be sent to that destination based on its address.

Initially, IP defined the IP address as a 32-bit number known as an **IPv4 address**. With the growth of the internet, the total number of IP addresses in a network has been exhausted. To address this issue, a new version of the IP protocol devised a 128-bit numbering scheme for IP addresses. A 128-bit IP address is also known as an **IPv6 address**.

In the next few sections, we'll take a closer look at the networking constructs that play an important role in IP addresses, such as IPv4 and IPv6 address formats, network classes, subnetworks, and broadcast addresses.

IPv4 addresses

An **IPv4 address** is a 32-bit number (4 bytes) usually expressed as four groups of 1-byte (8 bits) numbers, separated by a dot (.). Each number in these four groups is an integer between 0 and 255. An example of an IPv4 address is 192.168.1.53.

The following figure shows a binary representation of an IPv4 address:

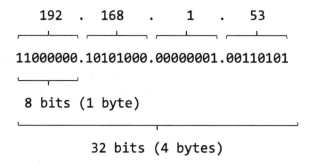

Figure 7.4 – Network classes

The IPv4 address space is limited to 4,294,967,296 (2^32) addresses (roughly 4 billion). Of these, approximately 18 million are reserved for special purposes (for example, private networks), and about 270 million are multicast addresses.

A **multicast address** is a logical identifier of a group of IP addresses. For more information on multicast addresses, please refer to *RFC 6308* (https://tools.ietf.org/html/rfc6308).

Network classes

In the early stages of the internet, the highest-order byte (first group) in the IPv4 address indicated the **network number**. The subsequent bytes further express the network hierarchy and subnetworks, with the lowest-order byte identifying the device itself. This scheme soon proved insufficient for network hierarchies and segregations as it only allowed for 256 (2^8) networks, denoted by the leading byte of the IPv4 address. As additional networks were added, each with its own identity, the IP address specification needed a special revision to accommodate a standard model. The *Classful Network* specification, which was introduced in 1981, addressed this problem by dividing the IPv4 address space into five classes based on the leading 4 bits of the address, as illustrated in the following figure:

Class	Leading bits	Start address	End address	Default subnet mask
Class A	0	0.0.0.0	127.255.255.255	255.0.0.0
Class B	10	128.0.0.0	191.255.255.255	255.255.0.0
Class C	110	192.0.0.0	223.255.255.255	255.255.255.0
Class D (multicast)	1110	224.0.0.0	239.255.255.255	Not defined
Class E (reserved)	1111	240.0.0.0	255.255.255.255	Not defined

Figure 7.5 – Network classes

For more information on network classes, please refer to *RFC 870* (https://tools.ietf.org/html/rfc870). In the preceding figure, the last column specifies the default subnet mask for each of these network classes. We'll look at subnets (or subnetworks) next.

Subnetworks

Subnetworks (or **subnets**) are logical subdivisions of an IP network. Subnets were introduced to identify devices that belong to the same network. The IP addresses of devices in the same network have an identical most-significant group. The subnet definition yields a logical division of an IP address into two fields: the **network identifier** and the **host identifier**. The numerical representation of the subnet is called a **subnet mask** or **netmask**. The following figure provides an example of a network identifier and a host identifier:

IP Address (192.168.1.53)	
Network Identifier	Host Identifier
192.168.1	53

Figure 7.6 – Subnet with network and host identifiers

With our IPv4 address (192.168.1.53), we could devise a network identifier of 192.168.1, where the host identifier is 53. The resulting subnet mask would be as follows:

```
192.168.1.0
```

We dropped the least significant group in the subnet mask, representing the host identifier (53), and replaced it with 0. Here, 0 indicates the starting address in the subnet. In other words, any host identifier value in the range of 0 to 255 is allowed in the subnetwork. For example, 192.168.1.92 is a valid (and accepted) IP address in the 192.168.1.0 network.

An alternative representation of subnets uses so-called **Classless Inter-Domain Routing (CIDR)** notation. CIDR represents an IP address as the network address (*prefix*) followed by a slash (/) and the *bit-length* of the prefix. In our case, the CIDR notation of the 192.168.1.0 subnet is this:

```
192.168.1.0/24
```

The first three groups in the network address make up *3 x 8 = 24* bits, hence the /24 notation.

Usually, **subnets** are planned with the host identifier address as a starting point. Back to our example, suppose we wanted our host identifier addresses in the network to start with 100 and end with 125. Let's look at how we can achieve this.

First, let's see the binary representation of 192.168.1.100:

```
11000000.10101000.00000001.01100100
```

As you can see, the last group, highlighted in the preceding sequence, represents the host identifier (100). Remember that we want the network to start with 100 and end with 125. This means that the closest binary value to the reserved 99 addresses that would not be permitted in our subnet is *96 = 64 + 32*. The equivalent binary value for it is as follows:

```
11100000
```

In other words, the three most significant bits in the host identifier are reserved. **Reserved bits** in the subnet representation are shown as 1. These bits would be added to the 24 already reserved bits of the network address (192.168.1), accounting in total for *27 = 24 + 3* bits. Here's the equivalent representation:

```
11111111.11111111.11111111.11100000
```

Consequently, the resulting netmask is as follows:

```
255.255.255.224
```

The CIDR notation of the corresponding subnet is shown here:

```
192.168.1.96/27
```

The remaining five bits in the host identifier's group account for $2\wedge5 = 32$ possible addresses in the subnet, starting with 97. This would limit the maximum host identifier value to $127 = 96 + 32 - 1$ (we subtract 1 to account for the starting number of 97 included in the total of 32). In this range of 32 addresses, the last IP address is reserved as a **broadcast address**, as shown here:

```
192.168.1.127
```

A broadcast address is reserved as the highest number in a network or subnet, when applicable. Back to our example, excluding the broadcast address, the maximum host IP address in the subnet is as follows:

```
192.168.1.126
```

You can learn more about subnets in *RFC 1918* (https://tools.ietf.org/html/rfc1918). Since we mentioned the broadcast address, let's have a quick look at it.

Broadcast addresses

A **broadcast address** is a reserved IP address in a network or subnetwork that's used to transmit a collective message (data) to all devices belonging to the network. The broadcast address is the last IP address in the network or subnet, when applicable.

For example, the broadcast address of the 192.168.1.0/24 network is 192.168.1.255. In our example in the previous section, the broadcast address of the 192.168.1.96/27 subnet is 192.168.1.127 ($127 = 96 + 32 - 1$).

For more information on broadcast addresses, you can refer to https://www.sciencedirect.com/topics/computer-science/broadcast-address.

IPv6 addresses

An IPv6 address is a 128-bit number (16 bytes) that's usually expressed as up to eight groups of 2-byte (16 bits) numbers, separated by a column (:). Each number in these eight groups is a hexadecimal number, with values between 0000 and FFFF. Here's an example of an IPv6 address:

```
2001:0b8d:8a52:0000:0000:8b2d:0240:7235
```

An equivalent representation of the preceding IPv6 address is shown here:

```
2001:b8d:8a52::8b2d:240:7235/64
```

In the second representation, the leading zeros are omitted, and the all-zero groups (0000:0000) are collapsed into an empty group (::). The /64 notation at the end represents the **prefix length** of the IPv6 address. The IPv6 prefix length is the equivalent of the CIDR notation of IPv4 subnets. For IPv6, the prefix length is expressed as an integer value between 1 and 128.

In our case, with a prefix length of 64 (*4 x 16*) bits, the subnet looks like this:

```
2001:b8d:8a52::
```

The subnet represents the leading four groups (`2001`, `0b8d`, `8a52`, and `0000`), which results in a total of *4 x 16 = 64* bits. In the shortened representation of the IPv6 subnet, the leading zeros are omitted and the all-zero group is collapsed to `::`.

Subnetting with IPv6 is very similar to IPv4. We won't go into the details here since the related concepts were presented in the *IPv4 addresses* section. For more information about IPv6, please refer to *RFC 2460* (`https://tools.ietf.org/html/rfc2460`).

Now that you've become familiar with IP addresses, it is fitting to introduce some of the related network constructs that serve the software implementation of IP addresses – that is, sockets and ports.

Sockets and ports

A **socket** is a software data structure representing a network node for communication purposes. Although a programming concept, in Linux, a **network socket** is ultimately a file descriptor that's controlled via a network **application programming interface** (**API**). A socket is used by an application process for transmitting and receiving data. An application can create and delete sockets. A socket cannot be active (send or receive data) beyond the lifetime of the process that created the socket.

Network sockets operate at the *transport-layer* level in the OSI model. There are two endpoints to a socket connection – a sender and a receiver. Both the sender and receiver have an IP address. Consequently, a critical piece of information in the socket data structure is the *IP address* of the endpoint that owns the socket.

Both endpoints create and manage their sockets via the network processes using these sockets. The sender and receiver may agree upon using multiple connections to exchange data. Some of these connections may even run in parallel. How do we differentiate between these socket connections? The IP address by itself is not sufficient, and this is where **ports** come into play.

A **network port** is a logical construct that's used to identify a specific process or network service running on a host. A port is an integer value in the range of `0` and `65535`. Usually, ports in the range of `0` and `1024` are assigned to the most used services on a system. These ports are also called **well-known ports**. Here are a few examples of well-known ports and the related network service for each:

- `25`: SMTP
- `21`: FTP
- `22`: SSH
- `53`: DNS

- 67, 68: DHCP (client = 68, server = 67)

- 80: HTTP

- 443: **HTTP Secure (HTTPS)**

Port numbers beyond 1024 are for general use and are also known as **ephemeral ports**.

A port is always associated with an IP address. Ultimately, a socket is a combination of an IP address and a port. For more information on network sockets, you can refer to *RFC 147* (https://tools.ietf.org/html/rfc147). For well-known ports, see *RFC 1340* (https://tools.ietf.org/html/rfc1340).

Now, let's put the knowledge we've gained so far to work by looking at how to configure the local networking stack in Linux.

Linux network configuration

This section describes the TCP/IP **network configuration** for Ubuntu and Fedora platforms, using their latest released versions to date. The same concepts would apply to most Linux distributions, albeit some of the network configuration utilities and files involved could be different.

We can use the ip command-line utility to retrieve the system's current IP addresses, as follows:

```
ip addr show
```

An example of the output is shown here:

```
packt@neptune:~$ ip addr show
1: lo: <LOOPBACK,UP,LOWER_UP> mtu 65536 qdisc noqueue state UNKNOWN group defaul
t qlen 1000
    link/loopback 00:00:00:00:00:00 brd 00:00:00:00:00:00
    inet 127.0.0.1/8 scope host lo
       valid_lft forever preferred_lft forever
    inet6 ::1/128 scope host
       valid_lft forever preferred_lft forever
2: enp1s0: <BROADCAST,MULTICAST,UP,LOWER_UP> mtu 1500 qdisc fq_codel state UP gr
oup default qlen 1000
    link/ether 52:54:00:d6:7d:69 brd ff:ff:ff:ff:ff:ff
    inet 192.168.122.117/24 metric 100 brd 192.168.122.255 scope global dynamic
enp1s0
       valid_lft 3071sec preferred_lft 3071sec
    inet6 fe80::5054:ff:fed6:7d69/64 scope link
       valid_lft forever preferred_lft forever
```

Figure 7.7 – Retrieving the current IP addresses with the ip command

We've highlighted some relevant information here, such as the network interface ID (2: enp1s0) and the IP address with the subnet prefix (192.168.122.117/24).

We'll look at Ubuntu's network configuration next. At the time of writing this book, the released version of Ubuntu is 22.04.2 LTS.

Ubuntu network configuration

Ubuntu 22.04 provides the `netplan` command-line utility for easy network configuration. `netplan` uses a **YAML Ain't Markup Language (YAML)** configuration file to generate the network interface bindings. The `netplan` configuration file(s) is in the `/etc/netplan/` directory, and we can access it by using the following command:

```
ls /etc/netplan/
```

In our case, the configuration file is `00-installer-config.yaml`.

Changing the network configuration involves editing the `netplan` YAML configuration file. As good practice, we should always make a backup of the current configuration file before making changes. Changing a network configuration would most commonly involve setting up either a dynamic or a static IP address. We will show you how to configure both types in the next few sections. We'll look at dynamic IP addressing first.

Dynamic IP configuration

To enable a dynamic (DHCP) IP address, we must edit the `netplan` configuration file and set the `dhcp4` attribute to `true` (as shown in *Figure 7.8*) for the network interface of our choice (`ens33`, in our case). Open the `00-installer-config.yaml` file with your text editor of choice (nano, in our case):

```
sudo nano /etc/netplan/00-installer-config.yaml
```

Here's the related configuration excerpt, with the relevant points highlighted:

Figure 7.8 – Enabling DHCP in the netplan configuration

After saving the configuration file, we can test the related changes with the following command:

```
sudo netplan try
```

We'll get the following response:

```
packt@neptune:~$ sudo netplan try
Do you want to keep these settings?


Press ENTER before the timeout to accept the new configuration


Changes will revert in 116 seconds
Configuration accepted.
```

Figure 7.9 – Testing and accepting the netplan configuration changes

The `netplan` keyword validates the new configuration and prompts the user to accept the changes. The following command applies the current changes to the system:

```
sudo netplan apply
```

Next, we will configure a static IP address using `netplan`.

Static IP configuration

To set the static IP address of a network interface, we start by editing the `netplan` configuration YAML file, as follows:

```
sudo nano /etc/netplan/00-installer-config.yaml
```

Here's a configuration example with a static IP address of `192.168.122.22/24`:

```
  GNU nano 6.2                     /etc/netplan/00-installer-config.yaml *
# This is the network config written by 'subiquity'
network:
  ethernets:
    enp1s0:
      dhcp4: false
      addresses:
        - 192.168.122.22/24
      gateway4: 192.168.122.1
      nameservers:
        addresses: [8.8.8.8, 8.8.4.4]
  version: 2
```

Figure 7.10 – Static IP configuration example with netplan

After saving the configuration, we can test and accept it, and then apply changes, as we did in the *Dynamic IP* section, with the following commands:

```
sudo netplan try
sudo netplan apply
```

For more information on the `netplan` command-line utility, see `netplan --help` or the related system manual (`man netplan`).

We'll look at the Fedora network configuration next. At the time of writing, the current released version of Fedora is 37.

Fedora/RHEL network configuration

Starting with Fedora 33 and RHEL 9, network configuration files are *no longer* kept in the `/etc/sysconfig/network-scripts/` directory. To learn more about the new configuration options, read the following file:

```
cat /etc/sysconfig/network-scripts/readme-ifcfg-rh.txt
```

The preferred method to configure the network in Fedora/RHEL is to use the `nmcli` utility. This location is deprecated and no longer used by NetworkManager in Fedora; it can still be used, but we do not recommend it. The new NetworkManager keyfiles are stored inside the `/etc/NetworkManager/system-connections/` directory.

Let's use some basic `nmcli` commands to view information about our connections. To learn about `nmcli`, read the related manual pages. First, let's find information about our active connection using the following command:

```
nmcli connection show
```

The output will show basic information about the name of the connection, UUID, type, and the device used. The following screenshot shows the relevant information on our Fedora 37 VM:

```
[packt@saturn ~]$ nmcli connection show
NAME                UUID                                  TYPE      DEVICE
Wired connection 1  ce007bd0-cc92-3a30-a367-95ecbf728ab7  ethernet  enp1s0
```

Figure 7.11 – Using nmcli to view connection information

Similar to Ubuntu, when using Fedora/RHEL, changing a network configuration would most commonly involve setting up either a dynamic or a static IP address. We will show you how to configure both types in the following sections. Let's look at dynamic IP addressing first.

Dynamic IP configuration

To configure a dynamic IP address using ncmli, we can run the following command:

```
sudo nmcli connection modify 'Wired connection 1' ipv4.method auto
```

The ipv4.method auto directive enables DHCP. There is no output from the command; after execution, you will be returned to the prompt again. You can check if the command worked by viewing the /etc/NetworkManager/system-connections/ directory. In our case, there is a new keyfile inside. It has the same name as our connection. The following is an excerpt:

```
[packt@saturn ~]$ sudo cat /etc/NetworkManager/system-connections/Wired\ connect
ion\ 1.nmconnection
[sudo] password for packt:
[connection]
id=Wired connection 1
uuid=ce007bd0-cc92-3a30-a367-95ecbf728ab7
type=ethernet
autoconnect-priority=-999
interface-name=enp1s0
timestamp=1679137326

[ethernet]

[ipv4]
method=auto

[ipv6]
addr-gen-mode=default
method=auto
```

Figure 7.12 – New configuration keyfile

Next, we'll configure a static IP address.

Static IP configuration

To perform the equivalent static IP address changes using ncmli, we need to run multiple commands. First, we must set the static IP address, as follows:

```
sudo nmcli connection modify 'Wired connection 1' ipv4.address
192.168.122.3/24
```

If no previous static IP address has been configured, we recommend saving the preceding change before proceeding with the next steps. The changes can be saved with the following code:

```
sudo nmcli connection down 'Wired connection 1'
sudo nmcli connection up 'Wired connection 1'
```

Next, we must set the gateway and DNS IP addresses, as follows:

```
sudo nmcli connection modify 'Wired connection 1' ipv4.gateway
192.168.122.1
sudo nmcli connection modify 'Wired connection 1' ipv4.dns 8.8.8.8
```

Finally, we must disable DHCP with the following code:

```
sudo nmcli connection modify 'Wired connection 1' ipv4.method manual
```

After making these changes, we need to restart the `'Wired connection 1'` network interface with the following code:

```
sudo nmcli connection down 'Wired connection 1'
sudo nmcli connection up 'Wired connection 1'
```

Now, let's see the results of all the commands we've performed. After bringing the connection up again, let's check the new IP address and the contents of the network keyfile. The following figure shows the new IP we assigned to the system (`192.168.122.3`) by using the `ip addr show` command:

```
2: enp1s0: <BROADCAST,MULTICAST,UP,LOWER_UP> mtu 1500 qdisc fq_codel state UP gr
oup default qlen 1000
    link/ether 52:54:00:37:a2:73 brd ff:ff:ff:ff:ff:ff
    inet 192.168.122.3/24 brd 192.168.122.255 scope global noprefixroute enp1s0
       valid_lft forever preferred_lft forever
    inet6 fe80::d78a:3dd9:7af7:c8d2/64 scope link noprefixroute
       valid_lft forever preferred_lft forever
```

Figure 7.13 – Checking the new IP address

Now, let's view the contents of the network keyfile to see the changes that were made for static IP configuration. Remember that the location of the file is `/etc/NetworkManager/system-connections/`:

```
[connection]
id=Wired connection 1
uuid=ce007bd0-cc92-3a30-a367-95ecbf728ab7
type=ethernet
autoconnect-priority=-999
interface-name=enp1s0
timestamp=1679147993

[ethernet]

[ipv4]
address1=192.168.122.3/24,192.168.122.1
dns=8.8.8.8;
method=manual
```

Figure 7.14 – New keyfile configuration for the static IP address

The nmcli utility is a powerful and useful one. At the end of this chapter, we will provide you with some useful links for learning more about it. Next, we'll take a look at how to configure network services on openSUSE.

openSUSE network configuration

openSUSE provides several tools for network configuration: **Wicked** and NetworkManager. According to the official SUSE documentation, Wicked is used for all types of machines, from servers to laptops and workstations, whereas NetworkManager is used only for laptop and workstation setup and is not used for server setup. However, in openSUSE Leap, Wicked is set up by default on both desktop or server configurations, and NetworkManager is set up by default on laptop configurations.

For example, on our main workstation (which is a laptop), if we want to see which service is running by default on openSUSE Leap, we can use the following command:

```
sudo systemctl status network
```

The output will show us which service is running, and in our case, it is NetworkManager:

```
alexandru@localhost:~> sudo systemctl status network
[sudo] password for root:
● NetworkManager.service - Network Manager
     Loaded: loaded (/usr/lib/systemd/system/NetworkManager.service; enabled; v▶
   Drop-In: /usr/lib/systemd/system/NetworkManager.service.d
              └─NetworkManager-ovs.conf
     Active: active (running) since Sun 2023-03-19 12:06:46 EET; 33min ago
       Docs: man:NetworkManager(8)
   Main PID: 1387 (NetworkManager)
```

Figure 7.15 – Checking which network service is running in openSUSE

When running the same command inside an openSUSE Leap server VM, the result is different. The output shows that Wicked is running by default. The following screenshot shows an example:

```
packt@localhost:~> sudo systemctl status network
● wicked.service - wicked managed network interfaces
     Loaded: loaded (/usr/lib/systemd/system/wicked.service; enabled; vendor pr▶
     Active: active (exited) since Sun 2023-03-19 13:42:07 EET; 2min 18s ago
   Main PID: 769 (code=exited, status=0/SUCCESS)
```

Figure 7.16 – Wicked is running inside the openSUSE server

As a result, we will perform all the examples in this section on an openSUSE Leap server VM, thus using Wicked as the default network configuration tool. In the next section, we will configure dynamic IP on an openSUSE machine.

Dynamic IP configuration

Before setting anything up, let's check for active connections and devices. We can do this by using the following command:

```
wicked show all
```

The output will show all the active devices. The following screenshot shows an excerpt from the output on our machine:

```
eth0            up
      link:     #2, state up, mtu 1500
      type:     ethernet, hwaddr 52:54:00:dc:4e:e0
      config:   compat:suse:/etc/sysconfig/network/ifcfg-eth0
      leases:   ipv4 dhcp granted
      leases:   ipv6 dhcp requesting
      addr:     ipv4 192.168.122.146/24 [dhcp]
      route:    ipv4 default via 192.168.122.1 proto dhcp
```

Figure 7.17 – Information about active devices

There are two active connections, one is loopback (lo) and the other is on the ethernet port (eth0). We will only show information related to eth0. The location where Wicked stores configuration files in openSUSE is /etc/sysconfig/network. If we do a listing of that directory, we will see that it is already populated with configuration files for existing connections:

```
packt@localhost:~> ls -la /etc/sysconfig/network/
total 64
drwxr-xr-x 1 root root   176 Mar  3 21:00 .
drwxr-xr-x 1 root root   584 Mar 11 14:18 ..
-rw-r--r-- 1 root root  9691 Mar  3 21:00 config
-rw-r--r-- 1 root root 15678 Mar  3 21:00 dhcp
-rw------- 1 root root    46 Mar  3 21:00 ifcfg-eth0
-rw-r--r-- 1 root root    34 Mar  3 21:00 ifcfg-eth0.bak
-rw------- 1 root root   147 Mar  3 21:00 ifcfg-lo
-rw-r--r-- 1 root root 21738 Aug  1  2022 ifcfg.template
drwxr-xr-x 1 root root     0 Mar 15  2022 if-down.d
drwxr-xr-x 1 root root     0 Mar 15  2022 if-up.d
drwx------ 1 root root     0 Mar 15  2022 providers
drwxr-xr-x 1 root root    38 Mar  3 20:59 scripts
```

Figure 7.18 – Location of the Wicked configuration files

In our case, and maybe it will be the same for you, the file we are interested in is called ifcfg-eth0; we can open it with a text editor or concatenate it. Let's take a look at the contents of the file:

```
  GNU nano 6.3              /etc/sysconfig/network/ifcfg-eth0
BOOTPROTO='dhcp'
STARTMODE='auto'
ZONE=public
```

Figure 7.19 – Information provided by the configuration file

As shown in the preceding screenshot, the information provided is rather scarce but relevant. For a more detailed output, we can use the following command:

```
sudo wicked show-config
```

This will provide much more relevant information directly to the monitor. The following screenshot provides an excerpt from our output, with detailed IPv4 DHCP information:

```
<ipv4>
  <enabled>true</enabled>
  <arp-verify>true</arp-verify>
</ipv4>
<ipv4:dhcp>
  <enabled>true</enabled>
  <flags>group</flags>
  <update>default-route,hostname,dns,nis,ntp,nds,mtu,tz,boot</update>
  <defer-timeout>15</defer-timeout>
  <recover-lease>true</recover-lease>
  <release-lease>false</release-lease>
</ipv4:dhcp>
```

Figure 7.20 – Detailed information provided by Wicked

To better understand this output, we recommend reading the `config` file and, if available, the `dhcp` files inside the `/etc/sysconfig/network` directory. These files provide information about specific variables and default parameters needed for configuring the network devices.

Dynamic IP addresses are usually set up by default when installing the operating system. If yours is not configured, all you need to do is create a configuration file inside `/etc/sysconfig/network` and give it a relevant name based on the device you are using to connect to the network, such as `ifcfg-eth0`. Inside that file, you will have to provide just three lines, as seen in *Figure 7.19*. The following commands are needed for the actions described in this paragraph:

- Check your device name using the `ip addr` command:

    ```
    ip addr show
    ```

- Create a configuration file inside the `/etc/sysconfig/network` directory:

    ```
    sudo nano /etc/sysconfig/network/ifcfg-eth0
    ```

- Provide relevant information for the DHCP configuration:

    ```
    BOOTPROTO='dhcp'
    STARTMODE='auto'
    ZONE=public
    ```

- Restart the Wicked service:

```
sudo systemctl restart wicked
```

- Check for connectivity by using either a web browser on your system or the `ping` command. Here's an example:

```
ping google.com
```

In the following section, we will show you how to set up a static IP configuration.

Static IP configuration

To set up a static IP configuration, you would need to manually provide variables for the configuration files. These files are the same ones that were presented in the previous section. The location of the files is `/etc/sysconfig/network`. For example, you can create a new file for the eth0 device connection and provide the information you want. Let's look at an example of using our openSUSE Leap server VM. However, before doing this, we advise you to open the manual pages for the `ifcfg` utility as they provide valuable information on the variables used for this exercise.

Therefore, we will set the `ifcfg` configuration file as follows:

- First, we will check for the IP address and the network device name; in our case, the dynamically allocated IP is `192.168.122.146` and the device's name is eth0:

```
2: eth0: <BROADCAST,MULTICAST,UP,LOWER_UP> mtu 1500 qdisc pfifo_fast state UP gr
oup default qlen 1000
    link/ether 52:54:00:dc:4e:e0 brd ff:ff:ff:ff:ff:ff
    altname enp1s0
    inet 192.168.122.146/24 brd 192.168.122.255 scope global eth0
       valid_lft forever preferred_lft forever
    inet6 fe80::5054:ff:fedc:4ee0/64 scope link
       valid_lft forever preferred_lft forever
```

Figure 7.21 – IP and device information

- Go to the `/etc/sysconfig/network` directory and edit the `ifcfg-eth0` file; we will use the following variables for static IP configuration:

  - `BOOTPROTO='static'`: This allows us to use a fixed IP address that will be provided by using the IPADDR variable

  - `STARTMODE='auto'`: The interface will be automatically enabled on boot

  - `IPADDR='192.168.122.144'`: The IP address we choose for the machine

  - `ZONE='public'`: The zone used by the `firewalld` utility

  - `PREFIXLEN='24'`: The number of bits in the IPADDR variable

This will look as follows:

```
GNU nano 6.3                                    ifcfg-eth0
BOOTPROTO='static'
STARTMODE='auto'
ZONE=public
IPADDR='192.168.122.144'
PREFIXLEN='24'
```

Figure 7.22 – New variables for static IP configuration

- Save the changes to the new file and restart the Wicked daemon:

```
sudo systemctl restart wickedd.service
```

- Enable the interface so that the changes appear:

```
sudo wicked ifup eth0
```

- Run the `ip addr` show command again to check for the new IP address:

```
2: eth0: <BROADCAST,MULTICAST,UP,LOWER_UP> mtu 1500 qdisc pfifo_fast state UP gr
oup default qlen 1000
    link/ether 52:54:00:dc:4e:e0 brd ff:ff:ff:ff:ff:ff
    altname enp1s0
    inet 192.168.122.146/24 brd 192.168.122.255 scope global eth0
       valid_lft forever preferred_lft forever
    inet 192.168.122.144/24 brd 192.168.122.255 scope global secondary eth0
       valid_lft forever preferred_lft forever
    inet6 fe80::5054:ff:fedc:4ee0/64 scope link
       valid_lft forever preferred_lft forever
```

Figure 7.23 – New IP address assigned to eth0

At this point, you know how to configure networking devices in all major Linux distributions, using their preferred utilities. We've merely scratched the surface of this matter, but we've provided sufficient information for you to start working with network interfaces in Linux. For more information, feel free to read the manual pages freely provided with your operating system. In the next section, we will approach the matter of hostname configuration.

Hostname configuration

To retrieve the current hostname on a Linux machine, we can use either the `hostname` or `hostnamectl` command, as follows:

```
hostname
```

The most convenient way to change the hostname is with the `hostnamectl` command. We can change the hostname to `earth` using the `set-hostname` parameter of the command:

```
sudo hostnamectl set-hostname earth
```

Let's verify the hostname change with the `hostname` command again. You could use the `hostnamectl` command to verify the hostname. The output of the `hostnamectl` command provides more detailed information compared to the `hostname` command, as shown in the following screenshot:

```
packt@neptune:~$ hostname
neptune
packt@neptune:~$ sudo hostnamectl set-hostname earth
packt@neptune:~$ hostname
earth
packt@neptune:~$ hostnamectl
   Static hostname: earth
         Icon name: computer-vm
           Chassis: vm
        Machine ID: 7c7f082fb11d431a9823a11ba9e87ad0
           Boot ID: f7eb64629ddf4424836760dfab2e9146
    Virtualization: kvm
  Operating System: Ubuntu 22.04.2 LTS
            Kernel: Linux 5.15.0-67-generic
      Architecture: x86-64
   Hardware Vendor: QEMU
    Hardware Model: Standard PC _Q35 + ICH9, 2009_
```

Figure 7.24 – Retrieving the current hostname with the different commands

Alternatively, we can use the `hostname` command to change the hostname *temporarily*, as follows:

```
sudo hostname jupiter
```

However, this change will not survive a reboot unless we also change the hostname in the `/etc/hostname` and `/etc/hosts` files. When editing these two files, change your hostname accordingly. The following screenshot shows the succession of commands:

```
packt@neptune:~$ hostname
earth
packt@neptune:~$ sudo hostname neptune
packt@neptune:~$ cat /etc/hostname
earth
packt@neptune:~$ sudo nano /etc/hostname
packt@neptune:~$ sudo nano /etc/hosts
packt@neptune:~$ hostname
neptune
```

Figure 7.25 – The /etc/hostname and /etc/hosts files

After the hostname reconfiguration, a logout followed by a login would usually reflect the changes. Hostnames are important for coherent network management, where each system on the network should have relevant hostnames set up. In the following section, you'll learn about network services in Linux.

Working with network services

In this section, we'll enumerate some of the most common network services running on Linux. Not all the services mentioned here are installed or enabled by default on your Linux platform of choice. *Chapter 9*, *Securing Linux*, and *Chapter 10*, *Disaster Recovery, Diagnostics, and Troubleshooting*, will dive deeper into how to install and configure some of them. Our focus in this section remains on what these network services are, how they work, and the networking protocols they use for communication.

A **network service** is typically a system process that implements application layer (OSI *Layer 7*) functionality for data communication purposes. Network services are usually designed as peer-to-peer or client-server architectures.

In peer-to-peer networking, multiple network nodes each run their own equally privileged instance of a network service while sharing and exchanging a common set of data. Take, for example, a network of DNS servers, all sharing and updating their domain name records.

Client-server networking usually involves one or more server nodes on a network and multiple clients communicating with any of these servers. An example of a client-server network service is SSH. An SSH client connects to a remote SSH server via a secure Terminal session, perhaps for remote administration purposes.

Each of the following subsections briefly describes a network service, and we encourage you to explore topics related to these network services in *Chapter 13* or other relevant titles recommended at the end of this chapter. Let's start with DHCP servers.

DHCP servers

A **DHCP server** uses the DHCP protocol to enable devices on a network to request an IP address that's been assigned dynamically. The DHCP protocol was briefly described in the *TCP/IP protocols* section earlier in this chapter.

A computer or device requesting a DHCP service sends out a broadcast message (or query) on the network to locate a DHCP server, which, in turn, provides the requested IP address and other information. Communication between the DHCP client (device) and the server uses the DHCP protocol.

The DHCP protocol's initial *discovery* workflow between a client and a server operates at the data link layer (*Layer 2*) in the OSI model. Since Layer 2 uses network frames as PDUs, the DHCP discovery packets cannot transcend the local network boundary. In other words, a DHCP client can only initiate communication with a *local* DHCP server.

After the initial *handshake* (on Layer 2), DHCP turns to UDP as its transport protocol, using datagram sockets (*Layer 4*). Since UDP is a connectionless protocol, a DHCP client and server exchange messages without a prior arrangement. Consequently, both endpoints (client and server) require a well-known DHCP communication port for the back-and-forth data exchange. These are the well-known ports 68 (for a DHCP server) and 67 (for a DHCP client).

A DHCP server maintains a collection of IP addresses and other client configuration data (such as MAC addresses and domain server addresses) for each device on the network requesting a DHCP service.

DHCP servers use a **leasing mechanism** to assign IP addresses dynamically. Leasing an IP address is subject to a **lease time**, either finite or infinite. When the lease of an IP address expires, the DHCP server may reassign it to a different client upon request. A device would hold on to its dynamic IP address by regularly requesting a **lease renewal** from the DHCP server. Failing to do so would result in the potential loss of the device's dynamic IP address. A late (or post-lease) DHCP request would possibly result in a new IP address being acquired if the previous address had already been allocated by the DHCP server.

A simple way to query the DHCP server from a Linux machine is by invoking the following command:

```
ip route
```

This is the output of the preceding command:

```
packt@neptune:~$ ip route
default via 192.168.122.1 dev enp1s0 proto dhcp src 192.168.122.117 metric 100
192.168.122.0/24 dev enp1s0 proto kernel scope link src 192.168.122.117 metric 1
00
192.168.122.1 dev enp1s0 proto dhcp scope link src 192.168.122.117 metric 100
```

Figure 7.26 – Querying the IP route for DHCP information

The first line of the output provides the DHCP server (192.168.122.1).

Chapter 13, *Configuring Linux Servers*, will further go into the practical details of installing and configuring a DHCP server.

For more information on DHCP, please refer to *RFC 2131* (https://tools.ietf.org/html/rfc2131).

DNS servers

A **Domain Name Server** (DNS), also known as a **name server**, provides a name-resolution mechanism by converting a hostname (such as wikipedia.org) into an IP address (such as 208.80.154.224). The name-resolution protocol is DNS, briefly described in the *TCP/IP protocols* section earlier in this chapter. In a DNS-managed TCP/IP network, computers and devices can also identify and communicate with each other via hostnames, not just IP addresses.

As a reasonable analogy, DNS very much resembles an address book. Hostnames are relatively easier to remember than IP addresses. Even in a local network, with only a few computers and devices connected, it would be rather difficult to identify (or memorize) any of the hosts by simply using their IP address. The internet relies on a globally distributed network of DNS servers.

There are four different types of DNS servers: **recursive servers**, **root servers**, **top-level domain (TLD) servers**, and **authoritative servers**. All these DNS server types work together to bring you the internet as you experience it in your browser.

A **recursive DNS server** is a resolver that helps you find the destination (IP) of a website you search for. When you perform a lookup operation, a recursive DNS server is connected to different DNS servers to find the IP address that you are looking for and return it to you in the form of a website. Recursive DNS lookups are faster as they cache every query that they perform. In a recursive type of query, the DNS server calls itself and does the recursion while still sending the request to another DNS server to find the answer.

In contrast, an **iterative DNS** lookup is done by every DNS server directly, without using caching. For example, in an iterative query, each DNS server responds with the address of another DNS server, until one of them has the matching IP address for the hostname in question and responds to the client. For more details on DNS server types, please check out the following Cloudflare learning solution: `https://www.cloudflare.com/learning/dns/what-is-dns/`.

DNS servers maintain (and possibly share) a collection of **database files**, also known as **zone files**, which are typically simple plaintext ASCII files that store the name and IP address mapping. In Linux, one such DNS resolver file is `/etc/resolv.conf`.

To query the DNS server managing the local machine, we can query the `/etc/resolv.conf` file by running the following code:

```
cat /etc/resolv.conf | grep nameserver
```

The preceding code yields the following output:

```
packt@neptune:~$ cat /etc/resolv.conf | grep nameserver
nameserver 127.0.0.53
packt@neptune:~$
```

Figure 7.27 – Querying DNS server using /etc/resolv.conf

A simple way to query name-server data for an arbitrary host on a network is by using the `nslookup` tool. If you don't have the `nslookup` utility installed on your system, you may do so with the commands outlined here.

On Ubuntu/Debian, run the following command:

```
sudo apt install dnsutils
```

On Fedora, run this command:

```
sudo dnf install bind-utils
```

For example, to query the name-server information for a computer named `neptune.local` in our local network, we can run the following command:

```
nslookup neptune.local
```

The output is shown here:

```
packt@neptune:~$ nslookup neptune.local
Server:         127.0.0.53
Address:        127.0.0.53#53

Name:   neptune.local
Address: 192.168.122.117
```

Figure 7.28 – Querying name-server information with nslookup

We can also use the `nslookup` tool interactively. For example, to query the name-server information for `wikipedia.org`, we can simply run the following command:

```
nslookup
```

Then, in the interactive prompt, we must enter `wikipedia.org`, as illustrated here:

```
packt@neptune:~$ nslookup
> wikipedia.org
Server:         127.0.0.53
Address:        127.0.0.53#53

Non-authoritative answer:
Name:   wikipedia.org
Address: 91.198.174.192
Name:   wikipedia.org
Address: 2620:0:862:ed1a::1
```

Figure 7.29 – Using the nslookup tool interactively

To exit the interactive shell mode, press *Ctrl + C*. Here's a brief explanation of the information shown in the preceding output:

- **Server (address)**: The loopback address (`127.0.0.53`) and port (`53`) of the DNS server running locally

- **Name**: The internet domain we're looking up (`wikipedia.org`)

- **Address**: The IPv4 (`91.198.174.192`) and IPv6 (`2620:0:862:ed1a::1`) addresses that correspond to the lookup domain (`wikipedia.org`) nslookup is also capable of reverse DNS search when providing an IP address. The following command retrieves the name server (dns.google) corresponding to the IP address 8.8.8.8:

```
nslookup 8.8.8.8
```

The preceding command yields the following output:

```
packt@neptune:~$ nslookup 8.8.8.8
8.8.8.8.in-addr.arpa    name = dns.google.

Authoritative answers can be found from:
```

Figure 7.30 – Reverse DNS search with nslookup

For more information on the nslookup tool, you can refer to the nslookup system reference manual (man nslookup).

Alternatively, we can use the dig command-line utility. If you don't have the dig utility installed on your system, you can do so by installing the dnsutils package on Ubuntu/Debian or bind-utils on Fedora platforms. The related commands for installing the packages were shown previously with nslookup.

For example, the following command retrieves the name-server information for the google.com domain:

```
dig google.com
```

This is the result (see the highlighted ANSWER SECTION):

```
;; QUESTION SECTION:
;google.com.                    IN      A

;; ANSWER SECTION:
google.com.           39        IN      A       172.217.169.206
```

Figure 7.31 – DNS lookup with dig

To perform a reverse DNS lookup with dig, we must specify the -x option, followed by an IP address (for example, 8.8.4.4), as follows:

```
dig -x 8.8.4.4
```

This command yields the following output (see the highlighted ANSWER SECTION):

```
;; QUESTION SECTION:
;4.4.8.8.in-addr.arpa.              IN       PTR

;; ANSWER SECTION:
4.4.8.8.in-addr.arpa.    25900   IN      PTR     dns.google.
```

Figure 7.32 – Reverse DNS lookup with dig

For more information about the dig command-line utility, please refer to the related system manual (man dig).

The DNS protocol operates at the application layer (*Layer 7*) in the OSI model. The standard DNS service's well-known port is 53.

Chapter 8, *Linux Shell Scripting*, will cover the practical details of installing and configuring a DNS server in more detail. For more information on DNS, you can refer to *RFC 1035* (https://www.ietf.org/rfc/rfc1035.txt).

The DHCP and DNS network services are arguably the closest to the TCP/IP networking stack while playing a crucial role when computers or devices are attached to a network. After all, without proper IP addressing and name resolution, there's no network communication.

There's a lot more to distributed networking and related application servers than just strictly the pure network management stack performed by DNS and DHCP servers. In the following sections, we'll take a quick tour of some of the most relevant application servers running across distributed Linux systems.

Authentication servers

Standalone Linux systems typically use the default authentication mechanism, where user credentials are stored in the local filesystem (such as /etc/passwd and /etc/shadow). We explored the related user authentication internals in *Chapter 4*, *Managing Users and Groups*. However, as we extend the authentication boundary beyond the local machine – for example, accessing a file or email server – having the user credentials shared between the remote and localhosts would become a serious security issue.

Ideally, we should have a centralized authentication endpoint across the network that's handled by a secure authentication server. User credentials should be validated using robust encryption mechanisms before users can access remote system resources.

Let's consider the secure access to a network share on an arbitrary file server. Suppose the access requires **Active Directory (AD)** user authentication. Creating the related mount (share) locally on a user's client machine will prompt for user credentials. The authentication request is made by the file server (on behalf of the client) to an authentication server. If the authentication succeeds, the server share becomes available to the client. The following diagram represents a simple remote authentication flow between a client and a server, using a **Lightweight Directory Access Protocol (LDAP)** authentication endpoint:

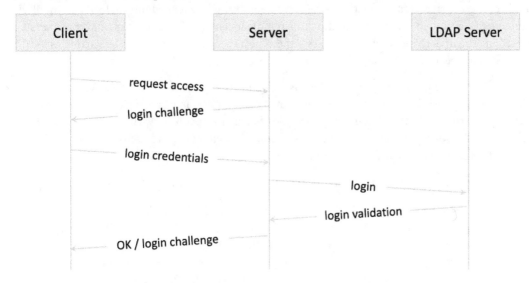

Figure 7.33 – Authentication workflow with LDAP

Here are some examples of standard secure authentication platforms (available for Linux):

- **Kerberos** (https://web.mit.edu/kerberos/)
- **LDAP** (https://www.redhat.com/en/topics/security/what-is-ldap-authentication)
- **Remote Authentication Dial-In User Service (RADIUS)** (https://freeradius.org/documentation/)
- **Diameter** (https://www.f5.com/glossary/diameter-protocol)
- **Terminal Access Controller Access-Control System (TACACS+)** (https://datatracker.ietf.org/doc/rfc8907/)

A Linux LDAP authentication server can be configured using OpenLDAP, which was covered in the first edition of this book.

In this section, we illustrated the authentication workflow with an example of using a file server. To remain on topic, we'll look at network file-sharing services next.

File sharing

In common networking terms, **file sharing** represents a client machine's ability to *mount* and access a remote filesystem belonging to a server, as if it were local. Applications running on the client machine would access the shared files directly on the server. For example, a text editor can load and modify a remote file, and then save it back to the same remote location, all in a seamless and transparent operation. The underlying remoting process – the appearance of a remote filesystem acting as local – is made possible by file-sharing services and protocols.

For every file-sharing network protocol, there is a corresponding client-server file-sharing platform. Although most network file servers (and clients) have cross-platform implementations, some operating system platforms are better suited for specific file-sharing protocols, as we'll see in the following subsections. Choosing between different file-server implementations and protocols is ultimately a matter of compatibility, security, and performance.

Here are some of the most common file-sharing protocols, with some brief descriptions for each:

- **Server Message Block** (**SMB**): The SMB protocol provides network discovery and file- and printer-sharing services. SMB also supports interprocess communication over a network. SMB is a relatively old protocol, developed by **International Business Machines Corporation** (**IBM**) in the 1980s. Eventually, Microsoft took over and made some considerable alterations to what became the current version through multiple revisions (SMB 1.0, 2.0, 2.1, 3.0, 3.0.2, and 3.1.1).

- **Common Internet File System** (**CIFS**): This protocol is a particular implementation of the SMB protocol. Due to the underlying protocol similarity, SMB clients can communicate with CIFS servers and vice versa. Though SMB and CIFS are idiomatically the same, their internal implementation of file locking, batch processing, and – ultimately – performance is quite different. Apart from legacy systems, CIFS is rarely used these days. SMB should always be preferred over CIFS, especially with the more recent revisions of SMB 2 or SMB 3.

- **Samba**: As with CIFS, Samba is another implementation of the SMB protocol. Samba provides file- and print-sharing services for Windows clients on a variety of server platforms. In other words, Windows clients can seamlessly access directories, files, and printers on a Linux Samba server, just as if they were communicating with a Windows server.

  As of version 4, Samba natively supports Microsoft AD and Windows NT domains. Essentially, a Linux Samba server can act as a domain controller on a Windows AD network. Consequently, user credentials on the Windows domain can transparently be used on the Linux server without being recreated, and then manually kept in sync with the AD users.

- **Network File System** (**NFS**): This protocol was developed by Sun Microsystems and essentially operates on the same premise as SMB – accessing files over a network as if they were local. NFS is not compatible with CIFS or SMB, meaning that NFS clients cannot communicate directly with SMB servers or vice versa.

- **Apple Filing Protocol** (**AFP**): The AFP is a proprietary file-sharing protocol designed by Apple and exclusively operates in macOS network environments. We should note that besides AFP, macOS systems also support standard file-sharing protocols, such as SMB and NFS.

Most of the time, NFS is the file-sharing protocol of choice within Linux networks. For mixed networking environments – such as Windows, Linux, and macOS interoperability – Samba and SMB are best suited for file sharing.

Some file-sharing protocols (such as SMB) also support print sharing and are used by print servers. We'll take a closer look at print sharing next.

Printer servers

A **printer server** (or **print server**) connects a printer to client machines (computers or mobile devices) on a network using a printing protocol. Printing protocols are responsible for the following remote printing tasks over a network:

- Discovering printers or print servers

- Querying printer status

- Sending, receiving, queueing, or canceling print jobs

- Querying print job status

Common printing protocols include the following:

- **Line Printer Daemon** (**LPD**) protocol

- **Generic protocols**, such as SMB and TELNET

- **Wireless printing**, such as AirPrint by Apple

- **Internet printing protocols**, such as Google Cloud Print

Among the generic printing protocols, SMB (also a file-sharing protocol) was previously described in the *File sharing* section. The TELNET communication protocol was described in the *Remote access* section.

File- and printer-sharing services are mostly about *sharing* documents, digital or printed, between computers on a network. When it comes to *exchanging* documents, additional network services come into play, such as *file transfer* and *email* services. We'll look at file transfer next.

File transfer

FTP is a standard network protocol for transferring files between computers on a network. FTP operates in a client-server environment, where an FTP client initiates a remote connection to an FTP server, and files are transferred in either direction. FTP maintains a **control connection** and one or more **data connections** between the client and the server. The control connection is generally established on the FTP server's port 21, and it's used for exchanging commands between the client and the server. Data connections are exclusively used for data transfer and are negotiated between the client and the server (through the control connection). Data connections usually involve ephemeral ports for inbound traffic, and they only stay open during the actual data transfer, closing immediately after the transfer completes.

FTP negotiates data connections in one of the following two modes:

- **Active mode**: The FTP client sends a PORT command to the FTP server, signaling that the client *actively* provides the inbound port number for data connections

- **Passive mode**: The FTP client sends a PASV command to the FTP server, indicating that the client *passively* awaits the server to supply the port number for inbound data connections

FTP is a relatively *messy* protocol when it comes to firewall configurations due to the dynamic nature of the data connections involved. The control connection port is usually well known (such as port 21 for insecure FTP) but data connections originate on a different port (usually 20) on either side, while on the receiving end, the inbound sockets are opened within a preconfigured ephemeral range (1024 to 65535).

FTP is most often implemented securely through either of the following approaches:

- **FTP over SSL (FTPS)**: SSL/TLS-encrypted FTP connection. The default FTPS control connection port is 990.

- **SSH File Transfer Protocol (SFTP)**: **FTP** over **SSH**. The default SFTP control connection port is 22. For more information on the SSH protocol and client-server connectivity, refer to *SSH* in the *Remote access* section, later in this chapter.

Next, we'll look at mail servers and the underlying email exchange protocols.

Mail servers

A **mail server** (or **email server**) is responsible for email delivery over a network. A mail server can either exchange emails between clients (users) on the same network (domain) – within a company or organization – or deliver emails to other mail servers, possibly beyond the local network, such as the internet.

An email exchange usually involves the following actors:

- An **email client** application (such as Outlook or Gmail)
- One or more **mail servers** (Exchange or Gmail server)
- The **recipients** involved in the email exchange – a *sender* and one or more *receivers*
- An **email protocol** that controls the communication between the email client and the mail servers

The most used email protocols are **POP3**, **IMAP**, and **SMTP**. Let's take a closer look at each of these protocols.

POP3

POP version 3 (**POP3**) is a standard email protocol for receiving and downloading emails from a remote mail server to a local email client. With POP3, emails are available for reading offline. After being downloaded, emails are usually removed from the POP3 server, thus saving up space. Modern-day POP3 mail client-server implementations (Gmail, Outlook, and others) also have the option of keeping email copies on the server. Persisting emails on the POP3 server becomes very important when users access emails from multiple locations (client applications).

The default POP3 ports are outlined here:

- `110`: For insecure (non-encrypted) POP3 connections
- `995`: For secure POP3 using SSL/TLS encryption

POP3 is a relatively old email protocol that's not always suitable for modern-day email communications. When users access their emails from multiple devices, IMAP is a better choice. We'll look at the IMAP email protocol next.

IMAP

IMAP is a standard email protocol for accessing emails on a remote IMAP mail server. With IMAP, emails are always retained on the mail server, while a copy of the emails is available for IMAP clients. A user can access emails on multiple devices, each with their IMAP client application.

The default IMAP ports are outlined here:

- `143`: For insecure (non-encrypted) IMAP connections
- `993`: For secure IMAP using SSL/TLS encryption

Both POP3 and IMAP are standard protocols for receiving emails. To send emails, SMTP comes into play. We'll take a look at the SMTP email protocol next.

SMTP

SMTP is a standard email protocol for sending emails over a network or the internet.

The default SMTP ports are outlined here:

- `25`: For insecure (non-encrypted) SMTP connections

- `465` or `587`: For secure SMTP using SSL/TLS encryption

When using or implementing any of the standard email protocols described in this section, it is always recommended to use the corresponding secure implementation with the most up-to-date TLS encryption, if possible. POP3, IMAP, and SMTP also support user authentication, an added layer of security – this is also recommended in commercial or enterprise-grade environments.

To get an idea of how the SMTP protocol operates, let's go through some of the initial steps for initiating an SMTP handshake with Google's Gmail SMTP server.

We will start by connecting to the Gmail SMTP server, using a secure (TLS) connection via the `openssl` command, as follows:

```
openssl s_client -starttls smtp -connect smtp.gmail.com:587
```

Here, we invoked the `openssl` command, simulated a client (`s_client`), started a TLS SMTP connection (`-starttls smtp`), and connected to the remote Gmail SMTP server on port `587` (`-connect smtp.gmail.com:587`).

The Gmail SMTP server responds with a relatively long TLS handshake block that ends with the following code:

```
---
No client certificate CA names sent
Peer signing digest: SHA256
Peer signature type: ECDSA
Server Temp Key: X25519, 253 bits
---
SSL handshake has read 4578 bytes and written 429 bytes
Verification: OK
---
New, TLSv1.3, Cipher is TLS_AES_256_GCM_SHA384
Server public key is 256 bit
Secure Renegotiation IS NOT supported
Compression: NONE
Expansion: NONE
No ALPN negotiated
Early data was not sent
Verify return code: 0 (ok)
---
250 SMTPUTF8
```

Figure 7.34 – Initial TLS handshake with a Gmail SMTP server

While still inside the `openssl` command's interactive prompt, we initiate the SMTP communication with a HELO command (spelled precisely as such). The HELO command *greets* the server. It is a specific SMTP command that starts the SMTP connection between a client and a server. There is also an EHLO variant, which is used for ESMTP service extensions. Google expects the following HELO greeting:

```
HELO hellogoogle
```

Another handshake follows, ending with 250 smtp.gmail.com at your service, as illustrated here:

```
                    Start Time: 1679236390
                    Timeout    : 7200 (sec)
                    Verify return code: 0 (ok)
                    Extended master secret: no
                    Max Early Data: 0
              ---
              read R BLOCK
              250 smtp.gmail.com at your service
```

Figure 7.35 – The Gmail SMTP server is ready for communication

Next, the Gmail SMTP server requires authentication via the AUTH LOGIN SMTP command. We won't go into further details, but the key point to be made here is that the SMTP protocol follows a plaintext command sequence between the client and the server. It's very important to adopt a secure (encrypted) SMTP communication channel using TLS. The same applies to any of the other email protocols (POP3 and IMAP).

So far, we've covered several network services, some of them spanning multiple networks or even the internet. Network packets carry data and destination addresses within the payload, but there are also synchronization signals between the communication endpoints, mostly to discern between sending and receiving workflows. The synchronization of network packets is based on timestamps. Reliable network communications would not be possible without a highly accurate time-synchronization between network nodes. We'll look at network timekeepers next.

NTP servers

NTP is a standard networking protocol for clock synchronization between computers on a network. NTP attempts to synchronize the system clock on participating computers within a few milliseconds of **Coordinated Universal Time (UTC)** – the world's time reference.

The NTP protocol's implementation usually assumes a client-server model. An NTP server acts as a time source on the network by either broadcasting or sending updated **timestamp datagrams** to clients. An NTP server continually adjusts its system clock according to well-known accurate time servers worldwide, using specialized algorithms to mitigate network latency.

A relatively easy way to check the NTP synchronization status on our Linux platform of choice is by using the `ntpstat` utility. `ntpstat` may not be installed by default on our system. On Ubuntu, we can install it with the following command:

```
sudo apt install ntpstat
```

On Fedora, we can install `ntpstat` with the following command:

```
sudo dnf install ntpstat
```

`ntpstat` requires an NTP server to be running locally. To set up a local NTP server, you will need to do the following (all examples shown here are for Ubuntu 22.04.2 LTS):

- Install the `ntp` package with the following command:

```
sudo apt install ntp
```

- Check for the `ntp` service's status:

```
sudo systemctl status ntp
```

- Enable the `ntp` service:

```
sudo systemctl enable ntp
```

- Modify the firewall settings:

```
sudo ufw allow from any to any port 123 proto udp
```

- Install the `ntpdate` package:

```
sudo apt install ntpdate
```

- Restart the `ntp` service:

```
sudo systemctl restart ntp
```

Before installing the `ntp` utility, take into account that Ubuntu is using another tool instead of `ntpd` by default, named `timesyncd`. When installing `ntpd`, the default utility will be disabled.

To query the NTP synchronization status, we can run the following command:

```
ntpstat
```

This is the output:

```
packt@neptune:~$ ntpstat
synchronised to NTP server (31.209.85.242) at stratum 2
   time correct to within 29 ms
   polling server every 64 s
```

Figure 7.36 – Querying the NTP synchronization status with ntpstat

ntpstat provides the IP address of the NTP server the system is synchronized with (31.209.85.242), the synchronization margin (29 milliseconds), and the time-update polling interval (64 seconds). To find out more about the NTP server, we can dig its IP address with the following command:

```
dig -x 31.209.85.242
```

It looks like it's one of the lwlcom time servers (ntp1.lwlcom.net), as shown here:

```
packt@neptune:~$ dig -x 31.209.85.242

; <<>> DiG 9.18.1-1ubuntu1.3-Ubuntu <<>> -x 31.209.85.242
;; global options: +cmd
;; Got answer:
;; ->>HEADER<<- opcode: QUERY, status: NOERROR, id: 49498
;; flags: qr rd ra; QUERY: 1, ANSWER: 1, AUTHORITY: 0, ADDITIONAL: 1

;; OPT PSEUDOSECTION:
; EDNS: version: 0, flags:; udp: 65494
;; QUESTION SECTION:
;242.85.209.31.in-addr.arpa.      IN       PTR

;; ANSWER SECTION:
242.85.209.31.in-addr.arpa. 2324 IN     PTR      ntp1.lwlcom.net.

;; Query time: 16 msec
;; SERVER: 127.0.0.53#53(127.0.0.53) (UDP)
;; WHEN: Sun Mar 19 15:04:57 UTC 2023
;; MSG SIZE  rcvd: 84
```

Figure 7.37 – Querying the NTP synchronization status with ntpstat

The NTP client-server communication uses UDP as the transport protocol on port 123. *Chapter 9, Securing Linux*, has a section dedicated to installing and configuring an NTP server. For more information on NTP, you can refer to https://en.wikipedia.org/wiki/Network_Time_Protocol.

With that, our brief journey into networking servers and protocols has come to an end. Everyday Linux administration tasks often require some sort of remote access to a system. There are many ways to access and manage computers remotely. The next section describes some of the most common remote-access facilities and related network protocols.

Remote access

Most Linux network services provide a relatively limited **remote management** interface, with their management **command-line interface (CLI)** utilities predominantly operating locally on the same system where the service runs. Consequently, the related administrative tasks assume local Terminal access. Direct console access to the system is sometimes not possible. This is when remote-access servers come into play to enable a virtual Terminal login session with the remote machine.

Let's look at some of the most common remote-access services and applications.

SSH

SSH is perhaps the most popular secure login protocol for remote access. SSH uses strong encryption, combined with user authentication mechanisms, for secure communication between a client and a server machine. SSH servers are relatively easy to install and configure, and the *Setting up an SSH server* section in *Chapter 13*, *Configuring Linux Servers*, is dedicated to describing the related steps. The default network port for SSH is 22.

SSH supports the following authentication types:

- Public-key authentication
- Password authentication
- Keyboard-interactive authentication

The following sections provide brief descriptions of these forms of SSH authentication.

Public-key authentication

Public-key authentication (or **SSH-key authentication**) is arguably the most common type of SSH authentication.

> **Important note**
> This section will use the terms *public-key* and *SSH-key* interchangeably, mostly to reflect the related SSH authentication nomenclature in the Linux community.

The SSH-key authentication mechanism uses a *certificate/key* pair – a **public** key (*certificate*) and a **private** key. An SSH certificate/key pair is usually created with the ssh-keygen tool, using standard encryption algorithms such as the **Rivest–Shamir–Adleman** algorithm (**RSA**) or the **Digital Signature Algorithm (DSA)**.

The SSH public-key authentication supports either **user-based authentication** or **host-based authentication** models. The two models differ in the ownership of the certificate/key pairs involved. With client authentication, each user has a certificate/key pair for SSH access. On the other hand, host authentication involves a single certificate/key pair per system (host).

Both SSH-key authentication models are illustrated and explained in the following sections. The basic SSH handshake and authentication workflows are the same for both models:

- First, the SSH client generates a secure certificate/key pair and shares its public key with the SSH server. This is a one-time operation for enabling public-key authentication.

- When a client initiates the SSH handshake, the server asks for the client's public key and verifies it against its allowed public keys. If there's a match, the SSH handshake succeeds, the server shares its public key with the client, and the SSH session is established.

- Further client-server communication follows standard encryption/decryption workflows. The client encrypts the data with its private key, while the server decrypts the data with the client's public key. When responding to the client, the server encrypts the data with its own private key, and the client decrypts the data with the server's public key.

SSH public-key authentication is also known as **passwordless authentication**, and it's frequently used in automation scripts where commands are executed over multiple remote SSH connections without prompting for a password.

Let's take a closer look at the user-based and host-based public-key authentication mechanisms:

- **User-based authentication**: This is the most common SSH public-key authentication mechanism. According to this model, every user connecting to a remote SSH server has its own SSH key. Multiple user accounts on the same host (or domain) would have different SSH keys, each with its own access to the remote SSH server, as suggested in the following figure:

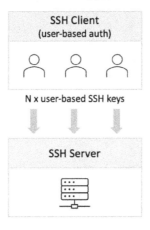

Figure 7.38 – User-based key authentication

- **Host-based authentication**: This is another form of SSH public-key authentication and involves a single SSH key per system (host) to connect to a remote SSH server, as illustrated in the following figure:

Figure 7.39 – Host-based key authentication

With host-based authentication, the underlying SSH key can only authenticate SSH sessions that originated from a single client host. Host-based authentication allows multiple users to connect from the same host to a remote SSH server. If a user attempts to use a host-based SSH key from a different machine than the one allowed by the SSH server, access will be denied.

Sometimes, a mix of the two public-key authentications is used – user- and host-based authentication –an approach that provides an increased level of security to SSH access.

When security is not critical, simpler SSH authentication mechanisms could be more suitable. Password authentication is one such mechanism.

Password authentication

Password authentication requires a simple set of credentials from the SSH client, such as a username and password. The SSH server validates the user credentials, either based on the local user accounts (in /etc/passwd) or select user accounts defined in the SSH server configuration (/etc/ssh/sshd_config). The SSH server configuration described in *Chapter 9, Securing Linux*, further elaborates on this subject.

Besides local authentication, SSH can also leverage remote authentication methods such as Kerberos, LDAP, RADIUS, and others. In such cases, the SSH server delegates the user authentication to a remote authentication server, as described in the *Authentication servers* section earlier in this chapter.

Password authentication requires either user interaction or some automated way to provide the required credentials. Another similar authentication mechanism is keyboard-interactive authentication, described next.

Keyboard-interactive authentication

Keyboard-interactive authentication is based on a dialogue of multiple challenge-response sequences between the SSH client (user) and the SSH server. This dialogue is a plaintext exchange of questions and answers, where the server may prompt the user for any number of challenges. In some respect, password authentication is a **single-challenge interactive authentication** mechanism.

The *interactive* connotation of this authentication method could lead us to think that user interaction would be mandatory for the related implementation. Not really. Keyboard-interactive authentication could also serve implementations of authentication mechanisms based on custom protocols, where the underlying message exchange would be modeled as an authentication protocol.

Before moving on to other remote access protocols, we should call out the wide use of SSH due to its security, versatility, and performance. However, SSH connectivity may not always be possible or adequate in specific scenarios. In such cases, *TELNET* may come to the rescue. We'll take a look at it next.

TELNET

TELNET is an application-layer protocol for bidirectional network communication that uses a plaintext CLI with a remote host. Historically, TELNET was among the first remote-connection protocols, but it always lacked secure implementation. SSH eventually became the standard way to log in from one computer to another, yet TELNET has its advantages over SSH when it comes to troubleshooting various application-layer protocols, such as web- or email-server communication. You will learn more about how to use TELNET in *Chapter 9, Securing Linux*.

TELNET and SSH are command-line-driven remote-access interfaces. There are cases when a direct desktop connection is needed to a remote machine through a **graphical user interface** (**GUI**). We'll look at desktop sharing next.

VNC

Virtual Network Computing (**VNC**) is a desktop-sharing platform that allows users to access and control a remote computer's GUI. VNC is a cross-platform client-server application. A VNC server running on a Linux machine, for example, allows desktop access to multiple VNC clients running on Windows or macOS systems. The VNC network communication uses the **Remote Framebuffer** (**RFB**) protocol, defined by *RFC 6143*. Setting up a VNC server is relatively simple. VNC assumes the presence of a graphical desktop system. More details on this will be provided in *Chapter 13, Configuring Linux Servers*.

This concludes our section about network services and protocols. We tried to cover the most common concepts about general-purpose network servers and applications, mostly operating in a client-server or distributed fashion. With each network server, we described the related network protocols and some of the internal aspects involved. *Chapter 9, Securing Linux*, and *Chapter 13, Configuring Linux Servers*, will showcase practical implementations for some of these network servers.

In the next section, our focus will turn to network security internals.

Understanding network security

Network security represents the processes, actions, and policies to prevent, monitor, and protect unauthorized access to computer networks. Network security paradigms span a vast array of technologies, tools, and practices. Here are a few important ones:

- **Access control**: Selectively restricting access based on user authentication and authorization mechanisms. Examples of access control include users, groups, and permissions. Some of the related concepts were covered in *Chapter 4, Managing Users and Groups*.

- **Application security**: Securing and protecting server and end user applications (email, web, and mobile apps). Examples of application security include **Security-Enhanced Linux (SELinux)**, strongly encrypted connections, antivirus, and anti-malware programs. We'll cover **SELinux** in *Chapter 10, Disaster Recovery, Diagnostics, and Troubleshooting*.

- **Endpoint security**: Securing and protecting servers and end user devices (smartphones, laptops, and desktop PCs) on the network. Examples of endpoint security include *firewalls* and various intrusion-detection mechanisms. We'll look at firewalls in *Chapter 10, Disaster Recovery, Diagnostics, and Troubleshooting*.

- **Network segmentation**: Partitioning computer networks into smaller segments or **virtual LANs (VLANs)**. This is not to be confused with subnetting, which is a logical division of networks through addressing.

- **VPNs**: Accessing corporate networks using a secure encrypted tunnel from public networks or the internet. We'll look at VPNs in more detail in *Chapter 9, Securing Linux*, and *Chapter 13, Configuring Linux Servers*.

In everyday Linux administration, setting up a network security perimeter should always follow the paradigms enumerated previously, roughly in the order listed. Starting with access-control mechanisms and ending with VPNs, securing a network takes an *inside-out* approach, from local systems and networks to firewalls, VLANs, and VPNs.

Summary

This chapter provided a relatively condensed view of basic Linux networking principles. We learned about network communication layers and protocols, IP addressing schemes, TCP/IP configurations, well-known network application servers, and VPN. A good grasp of networking paradigms will give Linux administrators a more comprehensive view of the distributed systems and underlying communication between the application endpoints involved.

Some of the theoretical aspects covered in this chapter will be taken for a practical spin in *Chapter 13, Configuring Linux Servers*, where we'll focus on real-world implementations of network servers. *Chapter 10, Disaster Recovery, Diagnostics, and Troubleshooting*, will further explore network security internals and practical Linux firewalls. Everything we have learned so far will serve as a good foundation for the assimilation of these upcoming chapters.

The following chapter will introduce you to Linux shell scripting, where you will learn about the most common shell features and how to use decisions, loops, variables, arrays, and functions.

Questions

Here's a quick quiz to outline and test some of the essential concepts covered in this chapter:

1. How does the OSI model compare to the TCP/IP model?

   Hint: *Figure 7.2* could be of help.

2. Think of a couple of TCP/IP protocols and try to see where and how they operate in some of the network administration tasks or applications you are familiar with.

3. At what networking layer does the HTTP protocol operate? How about DNS?

   Hint: Both operate on the same layer.

4. What is the network class for IP address `192.168.0.1`?

   Hint: Refer to *Figure 7.5*.

5. What is the network prefix that corresponds to network mask `255.255.0.0`?

   Hint: Check out *Figure 7.5* again.

6. How do you configure a static IP address using the `nmcli` utility?

   Hint: Use `connection modify`.

7. How do you change the hostname of a Linux machine?

   Hint: Use the `hostnamectl` utility.

8. What is the difference between the POP3 and IMAP email protocols?

9. How does SSH host-based authentication differ from user-based SSH key authentication?

10. What is the difference between SSH and TELNET?

Further reading

For more information about what was covered in this chapter, please refer to the following Packt titles:

- *Linux Administration Best Practices*, by Scott Alan Miller
- *Linux for Networking Professionals*, by Rob VandenBrink

8

Linux Shell Scripting

Knowing how to use the basics of Linux shell programming and the **command-line interface** (CLI) is essential for a modern-day Linux professional.

In this chapter, you will learn how to use the Linux shell's programming capabilities to automate different tasks in Linux. You will learn about the structure of a basic Linux shell script and how it is organized and executed. We'll explore most of the commands already available to you from the previous chapters, especially the ones for working with files and directories and input and output redirection. Along the way, we'll introduce you to writing scripts, the structure and complexity of shell programming, and how to use specialized tools such as sed and gawk. We hope that by the end of this chapter, you'll be comfortable using scripts in your day-to-day workflow and be ready for future, more advanced explorations.

We're going to cover the following main topics:

- Introducing shell features
- The structure of a shell script
- Decisions, loops, variables, arrays, and functions
- Using sed and (g)awk

Technical requirements

This chapter requires a working installation of a standard Linux distribution, on either server, desktop, PC, or **virtual machine** (VM). Our examples and case studies will use mainly Ubuntu/Debian and RHEL/Fedora platforms, but the commands and examples that will be explored are equally suitable for other Linux distributions, such as openSUSE/SLE.

Exploring the Linux shell

Back in *Chapter 2, The Linux Shell and Filesystem*, we introduced you to the shell by exploring the available virtual consoles, command types, and the filesystem. This gave you a fair foundation for what we are about to explore in this chapter. By now, with everything we have been showing you in this book, you are already well versed in using the command line; you know some of the most common and useful commands available in Linux as we explored file operations, package, user, and disk management, all the way up to network administration. All this knowledge will eventually be put to use in this chapter, where we will explore advanced shell features, shell variables, regular expressions, and how to take advantage of the powerful programming and automation features of the Bash shell.

In the next section, we will begin discovering the advanced features of the shell.

Bash shell features

The shell not only runs commands but also has many more features that make a system administrator's life more comfortable while at the command line. Some of these features include the use of **wildcards** and **metacharacters**, **brace expansion**, and **variables**. Apart from these, you will learn about the shell's PATH and aliases.

Before we proceed, let's dig into a little history about the standards the shell is based on. Back in the day, when UNIX emerged as an operating system, the need for a standard to oversee different variants appeared. Thus, the **Institute of Electrical and Electronics Engineers (IEEE)** created the **Portable Operating System Interface (POSIX)** as a family of different standards that were meant to assure compatibility between operating systems. Therefore, UNIX and Linux, as well as macOS (based on Darwin, the kernel of macOS derived from UNIX), AIX, HP-UX, and Oracle Solaris, are POSIX compliant. POSIX has different standards for the C language API, file format definitions, directory structures, environment variables definitions, locale specifications, character sets, and regular expressions.

With this short history lesson under our belts, let's proceed. In the next section, we will show you how to use shell wildcards and metacharacters.

Wildcards and metacharacters

In Linux, **wildcards** are used to match filenames. There are three main types of wildcards:

- **Asterisk** (*): This is used to match any string of none or more characters
- **Question mark** (?): This is used to match a single character
- **Brackets** ([ ]): This is used to match any of the characters inside brackets

Metacharacters are special characters that are used in Linux and any Unix-based system. These metacharacters are as follows:

Metacharacter	Description		Metacharacter	Description
>	Output redirection		<	Input redirection
>>	Output redirection – append		<<	Input redirection - append
*	File substitution wildcard		?	File substitution wildcard
[ ]	File substitution wildcard		;	Command execution sequence
|	Pipe for using multiple commands		( )	Group of commands in the execution sequence
||	Conditional execution (OR)		&&	Conditional execution (AND)
&	Run a command in the background		#	Use a command directly in the shell
$	Variable value expansion		\	The escape character
`cmd`	Command substitution		$(cmd)	Command substitution

Figure 8.1 – Metacharacter list

Let's look at two examples that use metacharacters for command substitution. We use the output of one command inside another command. This can be done in two ways, as shown in the following figure:

```
packt@neptune:~$ echo "Today is `date`"
Today is Mon Feb 27 02:09:18 PM UTC 2023
packt@neptune:~$ echo "Today is $(date)"
Today is Mon Feb 27 02:09:38 PM UTC 2023
packt@neptune:~$ ▮
```

Figure 8.2 – Example of command execution and substitution

The purpose of the preceding example is to show you how command substitution works in the shell, but perhaps we should explain further what the commands used do. We used two commands: echo and date. We used the output of the date command inside the output of the echo command. The echo command is one of the simplest commands in Linux as it prints the message between the quotes to the standard output. In our case, the message also consists of the date command, which outputs the current date of the system, in the format shown.

You can also combine two or more commands, and to do this in Linux, we use the pipe. The pipe sends the output of the first command that was used as the input for the second command, and so forth, depending on how many pipes you use.

In the following example, we're using the ls -l /etc command to do a long listing of the contents of the /etc directory; we will pipe this to the less command. Use it as shown in the following code:

```
ls -l /etc | less
```

The less command will show one display at a time, allowing you to see all the contents. You can use the arrow keys or the page up and page down keys to navigate through the output and see all the contents of the /etc directory.

The pipe and command substitution will be very useful, especially when you're working with complex commands or when scripting, as you will see later in this chapter when you learn how to create and use scripts.

Now, let's execute some commands in a sequence. After that, we will use metacharacters to group commands and redirect the output to a file. All this is shown in the following screenshot:

```
packt@neptune:~$ who; pwd;
packt     pts/0          2023-02-27 13:49 (192.168.124.1)
/home/packt
packt@neptune:~$ (who; pwd) > users
packt@neptune:~$ cat users
packt     pts/0          2023-02-27 13:49 (192.168.124.1)
/home/packt
packt@neptune:~$
```

Figure 8.3 – Example of command sequence execution

As you can see in the preceding output, the two commands that were executed on the first line can easily be grouped using brackets, and their output can be redirected to a file.

We used three types of metacharacters – the *command execution sequence* (;), the brackets for *grouping commands* in the execution sequence, and the *output redirection* (>) to redirect the output to a file. The file did not exist initially as it was created only when the command was executed. The last command we used was the cat command, which *concatenates* the contents of the newly created file.

The first two commands that were used were who, which prints information about the currently logged-in users to the standard output, and pwd, which prints the present working directory as the location we are in inside the filesystem. In the following section, we will show you how to use brace expansion with the shell.

Brace expansion

Curly brackets can also be used to expand the arguments of a command. **Braces** are not just limited to filenames, unlike a wildcard. They work with any type of string. Inside these braces, you can use a single string, a sequence, or several strings separated by commas.

In this section, we will show you some examples of using this type of expansion. First, we will use **brace expansion** to delete two files from one directory. Second, we will show you how to create multiple new files using brace expansion. Let's say that we have two files named report and new-report inside our present working directory and we want to delete them both at once. We can use the following command:

```
rm {report,new-report}
```

To create multiple files (five of them, for example) that share parts of their name, as in `file1`, `file2`, … `filen`, we can use the following command:

```
touch file{1..5}
```

The following screenshot shows the output of both these commands:

```
packt@neptune:~$ ls
new-report  report  users
packt@neptune:~$ rm {report,new-report}
packt@neptune:~$ ls
users
packt@neptune:~$ touch file{1..5}
packt@neptune:~$ ls
file1  file2  file3  file4  file5  users
packt@neptune:~$ 
```

Figure 8.4 – Examples of using brace expansion

> **Important note**
> Brace expansion is a powerful tool that adds flexibility and power to any system administrator's workflow. They will prove very useful when learning how to script, for example.

Now that we've created those files, it should be really easy for you to figure out how to use brace expansion to delete multiple files at once. Type the following command into your console and see what happens:

```
rm file{1..5}
```

It will delete all five files we created previously. Use the `ls` command to see the contents of the present working directory.

In the next section, we will talk about shell command aliases, what they are, and how to use them.

The shell's aliases

The Linux shell supports **aliases**, which are a very convenient way to create short commands as aliases for longer ones. For example, in Ubuntu, there is a predefined alias called `ll` that is shorthand for `ls -alF`. You can define your own aliases too. You can make them temporary or permanent, similar to variables. In the following example, we changed the alias for the `ll` command:

```
packt@neptune:~$ alias ll
alias ll='ls -alF'
packt@neptune:~$ alias ll='ls -l'
packt@neptune:~$ alias ll
alias ll='ls -l'
packt@neptune:~$ █
```

Figure 8.5 – Changing the alias of a command

This modification is only temporary, and it will revert to the default version after reboot or shell restart. If you want to make it permanent, you should edit the ~/.bashrc file and add the aliases you created previously inside the file. To do this, open the file with your preferred text editor and add the lines you used in the Terminal to the file. Save the file and execute it. Also, a better practice would be to add those lines to a new file called .bash_aliases. You can view the default contents of .bashrc for more information on how to use aliases.

> **Important note**
> The .bashrc file is a hidden script file that consists of different Terminal session configurations. Also, the file can contain different functions that can help the user overcome repetitive tasks. It is automatically executed when the user logs in, but it can also be manually executed by using the source .bashrc command.

In the next section, we will show you what shell variables are and how to use them.

Bash shell variables

The Bash shell uses different types of variables, in the same way you would use them in any programming language. The Bash shell has some built-in variables and indirect variables and offers the possibility to define your own variables as well.

Linux has two major types of shell variables: **global** and **local variables**. They are generally identical for every Linux distribution out there, with some exceptions. You will need to consult your distribution's documentation for any specific modifications to the environment variables.

We will walk you through the most widely used variables in Linux, starting with the built-in ones.

Built-in shell variables

Here is a short list of some of the standard built-in variables:

- HOME: The user's home directory (for example, /home/packt)
- LOGNAME: The user's login name (for example, packt)

- PWD: The shell's current working directory

- OLDPWD: The shell's previous working directory

- PATH: The shell's search path (list of directories separated by colons)

- SHELL: The path to the shell

- USER: The user's login name

- TERM: The type of the Terminal

To call a variable while in the shell, all you have to do is place a dollar sign, $, in front of the variable's name. Here is a short example that shows how to use the variables that we just listed:

```
packt@neptune:~$ echo $HOME
/home/packt
packt@neptune:~$ echo $LOGNAME
packt
packt@neptune:~$ echo $PWD
/home/packt
packt@neptune:~$ echo $OLDPWD

packt@neptune:~$ echo $PATH
/usr/local/sbin:/usr/local/bin:/usr/sbin:/usr/bin:/sbin:/bin:/usr/games:/usr/loc
al/games:/snap/bin
packt@neptune:~$ echo $SHELL
/bin/bash
packt@neptune:~$ echo $USER
packt
packt@neptune:~$ echo $TERM
xterm-256color
packt@neptune:~$
```

Figure 8.6 – Variable calling from the shell

You can also assign your own shell variables, as in the following example. Here, we're assigning the sysadmin string to a new variable called MYVAR and then printing it to standard output:

```
MYVAR=sysadmin; echo $MYVAR
```

The variables listed at the beginning of this section are just a part of all the variables available by default inside the shell. To see all the shell variables, use the printenv command. If the list is too long, you can redirect it to a file. In the following example, your variables list is inside the shell_variables file, and you can see it by concatenating or by editing inside a text editor such as Vim:

```
printenv > ~/shell_variables
```

Here, we use the tilde symbol (~) to specify the logged-in user's home directory. The shell's variables are only available inside the shell. If you want some variables to be known to other programs that are run by the shell, you must export them by using the export command. Once a variable is exported from the shell, it is known as an **environment variable**.

The shell's search path

The PATH variable is an essential one in Linux. It helps the shell know where all the programs are located. When you enter a command into your Bash shell, it first has to search for that command through the Linux filesystem. Some directories are already listed inside the PATH variable, but you can also add new ones. Your addition can be temporary or permanent, depending on how you do it. To make a directory's path available temporarily, simply add it to the PATH variable. In the following example, we're adding the /home/packt directory to PATH:

```
packt@neptune:~$ echo $PATH
/usr/local/sbin:/usr/local/bin:/usr/sbin:/usr/bin:/sbin:/bin:/usr/games:/usr/loc
al/games:/snap/bin
packt@neptune:~$ PATH=$PATH:/home/packt
packt@neptune:~$ echo $PATH
/usr/local/sbin:/usr/local/bin:/usr/sbin:/usr/bin:/sbin:/bin:/usr/games:/usr/loc
al/games:/snap/bin:/home/packt
packt@neptune:~$
```

Figure 8.7 – Adding a new location to PATH

To make any changes permanent, we must modify the PATH variable inside a file called ~/.bash_profile or ~/.bashrc.

> **Important note**
> Some distributions, such as openSUSE, add an extra bin directory inside the user's home directory. This is a place where you can put files that you want the shell to execute – for example, script files.

The shell's $PATH variable is important, especially when using scripts, as you will preferably have to create scripts inside a directory that is known by the shell. In the next section, we will show you how to create your first Bash scripts.

Basics of shell scripting

We have already covered important aspects of the Linux command line, shell variables, wildcards, and metacharacters. Now, we will start exploring what scripts are, how to create them, and how to use them in a Linux CLI. We will not use the graphical user interface, only the CLI, which we primarily used in our previous chapters. Let's start with some basic, but important, concepts about shell scripting.

First, let's learn what a **script** is. If we were to check the meaning of the term in a dictionary, the answer would be that a script is a series of instructions that are executed by a computer, mainly to automate a specific task. Instructions can easily be assimilated as commands too. Thus, a series of commands executed together by the shell can be considered a script. This is a very basic script, but it is a script. Let's look at how we can create a script file.

Creating a shell script file

The most appropriate way to write scripts is to create them in the form of a file, called a **shell script file**. In Linux, these types of files should use the .sh extension for clarity. However, this is not obligatory, because in Linux, files don't use extensions, unlike in Windows. The distinctive characteristic that makes a file considered a script is the *very first line* of text inside that file. In the case of a Bash shell script, this line is in the following format:

```
#!/bin/bash
```

When the file is opened and executed, the first line tells the shell's interpreter that it is dealing with a script file that, in our case, will be run by the Bash shell. If you are using a different shell, this first line will point to it. The use of the hashtag (#) inside a shell script file denotes a commented line, except for this very first line, where it is used, combined with the exclamation mark (!), to point to the shell's interpreter. The #! combination is also called the **shebang**.

Let's create a basic script file. We will use the following code:

```
#!/bin/bash
whoami
who
date
uptime
```

Here, we used four different commands in our first, basic script. We used a separate line for each command, but there is another way to write it: by putting all commands on the same line and using semicolons to separate them. However, for clarity, it is useful to use different lines.

Now that we have our first script, let's run it. We created the script file inside our home directory under the name basic-script.sh. Let's try and run it by simply invoking its name at the command line:

```
$ basic-script.sh
```

We will be prompted with an error, as shown in the following screenshot:

```
packt@neptune:~$ ls -la basic-script.sh
-rw-rw-r-- 1 packt packt 35 Mar 26 06:53 basic-script.sh
packt@neptune:~$ basic-script.sh
basic-script.sh: command not found
```

Figure 8.8 – Error upon running the new script

You might be wondering why we get this error. It is because the shell does not know about your script. It cannot find it inside its PATH variable. As you might remember from the previous section, PATH is a variable that the shell uses to find the location of specific files to run. To overcome this error, we have two options:

- We can add the directory in which our script resides to the shell's path

- We can use a relative or absolute path when we invoke the script at the command line

We will use the second method as it is more convenient. However, you can use the first method as a good practice exercise and try to add your directory's location to the shell's PATH variable. Let's invoke the script file with its location:

```
$ ./basic-script.sh
```

We will get another error, this time a different one, saying Permission denied. This is because we do not have permission to execute the file. When we created the file inside our Ubuntu machine, it only got read and write permissions for the file's owner and its group because of the default umask value. To change that, we will need to make the file executable by using the following command:

```
$ chmod u+x basic-script.sh
```

Once we've set the executable permissions on the file, we can run it again, and this time, the script will be executed. The output will show that every command inside our script was executed:

```
packt@neptune:~$ ./basic-script.sh
-bash: ./basic-script.sh: Permission denied
packt@neptune:~$ chmod u+x basic-script.sh
packt@neptune:~$ ./basic-script.sh
packt
packt     tty1          2023-03-26 06:44
packt     pts/0         2023-03-26 06:45 (192.168.124.1)
Sun Mar 26 07:17:36 AM UTC 2023
 07:17:36 up 33 min,  2 users,  load average: 0.00, 0.00, 0.00
```

Figure 8.9 – Running an executable script file

As shown in the previous screenshot, the script was executed, and the output showed the result of each command inside. On the first line, we have the username (the output of the `whoami` command), on the second line, we have information about the logged-in users (the output of the `who` command), on the third line, we have information about the current date (the output of the `date` command), and on the last line, we have information about the current session (the output of the `uptime` command).

> **Important note**
>
> As a general rule, when writing scripts, we advise you to *use as many comments* as possible to detail each variable and parameter you choose. This is considered a good programming practice, which will make your code writing more enjoyable and relevant. Documenting your coding steps will make your scripts easier to read at a later time, both by yourself and by anyone else who might come across your code. We don't use many comments in the examples used in this book, but this is due to constraints regarding page count. Nevertheless, we encourage you to use them.

With that, you know how to create a shell script file and how to execute it. Let's proceed to more advanced topics now. In the next section, we will show you how to use variables in your scripts.

Variables in shell scripts

We introduced you to variables at the beginning of this chapter. Now, it is time to learn how to use them inside a script. To recap, let's see what kind of variables are used in Linux. We have **environment variables**, which are available from the shell, and **user-defined variables**, which are created by the users and are not directly available from the shell. These two types of variables can also be used inside scripts. You can see a complete list of environment variables in your system by using the `printenv` and/or `set` commands. We listed some of the most commonly used variables in the *Built-in shell variables* section earlier in this chapter.

Understanding naming conventions

Inside the Linux shell, the system's environment variables use only uppercase letters. Thus, the relevant naming considerations should be applied when creating user-specified variables. In this regard, there is not one single naming convention that applies. But you should take into consideration that the names of variables are *case-sensitive* and should be up to *20 characters* in length. The way to assign a value to a variable is by using the equals (=) sign.

If you plan on using only uppercase letters in the names of your variables, you should consider the disastrous effects this might have, considering that the environment variables only use uppercase letters. We would advise you to consider one of the following rules when creating variable names inside your shell:

- Use only lowercase letters, underscores, and numbers
- Capitalize the first letter of a word in the variable name

> **Important note**
>
> When considering name length, try not to use very long names; instead, use succinct and relevant names or abbreviations. This will make your script easier to read and understand.

Now, let's learn how to define and use our first variables inside a shell. We will explore this in the next section.

Defining and using variables

Let's create a new file called user-script.sh that will show relevant user information by using environment variables. After we create the file and enter the relevant code, we will make it executable and then we will run it. The following are the relevant commands:

```
packt@neptune:~$ touch user-script.sh
packt@neptune:~$ nano user-script.sh
packt@neptune:~$ cat user-script.sh
#!/bin/bash
echo "user id: $UID"
echo 'user name:' $USER
echo "user's home: $HOME"
echo 'user session:' $BASH
packt@neptune:~$ chmod u+x user-script.sh
packt@neptune:~$ ./user-script.sh
user id: 1000
user name: packt
user's home: /home/packt
user session: /bin/bash
```

Figure 8.10 – Using environment variables in a script

In the preceding figure, we used two different ways to show information with the echo command. When we used double quotes to show information, the environment variable was used inside the quoted string, and its value was displayed in the output. Keep in mind that when using single quotes, the value of the variable will not be passed through to the shell's interpreter. We used four different environment variables to show information about the user. Those variables were UID, USER, HOME, and BASH. This is a very basic and straightforward way to use shell variables inside scripts.

You can also use your own variables, not just the ones that are provided by the shell. A very useful feature of the shell's interpreter is that it can automatically determine the data type a variable is using. You should also know that the values of variables defined inside a shell script are only active so long as the shell is running, and they will be lost afterward. Let's create a new shell script and use our own variables this time. The following is the output:

```
packt@neptune:~$ nano user-variables.sh
packt@neptune:~$ cat user-variables.sh
#!/bin/bash
value=25
product='Shirt'
echo "The $product costs $value $"
packt@neptune:~$ chmod u+x user-variables.sh
packt@neptune:~$ ./user-variables.sh
The Shirt costs 25 $
```

Figure 8.11 – A basic script using user-defined variables

Here, we created a file called user-variables.sh and defined two variables, one called value, which we gave a value of 25, and another variable called product, with a value of Shirt. When we called the variables inside the echo command, we used the same callout sign as for environment variables.

Now that you know how to name, define, and use a variable, let's continue to more advanced topics. In the next section, we will show you how to use mathematical expressions inside your shell scripts.

Using mathematical expressions in shell scripts

The shell is a programming language, so it has built-in features to work with numbers. The Bash shell provides the expr command, which is used for different mathematical operations. To learn about all the operations that are supported, please visit the internal manual page for the expr command, as we will not provide them fully here:

```
man expr
```

However, we will show you how to use some of the operations that the expr command provides. Keep in mind that, as the manual says, you will need to escape (by using the backslash character, \) some of the characters used by the expr command, as they will be misinterpreted by the shell. Let's create a new script file and do some basic mathematical operations. Our new file is called math.sh and can be created using the following code:

```
packt@neptune:~$ nano math.sh
packt@neptune:~$ chmod u+x math.sh
packt@neptune:~$ ./math.sh
The total price is: 22
packt@neptune:~$ cat math.sh
#!/bin/bash
price=20
vat=2
total=$(expr $price + $vat)
echo "The total price is: $total"
```

Figure 8.12 – Using the expr command inside scripts

Besides the `expr` command, we can also use square brackets as a much simpler variant for mathematical operations. Let's modify the preceding script and replace the `expr` command:

```
packt@neptune:~$ cat math.sh
#!/bin/bash
price=20
vat=2
total=$[($price + $vat)]
echo "The total price is: $total"

packt@neptune:~$ ./math.sh
The total price is: 22
```

Figure 8.13 – Using square brackets for math operations

As shown in the previous example, we use integer values. You can try and use a floating-point value for the `vat` variable, for example, and you will see that an error will be displayed when running the script. This is because the shell only supports integer arithmetic operations. There are workarounds to overcome this limitation, and the most feasible is by using the Bash calculator, or the `bc` command.

> **Important note**
>
> If you want to have full support for floating-point operations inside your shell, you might want to consider using the **Z shell (Zsh)**. It is installed by default in some Linux distributions (Manjaro and Kali Linux) and on macOS. You can also install it in your distribution if you like.

Let's see how we can use the `bc` command inside our `math.sh` script. We will change the code as follows:

```
packt@neptune:~$ nano math.sh
packt@neptune:~$ ./math.sh
The total price is: 22.50
packt@neptune:~$ cat math.sh
#!/bin/bash
price=20
vat=2.50
total=$(echo "decs=2; $price + $vat" | bc )
echo "The total price is: $total"
```

Figure 8.14 – Using the bc command for floating-point operations

In the preceding example, we assigned a floating-point value to the `vat` variable and used the `bc` command to calculate a floating-point total. We can use the `bc` command inside a variable like so:

```
var=$(echo "option; expression" | bc)
```

The `option` value provides options for `bc` to use. In our case, we used a variable called `decs` (an arbitrary name we chose) to specify the number of decimals we would like to provide. The `expression` parameter specifies the operation we used, which in our case was addition. We piped the output of the `echo` command to the `bc` command and the result was assigned to the `var` variable.

Creating Bash shell scripts is more than doing math operations or giving a sequence of consecutive shell commands. Sometimes, decisions need to be made inside the shell, depending on the input provided and the output expected. This is where specific programming structures intervene. We will walk you through all of them in the next section.

Using programming structures

In this section, we will show you how to use **conditional** and **looping statements**. They can prove invaluable when creating advanced shell scripts. We will also show you how to use arrays, how input reading is used inside scripts, and how to format and print data for the output.

Using arrays in Bash

We showed you how to use variables in previous sections. Now, it is time to step up our game and show you how to make use of **arrays**, a more complex form of variable. Let's say that we need to work with multiple variables that may store similar information, such as filenames. Instead of using multiple variables in the form of `filename1`, `filename2`, `filename3` ... `filenameN`, we can create an array that will hold all the filenames. If you know other programming languages, arrays may already be familiar to you. But if you don't know any other programming languages, fear not, as Bash has a facile way of using arrays.

Let's start with an easy example. Let's say we have to work with different usernames. Instead of using different variables for each username, we can use an **indexed array**:

```
usernames=("paul" "janet" "mike" "john" "anna" "martha")
```

The elements inside an array start from index number 0 (zero). This is important to remember when we need to access the contents of the array. If we would like to access the third element from the usernames array (the `"mike"` string), we must use the following code:

```
echo ${usernames[2]}
```

The output will be `mike` (without quotes). To print out the entire array, use the following code:

```
echo ${usernames[*]} or echo ${usernames[@]}
```

To print out the size of the array, as in the number of elements, use the following code:

```
echo ${#usernames[@]} or echo ${#usernames[*]}
```

In our case, we have six elements inside, and the output will be 6.

Let's say we need to add a new username (`"alex"`) to the array. There are different ways to add it. If we just want to add it with no specified position from the beginning, we can use the following code:

```
usernames+=("alex")
```

The new username will be appended at the end of the array. At this point, the array contains unordered names, and we will need to arrange them in alphabetical order. We will cover this in the *Using looping statements* section, after which we will teach you about output formatting and different conditional and looping statements.

Alternatively, we can add a new element (`"zack"`, for example) at a specific position inside the array (let's say position 2) by using the following code:

```
usernames[1]="zack"
```

So far, we've only used strings inside arrays as an example. You can also use integers for indexed arrays. The built-in command to create an array is `declare`. To create an indexed array, you can use the following command:

```
declare -a array_name
```

You can also create associative arrays using the following command:

```
declare -A array_name
```

Associative arrays are based on key-value pairs of elements. The following is an example of an associative array declaration:

```
declare -A linux_distros=( [KDE]="openSUSE" [GNOME]="Fedora"
[Xfce]="Debian" [Cinnamon]="Mint" )
```

Presented inside square brackets are the keys that are used to map the values. Inside double quotes, we have the values. To print the values, you can use the same command you used for indexed arrays:

```
echo ${linux_distros[@]}
```

To print the keys, use the following command:

```
echo ${!linux_distros[@]}
```

The main difference between indexed and associative arrays is that indexed arrays are based on index value, where each element has a specific index position inside the array, whereas associative arrays use specific keys to map the values.

Arrays are important data structures inside Bash and we will make use of them later in this chapter when we discuss looping statements. But first, let's learn how to read input data inside a script, and how to format output data. In the next section, we will show you how to read data from standard input.

Reading input data

By default, the shell reads the input data from the standard input, which is the keyboard. To read from the standard input, you can use the `read` command. This command reads all input data provided until a new line is provided. This happens when you press the *Enter* key on your keyboard.

With the `read` command, you can provide one or more variables. If you use more variables, each word provided through standard input will be assigned to a variable. The following is an example:

```
packt@neptune:~$ read name
alexandru
packt@neptune:~$ echo $name
alexandru
packt@neptune:~$ read a b c d
Monday
packt@neptune:~$ echo $a
Monday
packt@neptune:~$ echo $b

packt@neptune:~$ read a b c d
Monday Tuesday Wednesday Thursday
packt@neptune:~$ echo $b
Tuesday
packt@neptune:~$ echo $a $b $c $d
Monday Tuesday Wednesday Thursday
```

Figure 8.15 – Using the read command for standard input

In the preceding screenshot, we used the `read` command with four variables called a, b, c, and d. When we first introduced the data, we only provided a value for the first variable, meaning that we hit *Enter* after entering the first word from the keyboard. Thus, we had only one value for a and no value for the others. When we used the `read` command for the second time, we provided values for every variable, thus hitting *Enter* after the word `Thursday`. This way, each variable received a relevant value. The `read` command has several options available, but you will have to read the manual to learn about them in detail. Similar to providing values from the standard input, the `read` command can receive input from a file by using redirection. For example, if we have a file called `week-days`, we can redirect its content to the `read` command:

```
packt@neptune:~$ nano week-days
packt@neptune:~$ cat week-days
Monday Tuesday Wednesday Thursday Friday Saturday Sunday
packt@neptune:~$ read d1 d2 d3 d4 d5 d6 d7 < week-days
packt@neptune:~$ echo $d1 $d2 $d3 $d4 $d5 $d6 $d7
Monday Tuesday Wednesday Thursday Friday Saturday Sunday
```

Figure 8.16 – Using read with file redirection

The read command is used for input reading when creating scripts. We showed you how to use the command on the command line, but we will come back to it later in this chapter when we talk about more advanced scripts. In the following section, we will introduce you to output data formats.

Formatting output data

In Linux, the standard output is directed by default to the monitor. For this task, you will have two commands you can use. One of them is the echo command, which we've used quite extensively in this book. The other command is called printf, and we will cover its use in this section.

The printf command is similar to the one used in the C programming language. A quick manual search for the printf command will show us the form in which it should be used:

```
printf FORMAT [ARGUMENT] …
```

All the arguments of the command are printed according to the format string provided. The format controls can have normal characters or **escape sequences**, containing backslash and letters. These escape sequences are clearly presented in the available manual. Briefly, some widely used sequences are as follows:

- \b: Backspace
- \e: Escape
- \f: Form feed
- \n: New line
- \r: Carriage return
- \t: Horizontal tab
- \v: Vertical tab

When using a backslash with printf, it should be escaped from the shell by using double quotes or another backslash. For more details on this, please refer to the manual.

Besides escape sequences, the `printf` command has format specifiers. Here are some details about what some of these format specifiers represent:

- `%s`: This is a string specifier and it's used for basic string output

- `%b`: This is a string specifier that allows escape sequence interpretation

- `%d`: This is an integer specifier that's used for integral values

- `%f`: This is similar to the integer specifier, but it's used for floating-point values

- `%x`: This is used for the hexadecimal values of integers and output padding

Now that you know the basics of the `printf` command, let's look at some examples of how to use it.

In the following figure, we're using `printf` format specifiers to show you the difference between using them and not using them:

```
packt@neptune:~$ printf "hello world"
hello worldpackt@neptune:~$ printf "%s\n" "hello world"
hello world
packt@neptune:~$ printf "%b\n" "First row" "Second row"
First row
Second row
```

Figure 8.17 – Basic usage of the printf command

As shown here, when using the default setting, `printf` prints the string inside the double quotes but without a new line at the end. When using the `%s` format specifier, the command prints the strings provided as arguments and interprets them as characters – in our case, the strings between double quotes. Using \n will create a new line after each string.

Let's use the `printf` command inside a script now. The following is an example of `printf` using the `%s` format specifier. Notice that we use the command using single quotes since the output is similar to when using double quotes:

```
packt@neptune:~$ nano user-data.sh
packt@neptune:~$ chmod u+x user-data.sh
packt@neptune:~$ ./user-data.sh
Provide your first name:
Alexandru
Provide your last name:
Calcatinge
Welcome: Alexandru Calcatinge
packt@neptune:~$ cat user-data.sh
#!/bin/bash
printf "Provide your first name:\n"
read FirstName
printf "Provide your last name:\n"
read LastName
printf 'Welcome: %s\n' "$FirstName $LastName"
```

Figure 8.18 – Using printf inside a script

The preceding figure shows a script that reads two variables from the standard input device and then shows both variables to the standard output (the monitor). We used the string specifier (%s) and the new line escape sequence (\n). Now, let's dig deeper into formatting output. In the following examples, we're using the new tab escape sequence (\t) together with the newline escape sequence (\n) and the string specifier. Take a look at the following figure and see how formatting works:

```
packt@neptune:~$ printf "%s\t%s\n" "No." "Item" "1" "Paper"
No.     Item
1       Paper
packt@neptune:~$ printf "%s\t%s\n" "No." "Item" "1" "Paper" "2" "Pen"
No.     Item
1       Paper
2       Pen
```

Figure 8.19 – Using tab and newline escape sequences

The example we just showed you is using escape sequences to mimic table formatting for the output. We can do this by using a script with more complex specifiers than the ones already used. In the following example, we're using the string (%s), integer (%d), and floating (%f) specifiers to format a table output:

```
packt@neptune:~$ nano format-output.sh
packt@neptune:~$ chmod u+x format-output.sh
packt@neptune:~$ cat format-output.sh
#!/bin/bash
separator===========================
separator=$separator$separator
header="\n %-10s %8s %10s %11s\n"
format=" %-10s %08d %10s %11.2f\n"
width=43
printf "$header" "PRODUCT" "ID" "ISLE" "PRICE"
printf "%$width.${width}s\n" "$separator"
printf "$format" \
Eggs 2876 D02 10 \
Meat 8748 M05 58.75 \
Cereals 3243 C11 25.5
packt@neptune:~$ ./format-output.sh

 PRODUCT          ID       ISLE       PRICE
 ===========================================
 Eggs        00002876       D02       10.00
 Meat        00008748       M05       58.75
 Cereals     00003243       C11       25.50
```

Figure 8.20 – Using complex specifiers and escape sequences for table formatting

Let's detail our `format-output.sh` script. We have a variable called `separator` that's used to print out the graphical border between the header and the contents. Then, we have the `header` and `format` variables, each using specifiers and sequences for formatting specifics. `header` starts with a new line (\n), followed by a string specifier with a length of 10 characters wide aligned to the left (`%-10s`), followed by eight characters wide aligned to the right (`%8s`), 10 characters wide aligned to the right (`%10s`), and 11 characters wide aligned to the right (`%11s`) with a new line at the end (\n). The `format` variable is used to format the contents of the table by using two string columns (using the `%s` specifier), one integer (`%d`), and one floating-point (`%f`) specifier. The integer value is used for the product ID and the floating-point value is used for the price. We use the `%08d` format specifier to print the ID, which means that the output will be 8 characters wide. The `0` character in front indicates that any empty spaces will be filled with zeros. This ensures that even when the ID number has less than eight digits, the remaining width will be padded with zeros to maintain the desired width of eight characters. The result is shown in the lower part of the preceding screenshot, where we have a table with products, their IDs, placement, and prices.

Thus, `printf` is a very versatile and powerful tool that can be used with great results insider your scripts. Now that you know the basic tools for input and output data formatting for Bash scripting, let's proceed to other useful and important structures that can be used.

In the next section, we will cover exit statuses.

Understanding exit statuses and testing structures

To use conditional and looping statements, we need to understand the **exit status** of a command. Usually, when a statement is running, the given condition is checked and tested so that we can see the validity of the command. The status of a command is stored inside a special parameter that has the following form: `$?`. The question mark is the place of an integer that will give the status of the command. For example, if the command's execution was successful, then the value of the question mark will be 0 (zero) and the parameter will show `$0`. If the command's execution was not successful, the question mark can have any value starting from 1 to 255. Most regularly, the error number is 1, so the parameter will be `$1`. These are also called **exit codes**.

Alongside exit codes, **testing structures** are also important for conditional and looping statements in Bash. These testing structures are usually the building blocks for the aforementioned statements. They are considered shell's keywords and are represented like so:

- `[[ ]]`: Double square brackets are used to test the true or false status of a command; it can perform operations on regular expressions too

- `(( ))`: Double brackets are used for arithmetic operations

- `test`: This keyword is used to evaluate expressions such as strings, integers, and file properties

> **Important note**
> The syntax of Bash requires spaces to be used before and after brackets – for example, `[ operation ]`.

In conditional statements, some other types of operators are used for testing. Let's take a look at some of the most commonly used conditional operators for **integer tests**:

- `-eg`: The equality check operator
- `-ne`: The inequality check operator
- `-lt`: The less than operator
- `-le`: The less than or equal to operator
- `-gt`: The greater than operator
- `-ge`: The greater than or equal operator

In addition, there are argument operators in Linux shell scripting. The `$0` variable represents the command used to run the script, while `$1` through `$n` represents the first through *n*th arguments passed to the command. For example, `$1` refers to the first argument, `$2` refers to the second argument, and so on, where `$n` represents the *n*th argument of the command.

Besides the operators shown in this section, basic mathematical operators are also currently used in conditional statements.

There are also testing structures for **strings**:

- `=`: Tests if strings are identical (`==` is also accepted)
- `!=`: Tests if strings are *NOT* identical
- `\<` and `\>`: Less than and greater are accepted for string comparison, but they must be escaped (we already used the backslash character)

There are also testing operators for **file types**, which are in the form of options:

- `-f`: Tests for a regular file
- `-d`: Tests for a directory
- `-h` or `-L`: Tests for a symbolic link
- `-e`: Testing for a file's existence

Here are some other operators that are used for testing:

- -a: The logical AND

- -o: The logical OR

- -z: To check if an input string was entered

Testing operators are complex and useful, so it's very important to learn them.

In the next section, we will cover Bash conditional statements.

Using conditional if statements

Just like in any other programming language, Bash has conditional execution statements, such as if-then-fi, if-then-else-fi, and *nested* if, and conditional operators such as && (*AND*) and || (*OR*). We will show you how to use them in this section.

We will present the if statement in all its appearances (if-then, if-then-else, and nested if) in this section:

- In its most common form, the if-then-fi statement has the following syntax:

  ```
  if [condition]
  then
          commands
  fi
  ```

  This Bash if statement is running condition after the if keyword. If the command is completed successfully, meaning it has an exit status of zero, then it will run the commands that are listed after the then keyword.

- The if-then-else-fi statement is similar to if-then and has the following syntax:

  ```
  if [condition]
  then
          commands
  else
          commands
  fi
  ```

Similar to the simpler if-then statement, condition is run, and depending on its exit status, the results are different. If it completes successfully, the commands after the then keyword are executed, but if there is another exit status (non-zero), the commands after the else keyword are executed. This gives more options and alternatives, based on the result of the condition. There are situations when you would need to check for more conditions inside a single if-then command, so you can use nested if statements for this.

Now, let's discuss some basic conditional arguments that are used in `if` statements, together with some examples:

- In this example, we will check if the number a user is typing is even or odd. The script will take the input from the user by using the `read` command; then, it will check if what remains from its division by two is zero or not. This way, it determines if the number is odd or even. We will use the `if-then-else` statement for this example, together with the `read` and `printf` commands. The following screenshot shows the code and the execution's output:

```
packt@neptune:~$ nano even_odd.sh
packt@neptune:~$ chmod u+x even_odd.sh
packt@neptune:~$ cat even_odd.sh
#!/bin/bash
echo "Enter a number:"
read number
if [ $(( number % 2 )) == 0 ]
then
        printf "%s\n" "The number $number is even."
else
        printf "%s\n" "The number $number is odd."
fi
packt@neptune:~$ ./even_odd.sh
Enter a number:
10
The number 10 is even.
packt@neptune:~$ ./even_odd.sh
Enter a number:
5
The number 5 is odd.
```

Figure 8.21 – Script to determine an even or odd number

- The following script checks if a filename introduced by the user is indeed a file or not by using the `test -f` operator. We will introduce the absolute path of the file we want to run a check on. The script is called `testing_file.sh` and its code is shown in the following screenshot:

```
packt@neptune:~$ cat testing_file.sh
#!/bin/bash
#testing if a filename is indeed a file
echo "Enter a file name using absolute path:"
read filename
if [[ -z $filename ]]
then
        printf "%s\n" "no filename entered..."
        exit 1
else
        printf "The filename you entered is: %s\n" "$filename"
fi
printf "%s\n" "Testing if "$filename" is a file..."
test -f "$filename"
if (( $?==0 ))
then
        printf "%s %d\n" "The "$filename" represents a file. (0=true):" $?
else
        printf "%s %d\n" "The "$filename" is not a file. (1=false):" $?
fi
```

Figure 8.22 – Checking if a filename that's been introduced is a file

By running this script, you will be prompted to provide the filename and full path of an existing (or not) file. Let's do some tests. You will see the output shown in the following figure. We tested if the script is working correctly in three different scenarios: when we do not provide a filename, when we enter a correct filename, and when we enter the wrong filename:

```
packt@neptune:~$ ./testing_file.sh
Enter a file name using absolute path:

no filename entered...
packt@neptune:~$ ./testing_file.sh
Enter a file name using absolute path:
/etc/passwd
The filename you entered is: /etc/passwd
Testing if /etc/passwd is a file...
The /etc/passwd represents a file. (0=true): 0
packt@neptune:~$ ./testing_file.sh
Enter a file name using absolute path:
/home/test
The filename you entered is: /home/test
Testing if /home/test is a file...
The /home/test is not a file. (1=false): 1
```

Figure 8.23 – Running the file-checking script

Now that we've covered the basics of if conditional statement usage, let's proceed to other types of statements, such as looping statements.

Using looping statements

In Bash, **looping statements** use the `for`, `while`, and `until` commands, and we will show you how to use them in this section. Looping statements are used when repeating processes are needed, such as looping through several commands until a condition is met.

Using the for statement

As in any other programming language, the need for iterating appears when repetitive tasks have to be done. This means that some commands need to be repeated until condition(s) are met. This is similar in Bash as in any other programming language, and one of the commands to use is the `for` command. It has the following structure:

```
for var in list
do
      commands
done
```

If you did not have any interaction with such a statement before, we will help you understand what it means. The variables provided through the `var` parameter are assigned with a series of values provided through the `list` parameter, in a series of iterations. At the start of the iteration, the variable is set with the current (or starting) value in the list. Each iteration will use another value from the list, until the last item in the list. The number of items in the list will set the number of iterations. For each iteration, the commands inside the `commands` block will be executed. This is a basic loop we described.

Let's see some basic uses of the `for` command. We will loop through a statically declared array. This means that we will not use the input from our user; instead, we will specify the array directly inside the script. We will use a temporary variable (or counter) called i to iterate through the entire length of the array. We use `${array[@]}` to specify the array's length. The loop will stop when the counter (i) reaches this length. The following figure shows the script's code, the commands used to run it, and the output. Keep in mind that we provided an array that had values already ordered. This is not a sorting algorithm:

```
packt@neptune:~$ nano array_loop_1.sh
packt@neptune:~$ cat array_loop_1.sh
#!/bin/bash
array=(0 1 2 3 4 5 6)
#looping through the entire array
for i in "${array[@]}"
do
        echo $i
done
```
```
packt@neptune:~$ chmod u+x array_loop_1.sh
packt@neptune:~$ ./array_loop_1.sh
0
1
2
3
4
5
6
```

Figure 8.24 – Iterating through an array using the for statement

In the following example, we will bring back the discussion on arrays and use some of them inside a `for` statement. This time, we will show you how to sort an array. We will use most of the structures we've already learned about, such as input reading, output formatting, arrays, and `for` statements.

> **Important note**
>
> Sorting algorithms are outside the scope of this book. We will only use one type of sort (bubble) to show you how to use arrays and `for` statements and how powerful Bash can be. However, if you plan on doing any serious programming while using the shell, we advise you to use another programming language that is more suited for this type of action, such as Python. Python is incredibly versatile and can successfully be used for many administrative tasks.

Let's get back to our sorting issue. Let's say we have a random array that we would like to sort. We will use an array that has integer elements only. To make things more interesting, we will prompt the user to introduce the array elements from the standard input. The following figure shows the code of the script:

```
packt@neptune:~$ cat array_bubble_sort.sh
#!/bin/bash
#asking for array length
echo "total array elements:"
read n
#asking user to provide the numbers
echo "enter numbers:"
for (( i = 0; i < $n; i++ ))
do
        read num[$i]
done
#start the sorting
for (( i = 0; i < $n; i++ ))
do
        for (( j = $i; j < $n; j++ ))
        do
                if [ ${num[$i]} -gt ${num[$j]} ]
                then
                        k=${num[$i]}
                        num[$i]=${num[$j]}
                        num[$j]=$k
                fi
        done
done
#print sorted array
printf "%s\n" "Sorted array is:"
for (( i = 0; i < $n; i++ ))
do
        echo ${num[$i]}
done
```

Figure 8.25 – Using the bubble sort algorithm to sort an array

Let's explain the code. We used a variable, n, to specify the length of the array. Then, we used this variable to iterate through all the numbers provided by the user. In the first for statement, we iterate through all the numbers and carefully increase the counter (with the I variable) by each step (the i++ structure). The numbers provided by the user are then stored inside an array called num. When the sorting starts, we use two nested for statements and one if statement. We make use of a new counter called j, which is used to store the value of a new consecutive number inside the array. The if statement compares which of two consecutive numbers inside the array is greater, thus performing the switch between the first two elements inside the array. To perform the switch, we use a temporary counter called k to keep the value of the greater number to make the switch between the two numbers that are being compared. The loop is finished when all the numbers have been cycled through. The final for statement prints the contents of the new, sorted array.

The user input and the output of the command are shown here:

```
packt@neptune:~$ ./array_bubble_sort.sh
total array elements:
3
enter numbers:
45
24
56
Sorted array is:
24
45
56
```

Figure 8.26 – Showing the input and output for our sorting script

In the preceding example, bubble sort is working as follows:

- The first step is to compare the first two elements in the array, which are 45 and 24, and see which is greater; 45 is greater than 24, so the new array will be 24   45 56 (the algorithm swaps between 45 and 24).

- The second step is to compare the next two elements, which are now 45 and 56 (because 45 was greater than 24 and is now in the second position; as 45 is not greater than 56, their position will remain unchanged).

- The third step is to do one more pass through all the elements and still do the comparison.

> **Important note**
> Bubble sort is not an efficient sorting algorithm, but it was a good example of how to use arrays, `for` and `if` statements, input from the user, and output formatting. For more information on the bubble sort algorithm or any other type of sorting algorithm, we would advise a thorough online search or that you read the titles we have provided in the *Further reading* section at the end of this chapter.

Now that you know how to use the `for` statement, let's proceed to the `while` statement.

Using the while statement

The `while` loop is similar to the `for` loop, with the difference that it is somehow also a combination of the `if` statement. So long as a condition is true, the loop is executing the commands. The syntax is as follows:

```
while condition
do
      commands
done
```

The condition is tested every time an iteration is started. If the condition remains true, the exit status is zero, and the commands are executed until the condition changes its status. Let's see some examples.

In the following script, we're using a `while` statement to go through a list of numbers in descending order:

```
packt@neptune:~$ cat while_loop_1.sh
#!/bin/bash
#asking the user for the maximum value
printf "Provide the maximum value: "
read max
#starting the loop
printf "Listing numbers in descending order... \n"
while [ $max -gt 0 ]
do
        printf " %s" $max
        max=$[ $max - 1 ]
done
printf "%s\n"
packt@neptune:~$ ./while_loop_1.sh
Provide the maximum value: 10
Listing numbers in descending order...
 10 9 8 7 6 5 4 3 2 1
packt@neptune:~$ ./while_loop_1.sh
Provide the maximum value: 30
Listing numbers in descending order...
 30 29 28 27 26 25 24 23 22 21 20 19 18 17 16 15 14 13 12 11 10 9 8 7 6 5 4 3 2
 1
```

Figure 8.27 – Using a while statement

The `while` statement will evaluate the `[ $max -gt 0 ]` condition and iterate until the condition is false. This means that so long as the number you provide is greater than (`-gt`) zero, the commands will be executed. The commands inside the `while` loop are simply decreasing the number with every iteration. Otherwise, you will end up in an infinite loop. Thus, the value of the max variable will be lower by one point every time the `while` loop executes. We tested with two values, once with 10 and again with 30; you can see the output in *Figure 8.27*.

The `while` statement is very useful and straightforward, being a great addition to the `for` statement. Now, let's see the `until` statement.

Using the until statement

This looping structure is the opposite of `while`. It uses a condition that is false from the start, and while the condition remains false, the commands inside the structure will be executed. The syntax is as follows:

```
until condition
do
      commands
done
```

For a very quick example, let's redo the `while` loop from the previous example by using the `until` statement this time. Here's the code:

```
packt@neptune:~$ cat until_loop_1.sh
#!/bin/bash
#asking the user for the maximum value
printf "Provide the maximum value: "
read max
#starting the loop
printf "Listing numbers in descending order... \n"
until [ $max -eq 0 ]
do
        printf " %s" $max
        max=$[ $max - 1 ]
done
printf "%s\n"
```

Figure 8.28 – An example of an until statement

Can you spot the differences between the `until` and `while` loops? In the case of `until`, the iteration continues until the value of the variable is equal to zero, `[ $max -eq 0 ]`. The commands inside the `until` loop are the same as the ones used inside the `while` loop. The condition is different. The output, as you might expect, is the same as when using a `while` loop.

Before we move on and learn about more advanced programming structures, we'll provide some basic information about controlling the execution of a loop by using specific keywords.

Exiting loop statements

The two commands that are used in Bash to exit loops are `break` and `continue`. They are relatively straightforward. Whenever you want to exit a loop, you can use one of them. Let's use a simple script that iterates through a series of integer numbers until a specified value is reached and it exits the iteration. Here is the code:

```
packt@neptune:~$ cat break_loop.sh
#!/bin/bash
echo "Enter maximum sequence: "
read max
echo "Enter break value: "
read brk
echo "Starting the iteration..."
for (( i = 0; i <= $max; i++ ))
do
        echo $i
        if [ $i -eq $brk ]
        then
                break
        fi
done
```

Figure 8.29 – Exiting a loop using the break command

When executing, the user is asked to introduce the maximum value for the sequence and the value of break. The for loop goes through the sequence until the value of break is reached, and it exits the loop. We used the break command to exit the loop and started the iteration from zero. You can test the outcome with different values. The following is the output when using a value of 10 for the maximum sequence and a value of 5 for break:

```
packt@neptune:~$ ./break_loop.sh
Enter maximum sequence:
10
Enter break value:
5
Starting the iteration...
0
1
2
3
4
5
```

Figure 8.30 – Output of using the break script example

As you can see, the loop exits after 5 is reached. However, it shows the value of 5, it does not skip it. This can be fixed (it is not necessarily an issue, more of an algorithm design decision). Let's look at the following code:

```
packt@neptune:~$ cat break_loop_2.sh
#!/bin/bash
echo "Enter maximum sequence: "
read max
echo "Enter break value: "
read brk
echo "Starting the iteration..."
for (( i = 0; i <= $max; i++ ))
do
        if [ $i -eq $brk ]
        then
                break
        fi
echo $i
done
```

Figure 8.31 – Breaking loop optimized

For the breaking value to not be shown, we moved the echo $i command after the conditional if-then statement. This will prevent the script from showing the breaking value provided by the user. Both use cases are valid and they provide the same output, so the position of the output printing command is only relevant to your needs.

In the following example, we will show you how to use the continue command to exit a loop. The algorithm is similar to the one used in the break example, except this time, the value provided by the user will not be shown in the output. The break command will exit the loop when a condition is met, whereas the continue command will skip the rest of the command execution that is present after the condition, when a certain condition is met, and will continue to the next iteration of the loop sequence. This difference is sufficient for you to understand the differences between break and continue. Let's see the code for the same script, using the continue command:

```
packt@neptune:~$ cat continue_loop.sh
#!/bin/bash
echo "Enter maximum sequence: "
read max
echo "Enter the value to skip: "
read skp
echo "Starting the iteration..."
for (( i = 0; i <= $max; i++ ))
do
        if [ $i -eq $skp ]
        then
                continue
        fi
echo $i
done
```

Figure 8.32 – Using the continue command inside a loop

As you can see, the code is similar to what was used in the previous example. The only difference is the use of the `continue` command instead of `break`. Now, let's see the output that's obtained:

```
packt@neptune:~$ ./continue_loop.sh
Enter maximum sequence:
10
Enter the value to skip:
5
Starting the iteration...
0
1
2
3
4
6
7
8
9
10
```

Figure 8.33 – The output when using the continue command

As shown in the preceding figure, the number 5 is not shown, meaning that the loop skipped it when the `continue` command is used.

You now know quite a bit about scripting in Linux. You know how to use variables, arrays, if and looping statements, and even exiting loops. In the next section, we will show you how to use more advanced programming structures, such as functions.

Working with functions

As in most programming languages, **functions** prove useful when you need to use the same blocks of code multiple times inside a program. By creating functions for specific uses, you can call them anywhere in your script. In Bash, there are two ways to create a function. First, you can use the `function` keyword, followed by the function's name, as shown in the following syntax:

```
function name {
    commands
}
```

Alternatively, you can use parentheses after the function's name, as shown in the following syntax:

```
name () {
    commands
}
```

The name from the syntax is a unique name that the function will use throughout the script. The commands are represented by one or more shell commands that are executed by the function in their order of appearance. Simplified, you can look at functions as scripts inside scripts. Let's see some examples.

With the risk of being redundant, we will use one of the scripts we already created and use it as a function, just to show you how functions work, for starters. We will use the script that sorts numbers in descending order and make it a function. But before that, let's give you a word of caution regarding functions.

> **Important note**
>
> Functions must be created before they are called. Calling a function is the process of running it inside a script. If you create the function after you call it, the script will give you an error because Bash is a single-pass interpreter. A good practice is to create the functions at the beginning of a script. This way, they will be available whenever they're needed throughout the script.

So, here it is – our first function is shown in the following screenshot. As you can see, first, we created the sorting function, and then we called it:

```
packt@neptune:~$ nano function_first.sh
packt@neptune:~$ chmod u+x function_first.sh
packt@neptune:~$ ./function_first.sh
We will run our first function now...
Provide the maximum value: 5
Sorting numbers in descending order...
 5 4 3 2 1
The function ended...
packt@neptune:~$ cat function_first.sh
#!/bin/bash
#this is our first function
sorting () {
        printf "Provide the maximum value: "
        read max
        printf "Sorting numbers in descending order... \n"
        while [ $max -gt 0 ]
        do
                printf " %s" $max
           .    max=$[ $max - 1 ]
        done
        printf "%s\n"
}
#provide a message before calling the function called "sorting"
echo "We will run our first function now... "
sorting
echo "The function ended... "
```

Figure 8.34 – Running our first function

At this point, you know how to create and call a function inside a shell script, but there is much more to this matter than just that. We will try and give you all the necessary information about functions so that you will be able to use them in your scripts, but if you want to learn more, please consider the titles provided in the *Further reading* section.

In the next section, we will walk you through different function capabilities, such as output, variables, and array handling.

Advanced function capabilities

Every function inside the Bash shell, as stated before, works like a script by itself. This means that it can manage variables, arrays, and output in the same way as a script. In this section, we will show you how to use variables, arrays, and output inside functions.

Using variables inside functions

Both types of variables (global and local) can be used inside functions. Let's provide an overview of the differences between these two types of variables. The global ones are visible and available throughout the system, while the local ones are only available inside the function where they were declared. By default, all variables in Bash are defined as global variables, including the ones defined inside functions. To declare local variables inside functions, we can use the `local` keyword. Let's see a basic example to understand how this works:

```
packt@neptune:~$ nano variables_1.sh
packt@neptune:~$ chmod u+x variables_1.sh
packt@neptune:~$ ./variables_1.sh
variables BEFORE the function are: var1=1, var2=2
variables INSIDE the function are: var1=11, var2=22
variables AFTER executing the function are: var1=1, var2=22
packt@neptune:~$
packt@neptune:~$ cat variables_1.sh
#!/bin/bash
var1='1'
var2='2'

var_function () {
        local var1='11'
        var2='22'
        echo "variables INSIDE the function are: var1=$var1, var2=$var2"
}
echo "variables BEFORE the function are: var1=$var1, var2=$var2"
var_function
echo "variables AFTER executing the function are: var1=$var1, var2=$var2"
```

Figure 8.35 – Showing how local and global variables work in functions

The preceding figure shows how the variables were declared. For example, first, we declared the `var1='1'` and `var2='2'` variables. By default, they are set as global variables. Then, inside the `var_function` function, we modified the values of the two variables, but for one of them, we used the `local` keyword to define it local to the function. For the other one, we did not use the same keyword – we defined it as we did before the function. Thus, when printing the variables to the standard output after the function is run, only `var2` will keep the value given to it inside the variable, compared to `var1`, which was declared locally and had a different value only inside the function.

Using arrays inside functions

Unlike variables, arrays inside functions are somewhat problematic. There are two scenarios to consider: one when you need to pass arrays from the script to the function, and one when you would need to pass an array from the function back to the script. In the first case, you can't use the array as a function parameter because only the first value of the array will be used by the function. Thus, the convenient way is to break the array and then rebuild it inside the function, even though it sounds and proves unpractical. In the second case, the practice of handling arrays is similar to the first scenario as the function will output the values in the correct order and the script will reassemble the value into an array. Let's see an example:

```
packt@neptune:~$ cat arrays_in_functions.sh
#!/bin/bash
test_function_1 () {
        local new_array_1
        new_array_1=("$@")
        echo "New array: ${new_array_1[*]}"
}

test_function_2 () {
        local array_2
        local new_array_2
        local i_values
        local i
        array_2=($(echo "$@"))
        new_array_2=($(echo "$@"))
        i_values=$[ $# ]
        for (( i = 1; i <= $i_values; i++ ))
        do
                new_array_2[$i]=${array_2[$i]}
        done
        echo ${new_array_2[*]}
}

original_array_1=("John" "Claude" "Mike" "Anna")
echo "The original array: ${original_array_1[*]}"
test_function_1 ${original_array_1[*]}

original_array_2=(1 2 3 4 5 6)
echo "The original second array: ${original_array_2[*]}"
elements=$(echo ${original_array_2[*]})
new_array_2=($(test_function_2 $elements))
echo "New second array: ${new_array_2[*]}"
```

Figure 8.36 – Using arrays inside functions

In the preceding example, we used two functions, one for each of the scenarios described at the beginning of this subsection. The `test_function_1` function inside the script shows the way we can pass array elements to the function. The `test_function_2` function shows how arrays are being returned from functions. Here's the output:

```
packt@neptune:~$ ./arrays_in_functions.sh
The original array: John Claude Mike Anna
New array: John Claude Mike Anna
The original second array: 1 2 3 4 5 6
New second array: 1 2 3 4 5 6
```

Figure 8.37 – Output of using arrays in functions

At this point, you've learned how to create scripts and how to use arrays, variables, programming structures, and functions. Now, it's time to learn how to use `sed` and `(g)awk` both at the command line and in scripts.

Using sed and (g)awk commands

Both `sed` and `(g)awk` are advanced tools that are used for manipulating text files. `sed` is a stream editor and `awk` is a programming language. We also use the `gawk` reference (thus the letter g used inside parentheses) as it is the GNU implementation of `awk`, offering more features and extensions. Let's learn how to use both of them at the command line.

Using sed at the command line

`sed` is more than a simple command. It is a data stream editor that edits files based on a strict set of rules supplied beforehand. Based on these rules, the command reads the file line by line and the data inside the file is then manipulated. `sed` is a non-interactive stream editor that makes changes based on a script, and in this respect, it is well suited for editing more files at once or for doing mundane repetitive tasks. The `sed` command's general syntax is as follows:

```
sed OPTIONS… [SCRIPT] [FILE…]
```

The `sed` command uses different script subcommands, and one of the common subcommands that's used is for text substitution. There are many other use cases that we will not discuss here, but if you feel the need to learn more about the `sed` tool, there are plenty of great materials online and in print. For example, the following link could be useful: `https://www.ibm.com/docs/en/aix/7.2?topic=s-sed-command`.

The common syntax that's used for text substitution is as follows:

```
sed 's/regex/replacement/flag'
```

Here are some examples of the most common use cases of sed:

- Replace one name with another inside a text file. For this example, we will use a new file called poem in our home directory. Inside it, we generated a random poem. The task is to replace the name Jane with Elane from within the file. The letter g, as a flag of the command, specifies that the operation should be global – that is, it should be applied to the entire text document. Here is the result:

```
packt@neptune:~$ cat poem
Jane, Jane,
Happy Birthday, Jane.
There is no shame,
You are as bright as a flame.
packt@neptune:~$ sed 's/Jane/Elane/g' poem
Elane, Elane,
Happy Birthday, Elane.
There is no shame,
You are as bright as a flame.
packt@neptune:~$
```

Figure 8.38 – Using the sed command to replace a string in a text file

If you check the original file using the cat command, you will see that sed only delivered the changed name result to the standard output and did not make any changes to the original file. To make the changes to the file permanent, you will have to use the -i attribute.

- In the following example, we're adding new spaces at the beginning of each line and redirecting the output to a new file. We're using the same poem file as before. The beginning of a file is represented by the ^ character:

```
packt@neptune:~$ cat poem
Jane, Jane,
Happy Birthday, Jane.
There is no shame,
You are as bright as a flame.
packt@neptune:~$ sed 's/^/ /g' poem > poem-spaces
packt@neptune:~$ cat poem-spaces
 Jane, Jane,
 Happy Birthday, Jane.
 There is no shame,
 You are as bright as a flame.
packt@neptune:~$
```

Figure 8.39 – Using sed to add spaces

- We will use `sed` to show only the second line from the `poem` file and to show all the lines except for *line 2*:

```
packt@neptune:~$ sed -n 2p poem
Happy Birthday, Jane.
packt@neptune:~$ sed 2d poem
Jane, Jane,
There is no shame,
You are as bright as a flame.
packt@neptune:~$ 
```

Figure 8.40 – Using sed to show specific lines in a file

- Let's show only *lines 4 to 6* from a file – in our case, the `/etc/passwd` file:

```
packt@neptune:~$ sed -n 4,6p /etc/passwd
sys:x:3:3:sys:/dev:/usr/sbin/nologin
sync:x:4:65534:sync:/bin:/bin/sync
games:x:5:60:games:/usr/games:/usr/sbin/nologin
packt@neptune:~$ 
```

Figure 8.41 – Using sed to show a specific number of lines in a text file

- Here is a more practical exercise. We will show the contents of `/etc/apt/sources.list` from Ubuntu without the commented lines. To do this, use the following command:

```
sed '/^#/g' /etc/apt/sources.list
```

This command deletes the lines inside the file that start with the hashtag (#) character, represented by the `^#` characters inside the command. Those are the comments inside the file. We also use the `g` flag to specify that the operation is global for that file. The following is part of the output provided by the command. Use it on your Ubuntu system and analyze your output as well:

```
packt@neptune:~$ sed '/^#/g' /etc/apt/sources.list


deb http://ro.archive.ubuntu.com/ubuntu jammy main restricted



deb http://ro.archive.ubuntu.com/ubuntu jammy-updates main restricted
```

Figure 8.42 – Use of sed to show only lines with no comments

In the following subsection, we will explore the `awk` command at the command line.

Using awk from the command line

awk is much more than a simple command – it is a pattern-matching language. It is a full-fledged programming language that was the base for PERL. It is used for data extraction from text files, with a syntax similar to C. It sees a file as being composed of fields and records. The general structure of the awk command is as follows:

```
awk '/search pattern 1/ {actions} /search pattern 2/ {actions}' file
```

The true power of awk is beyond the scope of this chapter, so we will show no more than one simple example of its use that could prove practical for a future system administrator.

As an example, we will generate a list containing the names of all the packages installed by Ubuntu. We only want to print the name of each package, not all the other details. For this, we will use the following command:

```
sudo dpkg -l | awk '{print $2}' > package-list
```

This command is only showing the names of the packages that have been installed. Here is the output:

```
packt@neptune:~$ sudo dpkg -l | awk '{print $2}' > package-list
packt@neptune:~$ tail package-list
wireless-regdb
xauth
xdg-user-dirs
xfsprogs
xkb-data
xxd
xz-utils
zerofree
zlib1g:amd64
zstd
packt@neptune:~$
```

Figure 8.43 – Using awk to generate a list of package names

Generally, to see the installed packages in Ubuntu, we would run the dpkg -l command. In the preceding example, we piped the output of that command to the awk command, which printed the second column (field) from the dpkg -l output ('{print $2}'). Then, we redirected everything to a new file called package-list and used the tail command to see the last 10 lines of the newly created file.

Both sed and awk are very powerful tools, and we have merely scratched the surface of what they can do. Please feel free to dig deeper into these two awesome tools.

Using scripts to showcase interprocess communication

Interprocess communication (IPC) was introduced in *Chapter 5*. In this chapter, we will revisit the mechanism that can make use of scripts. To illustrate most of these communication mechanisms, we will build our examples using a model of **producer** and **consumer** processes. The producer and consumer share a common interface, where the producer writes some data that's read by the consumer. IPC mechanisms are usually implemented in distributed systems, built around more or less complex applications. Our examples will use simple **Bash scripts** (`producer.sh` and `consumer.sh`), thus mimicking the producer and consumer processes. We hope that the use of such simple models will still provide a reasonable analogy for real-world applications.

Now, let's look at shared storage, named and unnamed pipes, and sockets IPC mechanisms, all of which we introduced in *Chapter 5* but did not cover in detail.

Shared storage

In its simplest form, the **shared storage** of an IPC mechanism can be a simple file that's been saved to disk. The **producer** then writes to a file while the **consumer** reads from the same file. The producer and consumer data feeds are identical at any time. The two processes communicate via the shared `storage` file.

In this simple use case, the obvious challenge is the integrity of the read/write operations due to possible race conditions between the underlying operations. To avoid race conditions, the file must be locked during write operations to prevent overlapping I/O with another read or write action. To keep things simple, we're not going to resolve this problem in our naive examples, but we thought it's worth calling it out.

In our example, the producer writes a new set of data (`10` random UUID strings) every `5` seconds to the `storage` file. The following screenshot shows the producer's script:

```
packt@neptune:~$ cat producer.sh
#!/bin/bash
# producer.sh
STORAGE_FILE="./storage"
rm -f "${STORAGE_FILE}"
while true
do
        for (( i=1; i<=10; i++ ))
        do
                uid="$(uuidgen)"
                echo "${uid}"
                echo "${uid}" >> "${STORAGE_FILE}"
        done
        sleep 5s
done
```

Figure 8.44 – The producer script (using shared storage)

The consumer reads the content of the storage file every second. The following screenshot shows the consumer's script:

```
packt@neptune:~$ cat consumer.sh
#!/bin/bash
# consumer.sh
STORAGE_FILE="./storage"
while true
do
        while IFS= read -r line
        do
                echo "${line}"
        done < "${STORAGE_FILE}"
        sleep 1s
done
```

Figure 8.45 – The consumer script (using shared storage)

When running both scripts, the producer creates random strings and writes them to the storage file, and the consumer reads the producer's output from the same file. The output is shown in the following screenshot:

```
packt@neptune:~$ ./producer.sh          packt@neptune:~$ ./consumer.sh
47933b36-8ba6-422f-ba5f-5c8a927063d4 47933b36-8ba6-422f-ba5f-5c8a927063d4
305d29ad-fb28-453f-923e-7d97fa3f92f2 305d29ad-fb28-453f-923e-7d97fa3f92f2
e2da37d4-c839-4726-aff5-605aa9b07320 e2da37d4-c839-4726-aff5-605aa9b07320
72eadfef-574c-44b8-8627-4578ec8754e0 72eadfef-574c-44b8-8627-4578ec8754e0
7b014f35-b1e9-4737-bfd8-218fb742a8cc 7b014f35-b1e9-4737-bfd8-218fb742a8cc
ad8ec66e-0abe-43a9-a746-4e349d2e6dc9 ad8ec66e-0abe-43a9-a746-4e349d2e6dc9
6587ddcf-413c-421a-bc20-8ce88ce97ab4 6587ddcf-413c-421a-bc20-8ce88ce97ab4
d358483c-bfec-41fd-bfd4-d5f6ab338ba0 d358483c-bfec-41fd-bfd4-d5f6ab338ba0
9d8b7b02-9110-420b-ae0b-e0dde6cae9b5 9d8b7b02-9110-420b-ae0b-e0dde6cae9b5
5a946109-f4db-4146-b360-9299fb8b60cd 5a946109-f4db-4146-b360-9299fb8b60cd
^C                                      ^C
```

Figure 8.46 – The producer (left) and consumer (right) communicating through shared storage

Next, we will show you how unnamed pipes work.

Unnamed pipes

Unnamed or **anonymous** pipes, also known as **regular** pipes, feed the output of a process to the input of another one. Using our producer-consumer model, the simplest way to illustrate an unnamed pipe as an IPC mechanism between the two processes would be to do the following:

```
producer.sh | consumer.sh
```

The key element of the preceding illustration is the pipe (|) symbol. The left-hand side of the pipe produces an output that's fed directly to the right-hand side of the pipe for consumption. To accommodate the anonymous pipe IPC layer, we'll make two new scripts called `producer2.sh` and `consumer2.sh`. The code is shown in the following screenshot:

```
packt@neptune:~$ cat producer2.sh   packt@neptune:~$ cat consumer2.sh
#!/bin/bash                          #!/bin/bash
# producer 2                         # consumer 2
for (( i=1; i<=10; i++ ))            echo "Consumer data:"
do                                   echo "--------------"
        uid="$(uuidgen)"             if [ -t 0 ]
        echo "${uid}"                then
done                                         data="$*"
                                     else
                                             data=$(cat)
                                     fi
                                     echo "${data}"
```

Figure 8.47 – The producer2 (left) and consumer2 (right) scripts (using an unnamed pipe)

In our modified implementation, `producer2.sh` prints some data to the console (10 random UUID strings). `consumer2.sh` reads and displays either the data coming through the `/dev/stdin` pipe or the input arguments if the pipe is empty. *Line 6* in the `consumer2.sh` script checks the presence of piped data in `/dev/stdin` (0 for fd0):

```
if [ -t 0 ]
```

The output of the producer-consumer communication is shown in the following screenshot:

```
packt@neptune:~$ ./producer2.sh | ./consumer2.sh
Consumer data:
--------------
53ae71f3-2dc7-4304-b138-3ab67bc54284
a1e83d30-481c-4f10-ae1a-2530d451d2ed
6e8d3b09-74f1-4def-9db3-8fe9e34c6fc5
fcd3eae2-8e3c-4c19-92a9-d488b07de776
7088c4e7-2052-4350-b5f5-1da63ebb1daf
851387ad-e6b4-4e4b-8b66-8eb4ce93fcea
a361088d-cd38-40ca-8590-102f81aece43
b4691268-2a5e-43fb-b13b-74d01045fb48
cab386ef-39fb-4d00-990f-bb2ae3977994
8c35e22b-ed4e-47fe-b67c-f9198919ccfe
```

Figure 8.48 – The producer feeding data into a consumer through an unnamed pipe

The output clearly shows the data being printed out by the consumer process. (Note the "Consumer data:" header preceding the UUID strings.)

One of the problems with IPC anonymous pipes is that the data that's fed between the producer and consumer is not persisted through any kind of storage layer. If the producer or consumer processes are terminated, the pipe is gone, and the underlying data is lost. Named pipes solve this problem, as we will show you in the next section.

Named pipes

Named pipes, also known as **First In, First Outs (FIFOs)**, are similar to traditional (unnamed) pipes but substantially different in terms of their semantics. An unnamed pipe only persists for as long as the related process is running. However, a named pipe has backing storage and will last so long as the system is up, regardless of the running status of the processes attached to the related IPC channel.

Typically, a named pipe acts as a file, and it can be deleted when it's no longer being used. Let's modify our producer and consumer scripts so that we can use a named pipe as their IPC channel:

```
packt@neptune:~$ cat producer3.sh          packt@neptune:~$ cat consumer3.sh
#!/bin/bash                                 #!/bin/bash
# producer 3                                # consumer 3
PIPE="pipe.fifo"                            PIPE="pipe.fifo"
if [[ ! -p ${PIPE} ]]                       if [[ ! -p ${PIPE} ]]
then                                        then
        mkfifo ${PIPE}                              mkfifo ${PIPE}
fi                                          fi
while true                                  while true
do                                          do
        for (( i=1; i<=10; i++ ))                   if read line <${PIPE}
        do                                          then
                uid="$(uuidgen)"                            echo "${line}"
                echo "${uid}"                       fi
                echo "${uid}" > "${PIPE}"   done
                sleep 1s
        done
done
```

Figure 8.49 – The producer3 (left) and consumer3 (right) scripts (using named pipe)

The named pipe is pipe.fifo (*line 3* in both scripts). The pipe file is created (if it's not already present) by either the producer or consumer when they start (*line 6*). The related command is mkfifo (see man mkfifo for more information).

The producer writes a random UUID to the named pipe every second (*line 14* in `producer3.sh`), where the consumer immediately reads it (*lines 10* to *12* in `consumer3.sh`):

```
packt@neptune:~$ ./producer3.sh
fafeea38-6e27-4895-8fa8-843d7ff08e0a
171feaa4-42e0-4cca-98bc-2ba38efb69e3
3e25d71d-041f-49a7-8156-bf3fbca58c64
9419ac87-3240-45ed-a8d4-cfea4d79be73
523f08db-54f9-488a-b3be-71de843ed16e
33758560-80b1-41df-82b9-8bf265c5807c
27881ee1-a728-47f4-9c3c-8aa51c291d7f
0b7007ac-9de3-4a6c-9fca-889ea232a941
^C
packt@neptune:~$ ./producer3.sh
0287a341-df1b-4f2e-ba32-723eb9fea3f8
932258fb-e6e7-4962-856d-e148f0878d63
537c482e-d571-4248-9153-8e2996530bf0
1ae8ac95-7b09-46bc-a91d-cd227d58c38d
8bc05d85-adce-47a5-bf23-a78bd9a4b705
56ec1ef6-be90-40e9-b6c2-96f9e26e92fc
4deb3b0e-6415-4e2d-9cef-fccd9e6d5d4a
^C
packt@neptune:~$
```

```
packt@neptune:~$ ./consumer3.sh
fafeea38-6e27-4895-8fa8-843d7ff08e0a
171feaa4-42e0-4cca-98bc-2ba38efb69e3
3e25d71d-041f-49a7-8156-bf3fbca58c64
9419ac87-3240-45ed-a8d4-cfea4d79be73
523f08db-54f9-488a-b3be-71de843ed16e
33758560-80b1-41df-82b9-8bf265c5807c
27881ee1-a728-47f4-9c3c-8aa51c291d7f
^C
packt@neptune:~$ ./consumer3.sh
0287a341-df1b-4f2e-ba32-723eb9fea3f8
932258fb-e6e7-4962-856d-e148f0878d63
537c482e-d571-4248-9153-8e2996530bf0
1ae8ac95-7b09-46bc-a91d-cd227d58c38d
8bc05d85-adce-47a5-bf23-a78bd9a4b705
56ec1ef6-be90-40e9-b6c2-96f9e26e92fc
4deb3b0e-6415-4e2d-9cef-fccd9e6d5d4a
d8cba6c3-45e9-4af0-b5c4-160a645a076a
```

Figure 8.50 – producer3 (left) and consumer3 (right) communicating through a named pipe

We started both scripts – the producer and the consumer – in an arbitrary order. After a while, we stopped (interrupted) the consumer (*step 1*). The producer continued to run but automatically stopped sending data to the pipe. Then, we started the consumer again. The producer immediately resumed sending data to the pipe. After a while, we stopped the producer (*step 2*). This time, the consumer became idle. After starting the producer again, both resumed normal operation, and data began flowing through the named pipe. This workflow has shown the persistence and resilience of the named pipe, regardless of the running status of the producer or consumer processes.

Named pipes are essentially queues, where data is queued and dequeued on a first-come-first-served basis. When more than two processes communicate on the IPC named pipe channel, the FIFO approach may not fit the bill, especially when specific processes demand a higher priority for data processing. Next, we will show you how sockets work.

Sockets

There are two types of IPC **socket-based facilities**:

- **IPC sockets**: Also known as Unix domain sockets
- **Network sockets**: **Transport Control Protocol** (**TCP**) and **User Datagram Protocol** (**UDP**) sockets

IPC sockets use a local file as a **socket address** and enable bidirectional communication between processes on the same host. On the other hand, **network sockets** extend the IPC data connectivity layer beyond the local machine via TCP/UDP networking. Apart from the obvious implementation differences, the IPC socket's and network socket's data communication channels behave the same.

Both sockets are configured as streams, support bidirectional communication, and emulate a client/server pattern. The socket's communication channel is active until it's closed on either end, thereby breaking the IPC connection.

Let's adapt our producer-consumer model to simulate an IPC socket (Unix domain socket) data connectivity layer. We'll use netcat to handle the underlying client/server IPC socket's connectivity. netcat is a powerful networking tool for reading and writing data using TCP, UDP, and ICP socket connections. If netcat is not installed by default on your Linux distribution of choice, you may look to install it as follows.

On Ubuntu/Debian, use the following command:

```
sudo apt install netcat
```

On Fedora/RHEL, use the following command:

```
sudo dnf install nmap
```

For more information about netcat, please refer to the related system reference manual (man netcat).

In the following example, we will use a producer4.sh file and a consumer4.sh file. The code for each file is shown in the following screenshot:

```
packt@neptune:~$ cat producer4.sh          packt@neptune:~$ cat consumer4.sh
#!/bin/bash                                 #!/bin/bash
# producer 4                                # consumer 4
SOCKET="/var/tmp/ipc.sock"                  SOCKET="/var/tmp/ipc.sock"
rm -rf "${SOCKET}"                          nc -U "${SOCKET}"
while true
do
        uuidgen;
        sleep 1s;
done | tee /dev/tty | nc -lU "${SOCKET}"
```

Figure 8.51 – The producer4 (left) and consumer4 (right) scripts (using IPC sockets)

The producer acts as the server by initiating a netcat listener endpoint using an IPC socket (the last line in producer4.sh):

```
nc -lU "${SOCKET}"
```

The `-l` option indicates the listener (server) mode, while the `-U "${SOCKET}"` option parameter specifies the IPC socket type (Unix domain socket). The consumer connects to the `netcat` server endpoint as a client with a similar command (the last line in `consumer4.sh`). The producer and consumer both use the same (shared) IPC socket file descriptor (`/var/tmp/ipc.sock`) for communication.

The producer sends random UUID strings every second to the consumer (the `while-do-done` structure in `producer4.sh`). The related output is captured in `stdout` with the `tee` command before being piped to `netcat`:

```
packt@neptune:~$ ./producer4.sh
2eb91382-1a1f-428d-a5ed-2a9d5d25f81c
70ce94d6-d289-4b56-ae9e-aca5ff7e248a
9a2c764f-da76-44e7-a25d-4373e9749270
48511d35-f7c6-472a-9132-f427a39c8576
02814d87-fec6-47ac-95aa-3ecd8532f004
626c0e4c-af43-45fd-8af0-1a6ca1b41251
59f151d6-6ac5-4e3a-9061-cf38ffcfc7d0
60298054-944a-4c6c-8706-2490d020216d
1793b022-a82e-4791-9d1e-743315ea16a6
^C
packt@neptune:~$
```

```
packt@neptune:~$ ./consumer4.sh
nc: unix connect failed: Connection refused
nc: /var/tmp/ipc.sock: Connection refused
packt@neptune:~$ ./consumer4.sh
2eb91382-1a1f-428d-a5ed-2a9d5d25f81c
70ce94d6-d289-4b56-ae9e-aca5ff7e248a
9a2c764f-da76-44e7-a25d-4373e9749270
48511d35-f7c6-472a-9132-f427a39c8576
02814d87-fec6-47ac-95aa-3ecd8532f004
626c0e4c-af43-45fd-8af0-1a6ca1b41251
59f151d6-6ac5-4e3a-9061-cf38ffcfc7d0
60298054-944a-4c6c-8706-2490d020216d
1793b022-a82e-4791-9d1e-743315ea16a6
packt@neptune:~$
```

Figure 8.52 – producer4 (left) and consumer4 (right) communicating through an IPC socket

The consumer gets all the messages (UUIDs) that have been generated by the producer. To show you that the consumer listens, we first started the consumer script, which generated two errors, so long as the producer was not sending data through the socket. Once we started the producer script, the consumer started to receive data. When we interrupted the producer, the consumer stopped immediately.

In our producer-consumer model, we used `netcat` for the IPC socket communication layer. Alternatively, we could use `socat`, a similar networking tool. In the next section, we will show you a quick example of using a script for a specific Linux administrative task. As a bonus, we will also show you how to build applications from source.

Scripting for administrative tasks

Scripting in a Linux operating system is mainly useful when it can help with mundane administrative tasks. This way, you can automate your workflow in ways that will make your job easier and more enjoyable. There are many use cases of shell scripts, and we will only provide you with a quick and easy example, hoping that it will suffice for understanding how a script can be used for a sysadmin task.

In the following sections, we will show you how to build a distribution-specific package from a source. This is something that should have been presented to you in *Chapter 4*, but at that time, you did not know how to create a script. In this chapter, we only used Ubuntu 22.04.2 LTS for our examples. In the following sections, we will use Fedora 37 Server Edition for our examples.

Creating scripts for system administrative tasks

In this section, we will show you a couple of scripts for administrative tasks. As we stated at the beginning of this chapter, a shell script is a sequence of Bash commands that are executed when the file is running. In the following subsections, we will create two scripts that will do two different administrative tasks.

An updating script example

This script will use the `dnf update` command to update the system at a specified time. It is a very basic script that runs just a simple command and shows some messages to standard output. Remember that we will be using a Fedora Server distribution this time. The simplest way would be to run the following command inside the script:

```
sudo dnf update -y
```

The issue is that it requires the `sudo` password. This defies the purpose of automation because the user must provide the password manually. Let's learn how to overcome this issue. First, let's see the code of the script:

```
[packt@saturn2 ~]$ cat /home/packt/update_script.sh
#!/bin/bash
# a simple update script
echo "Starting the update process..."
sudo dnf update -y
echo "System update is finished! Enjoy!"
```

Figure 8.53 – A simple update script

Now, if you want the command to be run without the `sudo` password, you will have to edit the `/etc/sudoers` file and modify/add some things.

> **Important note**
>
> Please take into consideration that this method will have system-wide effects, not only on the script you want to run. It is not considered a safe measure and we advise you to use it with extreme care and consideration on any production system.

Remove the comment before %wheel in the following line:

```
%wheel   ALL=(ALL)        NOPASSWD: ALL
```

This will provide a password-less action for every user that is in the wheel group. This should include the user you are using. If it wasn't inside the wheel group, you wouldn't be able to use sudo with it. In our case, the packt user is inside the wheel group. To test if it works, you can run the script as a regular user and see if the prompt for the sudo password will appear.

Now, we will have to schedule the script to run at a certain time. Don't forget to make your script file executable to be able to run it. As we are using a server distribution, we assume that this machine is running 24/7 without interruptions, so running at startup would make no sense. Furthermore, we want to ensure that the system is always up to date. To schedule the script, we will use cron and crontab. We will show you how they work in the next section.

Scheduling scripts in Linux with cron

Using crontab might look scary at first, but once you get to know it, you will find it very useful. Perhaps the most intimidating aspect of using cron jobs is the definition process, especially the **schedule** setup. However, a very useful example of how to set the cron date is provided inside the /etc/crontab file:

```
# Example of job definition:
# .--------------- minute (0 - 59)
# |  .------------- hour (0 - 23)
# |  |  .---------- day of month (1 - 31)
# |  |  |  .------- month (1 - 12) OR jan,feb,mar,apr ...
# |  |  |  |  .---- day of week (0 - 6) (Sunday=0 or 7) OR sun,mon,tue,wed,thu,fri,sat
# |  |  |  |  |
# *  *  *  *  * user-name  command to be executed
```

Figure 8.54 – Example of a cron job definition in /etc/crontab

We believe that the preceding screenshot is self-explanatory. Now, let's set up a new cron job for our updating script. We will use the crontab -e command. This command will use the default shell text editor, which in our case (in Fedora) is Vim. Running the crontab -e command will start a new Vim instance where the job should be written. Here is our code:

```
00 23 * * 0 packt /home/packt/update_script.sh
```

Let's explain this. In the preceding example, we set the new update script file to run at 23:00 every Sunday. The user that is running it is packt.

Once the line of code is created, you can check if the `cron` job was created by using the `crontab -l` command. If you want to see the `cron` jobs of certain users, you can use the following command:

```
sudo crontab -u packt -l
```

Here, `packt` is our user. The following snippet shows the code, which can be enhanced inside `crontab` with an output and error message redirection to `/dev/null`. This could be useful when we don't want to see the command's output or if any errors occur and we don't need to see them. The line would be modified as follows:

```
00 23 * * 0 packt /home/packt/update_script.sh > /dev/null 2>&1
```

`crontab` is a powerful tool that will prove of great help whenever you need to schedule tasks in Linux. However, it is not the only tool available for the job. Feel free to explore other tools available, such as the `at` command. Next, we will go through another short script for backing up files.

A backup script example

Another common use for scripting is for **backing up** files. We will create a new script for this task and we will schedule it according to our needs. The script's code is shown in the following screenshot:

```
[packt@saturn2 ~]$ cat backup_script.sh
#!/bin/bash
#which directories to backup
backup_dirs="/home/packt"
#destination
destination="/mnt/backup"
#the archive file
date_backup=$(date +"%Y-%m-%d")
hostname=$(hostname)
file="$date_backup-$hostname.tgz"
printf "%s\n" "Backing up $backup_dirs to $destination/$file"
#backing up with tar
tar czf $destination/$file $backup_dirs
printf "%s\n" "Backup finished..."
#listing the backup destination
ls -lh $destination
```

Figure 8.55 – A short backup script

The code is backing up the `/home/packt` directory to the `/mnt/backup` directory. The contents of `/home/packt` will be archived using the `tar` command and saved as `.tgz` files using the current date and hostname for the filename.

> **Important note**
>
> Using the date format can be daunting and intimidating at first, but knowing how to use it in your scripts will prove invaluable. Use the `date --help` command for more information.

In the next subsection, we will show you how to create a small random password generator in Bash.

A random password generator script

Keeping your online or local accounts secure is extremely important, so secure passwords should be used as a general rule. We will provide you with an example of a script that generates random passwords.

There are many password generators available to use in Linux, but we thought that it would be fun if you created such a small script by yourself. One default password-generating app available in Bash is pwmake, for example. However, we will create our own password-generating script. We will use openssl and an encoding mechanism called base64. For more information, go to https://developer.mozilla.org/en-US/docs/Glossary/Base64. Keep in mind that there are many other ways to generate random characters in Linux, one highly used being the /dev/urandom pseudo-random number generator. Feel free to explore as many ways as you like. In the meantime, here is our code for the password-generating script:

```
[packt@saturn2 ~]$ cat passgen_script.sh
#!/bin/bash
printf "\n"
printf "%s\n" "*** Random password generator ***"
printf "\n"
printf "%s" "Number of characters (we recommend >8): "
read n
printf "%s" "How many passwords you want to generate? "
read p
printf "\n"
for (( i=0 ; i<$p ; i++ ))
do
        if [ $n -le 8 ]
        then
                echo "The password is too short. Try again please!"
                exit 1
        else
                openssl rand -base64 $n
        fi
done
printf "\n"
```

Figure 8.56 – Password-generating script

When running the script, you will be prompted to provide the number of characters you want to use and the number of passwords to be generated:

```
*** Random password generator ***

Number of characters (we recommend >8): 12
How many passwords you want to generate? 2

f1YT+q3LpxmdYhsn
iXIQkZ+pLuglP8K2
```

Figure 8.57 – The output of running the password-generating script

Scripting is an invaluable task you should master. We barely scratched the surface of shell scripting, but the information in this chapter should give you a good start so that you can start developing sysadmin scripts.

In the next subsection, we will show you how to package your scripts into full-fledged apps that can be installed on the Linux command line. This is an addition to *Chapter 3*, where you learned about Linux package management.

Packaging scripts

Bash scripts are pieces of software like any other, so they can be deployed with Linux distributions as platform-specific packages. Just like you would package any other piece of software code, you can package a piece of shell scripting code. In this section, as an add-on to the knowledge you gathered in *Chapter 3*, we will show you how to package a Bash script. As stated before, the information provided here can easily be used for other software sources (usually, in Linux, there is C/C++, Python, Rust, Java, or Go). In the next subsection, we will show you how to create an RPM package for RHEL-based distributions. We will use Fedora Linux 37 in our example.

Creating RPM packages from source

To create an RPM package, we will use the password generator script we developed in the previous section. Before going into more details, we'll provide a short word on programming language types and where Bash fits in.

> **Important note**
>
> Usually, software programs are developed using human-readable source code. This code needs to be translated into machine code so that the computer will understand it. There are several large generic types of programming languages: **interpreted** (such as Python or Bash – which is a CLI language but still considered an interpreted language) and **compiled** (such as C/C++, Java, and Go) are the widely known ones. The Bash source code is executed line by line, without prior compilation into specific machine code. For more information, check out https://en.wikipedia.org/wiki/List_of_programming_languages_by_type.

Often, the software source code is distributed in the form of compressed archives (`.tar.gz` files or tarballs) that are then packaged into RPM packages. The archive usually consists of the source code file and a license file. This license file offers information about the type of license the software is distributed with. In the case of **free and open source software** (**FOSS**), the license is usually GPLv3 or GLPLv3, but other types such as the MIT license or Apache and BSD licenses are also used.

> **Important note**
>
> For detailed information on FOSS license types, check out `https://en.wikipedia.org/wiki/Comparison_of_free_and_open-source_software_licenses`.

The following are the necessary steps for creating an RPM package from a Bash script:

1. **Create a directory**: First, we will create a new directory where all the specific files will be stored. The directory will be named `passgen-0.1`.

2. **Create a license file**: For our Bash script, we will create a license file to use with the package. The file will be named `LICENSE.txt` and placed inside the newly created directory. We will use the GPLv3 open source license. The text to be added to your file can be found under the *How to Apply These Terms to Your New Programs* section at `https://www.gnu.org/licenses`.

3. **Move the Bash script inside the directory**: We will also copy the `passgen_script.sh` file inside the new directory and change its name to `passgen-0.1.sh`.

4. **Add the script to the system**: We will add the `passgen-0.1.sh` script to the Filesystem Hierarchy Standard `$PATH` using the `install` command. We use the `install` command because our simple Bash script does not need any dependencies:

    ```
    sudo install -m 0755 passgen-0.1.sh /usr/bin/passgen
    ```

    This will ensure that we can run the `passgen` script without using the full path.

5. **Create the tarball**: Once both the source code and the license files are ready, we will create a `tar.gz` archive with the following command:

    ```
    tar -cvzf passgen-0.1.tar.gz passgen-0.1.sh LICENSE.txt
    ```

6. **Install specific RPM packaging utilities**: To create RPM packages, we need some specific utilities, such as the `rpmdevtools` package. We can install it using the following command:

    ```
    sudo dnf install rpmdevtools
    ```

    This will install all additional packages and dependencies to set up the packaging workspace.

7. **Set up the workspace**: To set up the workspace, we will run the following application:

    ```
    rpmdev-setuptree
    ```

This will create a new `rpmbuild` directory and sub-directories inside your home directory. The new `rpmbuild` directory has the following structure:

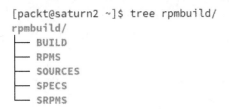

```
[packt@saturn2 ~]$ tree rpmbuild/
rpmbuild/
├── BUILD
├── RPMS
├── SOURCES
├── SPECS
└── SRPMS
```

Figure 8.58 – The rpmbuild's directory structure

The `BUILD` directory contains information about the build process; the `RPMS` directory contains binary RPMs; the `SOURCES` directory contains the tarball of the compressed source code; the `SPECS` directory contains the SPEC file; and the `SRPMS` directory contains source RPMs.

8. **Add the tarball to the ~/rpmbuild/SOURCES directory**: We will add the compressed file we created earlier to the `~/rpmbuild/SOURCES` directory with the following command (from within the `passgen-0.1` directory):

```
cp passgen-0.1.tar.gz ~/rpmbuild/SOURCES/
```

Now, the source file tarball is in the right place.

9. **Configure a new SPEC file**: First, we will create a new `SPEC` file by running the `rpmdev-newspec` command from inside the `~/rpmbuild/SPECS` directory:

```
rpmdev-newspec passgen
```

You can list the contents of the `~/rpmbuild/SPECS/` directory, after which you will see that a new file called `passgen.spec` was created.

The new `SPEC` file contains automatically generated lines with specific RPM macros defined. We will not get into much detail about macros, but you can find more information at `https://rpm-software-management.github.io/rpm/manual/macros.html`. As Bash is an interpreted language, some default specifications from the `SPEC` file are not needed, such as `BuildRequires`, which was deleted. For the `%build` section, we did not provide any information as Bash does not need anything specific. The `SPEC` file is shown in the following screenshot:

```
[packt@saturn2 SPECS]$ cat passgen.spec
Name:           passgen
Version:        0.1
Release:        %autorelease
Summary:        A bash password generator script

License:        GPLv3+
URL:            https://www.example.com/%{name}
Source0:        %{name}-%{version}.tar.gz
BuildRoot:      %(mktemp -ud %{_tmppath}/%{name}-%{version}-XXXXXX)

Requires:       bash

BuildArch:      noarch

%description
This is a longer description for the passwoed generator implemented in bash.

%prep
%setup -c

%build

%install
mkdir -p %{buildroot}/%{_bindir}
install -m 0755 %{name}-%{version}.sh %{buildroot}/%{_bindir}/%{name}

%files
%license LICENSE.txt
%{_bindir}/%{name}

%changelog
* Sun Apr 16 2023 packt
-
```

Figure 8.59 – The SPEC file's entries

10. **Build the RPM package**: The RPMs are built based on the specifications inside the SPEC file, but there are other use cases, such as building an RPM from a **source RPM (SRPM)**, for example. We will show you how to build a binary RPM from sources. In all of the cases outlined, the command to use is rpmbuild, but the options are different. When building source RPMs, we will use the -bs option, when rebuilding RPMs from source, we will use the --rebuild option, and when building binary RPMs from source, we will use the -bb option. In our case, we will create a binary from source and use the following command:

```
rpmbuild -bb ~/rpmbuild/SPECS/passgen.spec
```

The build was successful and we can verify if the new .rpm file was created. We can check this at ~/rpmbuild/RPMS/, where we will have a new directory based on the CPU architecture. In our case, we will have a new noarch directory that contains the .rpm file for our password generator. The following is the output:

```
[packt@saturn2 ~]$ tree ~/rpmbuild/RPMS/
/home/packt/rpmbuild/RPMS/
└── noarch
    └── passgen-0.1-1.fc37.noarch.rpm

2 directories, 1 file
```

Figure 8.60 – The new RPM binary package

Here you are, building your very first RPM binary package from a Bash script file! You can do this for any type of source file you might develop. Building binary packages is not a very difficult task, and with good documentation about the specifics of macros used in the SPEC file, you are good to go. More information about the available documentation on this matter can be found in the *Further reading* section.

Summary

In this chapter, you learned how to create Bash scripts in Linux. You now know about shell variables and script variables, as well as how to use programming structures such as loops, conditionals, and arrays inside scripts. You now further understand how interprocess communication works. The skills you have learned will help you create scripts in any Linux distribution. When you are creating scripts, you will put your text editor knowledge into action too. You will use the skills that you've learned regarding Bash scripting in many aspects of your everyday job as a system administrator too.

In the next chapter, you will learn how to manage security in Linux, the access control mechanisms, AppArmor and SELinux, and firewalls. This skill is important for any administrator and must be part of any advanced training.

Questions

In this chapter, we covered Linux Bash scripting. Here are some questions for you to test your knowledge and for further practice:

1. What are arrays and how are they used in Bash scripts? Can there be hybrid types?

   Hint: Think of their types, how they are defined, and how they are used.

2. What is an infinite loop?

   Hint: This is something you would not like to use but should know how to escape if needed.

3. How many types of loops can be used in a Bash script?

    Hint: Not that many, but more than conditional loops.

4. Find out how to build a DEB binary package.

    Hint: Use the examples from Debian, which can be found at `https://www.debian.org/doc/manuals/maint-guide/build.en.html` and `https://wiki.debian.org/HowToPackageForDebian`.

Further reading

For more information about what was covered in this chapter, please refer to the following resources:

- *Linux Administration Best Practices*, by Scott Alan Miller, published by Packt

- *Linux Command Line and Shell Scripting Techniques*, by Vedran Dakic and Jasmin Redzepagic, published by Packt

- Official documentation from `https://access.redhat.com/documentation/en-us/red_hat_enterprise_linux/9/html/packaging_and_distributing_software/index`, `https://docs.fedoraproject.org/en-US/packaging-guidelines/RPMMacros/` (RPM macros), and `rpm.org`

9

Securing Linux

Securing a Linux machine is usually a balancing act. The endgame is essentially protecting data from unwanted access. While there are many ways to achieve this goal, we should adopt the methods that yield maximum protection, along with the most efficient system administration. Gauging the attack and vulnerability surfaces, both internal and external, is always a good start. The rest of the work is building fences and putting on armor—not too high and not too heavy. The outer fence is a **network firewall**. Internally, at the system level, we build **application security policies**. This chapter introduces both, albeit the art of the balancing act is left to you.

In the first part of this chapter, we'll look at **access control mechanisms** (ACMs) and the related security modules—**Security-Enhanced Linux** (**SELinux**) and **AppArmor**. In the second part, we will explore packet filtering frameworks and firewall solutions.

After completing this chapter, you will have become acquainted with the tools for designing and managing application security frameworks and firewalls—a first solid step to securing a Linux system.

Here's a brief overview of the topics that will be covered in this chapter:

- Understanding Linux security—An overview of the ACMs available in the Linux kernel

- Introducing SELinux—An in-depth look at the Linux kernel security framework for managing access control policies

- Introducing AppArmor—A relatively new security module that controls application capabilities based on security profiles

- Working with firewalls—A comprehensive overview of firewall modules, including **Netfilter**, `iptables`, `nftables`, `firewalld`, and the **Uncomplicated Firewall** (`ufw`)

Technical requirements

This chapter covers a relatively vast array of topics, some of which will be covered with extensive command-line operations. We recommend that you use both a Fedora and an Ubuntu platform with Terminal or SSH access. Direct console access to the systems is highly preferable due to the possibly disruptive way of altering firewall rules.

Understanding Linux security

One significant consideration for securing a computer system or network is the means for system administrators to control how users and processes can access various resources, such as files, devices, and interfaces, across systems. The Linux kernel provides a handful of such mechanisms, collectively referred to as ACMs. Let's describe them briefly:

- **Discretionary access control (DAC)** is the typical ACM related to filesystem objects, including files, directories, and devices. Such access is at the discretion of the object's owner when managing permissions. DAC controls access to *objects* based on the identity of users and groups (*subjects*). Depending on a subject's access permissions, they could also pass permissions to other subjects —an administrator managing regular users, for example.

- **Access control lists (ACLs)** provide control over which subjects (such as users and groups) have access to specific filesystem objects (such as files and directories).

- **Mandatory access control (MAC)** provides different access control levels to subjects over the objects they own. Unlike DAC, where users have full control over the filesystem objects they own, MAC adds additional labels, or categories, to all filesystem objects. Consequently, subjects must have the appropriate access to these categories to interact with the objects labeled as such. MAC is enforced by *SELinux* on **Red Hat Enterprise Linux** (**RHEL**)/Fedora and *AppArmor* on Ubuntu/Debian/openSUSE.

- **Role-based access control (RBAC)** is an alternative to the permission-based access control of filesystem objects. Instead of permissions, a system administrator assigns *roles* that have access to a specific filesystem object. Roles could be based on some business or functional criteria and may have different access levels to objects.

  In contrast to DAC or MAC, where subjects have access to objects based strictly on the permissions involved, the RBAC model represents a logical abstraction over MAC or DAC, where the subjects must be members of a specific group or role before interacting with objects.

- **Multi-level security (MLS)** is a specific MAC scheme where the *subjects* are processes and the *objects* are files, sockets, and other similar system resources.

- **Multi-category security (MCS)** is an improved version of SELinux that allows users to label files with *categories*. MCS reuses much of the MLS framework in SELinux.

Wrapping up our brief discussion on ACMs, we should note that we covered some of the internals of DAC and ACL in *Chapter 4, Managing Users and Groups*, particularly in the *Managing permissions* section.

Next, we'll turn our attention to SELinux—a first-class citizen for MAC implementations.

Introducing SELinux

SELinux is a security framework in the Linux kernel for managing the access control policies of system resources. It supports a combination of the MAC, RBAC, and MLS models that were described in the previous section. SELinux is a set of kernel-space security modules and user-space command-line utilities, and it provides a mechanism for system administrators to have control over *who* can access *what* on the system. SELinux is designed to also protect a system against possible misconfigurations and potentially compromised processes.

SELinux was introduced by the **National Security Agency** (**NSA**) as a collection of **Linux Security Modules** (**LSM**) with kernel updates. SELinux was eventually released to the open source community in 2000 and became part of Linux starting with the 2.6 kernel series in 2003.

So, how does SELinux work? We'll look at this in the next section. We will use Fedora 37 Server Edition for all our examples.

Working with SELinux

SELinux uses **security policies** to define various access control levels for applications, processes, and files on a system. A security policy is a set of rules describing what can or cannot be accessed.

SELinux operates with **subjects** and **objects**. When a specific application or process (the *subject*) requests access to a file (the *object*), SELinux checks the required permissions involved in the request and enforces the related access control. The permissions for subjects and objects are stored in a lookup table known as the **Access Vector Cache** (**AVC**). The AVC is generated based on the **SELinux policy database**.

A typical SELinux policy consists of the following resources (files), each reflecting a specific aspect of the security policy:

- **Type enforcement**: Actions that have been granted or denied for the policy (such as read or write access to a file)
- **Interface**: The application interface the policy interacts with (such as logging)
- **File contexts**: The system resources associated with the policy (such as log files)

These policy files are compiled together using SELinux build tools to produce a specific **security policy**. The policy is loaded into the kernel, added to the SELinux policy database, and made active without a system reboot.

When creating SELinux policies, we usually test them in *permissive* mode first, where violations are logged but still allowed. When violations occur, the `audit2allow` utility in the SELinux toolset comes to the rescue. We use the log traces produced by `audit2allow` to create additional rules required by the policy to account for legitimate access permissions. SELinux violations are logged in `/var/log/messages` and are prefixed with `avc: denied`.

Before we learn how to create and manage a SELinux security policy, let's look at some higher-level operations for managing and controlling SELinux in everyday administration tasks.

Understanding SELinux modes

SELinux is either *enabled* or *disabled* in a system. When enabled, it operates in either of the following modes:

- `enforcing`: SELinux effectively monitors and controls security policies. In RHEL/Fedora, this mode is enabled by default.

- `permissive`: Security policies are actively monitored without enforcing access control. Policy violations are logged in `/var/log/messages`.

When SELinux is disabled, security policies are neither monitored nor enforced. The following command retrieves the current status of SELinux on the system:

```
sestatus
```

The output is as follows:

```
[packt@saturn2 ~]$ sestatus
SELinux status:                 enabled
SELinuxfs mount:                /sys/fs/selinux
SELinux root directory:         /etc/selinux
Loaded policy name:             targeted
Current mode:                   enforcing
Mode from config file:          enforcing
Policy MLS status:              enabled
Policy deny_unknown status:     allowed
Memory protection checking:     actual (secure)
Max kernel policy version:      33
```

Figure 9.1 – Getting the current status of SELinux

When SELinux is enabled, the following command retrieves the current mode:

```
getenforce
```

In `permissive` mode, we get the `enforcing` output.

To change from `enforcing` to `permissive` mode, we can run the following command:

```
sudo setenforce 0
```

The `getenforce` command will display `permissive` in this case. To switch back into `enforcing` mode, we can run the following command:

```
sudo setenforce 1
```

The SELinux mode can also be set by editing the `SELINUX` value in `/etc/selinux/config`. Possible values are documented in the configuration file.

> **Important note**
> Manually editing the SELinux configuration file requires a system reboot for changes to take effect.

With SELinux enabled, a system administrator may choose between the following SELinux policy levels by modifying the `SELINUXTYPE` value in `/etc/selinux/config`: `targeted`, `minimum`, and `mls`. The corresponding values are documented in the configuration file.

> **Important note**
> The default SELinux policy setting is `targeted`, and it's generally recommended not to change this setting, except for `mls`.

With the `targeted` policy in place, only processes that are specifically configured to use SELinux security policies can run in a *confined* (or restricted) domain. Such processes usually include system daemons (such as `dhcpd` and `sshd`) and well-known server applications (such as Apache and PostgreSQL). All other (non-targeted) processes run unrestricted and are usually labeled with the `unconfined_t` domain type.

To completely disable SELinux, we can edit the `/etc/selinux/config` file using a text editor of our choice (such as `sudo nano /etc/selinux/config`) and make the following change:

```
SELINUX=disabled
```

Alternatively, we can run the following command to change the SELinux mode from `enforcing` to `disabled`:

```
sudo sed -i 's/SELINUX=enforcing/SELINUX=disabled/g' /etc/selinux/
config
```

We can retrieve the current configuration with the following command:

```
cat /etc/selinux/config
```

With SELinux disabled, we get the following output (excerpt):

```
SELINUX=disabled
# SELINUXTYPE= can take one of these three values:
#      targeted - Targeted processes are protected,
#      minimum - Modification of targeted policy. Only selected processes are protect
ed.
#      mls - Multi Level Security protection.
SELINUXTYPE=targeted
```

Figure 9.2 – Disabling SELinux

We need to reboot the system for changes to take effect:

```
sudo systemctl reboot
```

Next, let's examine how access control decisions are made by introducing **SELinux contexts**.

Understanding SELinux contexts

With SELinux enabled, processes and files are labeled with a **context** containing additional SELinux-specific information, such as *user*, *role*, *type*, and *level* (optional). The context data serves for SELinux access control decisions.

SELinux adds the -Z option to the ls, ps, and other commands, thus displaying the security context of filesystem objects, processes, and more.

Let's create an arbitrary file and examine the related SELinux context:

```
touch afile
ls -Z afile
```

The output is as follows:

```
[packt@saturn2 ~]$ touch afile
[packt@saturn2 ~]$ ls -Z afile
unconfined_u:object_r:user_home_t:s0 afile
```

Figure 9.3 – Displaying the SELinux context of a file

The SELinux context has the following format—a sequence of four fields, separated by a colon (:):

```
USER:ROLE:TYPE:LEVEL
```

Now, let's take a look at the SELinux context fields:

- **SELinux user**: The SELinux user is an identity known to the policy that's authorized for a specific set of roles and has a particular level that's designated by an MLS/MCS range (see *SELinux level* in this list for more details). Every Linux user account is mapped to a corresponding SELinux user identity using an SELinux policy. This mechanism allows regular Linux users to inherit the policy restrictions associated with SELinux users.

  A process owned by a Linux user receives the mapped SELinux user's identity to assume the corresponding SELinux roles and levels.

  The following command displays a list of mappings between Linux accounts and their corresponding SELinux user identities. The command requires superuser privileges. Also, the `semanage` utility is available with the `policycoreutils` package, which you may need to install on your system:

  ```
  sudo semanage login -l
  ```

  The command yields the following output. The output may differ slightly from system to system:

  ```
  [packt@saturn2 ~]$ sudo semanage login -l

  Login Name          SELinux User          MLS/MCS Range          Service

  __default__         unconfined_u          s0-s0:c0.c1023         *
  root                unconfined_u          s0-s0:c0.c1023         *
  ```

  Figure 9.4 – Displaying the SELinux user mappings

  For more information on the `semanage` command-line utility, you may refer to the related system reference (`man semanage`, `man semanage-login`).

- **SELinux roles**: SELinux roles are part of the RBAC security model, and they are essentially RBAC attributes. In the SELinux context hierarchy, users are authorized for roles, and roles are authorized for types or domains. In the SELinux context terminology, **types** refer to filesystem object types and **domains** refer to process types (see more under *SELinux type* in this list).

  Take Linux processes, for example. The SELinux role serves as an intermediary access layer between domains and SELinux users. An *accessible* role determines which domain (that is, processes) can be accessed through that role. Ultimately, this mechanism controls which object types can be accessed by the process, thus minimizing the surface for privilege escalation attacks.

- **SELinux type**: The SELinux type is an attribute of SELinux *type enforcement*—a MAC security construct. For SELinux types, we refer to domains as process types and types as filesystem object types. SELinux security policies control how specific types can access each other—either with domain-to-type access or domain-to-domain interactions.

- **SELinux level**: The SELinux level is an attribute of the MLS/MCS schema and an optional field in the SELinux context. A level usually refers to the security clearance of a subject's access control to an object. Levels of clearance include `unclassified`, `confidential`, `secret`, and `top-secret` and are expressed as a **range**. An MLS range represents a pair of levels, defined as `low-high` if the levels differ or just `low` if the levels are identical. For example, a level of `s0-s0` is the same as `s0`. Each level represents a *sensitivity-category* pair, with categories being optional. When a category is specified, the level is defined as `sensitivity:category-set`; otherwise, it's defined as `sensitivity` only.

We are now familiar with SELinux contexts. We'll see them in action, starting with the SELinux contexts for users, next.

SELinux contexts for users

The following command displays the SELinux context associated with the current user:

```
id -Z
```

In our case, the output is as follows:

```
[packt@saturn2 ~]$ id -Z
unconfined_u:unconfined_r:unconfined_t:s0-s0:c0.c1023
```

Figure 9.5 – Displaying the current user's SELinux context

In RHEL/Fedora, Linux users are `unconfined` (unrestricted) by default, with the following context fields:

- `unconfined_u`: User identity
- `unconfined_r`: Role
- `unconfined_t`: Domain affinity
- `s0-s0`: MLS range (the equivalent of `s0`)
- `c0.c1023`: Category set, representing all categories (from `c0` to `c1023`)

Next, we'll examine the SELinux context for processes.

SELinux contexts for processes

The following command displays the SELinux context for current SSH processes:

```
ps -eZ | grep sshd
```

The command yields the following output:

```
[packt@saturn2 ~]$ ps -eZ | grep sshd
system_u:system_r:sshd_t:s0-s0:c0.c1023 794 ?    00:00:00 sshd
system_u:system_r:sshd_t:s0-s0:c0.c1023 910 ?    00:00:00 sshd
unconfined_u:unconfined_r:unconfined_t:s0-s0:c0.c1023 924 ? 00:00:00 sshd
```

Figure 9.6 – Displaying the SELinux context for SSH-related processes

From the output, we can infer that the first line refers to the sshd server process, which is running with the system_u user identity, system_r role, and sshd_t domain affinity. The second line refers to the current user's SSH session, hence the unconfined context. System daemons are usually associated with the system_u user and system_r role.

Before concluding this section on SELinux contexts, we'll examine the relatively common scenario of SELinux domain transitions, which is where a process in one domain accesses an object (or process) in a different domain.

SELinux domain transitions

Assuming an SELinux-secured process in one domain requests access to an object (or another process) in a different domain, SELinux **domain transitions** come into play. Unless there's a specific security policy allowing the related domain transition, SELinux would deny access.

An SELinux-protected process transitioning from one domain into another invokes the entrypoint type of the new domain. SELinux evaluates the related entrypoint permission and decides if the soliciting process can enter the new domain.

To illustrate a domain transition scenario, we will take the simple case of using the passwd utility when users change their password. The related operation involves the interaction between the passwd process and the /etc/shadow (and possibly /etc/gshadow) file(s). When the user enters (and reenters) the password, passwd would hash and store the user's password in /etc/shadow.

Let's examine the SELinux domain affinities involved:

```
ls -Z /usr/bin/passwd
ls -Z /etc/shadow
```

The corresponding output is as follows:

```
[packt@saturn2 ~]$ ls -Z /usr/bin/passwd
system_u:object_r:passwd_exec_t:s0 /usr/bin/passwd
[packt@saturn2 ~]$
[packt@saturn2 ~]$ ls -Z /etc/shadow
system_u:object_r:shadow_t:s0 /etc/shadow
```

Figure 9.7 – Comparing the domain affinity context

The `passwd` utility is labeled with the `passwd_exec_t` type, while `/etc/shadow` is labeled with `shadow_t`. There must be a specific security policy chain that allows the related domain to transition from `passwd_exec_t` to `shadow_t`; otherwise, `passwd` will not work as expected.

Let's validate our assumption. We'll use the `sesearch` tool to query for our assumed security policy. The command utility is not installed by default on Fedora, so you will have to install the `setools-console` package first. Use the following command:

```
sudo dnf install setools-console -y
```

Now that the package is installed, we can use the following command:

```
sudo sesearch -s passwd_t -t shadow_t -p write --allow
```

Here's a brief explanation of the preceding command:

- `sesearch`: Searches the SELinux policy database
- `-s passwd_t`: Finds policy rules with `passwd_t` as their source type or role
- `-t shadow_t`: Finds policy rules with `shadow_t` as their target type or role
- `-p write`: Finds policy rules with `write` permissions
- `--allow`: Finds policy rules that allow the queried permissions (specified with `-p`)

The output of the preceding command is as follows:

```
[packt@saturn2 ~]$ sudo sesearch -s passwd_t -t shadow_t -p write --allow
allow passwd_t shadow_t:file { append create getattr ioctl link lock map open read r
elabelfrom relabelto rename setattr unlink watch watch_reads write };
```

Figure 9.8 – Querying SELinux policies

Here, we can see the `append create` permissions, as we correctly assumed.

How did we pick the `passwd_t` source type instead of `passwd_exec_t`? By definition, the *domain* type corresponding to the *executable file* type, `passwd_exec_t`, is `passwd_t`. If we were not sure about *who* has write permissions to the `shadow_t` file types, we could have simply excluded the source type (`-s passwd_t`) in the `sesearch` query and parsed the output (for example, using `grep passwd`).

The use of the `sesearch` tool is very convenient when we're querying security policies. There are a handful of similar tools for troubleshooting or managing the SELinux configuration and policies. One of the most notable SELinux command-line utilities is `semanage` for managing SELinux policies. We'll examine this in the *Managing SELinux policies* section. But first, let's look at the necessary steps for creating an SELinux security policy.

Creating an SELinux security policy

For the examples in this section, we will use a program developed in the C programming language. This means that we will have to compile it, which is different than what we did in the previous chapter. In order to be able to compile C code, we will need to have the **GNU Compiler Collection (GCC)** on our system. We will install gcc on our Fedora system with the following command:

```
sudo dnf install gcc
```

Now, let's assume that we have a daemon called packtd and that we need to secure it to access /var/log/messages. For illustration purposes, the daemon has a straightforward implementation: periodically open the /var/log/messages file for writing. Use your favorite text editor (such as nano) to add the following content (C code) to a file. Let's name the file packtd.c:

```c
#include <unistd.h>
#include <stdio.h>

FILE *f;
char LOG_FILE[] = "/var/log/messages";

int main(void)
{
    while (1) {
    f = fopen(LOG_FILE, "w");
    sleep(10);
    fclose(f);
    }
}
```

Figure 9.9 – A simple daemon periodically checking logs

Let's compile and build packtd.c to generate the related binary executable (packtd):

```
gcc -o packtd packtd.c
```

The following is the result of the command used to compile the source code:

```
[packt@saturn2 ~]$ gcc -o packtd packtd.c
[packt@saturn2 ~]$ ls
backup_script.sh  packtd.c       passgen_script.sh  update_script.sh
packtd            passgen-0.1    rpmbuild
```

Figure 9.10 – Compiling the C source code

Now that the source code has been compiled, we are ready to proceed with the steps for creating the `packtd` daemon and the required SELinux security policy. This exercise is equally useful for SELinux administration and for creating a `systemd` daemon. Please refer to *Chapter 5* if you need to refresh your memory on daemons. Now, let's discuss the steps for creating a daemon and a security policy.

Installing the daemon

First, we must create a `systemd` unit file for the `packtd` daemon. You may use your favorite text editor (such as `nano`) to create the related file. We will call this file `packtd.service`:

```
[packt@saturn2 ~]$ cat packtd.service
[Unit]
Description="Checking the logs"

[Service]
Type=simple
ExecStart=/usr/local/bin/packtd

[Install]
WantedBy=multi-user.target
```

Figure 9.11 – The packtd daemon file

Copy the files we created to their respective locations, such as `/usr/local/bin` for `packtd` and `/usr/lib/systemd/system/` for `packtd.service`:

```
sudo cp packtd /usr/local/bin/
sudo cp packtd.service /usr/lib/systemd/system/
```

At this point, we are ready to start our `packtd` daemon:

```
sudo systemctl start packtd
sudo systemctl status packtd
```

Let's make sure the `packtd` daemon is not confined or restricted yet by SELinux:

```
ps -efZ | grep packtd | grep -v grep
```

The `-Z` option parameter of `ps` retrieves the SELinux context for processes.

The output of all these commands is as follows:

```
[packt@saturn2 ~]$ sudo cp packtd /usr/local/bin/
[packt@saturn2 ~]$ sudo cp packtd.service /usr/lib/systemd/system/
[packt@saturn2 ~]$ sudo systemctl start packtd
[packt@saturn2 ~]$ sudo systemctl status packtd
● packtd.service - "Checking the logs"
    Loaded: loaded (/usr/lib/systemd/system/packtd.service; disabled; preset: >
    Active: active (running) since Wed 2023-04-19 14:26:29 EEST; 5s ago
  Main PID: 1365 (packtd)
     Tasks: 1 (limit: 2297)
    Memory: 180.0K
       CPU: 1ms
    CGroup: /system.slice/packtd.service
            └─1365 /usr/local/bin/packtd

Apr 19 14:26:29 saturn2 systemd[1]: Started packtd.service - "Checking the logs".
[packt@saturn2 ~]$ ps -efZ | grep packtd | grep -v grep
system_u:system_r:unconfined_service_t:s0 root 1365    1  0 14:26 ?        00:00:
00 /usr/local/bin/packtd
```

Figure 9.12 – Running status and confinement status of the packtd daemon

The unconfined_service_t security attribute suggests that packtd is not restricted by SELinux.

Next, we will generate security policy files for the packtd daemon.

Generating policy files

To build a security policy for packtd, we need to generate the related policy files. The SELinux tool for building security policies is sepolicy. Also, packaging the final security policy binary requires the rpm-build utility. These command-line utilities may not be available by default on your system, so you may have to install the related packages using the following command:

```
sudo dnf install -y policycoreutils-devel rpm-build
```

We will use the next command to generate policy files for packtd (no superuser privileges required):

```
sepolicy generate --init /usr/local/bin/packtd
```

The output is as follows:

```
[packt@saturn2 ~]$ sepolicy generate --init /usr/local/bin/packtd
Created the following files:
/home/packt/packtd.te # Type Enforcement file
/home/packt/packtd.if # Interface file
/home/packt/packtd.fc # File Contexts file
/home/packt/packtd_selinux.spec # Spec file
/home/packt/packtd.sh # Setup Script
```

Figure 9.13 – Generating policy files with sepolicy

Take a moment and look over the preceding screenshot. You will see that *five new files* have been created in your home directory. Keep this in mind, as we will use them during our setup process. Next, we need to rebuild the system policy so that it includes the custom `packtd` policy module.

Building the security policy

To build the security policy, we will now use the `packtd.sh` build script that was created in the previous step (see *Figure 9.13* for details). The following command requires superuser privileges since it installs the newly created policy on the system:

```
sudo ./packtd.sh
```

The build takes a relatively long time to complete and yields the following output (excerpt):

```
[packt@saturn2 ~]$ sudo ./packtd.sh
Building and Loading Policy
+ make -f /usr/share/selinux/devel/Makefile packtd.pp
Compiling targeted packtd module
Creating targeted packtd.pp policy package
rm tmp/packtd.mod tmp/packtd.mod.fc
+ /usr/sbin/semodule -i packtd.pp
+ sepolicy manpage -p . -d packtd_t
./packtd_selinux.8
+ /sbin/restorecon -F -R -v /usr/local/bin/packtd
```

Figure 9.14 – Building the security policy for packtd

Please note that the build script reinstates the default *SELinux* security context for `packtd` using the `restorecon` command (highlighted in the previous output). Now that we've built the security policy, we're ready to verify the related permissions.

Verifying the security policy

First, we need to restart the `packtd` daemon to account for the policy change:

```
sudo systemctl restart packtd
```

The `packtd` process should now reflect the new SELinux security context:

```
ps -efZ | grep packtd | grep -v grep
```

The output shows a new label (`packtd_t`) for our security context:

```
[packt@saturn2 ~]$ sudo systemctl restart packtd
[packt@saturn2 ~]$ ps -efZ | grep packtd | grep -v grep
system_u:system_r:packtd_t:s0    root      1781     1  0 17:06 ?        00:00:00
/usr/local/bin/packtd
```

Figure 9.15 – The new security policy for packtd

Since SELinux now controls our `packtd` daemon, we should see the related audit traces in `/var/log/messages`, where SELinux logs the system's activity. Let's look at the audit logs for any permission issues. The following command fetches the most recent events for AVC message types using the `ausearch` utility:

```
sudo ausearch -m AVC -ts recent
```

We will immediately notice that `packtd` has no read/write access to `/var/log/messages`:

```
[packt@saturn2 ~]$ sudo ausearch -m AVC -ts recent
----
time->Wed Apr 19 17:06:16 2023
type=AVC msg=audit(1681913176.568:332): avc:  denied  { write } for  pid=1759 comm="
packtd" name="messages" dev="dm-0" ino=232655 scontext=system_u:system_r:packtd_t:s0
 tcontext=system_u:object_r:var_log_t:s0 tclass=file permissive=1
----
time->Wed Apr 19 17:06:16 2023
type=AVC msg=audit(1681913176.568:333): avc:  denied  { open } for  pid=1759 comm="p
acktd" path="/var/log/messages" dev="dm-0" ino=232655 scontext=system_u:system_r:pac
ktd_t:s0 tcontext=system_u:object_r:var_log_t:s0 tclass=file permissive=1
```

Figure 9.16 – No read/write access for packtd

To further inquire about the permissions needed by `packtd`, we will feed the output of `ausearch` into `audit2allow`, a tool for generating the required security policy stubs:

```
sudo ausearch -m AVC -ts recent | audit2allow -R
```

The output provides the code macro we're looking for:

```
[packt@saturn2 ~]$ sudo ausearch -m AVC -ts recent | audit2allow -R

require {
        type packtd_t;
}

#============= packtd_t ==============
logging_rw_generic_logs(packtd_t)
```

Figure 9.17 – Querying the missing permissions for packtd

The `-R` (`--reference`) option of `audit2allow` invokes a stub generation task, which could sometimes yield inaccurate or incomplete results. In such cases, it may take a few iterations to update, rebuild, and verify the related security policies. Let's proceed with the required changes, as suggested in the output shown in the preceding screenshot. We'll edit the *type enforcement* file (`packtd.te`) generated previously and add the lines (copy/paste) exactly, as indicated by the output of `audit2allow`. The contents of the file are shown in the following screenshot (excerpt). The lines to be added by us are highlighted:

```
domain_use_interactive_fds(packtd_t)

files_read_etc_files(packtd_t)

miscfiles_read_localization(packtd_t)

require {
        type packtd_t;
}
#============= packtd_t =============
logging_rw_generic_logs(packtd_t)
```

Figure 9.18 – Editing the packtd.te file

After saving the file, we need to rebuild the security policy, restart the `packtd` daemon, and verify the audit logs. We're reiterating the last three steps in our overall procedure:

```
sudo ./packtd.sh
sudo systemctl restart packtd
sudo ausearch -m AVC -ts recent | audit2allow -R
```

This time, the SELinux audit should come out clean:

```
[packt@saturn2 ~]$ sudo systemctl restart packtd
[packt@saturn2 ~]$ sudo ausearch -m AVC -ts recent | audit2allow -R
<no matches>
Nothing to do
```

Figure 9.19 – No more permission issues for packtd

Sometimes, it may take a little while for `ausearch` to refresh its `recent` buffer. Alternatively, we can specify a starting timestamp to analyze from, such as after we've updated the security policy, using a relatively recent timestamp:

```
sudo ausearch --start 04/19/2023 '17:30:00' | audit2allow -R
```

Now that we've created our own SELinux security policy, let's understand how it can be managed.

Managing SELinux policies

SELinux provides several utilities for managing security policies and modules, some of which will be briefly described in the *Troubleshooting SELinux issues* section. Examining each of these tools is beyond the scope of this chapter, but we'll take `semanage` for a quick spin to reflect on some use cases involving security policy management.

The general syntax of the `semanage` command is as follows:

```
semanage TARGET [OPTIONS]
```

`TARGET` usually denotes a specific namespace for policy definitions (for example, `login`, `user`, `port`, `fcontext`, `boolean`, `permissive`, and so on). Let's look at a few examples to get an idea of how `semanage` works.

Enabling secure binding on custom ports

Let's assume we want to enable SELinux for a custom SSH port instead of the default `22`. We can retrieve the current security records (labels) on the SSH port with the following command:

```
sudo semanage port -l | grep ssh
```

For a default configuration, we will get the output shown in *line 2* in *Figure 9.20*.

If we want to enable SSH on a different port (such as `2222`), first, we need to configure the related service (`sshd`) to listen on a different port (shown in *Chapter 13*). We won't go into those details here. Here, we need to enable the secure binding on the new port with the following command:

```
sudo semanage port -a -t ssh_port_t -p tcp 2222
```

Here's a brief explanation of the preceding command:

* `-a` (`--add`): Adds a new record (label) for the given type
* `-t ssh_port_t`: The SELinux type of the object
* `-p tcp`: The network protocol associated with the port

As a result of the previous command and the output for the default configuration, the new security policy for the `ssh_port_t` type looks like this:

```
[packt@saturn2 ~]$ sudo semanage port -l | grep ssh
ssh_port_t                      tcp       22
[packt@saturn2 ~]$ sudo semanage port -a -t ssh_port_t -p tcp 2222
[packt@saturn2 ~]$ sudo semanage port -l | grep ssh
ssh_port_t                      tcp       2222, 22
```

Figure 9.20 – Querying and changing the SELinux security label for the SSH port

We could arguably delete the old security label (for port 22), but that won't really matter if we disable port 22. If we want to delete a port security record, we can do so with the following command:

```
sudo semanage port -d -p tcp 22
```

We used the -d (--delete) option to remove the related security label. To view the local customization for our semanage port policies, we can invoke the -C (--locallist) option:

```
sudo semanage port -l -C
```

For more information on semanage port, you may refer to the related system reference (man semanage port). Next, we'll look at how to modify security permissions for specific server applications.

Modifying security permissions for targeted services

semanage uses the boolean namespace to toggle specific features of targeted services on and off. A targeted service is a daemon with built-in SELinux protection. In the following example, we want to enable FTP over HTTP connections. By default, this security feature of Apache (httpd) is turned off. Installation of the httpd server is shown in *Chapter 13*. Let's query the related httpd security policies with the following command:

```
sudo semanage boolean -l | grep httpd | grep ftp
```

We get the following output:

```
[packt@saturn2 ~]$ sudo semanage boolean -l | grep httpd | grep ftp
httpd_can_connect_ftp          (off  ,   off)  Allow httpd to act as a FTP client con
necting to the ftp port and ephemeral ports
httpd_enable_ftp_server        (off  ,   off)  Allow httpd to act as a FTP server by
listening on the ftp port.
```

Figure 9.21 – Querying httpd policies related to FTP

As we can see, the related feature—httpd_enable_ftp_server—is turned off by default. The current and persisted states are currently off: (off, off). We can enable it with the following command:

```
sudo semanage boolean -m --on httpd_enable_ftp_server
```

To view the local customizations of the semanage boolean policies, we can invoke the -C (--locallist) option:

```
sudo semanage boolean -l -C
```

The new configuration now looks like this:

```
[packt@saturn2 ~]$ sudo semanage boolean -m --on httpd_enable_ftp_server
[packt@saturn2 ~]$ sudo semanage boolean -l -C
SELinux boolean                 State  Default Description

httpd_enable_ftp_server         (on   ,   on)  Allow httpd to act as a FTP server by
listening on the ftp port.
```

Figure 9.22 – Enabling the security policy for FTP over HTTP

In the preceding example, we used the -m (--modify) option with the semanage boolean command to toggle the httpd_enable_ftp_server feature.

For more information on semanage boolean, you may refer to the related system reference (man semanage boolean). Now, let's learn how to modify the security context of specific server applications.

Modifying security contexts for targeted services

In this example, we want to secure SSH keys stored in a custom location on the local system. Since we're targeting a filesystem-related security policy, we will use the fcontext (file context) namespace with semanage.

The following command queries the file context security settings for sshd:

```
sudo semanage fcontext -l | grep sshd
```

Here's a relevant excerpt from the output:

```
[packt@saturn2 ~]$ sudo semanage fcontext -l | grep sshd
/etc/rc\.d/init\.d/sshd                     regular file    system_u:object_r:sshd_initrc_exec_t:s0
/etc/ssh/primes                             regular file    system_u:object_r:sshd_key_t:s0
/etc/ssh/ssh_host.*_key                     regular file    system_u:object_r:sshd_key_t:s0
/etc/ssh/ssh_host.*_key\.pub                regular file    system_u:object_r:sshd_key_t:s0
/usr/lib/systemd/system/sshd-keygen.*       regular file    system_u:object_r:sshd_keygen_unit_file_t:s0
/usr/lib/systemd/system/sshd.*              regular file    system_u:object_r:sshd_unit_file_t:s0
/usr/libexec/openssh/sshd-keygen            regular file    system_u:object_r:sshd_keygen_exec_t:s0
/usr/sbin/gsisshd                           regular file    system_u:object_r:sshd_exec_t:s0
/usr/sbin/sshd                              regular file    system_u:object_r:sshd_exec_t:s0
/usr/sbin/sshd-keygen                       regular file    system_u:object_r:sshd_keygen_exec_t:s0
/var/empty/sshd/etc/localtime               regular file    system_u:object_r:locale_t:s0
/var/run/sshd\.init\.pid                    regular file    system_u:object_r:sshd_var_run_t:s0
/var/run/sshd\.pid                          regular file    system_u:object_r:sshd_var_run_t:s0
```

Figure 9.23 – The security context of SSH keys

The following command also adds the /etc/ssh/keys/ path to the secure locations associated with the sshd_key_t context type:

```
sudo semanage fcontext -a -t sshd_key_t '/etc/ssh/keys(/.*)?'
```

The '`/etc/ssh/keys(/.*)?`' regular expression matches any files in the `/etc/ssh/keys/` directory, including subdirectories at any nested level. To view the local customizations of the `semanage fcontext` policies, we can invoke the `-C` (`--locallist`) option:

```
sudo semanage fcontext -l -CWe should see our new security context:
```

```
[packt@saturn2 ~]$ sudo semanage fcontext -a -t sshd_key_t '/etc/ssh/keys(/.*)?'
[packt@saturn2 ~]$ sudo semanage fcontext -l -C
SELinux fcontext                              type              Context

/etc/ssh/keys(/.*)?                           all files         system_u:object_r:sshd
_key_t:s0
```

Figure 9.24 – The modified security context of our SSH keys

We should also initialize the filesystem security context of the `/etc/ssh/keys` directory (if we've already created it; otherwise, we would get an error message):

```
sudo restorecon -r /etc/ssh/keys
```

`restorecon` is an SELinux utility for restoring the default security context to a filesystem object. The `-r` (or `-R`) option specifies a recursive action on the related path.

For more information on `semanage fcontext`, you may refer to the related system reference (`man semanage fcontext`). Next, we'll look at enabling the `permissive` mode of specific server applications.

Enabling permissive mode for targeted services

Earlier in this chapter, we created a custom daemon (`packtd`) with its security policy. See the related topic in the *Creating an SELinux security policy* section earlier in this chapter. During the entire process, we were able to run and test with `packtd` without having the daemon shut down by SELinux due to non-compliance. Our Linux system runs SELinux in `enforcing` mode (by default) and is not permissive. See the *Understanding SELinux modes* section for more information on `enforcing` and `permissive` modes.

By default, SELinux is permissive to any *untargeted* type in the system. By *untargeted*, we mean a domain (type) that hasn't been forced into a restrictive (or confined) mode yet.

When we built the security policy for our `packtd` daemon, we let the related SELinux build tools generate the default type enforcement file (`packt.te`) and other resources for our domain. A quick look at the `packt.te` file shows that our `packtd_t` type is `permissive`:

```
cat packt.te
```

Here's the relevant excerpt from the file:

```
type packtd_t;
type packtd_exec_t;
init_daemon_domain(packtd_t, packtd_exec_t)

permissive packtd_t;
```

Figure 9.25 – The packtd_t domain is permissive

So, the `packtd_t` domain is permissive by nature. The only way to confine `packtd` is to remove the `permissive` line from the `packtd.te` file and rebuild the related security policy. We will leave that as an exercise for you. The case we wanted to make here was to present a possibly misbehaving—in our case, `permissive`—domain that we can *catch* by managing `permissive` types with the `semanage permissive` command.

To manage `permissive` mode for individual targets, we can use the `semanage` command with our `permissive` namespace. The following command lists all the domains (types) currently in `permissive` mode:

```
sudo semanage permissive -l
```

In our case, we have the built-in `packtd_t` domain, which is `permissive`:

```
[packt@saturn2 ~]$ sudo semanage permissive -l

Builtin Permissive Types

packtd_t
```

Figure 9.26 – Displaying permissive types

In general, it is unlikely that a default SELinux configuration would have any `permissive` types.

We can use the `semanage permissive` command to temporarily place a restricted domain into `permissive` mode while testing or troubleshooting a specific functionality. For example, the following command sets the Apache (`httpd`) daemon in `permissive` mode:

```
sudo semanage permissive -a httpd_t
```

When we query for `permissive` types, we get the following result:

```
[packt@saturn2 ~]$ sudo semanage permissive -a httpd_t
[packt@saturn2 ~]$ sudo semanage permissive -l

Builtin Permissive Types

packtd_t

Customized Permissive Types

httpd_t
```

Figure 9.27 – Customized permissive types

Domains or types that are made permissive with the `semanage permissive` command will show up as `Customized Permissive Types`.

To revert the `httpd_t` domain to the confined (restricted) state, we can invoke the `semanage permissive` command with the `-d (--delete)` option:

```
sudo semanage permissive -d httpd_t
```

The output of the command is shown here:

```
[packt@saturn2 ~]$ sudo semanage permissive -d httpd_t
libsemanage.semanage_direct_remove_key: Removing last permissive_httpd_t module (no other pe
rmissive_httpd_t module exists at another priority).
```

Figure 9.28 – Reverting permissive types

Note that we cannot confine built-in `permissive` types with the `semanage` command. As we mentioned previously, the `packtd_t` domain is permissive by nature and cannot be restricted.

At this point, we have a basic understanding of SELinux security policy internals. Next, we'll turn to some higher-level operations for managing and controlling SELinux in everyday administration tasks.

Troubleshooting SELinux issues

Even during our relatively brief journey of exploring SELinux, we used a handful of tools and means to inspect some internal workings of security policies and access control between subjects (users and processes) and objects (files). SELinux's problems usually come down to action being denied, either between specific subjects or between a subject and some objects. SELinux-related issues are not always obvious or easy to troubleshoot, but knowing about the tools that can help is already a good start for tackling these issues.

Here are some of these tools, briefly explained:

- `/var/log/messages`: The log file containing SELinux access control traces and policy violations
- `audit2allow`: Generates SELinux policy rules from the log traces corresponding to denied operations
- `audit2why`: Provides user-friendly translations of SELinux audit messages of policy violations
- `ausearch`: Queries `/var/log/messages` for policy violations
- `ls -Z`: Lists filesystem objects with their corresponding SELinux context
- `ps -Z`: Lists processes with their corresponding SELinux context
- `restorecon`: Restores the default SELinux context for filesystem objects
- `seinfo`: Provides general information about SELinux security policies
- `semanage`: Manages and provides insight into SELinux policies
- `semodule`: Manages SELinux policy modules
- `sepolicy`: Inspects SELinux policies
- `sesearch`: Queries the SELinux policy database

For most of these tools, there is a corresponding system reference (such as `man sesearch`) that provides detailed information about using the tool. Beyond these tools, you can also explore the vast documentation SELinux has to offer. Here's how.

Accessing SELinux documentation

SELinux has extensive documentation, available as an RHEL/Fedora installable package or online at `https://access.redhat.com/documentation/en-us/red_hat_enterprise_linux/9/html/using_selinux/index` (for RHEL 9).

The following command installs the SELinux documentation on RHEL 9 systems:

```
sudo dnf install -y selinux-policy-doc.noarch
```

You can browse a particular SELinux topic with (for example) the following command:

```
man -k selinux | grep httpd
```

SELinux is among the most established and highly customizable security frameworks in the Linux kernel. However, its relatively vast domain and inherent complexity may appear overwhelming to many. Sometimes, even for seasoned system administrators, the choice of a Linux distribution could hang in the balance based on the underlying security module. SELinux is mostly available on RHEL/Fedora platforms, but it is also available as an option on **SUSE Linux Enterprise** (**SLE**). Google's Android also has SELinux available, and Debian also has it as an available option. Another relatively lighter and more efficient security framework is **AppArmor**, and it is available by default on Ubuntu, Debian, and openSUSE. Let us explore it in the next section.

Introducing AppArmor

AppArmor is a Linux security module based on the MAC model that confines applications to a limited set of resources. AppArmor uses an access control mechanism based on security profiles that have been loaded into the Linux kernel. Each profile contains a collection of rules for accessing various system resources. AppArmor can be configured to either enforce access control or just complain about access control violations.

AppArmor proactively protects applications and operating system resources from internal and external threats, including zero-day attacks, by preventing both known and unknown vulnerabilities from being exploited.

AppArmor has been built into the mainline Linux kernel since version 2.6.36 and is currently shipped with Ubuntu, Debian, openSUSE, and similar distributions.

In the following sections. we'll use an Ubuntu Server 22.04 LTS environment to showcase a few practical examples with AppArmor. Most of the related command-line utilities will work the same on any platform with AppArmor installed.

Working with AppArmor

AppArmor command-line utilities usually require superuser privileges. The following command checks the current status of AppArmor:

```
sudo aa-status
```

Here's an excerpt from the command's output:

```
packt@neptune:~$ sudo aa-status
apparmor module is loaded.
32 profiles are loaded.
32 profiles are in enforce mode.
[...]
 0 profiles are in complain mode.
 0 profiles are in kill mode.
 0 profiles are in unconfined mode.
 1 processes have profiles defined.
 1 processes are in enforce mode.
   /usr/sbin/ntpd (770)
 0 processes are in complain mode.
 0 processes are unconfined but have a profile defined.
 0 processes are in mixed mode.
 0 processes are in kill mode.
```

Figure 9.29 – Getting the status of AppArmor

The `aa-status` (or `apparmor_status`) command provides a full list of the currently loaded AppArmor profiles (not shown in the preceding excerpt). We'll examine AppArmor profiles next.

Introducing AppArmor profiles

With AppArmor, processes are confined (or restricted) by profiles. AppArmor profiles are loaded upon system start and run either in `enforce` mode or `complain` mode. Let's explore these modes in some detail:

- `enforce` mode: AppArmor prevents applications running in `enforce` mode from performing restricted actions. Access violations are signaled with log entries in `syslog`. Ubuntu, by default, loads the application profiles in `enforce` mode.

- `complain` mode: Applications running in `complain` mode can take restricted actions, while AppArmor creates a log entry for the related violation. `complain` mode is ideal for testing AppArmor profiles. Potential errors or access violations can be caught and fixed before switching the profiles to `enforce` mode.

With these introductory notes in mind, let's create a simple application with an AppArmor profile.

Creating a profile

In this section, we'll create a simple application guarded by AppArmor. We hope this exercise will help you get a reasonable idea of the inner workings of AppArmor. Let's name this application `appackt`. We'll make it a simple script that creates a file, writes to it, and then deletes the file. The goal is to have AppArmor prevent our app from accessing any other paths in the local system. To try to make some sense of this, think of it as trivial log recycling.

Here's the `appackt` script, and please pardon the thrifty implementation:

```
packt@neptune:~$ cat appackt
#!/bin/bash
# Assuming ./log directory exists!
if [[ ! -d "./log" ]]
then
    echo "No log dir!"
    exit 1
fi
LOG_FILE="./log/appackt"
echo "Creating ${LOG_FILE}..."
touch ${LOG_FILE}
echo "Writing to ${LOG_FILE}..."
date +"%b %d %T ${HOSTNAME}: Hello from Packt!" >> ${LOG_FILE}
echo "Reading from ${LOG_FILE}..."
cat ${LOG_FILE}
echo "Deleting ${LOG_FILE}..."
rm ${LOG_FILE}
```

Figure 9.30 – The appackt script

We are assuming that the `log` directory already exists at the same location as the script:

```
mkdir ./log
```

Let's make the script executable and run it:

```
chmod a+x appackt
./appackt
```

The output is as follows:

```
packt@neptune:~$ chmod a+x appackt
packt@neptune:~$ ./appackt
Creating ./log/appackt...
Writing to ./log/appackt...
Reading from ./log/appackt...
Apr 20 17:22:09 neptune: Hello from Packt!
Deleting ./log/appackt...
```

Figure 9.31 – The output of the appackt script

Now, let's work on guarding and enforcing our script with AppArmor. Before we start, we need to install the `apparmor-utils` package—the **AppArmor toolset**:

```
sudo apt install -y apparmor-utils
```

We'll use a couple of tools to help create the profile:

- `aa-genprof`: Generates an AppArmor security profile
- `aa-logprof`: Updates an AppArmor security profile

We use `aa-genprof` to monitor our application at runtime and have AppArmor learn about it. In the process, we'll be prompted to acknowledge and choose the behavior that's required in specific circumstances.

Once the profile has been created, we'll use the `aa-logprof` utility to make further adjustments while testing in `complain` mode, should any violations occur.

Let's start with `aa-genprof`. We need two terminals: one for the `aa-genprof` monitoring session (in *Terminal 1*) and the other for running our script (in *Terminal 2*).

We will start with *Terminal 1* and run the following command:

```
sudo aa-genprof ./appackt
```

There is a first prompt waiting for us. Next, while the prompt in *Terminal 1* is waiting, we will switch to *Terminal 2* and run the following command:

```
./appackt
```

Now, we must go back to *Terminal 1* and answer the prompts sent by `aa-genprof`, as follows (output detailed in *Figure 9.32*):

- **Prompt 1**: Waiting to scan

  This prompt asks to scan the system log for AppArmor events in order to detect possible complaints (violations).

  Answer: S (S)can

- **Prompts 2 to 5**: Execute permissions for `/usr/bin/touch`, `/usr/bin/date`, `/usr/bin/cat`, and `/usr/bin/rm`

  This prompt requests execute permissions for all the processes running our app.

  Answer: I (I)nherit

- **Prompts 6 to 9**: Read/write permissions to `/dev/tty`, `/home/packt/log/appackt`, and `/etc/ld.so.cache`

  This prompt requests read/write permissions for the app to control different files.

  Answer: A (A)llow

- **Prompt 10**: Save changes

The prompt asks to save or review changes.

Answer: S (S)ave

```
1  [(S)can system log for AppArmor events] / (F)inish
   Reading log entries from /var/log/syslog.

     Profile:  /home/packt/appackt
     Execute:  /usr/bin/touch
     Severity: 3

2  (I)nherit / (C)hild / (N)amed / (X) ix On / (D)eny / Abo(r)t / (F)inish

     Profile:  /home/packt/appackt
     Execute:  /usr/bin/date
     Severity: unknown

3  (I)nherit / (C)hild / (P)rofile / (N)amed / (U)nconfined / (X) ix On / (D)eny / Abo(r)t / (F)inish

     Profile:  /home/packt/appackt
     Execute:  /usr/bin/cat
     Severity: unknown

4  (I)nherit / (C)hild / (N)amed / (X) ix On / (D)eny / Abo(r)t / (F)inish

     Profile:  /home/packt/appackt
     Execute:  /usr/bin/rm
     Severity: unknown

5  (I)nherit / (C)hild / (N)amed / (X) ix On / (D)eny / Abo(r)t / (F)inish
   Complain-mode changes:

     Profile:  /home/packt/appackt
     Path:     /dev/tty
     New Mode: rw
     Severity: 9

    [1 - include <abstractions/consoles>]
     2 - /dev/tty rw,
6  (A)llow / [(D)eny] / (I)gnore / (G)lob / Glob with (E)xtension / (N)ew / Audi(t) / Abo(r)t / (F)inish
   Adding include <abstractions/consoles> to profile.

     Profile:  /home/packt/appackt
     Path:     /home/packt/log/appackt
     New Mode: owner w
     Severity: 6

    [1 - owner /home/*/log/appackt w,]
     2 - owner /home/packt/log/appackt w,
7  (A)llow / [(D)eny] / (I)gnore / (G)lob / Glob with (E)xtension / (N)ew / Audi(t) / (O)wner permissions off / Abo(r)t / (F)inish
   Adding owner /home/*/log/appackt w, to profile.

     Profile:  /home/packt/appackt
     Path:     /etc/ld.so.cache
     New Mode: r
     Severity: 1

    [1 - /etc/ld.so.cache r,]
8  (A)llow / [(D)eny] / (I)gnore / (G)lob / Glob with (E)xtension / (N)ew / Audi(t) / Abo(r)t / (F)inish
   Adding /etc/ld.so.cache r, to profile.

     Profile:  /home/packt/appackt
     Path:     /home/packt/log/appackt
     Old Mode: owner w
     New Mode: owner r
     Severity: 4

    [1 - owner /home/*/log/appackt r,]
     2 - owner /home/packt/log/appackt r,
9  (A)llow / [(D)eny] / (I)gnore / (G)lob / Glob with (E)xtension / (N)ew / Audi(t) / (O)wner permissions off / Abo(r)t / (F)inish
   Adding owner /home/*/log/appackt r, to profile.

   = Changed Local Profiles =

   The following local profiles were changed. Would you like to save them?

    [1 - /home/packt/appackt]
10 (S)ave Changes / Save Selec(t)ed Profile / [(V)iew Changes] / View Changes b/w (C)lean profiles / Abo(r)t
   Writing updated profile for /home/packt/appackt.
```

Figure 9.32 – Running aa-genprof and setting the profile

At this point, we have finished scanning with `aa-genprof`, and we can answer the last prompt with `F (F)inish`:

```
The following local profiles were changed. Would you like to save them?

 [1 - /home/packt/appackt]
 (S)ave Changes / Save Selec(t)ed Profile / [(V)iew Changes] / View Changes b/w (C)lean profiles / Abo(r)t
 Writing updated profile for /home/packt/appackt.

 Profiling: /home/packt/appackt

 Please start the application to be profiled in
 another window and exercise its functionality now.

 Once completed, select the "Scan" option below in
 order to scan the system logs for AppArmor events.

 For each AppArmor event, you will be given the
 opportunity to choose whether the access should be
 allowed or denied.

 [(S)can system log for AppArmor events] / (F)inish
```

Figure 9.33 – Finishing the scanning

Our app (`appackt`) is now enforced by AppArmor in `enforce` mode (by default).

For the rest of the steps, we only need one terminal window. Let's run the `aa-logprof` command to further tune our `appackt` security profile if needed:

```
sudo aa-logprof
```

We'll get several prompts again, similar to the previous ones, asking for further permissions needed by our script or by other applications. The prompts alternate between `Inherit` and `Allow` answers, where appropriate. We won't go into the details here as it is beyond the scope of this book. By now, you should have a general idea about these prompts and their meaning. It's always recommended, though, to ponder upon the permissions asked and act accordingly.

We may have to run the `aa-logprof` command a couple of times because, with each iteration, new permissions will be discovered and addressed, depending on the child processes that are spawned by our script, and so on. Eventually, the `appackt` script will run successfully.

During the iterative process described previously, we may end up with a few unknown or orphaned entries in the AppArmor database, which are artifacts of our previous attempts to secure our application:

```
4 profiles are in complain mode.
  /home/packt/appackt//null-/usr/bin/cat
  /home/packt/appackt//null-/usr/bin/date
  /home/packt/appackt//null-/usr/bin/rm
  /home/packt/appackt//null-/usr/bin/touch
```

Figure 9.34 – Remnants of the iterative process

They will all be named according to the path of our application (/home/packt/appackt). We can clean up these entries with the following command:

```
sudo aa-remove-unknown
```

We can now verify that our app is indeed guarded with AppArmor:

```
sudo aa-status
```

The relevant excerpt from the output is as follows:

```
packt@neptune:~$ sudo aa-status
[sudo] password for packt:
apparmor module is loaded.
33 profiles are loaded.
33 profiles are in enforce mode.
  /home/packt/appackt
```

Figure 9.35 – appackt in complain mode

Our application (/home/packt/appackt) is shown, as expected, in enforce mode.

Next, we need to validate that our app complies with the security policies enforced by AppArmor. Let's edit the appackt script and change the LOG_FILE path in *line 6* of *Figure 9.35* to the following:

```
LOG_FILE="./logs/appackt"
```

We have changed the output directory from log to logs. Let's create a logs directory and run our app:

```
mkdir logs
./appackt
```

The preceding output suggests that `appackt` is attempting to access a path outside the permitted boundaries by AppArmor, thus validating our profile:

```
packt@neptune:~$ ./appackt
Creating ./logs/appackt...
touch: cannot touch './logs/appackt': Permission denied
Writing to ./logs/appackt...
./appackt: line 12: ./logs/appackt: Permission denied
Reading from ./logs/appackt...
cat: ./logs/appackt: No such file or directory
Deleting ./logs/appackt...
rm: cannot remove './logs/appackt': No such file or directory
```

Figure 9.36 – appackt acting outside security boundaries

Let's revert the preceding changes and have the `appackt` script act normally. Let's assume that our app is not yet running in `enforce` mode (but ours is already). We can change it to `enforce` profile mode with the following command:

```
sudo aa-enforce /home/packt/appackt
```

We can verify that our application is indeed running in `enforce` mode with the following command:

```
sudo aa-status
```

If we wanted to make further adjustments to our application and then test it with the related changes, we would have to change the profile mode to `complain` and then reiterate the steps described earlier in this section. The following command sets the application profile to `complain` mode:

```
sudo aa-complain /home/packt/appackt
```

AppArmor profiles are plain text files stored in the `/etc/apparmor.d/` directory. Creating or modifying AppArmor profiles usually involves manually editing the corresponding files or the procedure described in this section using the `aa-genprof` and `aa-logprof` tools.

Next, let's look at how to disable or enable AppArmor application profiles.

Disabling and enabling profiles

Sometimes, we may want to disable a problematic application profile while working on a better version. Here's how we do this.

First, we need to locate the application profile we want to disable (for example, `appackt`). The related file is in the `/etc/apparmor.d/` directory and it's named according to its full path, with dots (`.`) instead of slashes (`/`). In our case, the file is `/etc/apparmor.d/home.packt.appackt`, as seen in the following screenshot:

```
packt@neptune:~$ cd /etc/apparmor.d/
packt@neptune:/etc/apparmor.d$ ls
abi              home.packt.appackt  sbin.dhclient    usr.lib.snapd.snap-confine.real
abstractions     local               tunables         usr.sbin.ntpd
disable          lsb_release         usr.bin.man      usr.sbin.rsyslogd
force-complain   nvidia_modprobe     usr.bin.tcpdump
```

Figure 9.37 – Location of the AppArmor profile for appackt

To disable the profile, we must run the following commands:

```
sudo ln -s /etc/apparmor.d/home.packt.appackt /etc/apparmor.d/disable/
sudo apparmor_parser -R /etc/apparmor.d/home.packt.appackt
```

If we run the aa-status command, we won't see our appackt profile anymore. The related profile is still present in the filesystem, at /etc/apparmor.d/disable/home.packt.appackt.

In this situation, the appackt script is not enforced by any restrictions. To re-enable the related security profile, we can run the following commands:

```
sudo rm /etc/apparmor.d/disable/home.packt.appackt
sudo apparmor_parser -r /etc/apparmor.d/home.packt.appackt
```

The appackt profile should now show up in the aa-status output as running in enforce mode. All the previous commands and their output are shown in the following screenshot:

```
packt@neptune:~$ sudo ln -s /etc/apparmor.d/home.packt.appackt /etc/apparmor.d/disable/
[sudo] password for packt:
packt@neptune:~$ sudo apparmor_parser -R /etc/apparmor.d/home.packt.appackt
packt@neptune:~$ ls -l /etc/apparmor.d/disable/home.packt.appackt
lrwxrwxrwx 1 root root 34 Apr 20 19:37 /etc/apparmor.d/disable/home.packt.appackt -> /etc/
apparmor.d/home.packt.appackt
packt@neptune:~$ sudo rm /etc/apparmor.d/disable/home.packt.appackt
packt@neptune:~$ sudo apparmor_parser -r /etc/apparmor.d/home.packt.appackt
packt@neptune:~$ sudo aa-status
apparmor module is loaded.
33 profiles are loaded.
33 profiles are in enforce mode.
   /home/packt/appackt
```

Figure 9.38 – Disabling and enabling an AppArmor profile

To disable or enable the profile, we used the apparmor_parser command, besides the related filesystem operations. This utility assists with loading (-r, --replace) or unloading (-R, --remove) security profiles to and from the kernel.

Deleting AppArmor security profiles is functionally equivalent to disabling them. We can also choose to remove the related file from the filesystem altogether. If we delete a profile without removing it from the kernel first (with `apparmor_parser -R`), we can use the `aa-remove-unknown` command to clean up orphaned entries.

Let's conclude our relatively brief study of AppArmor internals with some final thoughts.

Final considerations

Working with AppArmor is relatively easier than SELinux, especially when it comes to generating security policies or switching back and forth between permissive and non-permissive mode. SELinux can only toggle the permissive context for the entire system, while AppArmor does it at the application level. On the other hand, there might be no choice between the two, as some major Linux distributions either support one or the other. AppArmor is used on Debian, Ubuntu, and openSUSE, while SELinux runs on RHEL/Fedora and SLE. Theoretically, you can always try to port the related kernel modules across distros, but that's not a trivial task.

As a final note, we should reiterate that in the big picture of Linux security, SELinux and AppArmor are ACMs that act locally on a system, at the application level. When it comes to securing applications and computer systems from the outside world, firewalls come into play. We'll look at firewalls next.

Working with firewalls

Traditionally, a **firewall** is a network security device that's placed between two networks. It monitors the network traffic and controls access to these networks. Generally speaking, a firewall protects a local network from unwanted intrusion or attacks from the outside. But a firewall can also block unsolicited locally originated traffic targeting the public internet. Technically, a firewall allows or blocks incoming and outgoing network traffic based on specific security rules.

For example, a firewall can block all but a select set of inbound networking protocols (such as SSH and HTTP/HTTPS). It may also block all but approved hosts within the local network from establishing specific outbound connections, such as allowing outbound **Simple Mail Transfer Protocol** (SMTP) connections that originated exclusively from the local email servers.

The following diagram shows a simple firewall deployment regulating traffic between a local network and the internet:

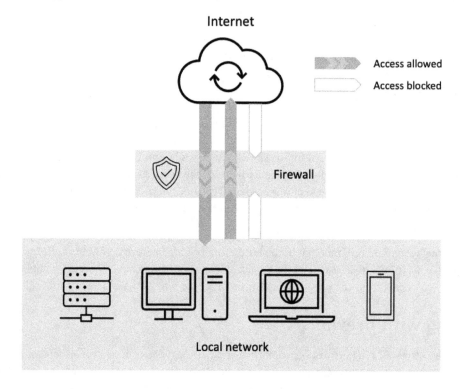

Figure 9.39 – A simple firewall diagram

The outgoing security rules prevent bad actors, such as compromised computers and untrustworthy individuals, from directing attacks on the public internet. The resulting protection benefits external networks, but it's ultimately essential for the organization as well. Thwarting hostile actions from the local network avoids them being flagged by **internet service providers** (**ISPs**) for unruly internet traffic.

Configuring a firewall usually requires a default security policy acting at a global scope, and then configuring specific exceptions to this general rule, based on port numbers (protocols), IP addresses, and other criteria.

In the following sections, we'll explore various firewall implementations and firewall managers. First, let's take a brief look under the hood at how a firewall monitors and controls network traffic by introducing the Linux firewall chain.

Understanding the firewall chain

At a high level, the TCP/IP stack in the Linux kernel usually performs the following workflows:

- Receives data from an application (process), serializes the data into network packets, and transmits the packets to a network destination, based on the respective IP address and port

- Receives data from the network, deserializes the network packets into application data, and delivers the application data to a process

Ideally, in these workflows, the Linux kernel shouldn't alter the network data in any specific way apart from shaping it due to TCP/IP protocols. However, with distributed and possibly insecure network environments, the data may need further scrutiny. The kernel should provide the necessary hooks to filter and alter the data packets further based on various criteria. This is where firewalls and other network security and intrusion detection tools come into play. They adapt to the kernel's TCP/IP packet filtering interface and perform the required monitoring and control of network packets. The blueprint of the Linux kernel's network packet filtering procedure is also known as the **firewall chain** or **firewalling chain**:

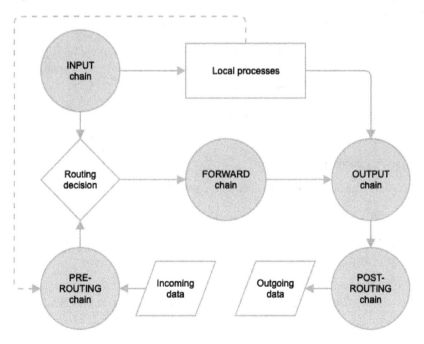

Figure 9.40 – The Linux firewall chain

When the incoming data enters the firewall packet filtering chain, a routing decision is made, depending on the packet's destination. Based on that routing decision, the packet can follow either the **INPUT** chain (for localhost) or the **FORWARD** chain (for a remote host). These chains may alter the incoming data in various ways via hooks that are implemented by network security tools or firewalls. By default, the kernel won't change the packets traversing the chains.

The **INPUT** chain ultimately feeds the packets into the **local application process** consuming the data. These local applications are usually user-space processes, such as network clients (for example, web browsers, SSH, and email clients) or network servers (for example, web and email servers). They may also include kernel space processes, such as the kernel's **Network File System** (**NFS**).

Both the **FORWARD** chain and the **local processes** route the data packets into the **OUTPUT** chain before placing them on the network.

Any of the chains can filter packets based on specific criteria, such as the following:

- The source or destination IP address
- The source or destination port
- The network interface involved in the data transaction

Each chain has a set of security rules that are matched against the input packet. If a rule matches, the kernel routes the data packet to the **target** specified by the rule. Some predefined targets include the following:

- ACCEPT: Accepts the data packet for further processing
- REJECT: Rejects the data packet
- DROP: Ignores the data packet
- QUEUE: Passes the data packet to a user-space process
- RETURN: Stops processing the data packet and passes the data back to the previous chain

For a full list of predefined targets, please refer to the `iptables-extensions` system reference (man `iptables-extensions`).

In the following sections, we'll explore some of the most common network security frameworks and tools based on the kernel's networking stack and firewall chain. We'll start with Netfilter—the Linux kernel's packet filtering system. Next, we'll look at `iptables`—the traditional interface for configuring Netfilter. `iptables` is a highly configurable and flexible firewall solution. Then, we'll briefly cover `nftables`, a tool that implements most of the complex functionality of `iptables` and wraps it into a relatively easy-to-use command-line interface. Finally, we'll take a step away from the kernel's immediate proximity of packet filtering frameworks and look at **firewall managers**—`firewalld` (RHEL/Fedora) and `ufw` (Debian/Ubuntu), two user-friendly frontends for configuring Linux firewalls on major Linux distros.

Let's start our journey with Netfilter.

Introducing Netfilter

Netfilter is a packet filtering framework in the Linux kernel that provides highly customizable handlers (or hooks) to control networking-related operations. These operations include the following:

- Accepting or rejecting packets
- Packet routing and forwarding
- **Network address translation** and **network address port translation (NAT/NAPT)**

Applications that implement the Netfilter framework use a set of callback functions built around hooks registered with kernel modules that manipulate the networking stack. These callback functions are further mapped to security rules and profiles, which control the behavior of every packet traversing the networking chain.

Firewall applications are first-class citizens of Netfilter framework implementations. Consequently, a good understanding of Netfilter hooks will help Linux power users and administrators create reliable firewall rules and policies.

We'll have a brief look at these Netfilter hooks next.

Netfilter hooks

As packets traverse the various chains in the networking stack, Netfilter triggers events for the kernel modules that are registered with the corresponding **hooks**. These events result in notifications in the module or packet filtering application (for example, the firewall) implementing the hooks. Next, the application takes control of the packet based on specific rules.

There are five Netfilter hooks available for packet filtering applications. Each corresponds to a networking chain, as illustrated in *Figure 9.40*:

- `NF_IP_PRE_ROUTING`: Triggered by incoming traffic upon entering the network stack and before any routing decisions are made about where to send the packet
- `NF_IP_LOCAL_IN`: Triggered after routing an incoming packet when the packet has a `localhost` destination
- `NF_IP_FORWARD`: Triggered after routing an incoming packet when the packet has a remote host destination
- `NF_IP_LOCAL_OUT`: Triggered by locally initiated outbound traffic entering the network stack
- `NF_IP_POST_ROUTING`: Triggered by outgoing or forwarded traffic, immediately after routing it and just before it exits the network stack

Kernel modules or applications registered with Netfilter hooks must provide a priority number to determine the order the modules are called in when the hook is triggered. This mechanism allows us to deterministically order multiple modules (or multiple instances of the same module) that have been registered with a specific hook. When a registered module is done processing a packet, it provides a decision to the Netfilter framework about what should be done with the packet.

The Netfilter framework's design and implementation is a community-driven collaborative project part of the **Free and Open Source Software (FOSS)** movement. As a good starting point for the Netfilter project, you may refer to `http://www.netfilter.org/`.

One of the most well-known implementations of Netfilter is `iptables`—a widely used firewall management tool that shares a direct interface with the Netfilter packet filtering framework. A practical examination of `iptables` would further reveal the functional aspects of Netfilter. Let's explore `iptables` next.

Working with iptables

`iptables` is a relatively low-level Linux firewall solution and command-line utility that uses Netfilter chains to control network traffic. `iptables` operates with **rules** associated with **chains**. A rule defines the criteria for matching the packets traversing a specific chain. `iptables` also uses **tables** to organize rules based on criteria or decision type. `iptables` defines the following tables:

- `filter`: The default table, which is used when we're deciding if packets should be allowed to traverse specific chains (`INPUT, FORWARD, OUTPUT`).

- `nat`: Used with packets that require a source or destination address/port translation. The table operates on the following chains: `PREROUTING, INPUT, OUTPUT`, and `POSTROUTING`.

- `mangle`: Used with specialized packet alterations involving IP headers, such as **maximum segment size (MSS)** or **time to live (TTL)**. The table supports the following chains: `PREROUTING, INPUT, FORWARD, OUTPUT`, and `POSTROUTING`.

- `raw`: Used when we're disabling connection tracking (`NOTRACK`) on specific packets, mainly for stateless processing and performance optimization purposes. The table relates to the `PREROUTING` and `OUTPUT` chains.

- `security`: Used for MAC when packets are subject to SELinux policy constraints. The table interacts with the `INPUT, FORWARD`, and `OUTPUT` chains.

The following diagram summarizes the tables with the corresponding chains supported in `iptables`:

Chains ➡ Tables ⬇	PREROUTING	INPUT	FORWARD	OUTPUT	POSTROUTING
filter		☑	☑	☑	
nat	☑	☑		☑	☑
mangle	☑	☑	☑	☑	☑
raw	☑			☑	
security		☑	☑	☑	

Figure 9.41 – Tables and chains in iptables

The chain traversal order of the packets in the kernel's networking stack is as follows:

- Incoming packets with localhost destination: PREROUTING | INPUT
- Incoming packets with remote host destination: PREROUTING | FORWARD | POSTROUTING
- Locally generated packets (by application processes): OUTPUT | POSTROUTING

Now that we're familiar with some introductory concepts, we can tackle a few practical examples to understand how `iptables` works.

The following examples use a Fedora 37 system, but they should work on every major Linux distribution. Please note that starting with RHEL 7, the default firewall management application is `firewalld` (discussed in the *Using firewall managers* section later in this chapter). If you want to use `iptables`, first, you need to disable `firewalld`:

```
sudo systemctl stop firewalld
sudo systemctl disable firewalld
sudo systemctl mask firewalld
```

Next, install the `iptables-services` package (on Fedora):

```
sudo dnf install iptables-services
```

The output of the preceding commands is shown here:

```
[packt@saturn2 ~]$ sudo systemctl stop firewalld
[packt@saturn2 ~]$ sudo systemctl disable firewalld
Removed "/etc/systemd/system/multi-user.target.wants/firewalld.service".
Removed "/etc/systemd/system/dbus-org.fedoraproject.FirewallD1.service".
[packt@saturn2 ~]$ sudo systemctl mask firewalld
Created symlink /etc/systemd/system/firewalld.service → /dev/null.
[packt@saturn2 ~]$ sudo dnf install iptables-services
Last metadata expiration check: 0:16:56 ago on Fri 21 Apr 2023 08:52:02 AM EEST.
Dependencies resolved.
================================================================================
 Package              Architecture    Version            Repository       Size
================================================================================
Installing:
 iptables-services    noarch          1.8.8-4.fc37       updates          17 k
Installing dependencies:
 iptables-utils       x86_64          1.8.8-4.fc37       updates          42 k
```

Figure 9.42 – Disabling firewalld and installing iptables on Fedora

> **Important note**
>
> On Ubuntu, you must install `iptables` using `sudo apt install iptables`.

Now, let's start configuring `iptables`.

Configuring iptables

The `iptables` command requires superuser privileges. First, let's check the current `iptables` configuration. The general syntax for retrieving the rules in a chain for a specific table is as follows:

```
sudo iptables -L [CHAIN] [-t TABLE]
```

The `-L` (`--list`) option lists the rules in a *chain*. The `-t` (`--table`) option specifies a table. The CHAIN and TABLE parameters are optional. If the CHAIN option is omitted, *all* chains and their related rules are considered within a table. When no TABLE option is specified, the `filter` table is assumed. Thus, the following command lists all the chains and rules for the `filter` table:

```
sudo iptables -L
```

On a system with a default firewall configuration, the output is as follows:

```
[packt@saturn2 ~]$ sudo iptables -L
Chain INPUT (policy ACCEPT)
target     prot opt source                destination

Chain FORWARD (policy ACCEPT)
target     prot opt source                destination

Chain OUTPUT (policy ACCEPT)
target     prot opt source                destination
```

Figure 9.43 – Listing the current configuration in iptables

We can be more specific—for example, by listing all the INPUT chain rules for the nat table with the following command:

```
sudo iptables -L INPUT -t nat
```

The -t (--table) option parameter is only required when iptables operations target something other than the default filter table.

> **Important note**
>
> Unless the -t (--table) option parameter is specified, iptables assumes the filter table by default.

When you're designing firewall rules from a clean slate, the following steps are generally recommended:

1. Flush any remnants in the current firewall configuration.
2. Set up a default firewall policy.
3. Create firewall rules, making sure the more specific (or restrictive) rules are placed first.
4. Save the configuration.

Let's briefly look at each of the preceding steps by creating a sample firewall configuration using the filter table:

1. **Flushing the existing configuration**: The following commands flush the rules from the filter table's chains (INPUT, FORWARD, and OUTPUT):

   ```
   sudo iptables -F INPUT
   sudo iptables -F FORWARD
   sudo iptables -F OUTPUT
   ```

   The preceding commands yield no output unless there is an error or you invoke the iptables command with the -v (--verbose) option.

The output is as follows:

```
[packt@saturn2 ~]$ sudo iptables -v -F INPUT
Flushing chain `INPUT'
[packt@saturn2 ~]$ sudo iptables -v -F FORWARD
Flushing chain `FORWARD'
[packt@saturn2 ~]$ sudo iptables -v -F OUTPUT
Flushing chain `OUTPUT'
```

Figure 9.44 – Flushing existing configuration in iptables

> **Important note**
>
> The flushing operation will delete all the rules in a specific chain. Please take into consideration that this kind of operation will disable your firewall. This can also lock you out of an SSH connection if you are using one, thus be careful when using the flushing operation.

2. **Setting up a default firewall policy**: By default, iptables allows all packets to pass through the networking (firewall) chain. A secure firewall configuration should use DROP as the default target for the relevant chains:

```
sudo iptables -P INPUT DROP
sudo iptables -P FORWARD DROP
sudo iptables -P OUTPUT DROP
```

The -P (--policy) option parameter sets the policy for a specific chain (such as INPUT) to the given target (for example, DROP). The DROP target makes the system gracefully ignore all packets.

At this point, if we were to save our firewall configuration, the system wouldn't accept any incoming or outgoing packets. So, we should be careful not to inadvertently drop our access to the system if we use SSH or don't have direct console access.

3. **Creating firewall rules**: Let's create some example firewall rules, such as accepting SSH, DNS, and HTTPS connections.

The following commands enable SSH access from a local network (192.168.0.0/24):

```
sudo iptables -A INPUT -p tcp --dport 22 -m state \
  --state NEW,ESTABLISHED -s 192.168.0.0/24 -j ACCEPT
sudo iptables -A OUTPUT -p tcp --sport 22 -m state \
  --state ESTABLISHED -s 192.168.0.0/24 -j ACCEPT
```

Let's explain the parameters that were used in the previous code block:

- -A INPUT: Specifies the chain (for example, INPUT) to append the rule to

- -p tcp: The networking protocol (for example, TCP or UDP) transporting the packets

- `--dport 22`: The destination port of the packets

- `--sport 22`: The source port of the packets

- `-m state`: The packet property we want to match (for example, `state`)

- `--state NEW,ESTABLISHED`: The state(s) of the packet to match

- `-s 192.168.0.0/24`: The source IP address/mask originating the packets

- `-j ACCEPT`: The target or what to do with the packets (such as `ACCEPT`, `DROP`, `REJECT`, and so on)

We used two commands to enable SSH access. The first allows incoming SSH traffic (`--dport 22`) for new and existing connections (`-m state --state NEW,ESTABLISHED`). The second command enables SSH response traffic (`--sport 22`) for existing connections (`-m state –state ESTABLISHED`).

Similarly, the following commands enable HTTPS traffic:

```
sudo iptables -A INPUT -p tcp --dport 443 -m state \
  --state NEW,ESTABLISHED -j ACCEPT
sudo iptables -A OUTPUT -p tcp --sport 443 -m state \
  --state ESTABLISHED,RELATED -j ACCEPT
```

To enable DNS traffic, we need to use the following commands:

```
sudo iptables -A INPUT -p udp --dport 53 -j ACCEPT
sudo iptables -A OUTPUT -p udp --sport 53 -j ACCEPT
```

For more information on the `iptables` option parameters, please refer to the following system reference manuals:

- `iptables` (man `iptables`)

- `iptables-extensions` (man `iptables-extensions`)

4. **Saving the configuration**: To save the current `iptables` configuration, we must run the following command:

```
sudo service iptables save
```

The output is as follows:

```
[packt@saturn2 ~]$ sudo service iptables save
iptables: Saving firewall rules to /etc/sysconfig/iptables: [  OK  ]
```

Figure 9.45 – Saving the iptables configuration

We can also dump the current configuration to a file (such as `iptables.config`) for later use with the following command:

```
sudo iptables-save -f iptables.config
```

The -f (--file) option parameter specifies the file to save (back up) the iptables configuration in. We can restore the saved iptables configuration later with the following command:

```
sudo iptables-restore ./iptables.config
```

Here, we can specify an arbitrary path to our iptables backup configuration file.

Exploring more complex rules and topics with iptables is beyond the scope of this chapter. The examples we've presented so far, accompanied by the theoretical introduction of iptables, should be a good start for everyone to explore more advanced configurations. Also, tools such as newly emerging nftables are getting a lot of traction in some of the more recent versions of Linux distributions, and firewall management tools such as ufw and firewalld are used out of the box in distros such as Fedora, RHEL, openSUSE or Ubuntu.

Next, we'll look at nftables, a relatively new framework that was designed and developed by the *Netfilter project*, built to eventually replace iptables.

Introducing nftables

nftables is a successor of iptables. nftables is a firewall management framework that supports packet filtering, NAT, and various packet shaping operations. nftables offers notable improvements in terms of features, convenience, and performance over previous packet filtering tools, such as the following:

- Lookup tables instead of linear processing of rules
- Rules are applied individually instead of processing a complete ruleset
- A unified framework for IPv4 and IPv6 protocols
- No protocol-specific extensions

The functional principles behind nftables generally follow the design patterns presented in earlier sections about firewall networking chains—that is, Netfilter and iptables. Just as with iptables, nftables uses tables to store chains. Each chain contains a set of rules for packet filtering actions.

nftables is the default packet filtering framework in Debian and RHEL/Fedora Linux distributions, replacing the old iptables (and related) tools. The command-line interface for manipulating the nftables configuration is nft. Yet some users prefer to use a more user-friendly frontend instead, such as firewalld (which recently added backend support for nftables). RHEL/Fedora, for example, uses firewalld as its default firewall management solution.

In this section, we'll show a few examples of how to use nftables and the related command-line utilities to perform simple firewall configuration tasks. For this purpose, we'll take an RHEL/Fedora distribution where we'll disable firewalld. Let's have a quick look at the preparatory steps required to run the examples in this section.

Prerequisites for our examples

If you have an RHEL 7 system, `nftables` is not installed by default. You can install it with the following command:

```
sudo yum install -y nftables
```

The examples in this section use a Fedora 37 distribution. To directly configure `nftables`, we need to disable `firewalld` and potentially `iptables` (if you ran the examples in the *Working with iptables* section). The steps for disabling `firewalld` were shown at the beginning of the *Configuring iptables* section.

Also, if you have `iptables` enabled, you need to stop and disable the related service with the following commands:

```
sudo systemctl stop iptables
sudo systemctl disable iptables
```

Next, we need to enable and start `nftables`:

```
sudo systemctl enable nftables
sudo systemctl start nftables
```

We can check the status of `nftables` with the following command:

```
sudo systemctl status nftables
```

The running status of `nftables` should be `active`, as seen here:

```
[packt@saturn2 ~]$ sudo systemctl enable nftables
Created symlink /etc/systemd/system/multi-user.target.wants/nftables.service → /usr/lib/sy
stemd/system/nftables.service.
[packt@saturn2 ~]$ sudo systemctl start nftables
[packt@saturn2 ~]$ sudo systemctl status nftables
• nftables.service - Netfilter Tables
     Loaded: loaded (/usr/lib/systemd/system/nftables.service; enabled; preset: disabled)
     Active: active (exited) since Fri 2023-04-21 09:44:43 EEST; 7s ago
       Docs: man:nft(8)
    Process: 1214 ExecStart=/sbin/nft -f /etc/sysconfig/nftables.conf (code=exited, statu>
   Main PID: 1214 (code=exited, status=0/SUCCESS)
        CPU: 5ms

Apr 21 09:44:43 saturn2 systemd[1]: Starting nftables.service - Netfilter Tables...
Apr 21 09:44:43 saturn2 systemd[1]: Finished nftables.service - Netfilter Tables.
lines 1-10/10 (END)
```

Figure 9.46 – Checking the status of nftables

At this point, we are ready to configure `nftables`. Let's work with a few examples in the next section.

Working with nftables

`ntftables` loads its configuration from `/etc/sysconfig/nftables.conf`. We can display the content of the configuration file with the following command:

```
sudo cat /etc/sysconfig/nftables.conf
```

A default `nftables` configuration has no active entries in `nftables.conf`, except for a few comments:

```
[packt@saturn2 ~]$ sudo cat /etc/sysconfig/nftables.conf
# Uncomment the include statement here to load the default config sample
# in /etc/nftables for nftables service.

#include "/etc/nftables/main.nft"

# To customize, either edit the samples in /etc/nftables, append further
# commands to the end of this file or overwrite it after first service
# start by calling: 'nft list ruleset >/etc/sysconfig/nftables.conf'.
```

Figure 9.47 – The default nftables configuration file

As the comments suggest, we have a few options for changing the `nftables` configuration:

- Directly edit the `nftables.conf` file

- Manually edit the `/etc/nftables/main.nft` configuration file, then uncomment the related line in `nftables.conf`

- Use the `nft` command-line utility to edit the rules and then dump the current configuration into `nftables.conf`

Regardless of the approach taken, we need to reload the updated configuration by restarting the `nftables` service. In this section, we'll use `nft` command-line examples to change the `nftables` configuration. Power users usually write `nft` configuration scripts, but it's best to learn the basic steps first.

The following command displays all the rules in the current configuration:

```
sudo nft list ruleset
```

Your system may already have some default rules set up. You may choose to do a backup of the related configuration (for example, `/etc/sysconfig/nftables.conf` and `/etc/nftables/main.nft`) before proceeding with the next steps.

The following command will flush any preexisting rules:

```
sudo nft flush ruleset
```

At this point, we have an empty configuration. Let's design a simple firewall that accepts SSH, HTTP, and HTTPS traffic, blocking anything else.

Accepting SSH, HTTP, and HTTPS traffic

First, we need to create a table and a chain. The following command creates a table named `packt_table`:

```
sudo nft add table inet packt_table
```

Next, we'll create a chain called `packt_chain` within `packt_table`:

```
sudo nft add chain inet packt_table packt_chain { type filter hook
input priority 0 \; }
```

Now, we can start adding rules to `packt_chain`. Allow SSH, HTTP, and HTTPS access with the following rule:

```
sudo nft add rule inet packt_table packt_chain tcp dport {ssh, http,
https} accept
```

Let's also enable ICMP (`ping`):

```
sudo nft add rule inet packt_table packt_chain ip protocol icmp accept
```

Finally, we will reject everything else:

```
sudo nft add rule inet packt_table packt_chain reject with icmp type
port-unreachable
```

Now, let's have a look at our new configuration:

```
sudo nft list ruleset
```

The output is as follows:

```
[packt@saturn2 ~]$ sudo nft list ruleset
table ip filter {
        chain INPUT {
                type filter hook input priority filter; policy accept;
        }

        chain FORWARD {
                type filter hook forward priority filter; policy accept;
        }

        chain OUTPUT {
                type filter hook output priority filter; policy accept;
        }
}
table inet packt_table {
        chain packt_chain {
                type filter hook input priority filter; policy accept;
                tcp dport { 22, 80, 443 } accept
                ip protocol icmp accept
                reject with icmp port-unreachable
        }
}
```

Figure 9.48 – A simple firewall configuration with nftables

The output suggests the following settings for our input chain (packt_chain):

- Allow TCP traffic on destination ports 22, 80, and 443 (tcp dport { 22, 80, 443 } accept)

- Allow ping requests (ip protocol icmp accept)

- Reject everything else (meta nfproto ipv4 reject)

Next, we will save the current configuration to /etc/nftables/packt.nft:

```
sudo nft list ruleset | sudo tee /etc/nftables/packt.nft
```

Finally, we will point the current nftables configuration to /etc/nftables/packt.nft in the /etc/sysconfig/nftables.conf file by adding the following line:

```
include "/etc/nftables/packt.nft"
```

We will use vim (or your editor of choice) to make this change:

```
sudo vim /etc/sysconfig/nftables.conf
```

The new `nftables.conf` file now contains the reference to our `packt.nft` configuration file:

```
# Uncomment the include statement here to load the default config sample
# in /etc/nftables for nftables service.

#include "/etc/nftables/main.nft"

# To customize, either edit the samples in /etc/nftables, append further
# commands to the end of this file or overwrite it after first service
# start by calling: 'nft list ruleset >/etc/sysconfig/nftables.conf'.

include "/etc/nftables/packt.nft"
```

Figure 9.49 – Including the new configuration in nftables.conf

The following command reloads the new `nftables` configuration:

```
sudo systemctl restart nftables
```

After this exercise, you can quickly write a script for configuring `nftables` using the output of the `nft list ruleset` command. As a matter of fact, we just did that with the `/etc/nftables/packt.nft` configuration file.

With that, we will conclude our examination of packet filtering frameworks and the related command-line utilities. They enable power users to have granular control over every functional aspect of underlying network chains and rules. Yet, some Linux administrators may find the use of such tools overwhelming and turn to relatively simpler firewall management utilities instead. So, next, we'll look at a couple of native Linux firewall management tools that provide a more streamlined and user-friendly command-line interface for configuring and managing firewalls.

Using firewall managers

Firewall managers are command-line utilities with a relatively easy-to-use configuration interface of firewall security rules. Generally, these tools require superuser privileges, and they are a significant asset for Linux system administrators.

In the following sections, we'll present two of the most common firewall managers that are widely used across modern-day Linux distributions:

- `firewalld`: On RHEL/Fedora platforms
- `ufw`: On Ubuntu/Debian platforms

Firewall managers are similar to other network security tools (such as `iptables`, Netfilter, and `nftables`), with the main difference being that they offer a more streamlined user experience for firewall security. An essential benefit of using a firewall manager is the convenience of not having to restart network daemons when you're operating various security configuration changes.

Let's start with `firewalld`, the default firewall manager for RHEL/Fedora.

Using firewalld

`firewalld` is the default firewall management utility for a variety of Linux distributions, including the following:

- RHEL 7 (and newer)
- openSUSE 15 (and newer)
- Fedora 18 (and newer)

On RHEL, if `firewalld` is not present, we can install it with the following command:

```
sudo yum install -y firewalld
```

You may also have to enable the `firewalld` daemon at startup with the following command:

```
sudo systemctl enable firewalld
```

If you use the same system you used to execute previous examples with `iptables` and `nftables`, remember that we had to disable `firewalld` at the beginning on our Fedora distribution. Now, it is time to re-enable it. We will use the following commands to do so:

```
[packt@saturn2 ~]$ sudo systemctl enable firewalld
Failed to enable unit: Unit file /etc/systemd/system/firewalld.service is masked.
[packt@saturn2 ~]$ sudo systemctl unmask firewalld
Removed "/etc/systemd/system/firewalld.service".
[packt@saturn2 ~]$ sudo systemctl enable firewalld
Created symlink /etc/systemd/system/dbus-org.fedoraproject.FirewallD1.service → /usr/lib/s
ystemd/system/firewalld.service.
Created symlink /etc/systemd/system/multi-user.target.wants/firewalld.service → /usr/lib/s
ystemd/system/firewalld.service.
[packt@saturn2 ~]$ sudo systemctl start firewalld
[packt@saturn2 ~]$ sudo systemctl status firewalld
● firewalld.service - firewalld - dynamic firewall daemon
     Loaded: loaded (/usr/lib/systemd/system/firewalld.service; enabled; preset: enabled)
     Active: active (running) since Fri 2023-04-21 10:04:12 EEST; 6s ago
       Docs: man:firewalld(1)
   Main PID: 1398 (firewalld)
      Tasks: 2 (limit: 2297)
     Memory: 23.8M
        CPU: 179ms
     CGroup: /system.slice/firewalld.service
             └─1398 /usr/bin/python3 -sP /usr/sbin/firewalld --nofork --nopid

Apr 21 10:04:11 saturn2 systemd[1]: Starting firewalld.service - firewalld - dynamic fire
Apr 21 10:04:12 saturn2 systemd[1]: Started firewalld.service - firewalld - dynamic firew
lines 1-13/13 (END)
```

Figure 9.50 – Re-enabling firewalld

`firewalld` has a set of command-line utilities for different tasks:

- `firewall-cmd`: The primary command-line tool of `firewalld`
- `firewall-offline-cmd`: Used for configuring `firewalld` while it's offline (not running)
- `firewall-config`: A graphical user interface tool for configuring `firewalld`
- `firewall-applet`: A system-tray app for providing essential information about `firewalld` (such as running status, connections, and so on)

In this section, we will look at a few practical examples of using the `firewall-cmd` utility. For any of the other utilities, you may refer to the related system reference manual (such as `man firewall-config`) for more information.

`firewalld` (and `firewalld-cmd`, for that matter) operates with a few key concepts related to monitoring and controlling network packets: *zones*, *rules*, and *targets*.

Understanding firewalld zones

Zones are the top organizational units of the `firewalld` configuration. A network packet monitored by `firewalld` belongs to a zone if it matches the network interface or IP address/netmask source associated with the zone. The following command lists the names of the predefined zones:

```
sudo firewall-cmd --get-zones
```

For detailed information about all the zones that have currently been configured, we can run the following command:

```
sudo firewall-cmd --list-all-zones
```

Here's an excerpt of the related output:

```
[packt@saturn2 ~]$ sudo firewall-cmd --get-zones
FedoraServer FedoraWorkstation block dmz drop external home internal nm-shared public trus
ted work
[packt@saturn2 ~]$
[packt@saturn2 ~]$ sudo firewall-cmd --list-all-zones
FedoraServer (active)
  target: default
  icmp-block-inversion: no
  interfaces: enp1s0
  sources:
  services: cockpit dhcpv6-client ssh
  ports:
  protocols:
  forward: yes
  masquerade: no
  forward-ports:
  source-ports:
  icmp-blocks:
  rich rules:
```

Figure 9.51 – Listing firewalld zones

The preceding output illustrates the default (active) zone in Fedora 37 Server Edition with its own attributes, some of which will be explained next. Zones associated with an interface and a source are known as **active zones**. The following command retrieves the active zones:

```
sudo firewall-cmd --get-active-zones
```

The output, in our case, is as follows:

```
[packt@saturn2 ~]$ sudo firewall-cmd --get-active-zones
FedoraServer
  interfaces: enp1s0
```

Figure 9.52 – The firewalld active zones

Interfaces represent the network adapters that are attached to the localhost. Active interfaces are assigned to either the default zone or a user-defined zone. An interface cannot be assigned to multiple zones.

Sources are incoming IP addresses or address ranges, and they can also be assigned to zones. A single source or multiple overlapping IP address ranges cannot be assigned to more than one zone. Doing so would result in undefined behavior, as it would be unclear which rule takes precedence for the related zone.

By default, `firewalld` assigns all network interfaces to the `public` zone without associating any sources with it. Also, by default, `public` is the only active zone and thus the default zone. The following command displays the default zone:

```
sudo firewall-cmd --get-default-zone
```

The default output is as follows:

```
[packt@saturn2 ~]$ sudo firewall-cmd --get-default-zone
FedoraServer
```

Figure 9.53 – Displaying the default zone in firewalld

Specifying a source for a zone is optional. Consequently, for every data packet, there will be a zone with a matching network interface. However, there won't necessarily be a zone with a matching source. This paradigm would play an essential role in the order in which the matching rules are evaluated. We'll discuss the related topic in the *Understanding rule precedence* section. But first, let's get acquainted with `firewalld` rules.

Understanding firewalld rules

Rules or **rich rules** that are defined in the `firewalld` configuration represent the configuration settings for controlling the data packets associated with a specific zone. Usually, a rule would decide whether a packet is accepted or rejected, based on some predefined criteria.

For example, to block `ping` requests (ICMP protocol) for the `FedoraServer` zone, we can add the following `rich-rule` attribute:

```
sudo firewall-cmd --zone=FedoraServer --add-rich-rule='rule protocol
value="icmp" reject'
```

We can retrieve the `FedoraServer` zone information with the following command:

```
sudo firewall-cmd --info-zone=public
```

The `rich-rule` attribute reflects the updated configuration:

```
[packt@saturn2 ~]$ sudo firewall-cmd --get-default-zone
FedoraServer
[packt@saturn2 ~]$
[packt@saturn2 ~]$ sudo firewall-cmd --zone=FedoraServer --add-rich-rule='rule protocol va
lue="icmp" reject'
success
[packt@saturn2 ~]$ sudo firewall-cmd --info-zone=FedoraServer
FedoraServer (active)
  target: default
  icmp-block-inversion: no
  interfaces: enp1s0
  sources:
  services: cockpit dhcpv6-client ssh
  ports:
  protocols:
  forward: yes
  masquerade: no
  forward-ports:
  source-ports:
  icmp-blocks:
  rich rules:
        rule protocol value="icmp" reject
```

Figure 9.54 – Getting the FedoraServer zone configuration with firewalld

At this point, our host won't respond anymore to `ping` (ICMP) requests. We can remove the `rich-rule` attribute we just added with the following command:

```
sudo firewall-cmd --zone=FedoraServer --remove-rich-rule='rule
protocol value="icmp" reject'
```

Alternatively, we can enable ICMP access with the following command:

```
sudo firewall-cmd --zone=FedoraServer --add-rich-rule='rule protocol
value="icmp" accept'
```

Please note that changes that are made without the `--permanent` option of the `firewall-cmd` utility are transient and won't persist after a system or `firewalld` restart.

When no rich rules are defined or matched for a zone, `firewalld` uses the zone's target to control the packet's behavior. Let's look at targets next.

Understanding firewalld targets

When a packet matches a specific zone, `firewalld` controls the packet's behavior based on the corresponding zone's rich rules. If there are no rich rules defined, or none of the rich rules matches the data packet, the packet's behavior is ultimately determined by the **target** associated with the zone. Possible target values are as follows:

- `ACCEPT`: Accepts the packet
- `REJECT`: Rejects the packet and responds with a reject reply
- `DROP`: Drops the packet without a reply
- `default`: Defers to the default behavior of `firewalld`

Zones, rules, and targets are key configuration elements used by `firewalld` when analyzing and handling data packets. Packets are matched using zones and then acted upon using either rules or targets. Due to the dual nature of zones—based on network interfaces and IP address/range sources—`firewalld` follows a specific order (or precedence) when calculating the matching criteria. We'll look at this next.

Understanding rule precedence

Let's define the terminology first. We'll refer to the zones associated with interfaces as **interface zones**. The zones associated with sources are known as **source zones**. Since zones can have both interfaces and sources assigned to them, a zone can act as either an interface zone, a source zone, or both.

`firewalld` handles a data packet in the following order:

1. It checks the corresponding source zone. There will be, at most, one such zone (since sources can only be associated with a single zone). If there is a match, the packet is handled according to the rules or target associated with the zone. Otherwise, data packet analysis follows as the next step.

2. It checks the corresponding interface zone. Exactly one such zone would (always) exist. If we have a match, the packet is handled according to the zone's rules or target. Otherwise, the packet validation follows as the next step.

Let's assume the default target of `firewalld`—it accepts ICMP packets and rejects everything else. The key takeaway from the preceding validation workflow is that source zones have precedence over interface zones. A typical design pattern for multi-zone `firewalld` configurations defines the following zones:

- **Privileged source zone**: Elevated system access from select IP addresses
- **Restrictive interface zone**: Limited access for everyone else

Let's explore some more potentially useful examples using the `firewall-cmd` utility.

The following command displays services enabled in the firewall:

```
sudo firewall-cmd --list-services
```

The following command enables HTTPS access (port 443):

```
sudo firewall-cmd --zone=FedoraServer --add-service=https
```

To add a user-defined service or port (for example, 8443), we can run the following command:

```
sudo firewall-cmd --zone=FedoraServer --add-port=8443/tcp
```

The following command lists the open ports in the firewall:

```
sudo firewall-cmd --list-ports
```

Invoking the `firewall-cmd` command without the `--permanent` option results in transient changes that won't persist after a system (or `firewalld`) restart. To reload the previously saved (permanent) configuration of `firewalld`, we can run the following command:

```
sudo firewall-cmd --reload
```

For more information on `firewalld`, refer to the related system reference (`man firewalld`) or `https://www.firewalld.org`.

Using ufw

`ufw` is the default firewall manager in Ubuntu. `ufw` provides a relatively simple management framework for `iptables` and Netfilter and an easy-to-use command-line interface for manipulating the firewall.

Let's look at a few examples of using `ufw`. Please note that the `ufw` command-line utility needs superuser privileges. The following command reports the status of `ufw`:

```
sudo ufw status
```

By default, `ufw` is `inactive` (disabled). We can enable `ufw` with the following command:

```
sudo ufw enable
```

Always be careful when you enable the firewall or perform any changes that may affect your access to the system. By default, when enabled, `ufw` will block all incoming access except `ping` (ICMP) requests. If you're logged in with SSH, you may get a prompt warning you that the SSH connection could be lost while trying to enable `ufw`. To play it safe, you may want to abort the preceding operation by pressing n (No) and enabling SSH access in the firewall first:

```
sudo ufw allow ssh
```

If SSH access is already enabled, the output suggests that the related security rule will not be added. If not, the rule will be added.

At this point, you can safely enable ufw without fearing that your current or existing SSH connections will be dropped. Upon enabling ufw, we get the same prompt as before, but this time, we can press y (Yes).

To check upon a detailed status of the firewall, you can run the following command:

```
sudo ufw status verbose
```

The output for running all these commands is shown in the following screenshot:

```
packt@neptune:~$ sudo ufw status
[sudo] password for packt:
Status: inactive
packt@neptune:~$ sudo ufw enable
Command may disrupt existing ssh connections. Proceed with operation (y|n)? n
Aborted
packt@neptune:~$ sudo ufw allow ssh
Rules updated
Rules updated (v6)
packt@neptune:~$ sudo ufw enable
Command may disrupt existing ssh connections. Proceed with operation (y|n)? y
Firewall is active and enabled on system startup
packt@neptune:~$ sudo ufw status verbose
Status: active
Logging: on (low)
Default: deny (incoming), allow (outgoing), disabled (routed)
New profiles: skip

To                         Action      From
--                         ------      ----
123/udp                    ALLOW IN    Anywhere
22/tcp                     ALLOW IN    Anywhere
123/udp (v6)               ALLOW IN    Anywhere (v6)
22/tcp (v6)                ALLOW IN    Anywhere (v6)
```

Figure 9.55 – Enabling ufw, allowing ssh, and detailed status of ufw

It's always recommended to check your firewall settings to ensure that inadvertent access to the system is not allowed.

We can list the current application security profiles with the following command:

```
sudo ufw app list
```

In our case, only OpenSSH is available, activated when we allowed SSH connections earlier in this section.

Let us add other services, such as HTTP (port 80) and HTTPS (port 443), used by Apache and nginx. This can be achieved in several different ways. We can either use port numbers (80, 443), we can use service names as an alternate way (http, https), or we can specify web server names directly (Apache Full, Nginx Full). Details are shown in *Figure 9.56*.

To remove a specific service's access (such as HTTP), we can run the following command:

```
sudo ufw deny http
```

The output shows that a new rule has been added. A subsequent detailed status check would show that access to port 80/tcp has been denied. Yet, the resulting status is somewhat convoluted. In the following screenshot, we can see the output of adding and removing the commands that were just discussed:

```
packt@neptune:~$ sudo ufw allow http
Rule added
Rule added (v6)
packt@neptune:~$ sudo ufw allow https
Rule added
Rule added (v6)
packt@neptune:~$ sudo ufw status verbose
Status: active
Logging: on (low)
Default: deny (incoming), allow (outgoing), disabled (routed)
New profiles: skip

To                         Action      From
--                         ------      ----
123/udp                    ALLOW IN    Anywhere
22/tcp                     ALLOW IN    Anywhere
80/tcp                     ALLOW IN    Anywhere
443                        ALLOW IN    Anywhere
123/udp (v6)               ALLOW IN    Anywhere (v6)
22/tcp (v6)                ALLOW IN    Anywhere (v6)
80/tcp (v6)                ALLOW IN    Anywhere (v6)
443 (v6)                   ALLOW IN    Anywhere (v6)

packt@neptune:~$ sudo ufw deny http
Rule updated
Rule updated (v6)
packt@neptune:~$ sudo ufw status verbose
Status: active
Logging: on (low)
Default: deny (incoming), allow (outgoing), disabled (routed)
New profiles: skip

To                         Action      From
--                         ------      ----
123/udp                    ALLOW IN    Anywhere
22/tcp                     ALLOW IN    Anywhere
80/tcp                     DENY IN     Anywhere
443                        ALLOW IN    Anywhere
123/udp (v6)               ALLOW IN    Anywhere (v6)
22/tcp (v6)                ALLOW IN    Anywhere (v6)
80/tcp (v6)                DENY IN     Anywhere (v6)
443 (v6)                   ALLOW IN    Anywhere (v6)
```

Figure 9.56 – Adding and denying rules in ufw

To reinstate the rules in the right order, let's get a numbered output of the rule list first:

```
sudo ufw status numbered
```

The output yields the following result:

```
packt@neptune:~$ sudo ufw status numbered
Status: active

     To                      Action      From
     --                      ------      ----
[ 1] 123/udp                 ALLOW IN    Anywhere
[ 2] 22/tcp                  ALLOW IN    Anywhere
[ 3] 80/tcp                  DENY IN     Anywhere
[ 4] 443                     ALLOW IN    Anywhere
[ 5] 123/udp (v6)            ALLOW IN    Anywhere (v6)
[ 6] 22/tcp (v6)             ALLOW IN    Anywhere (v6)
[ 7] 80/tcp (v6)             DENY IN     Anywhere (v6)
[ 8] 443 (v6)                ALLOW IN    Anywhere (v6)
```

Figure 9.57 – Numbered list of rules in ufw

The order of the rules is suggested by sequence numbers. Always put more specific (restrictive) rules first. As rules are being added or changed, you may need to delete old entries or rearrange their order to ensure that the rules are appropriately placed and evaluated.

Alternatively, we could use the insert option to add a specific rule at a given position. For example, the following command places the 80/tcp DENY rule in the second position:

```
sudo ufw insert 2 deny http
```

Let's look at a few more examples of using ufw. The following command enables SSH access (port 22) for all protocols (any) from a specific source address range (192.168.0.0/24):

```
sudo ufw allow from 192.168.0.0/24 to any port 22
```

The following command enables ufw logging:

```
sudo ufw logging on
```

The corresponding log traces are usually in /var/log/syslog:

```
grep -i ufw /var/log/syslog
```

To disable ufw logging, run the following command:

```
sudo ufw logging off
```

The following command reverts `ufw` to the system's defaults:

```
sudo ufw reset
```

The preceding command results in removing all rules and disabling `ufw`.

For more information about `ufw`, you may wish to explore the *UFW Community Help* wiki at `https://help.ubuntu.com/community/UFW` or the related system reference (`man ufw`).

The use of firewall management tools such as `ufw` and `firewalld` may have more appeal to some Linux administrators, compared with lower-level packet filtering utilities (for example, Netfilter, `iptables`, and `nftables`). One of the arguments for choosing one tool over the other, besides platform considerations, is related to scripting and automation capabilities. Some power users may consider the `nft` command-line utility the tool of choice for designing their firewall rules, due to the granular control provided by `nftables`. Other users may be inclined to use `iptables`, especially on older legacy platforms. In the end, it's a matter of choice or preference, as all of these tools are capable of configuring and managing a firewall to roughly the same extent.

Let's wrap up our chapter with some final considerations.

Summary

The relatively vast content of this chapter may appear overwhelming. A key takeaway should be the focus on the frameworks (modules). If we're discussing firewalls, we should look at packet filtering frameworks such as `iptables`, Netfilter, and `nftables`. For access control, we have security modules such as SELinux and AppArmor. We covered some of the pros and cons of each. The pivoting choice, possibly deciding the Linux distro, is between AppArmor and SELinux. One is perhaps swifter than the other, with the related administration effort hanging in the balance. For example, choosing AppArmor would narrow down the major Linux distributions to Ubuntu, Debian, and openSUSE. The distro choice, in turn, would further dictate the available firewall management solutions, and so on.

Mastering the application security frameworks and firewall management tools will help you keep your systems safe with minimal effort. As with any typical Linux system administration task, there are many ways of securing your system. We hope that you will build upon the exploratory knowledge and tools presented in this chapter to make a balanced decision regarding keeping your systems secure.

The next chapter will add a further notch to the safety and protection of your system by introducing **disaster recovery (DR)**, diagnostics, and troubleshooting practices.

Exercises

Here's a brief quiz about some of the essential concepts that were covered in this chapter:

1. Enumerate at least a couple of ACMs that are used in Linux.

    Hint: DAC, ACL, MAC, RBAC, MLS, MCS

2. Enumerate the fields of the SELinux security context.

    Hint: user, role, type, level

3. What is a domain in SELinux?

    Hint: Type assigned to a process

4. Can you think of a significant difference between SELinux and AppArmor in terms of enforcing security policies?

    Hint: SELinux uses policies based on file labels, while AppArmor uses security policies based on paths.

5. How do we toggle an AppArmor application profile between the `enforce` and `complain` modes?

    Hint: Using `aa-enforce` and `aa-complain`

6. How many chains can you think of in the Linux kernel networking stack?

    Hint: *Figure 9.41* could help you.

7. What is the default firewall management solution in RHEL/Fedora? How about Ubuntu?

    Hint: `firewalld` (Fedora) and `ufw` (Ubuntu)

Further reading

Please refer to the following Packt books for more information about the topics that were covered in this chapter:

- *Mastering Linux Security and Hardening – Second Edition* by Donald A. Tevault, Packt Publishing
- *Practical Linux Security Cookbook – Second Edition* by Tajinder Kalsi, Packt Publishing

10

Disaster Recovery, Diagnostics, and Troubleshooting

In this chapter, you will learn how to do a system backup and restore in a disaster recovery scenario, and how to **diagnose** and **troubleshoot** a common array of problems. These are skills that each Linux system administrator needs to have if they wish to be prepared for worst-case scenarios such as power outages, theft, or hardware failure. The world's IT backbone runs on Linux and we need to be prepared for anything that life throws at us.

In this chapter, we're going to cover the following main topics:

- Planning for disaster recovery
- Backing up and restoring the system
- Introducing common Linux diagnostic tools for troubleshooting

Technical requirements

No special technical requirements are needed for this chapter, just a working installation of Linux on your system or even two different working systems on your local network for some of the examples used. Ubuntu and Fedora are equally suitable for this chapter's exercises, but in this chapter, we'll be using Ubuntu 22.04.2 LTS Server and Desktop editions.

Planning for disaster recovery

Managing risks is an important asset for every business or individual. The responsibility of this is tremendous for everyone involved in system administration. For all businesses, managing risks should be part of a wider **risk management strategy**. There are various types of risks in IT, starting from natural hazards directly impacting data centers or business locations, all the way up to cyber security threats. IT's footprint inside a company has exponentially grown in the last decade. Nowadays, there is no activity that does not involve some sort of IT operations being behind it, be it inside small businesses, big corporations, government agencies, or the health and education public sectors, just to give a few examples. Each activity is unique in its own way, so it needs a specific type of assessment. Unfortunately, with regard to the information security field, risk management has largely evolved into a one-size-fits-all practice, based on checklists that should be implemented by IT management. Let's begin with a brief introduction to risk management before moving on to learning how we can assess risk.

A brief introduction to risk management

What is **risk management**? In a nutshell, it is comprised of specific operations that are set to mitigate any possible threat that could impact the overall continuity of a business. The risk management process is crucial for every IT department.

Risk management frameworks initially arose in the United States due to the **Federal Information Systems Modernization Act (FISMA)** laws, which started in 2002. This was the time when the United States **National Institute of Standards and Technology (NIST)** began to create new standards and methods for cyber security assessments among all US government agencies. Therefore, security certifications and compliances are of utmost importance for every Linux distribution provider that sees itself as a worthy competitor in the corporate and governmental space. Similar to the US certification bodies discussed previously, there are other agencies in the UK and Russia that develop specific security certifications. In this respect, all major Linux distributions from Red Hat, SUSE, and Canonical have certifications from NIST, the UK's **National Cyber Security Centre (NCSC)**, or Russia's **Federal Service for Technic and Export Control (FSTEC)**.

The risk management framework, according to NIST SP 800-37r2 (see the official NIST website at `https://csrc.nist.gov/publications/detail/sp/800-37/rev-2/final`), has seven steps, starting with preparing for the framework's execution, up to monitoring the organization's systems on a daily basis. We will not discuss those steps in detail; instead, we will provide a link at the end of this chapter for NIST's official documentation. In a nutshell, the risk management framework is comprised of several important branches, such as the following:

- **Inventory**: A thorough inventory of all available systems that are on-premises, and a list of all software solutions

- **System categorization**: Assesses the impact level for each data type that's used with regard to availability, integrity, and confidentiality

- **Security control**: Subject to detailed procedures with regard to hundreds of computer systems' security – a compendium of NIST security controls can be found under SP800-53r4 (the following is a link to the official NIST website: `https://csrc.nist.gov/publications/detail/sp/800-53/rev-4/final`)

- **Risk assessment**: A series of steps that cover threat source identification, vulnerability identification, impact determination, information sharing, risk monitoring, and periodical updates

- **System security plan**: A report based on every security control and how future actions are assessed, including their implementation and effectiveness

- **Certification, accreditation, assessment, and authorization**: The process of reviewing security assessments and highlighting security issues and effective resolutions that are detailed in a future plan of action

- **Plan of action**: A tool that's used to track security weaknesses and apply the correct response procedures

There are many types of risks when it comes to information technology, including hardware failure, software errors, spam and viruses, human error, and natural disasters (fires, floods, earthquakes, hurricanes, and so on). There are also risks of a more criminal nature, including security breaches, employee dishonesty, corporate espionage, or anything else that could be considered a cybercrime. These risks can be addressed by implementing an appropriate risk management strategy. As a basis, such a strategy should have five distinct steps:

1. **Identifying risk**: Identifying possible threats and vulnerabilities that could impact your ongoing IT operations.

2. **Analyzing risk**: Deciding how big or small it is, based on thorough studies.

3. **Evaluating risk**: Evaluating the impact that it could have on your operations; the immediate action is to respond to the risk based on the impact it has. This calls for real actions to be performed at every level of your operations.

4. **Responding to risk**: Activating your **disaster recovery plans (DRPs)**, combined with strategies for prevention and mitigation.

5. **Monitoring and reviewing risk**: Triggering a drastic monitoring and reviewing strategy will ensure that all the IT teams know how to respond to the risk and have the tools and abilities to isolate it and enforce the company's infrastructure.

Risk assessment is extremely important to any business and should be taken very seriously by IT management. Now that we've tackled some concepts of risk management, it is time to explain what it really is.

Risk calculation

Risk assessment, also known as **risk calculation** or **risk analysis**, refers to the action of finding and calculating solutions to possible threats and vulnerabilities. The following are some basic terms you should know when you talk about risk impact:

- The **annual loss expectancy (ALE)** defines the loss that's expected in 1 year.

- The **single loss expectancy (SLE)** represents how much loss is expected at any given time.

- The **annual rate of occurrence (ARO)** is the likeliness of a risky event occurring within 1 year.

- The **risk calculation formula** is *SLE x ARO = ALE*. There is a monetary value that each element of the formula will provide, so the final result is also expressed as a monetary value. This is a formula that is useful to know.

- The **mean time between failures (MTBF)** is used to measure the time between anticipated and reparable failures.

- The **mean time to failure (MTTF)** is the average time the system can operate before experiencing an irreparable failure.

- The **mean time to restore (MTTR)** measures the time needed to repair an affected system.

- The **recovery time objective (RTO)** represents the maximum time that's allocated for downtime.

- The **recovery point objective (RPO)** defines the time when a system needs to be restored.

Knowing those terms will help you understand risk assessments so that you can perform a well-documented assessment if or when needed. Risk assessment is based on two major types of actions (or better said, strategies):

- **Proactive actions**:

  - **Risk avoidance**: Based on risk identification and finding a quick solution to avoid its occurrence

  - **Risk mitigation**: Based on actions taken to reduce the occurrence of a possible risk

  - **Risk transference**: Transferring the risk's possible outcome with an external entity

  - **Risk deterrence**: Based on specific systems and policies that should discourage any attacker from exploiting the system

- **Non-active actions**:

  - **Risk acceptance**: Accepting the risk if the other proactive actions could exceed the cost of the harm that's done by the risk

The strategies described here can be applied to the risk associated with generic, on-premises computing, but nowadays, cloud computing is slowly and surely taking over the world. So, how could these risk strategies apply to cloud computing? In cloud computing, you use the infrastructure of a third party, but with your own data. Even though we will start discussing Linux in the cloud in *Chapter 14, Short Introduction to Computing*, there are some concepts that we will introduce now. As we mentioned earlier, the cloud is taking the infrastructure operations from your on-premises environment to a larger player, such as Amazon, Microsoft, or Google. This could generally be seen as outsourcing. This means that some risks that were a threat when you were running services on-premises are now transferred to third parties.

There are three major cloud paradigms that are now buzzwords all over technology media:

- **Software as a service (SaaS)**: This is a software solution for companies looking to reduce IT costs and rely on software subscriptions. Some examples of SaaS solutions are **Slack**, **Microsoft 365**, **Google Apps**, and **Dropbox**, among others.

- **Platform as a service (PaaS)**: The way you get software applications to your clients using another's infrastructure, runtimes, and dependencies is also known as an application platform. This can be on a public cloud, on a private cloud, or on a hybrid solution. Some examples of PaaS are **Microsoft Azure**, **AWS Lambda**, **Google App Engine**, **SAP Cloud Platform**, **Heroku**, and **Red Hat OpenShift**.

- **Infrastructure as a service (IaaS)**: These are services that are run online and provide high-level **application programming interfaces (APIs)**. A notable example is **OpenStack**.

Details about all these technologies will be provided in *Chapter 14, Short Introduction to Computing*, but for this chapter's purpose, we have provided enough information. Major risks regarding cloud computing are concerned with data integration and compatibility. Those are among the risks that you must still overcome since most of the other risks are no longer your concern as they are transferred to the third party managing the infrastructure.

Risk calculation can be managed in different ways, depending on the IT scenario a company uses. When you're using the on-premises scenario and you're managing all the components in-house, risk assessments become quite challenging. When you're using the IaaS, PaaS, and SaaS scenarios, risk assessment becomes less challenging as responsibilities are gradually transferred to an external entity.

Risk assessment should always be taken seriously by any individual concerned with the safety of their network and systems and by any IT manager. This is when a DRP comes into action. The foundation of a good DRP and strategy is having an effective risk assessment.

Designing a DRP

A DRP is structured around the steps that should be taken when an incident occurs. In most cases, the DRP is part of a **business continuity plan**. This determines how a company should continue to operate based on a functioning infrastructure.

Every DRP needs to start from an accurate **hardware inventory**, followed by a **software applications inventory** and a separate **data inventory**. The most important part of this is the strategy that's designed to back up all the information that's used.

In terms of the hardware that's used, there must be a clear policy for standardized hardware. This will ensure that faulty hardware can easily be replaced. This kind of policy ensures that everything works and is optimized. Standardized hardware surely has good driver support, and this is very important in the Linux world. Nevertheless, using standardized hardware will tremendously limit practices such as **bring your own device (BYOD)**, since employees only need to use the hardware provided by their employer. Using standardized hardware comes with using specific software applications that have been set up and configured by the company's IT department, with limited input available from the user.

The IT department's responsibility is huge, and it plays an important role in designing the **IT recovery strategies** as part of a DRP. Key tolerances for downtime and loss of data should be defined based on the minimal acceptable RPO and RTO.

Deciding on the **roles** regarding who is responsible for what is another key step of a good DRP. This way, the response time for implementing the plan will be dramatically reduced and everyone will know their own responsibilities in case any risks arise. In this case, having a good **communication strategy** is critical. Enforcing clear procedures for every level of the organizational pyramid will provide clear communication, centralized decisions, and a succession plan for backup personnel.

DRPs need to be thoroughly tested at least twice a year to prove their efficiency. Unplanned downtime and outages can negatively impact a business, both on-premises and in any multi-cloud environment. Being prepared for worst-case scenarios is important. Therefore, in the following sections, we will show you some of the best tools and practices for backing up and restoring a Linux system.

Backing up and restoring the system

Disasters can occur at any time. Risk is everywhere. In this respect, backing up your system is of utmost importance and needs to be done regularly. It is always better to practice good prevention than to recover from data loss and learn this the hard way.

Backup and **recovery** need to be done based on a well-thought-out strategy and need to take the RTO and RPO factors into consideration. The RTO should answer basic questions such as how fast to recover lost data and how this will affect the business operations, while the RPO should answer questions such as how much of your data you can afford to lose.

There are different types and methods of backup. The following are some examples:

Types of Backup		Methods of Backup	
Full backup	Backing up all the files in the destination target	**Manual backup**	User initiated, not necessarily on a reliable schedule
Incremental backup	Backing up all the files that changed from the last backup	**Local automated backup**	Automated backup, on a schedule, more reliable, targeting external drives
Differential backup	Backing up all the files that changed from the previous full backup	**Remote automated backup**	Automated backup, on a schedule, targeting external drives over the network

Figure 10.1 – Backup methods and types

When doing a backup, keep the following rules in mind:

- The **321 rule** means that you should always have at least three copies of your data, with two copies on two different media at separate locations and one backup always being kept off-site (at a different geographical location). This is also known as the **rule of three**; it can be adapted to anything, such as 312, 322, 311, or 323.

- **Backup checking** is extremely relevant and is overlooked most of the time. It checks the data's integrity and usefulness.

- **Clear and documented backup strategy and procedures** are beneficial to everyone in the IT team who is using the same practices.

In the next section, we will look at some well-known tools for full Linux system backups, starting with the ones that are integrated inside the operating system to third-party solutions that are equally suited for both home and enterprise use.

Disk cloning solutions

A good option for a backup is to clone the entire hard drive or several partitions that hold sensitive data. Linux offers a plethora of versatile tools for this job. Among those are the dd command, the ddrescue command, and the **Relax-and-Recover (ReaR)** software tool. Let's look at these in detail in the following sections.

The dd command

One of the most well-known disk backup commands is the dd command. We discussed this previously in *Chapter 6, Working with Disks and Filesystems*. Let's recap how it is used in a backup and restore scenario. The dd command is used to copy block by block, regardless of the filesystem type, from a source to a destination.

Let's learn how to clone an entire disk. We have a virtual machine on our system that has a 20 GB drive that we want to back up on a 128 GB USB pen drive. The procedures we are going to show you will work on bare metal too.

First, we will run the sudo fdisk -l command to verify that the disk sizes are correct. The output will show us information about both our local drive and the USB pen drive, among other information, depending on your system.

Now that we know what the sizes are and that the source can fit into the destination, we will proceed to cloning the entire virtual disk. We will clone the source disk, /dev/vda, to the destination disk, /dev/sda (the operation could take a while):

```
packt@neptune:~$ sudo dd if=/dev/vda of=/dev/sda conv=noerror,sync status=progress
2245710336 bytes (2.2 GB, 2.1 GiB) copied, 175 s, 12.8 MB/s
```

Figure 10.2 – Using dd to clone an entire hard drive

The options shown in the preceding command are as follows:

- if=/dev/vda represents the input file, which, in our case, is the source hard drive
- of=/dev/sda represents the output file, which is the destination USB drive
- conv=noerror represents the instruction that allows the command to continue ignoring errors
- sync represents the instruction to fill the input error blocks with zeros so that the data offset will always be synced
- status=progress shows statistics about the transfer process

Please keep in mind that this operation could take a while to finish. On our system, it took 200 minutes to complete. We took the preceding screenshot while the operation was at the beginning. In the following section, we will show you how to use ddrescue.

The ddrescue command

The ddrescue command is yet another tool you can use to clone your disk. This tool copies from one device or file to another one, trying to copy only the good and healthy parts the first time. If your disk is failing, you might want to use ddrescue twice since, the first time, it will copy only the good sectors and map the errors to a destination file. The second time, it will copy only the bad sectors, so it is better to add an option for several read attempts just to be sure.

On Ubuntu, the `ddrescue` utility is not installed by default. To install it, use the following `apt` command:

```
sudo apt install gddrescue
```

We will use `ddrescue` on the same system we used previously and clone the same drive. The command for this is as follows:

```
sudo ddrescue -n /dev/vda /dev/sda rescue.map --force
```

The output is as follows:

```
packt@neptune:~$ sudo ddrescue -n /dev/vda /dev/sda rescue.map --force
GNU ddrescue 1.23
Press Ctrl-C to interrupt
      ipos:    8800 MB, non-trimmed:       0 B,  current rate:   7340 kB/s
      opos:    8800 MB, non-scraped:       0 B,  average rate: 18258 kB/s
  non-tried:  12674 MB,  bad-sector:       0 B,    error rate:      0 B/s
   rescued:    8800 MB,   bad areas:       0,      run time:    8m  2s
pct rescued:   40.98%, read errors:        0,  remaining time:       7m
                             time since last successful read:        0s
Copying non-tried blocks... Pass 1 (forwards)█
```

Figure 10.3 – Using ddrescue to clone the hard drive

We used the `ddrescue` command with the `--force` option to make sure that everything on the destination will be overwritten. This operation is time-consuming too, so be prepared for a lengthy wait. In our case, it took almost 1 hour to finish. Next, we will show you how to use another useful tool, the ReaR utility.

Using ReaR

ReaR is a powerful disaster recovery and system migration tool written in Bash. It is used by enterprise-ready distributions such as RHEL and SLES, and can also be installed on Ubuntu. It was designed to be easy to use and set up. It is integrated with the local bootloader, with the `cron` scheduler, or monitoring tools such as **Nagios**. For more details on this tool, visit the official website at `http://relax-and-recover.org/about/`.

To install it on Ubuntu, use the following command:

```
sudo apt install rear
```

Once the packages have been installed, you will need to know the location of the main configuration file, which is `/etc/rear/local.conf`, and all the configuration options should be written inside it. ReaR makes ISO files by default, but it also supports Samba (CIFS), USB, and NFS as backup destinations. Next, we will show you how to use ReaR to back up to a local NFS server.

Backing up to a local NFS server using ReaR

As an example, we will show you how to back up to an NFS server. As specified in the *Technical requirements* section, you would need to have at least two systems available on your network for this exercise: an NFS server set up on one of the machines (as a backup server) and a second system as the production machine to be backed up. ReaR should be installed on both of them. Perform the following steps:

1. First, we must configure the NFS server accordingly (the operation is covered in *Chapter 13, Configuring Linux Servers*). For extensive information on setting up an NFS server, please refer to *Chapter 13*; here, we only cover it briefly. The configuration file for NFS is `/etc/exports` and it stores information about the share's location. Before you add any new information about the ReaR backup share's location, add a new directory. We will consider the `/home/export/` directory for our NFS setup. Inside that directory, we will create a new one for our ReaR backups. The command to create the new directory is as follows:

    ```
    sudo mkdir /home/export/rear
    ```

2. Now, change the ownership of the directory. If the owner remains `root`, ReaR will not have permission to write the backup to this location. Change the ownership using the following command:

    ```
    sudo chown -R nobody:nogroup /home/export/rear/
    ```

3. Once the directory has been created, open the `/etc/exports` file with your favorite editor and add a new line for the backup directory. The line should look like the following:

    ```
    /home/export/rear 192.168.124.0/24(rw,sync,no_subtree_check)
    ```

    Use your local network's IP range, not the one we used.

4. Once the new line has been introduced, restart the NFS service and run the `exportfs` command using the `-s` option:

    ```
    sudo systemctl restart nfs-kernel-server.service
    ```

5. After setting up the NFS server, go to the local machine and start editing the ReaR configuration file so that you can use the backup server. Edit the `/etc/rear/local.conf` file and add the lines shown in the following output. Use your own system's IP address, not the one we used. The code should look like the following:

    ```
    OUTPUT=ISO
    OUTPUT_URL=nfs://192.168.124.112/home/export/rear
    BACKUP=NETFS
    BACKUP_URL=nfs://192.168.124.112/home/export/rear
    ```

Backing up and restoring the system   393

The lines shown in the preceding code represent the following:

- OUTPUT: The bootable image type, which, in our case, is ISO
- OUTPUT_URL: The backup target, which can represent NFS, CIFS, FTP, RSYNC, or file
- BACKUP: The backup method used, which, in our case, is NETFS, the default ReaR method
- BACKUP_URL: The backup target's location

6. Now, run the mkbackup command with the -v and -d options:

```
sudo rear -v -d mkbackup
```

The output will be large, so we will not show it to you here. The command will take a significant time to finish. Once it has finished, you can check the NFS directory to view its output. The backup should be in there.

There are several files written on the NFS server. Among those, the one called rear-neptune.iso is the actual backup and the one that will be used in case a system restore is needed. There is also a file called backup.tar.gz, which contains all the files from our local machine.

> **Important note**
> The naming convention of ReaR is as follows. The name will consist of the term rear-, followed by the system's hostname and the .iso extension. Our system's hostname is neptune, which is why the backup file is called rear-neptune.iso in our case.

Once the backup has been written on the NFS server, you will be able to restore the system by using a USB disk or DVD with the ISO image that was written on the NFS server.

Backing up to USB using ReaR

There is also the option of directly backing up on the USB disk. Here are the steps to be followed:

1. Insert a disk into the USB port and format it by using the following command:

```
sudo rear format /dev/sda
```

The command will take a significant time to complete. The output is as follows:

```
packt@neptune:~$ sudo rear format /dev/sda
USB device /dev/sda is not formatted with ext2/3/4 or btrfs filesystem
Type exactly 'Yes' to format /dev/sda with ext3 filesystem
(default 'No' timeout 300 seconds)
Yes
```

Figure 10.4 – Formatting the USB disk with ReaR

2. Now, we need to modify the `/etc/rear/local.conf` file and adapt it so that it uses the USB as the backup destination. The new lines we will add should look as follows:

```
OUTPUT=USB
BACKUP_URL="usb:///dev/disk/by-label/REAR-000"
```

3. To understand the last line of code, you can run the following command:

`sudo ls -la /dev/disk/by-label/`

The output shows that `/dev/disk/by-label/REAR-000` is a link to `/dev/sda1` (in our case):

```
packt@neptune:~$ sudo ls -la /dev/disk/by-label/
total 0
drwxr-xr-x 2 root root  60 Apr 25 19:09 .
drwxr-xr-x 8 root root 160 Apr 25 19:09 ..
lrwxrwxrwx 1 root root  10 Apr 25 19:09 REAR-000 -> ../../sda1
```

Figure 10.5 – Checking the URL location from the ReaR configuration file

4. To back up the system on the USB disk, run the following command:

`sudo rear -v mkbackup`

The operation will take a considerable amount of time to run, so just be patient. Once it has finished, the ISO and the `tar.gz` files will be on the USB drive.

5. To recover the system, you will need to boot from the USB drive and select the first option, which says `Recover "hostname"`, where `"hostname"` is the hostname of the computer you backed up.

System backup and recovery are two very important tasks that should be indispensable to any Linux system administrator. Knowing how to execute those tasks can save data, time, and money for both the company and the client. Minimal downtime and having a quick, effective response should be the most important assets on every **Chief Technology Officer's (CTO's)** table. Backup and recovery strategies should always have a strong foundation in terms of good mitigation practices. In this respect, a strong diagnostics toolset and troubleshooting knowledge will always come in handy for every system administrator. This is why, in the next section, we will show you some of the best diagnostic tools in Linux.

Introducing common Linux diagnostic tools for troubleshooting

The openness of Linux is one of its best assets. This opened the door to an extensive number of solutions that can be used for any task at hand. Hence, many diagnostic tools are available to Linux system administrators. Depending on which part of your system you would like to diagnose, there are several tools available. Troubleshooting is essentially problem-solving based on diagnostics generated by specific tools. To reduce the number of diagnostic tools to cover, we will narrow down the issues to the following categories for this section:

- Boot issues
- General system issues
- Network issues
- Hardware issues

There are specific diagnostic tools for each of these categories. We will start by showing you some of the most widely used ones.

Tools for troubleshooting boot issues

To understand the issues that may affect the boot process, it is important to know how the boot process works. We have not covered this in detail yet, so pay attention to everything that we will tell you.

The boot process

All the major Linux distributions, such as Ubuntu, OpenSUSE, Debian, Fedora, and RHEL, use **Grand Unified Bootloader version 2** (**GRUB2**) as their default bootloader and `systemd` as their default init system. Until GRUB2 initialization and the `systemd` startup were put in place, the Linux boot process had several more stages.

The boot order is as follows:

1. The **Basic Input Output System (BIOS) Power-On Self-Test (POST)**
2. GRUB2 bootloader initialization
3. GNU/Linux kernel initialization
4. `systemd init` system initialization

BIOS POST is a process specific to hardware initialization and testing, and it is similar for every PC, regardless of whether it is using Linux or Windows. The BIOS makes sure that every hardware component inside the PC is working properly. When the BIOS fails to start, there is usually a hardware problem or incompatibility issue. The BIOS searches for the disk's boot record, such as the **master boot record** (**MBR**) or **GUID Partition Table** (**GPT**), and loads it into memory.

GRUB2 initialization is where Linux starts to kick in. This is the stage when the system loads the kernel into memory. It can choose between several different kernels in case there's more than one operating system available. Once the kernel has been loaded into memory, it takes control of the boot process.

The kernel is a self-extracting archive. Once extracted, it runs into the memory and loads the `init` system, the parent of all the other processes on Linux.

The `init` system, called `systemd`, starts by mounting the filesystems and accessing all the available configuration files.

During the boot process, issues may appear. In the next section, we will discuss what to do if disaster strikes and your bootloader won't start.

Repairing GRUB2

If GRUB2 breaks, you will not be able to access your system. This calls for a GRUB repair. At this stage, a live bootable USB drive will save you. The following steps are an exercise that could count as an experiment. In our case, we have an Ubuntu 22.04 LTS Desktop edition live disk, and we will use it for this example. However, you can use any Linux distribution you like, not necessarily Ubuntu. The point is that you would need a live bootable USB drive with Linux on it. Here are the steps you should follow:

1. Plug in the Ubuntu 22.04 live disk drive and boot the system.

2. Open the BIOS, select the bootable disk as the main boot device, and restart it.

3. Select the **Try Ubuntu** option.

4. Once inside the Ubuntu instance, open Terminal, enter the `sudo fdisk -l` command, and check your disks and partitions.

5. Select the one that GRUB2 is installed on and use the following command (use the disk names as provided by your system; don't copy/paste our example):

    ```
    sudo mount -t ext4 /dev/sda1 /mnt
    ```

6. Install GRUB2 using the following commands:

    ```
    sudo chroot /mnt
    grub-install /dev/sda
    grub-install -recheck /dev/sda
    update-grub
    ```

7. Unmount the partition using the following commands:

    ```
    exit
    sudo unmount /mnt
    ```

8. Reboot the computer.

Dealing with bootloaders is extremely sensitive. Pay attention to all the details and take care of all the commands you type in. If not, everything could go sideways. In the next section, we will show you some diagnostic tools for general system issues.

Tools for troubleshooting general system issues

System issues can be of different types and complexities. Knowing the tools to deal with them is of utmost importance. In this section, we will cover the default tools provided by the Linux distribution. Basic troubleshooting knowledge is necessary for any Linux system administrator as issues can – and will – occur during regular operations.

What could general system issues mean? Well, basically, these are issues regarding disk space, memory usage, system load, and running processes.

Commands for disk-related issues

Disks, be they HDDs or SSDs, are an important part of the system. They provide the necessary space for your data, files, and software of any type, including the operating system. We will not discuss hardware-related issues as this will be the subject of a future section in this chapter called *Tools for troubleshooting hardware issues*. Instead, we will cover issues related to **disk space**. The most common diagnostic tools for this are already installed on any Linux system, and they are represented by the following commands:

- du: A utility that shows disk space utilization for files and directories
- df: A utility that shows the disk usage for directories

The following is an example of using the df utility with the -h (human-readable) option:

```
df -h
```

If one of the disks runs out of space, it will be shown in the output. This is not an issue in our case, but the tool is still relevant for finding out which of the available disks is having issues with the free available space.

When a disk is full, or almost full, there are several fixes that can be applied. If you have to delete some of the files, we advise you to delete them from your /home directory. Try not to delete important system files. The following are some ideas for troubleshooting available space issues:

- Delete the unnecessary files using the rm command (optionally using, with caution, the -rf option) or the rmdir command
- Move files to an external drive (or to the cloud) using the rsync command
- Find which directories use the most space in your /home directory

The following is an example of using the du utility to find the largest directories inside the /home directory. We are using two pipes to transfer the output of the du command to the sort command and finally to the head command with the option of 5 (because we want to show the five largest directories, not all of them):

```
packt@neptune:~$ sudo du -h /home | sort -rh | head -5
181M    /home/packt
181M    /home
16K     /home/alex
12K     /home/packt/reports
12K     /home/packt/.local
```

Figure 10.6 – Finding the largest directories in your /home directory

Another troubleshooting scenario is with regard to the number of inodes being used, not with the space on a disk. In this case, you can use the df -i command to see whether you've run out of inodes:

```
packt@neptune:~$ df -i
Filesystem                          Inodes  IUsed  IFree IUse% Mounted on
tmpfs                               252890    810 252080    1% /run
/dev/mapper/ubuntu--vg-ubuntu--lv   655360 120212 535148   19% /
tmpfs                               252890      1 252889    1% /dev/shm
tmpfs                               252890      3 252887    1% /run/lock
tmpfs                                50578     25  50553    1% /run/user/1000
```

Figure 10.7 – inode usage statistics

The output in the preceding screenshot shows basic information about the inode usage on the system. You will see the total numbers of inodes on different filesystems, how many inodes are in use (as a number and as a percentage), and how many are free.

Besides the commands shown here, which are the defaults for every Linux distribution, there are many other open source tools for disk space issues, such as **pydf**, **parted**, **sfdisk**, **iostat**, and the GUI-based **GParted** application.

In the next section, we will show you how to use commands to verify possible memory issues.

Commands for memory usage issues

Memory overload, together with CPU loading and disk usage, are responsible for overall system performance. Checking system load with specific tools is of utmost importance. The default tool for checking RAM statistics in Linux is called free and it can be accessed in any major distribution. In the following example, we will use the -h option for a human-readable output:

```
packt@neptune:~$ free -h
              total        used        free      shared  buff/cache   available
Mem:          1.9Gi       251Mi       745Mi       1.0Mi       978Mi       1.5Gi
Swap:         1.8Gi       0.0Ki       1.8Gi
```

Figure 10.8 – Using the free command in Linux

As shown in the preceding screenshot, using the `free` command (with the `-h` option for human-readable output) shows the following:

- `total`: The total amount of memory
- `used`: The used memory, which is calculated as the total memory minus the buffered, cache, and free memory
- `free`: The free or unused memory
- `shared`: The memory used by `tmpfs`
- `buff/cache`: The memory used by kernel buffers and the page cache
- `available`: The amount of memory available for new applications

This way, you can find specific issues related to higher memory usage. Constantly checking memory usage on servers is important to see whether resources are being used efficiently.

Another way to check for memory usage is to use the `top` command, as shown in the following screenshot:

```
top - 19:45:13 up  1:37,  2 users, . load average: 0.00, 0.00, 0.06
Tasks: 135 total,   1 running, 134 sleeping,   0 stopped,   0 zombie
%Cpu(s):  0.0 us,  0.0 sy,  0.0 ni, 98.7 id,  1.3 wa,  0.0 hi,  0.0 si,  0.0 st
MiB Mem :   1975.7 total,    745.3 free,    251.2 used,    979.2 buff/cache
MiB Swap:   1840.0 total,   1839.7 free,      0.3 used.   1534.1 avail Mem
```

PID	USER	PR	NI	VIRT	RES	SHR	S	%CPU	%MEM	TIME+	COMMAND
4157	root	20	0	0	0	0	I	0.3	0.0	0:00.15	kworker/0:2-events
1	root	20	0	167828	13072	8028	S	0.0	0.6	0:01.74	systemd
2	root	20	0	0	0	0	S	0.0	0.0	0:00.00	kthreadd
3	root	0	-20	0	0	0	I	0.0	0.0	0:00.00	rcu_gp
4	root	0	-20	0	0	0	I	0.0	0.0	0:00.00	rcu_par_gp
5	root	0	-20	0	0	0	I	0.0	0.0	0:00.00	slub_flushwq
6	root	0	-20	0	0	0	I	0.0	0.0	0:00.00	netns
8	root	0	-20	0	0	0	I	0.0	0.0	0:00.00	kworker/0:0H-even+
10	root	0	-20	0	0	0	I	0.0	0.0	0:00.00	mm_percpu_wq
11	root	20	0	0	0	0	S	0.0	0.0	0:00.00	rcu_tasks_rude_
12	root	20	0	0	0	0	S	0.0	0.0	0:00.00	rcu_tasks_trace

Figure 10.9 – Using the top command to check memory usage

While using the `top` command, there are several sections available on screen. The output is dynamic, in the sense that it constantly changes, showing real-time information about the processes running on the system. The `memory` section shows information about total memory used, as well as free and buffered memory. All the information is shown in megabytes by default so that it's easier to read and understand.

Another command that shows information about memory (and other valuable system information) is `vmstat`:

```
packt@neptune:~$ vmstat
procs -----------memory---------- ---swap-- -----io---- -system-- ------cpu-----
 r  b   swpd   free   buff  cache   si   so    bi    bo   in   cs us sy id wa st
 1  0    268 763164 552328 450412    0    0  1616  1418  511 1045  0  1 85 14  0
```

Figure 10.10 – Using vmstat with no options

By default, `vmstat` shows information about processes, memory, swap, disk, and CPU usage. The memory information is shown starting from the second column and contains the following details:

- `swpd`: How much virtual memory is being used
- `free`: How much memory is free
- `buff`: How much memory is being used for buffering
- `cache`: How much memory is being used for caching

The `vmstat` command has several options available. To learn about all the options and what all the columns from the output represent, visit the respective pages in the manual using the following command:

```
man vmstat
```

The options that can be used with `vmstat` to show different information about memory are `-a` and `-s`. By using `vmstat  -a`, the output will show the active and inactive memory:

```
packt@neptune:~$ vmstat -a
procs -----------memory---------- ---swap-- -----io---- -system-- ------cpu-----
 r  b   swpd   free  inact active   si   so    bi    bo   in   cs us sy id wa st
 2  0    268 762912 700560 301296    0    0  1589  1393  503 1028  0  1 86 13  0
```

Figure 10.11 – Using vmstat -a to show the active and inactive memory

Using `vmstat  -s` will show detailed memory, CPU, and disk statistics.

All the commands discussed in this section are essential for troubleshooting any memory issues. There might be others you can use, but these are the ones you will find by default on any Linux distribution.

Nevertheless, there is one more that deserves to be mentioned in this section: the `sar` command. This can be installed in Ubuntu through the `sysstat` package. Therefore, install the package using the following command:

```
sudo apt install sysstat
```

Once the package has been installed, to be able to use the `sar` command to show detailed statistics about the system's memory usage, you will need to enable the `sysstat` service. It needs to be active to collect data. By default, the service runs every 10 minutes and saves the logs inside the `/var/log/sysstat/saXX` directory. Every directory is named after the day the service runs on. For example, if we were to run the `sar` command on April 25, the service would look for data inside `/var/log/sysstat/sa25`. We ran the `sar` command on April 25 before starting the service, and an error occurred. Thus, to enable data collection, first, we will start and enable the `sysstat` service, then we will run the application. With the `sar` command, you can generate different reports in real time. For example, if we want to generate a memory report times every two seconds, we will use the `-r` option:

```
packt@neptune:~$ sar
Cannot open /var/log/sysstat/sa25: No such file or directory
Please check if data collecting is enabled
packt@neptune:~$ sudo systemctl start sysstat
packt@neptune:~$ sudo systemctl enable sysstat
Synchronizing state of sysstat.service with SysV service script with /lib/systemd/systemd-sysv-install.
Executing: /lib/systemd/systemd-sysv-install enable sysstat
Created symlink /etc/systemd/system/multi-user.target.wants/sysstat.service → /lib/systemd/system/sysstat.service.
Created symlink /etc/systemd/system/sysstat.service.wants/sysstat-collect.timer → /lib/systemd/system/sysstat-collect.timer.
Created symlink /etc/systemd/system/sysstat.service.wants/sysstat-summary.timer → /lib/systemd/system/sysstat-summary.timer.
packt@neptune:~$ sudo sar -r 2 5
Linux 5.15.0-70-generic (neptune)        04/25/2023      _x86_64_        (2 CPU)

07:52:29 PM kbmemfree   kbavail kbmemused %memused kbbuffers  kbcached  kbcommit  %commit  kbactive   kbinact   kbdirty
07:52:31 PM    820640   1564124    219720    10.86    491816    338824    597344    15.29    316524    622284       248
07:52:33 PM    820640   1564124    219732    10.86    491816    338824    597344    15.29    316524    622284       248
07:52:35 PM    820640   1564124    219732    10.86    491824    338816    597344    15.29    316524    622288       244
07:52:37 PM    820640   1564124    219724    10.86    491824    338824    597344    15.29    316524    622288       244
07:52:39 PM    820640   1564124    219720    10.86    491824    338824    597344    15.29    316524    622288       244
Average:       820640   1564124    219726    10.86    491821    338822    597344    15.29    316524    622286       246
```

Figure 10.12 – Starting and enabling the service and running sar

The service's name is **system activity data collector** (`sadc`) and it uses the `sysstat` name for the package and service.

> **Important note**
> In the event of a system reboot, the service might not restart by default, even though the preceding commands were executed. To overcome this, on Ubuntu, you should edit the `/etc/default/sysstat` file and change the `ENABLED` status from `false` to `true`.

The output shown in *Figure 10.12* will write one line every two seconds, five times in a row, and an average line at the end. It is a powerful tool that can be used for more than just memory statistics. There are options for CPU and disk statistics as well.

Overall, in this section, we covered the most important tools to use for troubleshooting memory issues. In the next section, we will cover tools to use for general system load issues.

Commands for system load issues

Similar to what we covered in the previous sections, in this section, we will discuss **system load** issues. Some of the tools that were used for other types of issues can be used for system load issues too. For example, the top command is one of the most widely used when we're trying to determine the sluggishness of a system. All the other tools, such as vmstat and sar, can also be used for CPU and system load troubleshooting.

A basic command for troubleshooting system load is uptime:

```
packt@neptune:~$ uptime
 20:01:48 up  1:53,  2 users,  load average: 0.00, 0.00, 0.00
```

Figure 10.13 – Using uptime for checking system load

The uptime output shows three values at the end. Those values represent the load averages for 1, 5, and 15 minutes. The load average can give you a fair image of what happens with the system's processes.

If you have a single CPU system, a load average of 1 means that that CPU is under full load. If the number is higher, this means that the load is much higher than the CPU can handle, and this will probably put a lot of stress on your system. Because of this, processes will take longer to execute and the system's overall performance will be affected.

A high load average means that there are applications that run multiple threads simultaneously at once. Nevertheless, some load issues are not only the result of an overcrowded CPU – they can be the combined effect of CPU load, disk I/O load, and memory load. In this case, the Swiss Army knife for troubleshooting system load issues is the top command. The output of the top command constantly changes in real time, based on the system's load.

By default, top sorts processes by how much CPU they use. It runs in interactive mode and, sometimes, the output is difficult to see on the screen. You can redirect the output to a file and use the command in batch mode using the -b option. This mode only updates the command a specified number of times. To run top in batch mode, run the following command:

```
top -b -n 1 | tee top-command-output
```

The `top` command could be a little intimidating for inexperienced Linux users. The output is highlighted in the following screenshot:

```
packt@neptune:~$ top -b -n 1 | tee top-command-output
top - 15:20:30 up 3 min,  2 users,  load average: 0.21, 0.17, 0.07
Tasks: 154 total,   1 running, 153 sleeping,    0 stopped,   0 zombie
%Cpu(s):  0.0 us,  0.0 sy,  0.0 ni,100.0 id,  0.0 wa,  0.0 hi,  0.0 si,  0.0 st
MiB Mem :   3911.9 total,   1135.6 free,    244.9 used,   2531.5 buff/cache
MiB Swap:   1840.0 total,   1840.0 free,      0.0 used.   3413.7 avail Mem

    PID USER      PR  NI    VIRT    RES    SHR S  %CPU  %MEM     TIME+ COMMAND
      1 root      20   0  167740  13212   8256 S   0.0   0.3   0:02.94 systemd
      2 root      20   0       0      0      0 S   0.0   0.0   0:00.00 kthreadd
      3 root       0 -20       0      0      0 I   0.0   0.0   0:00.00 rcu_gp
      4 root       0 -20       0      0      0 I   0.0   0.0   0:00.00 rcu_par_gp
      5 root       0 -20       0      0      0 I   0.0   0.0   0:00.00 slub_flushwq
```

Figure 10.14 – The output of the top command

Let's look at what the output means:

- `us`: User CPU time

- `sy`: System CPU time

- `ni`: Nice CPU time

- `id`: Idle CPU time

- `wa`: Input/output wait time

- `hi`: CPU hardware interrupts time

- `si`: CPU software interrupts time

- `st`: CPU steal time

Another useful tool for troubleshooting CPU usage and hard drive input/output time is `iostat`:

```
packt@neptune:~$ iostat
Linux 5.15.0-70-generic (neptune)       04/25/2023      _x86_64_        (2 CPU)

avg-cpu:  %user   %nice %system %iowait  %steal   %idle
           0.10    0.01    0.82   11.40    0.01   87.67

Device            tps    kB_read/s    kB_wrtn/s    kB_dscd/s     kB_read    kB_wrtn    kB_dscd
dm-0             8.14        78.94        39.11       446.01      558397     276624    3154984
loop0            0.05         0.16         0.00         0.00        1098          0          0
loop1            0.05         0.16         0.00         0.00        1113          0          0
loop10           0.20         0.59         0.00         0.00        4183          0          0
loop11           0.08         0.32         0.00         0.00        2270          0          0
loop12           0.00         0.00         0.00         0.00          14          0          0
loop2            0.05         0.16         0.00         0.00        1140          0          0
loop3            0.08         0.41         0.00         0.00        2885          0          0
loop4            0.00         0.00         0.00         0.00          17          0          0
loop5            0.09         0.32         0.00         0.00        2296          0          0
loop6            0.01         0.18         0.00         0.00        1287          0          0
loop7            0.01         0.18         0.00         0.00        1308          0          0
loop8            0.13         4.62         0.00         0.00       32652          0          0
loop9            0.01         0.07         0.00         0.00         502          0          0
sda            155.27       616.49      2329.90         0.00     4360936   16481240          0
vda             21.32      2068.83        39.13       446.01    14634494     276780    3154984
```

Figure 10.15 – The output of iostat

The CPU statistics are similar to the ones from the output of the `top` command shown earlier. The I/O statistics are shown below the CPU statistic and here is what each column represents:

- `tps`: Transfers per second to the device (I/O requests)
- `kB_read/s`: Amount of data read from the device (in terms of the number of blocks – kilobytes)
- `kB_wrtn/s`: Amount of data written to the device (in terms of the number of blocks – kilobytes)
- `kB_dscd/s`: Amount of data discarded for the device (in kilobytes)
- `kB_read`: Total number of blocks read
- `kB_wrtn`: Total number of blocks written
- `kB_dscd`: Total number of blocks discarded

For more details about the `iostat` command, read the respective manual pages by using the following command:

```
man iostat
```

Besides the `iostat` command, there is another one that you could use, called `iotop`. It is not installed by default on Ubuntu, but you can install it with the following command:

```
sudo apt install iotop
```

Once the package has been installed, you will need `sudo` privileges to run it:

```
sudo iotop
```

The output is as shown in the following screenshot:

```
Total DISK READ:        0.00 B/s | Total DISK WRITE:        0.00 B/s
Current DISK READ:      0.00 B/s | Current DISK WRITE:      0.00 B/s
   TID  PRIO  USER     DISK READ  DISK WRITE  SWAPIN     IO>    COMMAND
     1 be/4 root        0.00 B/s    0.00 B/s ?unavailable?  init
     2 be/4 root        0.00 B/s    0.00 B/s ?unavailable?  [kthreadd]
     3 be/0 root        0.00 B/s    0.00 B/s ?unavailable?  [rcu_gp]
     4 be/0 root        0.00 B/s    0.00 B/s ?unavailable?  [rcu_par_gp]
     5 be/0 root        0.00 B/s    0.00 B/s ?unavailable?  [slub_flushwq]
     6 be/0 root        0.00 B/s    0.00 B/s ?unavailable?  [netns]
     8 be/0 root        0.00 B/s    0.00 B/s ?unavailable?  [kworker/0:0H~vents_highpri]
    10 be/0 root        0.00 B/s    0.00 B/s ?unavailable?  [mm_percpu_wq]
    11 be/4 root        0.00 B/s    0.00 B/s ?unavailable?  [rcu_tasks_rude_]
 keys:   any: refresh  q: quit  i: ionice  o: active  p: procs  a: accum
 sort:   r: asc  left: SWAPIN  right: COMMAND  home: TID  end: COMMAND
CONFIG_TASK_DELAY_ACCT not enabled in kernel, cannot determine SWAPIN and IO %
```

Figure 10.16 – Running the iotop command

You can also run the `sysstat` service to troubleshoot system load issues, similar to how we used it for troubleshooting memory issues.

By default, `sar` will output the CPU statistics for the current day:

```
packt@neptune:~$ sudo sar 2 5
Linux 5.15.0-70-generic (neptune)        04/25/2023        _x86_64_        (2 CPU)

08:14:17 PM     CPU     %user     %nice   %system   %iowait    %steal     %idle
08:14:19 PM     all      0.00      0.00      0.00      0.00      0.00    100.00
08:14:21 PM     all      0.00      0.00      0.25      0.00      0.00     99.75
08:14:23 PM     all      0.00      0.00      0.00      2.25      0.00     97.75
08:14:25 PM     all      0.00      0.00      0.00      0.00      0.00    100.00
08:14:27 PM     all      0.00      0.00      0.00      0.00      0.00    100.00
Average:        all      0.00      0.00      0.05      0.45      0.00     99.50
```

Figure 10.17 – Running sar for CPU load troubleshooting

In the preceding screenshot, `sar` ran five times, every two seconds. Our local network servers are not under heavy load at this time, but you can imagine that the output would be different when the command is run on a heavily used server. As we pointed out in the previous section, the `sar` command has several options that could prove useful in finding solutions to potential problems. Run the `man sar` command to view the manual page containing all the available options.

There are many other tools that could be used for general system troubleshooting. We barely scratched the surface of this subject with the tools shown in this section. We advise you to search for more tools designed for general system troubleshooting if you feel the need to do so. Otherwise, the ones presented here are sufficient for you to generate a viable report about possible system issues.

Network-specific issues will be covered in the next section.

Tools for troubleshooting network issues

Quite often, due to the complexities of a network, issues tend to appear. Networks are essential for everyday living. We use them everywhere, from our wireless smartwatch to our smartphone, to our computer, and up to the cloud. Everything is connected worldwide to make our lives better and a systems administrator's life a little bit harder. In this interconnected world, things can go sideways quite easily, and network issues need troubleshooting.

Troubleshooting **network issues** is almost 80% of a system administrator's job – probably even more. This number is not backed up by any official studies but more of a hands-on experience insight. Since most of the server and cloud issues are related to networking, an optimal working network means reduced downtime and happy clients and system administrators.

The tools we will cover in this section are the defaults on all major Linux distributions. All these tools were discussed in *Chapter 7, Networking with Linux*, and *Chapter 9, Securing Linux*, or will be discussed in *Chapter 13, Configuring Linux Servers*, so we will only name them again from a problem-solving standpoint. Let's break down the tools we should use on specific TCP/IP layers. Remember how many layers there are in the TCP/IP model? There are five layers available, and we will start from layer 1. As a good practice, troubleshooting a network is best done through the stack, starting from the application layer all the way to the physical layer.

Diagnosing the physical layer (layer 1)

One of the basic testing tools and one of the first to be used by most system administrators is the `ping` command. The name comes from **packet internet groper** and it provides a basic connectivity test. Let's do a test on one of our local servers to see whether everything is working fine. We will run four tests using the `-c` option of the `ping` command. The output is as follows:

```
packt@neptune:~$ ping -c 4 google.com
PING google.com (142.250.181.238) 56(84) bytes of data.
64 bytes from fra16s56-in-f14.1e100.net (142.250.181.238): icmp_seq=1 ttl=51 time=34.7 ms
64 bytes from fra16s56-in-f14.1e100.net (142.250.181.238): icmp_seq=2 ttl=51 time=32.9 ms
64 bytes from fra16s56-in-f14.1e100.net (142.250.181.238): icmp_seq=3 ttl=51 time=35.2 ms
64 bytes from fra16s56-in-f14.1e100.net (142.250.181.238): icmp_seq=4 ttl=51 time=33.1 ms

--- google.com ping statistics ---
4 packets transmitted, 4 received, 0% packet loss, time 3005ms
rtt min/avg/max/mdev = 32.948/33.978/35.178/0.967 ms
```

Figure 10.18 – Running a basic test using the ping command

Ping is sending simple ICMP packets to the destination (in our case, it was `google.com`) and is waiting for a response. Once it is received and no packets are lost, this means that everything is working fine. The `ping` command can be used to test connections to local network systems, as well as remote networks. It is the first tool that's used to test and isolate possible problems.

There are times when a simple test with the `ping` command is not enough. In this case, another versatile command is the `ip` command. You can use it to check whether there are any issues with the physical layer:

```
ip link show
```

You will see the output as follows:

```
packt@neptune:~$ ip link show
1: lo: <LOOPBACK,UP,LOWER_UP> mtu 65536 qdisc noqueue state UNKNOWN mode DEFAULT group def
ault qlen 1000
    link/loopback 00:00:00:00:00:00 brd 00:00:00:00:00:00
2: enp1s0: <BROADCAST,MULTICAST,UP,LOWER_UP> mtu 1500 qdisc fq_codel state UP mode DEFAULT
 group default qlen 1000
    link/ether ▮▮▮▮▮▮▮▮▮▮▮▮▮▮▮▮ brd ff:ff:ff:ff:ff:ff
```

Figure 10.19 – Showing the state of the physical interfaces with the ip command

In the preceding screenshot, you can see that the Ethernet interface is running well (`state UP`). As we are running on a virtual machine, we do not have a wireless connection. If we were to use a laptop, for example, the wireless connection would have been visible, showing something such as `wlp0s20f3`.

If any of the interfaces is not working, for example, the wireless one, the output of the preceding command would show `state DOWN`. In our case, we will bring the wireless interface up using the following command:

```
ip link set wlp0s20f3 up
```

Once executed, you can check the state of the interface by running the `ip` command once again:

```
ip link show
```

If you have direct access to a bare metal system, maybe a server, you can directly check whether the wires are connected. If, by any chance, you are using a wireless connection (not recommended), you will need to use the ip command.

Another useful tool for layer 1 is ethtool. On Ubuntu 22.04.2 LTS, it is installed by default. To check the Ethernet interface, run the following command by using the connection's name (you've seen it while using the ip command):

```
ethtool enp1s0
```

By using ethtool, we can check whether a connection has negotiated the correct speed. In the output of the command (which we will not show here), you would see that the system has correctly negotiated a full 1,000 Mbps full-duplex connection, for example (it may differ in your case). In the next section, we will show you how to diagnose the layer 2 stack.

Diagnosing the data link layer (layer 2)

The second layer in the TCP/IP stack is called the **data link layer**. It is generally responsible for local area network connectivity. Most of the issues that can occur at this stage happen due to improper IP to MAC address mapping. Some of the tools that can be used in this instance include the ip command and the arp command. The arp command, which comes from the **Address Resolution Protocol (ARP)**, is used to map IP addresses (layer 3) with MAC addresses (layer 2). In Ubuntu, the arp command is available through the net-tools package. First, proceed and install it using the following command:

```
sudo apt install net-tools
```

To check the entries inside the ARP table, you can use the arp command with the -a (all) option. As we are running on a virtual machine, we will have only one entry. As a comparison, we run the same command on our host system, this time having three entries, one for the wireless connection, one for the wired connection, and another for the virtual bridge connection used by KVM. The following is an example:

```
packt@neptune:~$ arp -a
fedora (192.168.124.1) at 52:54:00:4c:07:aa [ether] on enp1s0
packt@neptune:~$
```

```
[alexandru@fedora ~]$ arp -a
_gateway (192.168.0.1) at                    [ether] on enp46s0
_gateway (192.168.0.1) at                    [ether] on wlo1
? (192.168.124.112) at 52:54:00:c2:77:7f [ether] on virbr0
[alexandru@fedora ~]$
```

Figure 10.20 – Using the arp command to map the ARP entries

The output of the `arp` command will show all the connected devices, with details about their IP and MAC addresses. Note that the MAC addresses have been blurred for privacy reasons.

Similar to the `arp` command, you can use the `ip neighbor show` command, as shown in the following screenshot. We will use our host system, not the virtual machine:

```
🖥 packt@neptune: ~                                    alexandru@fedora:~                    ✕

[alexandru@fedora ~]$ ip neighbor show
192.168.0.1 dev enp46s0 lladdr                    DELAY
192.168.0.1 dev wlo1 lladdr                       STALE
192.168.124.112 dev virbr0 lladdr 52:54:00:c2:77:7f REACHABLE
```

Figure 10.21 – Listing the ARP entries using the ip command

The `ip` command can be used to delete entries from the ARP list, like so:

```
ip neighbor delete 192.168.124.112 dev virbr0
```

We used the command to delete the virtual bridge connection, using its IP address and name from the list as shown in *Figure 10.21*.

Both the `arp` and `ip` commands have a similar output. They are powerful commands and very useful for troubleshooting possible layer 2 issues. In the next section, we will show you how to diagnose the layer 3 stack.

Diagnosing the internet layer (layer 3)

On the internet layer, layer 3, we are working with IP addresses only. We already know about the tools to use here, such as the `ip` command, the `ping` command, the `traceroute` command, and the `nslookup` command. Since we've already covered the `ip` and `ping` commands, we will only discuss how to use `traceroute` and `nslookup` here. The `traceroute` command is not installed by default in Ubuntu. You will have to install it using the following command:

```
sudo apt install traceroute
```

The `nslookup` package is already available in Ubuntu by default. First, to check for the routing table to see the list of gateways for different routes, we can use the `ip route show` command:

```
packt@neptune:~$ ip route show
default via 192.168.124.1 dev enp1s0 proto dhcp src 192.168.124.112 metric 100
192.168.124.0/24 dev enp1s0 proto kernel scope link src 192.168.124.112 metric 100
192.168.124.1 dev enp1s0 proto dhcp scope link src 192.168.124.112 metric 100
```

Figure 10.22 – Showing the routing table using the "ip route show" command

The `ip route show` command is showing the default gateway. An issue would be if it is missing or incorrectly configured.

The `traceroute` tool is used to check the path of traffic from the source to the destination. The following output shows the path of packets traveling from our local gateway to Google's servers:

```
packt@neptune:~$ traceroute google.com
traceroute to google.com (142.250.181.238), 30 hops max, 60 byte packets
 1  fedora (192.168.124.1)  0.689 ms  0.641 ms  0.628 ms
 2  _gateway (192.168.0.1)  0.949 ms  0.967 ms  1.117 ms
 3                          3.644 ms  3.630 ms  3.613 ms
 4          .    .ro (         )  7.159 ms  7.550 ms  7.683 ms
 5              .    .ro (          )  5.248 ms  6.460 ms  6.887 ms
 6      .      .ro ('         )  8.463 ms  5.468 ms  5.430 ms
 7         .      .ro (        )  5.940 ms  7.417 ms  7.783 ms
 8  bucuresti.nxdata.br01.      .ro (81.22.150.2)  6.869 ms  8.687 ms  8.904 ms
 9  10.19.141.193 (10.19.141.193)  5.944 ms  8.166 ms  5.859 ms
10  * * *
```

Figure 10.23 – Using traceroute for path tracing

Packets don't usually have the same route when they're sending and coming back to the source. Packets are sent to gateways to be processed and sent to the destination on a certain route. When packets exceed the local network, their route can be inaccurately represented by the `traceroute` tool, since the packets it relies on could be filtered by many of the gateways on the path (*ICMP TTL Exceeded* packets are generally filtered).

Similar to `traceroute`, there is a newer tool called `tracepath`. It is installed by default on Ubuntu and is a replacement for `traceroute`. Both `traceroute` and `tracepath` use the UDP ports for tracking by default. The `tracepath` command can also be used with the `-n` option to show the IP address instead of the hostname. The following is an example of this:

```
packt@neptune:~$ tracepath google.com
 1?: [LOCALHOST]                       pmtu 1500
 1:  fedora                                        0.301ms
 1:  fedora                                        0.547ms
 2:  _gateway                                      1.589ms
 3:                                                2.763ms
 4:                                                2.880ms pmtu 1492
 4:                      .ro                       7.319ms
 5:                   .ro                          4.098ms
 6:                  .ro                           6.181ms
 7:                 .ro                            5.171ms
 8:  bucuresti.nxdata.br01.       .ro              5.216ms
 9:  10.19.141.193                                 4.205ms
```

Figure 10.24 – Using the tracepath command

Checking further network issues could lead to faulty DNS resolution, where a host can only be accessed by the IP address and not by the hostname. To troubleshoot this, even if it is not a layer 3 protocol, you could use the `nslookup` command, combined with the `ping` command.

If the `nslookup` command has the same IP output as the `ping` command, it means that everything is fine. If a different IP address shows up in the output, then you have an issue with your host's configuration. In the next section, we will show you how to diagnose both the layer 4 and layer 5 stacks.

Diagnosing the transport and application layers (layers 4 and 5)

The last two layers, layer 4 (**transport layer**) and layer 5 (**application layer**), mainly provide host-to-host communication services for applications. This is why we will cover them in a condensed manner. Two of the most well-known protocols from layer 4 are the **Transmission Control Protocol** (**TCP**) and the **User Datagram Protocol** (**UDP**), and both are used and implemented inside every operating system available. TCP and UDP cover all the traffic on the internet. One important tool for troubleshooting layer 4 issues is the `ss` command (where `ss` is short for **socket statistics**).

The `ss` command is a recent replacement for `netstat` and is used to see the list of all network sockets. As such, a list can have a significant size, so you could use several command options to reduce it.

For example, you could use the `-t` option to see only the TCP sockets, the `-u` option for UDP sockets, and `-x` for Unix sockets. Thus, to see TCP and UDP socket information, we will use the `ss` command with the `-t` option. Furthermore, to see all the listening sockets on your system, you can use the `-l` option. This one, combined with the `-u` and `-t` options, will show you all the UDP and TCP listening sockets on your system. The following is an excerpt from a much longer list:

```
packt@neptune:~$ ss -t
State   Recv-Q   Send-Q        Local Address:Port        Peer Address:Port      Process
ESTAB   0        0             192.168.124.112:ssh       192.168.124.1:55860
packt@neptune:~$ ss -ltu
Netid State   Recv-Q Send-Q                         Local Address:Port       Peer Address:Port Process

udp   UNCONN 0        0                             127.0.0.53%lo:domain       0.0.0.0:*

udp   UNCONN 0        0                    192.168.124.112%enp1s0:bootpc       0.0.0.0:*
```

Figure 10.25 – Using the ss command to list TCP and UDP sockets and all listening sockets

The `ss` command is important for network troubleshooting when you want to verify the available sockets and the ones that are in the `LISTEN` state, for example. Another use is for the `TIME_WAIT` state, and in this case, you can use the command as shown in the following screenshot:

```
alexandru@debian:~$ ss -o state time-wait
Netid    Recv-Q    Send-Q       Local Address:Port              Peer Address:Port     Process

icmp6    0         0                      *:ipv6-icmp                    *:*

icmp6    0         0                      *:ipv6-icmp                    *:*

tcp      0         0            192.168.0.211:59832                                    timer:(timewait,8.248ms,0)

tcp      0         0            192.168.0.211:33312                                    timer:(timewait,9.244ms,0)

tcp      0         0            192.168.0.211:59836                                    timer:(timewait,8.244ms,0)

tcp      0         0            192.168.0.211:42274                                    timer:(timewait,6.212ms,0)

tcp      0         0            192.168.0.211:33296                                    timer:(timewait,9.240ms,0)
```

Figure 10.26 – Showing the TIME_WAIT ports with the ss command

We used the ss command with the -o option and the state time-wait argument. The TIME_WAIT state is achieved when a socket closes for a short time.

For more information on this state, you can visit the following link: https://vincent.bernat.ch/en/blog/2014-tcp-time-wait-state-linux.

The ss tool should not be missing from a system administrator's toolbox. Layer 5, the application layer, comprises protocols used by applications, and we will remember protocols such as the **Dynamic Host Configuration Protocol (DHCP)**, the **Hypertext Transfer Protocol (HTTP)**, and the **File Transfer Protocol (FTP)**. Since diagnosing layer 5 is mainly an application troubleshooting process, this will not be covered in this section.

In the next section, we will discuss troubleshooting hardware issues.

Tools for troubleshooting hardware issues

The first step in troubleshooting hardware issues is to check your hardware. A very good tool to see details about the system's hardware is the dmidecode command. This command is used to read details about each hardware component in a human-readable format. Each piece of hardware has a specific DMI code, depending on its type. This code is specific to the **System Management Basic Input/Output System (SMBIOS)**. There are 45 codes that are used by the SMBIOS. More information about the codes can be obtained at https://www.thegeekstuff.com/2008/11/how-to-get-hardware-information-on-linux-using-dmidecode-command/.

To view details about the system's memory, you can use the dmidecode command with the -t option (from TYPE) and code 17, which corresponds to the memory device code from SMBIOS. An example from our virtual machine is as follows:

```
packt@neptune:~$ sudo dmidecode -t 17
[sudo] password for packt:
# dmidecode 3.3
Getting SMBIOS data from sysfs.
SMBIOS 2.8 present.

Handle 0x1100, DMI type 17, 40 bytes
Memory Device
        Array Handle: 0x1000
        Error Information Handle: Not Provided
        Total Width: Unknown
        Data Width: Unknown
        Size: 2 GB
        Form Factor: DIMM
```

Figure 10.27 – Using dmidecode to view information about memory

To see details about other hardware components, use the command with the specific code.

Other quick troubleshooting tools include commands such as `lspci`, `lsblk`, and `lscpu`. The output of the `lsblk` command shows information about the disks and partitions being used on the system. The `lscpu` command will show details about the CPU.

Also, when you're troubleshooting hardware issues, taking a quick look at the kernel's logs could prove useful. To do this, use the `dmesg` command. You can use the `dmesg | more` command to have more control over the output.

As you've seen in this section, hardware troubleshooting is just as important and challenging as all other types of troubleshooting. Solving hardware-related issues is an integral part of any system administrator's job. This involves constantly checking hardware components, replacing the faulty parts with new ones, and making sure that they run smoothly.

Summary

In this chapter, we emphasized the importance of disaster recovery planning, backup and restore strategies, and troubleshooting various system issues. Every system administrator should be able to put their knowledge into practice when disaster strikes. Different types of failures will eventually hit the running servers, so solutions should be found as soon as possible to ensure minimal downtime and to prevent data loss.

This chapter represented the culmination of the *Advanced Linux Administration* section of this book. In the next chapter, we will introduce you to **server administration**, with emphasis on KVM virtual machine management, Docker containers, and different types of Linux server configuration.

Questions

Troubleshooting is problem-solving at its best. Before we dive into the server section, let's test your troubleshooting knowledge:

1.   Try to draft a DRP for your private network or small business.

2.   Back up your entire system using the 321 rule.

3.   Find out what your system's top 10 processes are that use CPU the most.

4.   Find out what your system's top 10 processes are that use RAM the most.

Further reading

- Ubuntu LTS official documentation: `https://ubuntu.com/server/docs`

- RHEL official documentation: `https://access.redhat.com/documentation/en-us/red_hat_enterprise_linux/9/`

- SUSE official documentation: `https://documentation.suse.com/`

Part 3:
Server Administration

In this third part, you will learn about advanced Linux server administration tasks by setting up different types of servers, as well as working with and managing virtual machines and Docker containers.

This part has the following chapters:

- *Chapter 11, Working with Virtual Machines*
- *Chapter 12, Managing Containers with Docker*
- *Chapter 13, Configuring Linux Servers*

11

Working with Virtual Machines

In this chapter, you will learn about **virtual machines** (**VMs**) on Linux. For starters, you will learn how virtualization works and how to create and use VMs. You will learn about one of the most widely used virtualization and hypervisor technologies on Linux, called **Kernel-based Virtual Machine** (**KVM**). The topics in this chapter will prepare you for the future of Linux, as it is the foundation of every modern cloud technology. If you wish to remain up to date in a constantly changing landscape, this chapter will be an essential starting point for your journey.

In this chapter, we're going to cover the following main topics:

- Introduction to virtualization on Linux
- Understanding Linux KVM
- Working with basic KVM commands
- Advanced KVM management
- Provisioning VMs using cloud-init
- Public key authentication with SSH

Technical requirements

No special technical requirements are needed, just a working installation of Linux on your system. We will mainly use Debian GNU/Linux 12 for our examples, but we will also show you how to install KVM in Fedora and openSUSE.

Introduction to virtualization on Linux

Virtualization is a way to make more efficient use of computer hardware. It is basically an abstraction layer that takes advantage of the computer's resources. In this section, you will learn about the types of VMs, how they work on Linux, and how to deploy and manage them.

Efficiency in resource usage

The abstraction layer that virtualization uses is a software layer that allows more efficient use of all the computer's components. This in turn allows better use of all the physical machine's capabilities and resources.

Before going any further into virtualization, let's give you an example. In our testing laboratory, we have several physical machines, in the form of laptops and small form factor desktop computers (Intel NUCs) that we use as servers. Each of the systems has significant resources available, more than enough to run the services we need. For instance, our least performant systems are a 5th-generation Intel NUC with an Intel i3 CPU with four processing cores and 16 GB of RAM and a 7th-generation Intel NUC with a four-core Intel Pentium and 12 GB of RAM. Those two systems have plenty of resources that could be more efficiently used by using VMs.

For running a local web service or any kind of server on our local network, those resources can be split between various VMs with ease. For example, each physical system could host four different VMs, each using a single CPU core, and at least 2 GB of memory and all the necessary storage capacities. This way, one single machine will work as if there were four different ones. This is way more efficient than using individual machines for separate tasks.

In the following diagram, we are comparing the load on a single computer versus the same load divided between several VMs. This way of using the same hardware resources is more efficient:

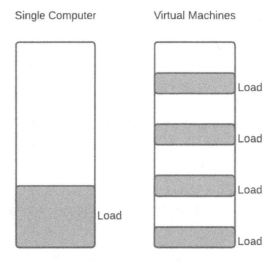

Figure 11.1 – Comparison between single computer use and using multiple VMs

Nonetheless, as we will use the hypervisor on top of a host OS, we will have to keep some resources for the OS's use, so the number of VMs will be smaller. Here is a diagram of how the VMs work on a host OS:

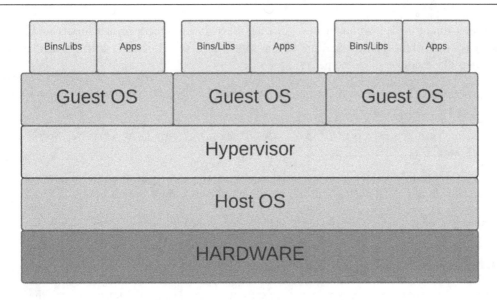

Figure 11.2 – How virtualization works on a host OS

The preceding diagram shows the scheme of how virtualization works when used on a host OS. As we will see in the following sections, it is not the only type of virtualization.

It is important to note that efficiency is not related solely to the hardware resources used. A significant aspect of the efficient use of hardware in data centers is related to increased energy efficiency and a reduction of the carbon footprint. In this respect, virtualization has played a major role for many decades in changing the usage patterns of servers inside data centers. Overall, virtualization and containerization are significant players in the fight against climate change.

In the following sections, we will give you a short introduction to hypervisors and VMs.

Introduction to hypervisors

The software layer that virtualization is based on is called a **hypervisor**. The physical resources are divided and used as virtual computers, better known as VMs. By using VMs, the limits of physical hardware are overcome by the process of **emulation**. This has a lot of advantages, enabling the hardware to be used more effectively.

> **Important note**
>
> The process of emulation is basically an imitation process through which a piece of software replicates (or imitates) the functions of another system. In our case, the hypervisor (the virtualization software layer) is simulating the use of hardware as if it were a different system altogether. This allows the hardware resources a computer has to be used more effectively.

Hypervisors can be used either on top of an existing OS (*type 2*) or directly on bare metal (hardware) (*type 1*). For each of these types, there are various solutions that can be used, particularly on Linux. For a Linux OS, examples of each type are as follows:

- Examples of hypervisors that run on top of a host OS (type 2) are Oracle VirtualBox and VMware Workstation/Fusion

- Examples of hypervisors that run directly on bare metal (type 1) are Citrix Xen Server and VMware ESXi

- KVM is mostly classified as a bare-metal hypervisor (type 1), while its underlying system is a full OS, thus it is classified as a host hypervisor at the same time (type 2)

In this chapter, we will exclusively use KVM as the hypervisor of choice.

Understanding Linux KVMs

A VM is similar to a standalone computer. It is a software-based emulator that has access to the host computer's resources. It uses the host's CPU, RAM, storage, networking interface(s), and ports. Not only that, but it is a virtual environment that has the same functions as a physical computer; it is also seen as a virtual computer.

The resources for each VM are managed by the hypervisor. It can relocate resources between existing VMs or create new VMs. The VMs are isolated from each other and from the host computer. As multiple VMs can exist on a single computer, each VM can use different guest OSes. For example, if you use a Windows machine and want to try out Linux, a popular solution would be to create a VM with the Linux distribution that you want to try. The same goes for Mac users, too. An OS installed inside a VM runs similarly to an OS installed on bare metal. The user experience could vary from one hypervisor to the other, and so could the resource efficiency and response times. From our experience, we prefer running VMs from KVM rather than running from any other hypervisor, mainly because of the comprehensive **command-line interface** (**CLI**). However, use cases could be different from one user to another.

Choosing the hypervisor

In this chapter, we chose the KVM hypervisor. As an optional solution, if you use the GNOME desktop environment, you will have access to GNOME Boxes. As both KVM and GNOME Boxes are directly available from Linux repositories, we consider them to be the better solutions for newcomers to Linux. Both KVM and GNOME Boxes share parts of `libvirt` and `qemu` code (to be detailed in the next section), and in this respect, we consider them to both be the same hypervisor, which is KVM.

In *Chapter 1, Installing Linux*, you first encountered the use of a hypervisor to set up a Linux VM. We showed you how to use VMware solutions and VirtualBox to set up a Linux VM. The details used then should be sufficient for any user, whether they are experienced or a newbie. VirtualBox has several features that make it a fair candidate for your hypervisor solution, but in our opinion, it still lacks the finesse of KVM. In the next section, we will walk you through KVM.

Using the KVM hypervisor

The KVM hypervisor is an open source virtualization project available on all major Linux distributions. It is a modern hypervisor that uses specific kernel modules to take advantage of all the benefits that the Linux kernel has to offer, including memory support, scheduler, nested virtualization, GPU pass-through, and so on.

KVM in detail – QEMU and libvirt

KVM uses **Quick Emulator** (**QEMU**) as the emulator software for all the hardware components and peripherals. The main management tool and daemon that controls the hypervisor and also the **Application Programming Interface** (**API**) for KVM is called libvirt. The KVM's interface with libvirt, specifically in GNOME, is virt-manager. The CLI for libvirt is called virsh.

The libvirt API provides a common library for managing VMs. It is the management layer for VM creation, modification, and provision. It is running in the background as a daemon called libvirtd that manages the connections with the hypervisor at the client's request.

QEMU is both an emulator and a virtualizer. When used as an emulator, QEMU uses **dynamic binary translation** methods to operate. This means that it can use different types of OS on the host machine, even if they are designed for different architectures. Dynamic binary translations are used in **software-based virtualization**, where hardware is emulated to execute instructions in virtualized environments. This way, QEMU emulates the machine's CPU, using a specific binary translator method called **Tiny Code Generator** (**TCG**), which transforms the binary code for different types of architectures.

When used as a virtualizer, QEMU uses what is known as a **hardware-based virtualization**, where the binary translation is not used, because the instructions are executed directly on the host CPU. The differences between software- and hardware-assisted virtualization are shown in the following diagram:

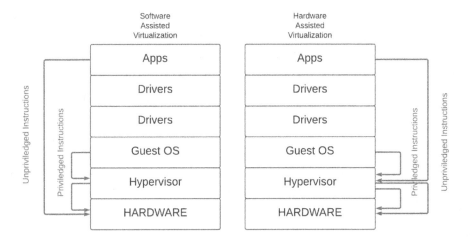

Figure 11.3 – Comparison between software- and hardware-assisted virtualization

As you can see in the diagram, instructions have different paths when using software- and hardware-assisted virtualization. In software-assisted virtualization, when dynamic binary translations are used, the user's unprivileged instructions are sent directly to the hardware, while the guest OS privileged instructions are first sent to the hypervisor before getting to the hardware. In hardware-assisted virtualization, the user's unprivileged instructions are sent to the hypervisor first, and then sent to the hardware, while the privileged instructions from the guest OS have the same path as in software-assisted virtualization. This ensures a certain level of isolation for the guest OS, thereby achieving better performance and less complexity.

In the following section, we will show you how to install and configure QEMU on a Debian 12 machine. We consider Debian to be a sufficiently lightweight distribution, offering the necessary stability for a virtualization host OS. Some commands can be replicated on Ubuntu as well.

Installing the hypervisor on major Linux distributions

Installing QEMU is a straightforward task. All you need to do is to run the package installer utility of your distribution, with some specified package names. In our case, we will show you how to install it on major Linux distributions such as Debian/Ubuntu, Fedora, and openSUSE:

- **Installing on Debian/Ubuntu Linux**

  Run the following command:

  ```
  sudo apt install qemu-kvm libvirt-clients libvirt-daemon-system
  bridge-utils virtinst libvirt-daemon virt-manager
  ```

- **Installing on Fedora Linux**

  Run the following command:

  ```
  sudo dnf group install --with-optional virtualization
  ```

- **Installing on openSUSE Linux**

  Run the following commands:

  ```
  sudo zypper install -t pattern kvm_server kvm_tools
  sudo zypper install libvirt-daemon
  ```

Once all the necessary packages are installed, you can enable and start the `libvirtd` daemon with the following commands (valid for all Linux distributions showcased in this section):

```
sudo systemctl start libvirtd
sudo systemctl enable libvirtd
```

Once the packages are installed and the daemon is started and enabled, a safe action to take is to check whether your machine is compatible with KVM requirements. To do this, use the `virt-host-validate` command as a root user or by using `sudo`. We are running the command on a Debian GNU/Linux 12 host, but it can be used on other Linux distributions as well:

```
sudo virt-host-validate
```

Once the command is running, you may receive a couple of errors or warnings regarding QEMU or **Linux Containers (LXC)** – which is a technology used to run isolated systems, similar to how KVM works – depending on your system (there's more on LXC in *Chapter 12*). In our case, the output shows one error regarding LXC compatibility, as shown in the following screenshot:

```
packt@debian:~$ sudo virt-host-validate
[sudo] password for packt:
  QEMU: Checking for hardware virtualization                        : PASS
  QEMU: Checking if device /dev/kvm exists                          : PASS
  QEMU: Checking if device /dev/kvm is accessible                   : PASS
  QEMU: Checking if device /dev/vhost-net exists                    : PASS
  QEMU: Checking if device /dev/net/tun exists                      : PASS
  QEMU: Checking for cgroup 'cpu' controller support                : PASS
  QEMU: Checking for cgroup 'cpuacct' controller support            : PASS
  QEMU: Checking for cgroup 'cpuset' controller support             : PASS
  QEMU: Checking for cgroup 'memory' controller support             : PASS
  QEMU: Checking for cgroup 'devices' controller support            : PASS
  QEMU: Checking for cgroup 'blkio' controller support              : PASS
  QEMU: Checking for device assignment IOMMU support                : PASS
  QEMU: Checking if IOMMU is enabled by kernel                      : PASS
  QEMU: Checking for secure guest support                           : WARN
(Unknown if this platform has Secure Guest support)
  LXC: Checking for Linux >= 2.6.26                                 : PASS
  LXC: Checking for namespace ipc                                   : PASS
  LXC: Checking for namespace mnt                                   : PASS
  LXC: Checking for namespace pid                                   : PASS
  LXC: Checking for namespace uts                                   : PASS
  LXC: Checking for namespace net                                   : PASS
  LXC: Checking for namespace user                                  : PASS
  LXC: Checking for cgroup 'cpu' controller support                 : PASS
  LXC: Checking for cgroup 'cpuacct' controller support             : PASS
  LXC: Checking for cgroup 'cpuset' controller support              : PASS
  LXC: Checking for cgroup 'memory' controller support              : PASS
  LXC: Checking for cgroup 'devices' controller support             : PASS
  LXC: Checking for cgroup 'freezer' controller support             : FAIL
(Enable 'freezer' in kernel Kconfig file or mount/enable cgroup controller in your s
ystem)
  LXC: Checking for cgroup 'blkio' controller support               : PASS
  LXC: Checking if device /sys/fs/fuse/connections exists           : PASS
```

Figure 11.4 – Running the host validation program

However, this error will not limit our use of `libvirt` and QEMU, so we do not intend to resolve it here.

After seeing that there are no compatibility issues regarding QEMU, we can proceed to creating our first VM using the CLI. Thus, we will start using KVM-specific commands.

Working with basic KVM commands

One of the first commands that you will use when working with KVM is the one used for creating a VM. Other commands, as shown in the following sections, are the ones used to start, stop, delete, or pause an already existing VM.

Creating a VM using the command line

Before creating our first VM using `libvirt`, we must check and see whether our default bridge network configuration was created. We can verify this by using the following command:

```
sudo virsh net-list
```

This command shows if the default bridge configuration was created and if it is running. In our case, the bridge connection is not running, thus we will need to set it up ourselves. The command used to start the default bridge network is as follows:

```
sudo virsh net-start default
```

Once it has been started, the network bridge is not set up for automatic start, thus we will use the following command to set it for automatic start:

```
sudo virsh net-autostart default
```

Now, the output is as follows:

```
packt@debian:~$ sudo virsh net-start default
Network default started

packt@debian:~$ sudo virsh net-list
 Name       State     Autostart    Persistent
--------------------------------------------------
 default    active    no           yes

packt@debian:~$ sudo virsh net-autostart default
Network default marked as autostarted

packt@debian:~$ sudo virsh net-list
 Name       State     Autostart    Persistent
--------------------------------------------------
 default    active    yes          yes
```

Figure 11.5 – Enabling the default bridge connection

Now that the default bridge connection has been enabled and set for `autostart`, we can create our first VM. In order to create a VM, follow these steps:

1. First, we will need to download the image file of the OS to use inside the VM. For our example, we will create a new VM with Ubuntu 22.04.2 LTS server edition. We can download the ISO image with the following command:

```
wget https://releases.ubuntu.com/22.04.2/ubuntu-22.04.2-live-
server-amd64.iso
```

2. The download location will be inside your present working directory, thus you may want to move it to another location, otherwise the hypervisor will not have permission to access your ISO file. The location you should move the ISO file is `/var/lib/libvirt/images`.

3. Once the Ubuntu image is downloaded, we will use the `virt-install` command to create the first VM on our host system. We will create one VM that will use a single **virtual CPU** (**vCPU**), 2 GB of RAM, and 20 GB of storage.

   The `virt-install` command used is the following (run as root):

```
virt-install --virt-type=kvm --name ubuntu-vm1 --vcpus=2
--memory=2048 --os-variant=ubuntufocal --cdrom=/var/lib/libvirt/
images/ubuntu-22.04.2-live-server-amd64.iso --network=default
--disk size=20
```

It has the following mandatory arguments:

- `--virt-type`: Type of the new VM
- `--name`: The name of the new VM
- `--memory`: The amount of RAM used by the VM
- `--vcpus`: The number of virtual CPUs used by the new VM
- `--disk size`: The amount of storage used
- `--os-variant`: The type of guest OS
- `--network`: The bridge network used
- `--cdrom`: The location of the guest OS ISO file

The command will start a new `virt-viewer` window, which will start the OS installation process. Similarly, by using the command with the `–graphics=vnc` argument, `virt-install` will start `virt-viewer`, which is the default tool for displaying the graphical console using the VNC protocol.

Simply knowing how to create a VM is not sufficient for a system administrator. This is why, in the next section, we will show you some basic VM management tools to use.

Basic VM management

The basic VM tasks can be done using the `virsh` command when using the CLI, or Virtual Machine Manager when using a graphical user interface. In the following, we will show you the basic commands to use while inside a CLI.

To list the existing VM guests, use the `virsh list` command:

```
sudo virsh list
```

Be aware that listing the VMs cannot be done by just anyone. This is why the following note needs to be considered.

> **Important note**
> When trying to list the existing guest VMs, you will not get a valid output when using a regular user. You will need to be logged in as `root` or use `sudo` to see the list of VMs.

The following screenshot shows some basic commands used to manage VMs, together with their output:

```
packt@debian:~$ sudo virsh list
 Id   Name         State
-----------------------------
 5    ubuntu-vm1   running

packt@debian:~$ sudo virsh destroy ubuntu-vm1
Domain 'ubuntu-vm1' destroyed

packt@debian:~$ sudo virsh list
 Id   Name   State
--------------------

packt@debian:~$ sudo virsh start ubuntu-vm1
Domain 'ubuntu-vm1' started

packt@debian:~$ sudo virsh list
 Id   Name         State
-----------------------------
 6    ubuntu-vm1   running

packt@debian:~$ sudo virsh reboot ubuntu-vm1
Domain 'ubuntu-vm1' is being rebooted

packt@debian:~$ sudo virsh list
 Id   Name         State
-----------------------------
 6    ubuntu-vm1   running

packt@debian:~$ sudo virsh suspend ubuntu-vm1
Domain 'ubuntu-vm1' suspended

packt@debian:~$ sudo virsh resume ubuntu-vm1
Domain 'ubuntu-vm1' resumed

packt@debian:~$ sudo virsh list
 Id   Name         State
-----------------------------
 6    ubuntu-vm1   running
```

Figure 11.6 – Commands for VM management

Here is a short explanation of the commands you see in the preceding figure. To change the state of a VM, such as starting, stopping, and pausing, use the following commands:

- **To force stop a VM**: `sudo virsh destroy ubuntu-vm1`
- **To reboot a VM**: `sudo virsh reboot ubuntu-vm1`
- **To pause (suspend) a VM**: `sudo virsh suspend ubuntu-vm1`
- **To start a VM**: `sudo virsh start ubuntu-vm1`
- **To resume an already suspended (paused) VM**: `sudo virsh resume ubuntu-vm1`
- **To completely delete a VM guest**: `sudo virsh undefine ubuntu-vm1`

For all the options available for `virsh`, please refer to the manual pages using the following command:

```
man virsh
```

The command-line tools for managing VMs are powerful and offer various options. If we consider the fact that, most of the time, a system administrator will be using the CLI rather than the GUI, the ability to use command-line tools is of the utmost importance.

In the following section, we will show you some advanced KVM management practices.

Advanced KVM management

Using KVM is so much more than just creating VMs and starting or stopping them. VM management can be much more complex, starting with VM automated installation, storage and resources management, and up to VM orchestration. Some of these topics are out of the scope of this book, but we will still show you how to master your VMs on your Linux-powered systems.

By now, we only have one VM. For the purpose of the exercises in this section, we will create two more VMs, all running the same Ubuntu OS that we used for the first VM. We will create `ubuntu-vm2` and `ubuntu-vm3` VMs using the following commands:

- For `ubuntu-vm2`:

```
sudo virt-install --virt-type=kvm --name ubuntu-vm2 --vcpus=2
--memory=2048 --os-variant=ubuntufocal --cdrom=/var/lib/libvirt/
images/ubuntu-22.04.2-live-server-amd64.iso --network=default
--disk size=20 --noautoconsole
```

- For `ubuntu-vm3`:

```
sudo virt-install --virt-type=kvm --name ubuntu-vm3 --vcpus=2
--memory=2048 --os-variant=ubuntufocal --cdrom=/var/lib/libvirt/
images/ubuntu-22.04.2-live-server-amd64.iso --network=default
--disk size=20 --noautoconsole
```

Now, we have three VMs running on our system and we can begin managing them. In the next section, we will show you how to find out the IP of a VM and how to connect to it.

Connecting to a VM

Most of the time, we would like to connect to a running VM from a terminal and not use the integrated console provided by the VM manager. In order to be able to do this, we will need to know the VM's IP address. A simple run of the `ip neighbor` command will show us all the IP addresses on our local network, but this will not provide the relevant information we need, such as the VM's name.

On our system, when running the `ip neighbor` command, the output is as follows:

```
alexandru@debian:~$ ip neighbor
192.168.122.129 dev virbr0 lladdr 52:54:00:3b:56:e5 STALE
192.168.0.1 dev enp5s0 lladdr                       STALE
192.168.0.1 dev wlp3s0 lladdr                       STALE
192.168.122.30 dev virbr0 lladdr 52:54:00:20:fe:4a STALE
192.168.122.75 dev virbr0 lladdr 52:54:00:d4:24:e8 STALE
```

Figure 11.7 – Viewing the IP addresses on the local network

From the output, we can see that three of the IP addresses are from the default virtual network that is set up by KVM (`virbr0`). This is the first information that tells us the IP addresses used by our VMs. But which IP is which VM? To find out more information, we will use the following commands:

```
sudo virsh list --all
```

The preceding command is used to list all the existing VMs. The output (as seen in *Figure 11.8*) shows the names of the VMs. In order to see the IP addresses associated with each one, we will use the following command:

```
sudo virsh domifaddr [vm name]
```

The [vm name] represents one of the VM names from the virsh list command's output. In the following screenshot, you can see the output of the previous commands:

```
alexandru@debian:~$ sudo virsh list --all
 Id   Name         State
---------------------------------
 1    ubuntu-vm1   running
 4    ubuntu-vm2   running
 5    ubuntu-vm3   running

alexandru@debian:~$ sudo virsh domifaddr ubuntu-vm1
 Name         MAC address         Protocol      Address
----------------------------------------------------------------------
 vnet0        52:54:00:3b:56:e5   ipv4          192.168.122.129/24

alexandru@debian:~$ sudo virsh domifaddr ubuntu-vm2
 Name         MAC address         Protocol      Address
----------------------------------------------------------------------
 vnet3        52:54:00:20:fe:4a   ipv4          192.168.122.30/24

alexandru@debian:~$ sudo virsh domifaddr ubuntu-vm3
 Name         MAC address         Protocol      Address
----------------------------------------------------------------------
 vnet4        52:54:00:d4:24:e8   ipv4          192.168.122.75/24
```

Figure 11.8 – Showing the IP addresses for VMs

Now that we know the IP addresses of every VM we created, we can connect to any of the VMs using SSH (more on installing and configuring SSH in *Chapter 13*). Considering that we already have openSSH installed on both our host system and the target VM, the simplest way to connect using SSH is as follows:

```
alexandru@debian:~$ ssh packt@192.168.122.129
The authenticity of host '192.168.122.129 (192.168.122.129)' can't be establishe
d.
ED25519 key fingerprint is SHA256:/K8iA4WMXxtaras1g/n8Kr0oaAGGYqsPMH/ZmsxUdNA.
This key is not known by any other names.
Are you sure you want to continue connecting (yes/no/[fingerprint])? yes
Warning: Permanently added '192.168.122.129' (ED25519) to the list of known host
s.
packt@192.168.122.129's password:
```

Figure 11.9 – Connect to a VM through SSH

Another way to connect to a VM is by using the virt-viewer command:

```
virt-viewer --connect qemu:///system ubuntu-vm1
```

This command will open a new console window using the virt-viewer utility and connect to the VM you specify (in our case, ubuntu-vm1 again) without using the SSH protocol:

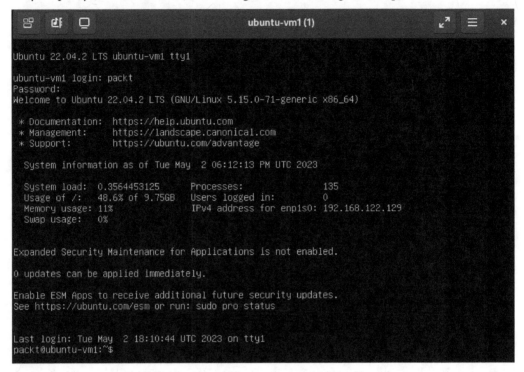

Figure 11.10 – Connecting to VM using virt-viewer

> **Important note**
>
> The connection remains active inside the terminal where you initiated the command. Thus, if you press *Ctrl + C*, the connection will be terminated and the new console window will close. Take into consideration that only the connection will be terminated and the VM will still be running.

We have shown you how to use the command line to create VMs, for basic management, and to connect to a virtual machine. However, you can also use GUI tools. All modern Linux distributions that use GNOME as the desktop environment will offer at least two useful tools: the Virtual Machine Manager and GNOME Boxes. The former is simply the GUI for libvirt, and the latter is a new and simple way to provision VMs for immediate use inside GNOME based on QEMU/KVM technology. We will let you discover these GUI tools as they are pretty straightforward and not difficult to use. You could start creating new VMs using the Virtual Machine Manager. In the next section, we will show you how to clone VMs.

Cloning VMs

We have already created three different VMs on our host system. However, there are times when you might want to clone an existing VM instead of creating a new one.

Before starting to clone a VM, we need to stop or suspend it. We will do this using the `suspend` or the `shutdown` commands. We will stop one of our VMs, as shown:

```
sudo virsh shutdown ubuntu-vm1
```

This command will shut down the `ubuntu-vm1` VM. In order to clone it, we will use the `virt-clone` command. Let's say that we want to name the clone `ubuntu-vm1-clone1`. We will use the following command:

```
sudo virt-clone --original ubuntu-vm1 --name ubuntu-vm1-clone1 --auto-
clone
```

The output of the command is shown in the following screenshot:

```
alexandru@debian:~$ sudo virsh list --all
 Id   Name          State
---------------------------
 2    ubuntu-vm2    running
 3    ubuntu-vm3    running
 -    ubuntu-vm1    shut off

alexandru@debian:~$ sudo virt-clone --original ubuntu-vm1 --name ubuntu-vm1-clone1 --auto-clone
Allocating 'ubuntu-vm1-clone1.qcow2'                    | 3.9 GB  00:04 ...

Clone 'ubuntu-vm1-clone1' created successfully.
alexandru@debian:~$ sudo virsh list --all
 Id   Name              State
-----------------------------------
 2    ubuntu-vm2        running
 3    ubuntu-vm3        running
 -    ubuntu-vm1        shut off
 -    ubuntu-vm1-clone1 shut off
```

Figure 11.11 – Cloning virtual machines using virt-clone

Now that the clone has been created, we can start it using the `virsh start` command. Cloning a VM will also *transfer* all the original VM's configuration regarding the number of vCPUs, RAM, bridge networking configuration, the same MAC address, and even the same IP address. This can become a real headache and needs to be solved.

One way to solve this is to directly connect to the VM's console (not through SSH) and run the `ip addr show` command. This will enable the DHCP client to automatically assign an IP address to the host. In the next section, we will show you another useful way to manage cloning with VM templates.

Creating VM templates

Another useful way to overcome the issue described in the previous section is to first create a VM template before cloning. By creating a template, you make sure that all the configuration files will not persist, including MAC and IP configuration, user settings, or SSH host keys.

To create a template, follow these steps:

1. We will use the `virt-sysprep` utility. In Debian 12, we will install the `libguestfs-tools` utility, which contains the `virt-sysprep`, using the following command:

    ```
    sudo apt install libguestfs-tools
    ```

2. Now that the utility is installed, we will use it to create a template. But first, we will create a new VM running Ubuntu and use it as a template. We will use the following command to create the new VM:

    ```
    sudo virt-install --virt-type=kvm --name ubuntu-template
    --vcpus=2 --memory=2048 --os-variant=ubuntufocal --cdrom=/
    var/lib/libvirt/images/ubuntu-22.04.2-live-server-amd64.iso
    --network=default --disk size=20 -noautoconsole
    ```

3. After finishing the OS installation, make sure that it is up to date with all the available packages.

4. Proceed only after ensuring that the VM is turned off. As a precautionary method, you could first copy the file with a different name:

    ```
    sudo cp /var/lib/libvirt/images/ubuntu-template.qcow2 /var/lib/
    libvirt/images/ubuntu-back-template.qcow2
    ```

5. Now you can prepare the new VM instance with the `virt-sysprep` utility:

    ```
    sudo virt-sysprep -d ubuntu-template
    ```

The `virt-sysprep` command is preparing the VM by resetting all the configuration files that might have been created. The following is an excerpt from the output:

```
alexandru@debian:~$ sudo virt-sysprep -d ubuntu-template
[   0.0] Examining the guest ...
[   6.9] Performing "abrt-data" ...
[   6.9] Performing "backup-files" ...
[   7.2] Performing "bash-history" ...
[   7.2] Performing "blkid-tab" ...
[   7.3] Performing "crash-data" ...
[   7.3] Performing "cron-spool" ...
[   7.3] Performing "dhcp-client-state" ...
[   7.3] Performing "dhcp-server-state" ...
[   7.3] Performing "dovecot-data" ...
[   7.3] Performing "ipa-client" ...
[   7.3] Performing "kerberos-hostkeytab" ...
[   7.4] Performing "logfiles" ...
[   7.5] Performing "machine-id" ...
[   7.5] Performing "mail-spool" ...
[   7.5] Performing "net-hostname" ...
[   7.5] Performing "net-hwaddr" ...
[   7.6] Performing "net-nmconn" ...
```

Figure 11.12 – Creating a template with virt-sysprep

6. Now that the template is prepared, you can do either of the following:

    *   Undefine the domain by using the `virsh undefine` command. This command removes the configuration of the VM but leaves the `qcow2` file that it created so that you could use it when creating a new VM.

    *   Keep the VM (in our case, the one named `ubuntu-template`) and use it as a clone template, as intended.

    The choice is yours, but we are inclined towards the second option, as it is already configured and thus is much easier to use. When using only the `qcow2` file, you still have to configure (setting CPUs, RAM, networking, etc.) the VM prior to using it.

Now that you know how to clone a VM and how to create templates, let's see other ways to manage VMs. In the next section, we will show you how to obtain information about the VMs you work with, from the command line.

Obtaining VM and host resource information

When you're working at the command line, some information is not as visible as when working with the GUI tools. To see if we still have the necessary sources for creating new VMs, we will need to use the `virsh nodeinfo` command to obtain information about the host machine:

```
alexandru@debian:~$ sudo virsh nodeinfo
CPU model:          x86_64
CPU(s):             16
CPU frequency:      3197 MHz
CPU socket(s):      1
Core(s) per socket: 8
Thread(s) per core: 2
NUMA cell(s):       1
Memory size:        48113628 KiB
```

Figure 11.13 – Finding host information with the nodeinfo command

In our case, as seen in the preceding image, the host has 16 vCPUs available and 48 GB of RAM, meaning that we still have resources available for some new VMs. We know that when we created the VMs we allocated 2 vCPUs and 2 GB of RAM for each one. As we now have five VMs (as shown in the following image), it means that we use 10 out of 16 vCPUs and 10 GB out of 48 GB RAM:

```
alexandru@debian:~$ sudo virsh list --all
 Id    Name                State
-----------------------------------
 -     ubuntu-template     shut off
 -     ubuntu-vm1          shut off
 -     ubuntu-vm1-clone1   shut off
 -     ubuntu-vm2          shut off
 -     ubuntu-vm3          shut off
```

Figure 11.14 – Listing the existing VMs

But what if we do not know how many resources the existing VMs use? There is a command that can help us with that. It is called virsh dominfo. Let's see the resources that one of our VMs is using, for example, ubuntu-vm1:

```
alexandru@debian:~$ sudo virsh dominfo ubuntu-vm1
Id:              -
Name:            ubuntu-vm1
UUID:            e55f3253-0e71-441e-b7c5-e7bc8d4b9f43
OS Type:         hvm
State:           shut off
CPU(s):          2
Max memory:      2097152 KiB
Used memory:     2097152 KiB
Persistent:      yes
Autostart:       disable
Managed save:    no
Security model:  apparmor
Security DOI:    0
```

Figure 11.15 – Showing the VMs' resource usage

In the preceding image, you can see that our VM is using 2 vCPUs and 2 GB of RAM. You can check the resource usage for every VM that you manage. Besides vCPUs and RAM, you can also manage virtual disks for existing VMs. To see the disk usage for a VM you can use the `virt-df` command:

```
alexandru@debian:~$ sudo virt-df -d ubuntu-vm1
Filesystem                          1K-blocks       Used  Available  Use%
ubuntu-vm1:/dev/sda2                  1790136     132868    1548008    8%
ubuntu-vm1:/dev/ubuntu-vg/ubuntu-lv  10218772    4922772    4755328   49%
alexandru@debian:~$ sudo virt-df -h -d ubuntu-vm1
Filesystem                             Size       Used  Available  Use%
ubuntu-vm1:/dev/sda2                   1.7G       130M       1.5G    8%
ubuntu-vm1:/dev/ubuntu-vg/ubuntu-lv    9.7G       4.7G       4.5G   49%
```

Figure 11.16 – Showing disk usage for a VM

We have used the `-d` option for showing `libvirt` domain guests and the `-h` option to show the results in a human-readable format. The `virt-df` command is similar to the `df` command (see *Chapter 6*).

Knowing the resource usage is the first step in managing the resources that you have. In the following section, we will show you how to change the amount of resources a VM is using.

Managing VM resource usage

As shown earlier, knowing how many resources a VM is using can prove of great value. You would need to be able to modify the resources already in use if you run out of resources. You have tools available to modify the amount of vCPUs and RAM an existing VM is using. For example, let's change the resources for our `ubuntu-vm1-clone1` VM from 2 vCPUs to 1 vCPU and from 2 GB of RAM to 1 GB of RAM. The command we will use is `virsh setvcpus`, and we will use it as follows:

```
alexandru@debian:~$ sudo virsh setvcpus --domain ubuntu-vm1-clone1 --maximum 1 --config

alexandru@debian:~$ sudo virsh setvcpus --domain ubuntu-vm1-clone1 --count 1 --config
```

Figure 11.17 – Changing the vCPU count for a VM

We can also change the amount of RAM used with the `virsh setmem` and `virsh setmaxmem` commands:

```
alexandru@debian:~$ sudo virsh setmaxmem ubuntu-vm1-clone1 1G --config

alexandru@debian:~$ sudo virsh setmem ubuntu-vm1-clone1 1G --config
```

Figure 11.18 – Changing the memory used by a VM

We can now check the resources used by the `ubuntu-vm1-clone1` VM using the `virsh dominfo` command, as shown in the following screenshot:

```
alexandru@debian:~$ sudo virsh dominfo ubuntu-vm1-clone1
Id:             -
Name:           ubuntu-vm1-clone1
UUID:           86f38f9f-08d7-49da-922c-fc6b31b16f9f
OS Type:        hvm
State:          shut off
CPU(s):         1
Max memory:     1048576 KiB
Used memory:    1048576 KiB
Persistent:     yes
Autostart:      disable
Managed save:   no
Security model: apparmor
Security DOI:   0
```

Figure 11.19 – Checking the resources for a VM

As you can see, the resources used by the VM have been changed according to your new settings. Now that you know how to manage KVMs, which is a required asset for a Linux system administrator. In the next section, we will show you how to automate KVM VM provisioning using **cloud-init**.

Provisioning VMs using cloud-init

When you're dealing with only one VM, things can be relatively simple. But when we have to create hundreds of VMs, manual creation can be daunting. One useful tool you can use for such a task is **cloud-init**. Another tool that is suitable for this kind of task is **Ansible** (there's more on Ansible in *Chapter 17*). In this section, we will cover only cloud-init. It was developed by Canonical to be used as a tool for configuring VM instances on cloud platforms, and it is written in Python. Currently, it is considered an industry standard for provisioning cloud images. In the next subsection, we will briefly explain to you how cloud-init works.

Understanding how cloud-init works

According to the official cloud-init documentation, it is based on several configuration sources, specific boot stages, user data formats, vendor data, and instance metadata. The concept of boot stages is specific to cloud-init architecture, as it configures the entire instance during specific stages of the boot process. It provides a way for managing completely working instances that have networking, boot sequence, and local configuration files configured.

Cloud-init is available on most widely used Linux distributions, such as Ubuntu, Debian, Red Hat Enterprise Linux, Fedora, SUSE, and openSUSE. We will use one of our Debian 12 systems as a host and install and configure cloud-init on it. We will show you how in the following subsection.

Installing and configuring cloud-init

Even if its main purpose is to be used for cloud deployments, cloud-init can also be used locally. We will use it to deploy VMs on our local system. As a prerequisite for using cloud-init, a hypervisor should already be installed on your system, such as KVM. For the guest image, cloud-init uses specific cloud images that are already available from almost every Linux distribution provider. For example, we are planning on deploying Ubuntu VMs, thus we will need Ubuntu-optimized cloud images, which are available at `https://cloud-images.ubuntu.com/`. Let's look at the steps required to prepare the image for deployment:

1. First, we will install the `cloud-image-utils` additional package and then the `cloud-init` package:

```
sudo apt install cloud-image-utils cloud-init
```

2. The next step is to create a new directory for the new cloud images:

```
mkdir local-cloud-images && cd local-cloud-images
```

3. The next step is to download the cloud image:

```
wget https://cloud-images.ubuntu.com/jammy/current/jammy-server-cloudimg-amd64.img
```

4. Then we get details for the cloud image file:

```
qemu-img info jammy-server-cloudimg-amd64.img
```

5. Then we resize the image:

```
qemu-img resize jammy-server-cloudimg-amd64.img 15G
```

6. Create a new image as a `.qcow2` base image:

```
qemu-img create -f qcow2 -F qcow2 -b jammy-server-cloudimg-amd64.img ubuntu.qcow2 15G
```

7. Copy the images to the `libvirt` directory:

```
sudo cp ubuntu.qcow2 /var/lib/libvirt/images/
```

Right now, we have the images ready for use. Some more steps are needed for the cloud-init configuration. We will need to create local files for metadata (called `meta-data`) and another file for user data (called `user-data`). They are **Yet Another Markup Language (YAML)** files so you will need to use the YAML syntax.

8. We will create a new directory (inside `/var/lib/libvirt/image/`) to store the new configuration files. We will use the following commands as root:

```
mkdir cloud-init && cd cloud-init/ && touch user-data && touch
meta-data && touch network-config
```

9. The `meta-data` file will not be populated just yet. We will edit the `user-data` file first.

> **Important note**
> At this point, we will need a pair of SSH keys to use to connect with the new VM we plan to create. As we have not shown you yet how to work with SSH keys, we will provide you with the needed information in the next subsection. Go ahead and read the *Public key authentication with SSH* section, then get back to this point, where we will continue configuring our cloud-init files.

Let's create the `user-data` file and add the following information:

```
alexandru@debian:~/local-cloud-images/cloud-init$ cat user-data
#cloud-config

hostname: ubuntu-vm1
fqdn: ubuntu-vm1.localdomain
manage_etc_hosts: true

ssh_pwauth: false
disable_root: true

users:
  - name: packt
    home: /home/packt
    shell: /bin/bash
    groups: sudo
    sudo: ALL=(ALL) NOPASSWD:ALL
    ssh-authorized-keys:
      - ssh-rsa AAAAB3NzaC1yc2EAAAADAQABAAABgQCnPsaGTuyBIZ3+fSLgHntaC3RUnc2ucoCC
e0QDUTV9Y/B2gLt8deZYfoCue06Gp1cA1SK7E4hei0vkuIpUlm0isbDiQaBEpAzSGwzw6nA9QsNbw0RS
op/PM1KZPdKST20zG8kNYVdlp1P2mc8WA8utZzOvJn224cG0/WWW7nO4fxiuz+rn8QkOfFMEnTtvjV5t
3e/b8oPP3gVK6bgxCipG88+aUfPX7d4yoQqDQuoCpLSulnmlvEWV1TP4qjJXAxU6t6E1R624W4UVIdcF
agQpQEHLw/G6aj9mIzVFAgCwxuQfZi8dGiZi5xyfDEuGMX5J1kIGW/NQclfX7/IU4gSRRDH66D5Ae54X
9ciYR1dU39gV3Md2r7ZBLjsJTaaj3jbspWgH2uByzM0aUz6N30D+srFXAP91nGqMor6JAhMHZVnlhidu
mbehy9oKT0M5JjDJH3p7aFxSt+CSmSEYwCA0kG2d7/AqrmgsTSmGiAz4A5o+KbYuix3Aj2b17dUa92s=
 alexandru@debian
```

Figure 11.20 – The user-data file contents

10. After the `user-data` file editing is finished, we can continue and create a disk image that will contain the configuration files. We will use the `cloud-localds` command from the `cloud-image-utils` package we installed earlier:

```
cloud-localds -v ubuntu-provisioning.qcow2 user-data meta-data
```

11. Now, we have created a new disk image based on the `user-data` file we created. The preparations are finished and we can start deploying. We will deploy our VM using the following command:

```
sudo virt-install --name vm01 --virt-type kvm --vcpus 1
--memory 2048 --disk path=/var/lib/libvirt/images/ubuntu.
qcow2,device=disk --disk path=/var/lib/libvirt/images/cloud-
init/ubuntu-provisioning.qcow2,device=cdrom --os-type linux
--os-variant generic --import --network network=default
--noautoconsole
```

12. If you get any errors regarding the network activation, you might have to use the following commands to activate the default network:

```
sudo virsh net-start default && sudo virsh net-autostart default
```

13. After running the `virt-install` command, the output will be as shown as follows:

```
alexandru@debian:~$ sudo virt-install --name vm01 --virt-type kvm --vcpus 1 --me
mory 2048 --disk path=/var/lib/libvirt/images/ubuntu.qcow2,device=disk --disk pa
th=/var/lib/libvirt/images/cloud-init/ubuntu-provisioning.qcow2,device=cdrom --o
s-type linux --os-variant generic --import --network network=default --noautocon
sole
WARNING  --os-type is deprecated and does nothing. Please stop using it.
WARNING  Using --osinfo generic, VM performance may suffer. Specify an accurate
OS for optimal results.

Starting install...
Creating domain...                                      |    0 B  00:00
Domain creation completed.
```

Figure 11.21 – Creating a new VM

14. We now have deployed a new VM using cloud-init. We can verify that it is running by using the `sudo virsh list` command or by using the Virtual Manager GUI. We will verify if the VM is running, we will find out the IP address and connect to it using SSH. We will use the following commands: `sudo virsh list` to check the state of the VM, `sudo virsh domifaddr vm01` to find its IP, and `ssh packt@192.168.122.32` to connect to it. The output is shown in the following screenshot:

```
alexandru@debian:~$ sudo virsh list
 Id   Name   State
----------------------
 2    vm01   running

alexandru@debian:~$ sudo virsh domifaddr vm01
 Name         MAC address         Protocol    Address
-------------------------------------------------------------------------
 vnet0        52:54:00:35:e6:8e   ipv4        192.168.122.32/24

alexandru@debian:~$ ssh packt@192.168.122.32
The authenticity of host '192.168.122.32 (192.168.122.32)' can't be established.
ED25519 key fingerprint is SHA256:oNFhrgESf4jFhh8VmolfCerb7lVXwpejXoaTyj9QNP4.
This key is not known by any other names.
Are you sure you want to continue connecting (yes/no/[fingerprint])? yes
Warning: Permanently added '192.168.122.32' (ED25519) to the list of known hosts
.
Welcome to Ubuntu 22.04.2 LTS (GNU/Linux 5.15.0-71-generic x86_64)
```

Figure 11.22 – Connecting to the new VM using SSH

We have successfully created and connected to a new VM using cloud-init. After finishing this section, you now possess the ability to deploy VMs using cloud-init. However, we have only scratched the surface of what cloud-init can do, so if you feel like you would like to learn more about it, please use the official documentation or any of the titles provided in the *Further reading* section at the end of the chapter.

In the next section, we will show you how to use public key authentication with SSH.

Public key authentication with SSH

Public key authentication is a secure way to log in to a virtual private server or a cloud instance through SSH. It provides better security and cryptographic strength than any strong password in use. When setting up SSH key authentication, we generate a pair of two keys, a private and a public key. From those two keys, the private key will be stored on the local machine, and the public key will be used on the host VM. The keys are stored inside the .ssh directory in your user's home directory. To generate a new pair of keys, you will have to use the ssh-keygen command.

It can be used with options, the most relevant ones being: -t to specify the type of encryption algorithm used, -b to specify the number of bits. Used with no option, the ssh-keygen command will use the RSA encryption algorithm and a 3,072-bit key. The following is the output for using the command as is:

```
alexandru@debian:~$ ssh-keygen
Generating public/private rsa key pair.
Enter file in which to save the key (/home/alexandru/.ssh/id_rsa):
Enter passphrase (empty for no passphrase):
Enter same passphrase again:
Your identification has been saved in /home/alexandru/.ssh/id_rsa
Your public key has been saved in /home/alexandru/.ssh/id_rsa.pub
The key fingerprint is:
SHA256:Vokl2Ihnas9XXFoiOFI1XRXsQfR6SQbpD5y62Cg7K7M alexandru@debian
The key's randomart image is:
+---[RSA 3072]----+
|       o.*+....**. |
|      o B o=o.o.+. |
|      = ..oo=o..+.|
|     o    .+  =+..|
|    . o  S.  . +..|
|       o..     o |
|        . + .     |
|     o o o o     |
|     E+o=         |
+----[SHA256]-----+
```

Figure 11.23 – Using the ssh-keygen to create a pair of SSH keys

As mentioned earlier, the two keys are stored inside the `.ssh` directory. One will be called `id_rsa` and the other `id_rsa.pub`. For our use case, configuring cloud-init, we will need to use the public key. Thus, we will need to concatenate the contents of the `id_rsa.pub` file and copy the key. In our case, the contents are as follows:

```
alexandru@debian:~$ cd .ssh/
alexandru@debian:~/.ssh$ ls -la
total 16
drwx------  2 alexandru alexandru 4096 May 15 22:28 .
drwx------ 21 alexandru alexandru 4096 May 15 18:56 ..
-rw-------  1 alexandru alexandru 2602 May 15 22:28 id_rsa
-rw-r--r--  1 alexandru alexandru  570 May 15 22:28 id_rsa.pub
alexandru@debian:~/.ssh$ cat id_rsa.pub
ssh-rsa AAAAB3NzaC1yc2EAAAADAQABAAABgQCnPsaGTuyBIZ3+fSLgHntaC3RUnc2ucoCCe0QDUTV9
Y/B2gLt8deZYfoCue06Gp1cA1SK7E4hei0vkuIpUlm0isbDiQaBEpAzSGwzw6nA9QsNbw0RSop/PMlKZ
PdKST20zG8kNYVdlp1P2mc8WA8utZzOvJn224cG0/WWW7nO4fxiuz+rn8QkOfFMEnTtvjV5t3e/b8oPP
3gVK6bgxCipG88+aUfPX7d4yoQqDQuoCpLSulnmlvEWV1TP4qjJXAxU6t6E1R624W4UVIdcFagQpQEHL
w/G6aj9mIzVFAgCwxuQfZi8dGiZi5xyfDEuGMX5J1kIGW/NQclfX7/IU4gSRRDH66D5Ae54X9ciYR1dU
39gV3Md2r7ZBLjsJTaaj3jbspWgH2uByzM0aUz6N30D+srFXAP91nGqMor6JAhMHZVnlhidumbehy9oK
T0M5JjDJH3p7aFxSt+CSmSEYwCA0kG2d7/AqrmgsTSmGiAz4A5o+KbYuix3Aj2b17dUa92s= alexand
ru@debian
```

Figure 11.24 – The SSH public key

However, if we need to use those keys to connect to a cloud instance of a virtual private server or a VM, the public key needs to be safely copied to that machine or instance. For this, we will use the `ssh-copy-id` command. When using the command, we will need to provide a username and an IP address or hostname for the destination machine. For example, if we were to copy the SSH public key to a VM that has the IP `192.168.122.48` and a user `packt`, we would use the following command:

```
ssh-copy-id packt@192.168.122.48
```

More details on how to install and configure an SSH server will be provided in *Chapter 13*. The information shown here is sufficient for our cloud-init task.

Virtualization is an important part of computing, providing the technology needed to take advantage of the tremendous computing power that modern systems provide. It gives you the ability to get the most out of your investment in hardware technology.

Summary

In this chapter, we emphasized the importance of virtualization on a Linux system. We showed you how to create and manage VMs using KVM. You know how to clone, template, and manage resources for VMs; and you know how virtualization works and how to install the QEMU/KVM hypervisor on Linux. With those assets, you are prepared to start your path into virtualization with no fears.

In the next chapter, we will introduce you to Docker container technologies.

Exercises

Here's a brief quiz about some of the essential concepts that were covered in this chapter:

1. Enumerate and describe the types of hypervisors.
2. Practice by installing a hypervisor on many Linux hosts.
3. Verify whether your hypervisor is working correctly.

   Hint: Use `virt-host-validate`.
4. Can you think of significant differences between major hypervisors?

   Hint: Test KVM and VirtualBox for example, and make a comparison.
5. How can you find the IP addresses of VMs?

   Hint: Use the `virsh domifaddr` command.

Further reading

For more information on the topics covered in this chapter, you can refer to the following Packt books:

- *Mastering KVM Virtualization – Second Edition*, Vedran Dakic, Humble Devassy Chirammal, Prasad Mukhedkar, Anil Vettathu

- *KVM Virtualization Cookbook*, Konstantin Ivanov

For detailed information about the inner workings of cloud-init, visit the official documentation website at `https://cloudinit.readthedocs.io/en/latest/explanation/index.html`.

12

Managing Containers with Docker

In this chapter, you will learn about one of the most well-known tools for creating and managing containers – **Docker**. The topics in this chapter will prepare you for the future of Linux, as it is the foundation of every modern cloud technology. If you wish to remain up to date in a constantly changing landscape, this chapter will be the essential starting point for your journey.

In this chapter, we're going to cover the following main topics:

- Understanding Linux containers
- Working with Docker
- Working with **Dockerfiles**
- Deploying a containerized application with Docker

Technical requirements

No specific technical requirements are needed, just a working installation of Linux on your system. Both Ubuntu/Debian and Fedora/RHEL are equally suitable for this chapter's exercises. We will use Debian GNU/Linux 12 for most of our examples, but where appropriate, we will discuss the specifics of Fedora Linux installation and use.

Understanding Linux containers

As we have demonstrated in the previous chapter, there are two main types of virtualization: **virtual machine (VM)-based** and **container-based**. We discussed VM-based virtualization in the previous chapter, and now it is time to explain what containers are. At a very basic, conceptual level, containers are similar to VMs. They have similar purposes – allowing an isolated environment to run – but they are different in so many ways that they can hardly be called similar. Let's compare these two concepts in more detail.

Comparing containers and VMs

As you already know, a VM emulates the machine's hardware and uses it as if there were several machines available. By comparison, containers do not replicate the physical machine's hardware; they do not emulate anything.

A container shares the base OS kernel with shared libraries and binaries needed for certain applications to run. The applications are contained inside the container, isolated from the rest of the system. They also share a network interface with the host to offer similar connectivity to a VM.

Containers run on top of a **container engine**. Container engines offer OS-level virtualization, used to deploy and test applications by using only the requisite libraries and dependencies. This way, containers make sure that applications can run on any machine by providing the same expected behavior as intended by the developer. The following is a visual comparison between containers and VMs:

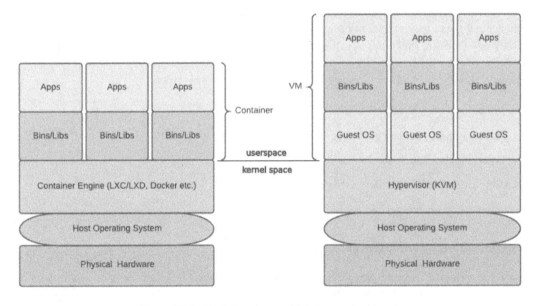

Figure 12.1 – Containers versus VMs (general scheme)

As you can see, the containers only use the **userspace**, sharing the underlying OS-level architecture.

Historically speaking, containerization has been around for some time now. With the Unix OS, **chroot** has been the tool used for containerization since 1982.

On Linux, some of the newest and most frequently used tools are **Linux containers** (**LXC**), with **LXD** as a newer and extended version of the former, introduced in 2008, and Docker, introduced in 2013. Why this LXC/LXD nomenclature? Well, LXC was the first kid on the containers block, with LXD being a newer, redesigned version of it.

In the next section, we will dissect the underlying container technology.

Understanding the underlying container technology

As mentioned earlier, LXC was one of the earliest forms of containers, introduced 12 years ago. The newer form of containers, and the ones that changed the entire container landscape and started all the DevOps hype (more on this in *Chapter 14*), is called Docker. Containers do not abstract the hardware level as hypervisors do. They use a specific userspace interface that benefits from the kernel's techniques to isolate specific resources. By using Linux containers, you can replicate a default Linux system without using a different kernel, as you would do by using a VM.

What made LXC appealing when it first appeared were the APIs it uses for multiple programming languages, including Python 3, Go, Ruby, and Haskell. So, even though LXC is no longer that popular, it is still worth knowing. Docker has taken the crown and center stage in container engine usage. We will not use LXC/LXD in our examples, but we will still discuss it for backward compatibility purposes. As of the time of writing this book, there are two supported versions of LXC, version 4.0, with support until June 2025, and version 5.0, with support until June 2027.

According to its developers, LXC uses features to create an isolated environment that is as close as possible to a default Linux installation. Among the kernel technologies that it uses, we could bring up the most important one, which is the backbone of any container inside Linux: kernel **namespaces** and **cgroups**. Besides those, there are still chroots and security profiles for both AppArmor and SELinux.

Let's now explain these basic features that Linux containers use.

Linux namespaces

What are **Linux namespaces**? In a nutshell, namespaces are kernel global system resources responsible for the isolation that containers provide. Namespaces wrap a global system resource inside an abstraction layer. This process fools any app process that is running inside the namespace into believing that the resource it is using is its own. A namespace provides isolation at a logical level inside the kernel and also provides visibility for any running processes.

To better understand how namespaces work, think of any user on a Linux system and how it can view different system resources and processes. As a user, you can see the global system resources, the running processes, other users, and kernel modules, for example. This amount of transparency could be harmful when wanting to use containers as virtualized environments at the OS level. As it cannot provide the encapsulation and emulation level of a VM, the container engine must overcome this somehow, and the kernel's low-level mechanisms of virtualization of the environment come in the form of namespaces and cgroups.

There are several types of namespaces inside the Linux kernel, and we will describe them briefly:

- **Mount**: They restrict visibility for available filesystem mount points within a single namespace so that processes from that namespace have visibility of the filesystem list; processes can have their own root filesystem and different private or shared mounts

- **Unix Time Sharing** (**UTS**): This isolates the system's hostname and domain name

- **Interprocess Communication** (**IPC**): This allows processes to have their own IPC shared memory, queues, and semaphores

- **Process Identification**: This allows mapping of **process IDs** (**PIDs**) with the possibility of a process with PID 1 (the root of the process tree) to spin off a new tree with its own root process; processes inside a PID namespace only see the processes inside the same PID namespace

- **Network**: Abstraction at the network protocol level; processes inside a network namespace have a private network stack with private network interfaces, routing tables, sockets, and iptables rules

- **User**: This allows mapping of UID and GID, including root UID 0 as a non-privileged user

- **cgroup**: A cgroup namespace process can see filesystem paths relative to the root of the namespace

The namespaces can be viewed by using the `lsns` command in Linux. The following is an excerpt from the command's output:

```
alexandru@debian:~$ lsns
        NS TYPE    NPROCS    PID USER      COMMAND
4026531834 time       141   5097 alexandru /lib/systemd/systemd --user
4026531835 cgroup     141   5097 alexandru /lib/systemd/systemd --user
4026531836 pid        116   5097 alexandru /lib/systemd/systemd --user
4026531837 user        89   5097 alexandru /lib/systemd/systemd --user
4026531838 uts        141   5097 alexandru /lib/systemd/systemd --user
4026531839 ipc        115   5097 alexandru /lib/systemd/systemd --user
4026531840 net        115   5097 alexandru /lib/systemd/systemd --user
4026531841 mnt        113   5097 alexandru /lib/systemd/systemd --user
```

Figure 12.2 – Using lsns to view the available namespaces

In the following section, we will break down cgroups as the second major building block of containers.

Linux cgroups

What are cgroups? Their name comes from **control groups**, and they are kernel features that restrict and manage resource allocation to processes. Cgroups control how memory, CPU, I/O, and network are used. They provide a mechanism that determines specific sets of tasks that limit how many resources a process can use. They are based on the concept of **hierarchies**. Every child group will inherit the attributes of its parent group, and multiple cgroups hierarchies can exist at the same time in one system.

Cgroups and namespaces combined are creating the isolation that containers are built upon. By using cgroups and namespaces, resources are allocated and managed for each container separately. Compared to VMs, containers are lightweight and run as isolated entities.

As stated earlier, there are two types of containers used, LXC and Docker. As we have already discussed LXC, let us see in the following section what Docker is.

Understanding Docker

Docker, similar to LXC/LXD, is based, among other technologies, on kernel namespaces and cgroups. Docker is a platform that is used for developing and shipping applications. The Docker platform provides the underlying infrastructure for containers to operate securely. Docker containers are lightweight entities that run directly on the host's kernel. The platform offers features such as tools to create and manage isolated, containerized applications. Thus, the container is the base unit used for application development, testing, and distribution. When apps are production-ready and fit for deployment, they can be shipped as containers or as orchestrated services (we will discuss orchestration in *Chapter 16, Deploying Applications with Kubernetes*).

In the following diagram, we will show you how the Docker architecture works:

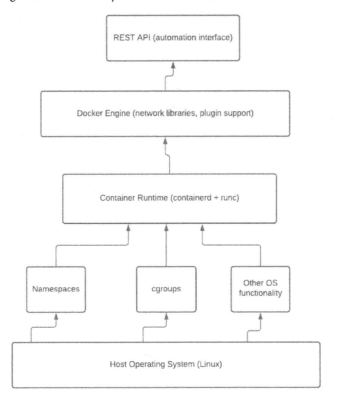

Figure 12.3 – Docker architecture

Let's explain the preceding diagram. Docker uses both namespaces and cgroups available in the Linux kernel, and is split into two major components:

- **Container runtime**: The overseeing authoritative structure that governs the specification for container runtimes is called the **Open Container Initiative (OCI)** and defines the open industry standards for containers. The container runtime is split into the following for namespaces and cgroups management:

  - **containerd** is responsible for downloading Docker images and then running them.

  - The **runc** component follows OCI specifications and is responsible for managing namespaces and cgroups for each container.

 According to the OCI, the runtime specification defines how to download an image, unpack it, and run it using a specific filesystem bundle. The OCI is part of the Linux Foundation. Docker donated `runc` and `containerd` to *Cloud Native Computing Foundation* so that more organizations would be able to contribute to both. The following is a diagram showing the details of the Docker architecture, with the core components, the Docker engine and the container runtime, being shown in detail:

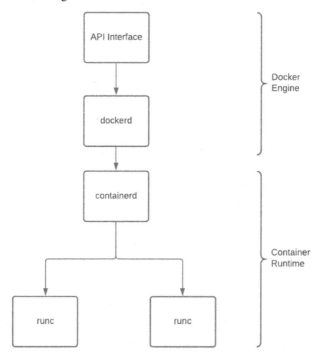

Figure 12.4 – Docker architecture details

- The **Docker engine**: This engine is what is split into the **dockerd** daemon, the **API** interface, and the **command-line interface (CLI)**. The Docker engine comprises the API interface and the dockerd daemon, while the container runtime has two main components – the **containerd** daemon and **runc** for namespaces and cgroups management. Besides the components listed in the previous point, a number of other components are used to run and deploy Docker containers. Docker has a client-server architecture and the workflow involves a **host**, or server daemon, a **client**, and a **registry**. The host consists of images and containers (downloaded from the registry), and the client provides the commands needed to manage containers.

The workflow of these components is as follows:

- The dockerd daemon listens for API requests to manage services and objects (such as images, containers, networks, and volumes).

- The client is the way for users to interact with the daemon through the API.

- The registries store images, and Docker Hub is a public registry for anyone to use freely. In addition to this, there are private registries that can be used.

The following is a graphical representation of Docker's workflow, showing the client component, the API, and the daemon:

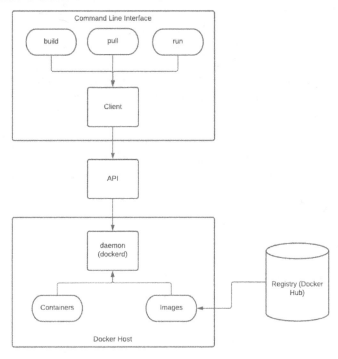

Figure 12.5 – Docker workflow

Docker may seem difficult, even disarming, to a beginner. All the different components that work together, all those new typologies, and specific workflows are complicated. Do you feel like you know how Docker works just after reading this section? Of course not. The process of learning Docker has just begun. Having a strong foundation on which to build your Docker knowledge is extremely important. This is why, in the next section, we will show you how to use Docker.

Working with Docker

We will use Debian GNU/Linux 12 for this section's exercises, installed on a VM with 2 vCPUs and 2 GB of RAM as a host. But before we start installing Docker, let's go into a little detail about how Docker, as an entity, operates, to help us identify which version to choose for our use case.

Which Docker version to choose?

In order for the business to be viable, the corporation behind Docker (the Docker corporation) offers a series of products, all revolving around their primary product, Docker. In the past, it had two different products available, the Docker **Community Edition** (**CE**) and the Docker **Enterprise Edition** (**EE**). Out of these two, only the EE version was responsible for the revenue of Docker.

Recently, the portfolio evolved to different products and offerings, such as **Docker Personal**, **Docker Pro**, **Docker Team**, and **Docker Business**. Among those, only Docker Personal is free to use; the other three products are subscription-based. Docker Personal is suitable for individual developers, education, and open source communities, but has some limitations (which can be seen here: `https://www.docker.com/products/personal/`). Using Docker Personal implies the existence of a Docker user account, and it includes Docker Desktop for Linux (and all other major platforms) and Docker Engine for servers.

On the server side, Docker Engine is available for **x86** and **arm** architectures using both `.deb` and `.rpm` package formats and is available for Ubuntu, Debian, Fedora, and CentOS. For our examples, we will use Docker Personal. We will show you how to install Docker in the next section.

Installing Docker

Depending on the version of your preferred Linux distribution that you choose, the package available inside the official repository may be out of date. Nevertheless, you have two options: one is to use the official package from our Linux distribution's own repository, and the other is to download the latest available version from the official Docker website.

As we are using a fresh system, with no prior Docker installation, we will not need to worry about older versions of the software and possible incompatibilities with the new versions. We will use Docker's `apt` repository, which will ensure that our package versions will always be up to date. Remember that we are using a Debian host.

The procedure to install Docker is as follows:

1. First, add the requisite certificates for the Docker repository using the following commands:

```
sudo apt update -y && sudo apt install ca-certificates curl
gnupg
```

2. In order to use the official Docker repository, you will need to add the Docker GPG key. For this, use the following commands:

```
sudo install -m 0755 -d /etc/apt/keyrings
curl -fsSL https://download.docker.com/linux/debian/gpg | sudo
gpg --dearmor -o /etc/apt/keyrings/docker.gpg
sudo chmod a+r /etc/apt/keyrings/docker.gpg
```

3. Set up the repository needed to install the version of Docker we want:

```
echo "deb [arch=$(dpkg --print-architecture) signed-by=/etc/apt/
keyrings/docker.gpg] https://download.docker.com/linux/debian
$(. /etc/os-release && echo "$VERSION_CODENAME") stable" | sudo
tee /etc/apt/sources.list.d/docker.list > /dev/null
```

4. The next logical step is to update the repository list. When you do this, you should see the official Docker repository. Use the following command:

```
sudo apt update -y
```

5. Install the Docker packages. In our case, we will install the latest packages available using the following command:

```
sudo apt install docker-ce docker-ce-cli containerd.io docker-
buildx-plugin docker-compose-plugin
```

6. To verify that you installed the packages from the official Docker repository and not the ones from the Debian repositories, run the following command:

```
apt-cache policy docker-ce
```

If the output shows the source from the `docker.com` website, this means that the source repository is the official Docker one:

```
packt@debian:~$ apt-cache policy docker-ce
docker-ce:
  Installed: 5:23.0.6-1~debian.12~bookworm
  Candidate: 5:23.0.6-1~debian.12~bookworm
  Version table:
 *** 5:23.0.6-1~debian.12~bookworm 500
        500 https://download.docker.com/linux/debian bookworm/stable amd64 Packages
        100 /var/lib/dpkg/status
     5:23.0.5-1~debian.12~bookworm 500
        500 https://download.docker.com/linux/debian bookworm/stable amd64 Packages
     5:23.0.4-1~debian.12~bookworm 500
        500 https://download.docker.com/linux/debian bookworm/stable amd64 Packages
     5:23.0.3-1~debian.12~bookworm 500
        500 https://download.docker.com/linux/debian bookworm/stable amd64 Packages
     5:23.0.2-1~debian.12~bookworm 500
        500 https://download.docker.com/linux/debian bookworm/stable amd64 Packages
     5:23.0.1-1~debian.12~bookworm 500
        500 https://download.docker.com/linux/debian bookworm/stable amd64 Packages
     5:23.0.0-1~debian.12~bookworm 500
        500 https://download.docker.com/linux/debian bookworm/stable amd64 Packages
```

Figure 12.6 – Verifying the source repository

7. Check the status of the Docker daemon. It should be started right after installation:

    ```
    sudo systemctl status docker
    ```

    If everything went without issues, the output should show that the Docker daemon is running.

8. At the time of installation, a group called `docker` is created. In order to be able to use Docker, your user should be added to the `docker` group. The existing groups in Linux are inside the `/etc/group` file. You can list the last lines (new groups are appended at the end of the file) to see the `docker` group as the last one created:

    ```
    tail /etc/group
    ```

    You can either add your existing user or create a new one. We will add our already existing user. Add the user with the following command:

    ```
    sudo usermod -aG docker ${USER}
    ```

9. After you add the user, log out and back in again and check whether you were added to the new group with the following command:

    ```
    groups
    ```

10. You have completed the installation of Docker. Now you can enable the Docker daemon to begin at system startup:

    ```
    sudo systemctl enable docker
    ```

Installing Docker is only the first step. Now let's explore what we can do with it. In the following section, you will learn about the commands available in Docker.

Using some Docker commands

Working with Docker means using its CLI. It has a significant number of sub-commands available. If you want to see them all, you should run the `docker --help` command. There are two main command groups shown:

- The first group shows the management commands
- The second group shows the regular commands

We will not discuss all the commands in this section. We will only focus on the ones that you will need to get started with Docker.

Before learning anything about the commands, let's first perform a test to see whether the installation is working. We will use the `docker run` command to check whether we can access Docker Hub and run containers. Our testing command will be the following:

```
sudo docker run hello-world
```

This command downloads an image from Docker Hub and runs it as a container. The following is a screenshot of the output:

```
packt@debian:~$ sudo docker run hello-world
Unable to find image 'hello-world:latest' locally
latest: Pulling from library/hello-world
719385e32844: Pull complete
Digest: sha256:9eabfcf6034695c4f6208296be9090b0a3487e20fb6a5cb056525242621cf73d
Status: Downloaded newer image for hello-world:latest

Hello from Docker!
This message shows that your installation appears to be working correctly.

To generate this message, Docker took the following steps:
 1. The Docker client contacted the Docker daemon.
 2. The Docker daemon pulled the "hello-world" image from the Docker Hub.
    (amd64)
 3. The Docker daemon created a new container from that image which runs the
    executable that produces the output you are currently reading.
 4. The Docker daemon streamed that output to the Docker client, which sent it
    to your terminal.

To try something more ambitious, you can run an Ubuntu container with:
 $ docker run -it ubuntu bash

Share images, automate workflows, and more with a free Docker ID:
 https://hub.docker.com/

For more examples and ideas, visit:
 https://docs.docker.com/get-started/
```

Figure 12.7 – Running the first docker run command

The preceding screenshot is self-explanatory and a nice touch from the Docker team. It explains what the command did in the background using clear and easy-to-understand language. By running the `docker run` command, you both learn about the workflow and the success of the installation. Also, it is one of the basic Docker commands that you will use relatively often.

Let's now dig deeper and search for other images available on Docker Hub. Let's search for an Ubuntu image to run containers on. To search for the image, we will use the `docker search` command:

```
docker search ubuntu
```

The output of the command should list all the Ubuntu images available inside Docker Hub:

```
packt@debian:~$ docker search ubuntu
NAME                              DESCRIPTION                                STARS    OFFICIAL    AUTOMATED
ubuntu                            Ubuntu is a Debian-based Linux operating sys…   15927   [OK]
websphere-liberty                 WebSphere Liberty multi-architecture images …   293     [OK]
open-liberty                      Open Liberty multi-architecture images based…   59      [OK]
neurodebian    ·                  NeuroDebian provides neuroscience research s…   99      [OK]
ubuntu-debootstrap                DEPRECATED; use "ubuntu" instead                51      [OK]
ubuntu-upstart                    DEPRECATED, as is Upstart (find other proces…   114     [OK]
ubuntu/nginx                      Nginx, a high-performance reverse proxy & we…   89
ubuntu/cortex                     Cortex provides storage for Prometheus. Long…   3
ubuntu/squid                      Squid is a caching proxy for the Web. Long-t…   56
ubuntu/apache2                    Apache, a secure & extensible open-source HT…   58
ubuntu/mysql                      MySQL open source fast, stable, multi-thread…   59
ubuntu/kafka                      Apache Kafka, a distributed event streaming …   31
ubuntu/bind9                      BIND 9 is a very flexible, full-featured DNS…   51
ubuntu/redis                      Redis, an open source key-value store. Long-…   18
ubuntu/prometheus                 Prometheus is a systems and service monitori…   40
ubuntu/postgres                   PostgreSQL is an open source object-relation…   27
ubuntu/zookeeper                  ZooKeeper maintains configuration informatio…   5
ubuntu/grafana                    Grafana, a feature rich metrics dashboard & …   9
ubuntu/memcached                  Memcached, in-memory keyvalue store for smal…   5
ubuntu/prometheus-alertmanager    Alertmanager handles client alerts from Prom…   8
ubuntu/dotnet-deps                Chiselled Ubuntu for self-contained .NET & A…   8
ubuntu/dotnet-runtime             Chiselled Ubuntu runtime image for .NET apps…   5
ubuntu/dotnet-aspnet              Chiselled Ubuntu runtime image for ASP.NET a…   6
ubuntu/cassandra                  Cassandra, an open source NoSQL distributed …   2
ubuntu/telegraf                   Telegraf collects, processes, aggregates & w…   4
```

Figure 12.8 – Searching for the Ubuntu image

As you can see, the output has five columns:

- **NAME**: The first column shows the image's name

- **DESCRIPTION**: The second column shows the description, which is a short text providing information about a specific image

- **STARS**: The third column shows the number of stars it has (representing popularity based on user opinion)

- **OFFICIAL**: The fourth column shows whether that image is an official one supported by the company behind the distribution/software

- **AUTOMATED**: The fifth column shows whether the image has automated scripts

Once you find the image you are looking for, you can download it onto your system using the `docker pull` command. Let us download the first image from the list shown in the preceding screenshot, the one called `ubuntu`. We will use the following command:

```
docker pull ubuntu
```

With this command, the `ubuntu` image is downloaded locally onto your computer. Now, containers can be run using this image. To list the images that are already available on your computer, run the `docker images` command:

```
packt@debian:~$ docker images
REPOSITORY    TAG       IMAGE ID       CREATED       SIZE
hello-world   latest    9c7a54a9a43c   4 days ago    13.3kB
ubuntu        latest    3b418d7b466a   13 days ago   77.8MB
```

Figure 12.9 – Running the docker images command

Please note the small size of the Ubuntu Docker image. You may be wondering why it is so small. This is because Docker images contain only the base and minimum packages needed to run. This makes the container running on the image extremely efficient in resource usage.

The few commands we showed you in this section are the most basic ones needed to start using Docker. Now that you know how to download an image, let's show you how to manage Docker containers.

Managing Docker containers

In this section, we will learn how to run, list, start, stop, and remove Docker containers, and also how to manage networking.

Running containers

We will use the Ubuntu image that we just downloaded. To run it, we will use the `docker run` command with two arguments, `-i` for interactive output and `-t` for starting a pseudo TTY, which will give us interactive access to the shell:

```
docker run -it ubuntu
```

You will notice that your command prompt will change. Now it will contain the container ID. The user, by default, is the root user. Basically, you are now inside an Ubuntu image, so you can use it exactly as you would use any Ubuntu command line. You can update the repository, install the requisite applications, remove unnecessary apps, and so on. Any changes that you make to the container image stay inside the container. To exit the container, simply type `exit`. Now, we will show you how to list containers, but before we do that, we should ask you not to close the terminal in which the Ubuntu-based container is currently running.

Listing containers

You can open a new terminal on your system and check to see how many Docker containers are actively running, using the docker ps command.

In the command's output, you will see the ID of the container that is running in the other terminal. There are also details about the command that runs inside the container and the creation time.

There are a couple of arguments that you can use with the docker ps command:

- If you want to see all active and inactive containers, use the docker ps -a command
- If you want to see the latest created container, use the docker ps -l command

The following is the output of all three variants of the docker ps command:

```
packt@debian:~$ docker ps
CONTAINER ID   IMAGE        COMMAND       CREATED         STATUS          PORTS         NAMES
f02e14e61e2b   ubuntu       "/bin/bash"   3 minutes ago   Up 3 minutes                  amazing_hopper
packt@debian:~$ docker ps -a
CONTAINER ID   IMAGE         COMMAND       CREATED           STATUS                     PORTS         NAMES
f02e14e61e2b   ubuntu        "/bin/bash"   3 minutes ago     Up 3 minutes                             amazing_hopper
3a340db56d48   hello-world   "/hello"      About an hour ago Exited (0) About an hour ago             recursing_murdock
packt@debian:~$ docker ps -l
CONTAINER ID   IMAGE        COMMAND       CREATED         STATUS          PORTS         NAMES
f02e14e61e2b   ubuntu       "/bin/bash"   3 minutes ago   Up 3 minutes                  amazing_hopper
```

Figure 12.10 – Listing containers with the docker ps command

In the output, you will also see names assigned to containers, such as amazing_hopper or recursing_murdock. Those are random names automatically given to containers by the daemon. Now, we will learn how to start, stop, and remove running containers.

Starting, stopping, and removing running containers

When managing containers, such as starting and stopping, you can refer to them by using the container ID or the name assigned by Docker. Let's now show you how to start, stop, and remove a container.

To start a Docker container, use the docker start command, followed by the name or ID of the container. Here is an example:

```
docker start amazing_hopper
```

To stop a container, use the docker stop command, followed by the name of the ID of the container. Here is an example:

```
docker stop amazing_hopper
```

In our case, the Ubuntu container, named `amazing_hopper`, is already running, so the `start` command will not do anything. But the `stop` command will stop the container. After stopping, if you run the `docker ps` command, there will be no more containers in the list.

Let's take a look at the output of both these commands:

```
packt@debian:~$ docker start amazing_hopper
amazing_hopper
packt@debian:~$ docker ps
CONTAINER ID    IMAGE       COMMAND        CREATED          STATUS        PORTS        NAME
S
f02e14e61e2b    ubuntu      "/bin/bash"    14 minutes ago   Up 3 seconds               amaz
ing_hopper
packt@debian:~$ docker stop amazing_hopper
amazing_hopper
packt@debian:~$ docker ps
CONTAINER ID    IMAGE       COMMAND     CREATED    STATUS     PORTS      NAMES
```

Figure 12.11 – Starting and stopping containers

To remove a container, you can use the `docker rm` command. For example, if we would like to remove the initial `hello-world` container (also called `recursing_murdock` in our case), we will use the following command:

```
docker rm recursing_murdock
```

Once you remove the container, any changes that you made and you did not save (commit) will be lost. Let us show you how to commit changes you made in a container to the Docker image. This means that you will save a specific state of a container as a new Docker image.

> **Important note**
> Please take into consideration that removing a container will not erase the existing image downloaded from Docker Hub.

Let's say that you would like to develop, test, and deploy a Python application on Ubuntu. The default Docker image of Ubuntu doesn't have Python installed.

Next, we will show you how to troubleshoot Docker networking and how to commit a new image.

Docker networking and committing a new image

The scenario for this section's exercise is that you would like to modify the existing Ubuntu image by installing the Python packages that you need for your application. To do this, we follow these steps:

1. First, we start the container and check to see whether Python is installed or not:

```
packt@debian:~$ docker images
REPOSITORY    TAG       IMAGE ID       CREATED       SIZE
hello-world   latest    9c7a54a9a43c   4 days ago    13.3kB
ubuntu        latest    3b418d7b466a   13 days ago   77.8MB
packt@debian:~$ docker run -it ubuntu
root@ff4bda7abc90:/# python -v
bash: python: command not found
root@ff4bda7abc90:/# python3 -v
bash: python3: command not found
```

Figure 12.12 – Checking for Python inside the container

2. We check for both Python 2 and Python 3, but neither version is installed on the image. As we want to use the latest version of the programming language, we will use the following command to install Python 3 support (running as root):

```
apt install python3
```

In doing so, you will get in contact with Docker networking for the first time, as the container needs to reach out to the official Ubuntu repositories in order to download and install the packages you need. It might be the case for you, too, as it was in ours, that when trying to install Python, you will be greeted with an error, such as the one shown in the following screenshot:

```
Reading package lists... Done
Building dependency tree... Done
Reading state information... Done
E: Unable to locate package python3
```

Figure 12.13 – Error while trying to install Python

This error shows that the package named `python3` cannot be located, meaning that our container does not have access to the repositories. A quick thought would be that there is something wrong with Docker's networking. In order to troubleshoot this, we have a useful command called `docker network`. It is used to manage network connections for the Docker container. In our case, the fault for the error message could be a missing connection between the container and the network. In this case, we can investigate first with the `docker network ls` command:

```
docker network ls
```

This command will show all the active networks that are used by Docker. In our case, when running the preceding command, we can see that there are three available networks for Docker, each with a network ID and a name assigned to it:

```
packt@debian:~$ docker network ls
NETWORK ID      NAME      DRIVER    SCOPE
f8b50039d02e    bridge    bridge    local
2d35dbd91efc    host      host      local
4ae4f24c96be    none      null      local
```

Figure 12.14 – Showing the available networks

> **Important note**
>
> The issue described in this example may not appear in your case. However, it is a good exercise to show you how to use the `docker network` command in action.

3. Before starting to solve our issue, let us see once again what the containers are that are running and what their given names are. As we started the new container once again, it should have another ID and name. We will use the following command:

    ```
    docker ps
    ```

4. Now, in order to try and solve our issue, we will connect the Ubuntu container that we use (name according to your output from the `docker ps` command) to the `bridge` network. This will be done with the following command:

    ```
    docker network connect bridge [container_name]
    ```

5. Running the command will not show any kind of output, but we will test the result by running the command to update the repositories inside the container to see that it works:

    ```
    apt update -y
    ```

    The output of the command shows that the repositories are accessible from our container, meaning that we can now install Python. The following screenshot shows an excerpt of the output:

```
Get:1 http://archive.ubuntu.com/ubuntu jammy InRelease [270 kB]
Get:2 http://security.ubuntu.com/ubuntu jammy-security InRelease [110 kB]
Get:3 http://archive.ubuntu.com/ubuntu jammy-updates InRelease [119 kB]
Get:4 http://security.ubuntu.com/ubuntu jammy-security/main amd64 Packages [597 kB]
Get:5 http://archive.ubuntu.com/ubuntu jammy-backports InRelease [108 kB]
```

Figure 12.15 – Proof that the network connection is working

By connecting a container to a network, it will be able to communicate with other containers on the same network too.

6. Now, before going further with our Python installation, we would like to show you that there is a command that we can use to automatically connect a container to a network when starting the container:

```
docker run -itd --network=bridge [container_name]
```

In our example, we provide two arguments, the network name (bridge) and the container's name. We used the -i option for interactive output, the -t option for opening a pseudo TTY, and the -d option for detaching the container and running in the background.

7. Now, let us proceed with our initial Python installation. We can once again run the following command:

```
apt install python3
```

This time, the command will not give any errors and it will proceed with the installation. The following is an excerpt from the command's output:

```
Reading package lists... Done
Building dependency tree... Done
Reading state information... Done
The following additional packages will be installed:
  libexpat1 libmpdec3 libpython3-stdlib libpython3.10-minimal libpython3.10-stdlib
  libreadline8 libsqlite3-0 media-types python3-minimal python3.10
  python3.10-minimal readline-common
Suggested packages:
  python3-doc python3-tk python3-venv python3.10-venv python3.10-doc binutils
  binfmt-support readline-doc
The following NEW packages will be installed:
  libexpat1 libmpdec3 libpython3-stdlib libpython3.10-minimal libpython3.10-stdlib
  libreadline8 libsqlite3-0 media-types python3 python3-minimal python3.10
  python3.10-minimal readline-common
0 upgraded, 13 newly installed, 0 to remove and 0 not upgraded.
```

Figure 12.16 – Installing Python packages inside a Docker container

8. Now, with Python 3 installed and the necessary modifications made to the image used inside the container, we can save the instance of the container to a new Docker image. For this, we will use the following command:

```
docker commit -m "added python3 to ubuntu" -a "packt user"
260ead99f7ca packt/ubuntu-python3
```

Make sure that you use your own container ID with the preceding command; don't use the one from our example. When using this command, you will save the new image onto your local computer, but there is also the possibility to save it to Docker Hub for others to use, too. To save to Docker Hub, you will need to have an active Docker user account created.

We used the -m option to add a comment that details our commit process and the -a option to specify the account user and the ID of the base image we used, in our case, the ID of the running container. The following screenshot shows a series of commands to help you to understand the process better:

```
packt@debian:~$ docker ps
CONTAINER ID    IMAGE      COMMAND        CREATED        STATUS          PORTS       NAMES
260ead99f7ca    ubuntu     "/bin/bash"    35 seconds ago Up 34 seconds               peaceful_euler
packt@debian:~$ docker commit -m "added python3 to ubuntu" -a "packt user" 260ead99f7ca packt/ub
untu-python3
sha256:d02e16cc3a1f3d976cd97347d57c9ec7869a303c4a8b14d014e8c744b9720a90
packt@debian:~$ docker images
REPOSITORY              TAG       IMAGE ID       CREATED        SIZE
packt/ubuntu-python3    latest    d02e16cc3a1f   4 seconds ago  149MB
hello-world             latest    9c7a54a9a43c   6 days ago     13.3kB
ubuntu                  latest    3b418d7b466a   2 weeks ago    77.8MB
```

Figure 12.17 – A new image committed locally

As shown in the preceding screenshot, we first used the docker ps command to see the ID of the container we are running, then we used the docker commit command (with the options described earlier) to save the new image locally. Notice the increased size of the image we just saved. Installing Python 3 more than doubled the size of the initial Ubuntu image. The last command used was docker images, to see the existing images, including the one we just created (ubuntu-python3).

By now, you have learned how to use extremely basic Docker commands for opening, running, and saving containers. In the next section, we will introduce you to Dockerfiles and the process of building container images.

Working with Dockerfiles

Before starting to work with Dockerfiles, let's see what a Dockerfile is. It is a text file that consists of instructions defined by the user for Docker to execute, and respecting some basic structure, such as the following:

```
INSTRUCTION arguments
```

The Dockerfile is mainly used for creating new container images. This file is used by Docker to automatically build images based on the information the user provides inside the file. There are some keywords that define a Dockerfile. Those keywords, which are referred to as instructions, are as follows:

- FROM: This must be the first instruction inside a Dockerfile as it tells Docker what the image is that you build upon

- LABEL: This instruction adds some more information, such as a description, or anything that could help describe the new image you are creating; the use of such instructions needs to be limited

- RUN: This is the instruction that offers direct interaction with the image, the place where commands or scripts to be run inside the image are written

- ADD: This instruction is used to transfer files inside the image; it copies files or directories to the filesystem of the image

- COPY: This instruction is similar to ADD, as it is also used to copy files or directories from one source to the image's filesystem

- CMD: This instruction can occur only once in a Dockerfile, as it provides defaults for an image that is executed

- USER: This instruction is used to set a username that will be used when a command is executed; it can be used on the RUN or CMD instructions

- WORKDIR: This instruction will set the default working directory for other instructions inside a Dockerfile, such as RUN, CMD, COPY, ADD, or ENTRYPOINT

- ENTRYPOINT: This instruction is used to configure containers that will run as executables

The instructions listed here are just the ones that are usually used in a Dockerfile, but they do not represent all the instructions available. You can visit https://docs.docker.com/engine/reference/builder/ for a complete listing of all the instructions available for a Dockerfile. In the next section, we will show you how to build a container image using a Dockerfile.

Building container images from Dockerfiles

In this section, we will create a Dockerfile that will be used for building a new Docker container image. Let us present the scenario on which our exercise is built. Similar to the exercise used in the *Docker networking and committing a new image* section, we will prepare an image for the Python programming environment. In order to create the new Docker image, we will first need to create the Dockerfile. The following are the steps to take:

1. Create a new directory inside your home directory using the following command:

    ```
    mkdir ~/my_docker_images && cd ~/my_docker_images
    ```

2. Create a new file inside the new directory:

    ```
    touch py_env_dockerfile
    ```

3. Open and edit the new Dockerfile. Now, let us dissect the contents of the new Dockerfile. As stated earlier, we want to install the needed packages and dependencies for a Python 3 programming environment. This time we will use another base image, not Ubuntu. We will use a Debian Linux image (based on Debian 11). If you use the docker search debian command, the second image name on the output list will be the official Debian Linux image, called debian. We will use that. The contents of the Dockerfile are shown in the following screenshot:

```
packt@debian:~/my_docker_images$ cat py_env_dockerfile
FROM debian
MAINTAINER packt

RUN apt update -y
RUN apt upgrade -y
RUN apt install python3 -y
```

Figure 12.18 – Creating the Dockerfile

4. Now that the Dockerfile is created, we will run the docker build command to create the new Docker image. The command we used is as follows:

```
docker build ~/my_docker_images -f py_env_dockerfile -t pydeb
```

We used the -f option to specify the Dockerfile name and the -t option to specify the name of the image we want to create, in our case pydeb. In the next screenshot, you will see the output of the docker build command, showing all the steps needed to build the image, as specified in the Dockerfile. The build was successful:

```
packt@debian:~/my_docker_images$ docker build ~/my_docker_images -f py_env_dockerfile -t
pydeb
[+] Building 8.9s (8/8) FINISHED
 => [internal] load .dockerignore                                                 0.0s
 => => transferring context: 2B                                                   0.0s
 => [internal] load build definition from py_env_dockerfile                       0.0s
 => => transferring dockerfile: 140B                                              0.0s
 => [internal] load metadata for docker.io/library/debian:latest                  1.5s
 => [1/4] FROM docker.io/library/debian@sha256:63d62ae233b588d6b426b7b072d79d1306b  0.0s
 => CACHED [2/4] RUN apt update -y                                                0.0s
 => CACHED [3/4] RUN apt upgrade -y                                               0.0s
 => [4/4] RUN apt install python3 -y                                              7.1s
 => exporting to image                                                            0.2s
 => => exporting layers                                                           0.2s
 => => writing image sha256:5f925117827e3429cf77a6b7fa820b0ccfa656cabc8f38c2595e4b  0.0s
 => => naming to docker.io/library/pydeb                                          0.0s
packt@debian:~/my_docker_images$ docker images
REPOSITORY               TAG        IMAGE ID       CREATED          SIZE
pydeb                    latest     5f925117827e   4 minutes ago    175MB
packt/ubuntu-python3     latest     d02e16cc3a1f   6 hours ago      149MB
hello-world              latest     9c7a54a9a43c   7 days ago       13.3kB
ubuntu                   latest     3b418d7b466a   2 weeks ago      77.8MB
```

Figure 12.19 – Building a new custom image from a Dockerfile

We can verify if the image was created by using the docker images command. As shown in the preceding screenshot, the new pydeb image was successfully created.

5. We can use the new image and create a new container with the following command:

```
docker run -it pydeb
```

This will run a new container based on the pydeb images we just created.

6.   To verify the container running, open a new terminal window and run the docker ps command, as shown in the following screenshot:

```
packt@debian:~$ docker ps
CONTAINER ID    IMAGE     COMMAND    CREATED         STATUS          PORTS        NAMES
8d133fd5f7f8    pydeb     "bash"     29 seconds ago  Up 28 seconds                gifted_
chatelet
```

Figure 12.20 – New container based on our custom image

By now, you already know enough about Docker to feel comfortable using it in production. In the next section, we will show you how to use Docker to deploy a very basic application. We will make it so simple that the app to deploy will be a basic static presentation website.

Deploying a containerized application with Docker

So far, we have shown you how to use Docker and how to manage containers. Docker is so much more than that, but this is enough to get you started and make you want to learn more. Docker is a great tool for developers as it offers a streamlined way to deploy applications by removing the necessity to replicate development environments. In the next section, we will show you how to deploy a simple website using Docker.

Deploying a website using Docker

To deploy a website using Docker, follow these steps:

1.   We will use a free website template randomly downloaded from the internet (the download link is https://www.free-css.com/free-css-templates/page262/focus). We will copy the download location from the website and download the file inside our home directory using the wget utility:

```
wget https://www.free-css.com/assets/files/free-css-templates/
download/page262/focus.zip
```

2.   The new file is a compressed ZIP file, so we will have to extract it. We will use the unzip command:

```
unzip focus.zip
```

3.   The file has to be downloaded and extracted inside our home directory. You can use another directory, and we advise you to do so for clarity. We will create a new directory called docker_webapp inside the ~/my_docker_images directory created in the previous section, and move the extracted file inside of it. Therefore, the new location in our case will be the following:

```
~/my_docker_images/docker_webapp/focus
```

4. Once the files are moved to the desired location, we can proceed to create a Dockerfile inside the same directory. We will create a Dockerfile called `webapp_dockerfile` inside our present working directory. The contents of the Dockerfile are as follows:

```
FROM nginx
COPY . /usr/share/nginx/html
```

Figure 12.21 – Contents of a new Dockerfile

The file is simple and has only two lines:

- The first line, using the `FROM` keyword, specifies the base image that we will use, which will be the official NGINX image available on Docker Hub. As you will see in *Chapter 13*, NGINX is a widely used type of web server.

- The second line, using the `COPY` keyword, specifies the location where the contents of our present working directory will be copied inside the new container.

The following action builds the Docker image using the `docker build` command:

```
docker build ~/my_docker_images/docker_webapp/focus -f webapp_
dockerfile -t webapp
```

5. The new image was created, so we can now check for it using the `docker images` command. In our case, the output is as follows:

```
packt@debian:~$ docker images
REPOSITORY             TAG      IMAGE ID        CREATED          SIZE
webapp                 latest   c9b453caff52    49 seconds ago   144MB
pydeb                  latest   5f925117827e    13 hours ago     175MB
packt/ubuntu-python3   latest   d02e16cc3a1f    19 hours ago     149MB
hello-world            latest   9c7a54a9a43c    7 days ago       13.3kB
ubuntu                 latest   3b418d7b466a    2 weeks ago      77.8MB
```

Figure 12.22 – The new webapp Docker image was created

6. As the output shows, the new image called `webapp` was created, and we can start a new container using it. As we will need to access the container from the outside, we will need to open specific ports, and we will do that using the `-p` parameter inside the `docker run` command. We can either specify a single port or a range of ports. When specifying ports, we will give the ports for the container and for the host, too. We will use the `-d` parameter to detach the container and run it in the background. The command is as follows:

```
docker run -it -d -p 8080:80 webapp
```

The output is as follows:

```
packt@debian:~$ docker run -it -d -p 8080:80 webapp
1d5e08e9f4e55326fb57ff04e571c1aa7778afc656ef5025d4d081033059765f
```

Figure 12.23 – The output of the docker run command

We are exposing host port 8080 to port 80 on the container. We could have used both ports 80, but on the host, it might be occupied by other services.

7. You can now access the new containerized application by going to your web browser and typing the local IP address and port 8080 into the address bar. As we are using a VM and not the host, we will point to the VM's IP address, in our case 192.168.122.48, followed by the 8080 port. In the next screenshot, you will see our Docker-deployed website:

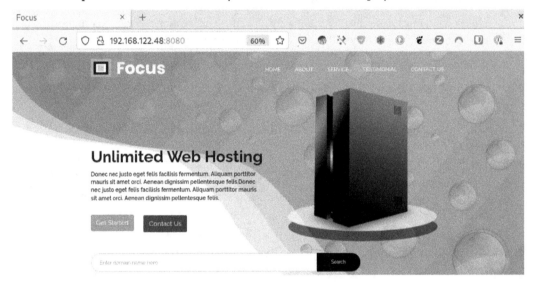

Figure 12.24 – Running the web app in our web browser

As you can see in the preceding image, the website is accessible from localhost. For deploying a website on a virtual private server, please visit *Chapter 13*.

Summary

In this chapter, we emphasized the importance of containerization. We showed you what containers are, how they work, and why they are so important. Containers are the foundation of the modern DevOps revolution, and you are now ready to use them. We also taught you about Docker, the basic commands for sleek use. You are now ready to start the cloud journey. Virtualization and container technologies are at the heart of cloud and server technologies.

In the next chapter, we will show you how to install and configure different Linux-based servers, such as web servers, DNS servers, DHCP servers, and mail servers.

Questions

Here's a brief quiz about some of the essential concepts that were covered in this chapter:

1. What is the major difference between containers and VMs?

    Hint: Revisit *Figure 12.1*.

2. How does container technology work?

3. What are the two major components of Docker architecture?

4. Which Docker command shows the running containers?

5. Which command is used for container network management?

    Hint: See the `docker network` command's help.

Further reading

For more information on the topics covered in this chapter, you can refer to the following Packt titles:

*   *Docker Quick Start Guide*, Earl Waud

*   *Mastering Docker – Fourth Edition*, Russ McKendrick

*   *Containerization with LXC*, Konstantin Ivanov

*   *A Developer's Essential Guide to Docker Compose*, Emmanouil Gkatziouras

13

Configuring Linux Servers

In this chapter, you will learn how to set up different types of Linux servers. This will include **Domain Name System (DNS)** servers, **Domain Host Configuration Protocol (DHCP)** servers, **Samba** or **Server Message Block/Common Internet File System (SMB/CIFS)** file servers, and **Network File System (NFS)** servers. All these servers, in one way or another, are powering the backbone of the World Wide Web. Even though we will not cover it here, you should know that the reason your computer is showing the exact time is because of a well-implemented **Network Time Protocol (NTP)** server. You can shop online and transfer files between your friends and colleagues thanks to effective DHCP, web, and file servers. Configuring the different types of Linux services that power all these servers represents the knowledge base for any Linux system administrator. In this edition of the book, we will only cover a select few of these Linux servers, those we consider the most important and major Linux servers currently. For further information, please refer to the *Further reading* section at the end of this chapter.

In this chapter, we're going to cover the following main topics:

- Introduction to Linux services

- Setting up an SSH server

- Setting up a DNS server

- Setting up a DHCP server

- Setting up an NFS server

- Setting up a Samba file server

Technical requirements

Basic knowledge of networking and Linux commands is required. You will need access to multiple working systems, preferably on premise or in the cloud. If this is not possible, you can use local virtual machines on your system. Furthermore, it would be useful to have a domain available for you to use too. We will use Ubuntu Server 22.04.2 LTS as the distribution of choice for this chapter's exercises and examples. Nevertheless, any other major Linux distribution—such as Fedora, RHEL, openSUSE, or Debian—is equally suitable for the tasks detailed in this chapter.

Introducing Linux services

Everything you have learned up until now will easily apply to any workstation or desktop/laptop running Linux. We have delved into advanced networking subjects that are meant to ease your learning path to becoming a seasoned Linux system administrator. Now we will enter the *server* territory as a natural path to the *cloud*, which will be discussed in detail in the last four chapters of this book.

A **Linux server**, compared to a Linux workstation, is a system that serves content over a network. While doing so, a server provides its hardware and software resources to different clients that are accessing it. For example, every time you enter a website address into your browser, a server is accessed. That particular type of server is a **web server**. When you print over the network in your workplace, you access a **print server**, and when you read your email, you access a **mail server**. All these are specialized systems that run a specific piece of software (sometimes called a service) that provides you, the client, with the data you requested. Usually, servers are very powerful systems that have lots of resources available for a client's use.

In contrast, a **workstation** (which is yet another powerful piece of hardware) is generally used for personal work, not for client access over a network. A workstation is used for intensive work, similar to any regular desktop or laptop system. In light of everything we have exposed up to now, the contents of this chapter and the following chapters are best suited for server use, but not limited to it.

You've probably already heard about setting up different Linux servers—such as a web server, a file server, or an email server—and have probably wondered why they are called that. They do not represent the hardware boxes that are the actual servers—they are basically services running on top of Linux. So what are Linux services? These are programs that run in the background. Inside the Linux world, those services are known as **daemons**. You were briefly introduced to daemons and the `init` process in *Chapter 5, Working with Processes, Daemons, and Signals*, when we discussed what processes, daemons, and signals are and how to manage them on Linux. The mother of all processes is the `init` process, which is among the first processes when Linux boots up. Currently, the latest version of Ubuntu (and also CentOS, Fedora, openSUSE, and others) uses `systemd` as the default `init` process.

We will refresh your memory by using some basic commands for working with services on Linux. If you want more information, please refer to *Chapter 5, Working with Processes, Daemons, and Signals*.

The first command we will remind you of is the `ps` command. We will use it to show the `init` process running, as follows:

```
ps -ef | less
```

The output on our Ubuntu 22.04.2 system is shown in the following screenshot:

```
UID          PID   PPID  C STIME TTY          TIME CMD
root           1      0  2 06:12 ?        00:00:03 /lib/systemd/systemd --syste
m --deserialize 35
```

Figure 13.1 – Showing the init process by using the ps command

By using the -e flag, we can generate information about all processes, except kernel-related ones, while the -f flag is used to generate a full listing.

In the process list shown, the first process is either the init process or systemd. Sometimes, on older operating systems (such as Ubuntu 20.04 or 18.04), it uses the init name for backward-compatibility issues, but to make sure that it really is systemd, you can use the manual pages of init for more details. When you type man init in the command line, the manual page shown is for systemd. As the parent of all services, systemd starts all the running processes in parallel as a way to make the boot process and service-time response more efficient. To see how efficient those processes are, you can run the systemd-analyze command.

A command we have frequently used, and one you should already know, is the systemctl command, which is the main command-line utility for working with systemd services (or daemons) on Linux.

As you know systemctl invokes **units**, which are system resources managed by systemd. Those units have several types, such as service, mount, socket, and others. To see those units listed by the time they take to start up, you can use the systemd-analyze blame command, as shown in the following screenshot:

```
packt@ch13:~$ systemd-analyze
Startup finished in 4.635s (kernel) + 10.161s (userspace) = 14.797s
graphical.target reached after 9.891s in userspace
packt@ch13:~$ systemd-analyze blame
2.974s snapd.seeded.service
1.349s cloud-config.service
1.040s snapd.apparmor.service
 975ms cloud-init.service
 942ms snapd.service
 620ms dev-mapper-ubuntu\x2d\x2dvg\x2dubuntu\x2d\x2dlv.device
 596ms pollinate.service
 477ms cloud-init-local.service
 427ms apparmor.service
```

Figure 13.2 – The systemd-analyze blame command

The output shows different types of units, such as *service*, *mount*, and *device*. The preceding screenshot is only an excerpt of the running units. To learn more about the systemctl command, feel free to use the manual pages, or go back to *Chapter 5* to refresh your memory.

This brief introduction to Linux services is only a refresher of the respective sections from *Chapter 5*, enough for you to start delving into setting up and configuring specific Linux services. In the following sections, we will show you how to manage some of the most important services on Linux, such as **SSH, DNS, DHCP, NTP, Samba, NFS, web, File Transfer Protocol (FTP)**, and **printing services**. Now, it's time to roll up your sleeves and configure them yourself. First, we will show you how to set up an SSH server on Ubuntu Linux.

Setting up SSH

We will configure SSH on a computer running Ubuntu Server 22.04.2 LTS as the host operating system. Throughout the entire book, we used SSH connections several times, and showed you how to create an SSH key pair in *Chapter 11*, *Working with Virtual Machines*, when we worked with cloud-init. This time, we will show you how to install **OpenSSH**, how to enable SSH, and how to modify some of its configuration defaults.

Installing and configuring OpenSSH on Ubuntu

In order to use SSH, the first thing we need to do is to install the `openssh` package. On Ubuntu, this can be done by using the following command:

```
sudo apt install openssh-server
```

Chances are that it is already installed on your system. If that is the case, you can go ahead and skip this step and go to the configuration files.

After installation, we can start and enable the `openssh` service with the following commands:

```
sudo systemctl enable ssh && sudo systemctl start ssh
```

For openSSH, the configuration file that we can work with is located under `/etc/ssh/sshd_config`. By default, this file already contains a lot of information, all we need to do is to open it with our text editor and start modifying the available options. Depending on what we want to achieve, the bare minimum configuration for SSH involves the following:

- Modify the remote root login options; this can be done by changing the line with the following code and setting the option accordingly:

  ```
  PermitRootLogin no
  ```

  In our case, we modified the default `prohibit-password` option to `no`, so that the root user will not be able to connect through SSH at all.

- Disable the SSH password authentication. This can be done by changing the following lines to `no`:

  ```
  PasswordAuthentication no
  PermitEmptyPasswords no
  ```

  Do this only after you copy your key pair on the remote machine and make sure you can use it. Otherwise, you won't be able to access your server.

- To allow public key authentication, you will need to uncomment the following line:

  ```
  PubkeyAuthentication yes
  ```

- We will quickly show the commands used in *Chapter 11* to enable public keys authentication, as a reminder:

```
ssh-keygen
ssh-copy-id user@host_IP
```

Instead of `user`, use the username from the remote server, and instead of `host_IP`, use the IP address of the remote server. Also, `ssh-keygen` can be used with several options, such as `-b` to specify the number of bits and `-t` to specify the algorithm type. After this, you can connect with the `ssh user@IP` command, which in our case is the following:

```
ssh packt@192.168.0.113
```

The configuration options presented here are the base minimum to start using SSH when working with a remote system or a virtual machine. However, OpenSSH is a very powerful tool that offers lots of options that you could explore. Here are two links that could help you in your endeavors: `https://ubuntu.com/server/docs/service-openssh` and `https://www.openssh.com/manual.html`. In the following section, we will show you how to set up a DNS server.

Setting up a DNS server

One of the most widely used DNS services is **Berkeley Internet Name Domain 9 (BIND 9)**. You can visit its official website at the following address: `https://www.isc.org/bind/`. Before continuing, let's underline the system configuration and goals. For this section, we will use a computer running on Ubuntu Server 22.04.2 LTS. On this system, we will create two types of servers, a **caching name server** and a **primary name server**, which you can use on your local network to manage hostnames and private IP addresses.

> **Important note**
>
> There are different DNS servers, such as **authoritative**, **caching**, or **forwarding** types; those are also called functional types. Among those, a caching DNS server is the one that always answers recursive requests from clients. Also, there are **relational server types**, such as primary and secondary DNS servers. Those are authoritative types, and are almost identical, with the only difference between the primary and the secondary being the location from which they get the zones' information. For more information on DNS, you can consult the following links: `https://www.digitalocean.com/community/tutorials/a-comparison-of-dns-server-types-how-to-choose-the-right-dns-configuration` and `https://www.digitalocean.com/community/tutorials/an-introduction-to-dns-terminology-components-and-concepts`.

There are other ways to do this, but for the purpose of showing you the basics of DNS setup, this configuration will suffice. If you would like a secondary server, you will need to have another spare system, or if you use **virtual private servers** (**VPSs**), they would have to be in the same data center and be using the same private network. In our case, however, we will use a local system on our small private network.

First, we will install the `bind9` package in Ubuntu by using the following command:

```
sudo apt install bind9 bind9utils bind9-doc
```

The preceding command will install all the packages needed for BIND9 to run.

Once the packages are installed, you can test them to see whether BIND works as expected. For this, we will use the `nslookup` command, as shown in the following screenshot, by using the local address (or *loopback* address):

```
packt@nuc5:~$ nslookup google.com 127.0.0.1
Server:        127.0.0.1
Address:       127.0.0.1#53

Non-authoritative answer:
Name:    google.com
Address:
Name:    google.com
Address:
```

Figure 13.3 – Checking to see whether BIND is working using nslookup

You can now start setting up the service, as you can see it is working. First, we will configure a caching DNS service. But before we start, we advise you to back up the following configuration files: `/etc/bind/named.conf`, `/etc/bind/named.conf.options`, `/etc/hosts`, and `/etc/resolv.conf`. Let's see how to create a caching server.

Caching a DNS service

The default behavior of BIND9 is as a caching server. This means that setting it up is quite straightforward. We will tweak the configuration file just a little, in order to make it work according to our requests:

1. After seeing that the installed packages work as intended, you can also configure the firewall to allow BIND9, using the following command:

    ```
    sudo ufw allow Bind9
    ```

2. In Ubuntu, you will have to alter the `/etc/bind/named.conf.options` file to add or delete different options. We will do that by opening it with the text editor. Inside the file, by default, are a few settings that have been set up, and a lot of commented lines with details on how to use the file. The `//` double slashes indicate that the respective lines are commented out. All the modifications will be done inside the `options` directive, between curly brackets, as it is the only existing directive by default.

The first thing to do, as we will only use **IP version 4 (IPv4)**, is to comment out the following line by adding two slashes:

```
// listen-on-v6 { any; };
```

3. You will have to add a list of IP addresses inside the `forwarders` directive. This line tells the server where to look in order to find addresses not cached locally. For simplicity, we will add the Google public DNS servers, but feel free to use your **Internet Service Provider's (ISP's)** DNS servers. Now, edit the `forwarders` directive to look like this:

```
forwarders {
        8.8.8.8;
        8.8.4.4;
          };
```

4. You can also add a directive defining the `allow-query` spectrum. This line tells the server which networks can be accepted for DNS queries. You can add your local network address. In our case, it will be the following:

```
allow-query {
        localhost;
        192.168.0.0/24;
          };
```

5. There is also a `listen-on` directive, where you can specify the networks the DNS server will work for. This applies for IPv4 addresses and is shown in the following code snippet:

```
listen-on {
        192.168.0.0/24;
        }
```

After the added options, the code you added should appear as in the following screenshot:

```
forwarders {
        8.8.8.8;
        8.8.4.4;
  };
allow-query {
        localhost;
        192.168.0.0/24;
  };
listen-on {
        192.168.0.0/24;
  };
```

Figure 13.4 – The final form of /etc/bind/named.conf.options after adding new options

6. Save the file and exit the editor. You can check the BIND9 configuration with the `named-checkconf` command. If there is no output, it means that the configuration of the file is correct. Restart the BIND9 service and optionally check its status.

7. Knowing that the BIND9 service is working fine, you can test the service from any other computer on the network with the `nslookup` command, as follows:

```
alexandru@debian:~$ nslookup google.com 192.168.0.113
Server:         192.168.0.113
Address:        192.168.0.113#53

Non-authoritative answer:
Name:    google.com
Address:
Name:    google.com
Address:
```

Figure 13.5 – Testing the BIND9 implementation

We used the command with the host's IP address, as seen in the previous screenshot. The output shows that the DNS service on our test machine is working fine. The test was conducted from a local ThinkPad on the same network.

You now have a working caching DNS server on your private network. In the next section, we will show you how to create a primary DNS server.

Creating a primary DNS server

In order to configure a primary DNS server, we will need a domain name that it will serve. For this section's purpose, we will use the `calcatinge.ro` domain name (when you try on your system, please use a domain name you own). We will have to create new zones for the BIND9 configuration, and we will add information to the `/etc/bind/named.conf.local` file about the ones we create. Right now, we will create a new zone for our `calcatinge.ro` domain.

> **Important note**
>
> What is a **DNS zone**? The short answer is that it is a part of a domain namespace associated with an entity responsible for maintaining it. Zones also offer a granular take on administrating different components. For more information on DNS zones, please refer to the following link: `https://ns1.com/resources/dns-zones-explained`.

In the following screenshot, you can see the contents of our configuration file, followed by details on each of the lines:

```
//
// Do any local configuration here
//

// Consider adding the 1918 zones here, if they are not used in your
// organization
//include "/etc/bind/zones.rfc1918";

zone "calcatinge.ro" {
        type master;
        file "/etc/bind/db.calcatinge.ro";
        allow-transfer { 192.168.0.113; };
        also-notify { 192.168.0.113; };
};
```

Figure 13.6 – New zone for our domain in /etc/bind/named.conf.local file

Now, let's explain the contents of a zone directive:

- First, we had to add the name of the domain that the zone will serve

- The type of the zone is set as master, but there are other types to use, such as slave, forward, or hint

- The file represents the path to the actual zone file that will be created

- In the allow-transfer list, the IPs of DNS servers that handle the zone are set

- In the also-notify list, the IPs of servers that will be notified about zone changes are indicated

Now, let's create a new zone for our chosen domain:

1. The following screenshot shows how we copied the db.local file under another name and used it for a new zone:

```
packt@nuc5:/etc/bind$ sudo cp db.local db.calcatinge.ro
packt@nuc5:/etc/bind$ ls
bind.keys  db.calcatinge.ro  named.conf.default-zones  zones.rfc1918
db.0       db.empty          named.conf.local
db.127     db.local          named.conf.options
db.255     named.conf        rndc.key
```

Figure 13.7 – Creating the zone file for our domain

2. The next step is to create the zone file, as indicated in the zone directive about calcatinge.ro. The details are shown in the preceding screenshot and as you can see, its location is /etc/bind/. Once the file is created using db.local as a template, you can open it with your favorite text editor and add information about your server IP and domain name. In the following screenshot, you can see the zone file for calcatinge.ro created on our machine:

```
;
; BIND data file for local loopback interface
;
$TTL    604800
@       IN      SOA     ns.calcatinge.ro. admin.calcatinge.ro. (
                             2          ; Serial
                        604800          ; Refresh
                         86400          ; Retry
                       2419200          ; Expire
                        604800 )        ; Negative Cache TTL
;
@       IN      NS      ns.calcatinge.ro.
@       IN      A       192.168.0.113
ns      IN      A       192.168.0.113
```

Figure 13.8 – Zone file information

3. The DNS records are introduced at the end of the file. Here are some details about the contents of the file:

    -   The table has a specific format that contains details about hostname (first column), class (second column), DNS record type (third column), and value (the last column).

    -   For the hostname, we entered @, which means that the entry of the record refers to the zone name from the file.

    -   The class is IN, which indicates that the network is the internet.

    -   DNS records types are A, NS, MX, CNAME, TXT, and SOA. A indicates the IP address of the domain name; NS indicates the IP address of the DNS server; MX is the address of the email server; CNAME is an alias (canonical name); and TXT has a custom entry, SOA, which indicates the authoritative name server for the zone, with details on the administrator, serial number, and refresh rates.

    -   The value in the last column most often comprises of the IP address or the hostname.

4. The next step is to restart the **Remote Name Daemon Control** (**RNDC**), which is a control utility inside BIND that controls the name server. The command to do that is shown here:

    ```
    sudo rndc reload
    ```

5. Now, you can check to see if the primary DNS server works. Try the nslookup command from another system on the network, as follows:

    ```
    nslookup calcatinge.ro 192.168.0.113
    ```

    The output of the preceding command will most certainly show that the local DNS server on the system with the indicated IP address has a working zone file. Your primary DNS server works as expected on your local network. Don't forget to use your IP inside the command.

It is always a good idea to create a secondary DNS server in case the first one stops working, which is why we will show you how to set up a second one in the following section.

Setting up a secondary DNS server

It comes as no surprise that the secondary DNS server should be set up on different hardware from the primary one, but on the same network. If you do it inside a data center, use a VPS in the same network as the first one. If you plan to experiment with it on your home private network, make sure you have another system at your disposal.

We will start another NUC system available that is also running Ubuntu Server 22.04.2 LTS. We will need to know its IP address in order to use it in our configuration. In our case, the IP of the new system is 192.168.0.140. This second machine needs to have BIND9 installed and configured too. Before setting up the secondary server, you will need to modify the configuration of the primary DNS server first.

Modifying the primary server configuration files

To modify the configuration of the primary DNS server and allow it to send the zone details to the secondary server, follow these steps:

1. You will have to open the /etc/bind/named.conf.local configuration file and add some new lines to it. We add the second server's IP address inside the allow-transfer and also-notify directives, as shown in the following screenshot:

```
//
// Do any local configuration here
//

// Consider adding the 1918 zones here, if they are not used in your
// organization
//include "/etc/bind/zones.rfc1918";

zone "calcatinge.ro" {
        type master;
        file "/etc/bind/db.calcatinge.ro";
        allow-transfer { 192.168.0.113; 192.168.0.140; };
        also-notify { 192.168.0.113; 192.168.0.140; };
};
```

Figure 13.9 – Adding the IP of the secondary DNS server

2. Save the file and restart the BIND9 service.

3. You will also need to open the /etc/bind/named.conf.options configuration file and add an access list parameter (acl "trusted") with all the accepted IP addresses on the network. In our case, the primary server has the address 192.168.0.113, and the

secondary server has the address `192.168.0.140`. Add this before the already existing `options` directive.

4. Inside the `options` directive block, below the comments, we also add the following directives:

```
recursion yes;
allow-recursion { trusted; };
listen-on { 192.168.0.113; };
allow-transfer { none; };
```

Figure 13.10 – Adding new directive inside /etc/bind/named.conf.options file

5. The configuration is finished, and we will restart the BIND9 service using the `systemctl` command, as follows:

```
sudo systemctl restart bind9.service
```

Before proceeding further, let's understand the directives used. The `recursion` directive has a boolean value (`yes` | `no`) and defines whether recursion and caching are allowed or not on the server. The default is `yes`, and thus the server will require DNS query recursion by solving all the attempts.

> **Important note**
> **Recursion** is also known as **recursive query**, which in the case of DNS refers to the way a name resolution is solved. The recursive mode represents the way a computer looks for a FQDN by inquiring first at the local cache data and the local DNS server. The request is clear and demands a precise answer, and the solution for that answer is the responsibility of the DNS server. Thus, the query initiated by the computer, which is a DNS client, to the DNS server is a recursive query.

The `allow-recursion` directive is referenced to a list of matching addresses of clients, in our case specified by a **trusted list**. The `listen-on` directive specifies the IP on which the server listens. And we also used the `allow-transfer` directive that provides a list of hosts that are allowed to transfer zone information (in our case, none). For more information about configuration options, please refer to the following link: `https://bind9.readthedocs.io/en/latest/reference.html#`.

Next, let's learn how to configure the secondary server.

Setting up the secondary server

On the secondary server, as stated earlier, you will need to install BIND9 too. Once it is installed, you will need to follow these steps:

1. Go to the `/etc/bind/named.conf.options` file and add the following lines in an `acl` directive, before the already existing `options` directive:

```
acl "trusted" {
        192.168.0.113;
        192.168.0.140;
};

options {
        directory "/var/cache/bind";
```

Figure 13.11 – Adding an acl directive on the secondary server

2. Also, add the following lines inside the `options` directive:

```
recursion yes;
allow-recursion { trusted; };
listen-on { 192.168.0.140; };
allow-transfer { none; };

forwarders {
        8.8.8.8;
        8.8.4.4;
};
```

Figure 13.12 – Adding new directives inside options

3. Now edit the `/etc/bind/named.conf.local` file and add the zones you want, but this time use the `secondary` type, as opposed to the `master` one used on the primary DNS server.

The following is a comparison between the two `/etc/bind/named.conf.local` files. On the left is the file on the primary DNS server, and on the right is the file on the secondary DNS server:

```
//                                                      //
// Do any local configuration here                      // Do any local configuration here
//                                                      //

// Consider adding the 1918 zones here, if they are not used in your   // Consider adding the 1918 zones here, if they are not used in your
// organization                                         // organization
//include "/etc/bind/zones.rfc1918";                    //include "/etc/bind/zones.rfc1918";

zone "calcatinge.ro" {                                  zone "calcatinge.ro" {
    type master;                                            type secondary;
    file "/etc/bind/db.calcatinge.ro";                      file "/etc/bind/db.calcatinge.ro";
    allow-transfer { 192.168.0.113; 192.168.0.140; };       primaries { 192.168.0.113; };
    also-notify { 192.168.0.113; 192.168.0.140; };      };
};
```

Figure 13.13 – Configuration files from primary (left) and secondary (right) servers

4. Now we can restart the BIND9 service and make sure that the firewall is allowing DNS connections on the second server with the following commands:

```
sudo ufw allow Bind9 && sudo systemctl restart bind9
```

Now you have two DNS servers set up and working, one primary and one secondary. In the following section, we will show you how to set up a local DHCP server.

Setting up a DHCP server

DHCP is a network service that is used to assign IP addresses to hosts on a network. The settings are enabled by the server, without any control from the host. Most commonly, the DHCP server provides the IP addresses and netmasks for clients, the default gateway IP, and the DNS server's IP address.

To install the DHCP service on Ubuntu, use the following command:

```
sudo apt install isc-dhcp-server
```

As a test system, we will use the same system on which we installed the DNS services in the previous section. After installation, we will configure two specific files. On an Ubuntu system, like ours, the default configuration will be set inside the /etc/dhcp/dhcpd.conf file, while the interfaces will be configured inside the /etc/default/isc-dhcp-server file:

1. We will first show you how to set up a basic local DHCP server. In this respect, we will alter the /etc/dhcp/dhcpd.conf file by adding the IP address pool. You can either uncomment one of the subnet directives already available inside the file, or you can add a new one, which is what we will do. Our existing subnet is 192.168.0.0/24, and we will add a new one for this new DHCP server, as shown in the following screenshot (for a refresher on networking, please refer to *Chapter 7, Networking with Linux*):

    ```
    subnet 192.168.1.0 netmask 255.255.255.0 {
            range 192.168.1.100 192.168.1.200;
            option routers 192.168.1.1;
            option domain-name-servers 192.168.1.2, 192.168.1.3;
            option domain-name "homecomputer.local";
            option broadcast-address 192.168.1.255;
    }
    ```

    Figure 13.14 – Defining a new subnet in /etc/dhcp/dhcpd.conf

2. Inside the same /etc/dhcp/dhcpd.conf file, you can uncomment the line that says authoritative;. The authoritative DHCP clause ensures that the server will automatically resolve any invalid IP numbers on the network and assign a new and valid IP to each new device registered without requiring the user's manual interaction.

3. Once the options are modified, you must specify the network interface name in the /etc/default/isc-dhcp-server file. This is needed for the server to know which network device to use. To do this, open the file with your preferred editor and add the interface's name. If you don't remember your interface name, run the ip addr show command and select the appropriate interface. In our case, the system we use has both Ethernet and wireless interfaces,

and we will choose the Ethernet interface for the DHCP server, which is `enp0s25`. Inside the `/etc/default/isc-dhcp-server` file, add the interface as follows:

```
INTERFACESv4="enp0s25"
```

4. Then, save the changes to the file and restart the DHCP service with the following command:

```
sudo systemctl restart isc-dhcp-server.service
```

Now, you have a working DHCP server on your system of choice. A DHCP server gives you some advantages in managing your local network, but there are times when you might not need to create a new one, as all the network routers provide a fully working DHCP service right out of the box.

> **Important note**
>
> To avoid conflicts, you might want to isolate the new DHCP server from your local network router. Your network router already has a fully functional DHCP server that will most likely conflict with the new one. In most cases, `isc-dhcp-server.service` will give you an error as an indication that it was not able to connect to any interface.

Taking the preceding note into consideration, when we check to see whether the DHCP service is running with the following command:

```
sudo systemctl status isc-dhcp-server.service
```

We received an error, as shown in the following screenshot:

```
× isc-dhcp-server.service - ISC DHCP IPv4 server
    Loaded: loaded (/lib/systemd/system/isc-dhcp-server.service; enabled; vendor preset: enabled)
    Active: failed (Result: exit-code) since Thu 2023-06-22 11:33:43 UTC; 31min ago
      Docs: man:dhcpd(8)
   Process: 1716 ExecStart=/bin/sh -ec      CONFIG_FILE=/etc/dhcp/dhcpd.conf;      if [ -f /etc/ltsp/dhcpd.conf ]; then CONFIG_FILE=/etc/ltsp/dhcpd.conf;█
  Main PID: 1716 (code=exited, status=1/FAILURE)
       CPU: 12ms

Jun 22 11:33:43 nuc5 dhcpd[1716]:
Jun 22 11:33:43 nuc5 dhcpd[1716]: Not configured to listen on any interfaces!
Jun 22 11:33:43 nuc5 dhcpd[1716]:
Jun 22 11:33:43 nuc5 dhcpd[1716]: If you think you have received this message due to a bug rather
Jun 22 11:33:43 nuc5 dhcpd[1716]: than a configuration issue please read the section on submitting
Jun 22 11:33:43 nuc5 dhcpd[1716]: bugs on either our web page at www.isc.org or in the README file
Jun 22 11:33:43 nuc5 dhcpd[1716]: before submitting a bug.  These pages explain the proper
Jun 22 11:33:43 nuc5 dhcpd[1716]: process and the information we find helpful for debugging.
Jun 22 11:33:43 nuc5 dhcpd[1716]:
Jun 22 11:33:43 nuc5 dhcpd[1716]: exiting.
```

Figure 13.15 – Error running the DHCP service

Once you isolate the machine from your local network and use it as a single DHCP server, the service will be running as intended.

In the next section, we will show you how to set up an NFS server on your local network.

Setting up an NFS server

NFS is a distributed filesystem used to share files over a network. To show you how it works, we will set up the NFS server on one of our machines on the network. We will use Ubuntu 22.04.2 LTS as the base for the NFS server. For more in-depth theoretical information about NFS, please refer to *Chapter 7, Networking with Linux*.

The NFS filesystem type is supported by any Linux and/or Unix environment and also by Windows, but with some limitations. For mostly-Windows client environments, we recommend using the Samba/ **Common Internet File System** (**CIFS**) protocol instead. Also, for those of you concerned about privacy and security, please keep in mind that the NFS protocol is not encrypted, thus any transfer of data is not protected by default.

Installing and configuring the NFS server

On our network, we will use an Ubuntu machine as a server and we will show you how to access the files from another Linux client. First, let's install and configure the server, as follows:

1. We will install the `nfs-kernel-server` package using the following command:

    ```
    sudo apt install nfs-kernel-server
    ```

2. Once the package is installed, you will have to start the service using the `systemctl` command, and then we will check its status. The commands are the following:

    ```
    sudo systemctl start nfs-kernel-server.service
    sudo systemctl enable nfs-kernel-server.service
    sudo systemctl status nfs-kernel-server.service
    ```

3. For a more efficient workflow inside our network, we will add all the directories to be exported inside a single parent directory on the server. As a general rule, you have two options for creating shared directories. You could export the already existing `/home` directory for all clients on the network, or you could make a dedicated shared directory from the start. You could create a new directory starting from the root, but you could also create your shared directory inside specific directories such as `/var`, `/mnt`, or `/srv`—it's your choice.

    We will create a new directory called `/home/export/shares` inside our `/home` directory using the following commands (make sure that you are already inside your `/home` directory if you want to use the command as is):

    ```
    sudo mkdir -p export/shares
    ```

4. Set permissions to 777 as we will not use **Lightweight Directory Access Protocol** (**LDAP**) authentication on the following example:

    ```
    sudo chmod 777 /home/export/shares/
    ```

5. The directory is now ready to be exported. We will add configuration options to the `/etc/exports` file. There are three configuration files for NFS (`/etc/default/nfs-kernel-server`, `/etc/default/nfs-common`, and `/etc/exports`) but we will only alter one of them. In the following screenshot, you will see the two files inside `/etc/default` and the default contents of the `/etc/exports` configuration file:

```
packt@nuc5:/home$ ls /etc/default
amd64-microcode  grub             keyboard            nfs-common         ssh
apport           grub.d           locale              nfs-kernel-server  ufw
console-setup    grub.ucf-dist    mdadm               open-iscsi         useradd
cron             intel-microcode  motd-news           pollinate
cryptdisks       irqbalance       named               rpcbind
dbus             isc-dhcp-server  networkd-dispatcher rsync
packt@nuc5:/home$ cat /etc/exports
# /etc/exports: the access control list for filesystems which may be exported
#               to NFS clients.  See exports(5).
#
# Example for NFSv2 and NFSv3:
# /srv/homes       hostname1(rw,sync,no_subtree_check) hostname2(ro,sync,no_subtree_check)
#
# Example for NFSv4:
# /srv/nfs4        gss/krb5i(rw,sync,fsid=0,crossmnt,no_subtree_check)
# /srv/nfs4/homes  gss/krb5i(rw,sync,no_subtree_check)
```

Figure 13.16 – The configuration files inside /etc/default and the
contents of the /etc/exports configuration file

Open the `/etc/exports` file with your preferred text editor and edit it according to your configuration. Inside the file, we will add lines for each shared directory. Before doing that, you might have noticed that inside the file there are two types of directives: one for NFS versions 2 and 3, and one for version 4. For more details about the differences between those versions, we encourage you to consult the following document: `https://archive.fosdem.org/2018/schedule/event/nfs3_to_nfs4/attachments/slides/2702/export/events/attachments/nfs3_to_nfs4/slides/2702/FOSDEM_Presentation_Final_pdf.pdf`.

6. Now let's start editing the configuration file. We will add a new line containing the directory, the IP address of the client, and configuration options. The general syntax is as follows:

```
/first/path/to/files  IP(options) [ IP(options)  IP(options)]
/second/path/to/files IP(options) [ IP(options)  IP(options)]
```

We share only one directory, hence the single line added. If you want all clients on the network to access the shares, you can add the subnet class (for example, `192.168.0.0/24`). Or, if you want only specific clients to access the shares, you should add their IPs. More clients will be added on the same line, separated by spaces. There are many options that you can add, and for a full list, we advise that you consult `https://linux.die.net/man/5/exports` or the local manual file with the `man exports` command. In our file, we added the following options:

- `rw` for both read and write access

- `sync` to force write changes to disk (this reduces the speed, though)

- `no_subtree_check` to prevent subtree checking, which is mainly a check to see whether the file is still available before the request

In a nutshell, here is the line we added to the file (please take into consideration that this is only a single line, with a space between `/home/export/shares` and the IP, and there is no space between the IP and the parentheses):

```
/home/export/shares    192.168.0.0/24(rw,sync,no_subtree_check)
```

7. After saving and closing the file, restart the service with the following command:

```
sudo systemctl restart nfs-kernel-server.service
```

8. Then, apply the configuration with the following command:

```
sudo exportfs -a
```

The `-a` options export all directories without specifying a path.

9. Once the service is restarted and running, you can set up a firewall to allow NFS access. For this, it is extremely useful to know that the port NFS is using port `2049` by default. As we allow all the systems from our network to access the shares, we will add the following new rule to the firewall:

```
sudo ufw allow nfs
```

10. Now that the new firewall rule has been added, we can run the following command to make sure that it is running according to our needs:

```
sudo ufw status
```

11. If your firewall is not actively running, you can use the following command to activate it:

```
sudo ufw enable
```

The output of the `ufw status` command is shown in the following screenshot:

```
packt@nuc5:/home$ sudo ufw status
Status: active

To                         Action       From
--                         ------       ----
Bind9                      ALLOW        Anywhere
2049                       ALLOW        Anywhere
Bind9 (v6)                 ALLOW        Anywhere (v6)
2049 (v6)                  ALLOW        Anywhere (v6)
```

Figure 13.17 – Showing the new firewall rule to allow NFS shares

In the preceding screenshot, you can see that after adding the new rule using the `sudo ufw allow nfs` command, port 2049 was added to the list of allowed rules.

The basic configuration of the server is now complete. In order to access the files, you will need to configure the clients too. We will show you how to do this in the next section.

Configuring the NFS client

As a client, we will use another system, a laptop running Debian GNU/Linux 12 Bookworm. First, we will have to install NFS on the client by using the following command:

```
sudo apt install nfs-common
```

Now that the needed packages are installed on the client too, we can create directories on the client to mount the shares to. We will create a new directory on the client, where the shares from the server will be mounted. This new directory will be `/home/shares`. We create it with the following command:

```
sudo mkdir /home/shares
```

Now that the new directory is created, we can mount the location from the server:

```
sudo mount 192.168.0.113:/home/export/shares /home/shares
```

With the preceding command, we mounted the shares from the server on the client using the `mount` command. We gave the location on the server as the first argument, followed by the location on the client as the second argument. We can also check to see whether everything went well by using the `df -h` command. The new mount is shown last in the `df` command's output. The following is a screenshot showing the commands used to create, mount, and check the new shares directory:

```
alexandru@debian:~$ sudo mkdir /home/shares
alexandru@debian:~$ sudo mount 192.168.0.113:/home/export/shares /home/shares
alexandru@debian:~$ df -h
Filesystem                      Size  Used Avail Use% Mounted on
udev                            12G      0   12G   0% /dev
tmpfs                           2.3G  2.2G  2.3G   1% /run
/dev/mapper/debian--vg-root     467G   11G  432G   3% /
tmpfs                           12G      0   12G   0% /dev/shm
tmpfs                           5.0M   16K  5.0M   1% /run/lock
/dev/nvme0n1p2                  456M   86M  345M  20% /boot
/dev/nvme0n1p1                  511M  5.9M  506M   2% /boot/efi
tmpfs                           2.3G  2.6M  2.3G   1% /run/user/1000
/dev/sdb1                        58G  3.5G   55G   7% /media/alexandru/book
/dev/sdc1                        58G  3.4G   54G   6% /media/alexandru/book2
/dev/sda1                       115G   50G   65G  44% /media/alexandru/Ventoy
192.168.0.113:/home/export/shares 98G 7.8G  86G   9% /home/shares
```

Figure 13.18 – Mounting the new shares directory on the client

At this point, we have finished the setup for the NFS shares. We now need to test the configuration to prove that it works.

Testing the NFS setup

Once the setup is finished on both server and client, you can test to see if everything works according to your expectations. In our test, we created several files named `testing_files` using the `packt` user on the server, and a file called `file` using the regular user `alexandru` on the client machine. The following is the output showing the contents of the `/home/shares` directory on our Debian local system:

Figure 13.19 – Testing the NFS on our local client

There you have it, the NFS server and client are working just fine. You can use the **graphical user interface** (**GUI**) on the client (as shown in the previous screenshot), and also the **command-line interface** (**CLI**) to access the NFS shares.

In the next section, we will show you how to configure a Samba/CIFS share that can be accessed by Windows clients on the network.

Setting up a Samba file server

The Samba server allows you to share files over a network where clients use different operating systems, such as Windows, macOS, and Linux. In this section, we will set up a Samba server on Ubuntu 22.04.2 LTS and access shares from different operating systems on the network. The SMB/CIFS protocol is developed by Microsoft; for more details, you can visit their developer pages at `https://docs.microsoft.com/en-us/windows/win32/fileio/microsoft-smb-protocol-and-cifs-protocol-overview`. Some information about the SMB/CIFS protocol can be found in

Chapter 7, *Networking with Linux*, too. In the following sub-sections we will show you how to install and configure it on your local network.

Installing and configuring Samba

The installation procedure has the following steps:

1. First, we will install Samba on the system using the following command:

   ```
   sudo apt install samba
   ```

2. Once Samba is installed, we can check whether the service is running as expected. We will run the following command for this:

   ```
   sudo systemctl status smbd.service
   ```

3. If the service is running as expected, we now continue and create a directory to share on the network. We will make a new directory inside our /home directory using the mkdir command, as follows:

   ```
   mkdir /home/packt/samba_shares
   ```

4. After creating the new directory, we will edit the Samba configuration file. This is located under /etc/samba/smb.conf. The configuration file has two major sections: a [global] section with general configuration settings, and a [shares] section that configures the shares' behavior. A safe practice is to back up the original configuration file before starting to modify it. We will do this with the following command:

   ```
   sudo mv /etc/samba/smb.conf /etc/samba/smb.conf.original
   ```

5. With the preceding command, we renamed the original configuration file and now, we will create a new file with the same name as the original one, smb.conf. Inside the configuration file, we will first create the [global] section with directives, as shown in the following screenshot:

```
[global]
server string = Local Samba File Server
workgroup = WORKGROUP
map to guest = Bad User
usershare allow guests = yes
interfaces = lo eno1
bind interfaces only = yes
server role = standalone server
hosts allow = 192.168.0.0/16
name resolve order = bcast host
```

Figure 13.20 – The smb.conf global directive

Let us briefly explain the content shown in the preceding screenshot:

- The first line sets a server name, in our case Local Samba File Server

- The second line sets the workgroup name, in our case the Windows default name, WORKGROUP

- The third line determines that it will not be necessary to have a Samba user account in order to access the shares (mapping the guest to Bad User)

- Guest users are allowed on the fourth line

- Then we set the interfaces used by Samba, which in our case will be the Ethernet connection (eno1) and the loopback (lo) interfaces (check your exact interface name with the ip addr show or ip link commands)

- We will set the server role and the hosts allowed (from the local pool)

- The last line sets the order the hostnames are checked, using the broadcast (bcast) method

6. Now we will create the [shares] directive and add the necessary configuration options for the shares. We will add details about the shared directory on our server, user details, and permissions. See the following screenshot for details:

```
[shares]
comment = Samba shares
path = /home/packt/samba_shares
create mask = 0664
force create mode = 0664
directory mask = 0775
force directory mode = 0775
public = yes
writable = yes
read only = no
guest ok = yes
browsable = yes
valid users = @packt @alex
```

Figure 13.21 – Adding information inside the shares.conf file

Let us briefly explain the contents of this directive:

- We first set a name for the shares

- Then we set the path of our local shared directory

- Next, we set the default permissions for the directory and files

- We also set the default mask values

- Finally, we set the shares as public, guest-user friendly, and writable

7. Once the modifications are done, we restart the service with the following command:

```
sudo systemctl restart smbd.service
```

8. Furthermore, we adjust the firewall rules to allow Samba using the following command:

```
sudo ufw allow samba
```

9. Once the firewall is set up, you can run the `testparm` command to test that the configuration has been done correctly, with no errors, as follows:

```
packt@nuc7:~$ testparm
Load smb config files from /etc/samba/smb.conf
Loaded services file OK.
Weak crypto is allowed

Server role: ROLE_STANDALONE

Press enter to see a dump of your service definitions

# Global parameters
[global]
        bind interfaces only = Yes
        interfaces = lo eno1
        map to guest = Bad User
        name resolve order = bcast host
        server role = standalone server
        server string = Local Samba File Server
        usershare allow guests = Yes
        idmap config * : backend = tdb
        hosts allow = 192.168.0.0/16


[shares]
        comment = Samba shares
        create mask = 0664
        directory mask = 0775
        force create mode = 0664
        force directory mode = 0775
        guest ok = Yes
        path = /home/packt/samba_shares
        read only = No
        valid users = @packt @alex
```

Figure 13.22 – Testing the Samba configuration

The output shows `Loaded services file OK`, which means that the configuration files have no syntax errors.

After the system is restarted and the firewall configured, we can proceed to setting up a Samba password for users who can access the shares. In the next section, we will create new Samba users and groups.

Creating Samba users

Each Samba server needs to have specific users that can access the shared directories and files. Those users need to be both Samba and system users, as this is necessary for users to be able to authenticate and to read and write system files. Let's assume that you need to create a local share for your small business or family group.

By creating local users specifically for using the Samba shares, you don't need them to act like actual users as they only need to be able to access the shares. However, local Samba users need to be local system users. In our case, we will use our local `packt` user to create a new user for Samba:

1. We use the following command to add the `packt` local user to Samba:

    ```
    sudo smbpasswd -a packt
    ```

2. As `packt` is our primary user, it is also the owner of the `samba_shares` directory created at the beginning of this section. We can change that with the following command:

    ```
    sudo chown -R nobody:nogroup /home/packt/samba_shares
    ```

3. But what if we wanted to use another system user? We can add a new local user called `alex` using the following command:

    ```
    sudo adduser alex
    ```

4. Then we add it to Samba with the following command:

    ```
    sudo smbpasswd -a alex
    ```

5. Now that it is added to Samba, we can alter the `smb.conf` file and add the users we would like to give permissions to Samba, such as `packt` and `alex` users. Let us open the `/etc/samba/smb.conf` file and add the following line inside the `[samba shares]` directive:

    ```
    valid users = @packt @alex
    ```

Before testing the new user's access to Samba, we will need to give the user `alex` access to the shared directory. To do this, we follow these steps:

1. We add the `acl` package in Ubuntu with the following command:

    ```
    sudo apt install acl
    ```

2. Then we use the `setfacl` command to set read, write, and execute permissions for the `/home/packt/samba_shares` directory. For this, we use the following command:

    ```
    sudo setfacl -R -m "u:alex:rwx" /home/packt/samba_shares
    ```

In the next section, we will show you how to access the Samba shares from different systems on the network.

Accessing the Samba shares

On your network, you can access the shares from Linux, macOS, or Windows. To make everything a little bit challenging—worthy of a Linux master!—we will show you how to access the Samba shares in Linux using the CLI only. We will let you find out for yourselves how to access them from the GUI or from a Windows or macOS client. To access the shares from the CLI, use the smbclient tool.

On a Linux system, you need to install the Samba client smbclient first. We will assume that you will have an Ubuntu or Debian Linux client, but the steps are similar for other Linux distributions too. On Ubuntu/Debian, first install the Samba client with the following command, but make sure that your repositories are updated before you do this:

```
sudo apt install smbclient
```

If you are running a Fedora/RHEL client, install the Samba client with the following command:

```
sudo dnf install samba-client
```

For example, let's access the shares of user packt from one of our local machines. Remember that the shares are on a local server running Ubuntu. We will use our local IP for the server and run the following code:

```
alexandru@debian:~$ smbclient //192.168.0.140/shares -U packt
Password for [WORKGROUP\packt]:
Try "help" to get a list of possible commands.
smb: \> ls
  .                                   D        0  Sat Jul  8 09:56:43 2023
  ..                                  D        0  Fri Jul  7 11:42:44 2023
  new_file                            N        0  Thu Jan  1 02:00:00 1970

            102626232 blocks of size 1024. 72091436 blocks available
smb: \>
```

Figure 13.23 – Accessing shares from a Linux CLI client

In the preceding screenshot, you can see that the Samba access was successful, and the user `packt` managed to access the Samba shares on the server. We used the `-U` option followed by the username to specify the name of the user we are connecting with. The location was given using the server's local IP, followed by the Samba `samba shares` name. Furthermore, if we would like to see the Samba services available on the server, we could use the `-L` option with the `smbclient` command, as follows:

```
alexandru@debian:~$ smbclient -L //192.168.0.140 -U packt
Password for [WORKGROUP\packt]:

        Sharename       Type        Comment
        ---------       ----        -------
        shares          Disk        Samba shares
        IPC$            IPC         IPC Service (Local Samba File Server)
```

Figure 13.24 – Listing the available services on the Samba server

Here we are, at the end of this chapter on configuring Linux servers. The servers showcased were considered important and relevant for any Linux sysadmin to know. However, there are many other types of Linux servers not covered due to page-count constraints. Nevertheless, there are plenty of resources you can find online. As a base, you can start with the official documentation for RHEL, Ubuntu, or Debian, which will cover most of the Linux server types that you should know. One server type that will prove useful to know how to configure is the web server. Feel free to explore any other resources that you find relevant and might not be included in the *Further reading* list.

Summary

In this chapter, we covered the installation and configuration processes for the most well-known services available for Linux. Knowing how to configure all the servers described in this chapter—from DNS to DHCP, Apache, and a printing server—is a minimum requirement for any Linux administrator.

By going through this chapter, you learned how to provide essential services for any Linux server. You learned how to set up and configure a web server using the Apache package; how to provide networked printing services to a small office or home office; how to run an FTP server and share files over TCP; how to share files with Windows clients on your network using the Samba/CIFS protocol; how to share files over Unix and Linux systems using the NFS file-sharing protocol; how to set up NTP to show an accurate time; and how to configure DNS and local DHCP servers. In a nutshell, you learned a lot in this chapter, and yet we have barely scratched the surface of Linux server administration.

In the next chapter, we will introduce you to cloud technologies.

Questions

Now that you have a clear view of how to manage some of the most widely used services in Linux, here are some exercises that will further contribute to your learning:

1. Try using a VPS for all the services detailed in this chapter, not on your local network.
2. Try setting up a LEMP stack on Ubuntu.
3. Test all the services described in this chapter using Fedora or RHEL-based distributions.

Further reading

For more information about the topics covered in the chapter, you can refer to the following links:

- Official Ubuntu documentation: `https://ubuntu.com/server/docs`
- RHEL official docs: `https://www.redhat.com/sysadmin/install-apache-web-server`
- NGINX official docs: `https://docs.nginx.com/nginx/admin-guide/installing-nginx/installing-nginx-open-source/`
- DigitalOcean official docs: `https://www.digitalocean.com/community/tutorials/how-to-install-the-apache-web-server-on-ubuntu-22-04`

Part 4: Cloud Administration

In this fourth part, you will learn about advanced concepts related to cloud computing. By the end of this part, you will be proficient in using specific tools such as Kubernetes and Ansible and deploying Linux to the AWS and Azure clouds.

This part has the following chapters:

- *Chapter 14, Short Introduction to Computing*
- *Chapter 15, Deploying to the Cloud with AWS and Azure*
- *Chapter 16, Deploying Applications with Kubernetes*
- *Chapter 17, Infrastructure and Automation with Ansible*

14

Short Introduction to Cloud Computing

In this chapter, you will learn the basics of **cloud computing** and will be presented with the core foundations of cloud infrastructure technologies. You will learn about the as-a-service solutions such as **Infrastructure as a Service (IaaS)**, **Platform as a Service (PaaS)**, **Software as a Service (SaaS)**, and **Containers as a Service (CaaS)**. You will be presented with the basics of cloud standards, **Development and Operations (DevOps)**, **continuous integration/continuous deployment (CI/CD)**, and **microservices**. A base knowledge of the cloud will offer at least a basic introduction to AWS, Azure, and other cloud solutions. By the end of this chapter, we will also introduce you to technologies such as **Ansible** and **Kubernetes**. This chapter will provide a concise theoretical introduction that will be the foundation for the following three cloud-related chapters, which will provide you with important practical knowledge on the many solutions presented here.

In this chapter, we're going to cover the following main topics:

- Introduction to cloud technologies
- Introducing IaaS solutions
- Introducing PaaS solutions
- Introducing CaaS solutions
- Introducing DevOps
- Exploring cloud management tools

Technical requirements

No special technical requirements are needed as this chapter is a purely theoretical one. All you need is a desire to learn about cloud technologies.

Introduction to cloud technologies

The term "cloud computing," or the simple alternative "cloud," is not missing from any tech enthusiast's or **Information Technology** (**IT**) professional's vocabulary these days. You don't even have to be involved in IT at all to hear (or even use) the term "cloud" relatively often. Today's computing landscape is changing at a rapid pace, and the pinnacle of this change is the cloud and the technologies behind it. According to the literature, the term "cloud computing" was used for the first time in 1996, in a business plan from Compaq (`https://www.technologyreview.com/2011/10/31/257406/who-coined-cloud-computing/`).

Cloud computing is a relatively old concept, even though it was not referred to using this term right from the beginning. It is a computing model that was used from the early days of computing. Back in the 1950s, for example, there were mainframe computers that were accessed from different terminals. This model is similar to modern cloud computing, where services are hosted and delivered over the internet to different terminals, from desktop computers to smartphones, tablets, or laptops. This model is based on technologies that are extremely complex and essential for anyone who wants to master them to know.

You might be wondering why we have an entire section dedicated to cloud computing and technologies inside a *Mastering Linux Administration* title. This is simply because Linux has taken over the cloud in the last decade, in the same way that Linux took over the internet and the high-performance computing landscape. According to the TOP500 association, the world's top 500 supercomputers all run on Linux (`https://top500.org/lists/top500/2020/11/`). Clouds need to have an operating system to operate on, but it doesn't have to be Linux. Nevertheless, Linux runs on almost 90% of public clouds (`https://www.redhat.com/en/resources/state-of-linux-in-public-cloud-for-enterprises`), mostly because its open source nature appeals to IT professionals inside the public and private sectors alike.

In the following section, we will tackle the subject of cloud standards and why it is good to know about them when planning to deploy or manage a cloud instance.

Exploring the cloud computing standards

Before going into more details about cloud computing, let's give you a short introduction to what cloud standards are and their importance in the overall contemporary cloud landscape. You may know that almost every activity in the wider **Information and Communications Technology** (**ICT**) spectrum is governed by some kind of standard or regulation.

Cloud computing is no wild land, and you will be surprised at how many associations, regulatory boards, and organizations are involved in developing standards and regulations for it. Covering all these institutions and standards is out of the scope of this book and chapter, but in the following sections, we will describe some of the most important and relevant ones (in our opinion) so that you can have an idea of their importance in keeping clouds together and web applications running.

International Organization for Standardization/International Electrotechnical Commission

Two of the most widely known standards entities are the **International Organization for Standardization (ISO)** and the **International Electrotechnical Commission (IEC)**, and they currently have 28 published and under-development standards on cloud computing and distributed platforms. They have a joint task group to develop standards for specific cloud core infrastructure, consumer application platforms, and services. Those standards are found under the responsibility of the **Joint Technical Committee 1 (JTC 1) subcommittee 38 (SC38)**, or **ISO/IEC JTC 1/SC 38** for short.

Examples of standards from ISO/IEC include the following:

- Cloud computing **service-level agreement (SLA)** frameworks:

  - ISO/IEC 19086-1:2016

  - ISO/IEC 19086-2:2018

  - ISO/IEC 19086-3:2017

- Cloud computing **service-oriented architecture (SOA)** frameworks:

  - ISO/IEC 18384-1:2016

  - ISO/IEC 18384-2:2016

  - ISO/IEC 18384-3:2016

- **Open Virtualization Format (OVF)** specifications:

  - ISO/IEC 17203:2017

- Cloud computing **data sharing agreement (DSA)** frameworks:

  - ISO/IEC CD 23751

- **Distributed application platforms and services (DAPS)** technical principles:

  - ISO/IEC TR 30102:2012

To take a closer look at those standards, please go to `https://www.iso.org/committee/601355/x/catalogue/`.

The Cloud Standards Coordination initiative

Next on our list of standards development entities is an initiative called the **Cloud Standards Coordination (CSC)**, created by the **European Commission (EC)**, together with specialized bodies.

Back in 2012, the EC, together with the **European Telecommunications Standards Institute (ETSI)**, launched the CSC to develop standards and policies for cloud security, interoperability, and portability. The initiative had two phases, with Phase 1 starting in 2012 and Phase 2 starting in 2015. The final reports of Phase 2 (version 2.1.1), were made public, as follows:

- Cloud computing users' needs (ETSI SR 003 381)

- Standards and Open Source (ETSI SR 003 382)

- Interoperability and Security (ETSI SR 003 391)

- Standards Maturity Assessment (ETSI SR 003 392)

For more details on each of those standards, access the following link: `http://csc.etsi.org/`.

National Institute of Standards and Technology

The list continues with one of the most widely known entities in standards development: the **United States (US) National Institute of Standards and Technology (NIST)**. This will not be the first time you will read about NIST in this book. It is the standards development body in the US Department of Commerce. The main objective of NIST is the standardization of security and interoperability inside US government agencies, so anyone interested in developing for those entities should take a look at the NIST cloud documentation. The NIST document that standardizes cloud computing is called NIST SP 500-291r2 and can be found at `http://csrc.nist.gov/publications/nistpubs/800-145/SP800-145.pdf`.

The International Telecommunication Union

We will close our shortlisting with one of the oldest—if not the oldest—standards development bodies, part of the **United Nations (UN)** organization: the **International Telecommunication Union (ITU)**. The ITU is a body inside the UN, and its main focus is to develop standards for communications, networking, and development. This agency was founded in 1865 and, among other things, it is responsible for global radio frequency spectrum and satellite orbit allocation. It is also responsible for the use of Morse code as a standard means of communication. When it comes to global information infrastructure, internet protocols, next-generation networks, **Internet of Things (IoT)**, and smart cities, the ITU has a lot of standards and recommendations available. To check them all out, have a look at the following link: `https://www.itu.int/rec/T-REC-Y/en`. To narrow down the document list from the aforementioned link, some specific cloud computing documents can be found using document codes, from Y.3505 up to Y.3531. The cloud computing standards were developed by the **Study Group 13 (SG13) Joint Coordination Activity on Cloud Computing (JCA-Cloud)** within the ITU.

Besides the entities described in this section, there are many others, including the following:

- The **Cloud Standards Customer Council (CSCC)**
- The **Distributed Management Task Force (DMTF)**
- The **Organization for the Advancement of Structured Information Standards (OASIS)**

The main reason for adopting standards for cloud computing is ease of use when it comes to either the **Cloud Service Provider (CSP)** or the client. Both categories need to have easy access to data, more so for CSPs and application developers, as easy access to data is translated into agility and interoperability. However, standards, besides being technically correct, need to be consistent and persistent. According to the literature, there are two main standards groups: ones that are established from practice, and ones that are being regulated. An important part of the cloud standards, from the second category, is the **application programming interfaces (APIs)**. Standardization of application frameworks, network protocols, and APIs guarantees success for everyone involved.

Understanding the cloud through API standards

APIs are sets of protocols, procedures, and functions: all the bricks needed to build a web-distributed application. Modern APIs emerged at the beginning of the 21st century, firstly as a theory in Roy Fielding's doctoral dissertation. Before the modern APIs, there were SOA standards and the **Simple Object Access Protocol (SOAP)**, based on **Extensible Markup Language (XML)**. Modern APIs are based on a new application architectural style, called **REpresentational State Transfer (REST)**.

REST APIs are based on a series of architectural styles, elements, connectors, and views that are clearly described by Roy Fielding in his thesis. There are six guiding constraints for an API to be RESTful, and they are as follows:

- Uniform user interfaces
- Client-server clear delineation
- Stateless operations
- Cacheable resources
- Layered system of servers
- Code on-demand execution

Following these guiding principles is far from following a standard, but REST provides them for developers as a high-level abstraction layer. Unless they are standardized, they will always remain great principles that generate confusion and frustration among developers.

The only organization that managed to standardize REST APIs for the cloud is the DMTF, through the **Cloud Infrastructure Management Interface (CIMI)** model and the RESTful **HyperText Transfer Protocol (HTTP)**-based protocol, in a document coded DSP0263 version 2.0.0, which can be downloaded from the following link: `https://www.dmtf.org/standards/cloud`.

There are other specifications that emerge as possible future standards for developers to use when designing REST APIs. Among those, there is the **OpenAPI Specification** (**OAS**), an industry standard that provides a language-agnostic description for API development (document available at `http://spec.openapis.org/oas/v3.0.3`), and **GraphQL**, as a query language and server-side runtime, with support for several programming languages such as Python, JavaScript, Scala, Ruby, and **PHP: Hypertext Preprocessor** (**PHP**).

REST managed to become the preferred API because it is easier to understand, more lightweight, and simple to write. It is more efficient, uses less bandwidth, supports many data formats, and uses **JavaScript Object Notation** (**JSON**) as the preferred data format. JSON is easy to read and write and offers better interoperability between applications written in different languages, such as JavaScript, Ruby, Python, and Java. By using JSON as the default data format for the API, it makes it friendly, scalable, and platform-agnostic.

APIs are everywhere on the web and in the cloud and are the base for SOA and microservices. For example, microservices use RESTful APIs to communicate between services by offering an optimized architecture for cloud-distributed resources.

Therefore, if you want to master cloud computing technologies, you should be open to embracing cloud standards. In the next section, we will discuss the cloud types and architecture.

Understanding the architecture of the cloud

The cloud's architectural design is similar to a building's architectural design. There is one design paradigm that governs the cloud—the one in which the design starts from a blank, clean drawing board where the architects put together different standardized components in order to achieve an architectural design. The final result is based on a certain architectural style. The same happens when designing the cloud's architecture.

The cloud is based on a client-server, layered, stateless, network-based architectural style. The REST APIs, SOA, microservices, and web technologies all are the base components that form the foundation of the cloud. The architecture of the cloud has been defined by NIST (`https://www.nist.gov/publications/nist-cloud-computing-reference-architecture`).

Some of the technologies behind the cloud have been discussed in *Chapter 11*, *Working with Virtual Machines*, and *Chapter 12*, *Managing Containers with Docker*. Indeed, both virtualization and containers are the foundation technologies of cloud computing.

Let's imagine a situation where you would like to have several Linux systems to deploy your apps. What you do first is go to a CSP and request the systems you need. The CSP will create the **virtual machines** (**VMs**) on its infrastructure, according to your needs, and will put all of them in the same network and share the credentials to access them with you. This way, you will have access to the systems you wanted, in exchange for a subscription fee that is billed either on a daily, monthly, or yearly basis or based on a resource-consumption basis. Most of the time, those CSP requests are done through a specific web interface, developed by the provider to best suit the needs of their users.

Everything that the cloud uses as technology is based on VMs and containers. Inside the cloud, everything is abstracted and automated. In the following section, we will provide you with information about the types of services that are available in the cloud.

Describing the types of infrastructure and services

No matter the type, each cloud has a specific architecture, just as we showed you in the previous section. It provides the blueprints for the foundation of cloud computing. The cloud architecture is the base for the cloud infrastructure, and the infrastructure is the base for cloud services. See how everything is connected? Let's now see what the infrastructure and services are with regard to the cloud.

There are four main **cloud infrastructure types**, as follows:

- **Public clouds**: These run on infrastructure owned by the provider and are available mostly off-premises; the largest public cloud providers are AWS, Microsoft Azure, and Google Cloud.

- **Private clouds**: These run specifically for individuals and groups with isolated access; they are available on both on-premises and off-premises hardware infrastructure. There are managed private clouds available, or dedicated private clouds.

- **Hybrid clouds**: These are both private and public clouds running inside connected environments, with resources available for potential on-demand scaling.

- **Multi-clouds**: These are more than one cloud running from more than one provider.

Besides the cloud infrastructure types, there are also four main **cloud service types**:

- **IaaS**: With an IaaS cloud service type, the cloud provider manages all hardware infrastructure such as servers and networking, plus virtualization and storage of data. The infrastructure is owned by the provider and rented by the user; in this case, the user needs to manage the operating system, the runtimes, automation, management solutions, and containers, together with the data and applications. IaaS is the backbone of every cloud computing service, as it provides all the resources.

- **CaaS**: This is considered to be a subset of IaaS; it has the same advantages as IaaS, only that the base consists of containers, not VMs, and it is better suited to deploying distributed systems and microservices architectures.

- **PaaS**: With a PaaS cloud service type, the hardware infrastructure, networking, and software platform are managed by the cloud provider; the user manages and owns the data and applications.

- **SaaS**: With a SaaS cloud service type, the cloud provider manages and owns the hardware, networking, software platform, management, and software applications. This type of service is also known for delivering web apps or mobile apps.

Besides these types of services, there is another one that we should bring into the discussion: **serverless computing** services. In contrast to what the name might suggest, serverless computing still implies the use of servers, but the infrastructure running them is not visible to users, who in most cases are developers. Serverless can also be referred to as **Function as a Service** (**FaaS**), and it provides an on-demand way to execute modular code, by letting developers update their code on the fly. Examples of this kind of service would be AWS Lambda, Azure Functions, and Google Cloud Functions. It is similar to SaaS; actually, it would fit right between PaaS and SaaS. It has no infrastructure management, is scalable, offers a faster way to market for app developers, and is efficient when it comes to the use of resources.

Now that you know the types of cloud infrastructure and services, you might wonder why you, your business, or anyone you know should migrate to cloud services. First of all, cloud computing is based on on-demand access to various resources that are hosted and managed by a CSP. This means that the infrastructure is owned or managed by the CSP and the user will be able to access the resources based on a subscription fee. Should you migrate to the cloud? We will discuss the advantages and disadvantages of migrating to the cloud in the next section.

Knowing the key features of cloud computing

Before deciding whether migrating to the cloud would be a good decision, you need to know the advantages and disadvantages of doing this. Cloud computing does provide some essential features, such as the following ones listed:

- **Cost savings**: There are reduced costs generated by the infrastructure setup, which is now managed by the CSP; this puts the user's focus on application development and running the business.

- **Speed**, **agility**, and **resource access**: All the resources are available from any place, just a few clicks away, at any time (dependent on internet connectivity and speed).

- **Reliability**: Resources are hosted in different locations, by providing good quality control, **disaster recovery** (**DR**) policies, and loss prevention; maintenance is done by the CSP, meaning that end users don't need to waste time and money doing this.

Besides the advantages (key features) listed previously, there are possible disadvantages too, such as the following:

- **Performance variations**: Performance may vary depending on the CSP you choose, but none of the big names out there (such as AWS, Azure, or GCP) have any significant performance issues. In these cases, performance is dictated by the local internet speed of the user, so it isn't a CSP problem after all. This might not be the case for other CSPs though.

- **Downtime**: Downtime could be an issue, but all major providers strive to offer 99.9% uptime. If disaster strikes, issues are solved in a matter of minutes—or in worst-case scenarios, in a matter of hours.

- **Lack of predictability**: There is a lack of predictability with regard to the CSP and its presence on the market, but rest assured that none of the big players will go away anytime soon.

Therefore, these are not game stoppers for anyone wanting to migrate to the cloud. In the next section, we will introduce you to some IaaS solutions.

Introducing IaaS solutions

IaaS is the backbone of cloud computing. It offers on-demand access to resources, such as compute, storage, network, and so on. The CSP uses hypervisors to provide IaaS solutions. In this section, we provide you with information about some of the most widely used IaaS solutions available. We will give you details about providers such as **Amazon Elastic Compute Cloud (Amazon EC2)**, and Microsoft Azure Virtual Machines as the big players, and **DigitalOcean** as a viable solution. We will tackle **OpenStack** too, for those interested in what it could offer.

Amazon EC2

The IaaS solution provided by AWS is called Amazon EC2. It provides a good infrastructure solution for anyone, from low-cost compute instances to a high-power **graphics processing unit** (**GPU**) for machine learning. AWS was the first provider of IaaS solutions 12 years ago and it is doing better than ever, even after the COVID-19 pandemic (`https://www.statista.com/chart/18819/worldwide-market-share-of-leading-cloud-infrastructure-service-providers/`).

When starting with Amazon EC2, you have several steps to fulfill:

- The first is the option to choose your **Amazon Machine Image** (**AMI**), which is basically a preconfigured image of either Linux or Windows. When it comes to Linux, you can choose between the following:

  - Amazon Linux 2 (based on CentOS/**Red Hat Enterprise Linux (RHEL)**)

  - RHEL 8/9

  - **SUSE Linux Enterprise Server (SLES)**

  - Ubuntu Server 20.04/22.04 **Long-Term Support (LTS)**

- You will need to choose your **instance type** from a really wide variety. To learn more about EC2 instances, visit `https://aws.amazon.com/ec2/instance-types/` and find out details about each one. EC2, for example, is the only provider that offers Mac instances, based on Mac mini. To use Linux, you can choose from low-end instances up to high-performance instances, depending on your needs.

- Amazon provides an **Elastic Block Store** (**EBS**) option with **solid-state drive** (**SSD**) and magnetic mediums available. You can select a custom value depending on your needs. EC2 is a flexible solution compared to other options. It has an easy-to-use and straightforward interface, and you will only pay for the time and resources you use. An example of how to deploy on EC2 will be provided to you in *Chapter 15, Deploying to the Cloud with AWS and Azure*.

Microsoft Azure Virtual Machines

Microsoft is the second biggest player in the cloud market, right after Amazon. Azure is the name of their cloud computing offering. Even though it is provided by Microsoft, Linux is the most widely used operating system on Azure (`https://www.zdnet.com/article/microsoft-developer-reveals-linux-is-now-more-used-on-azure-than-windows-server/`).

Azure's IaaS offering is called **Virtual Machines** and is similar to Amazon's offering; you can choose between many tiers. What is different about Microsoft's offering is the pricing model. They have a pay-as-you-go model, or a reservation-based instance, for one to three years. Microsoft's interface is totally different from Amazon's, and in our opinion might not be as straightforward as its competitor's, but you will get used to it eventually.

Microsoft offers several types of VM instances, from economical burstable VMs to powerful memory-optimized instances. The pay-as-you-go model offers a per-hour cost, and this could add to the final bill for those services, so choose with care based on your needs. When it comes to Linux distributions, you can choose from the following: CentOS, Debian, RHEL, SLES for SAP, openSUSE Leap, and Ubuntu Server.

Azure has a very powerful SaaS offering too, and this will make it a good option if you use other Azure services. An example of how to deploy to Azure will be provided to you in *Chapter 15, Deploying to the Cloud with AWS and Azure.*

Other strong IaaS offerings

DigitalOcean is another important player in the cloud market and it offers a strong IaaS solution. It has a straightforward interface and it helps you to create a cloud in a very short time. They call their VMs **droplets** and you create one in a matter of seconds. All you have to do is the following:

- Choose the image (Linux distribution)
- Select the plan, based on your **virtual CPU (vCPU)**, memory, and disk space needs
- Add storage blocks
- Choose your data center region, authentication method (password or **Secure Shell (SSH)** key), and hostname
- You can also assign droplets to certain projects you manage

DigitalOcean's interface is better looking and much more user friendly than its competitors. Following the example of DigitalOcean, other IaaS providers—such as **Linode** and **Hetzner**—provide a slim and friendly interface for creating virtual servers.

Linode is another strong competitor in the cloud market, offering powerful solutions. Their VMs are called Linodes. The interface is somewhere between DigitalOcean and Azure, with regard to their ease of use and appearance.

Another strong player, at least in the European market, is Hetzner, a Germany-based cloud provider. They offer a great balance between resources and cost, and similar solutions to the others mentioned in this section. They provide an interface similar to DigitalOcean that is really easy to explore, and the cloud instance will be deployed in a matter of seconds.

Similar to the offerings of DigitalOcean, Linode, and Hetzner, there is a relatively new offering from Amazon (starting in 2017), called **Lightsail**. This service was introduced in order to offer clients an easy way to deploy **virtual private servers** (**VPSs**) or VMs in the cloud. The interface is similar to that seen from the competition, but it comes with the full Amazon infrastructure reliability on top. Lightsail provides several distributions, together with application bundles. Deploying on AWS, using Lightsail, becomes more straightforward. It is a useful tool to lure in new users wanting a quick and secure solution for delivering their web apps.

There are other solutions available, such as Google's solution, called GCE, which is the IaaS solution from **Google Cloud Platform** (**GCP**). The GCP interface is very similar to the one on the Azure platform.

> **Important note**
> One interesting aspect of using GCP is that when you want to delete a project, the operation is not immediate, and the deletion is scheduled in one month's time. This could be seen as a safety net if the deletion was not intentional, and you need to roll back the project.

In the next section, we will detail some of the PaaS solutions.

Introducing PaaS solutions

PaaS is another form of cloud computing. Compared to IaaS, PaaS provides the hardware layer together with an application layer. The hardware and software are hosted by the CSP, with no need to manage them from the client side. Clients of PaaS solutions are, in the majority of cases, application developers. The CSPs that offer PaaS solutions are mostly the same as those that offer IaaS solutions. We have Amazon, Microsoft, and Google as the major PaaS providers. In the following subsections, we will discuss some PaaS solutions.

Amazon Elastic Beanstalk

Amazon offers the **Elastic Beanstalk** service, whose interface is straightforward. You can create a sample application or upload your own, and Beanstalk takes care of the rest, from deployment details to load balancing, scaling, and monitoring. You select the AWS EC2 hardware instances to deploy on.

Next, we will discuss another major player's offering: **Google App Engine**.

Google App Engine

Google's PaaS solution is Google App Engine, a fully managed serverless environment that is relatively easy to use, with support for a large number of programming languages. Google App Engine is a scalable solution with automatic security updates and managed infrastructure and monitoring. It offers solutions to connect to Google Cloud storage solutions and support for all major web programming languages such as Go, Node.js, Python, .NET, or Java. Google offers competitive pricing and an interface similar to the one we saw in their IaaS offering. Another major player with solid offerings is DigitalOcean, and we will discuss this next.

DigitalOcean App Platform

DigitalOcean offers a PaaS solution in the form of **App Platform**. It offers a straightforward interface, a direct connection with your GitHub or GitLab repository, and a fully managed infrastructure. DigitalOcean is on the same level as big players such as Amazon and Google, and with App Platform, it manages infrastructure, provisioning, databases, application runtimes and dependencies, and the underlying operating system. It offers support for popular programming languages and frameworks such as Python, Node.js, Django, Go, React, and Ruby. DigitalOcean App Platform uses open cloud-native standards, with automatic code analysis, container creation, and orchestration. A distinctive competence of this solution is the free *starter tier*, for deploying up to three static websites. For prototyping dynamic web apps, there is a *basic tier*, and for deploying professional apps on the market, there is a *professional tier* available. DigitalOcean's interface is pleasant and could be attractive to newcomers. Their pricing acts as an advantage too.

Open source PaaS solutions

Besides ready-to-use solutions from providers listed previously, there are open source PaaS solutions provided by **Cloud Foundry**, **Red Hat OpenShift**, **Heroku**, and others, all of which we will not detail in this section. Nevertheless, the three mentioned previously are worth at least a short introduction, so let's discuss them briefly:

- **Red Hat OpenShift**: This is a container platform for application deployments. Its base is a Linux distribution (RHEL) paired with a container runtime and solutions for networking, registry, authentication, and monitoring. OpenShift was designed to be a viable, hybrid PaaS solution with total Kubernetes integration (Kubernetes will be covered briefly in the following section, *Introducing CaaS solutions*, and in more detail in *Chapter 16, Deploying Applications with Kubernetes*). OpenShift took advantage of the CoreOS acquisition (discussed later on) by providing some unique solutions. The new CoreOS Tectonic container platform is merging with OpenShift to bring to the user the best of both worlds.

- **Cloud Foundry**: This is a cloud platform designed as an enterprise-ready PaaS solution. It is open source and can be deployed on different infrastructures, from on-premises to IaaS providers such as Google GCP, Amazon AWS, Azure, or OpenStack. It offers various developer frameworks and a choice of Cloud Foundry certified platforms, such as Atos Cloud Foundry, IBM Cloud Foundry, SAP Cloud Platform, SUSE Cloud Application Platform, and VMware Tanzu.

- **Heroku**: Heroku is a Salesforce company, and the platform was developed as an innovative PaaS. It is based on a container system called Dynos, which uses Linux-based containers run by a container management system, designed for scalability and agility. It offers fully managed data services with support for Postgres, Redis, Apache Kafka, and Heroku Runtime, a component responsible for container orchestration, scaling, and configuration management. Heroku also supports a plethora of programming languages, such as Node.js, Ruby, Python, Go, Scala, Clojure, and Java.

PaaS has many solutions for developers, helping them create and deploy an application by taking away the burden of managing the infrastructure. As you might have learned by now, many of the solutions described in this section rely on the use of containers. This is why, in the next section, we will detail a subset of IaaS called CaaS, where we will introduce you to container orchestration and container-specialized operating systems.

Introducing CaaS solutions

CaaS is a subset of the IaaS cloud service model. It lets customers use individual containers, clusters, and applications on top of a provider-managed infrastructure. CaaS can be used either on-premises or in the cloud, depending on the customer's needs. In a CaaS model, the container engines and orchestration are provided and managed by the CSP. A user's interaction with containers can be done either through an API or a web interface. The container orchestration platform used by the provider—mainly **Kubernetes** and **Docker**—is important and is a key differentiator between different solutions.

We covered containers (and VMs) in *Chapter 11, Working with Virtual Machines*, and *Chapter 12, Managing Containers with Docker*, without giving any detailed information about orchestration or container-specialized micro operating systems. We will now provide you with some more details on those subjects.

Introducing the Kubernetes container orchestration solution

Kubernetes is an open source project developed by Google to be used for the automatic deployment and scaling of containerized applications. It was written in the **Go** programming language. The name "Kubernetes" comes from Greek, and it refers to a ship's helmsman or captain. Kubernetes is a tool for automating container management together with infrastructure abstraction and service monitoring.

Many newcomers confuse Kubernetes with Docker, or vice versa. They are complementary tools, each used for a specific purpose. Docker creates a container (like a box) in which you want to deploy your application, and Kubernetes takes care of the containers (or boxes) once the applications are packed inside and deployed. Kubernetes provides a series of services that are essential to running containers, such as service discovery and load balancing, storage orchestration, automated backups and self-healing, and privacy. The Kubernetes architecture consists of several components that are crucial for any administrator to know. We will break them down for you in the next section.

Introducing the Kubernetes components

When you run Kubernetes, you mainly manage clusters of hosts, which are usually containers running Linux. In short, this means that when you run Kubernetes, you run clusters. Here is a list of the basic components found in Kubernetes:

- A **cluster** is the core of Kubernetes, as its sole purpose is to manage lots of clusters. Each cluster consists of at least a control plane and one or more nodes, each node running containers inside pods.

- A **control plane** consists of processes that control nodes. The components of a control plane are as follows:

  - **kube-apiserver**: This is the API server at the frontend of the control plane

  - **etcd**: This is the key-value store for all the data inside the cluster

  - **kube-scheduler**: This looks for pods that have no assigned node and connects them to a node to run

  - **kube-controller-manager**: This runs the controller processes, including the node controller, the replication controller, the endpoints controller, and the token controller

  - **cloud-controller-manager**: This is a tool that allows you to link your cluster to your cloud provider's API; it includes the node controller, the route controller, and the service controller

- **Nodes** are either a VM or a physical machine running services needed for pods. The node components run on every node and are responsible for maintaining the running pods. The components are as follows:

  - **kube-proxy**: This is responsible for network rules on each node

  - **kubelet**: This makes sure that each container is running inside a pod

- **Pods** are a collection of different containers running in the cluster. They are the components of the workload.

Kubernetes clusters are extremely complicated to master. Understanding the concepts around it needs a lot of practice and dedication. No matter how complex it is, Kubernetes does not do everything for you. You still have to choose the container runtime (supported runtimes are **Docker**, **containerd**, and **Container Runtime Interface** (**CRI**)-O), CI/CD tools, the storage solution, access control, and app services.

Managing Kubernetes clusters is out of the scope of this chapter, but you will learn about this in *Chapter 16*, *Deploying Applications with Kubernetes*. This short introduction was needed for you to understand the concepts and tools that Kubernetes uses.

Besides Kubernetes, there are several other container orchestration tools, such as **Docker Swarm**, **Apache Mesos**, and **Nomad** from HashiCorp. They are extremely powerful tools, used by many people around the world. We will not cover these in detail here, but we thought it would be useful to at least enumerate them at the end of this container orchestration section. In the next section, we will provide you with some information about container solutions in the cloud.

Deploying containers in the cloud

You can use container orchestration solutions in the cloud, and the following offerings are essential for this:

- **Amazon Elastic Container Service** (**ECS**): Amazon ECS is a fully managed service for orchestrating containers. It offers an optional, serverless solution (**AWS Fargate**) and is run inside by some of Amazon's key services, which ensures that the tool is tested and is secure enough for anyone to use.

- **Amazon Amazon Elastic Kubernetes Service** (**EKS**): Amazon also offers an EKS service for orchestrating Kubernetes applications. It is based on **Amazon EKS Distro** (**EKS-D**), which is a Kubernetes distribution developed by Amazon, based on the original open source Kubernetes. By using EKS-D, you can run Kubernetes either on-premises, on Amazon's own EC2 instances, or on VMware vSphere VMs.

- **Google Kubernetes Engine** (**GKE**): GKE offers pre-built deployment templates, with pod auto-scaling based on the CPU and memory usage. Scaling can be done across multiple pools, with enhanced security provided by GKE Sandbox. GKE Sandbox provides an extra layer of security by protecting the host kernel and running applications. Besides Google and Amazon, Microsoft offers a strong solution for container orchestration with AKS.

- **Microsoft Azure Kubernetes Service** (**AKS**): AKS is a managed service for deploying clusters of containerized applications. As with the other providers, Microsoft offers a fully managed solution by handling resource maintenance and health monitoring. The AKS nodes use Azure VMs to run and support different operating systems, such as Microsoft Windows Server images. It also offers free upgrades to the newest available Kubernetes images. Among other solutions, AKS offers GPU-enabled nodes, storage volume support, and special development tool integration with Microsoft's own Visual Studio Code.

After seeing some of the solutions available to deploy Kubernetes in the cloud and learning about the main components of Kubernetes and how they work, in the following section, we will discuss the importance of microservices in cloud computing.

Introducing microservices

A **microservice** is an architectural style used in application delivery. Over time, application delivery evolved from a monolithic model toward a decentralized one, all thanks to the evolution of cloud technologies. Starting with the historical launch of AWS in 2006, followed by the launch of Heroku in 2007 and Vagrant in 2010, application deployment started to change too, in order to take advantage of the new cloud offerings. Applications moved from having a single, large, and monolithic code base to a model where each application would benefit from different sets of services. This would make the code base more lightweight and dependent on different services.

Let us explain how a **monolithic application** differs from a **microservices architecture** application:

- A monolithic application model has all the functionalities inside a single process and it is deployed by simple replication on multiple servers. In comparison, a microservice architecture assumes that the application has its functionalities separated into different services. Those services are then distributed and scaled across different servers, depending on the user's needs.

- A microservices architecture has a modular-based approach. Each module will correspond to a specific service. Services work independently of one another and are connected through REST APIs based on the HTTP protocol. This means that each application functionality can be developed in different languages, depending on which one is better suited. This modular base can also take advantage of new container technologies.

- A microservices architecture is known for rapidly delivering complex applications. It has no technology or language lock-in; it offers independent scaling and updates for each service and component, with no disturbance to other running services; and it has a fail-proof architecture. The microservices model can be adapted to existing monolithic applications by breaking them down into individual, modular services. There is no need to rewrite the entire application, only splitting the entire code base into smaller parts. Microservices are optimized for DevOps and CI/CD practices, thanks to their modular approach.

In the next section, we will introduce you to DevOps practices and tools.

Introducing DevOps

DevOps is a culture. Its name comes from a combination of development and operations, and it envisions the practices and tools that are used to deliver rapidly. DevOps is about speed, agility, and time. We all know the phrase "time is money," and this applies very well to the IT sector. The ability to deliver services and applications at a high speed can make the difference between being successful as a business and being irrelevant in the market.

DevOps is a model of cooperation between different teams involved in delivering services and applications. This means that the entire life cycle, from development and testing, up to deployment and management, is done by teams that are equally involved at every stage. The DevOps model assumes that no team is operating in a closed environment, but rather operates transparently in order to achieve the agility they need to succeed. There is also a different DevOps model whereby security and quality assurance teams are equally involved in the development cycle. It is called **DevSecOps**.

Crucial for the DevOps model are the automated processes that are created using specific tools. This mindset of agility and speed determined the rise of a new name associated with DevOps, and that is CI/CD. The CI/CD mindset assures that every development step is continuous, with no interruptions. To support this mindset, new automation tools have emerged. Perhaps the most widely known is the open source automation tool, **Jenkins**. This is a modular tool and can be extended with the use of plugins. The ecosystem around the application is quite large, with hundreds of plugins available to choose from. Jenkins is written in Java and was designed to automate software development processes, from building and testing, up to delivery. One of the assets of Jenkins is the ability to create a pipeline through the use of specialized plugins. A pipeline is a tool that adds support for CD as an automated process to the application life cycle. Jenkins can be used either on-premises or in the cloud. It is also a viable solution for use as a SaaS offering.

The DevOps philosophy is not only related to application deployment; healthy CD and CI are closely tied to the state of infrastructure. In this respect, tools for cloud management such as Ansible, Puppet, and Chef are extremely useful for managing the infrastructure that supports application deployments. This is why configuration and management at the infrastructure level is extremely important. In the next section, you will learn about cloud infrastructure management.

Exploring cloud management tools

Today's software development and deployment relies on a plethora of physical systems and VMs. Managing all the related environments for development, testing, and production is a tedious task and involves the use of automated tools. The most widely used solutions for cloud infrastructure management are tools such as **Ansible**, **Puppet**, and **Chef Infra**. All these configuration management tools are powerful and reliable, and we will reserve *Chapter 17, Infrastructure and Automation with Ansible*, to teach you how to use only one of them: Ansible. Nevertheless, we will briefly introduce you to all of them in this section.

Ansible

Ansible is an open source project currently owned by Red Hat. It is considered a simple automation tool, used for diverse actions such as application deployment, configuration management, cloud provisioning, and service orchestration. It was developed in Python and uses the concept of nodes to define categories of systems, with a **control node** as the master machine running Ansible, and different

managed nodes as other machines that are controlled by the master. All the nodes are connected over SSH and controlled through an application called an **Ansible module**. Each module has a specific task to do on the managed nodes, and when the task is completed, it will be removed from that node.

The way modules are used is determined by an Ansible playbook. The playbook is written in **YAML** (a recursive acronym for **YAML Ain't Markup Language**), a language mostly used for configuration files. Ansible also uses the concept of **inventory**, where lists of the managed nodes are kept. When running commands on nodes, you can apply them based on the lists inside your inventory, based on **patterns**. Ansible will apply the commands on every node or group of nodes available in a certain pattern. Ansible is considered one of the easiest automation tools available. It supports Linux/Unix and Windows for client machines, but the master machine must be Linux/Unix.

Puppet

Puppet is one of the oldest automation tools available. Puppet's architecture is different from that of Ansible. It uses the concepts of **primary servers** and **agents**. Puppet works with infrastructure code written using **domain-specific language** (DSL) code specific to Puppet, based on the Ruby programming language. The code is written on the primary server, transferred to the agent, and then translated into commands that are executed on the system you want to manage. Puppet also has an inventory tool called **Facter**, which stores data about the agents, such as hostname, IP address, and operating system. Information stored is sent back to the primary server in the form of a **manifest**, which will then be transformed into a JSON document called a **catalog**. All the manifests are kept inside **modules**, which are tools that are used for specific tasks. Each module contains information in the form of code and data. This data is centralized and managed by a tool called **Hiera**. All the data that Puppet generates is stored inside databases and managed through APIs by every app that needs to manage it. Compared to Ansible, Puppet seems a lot more complex. Puppet's primary server supports only Linux/Unix.

Chef Infra

Chef Infra is another automation tool. It uses a client-server architecture. It uses the concepts of **cookbooks** and **recipes**. The main components are as follows:

- **Chef Server**: This is similar to a hub that handles all the configuration data. It is mainly used to upload cookbooks to the Chef Client.

- **Chef Client**: This is an application that is installed on every node from the infrastructure that you manage.

- **Chef Workstation**: The Chef Workstation manages cookbooks that are used for infrastructure administration.

Chef Infra uses the same Ruby-based code similar to Puppet called DSL. The server needs to be installed on Linux/Unix, and the client supports Windows too.

All the automation and configuration tools presented in this section use different architectures but do the same thing, which is to provide an abstraction layer that defines the desired state of the infrastructure. Each tool is a different beast, having its own strengths and weaknesses. Chef Infra and Puppet might have a steeper learning curve with their Ruby/DSL-based code, while Ansible could be easier to approach due to its simpler architecture and use of the Python programming language. Nevertheless, you can't go wrong with either one.

Summary

In this chapter, we introduced you to cloud computing by showing you some of the most important concepts, tools, and solutions used. This should be enough for you to start learning about cloud technologies, which is a very vast and complex subject. For more details, please refer to the *Further reading* section.

We talked about cloud standards, a significant and largely overlooked subject, and about the main cloud types and services. You now have an idea of what each as-a-service solution means and what the main differences are between them. You know what the most important solutions are and how they are provided by the main players in this field: Amazon, Google, and Microsoft. We introduced you to container orchestration with Kubernetes and how it works. You learned about APIs and minimal container-specialized operating systems and the DevOps culture, microservices, and infrastructure automation tools. You learned a lot in this chapter, but keep in mind that all these subjects have only scratched the surface of cloud computing.

In the next chapter, we will introduce you to the more practical side of cloud deployments. You will learn how to deploy Linux on major clouds such as AWS, Azure, and GCP.

Further reading

If you want to learn more about cloud technologies, please check out the following titles:

- *OpenStack for Architects – Second Edition* by Ben Silverman and Michael Solberg, Packt Publishing

- *Learning DevOps – Second Edition* by Mikael Krief, Packt Publishing

- *Design Microservices Architecture with Patterns and Principles [Video]* by Mehmet Ozkaya, Packt Publishing

- *Multi-Cloud Strategy for Cloud Architects – Second Edition* by Jeroen Mulder, Packt Publishing

- *Architecting Cloud-Native Serverless Solutions*, Safeer CM, Packt Publishing

15

Deploying to the Cloud with AWS and Azure

Recent years have seen a significant shift from on-premises computing platforms to private and public clouds. In an ever-changing and accelerating world, deploying and running applications in a highly scalable, efficient, and secure infrastructure is critical for businesses and organizations everywhere. On the other hand, the cost and expertise required to maintain the equivalent level of security and performance with on-premises computing resources become barely justifiable compared to current public cloud offerings. Businesses and teams, small and large, adopt public cloud services in increasing numbers, albeit large enterprises are relatively slow to make a move.

One of the best metaphors for cloud computing is application services *on tap*. Do you need more resources for your apps? Just *turn on the tap* and provision the virtual machines or instances in any number you require (scale horizontally). Or perhaps, for some instances, you require more CPUs or memory (scale vertically). When you no longer need resources, just *turn off the tap*.

Public cloud services provide all these functions at relatively low rates, taking away the operations overhead that you might otherwise have with maintaining the on-premises infrastructure accommodating such features.

This chapter will introduce you to **Amazon Web Service (AWS)** and **Microsoft Azure** – two major public cloud providers – and offer some practical guidance for deploying your applications in the cloud. In particular, we'll focus on typical cloud management workloads, using both the web administration console and the command-line interface.

By the end of this chapter, you'll know how to use the AWS web console and the AWS CLI, as well as the Azure web portal and the Azure CLI, to manage your cloud resources with the two most popular cloud providers of our time. You'll also learn how to make a prudent decision about creating and launching your resources in the cloud, striking a sensible balance between performance and cost.

We hope that Linux administrators – novice and experienced alike – will find the content in this chapter relevant and refreshing. Our focus is purely practical as we explore the AWS and Azure cloud workloads. We will refrain from comparing the two since such an endeavor would go beyond this chapter's scope. To make the journey less boring, we'll also steer away from keeping a perfect symmetry between describing AWS and Azure management tasks. We all know AWS blazed the trail into the public cloud realm first. Other major cloud providers followed, adopted, and occasionally improved the underlying paradigms and workflows. Since we'll be introducing AWS first, we'll cover more ground on some cloud provisioning concepts (such as Regions and **Availability Zones (AZs)**), which in many ways are very similar to what's available in Azure.

Finally, we'll leave the ultimate choice between using AWS or Azure up to you. We're giving you the map. The road is yours to take.

Here are some of the key topics you'll learn about:

- Working with AWS EC2
- Working with Microsoft Azure

Technical requirements

To complete the tasks in this chapter, you will require the following:

- AWS and Azure accounts if you want to follow along with the practical examples. Both cloud providers provide free subscriptions:

    - AWS free tier: `https://aws.amazon.com/free`

    - Microsoft Azure free account: `https://azure.microsoft.com/en-us/free/`

- A local machine with a Linux distribution of your choice to install and experiment with the AWS CLI and Azure CLI utilities.

- A modern web browser (such as Google Chrome or Mozilla Firefox) for the web-console-driven management tasks for both AWS and Azure. You can access the related portals on any platform.

- A Linux command-line terminal and intermediate-level proficiency using the shell to run the AWS and Azure CLI commands.

> **Important note**
> As you proceed, please make sure to shut down your EC2 instances or Azure virtual machines after you finish experimenting with them. Failure to do so may result in relatively high bills being generated for you.

With this, let's start with our first contender, AWS EC2.

Working with AWS EC2

AWS **Elastic Compute Cloud** (**EC2**) is a scalable computing infrastructure that allows users to lease virtual computing platforms and services to run their cloud applications. AWS EC2 has gained extreme popularity in recent years due to its outstanding performance and scalability combined with relatively cost-effective service plans. This section provides some basic functional knowledge to get you started with deploying and managing AWS EC2 instances running your applications. In particular, we'll introduce you to EC2 instance types, particularly how you can differentiate between various provisioning and related pricing tiers, how to use SSH to connect and SCP to transfer files to and from your EC2 instances, and how to work with the AWS CLI.

By the end of this section, you'll have a basic understanding of AWS EC2 and how to choose, deploy, and manage your EC2 instances.

Introducing and creating AWS EC2 instances

AWS EC2 provides various instance types, each with its provisioning, capacity, pricing, and use case models. Choosing between different EC2 instance types is not always trivial. This section will briefly describe each EC2 instance type, some pros and cons of using them, and how to choose the most cost-effective solution. With each instance type, we'll show you how to launch one using the AWS console.

We can look at EC2 instance types from two perspectives. When you decide on an EC2 instance, you'll have to consider both these factors. Let's look at each of these options briefly:

- **Provisioning**: The capacity and computing power of your EC2 instance. The main differentiating feature of each EC2 instance provisioning type is the computing power, which is expressed by vCPU (or CPU), memory (RAM), and storage (disk capacity).

  Some EC2 instance types also provide **graphical processing unit** (**GPU**) or **field programmable gate array** (**FPGA**) computing capabilities. A detailed view of EC2 instance provisioning types is beyond the scope of this chapter. You can explore the related information at `https://docs.aws.amazon.com/AWSEC2/latest/UserGuide/instance-types.html` or `https://aws.amazon.com/ec2/instance-types/`.

- **Pricing**: How much you pay for running your EC2 instance. At the time of writing, the EC2 instance types based on purchasing options are as follows:

  - **On-demand instances**: You pay for computing capacity per second, without long-term commitments

  - **Reserved instances**: These provide significant savings compared to on-demand instances if specific instance attributes are set for a long term, such as `type` and `region`

  - **Spot instances**: These EC2 instances are available for reuse at a lower price than on-demand instances

- **Dedicated instances**: These EC2 instances run in a **virtual private cloud** (**VPC**) assigned to a single-payer account

We'll cover each of these EC2 instance types in the following sections. For each of these types, we'll show an example of how to launch a corresponding instance.

However, before creating an instance, we'll look at another key concept regarding EC2 instances – **AZs**.

EC2 AZs

The AWS EC2 service is available in multiple locations around the globe, known as **Regions**. Here are some examples of Regions:

- **US West Oregon** (`us-west-2`)
- **Asia Pacific Mumbai** (`ap-south-1`)

EC2 defines multiple AZs in a Region, which are essentially one or more data centers. Regions are entirely isolated from each other in terms of the underlying infrastructure to provide fault tolerance and high availability. If a Region becomes unavailable, only the EC2 instances within the affected Region are unreachable. Other Regions with their EC2 instances will continue to work uninterrupted.

Similarly, AZs are connected while providing highly available and fault-tolerant EC2 services within a Region. Launching an EC2 instance creates it in the current Region selected in the AWS console. An AWS EC2 administrator may switch between different Regions when managing EC2 instances. Only instances within the selected Region are visible in the EC2 administration console. An EC2 administrator will usually choose a Region based on the geographical location of the users accessing the EC2 instance.

Now that we have preliminary knowledge of various EC2 instance types, let's look at on-demand instances.

EC2 on-demand instances

AWS EC2 **on-demand instances** use a *pay-as-you-go* pricing model for resource usage per second, without a long-time contract. On-demand instances are best suited for experimenting with uncertain workloads where the resource usage is not fully known (such as during development). The flexibility of these on-demand instances comes with a higher price than reserved instances, for example.

Let's launch an on-demand instance:

1. First, we must log into our AWS account console at `https://console.aws.amazon.com`. The following screenshot shows the default console view, where you will have information about the user (**1**), the Region (**2**), and the available – or recently visited – services (**3**):

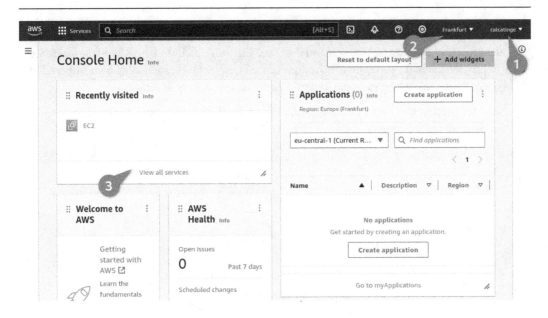

Figure 15.1 – The AWS management console

2. Next, we must select the EC2 service from the list on the left-hand side, as shown in the preceding screenshot. This will lead us to the EC2 dashboard interface, as follows:

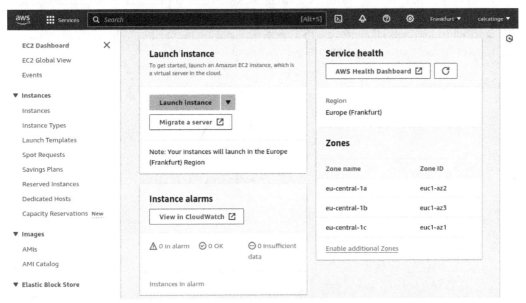

Figure 15.2 – The EC2 dashboard

The **Launch instance** button, as shown in the preceding screenshot, will begin the step-by-step process of creating our on-demand instance. This will lead us to a new interface where we can provide the main configuration options on our new instance, such as its name, operating system to use, instance type, login key pair, network, and storage settings.

3. Next, we need to choose a name and a tag. First, we will choose a name for our instance. In our case, we set the name to `aws_packt_testing_1`:

Launch an instance Info

Amazon EC2 allows you to create virtual machines, or instances, that run on the AWS Cloud. Quickly get started by following the simple steps below.

Name and tags Info

Name

| aws_packt_testing_1 | Add additional tags |

Figure 15.3 – Giving a name to the new EC2 instance

Alternatively, we can add a new tag. To do this, we must click **Add additional tags** to the right of the EC2 instance's name. Now, we can define key-value pairs to label or identify our instance. When we manage many EC2 instances, tags will help with user-friendly finding and filtering operations. For example, if we want to identify our EC2 instance as part of a *Packt* environment, we may create a tag with a key of `env` and a value of `packt`. We can add multiple tags (key-value pairs) to a given instance if we need to:

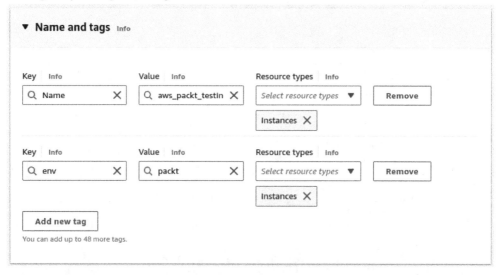

Figure 15.4 – Adding tags to an EC2 instance

4. Next, we must choose an operating system. We'll select Ubuntu 22.04 LTS as our Linux distribution for the new EC2 instance, as shown in the following screenshot:

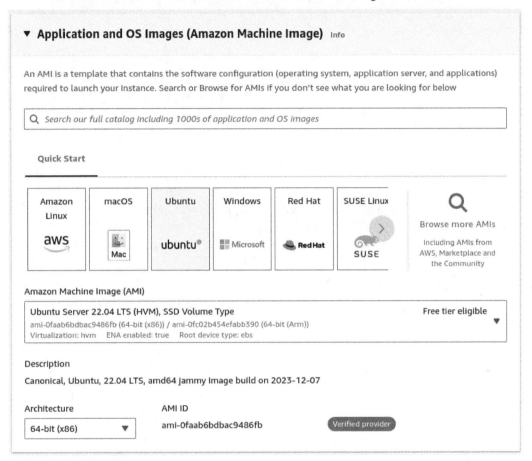

Figure 15.5 – Choosing the operating system for the EC2 instance

There are other operating systems to choose from, including macOS, Microsoft Windows, and Linux distributions such as Red Hat Enterprise Linux, SUSE Linux Enterprise, or Debian Linux, alongside Amazon Linux and Ubuntu.

5. Now, we can choose an instance type. Here, we'll select the instance type based on our provisioning needs. In our case, we will select the **t2.micro** type, with 1 vCPU and 1 GB of memory:

Figure 15.6 – Choosing an instance type – the t2.micro

6. Under **Network settings**, we will leave the default settings unchanged for now:

Figure 15.7 – Setting up the network for the new EC2 instance

7. The next step is to configure storage. By default, the EC2 instance provides an 8 GB SSD volume, but you can set it up to 30 GB while using the free tier. We will use it with the default 8 GB:

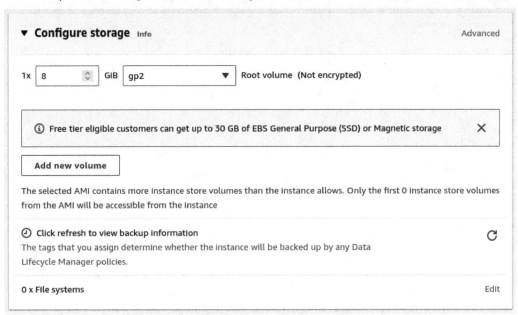

Figure 15.8 – Setting up storage for the EC2 instance

8. The last step before launching the new EC2 instance is to review the detailed summary provided and decide if there are any other changes to be made. Once the new instance has been tailored to our needs, we can create it by clicking on the **Launch instance** button, as shown in the following screenshot:

Figure 15.9 – Summary of the new EC2 instance and the Launch instance button

At this point, we are ready to launch our instance by pressing the **Launch instance** button. Alternatively, we could follow further configuration steps by revisiting the previous steps; otherwise, EC2 will assign some default values.

9. When launching the EC2 instance, we will be asked to create or select a certificate key pair for remote SSH access into our instance. This will highlight the key pair section on the screen, where we can click on the **Create new key pair** link. We will name the new key pair packt_ aws_key, select the **RSA** type and the **.pem** file format, and then click on the **Create key pair** button in the lower right corner:

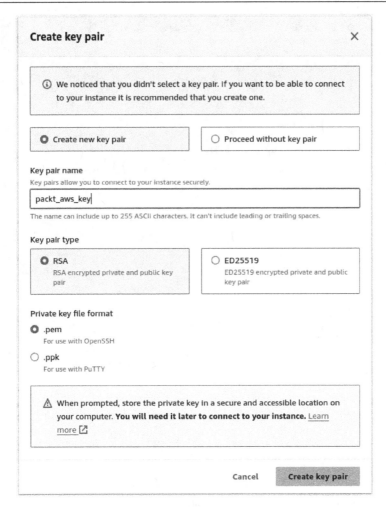

Figure 15.10 – Selecting or creating a certificate key pair for SSH access

You will be automatically asked to download the new .pem file to a location on your local machine.

10. Download the related file (packt-ec2.pem) to a secure location on your local machine, where you can use it with the ssh command to access your EC2 instance:

```
ssh -i aws/packt-ec2.pem ec2-user@EC2_INSTANCE
```

We'll look at how to connect via SSH to our EC2 instances later in this chapter.

11. Clicking the **Launch instance** button will create and launch our EC2 instance. The next screen will show a **View Instances** button, which will take you to the EC2 dashboard and show your instances in the current Region. You may also filter the view based on various instance properties, including tags. For example, by filtering by the env: packt tag, we'll get a view of the EC2 instance we just created:

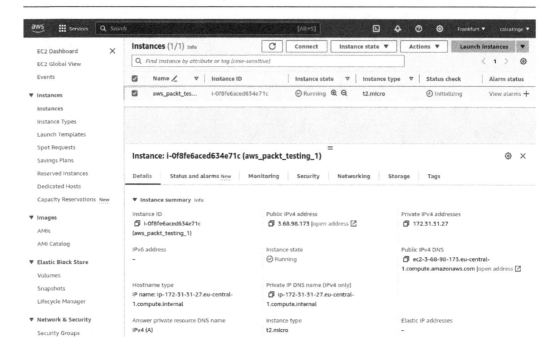

Figure 15.11 – An EC2 instance in the running state

For more information about on-demand instances, please visit `https://docs.aws.amazon.com/AWSEC2/latest/UserGuide/ec2-on-demand-instances.html`.

Now that we have learned the basics of launching an on-demand instance, let's look at reserved instances.

EC2 reserved instances

With **reserved instances**, we lease the EC2 computing capacity of a specific type for a specific amount of time. This length of time is called a **term** and can either be a 1-year or a 3-year commitment. Here are the main characteristics that need to be set upfront when purchasing reserved instances, as shown in *Figure 15.12*:

- **Platform**: An example of this is **Linux**.

- **Tenancy**: Running on **Default** (shared) or **Dedicated** hardware.

- **Offering Class**: These are the types of reserved instances that are available. The options are as follows:

    - **Standard**: A plain reserved instance with a well-defined set of options

    - **Convertible**: It allows specific changes, such as modifying the instance type (for example, from **t2.large** to **t2.xlarge**)

- **Instance Type**: An example of this is **t2.large**.

- **Term**: For example, **1 year.**

- **Payment option: All upfront, Partial upfront, No upfront.**

With each of these options and the different tiers within, your costs depend on the cloud computing resources involved and the duration of the service. For example, if you choose to pay all upfront, you'll get a better discount than otherwise. Choosing from among the options previously mentioned is ultimately an exercise in cost-saving and flexibility.

A close analogy to purchasing reserved instances is a *mobile telephone plan* – you decide on all the options you want, and then you commit a certain amount of time. With reserved instances, you get less flexibility in terms of making changes, but with significant savings in cost – sometimes up to 75%, compared to on-demand instances.

To launch a reserved instance, go to your EC2 dashboard in the AWS console and choose **Reserved Instances** under **Instances** in the left panel, then click on the **Purchase Reserved Instances** button. Here is an example of purchasing a reserved EC2 instance:

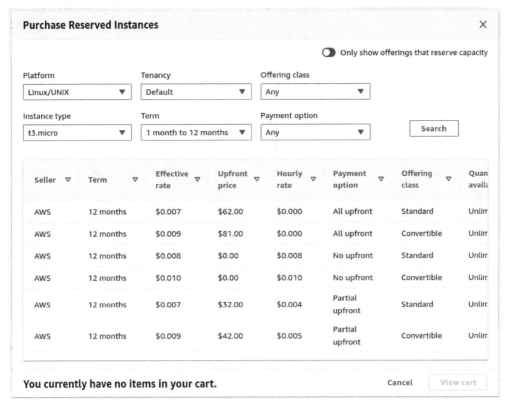

Figure 15.12 – Purchasing a reserved EC2 instance

For more information about EC2 reserved instances, please visit `https://docs.aws.amazon.com/AWSEC2/latest/UserGuide/ec2-reserved-instances.html`.

We have learned that reserved instances are a cost-effective alternative to on-demand EC2 instances. Now, let's take our journey further and look at yet another way to reduce the costs by using spot instances.

EC2 spot instances

A **spot instance** is an unused instance waiting to be leased. The amount of time a spot instance is vacant and at your disposal depends on the general availability of the requested capacity in EC2, given that the associated costs are not higher than the amount you are willing to pay for your spot instance. AWS advertises spot instances with an up to 90% discount compared to on-demand EC2 pricing.

The major caveat of using spot instances is the potential *no-vacancy* situation when the required capacity is no longer available at the initially agreed-upon rate. In such circumstances, the spot instance will shut down (and perhaps be leased elsewhere). AWS EC2 is kind enough to give a 2-minute warning before stopping the spot instance. This time should be used to properly tear down the application workflows running within the instance.

Spot instances are best suited for non-critical tasks, where application processing could be inadvertently interrupted at any moment and resumed later, without considerable damage or data loss. Such jobs may include data analysis, batch processing, and optional tasks.

To launch a spot instance, go to your **EC2** dashboard and choose **Spot Requests** in the left-hand menu. Under **Instances**, click on **Request Spot Instances** and follow the steps described in the *EC2 on-demand instances* section.

A detailed explanation of launching a spot instance is beyond the scope of this chapter. The AWS EC2 console does a great job of describing and assisting with the related options. For more information about spot instances, please visit `https://docs.aws.amazon.com/AWSEC2/latest/UserGuide/using-spot-instances.html`.

We know that by default, EC2 instances run on shared hardware, meaning that instances owned by multiple AWS customers share the same machine (or virtual machine). But what if you wanted to have a dedicated platform to run your EC2 instances? We'll look at dedicated instances next.

EC2 dedicated instances

Specific businesses require applications to run on dedicated hardware without them sharing the platform with anyone. AWS EC2 provides **dedicated hosts** and **dedicated instances** to accommodate this use case. As you may expect, dedicated instances would cost more than other instance types. So, why should we care about leasing such instances?

There are businesses – especially among financial, health, and governmental institutions – required by law to meet strict regulatory requirements for processing sensitive data or to acquire hardware-based licenses for running their applications.

With dedicated instances *without* a dedicated host, EC2 would guarantee that your applications run on a hypervisor exclusively dedicated to you, yet it would not enforce a fixed set of machines or hardware. In other words, some of your instances may run on different physical hosts. Choosing a dedicated host in addition to dedicated instances would always warrant a fully dedicated environment – hypervisors and hosts – for running your applications exclusively, without sharing the underlying platforms with other AWS customers.

To launch a dedicated instance, you can follow these steps:

1. Start with the same steps that you performed for launching an on-demand EC2 instance that were described earlier in this chapter, in the *EC2 on-demand instances* section.

2. You can add another step to the launching process. To do this, you must open the **Advanced details** drop-down section and scroll to the **Tenancy** option, where you must choose **Dedicated – run a dedicated instance**, as shown in the following screenshot:

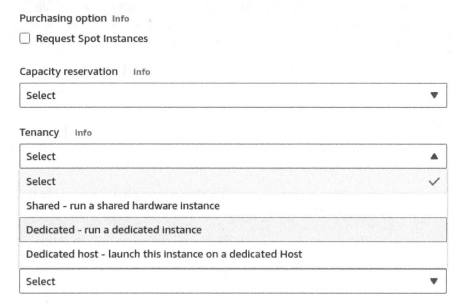

Figure 15.13 – Launching a dedicated EC2 instance

3. If you want to run your dedicated instance on a dedicated host, you must create a dedicated host first. To do this, on the **EC2** dashboard, navigate to **Instances | Dedicated Hosts**:

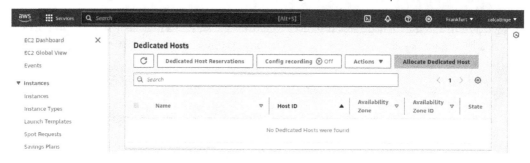

Figure 15.14 – Creating a dedicated EC2 host

4. Follow the EC2 wizard to allocate your dedicated host according to your preferences. After creating your host, you may launch your dedicated instance as described previously and choose the **Dedicated host – launch this instance on a dedicated Host** option for **Tenancy**, as shown in *step 2*.

For more information on dedicated hosts, please visit `https://aws.amazon.com/ec2/dedicated-hosts/`. For dedicated instances, see `https://aws.amazon.com/ec2/pricing/dedicated-instances/`.

We'll conclude our journey through AWS EC2 instance types here. For more information, please visit `https://docs.aws.amazon.com/AWSEC2/latest/UserGuide/Instances.html`.

Next, we'll look at one of the two essential EC2 deployment features that allow you to be proficient and resourceful when deploying and scaling your EC2 instances – **Amazon Machine Images** (**AMIs**) and **placement groups**. We will only discuss placement groups in this chapter. For more information about AMIs, please visit `https://docs.aws.amazon.com/AWSEC2/latest/UserGuide/AMIs.html`. Placement groups control how your instances are spread across the EC2 infrastructure for high availability and optimized workloads. We'll discuss this next.

Introducing AWS EC2 placement groups

Placement groups allow you to specify how your EC2 instances are placed across the underlying EC2 hardware or hypervisors, providing strategies to group or separate instances depending on your requirements. Placement groups are offered free of charge.

There are three types of placement groups to choose from. Let's quickly go through each of these types and look at their use cases:

- **Cluster placement groups**: With cluster placement groups, instances are placed within a single AZ (data center). They are best suited for low-latency, high-throughput communication between instances, but not with the outside world. Applications with high-performance computing or data replication would greatly benefit from cluster placement, but web servers, for example, not so much.

- **Spread placement groups**: When you launch multiple EC2 instances, there's always a possibility that they may end up running on the same physical machine or hypervisor. This may not be desirable when a single point of failure (such as hardware) would be critical for your applications. Spread placement groups provide hardware isolation between instances. In other words, if you launch multiple instances in a spread placement group, there's a guarantee that they will run on separate physical machines. In the rare case of an EC2 hardware failure, only one of your instances would be affected.

- **Partition placement groups**: Partition placement groups will group your instances in logical formations (partitions) with hardware isolation between the partitions, but not at the instance level. We can view this model as a hybrid between the cluster and spread placement groups. When you launch multiple instances within a partition placement group, EC2 will do its best to distribute the instances between partitions evenly. For example, if you had four partitions and 12 instances, EC2 would place three instances in each node (partition). We can look at a partition as a computing unit made of multiple instances. In the case of a hardware failure, the isolated partition instances can still communicate with each other but not across partitions. Partition placement groups support up to seven instances in a single logical partition.

To create a placement group, navigate to **Network & Security | Placement Groups** in your **EC2** dashboard's left menu and click on the **Create Placement Group** button. On the next screen, you must specify a name for the **Placement Group** option, as well as a **Placement Strategy** value. Optionally, you can add tags (key-value pairs) for organizing or identifying your placement group. When you're done, click the **Create group** button:

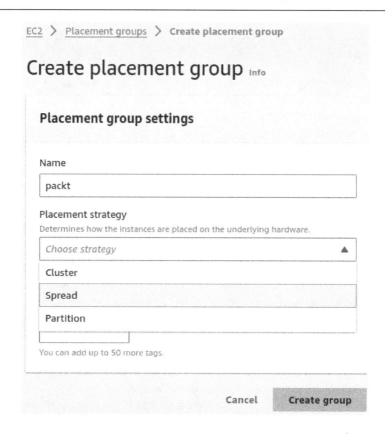

Figure 15.15 – Creating a placement group

For more information on EC2 placement groups, please visit `https://docs.aws.amazon.com/AWSEC2/latest/UserGuide/placement-groups.html`.

Now that we are familiar with various EC2 instance types, let's look at how to use our instances.

Using AWS EC2 instances

In this section, we'll briefly go through some essential operations and management concepts regarding your instances. First, we'll look at the life cycle of an EC2 instance.

The life cycle of an EC2 instance

When using or managing EC2 instances, it is important to understand the transitional stages, from launch to running to hibernation, shutdown, or termination. Each of these states affects billing and the way we access our instances:

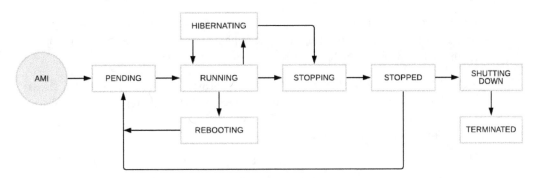

Figure 15.16 – The life cycle of an EC2 instance

Let's break this down:

- The **PENDING** state corresponds to the boot-up and initialization phase of our instance.

- Transitioning from **PENDING** to **RUNNING** is not always immediate, and it may take a while for the applications running within the instance to become responsive. EC2 starts billing our instance in the **RUNNING** state until transitioning to the **STOPPED** state.

- In the **RUNNING** state, we can reboot our instance if needed. During the **REBOOTING** state, EC2 always brings back our instance on the same host, whereas stopping and restarting doesn't always guarantee the same host for the instance.

- In the **STOPPED** state, we'll no longer be charged for the instance, but there will be costs related to any additional storage (other than the root volume) attached to the instance.

- When the instance is no longer required, we may choose between the **STOPPING** or **HIBERNATING** states. With **HIBERNATING**, we avoid the **PENDING** state's potential latency upon startup. If we no longer use the instance, we may decide to terminate it. Upon termination, there are no more charges related to the instance. When terminating an instance, it may still show up for a little while in the EC2 dashboard before it gets permanently removed.

We can connect to an EC2 instance in a running state using SSH. In the next section, we'll show you how.

Connecting to AWS EC2 instances

EC2 instances, in general, serve the purpose of running a specific application or a group of applications. The related platform's administration and maintenance usually require terminal access. The way to access these instances (or any other service) is determined by how AWS differentiates the available services into two different concepts, similar to the ones used in networking – control plane and data plane. These are concepts that represent how EC2 instances can be accessed:

- **Control plane (or management plane) access**: Using the AWS EC2 console and the SSH terminal, we perform administrative tasks on EC2 instances.

- **Data plane access**: Applications running on EC2 instances may also expose their specific endpoints (ports) for communicating with the outside world. EC2 uses security groups to control the related network traffic.

In this section, we'll briefly look at both control plane and data plane access. In particular, we'll discuss how to connect to an EC2 instance using SSH and how to use SCP for file transfer with EC2 instances.

Connecting via SSH to an EC2 instance

In control plane access mode, using SSH with our EC2 instance allows us to manage it like any on-premises machine on a network. The related SSH command is as follows:

```
ssh -i SSH_KEY ec2-user@EC2_INSTANCE
```

Let's break this down to understand it better:

- SSH_KEY represents the private key file on our local system that we created and downloaded when launching our instance. See the *EC2 on-demand instances* section for more details.

- ec2-user is the default user assigned by EC2 to our AMI Linux instance. Different AMIs may have different usernames to connect with. You should check with the AMI vendor of your choice about the default username to use with SSH. For example, when using **Amazon Linux**, the default username is ec2-user, when using **Ubuntu**, the default username is ubuntu, and when using **Debian**, the default username is admin.

- EC2_INSTANCE represents the public IP address or DNS name of our EC2 instance. You can find this in the EC2 dashboard for your instance:

Figure 15.17 – The public IP address and DNS name of an EC2 instance

In our case, the SSH command is as follows:

```
ssh -i packt_aws_key.pem ubuntu@3.68.98.173
```

However, before we connect, we need to set the right permissions for our `private key` file so that it's not publicly viewable:

```
chmod 400 packt_aws_key.pem
```

Failing to do this results in an unprotected key file error while attempting to connect.

A successful SSH connection to our EC2 instance yields the following output:

```
alexandru@debian:~$ chmod 400 packt_aws_key.pem
alexandru@debian:~$ ssh -i packt_aws_key.pem ubuntu@3.68.98.173
The authenticity of host '3.68.98.173 (3.68.98.173)' can't be established.
ED25519 key fingerprint is SHA256:OQpr2IsZyLfOvK9tLbikCGlbT5gU6qNI+S5ii6tcZUc.
This key is not known by any other names.
Are you sure you want to continue connecting (yes/no/[fingerprint])? yes
Warning: Permanently added '3.68.98.173' (ED25519) to the list of known hosts.
Welcome to Ubuntu 22.04.3 LTS (GNU/Linux 6.2.0-1017-aws x86_64)

 * Documentation:  https://help.ubuntu.com
 * Management:     https://landscape.canonical.com
 * Support:        https://ubuntu.com/advantage

  System information as of Tue Jan 16 09:35:00 UTC 2024

  System load:  0.0              Processes:             98
  Usage of /:   24.7% of 7.57GB  Users logged in:       0
  Memory usage: 23%              IPv4 address for eth0: 172.31.31.27
  Swap usage:   0%
```

Figure 15.18 – Connecting with SSH to an EC2 instance

At this point, we can interact with our EC2 instance as if it were a standard machine.

Next, let's look at how to transfer files from an EC2 instance.

Using SCP for file transfer

To transfer files to and from an EC2 instance in data plane access mode, we must use the `scp` utility. `scp` uses the **Secure Copy Protocol (SCP)** to securely transfer files between network hosts.

The following command copies a local file (`README.md`) to our remote EC2 instance (so it must be run from our machine, not the EC2 instance):

```
scp -i packt_aws_key.pem README.md ubuntu@3.68.98.173:~/
```

The file is copied to the `ubuntu` user's home folder (`/home/ubuntu`) on the EC2 instance. The reverse operation of transferring the `README.md` file from the remote instance to our local directory is as follows:

```
scp -i packt_aws_key.pem ubuntu@3.68.98.173:~/README.md .
```

Note that the `scp` command's invocation is similar to `ssh`, where we specify the private key file (`aws/packt-ec2.pem`) via the `-i` (identity file) parameter.

Next, we'll look at yet another critical aspect of managing and scaling EC2 instances – storage volumes.

Using EC2 storage volumes

Storage volumes are device mounts within an EC2 instance that provide additional disk capacity (at extra cost). You may need additional storage for large file caches or extensive logging, for example, or you may choose to mount network-attached storage for critical data shared between your EC2 instances. You can think of EC2 storage volumes as *modular hard drives*. You mount or unmount them based on your needs.

Two types of storage volumes are provided by EC2:

- **Instance store**
- **Elastic Block Store (EBS)**

Knowing how to use storage volumes allows you to make better decisions when scaling your applications as they grow. Let's look at instance store volumes first.

Introducing instance store volumes

Instance store volumes are disks that are directly (physically) attached to your EC2 instance. Consequently, the maximum size and number of instance store volumes you can connect to your instance are limited by the instance type. For example, a storage-optimized *i3* instance can have up to 8 x 1.9 TB SSD disks attached, while a general-purpose *m5d* instance may only grow up to four drives of 900 GB each. See `https://aws.amazon.com/ec2/instance-types/` for more information on instance capacity.

An instance store volume comes at no additional cost if it's the root volume – the volume with the operating system platform booting the instance.

Not all EC2 instance types support instance store volumes. For example, the general-purpose *t2* instance types only support EBS storage volumes. On the other hand, if you want to grow your storage beyond the maximum capacity allowed by the instance store, you'll have to use EBS volumes. We'll look at EBS volumes next.

Introducing EBS volumes

The data on instance store volumes only persists with your EC2 instance. If your instance stops or terminates, or there is a failure with it, all of your data is lost. To store and persist critical data with your EC2 instances, you'll have to choose EBS.

EBS volumes are flexible and high-performing network-attached storage devices that serve both the root volume system and additional volume mounts on your EC2 instance. An EBS root volume can only be attached to a single EC2 instance at a time while an EC2 instance can have multiple EBS volumes attached at any time. An EBS volume can also be attached to multiple EC2 instances at a time via *multi-attach*. For more information on EBS multi-attach, see `https://docs.aws.amazon.com/AWSEC2/latest/UserGuide/ebs-volumes-multi.html`.

When you create an EBS volume, it will be automatically replicated within the AZ of your instance to minimize latency and data loss. With EBS, you get live monitoring of drive health and stats via Amazon CloudWatch free of charge. EBS also supports encrypted data storage to meet the latest regulatory standards for data encryption.

EC2 storage volumes are backed by Amazon's **Simple Storage Service (S3)** or **Elastic File System (EFS)** infrastructure. For more information on the different EC2 storage types, please visit `https://docs.aws.amazon.com/AWSEC2/latest/UserGuide/Storage.html`.

Now, let's create and configure an EBS storage volume and attach it to our EC2 instance.

Configuring an EBS storage volume

Here are the steps we'll follow, starting with creating the EBS volume:

1. In the **EC2** dashboard, go to **Volumes** under **Elastic Block Store** in the left navigation pane, and click on the **Create Volume** button at the top:

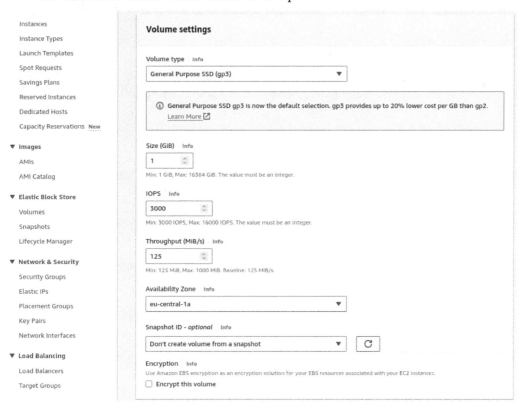

Figure 15.19 – Creating an EBS volume

2. Enter the values of your choice for **Volume Type, Size**, and **Availability Zone**. Make sure you choose the AZ where your EC2 instances are. You could also include a **Snapshot ID** value if you want to restore the volume from a previous EC2 instance backup (snapshot). We'll look at backup/restore using EBS snapshots later in this chapter.

3. Press the **Create Volume** button when you're done. You'll get a **Volume created successfully** message that specifies your new EBS volume ID if all goes well.

4. Click on **Volume ID** or select the volume from the left navigation pane, under **Elastic Block Store** and **Volumes**. Click on the **Actions** button and choose **Attach Volume**:

Figure 15.20 – Attaching the EBS volume to an EC2 instance

5. On the next screen, enter your EC2 instance ID (or name tag to search for it) in the **Instance** field:

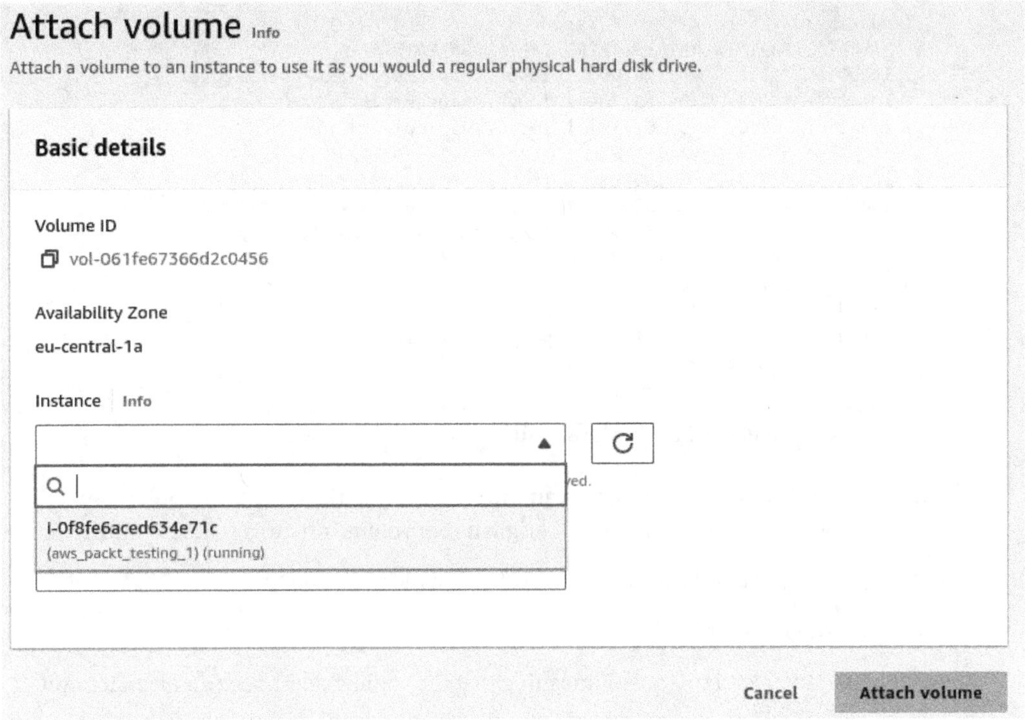

Attach volume Info

Attach a volume to an instance to use it as you would a regular physical hard disk drive.

Basic details

Volume ID

vol-061fe67366d2c0456

Availability Zone

eu-central-1a

Instance   Info

🔍 |

i-0f8fe6aced634e71c
(aws_packt_testing_1) (running)

Cancel   **Attach volume**

Figure 15.21 – Entering the EC2 instance ID to attach the volume

6. Press the **Attach volume** button when you're done. After a few moments, EC2 will initialize your EBS volume, and **State** will change to **in-use**. The volume device is now ready, but we need to format it with a filesystem so that it can be used.

7. Let's SSH into the EC2 instance where we attached the volume:

```
ssh -i packt_aws_key.pem ubuntu@3.68.98.173
```

8. Next, we must retrieve the drives that are available in our EC2 instance using the `lsblk` command-line utility to list the block devices:

```
lsblk
```

The output is as follows:

```
ubuntu@ip-172-31-31-27:~$ lsblk
NAME       MAJ:MIN RM    SIZE RO TYPE MOUNTPOINTS
loop0          7:0  0   24.9M  1 loop /snap/amazon-ssm-agent/7628
loop1          7:1  0   55.7M  1 loop /snap/core18/2812
loop2          7:2  0   63.5M  1 loop /snap/core20/2015
loop3          7:3  0  111.9M  1 loop /snap/lxd/24322
loop4          7:4  0   40.9M  1 loop /snap/snapd/20290
loop5          7:5  0   63.9M  1 loop /snap/core20/2105
loop6          7:6  0   40.4M  1 loop /snap/snapd/20671
xvda         202:0  0      8G  0 disk
├─xvda1      202:1  0    7.9G  0 part /
├─xvda14     202:14 0      4M  0 part
└─xvda15     202:15 0    106M  0 part /boot/efi
xvdf         202:80 0      1G  0 disk
ubuntu@ip-172-31-31-27:~$
```

Figure 15.22 – The local volumes in our EC2 instance

Looking at the size of the volumes, we can immediately tell the one we just added – xvdf with 1G. The other volume (xvda) is the original root volume of our t3.micro instance.

9. Now, let's check if our new EBS volume (xvdf) has a filesystem on it:

    sudo file -s /dev/xvdf

    The output is /dev/xvdf: data, meaning that the volume doesn't have a filesystem yet.

10. Let's build a filesystem on our volume using the mkfs (*make filesystem*) command-line utility:

    sudo mkfs -t xfs /dev/xvdf

    Here, we invoke the -t (--type) parameter with an xfs filesystem type. XFS is a high-performance journaled filesystem that's supported by most Linux distributions and is installed by default in some of them.

11. If we check the filesystem using the following command, we should see the filesystem details displayed instead of empty data:

    sudo file -s /dev/xvdf

The output of all the commands used to check and create a new filesystem is shown in the following screenshot:

```
ubuntu@ip-172-31-31-27:~$ sudo file -s /dev/xvdf
/dev/xvdf: data
ubuntu@ip-172-31-31-27:~$ sudo mkfs -t xfs /dev/xvdf
meta-data=/dev/xvdf              isize=512    agcount=4, agsize=65536 blks
         =                       sectsz=512   attr=2, projid32bit=1
         =                       crc=1        finobt=1, sparse=1, rmapbt=0
         =                       reflink=1    bigtime=0 inobtcount=0
data     =                       bsize=4096   blocks=262144, imaxpct=25
         =                       sunit=0      swidth=0 blks
naming   =version 2              bsize=4096   ascii-ci=0, ftype=1
log      =internal log           bsize=4096   blocks=2560, version=2
         =                       sectsz=512   sunit=0 blks, lazy-count=1
realtime =none                   extsz=4096   blocks=0, rtextents=0
ubuntu@ip-172-31-31-27:~$ sudo file -s /dev/xvdf
/dev/xvdf: SGI XFS filesystem data (blksz 4096, inosz 512, v2 dirs)
ubuntu@ip-172-31-31-27:~$
```

Figure 15.23 – Creating a new filesystem

The volume drive is now formatted.

12. Now, let's make it accessible to our local filesystem. We'll name our mount point `packt_drive` and create it in the root directory:

```
sudo mkdir /packt_drive
sudo mount /dev/xvdf /packt_drive
```

At this point, the EBS volume is mounted. Now, when we access the /packt directory, we're accessing the EBS volume:

```
ubuntu@ip-172-31-31-27:~$ sudo mkdir /packt_drive
ubuntu@ip-172-31-31-27:~$ sudo mount /dev/xvdf /packt_drive
ubuntu@ip-172-31-31-27:~$ cd /packt_drive/
ubuntu@ip-172-31-31-27:/packt_drive$ sudo touch README.md
ubuntu@ip-172-31-31-27:/packt_drive$ ls -la .
total 4
drwxr-xr-x  2 root root   23 Jan 16 17:03 .
drwxr-xr-x 20 root root 4096 Jan 16 17:02 ..
-rw-r--r--  1 root root    0 Jan 16 17:03 README.md
ubuntu@ip-172-31-31-27:/packt_drive$
```

Figure 15.24 – Accessing the EBS volume

Working with EBS volumes is similar to working with any volumes on Linux, so all the knowledge you've received from this chapter will be very useful when you're working with Amazon EC2 instances. Now, let's look at how to detach an EBS volume.

Detaching an EBS volume

Before detaching any EBS volume, you need to unmount it. In our case, as we are already in the terminal and using the volume, we will type the following command to unmount the volume we use:

```
sudo umount -d /dev/xvdf
```

Now that the volume has been unmounted, we can head to the EC2 dashboard and go to **Volumes**, select the corresponding **in-use** volume we want to detach, go to **Actions** in the top-right corner, and choose **Detach Volume**. Acknowledge the operation and wait for the volume to be detached.

We're now at the final step of our backup-restore procedure – that is, attaching the new volume containing the snapshot to our EC2 instance.

We'll conclude our exploration of the AWS EC2 console and related management operations here. For a comprehensive reference on EC2, please refer to the Amazon EC2 documentation at `https://docs.aws.amazon.com/ec2`.

The EC2 management tasks we've presented so far exclusively used the AWS web console. If you're looking to automate your EC2 workloads, you may want to adopt the AWS CLI, which we'll check out next.

Working with the AWS CLI

The AWS CLI is a unified tool for managing AWS resources. This tool was created so that we can manage all the AWS services from a terminal session on our local machine. Compared to the AWS web console, which offers visual tools through the web browser, the AWS CLI (as its name states) offers all the functionalities inside your terminal program on your machine. The AWS CLI is available for all major operating systems, such as Linux, macOS, and Windows. In the next section, we will show you how to install it on your Linux local machine.

Installing the AWS CLI

To install the AWS CLI, please visit `https://aws.amazon.com/cli/`. At the time of writing, the latest release of the AWS CLI is version 2. For the examples in this chapter, we'll be using a Debian machine to install the AWS CLI while following the instructions at `https://docs.aws.amazon.com/cli/latest/userguide/getting-started-install.html#cliv2-linux-install`. This resource link offers instructions for installing the AWS CLI on all major operating systems, not only Linux.

Follow these steps to install the AWS CLI on Linux:

1. We'll start by downloading the AWS CLI v2 package (`awscliv2.zip`):

    ```
    curl "https://awscli.amazonaws.com/awscli-exe-linux-x86_64.zip"
    -o "awscliv2.zip"
    ```

2. Next, we'll unzip and install the AWS CLI:

```
unzip awscliv2.zip
sudo ./aws/install
```

3. We should now have the `aws` command-line utility installed on our system. Let's check the version:

```
aws --version
```

In our case, the output shows that the version of the package is 2.15.10 at the time of writing.

4. You can start exploring the AWS CLI by invoking `help`:

```
aws help
```

To manage your AWS EC2 resources using the `aws` utility, first, you need to configure your local environment to establish the required trust with the AWS endpoint. We'll do that next.

Configuring the AWS CLI

To configure the local AWS environment on your local machine, you will have to set up your AWS access key. If you already have it, you can skip this part:

1. The AWS CLI configuration asks for your **AWS Access Key ID** and **AWS Secret Access Key** values. You can generate or retrieve these keys by logging into your AWS account.

2. Select the dropdown next to your account name in the top-right corner of the AWS web console and choose **Security Credentials**. If you haven't generated your access key yet, go to the **Access keys** tab and click on the **Create access key** button. You'll have to store your AWS key ID and secret in a safe place for later reuse.

3. Now that you have those keys, you can proceed to setting up AWS on your local machine. To configure the AWS environment, run the following command:

```
aws configure
```

The preceding command will prompt you for a few pieces of information, as suggested by the following output:

```
alexandru@debian:~$ aws configure
AWS Access Key ID [None]:
AWS Secret Access Key [None]:
Default region name [None]: eu-central-1
Default output format [None]:
```

Figure 15.25 – Configuring the local AWS CLI environment

4. In the AWS CLI configuration wizard, set **Default region name** to eu-central-1 (Frankfurt, in our case). You may want to enter the region of your choice or leave it as the default (None). If you don't have a default Region specified, you'll have to enter it every time you invoke the `aws` command.

At this point, we're ready to use the AWS CLI. Let's start by listing our EC2 instances.

Querying EC2 instances

The following command provides detailed information about EC2 instances:

```
aws ec2 describe-instances
```

The preceding command provides sizeable JSON output (too long to present in a screenshot), with the details of all the EC2 instances we own in our default Region (eu-central-1). Alternatively, we can specify the Region with the --region parameter:

```
aws ec2 describe-instances --region eu-central-1
```

We can get more creative and list only the EC2 instances matching a specific key-value tag, such as env: packt, that we previously tagged our instances with, using the --filters parameter:

```
aws ec2 describe-instances \
  --filters "Name=tag-key,Values=env" \
  --filters "Name=tag-value,Values=packt"
```

The first --filters parameter specifies the key (tag-key=env), while the second points to the value (tag-value=packt).

Combining the aws and jq (*JSON query*) commands, we can extract the JSON fields we want. For example, the following command lists the InstanceId, ImageId, and BlockDeviceMappings fields of the EC2 instances tagged with env:packt:

```
aws ec2 describe-instances \
  --filters "Name=tag-key,Values=env" \
  --filters "Name=tag-value,Values=packt" | \
  jq '.Reservations[].Instances[] | { InstanceId, ImageId,
BlockDeviceMappings }'
```

If the jq utility is not present on your Linux machine, install it with the following command:

```
sudo apt install -y jq # on Ubuntu/Debian
```

The output of the preceding `aws` command is as follows:

```
alexandru@debian:~$ aws ec2 describe-instances --filters "Name=tag-key,Values=env" --filters "Name=t
ag-value,Values=packt" | jq '.Reservations[].Instances[] | { InstanceId, ImageId, BlockDeviceMapping
s }'
{
  "InstanceId": "i-0f8fe6aced634e71c",
  "ImageId": "ami-0faab6bdbac9486fb",
  "BlockDeviceMappings": [
    {
      "DeviceName": "/dev/sda1",
      "Ebs": {
        "AttachTime": "2024-01-14T13:25:46+00:00",
        "DeleteOnTermination": true,
        "Status": "attached",
        "VolumeId": "vol-03d55241cf12c6772"
      }
    }
  ]
}
```

Figure 15.26 – Querying EC2 instances

Note the `DeviceName` properties in the output JSON, which reflect only one block device (this is `/dev/sdf` since we deleted the EBS volume we attached earlier).

We can filter the output of the `aws ec2 describe-instances` command by any property. For example, the following command filters our EC2 instances by the `image-id` AMI:

```
aws ec2 describe-instances \
  --filters "Name=image-id,Values=ami-0e999cbd62129e3b1"
```

Note that the property name that's used in the filter is a *hyphenated* transformation of the corresponding camel-cased JSON property: `image-id` versus `ImageId`. You have to keep this rule in mind when you write your filter queries.

Next, let's plan to launch a new EC2 instance of the same AMI type with our current machine and the same security group.

Creating an EC2 instance

Let's look at how we can create a new EC2 instance. To do this, we will need some prior information regarding the existing security group inside which we would like to create the new instance. The following command retrieves the security groups of the current instance (`i-0f8fe6aced634e71c`):

```
aws ec2 describe-instances \
  --filters "Name=instance-id,Values=i-0f8fe6aced634e71c" \
  --query "Reservations[].Instances[].SecurityGroups[]"
```

The output is as follows:

```
alexandru@debian:~$ aws ec2 describe-instances --filters "Name=instance-id,Values=i-0f8fe6aced634e71
c" --query "Reservations[].Instances[].SecurityGroups[]"
[
    {
        "GroupName": "launch-wizard-5",
        "GroupId": "sg-0aa7c8ef75503a9aa"
    }
]
```

Figure 15.27 – Retrieving the security groups of an EC2 instance

To retrieve `GroupId` directly, we could run the following:

```
aws ec2 describe-instances \
  --filters "Name=instance-id,Values=i-0f8fe6aced634e71c" \
  --query "Reservations[].Instances[].SecurityGroups[].GroupId"
```

In this case, the output would only show `GroupId`. Here, we used the `--query` parameter to specify the exact JSON path for the field we're looking for (`GroupId`):

```
Reservations[].Instances[].SecurityGroups[].GroupId
```

The use of the `--query` parameter somewhat resembles piping the output to the `jq` command, but it's less versatile.

We also need the AMI ID. To obtain this, navigate to your AWS EC2 console and then, from the left-hand side pane, go to **Images** | **AMI Catalog**. Look for **Ubuntu Server 22.04 LTS** and copy the AMI ID for the 64-bit version. In our case, it's `ami-0faab6bdbac9486fb`.

To launch a new instance with the AMI type of our choice and the security group ID, we must use the `aws ec2 run-instances` command:

```
aws ec2 run-instances --image-id ami-0faab6bdbac9486fb --count 1
--instance-type t3.micro --key-name packt_aws_key --security-group-ids
sg-0aa7c8ef75503a9aa –placement AvailabilityZone=eu-central-1b
```

Here's a brief explanation of the parameters:

- `image-id`: The AMI image ID (`ami-0faab6bdbac9486fb`); we're using the same AMI type (*Ubuntu Linux*) as with the previous instance we created in the AWS EC2 web console
- `count`: The number of instances to launch (`1`)
- `instance-type`: The EC2 instance type (`t3.micro`)
- `key-name`: The name of the SSH private key file (`packt_aws_key`) to use when connecting to our new instance; we're reusing the SSH key file we created with our first EC2 instance in the AWS web console

- `security-group-ids`: The security groups attached to our instance; we're reusing the security group attached to our current instance (`sg-0aa7c8ef75503a9aa`)

- `--placement`: The AZ to place our instance in (`AvailabilityZone=eu-central-1b`)

The command should run successfully and you will see the new EC2 instance running in your console. Here's a screenshot of our EC2 console and the two instances running:

Figure 15.28 – The new EC2 instance shown in the console

As you can see, our newly created EC2 instance has no name. Let's add a name and some tags to it using the command line.

Naming and tagging an EC2 instance

The following command names our new instance as `aws_packt_testing_2`:

```
aws ec2 create-tags --resources i-091e2f515d15c3b0b --tags
Key=Name,Value=aws_packt_testing_2
```

Now, we can add a tag to the new instance. Adding a name and a tag can be done in a single command, but for a better understanding, we've decided to use two different commands. Here's how to add a tag:

```
aws ec2 create-tags \
   --resources i-0e1692c9dfdf07a8d \
   --tags Key=env,Value=packt
```

Now, let's query the instance with the following command:

```
aws ec2 describe-instances \
   --filters "Name=tag-key,Values=env" \
   --filters "Name=tag-value,Values=packt" \
   --query "Reservations[].Instances[].InstanceId"
```

The output shows that our two EC2 instances have the same tag (`packt`):

```
alexandru@debian:~$ aws ec2 create-tags --resources i-091e2f515d15c3b0b --tags Key=Name,Value=aws_pa
ckt_testing_2
alexandru@debian:~$ aws ec2 create-tags --resources i-091e2f515d15c3b0b --tags Key=env,Value=packt
alexandru@debian:~$ aws ec2 describe-instances --filters "Name=tag-key,Values=env" --filters "Name=t
ag-value,Values=packt" --query "Reservations[].Instances[].InstanceId"
[
    "i-0f8fe6aced634e71c",
    "i-091e2f515d15c3b0b"
]
```

Figure 15.29 – Querying EC2 instance IDs by tag

If you check the EC2 console inside your browser, you will see the two instances. Now, the second instance has its new name shown (`aws_packt_testing_2`) and the **Instance ID** value for each one:

Figure 15.30 – Showing all instances in the EC2 console

Next, we'll show you how to terminate an EC2 instance from the command line.

Terminating an EC2 instance

To terminate an EC2 instance, we can use the `aws ec2 terminate-instance` command. Note that terminating an instance results in the instance being deleted. We cannot restart a terminated instance. We could use the `aws ec2 stop-instances` command to stop our instance until later use.

The following command will terminate the instance with the ID of `i-091e2f515d15c3b0b`:

```
aws ec2 terminate-instances --instance-ids i-091e2f515d15c3b0b
```

The output states that our instance is shutting-down (from a previously running state):

```
alexandru@debian:~$ aws ec2 terminate-instances --instance-ids i-091e2f515d15c3b0b
{
    "TerminatingInstances": [
        {
            "CurrentState": {
                "Code": 32,
                "Name": "shutting-down"
            },
            "InstanceId": "i-091e2f515d15c3b0b",
            "PreviousState": {
                "Code": 16,
                "Name": "running"
            }
        }
    ]
}
```

Figure 15.31 – Terminating an instance

The instance will eventually transition to the terminated state and will no longer be visible in the AWS EC2 console. The AWS CLI will still list it among the instances until EC2 finally disposes of it. According to AWS, terminated instances can still be visible up to an hour after termination. It's always a good practice to discard the instances in the terminated or shutting-down state when performing queries and management operations via the AWS CLI. The following screenshot of the EC2 console shows that the second EC2 instance is in a terminated state:

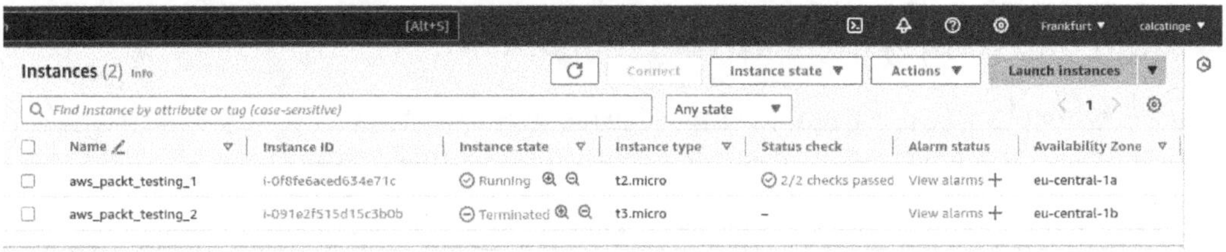

Figure 15.32 – Showing the terminated instance in the EC2 console

This is where we'll wrap up our journey regarding AWS EC2. Note that we've only scratched the surface of cloud management workloads in AWS.

The topics that were covered in this section provide a basic understanding of AWS EC2 cloud resources and help system administrators make better decisions when managing the related workloads. Power users may find the AWS CLI examples a good starting point for automating their cloud management workflows in EC2.

Now, let's turn our focus to our next public cloud services contender, Microsoft Azure.

Working with Microsoft Azure

Microsoft Azure, also known as **Azure**, is a public cloud service by Microsoft for building and deploying application services in the cloud. Azure provides a full offering of a highly scalable **Infrastructure-as-a-Service (IaaS)** at relatively low costs, accommodating a wide range of users and business requirements, from small teams to large commercial enterprises, including financial, health, and governmental institutions.

In this section, we'll explore some very basic deployment workflows using Azure, such as the following:

- Creating a Linux virtual machine
- Managing virtual machine sizes
- Adding additional storage to a virtual machine
- Working with the Azure CLI

Once you've created your free Azure account, go to `https://portal.azure.com` to access the Azure portal. You may want to enable the docked view of the portal navigation menu on the left for quick and easy access to your resources. Throughout this chapter, we'll use the docked view for our screen captures. Go to the **Portal settings** cog in the top-right corner and choose **Docked** for the default mode of the portal menu.

Now, let's create our first resource in Azure – an Ubuntu virtual machine.

Creating and deploying a virtual machine

We'll follow a step-by-step procedure, guided by the resource wizard in the Azure portal. Let's start with the first step, which is creating a compute resource for the virtual machine.

1. **Creating a compute resource**: Start by clicking on the **Create a resource** option in the left navigation menu or under **Azure services** in the main window. This will take us to the Azure Marketplace. Here, we can search for our resource of choice. You can either search for a relevant keyword or narrow down your selection based on the resource type you're looking for. Let's narrow down our selection by choosing **Compute**, then selecting **Ubuntu Server 22.04 LTS** from the available **Popular Marketplace products** options. You may click on **Learn more** for a detailed description of the image or click **Create**.

When we select **Ubuntu Server 22.04 LTS**, we'll be guided through the process of configuring and creating our new virtual machine. The setup page looks like this:

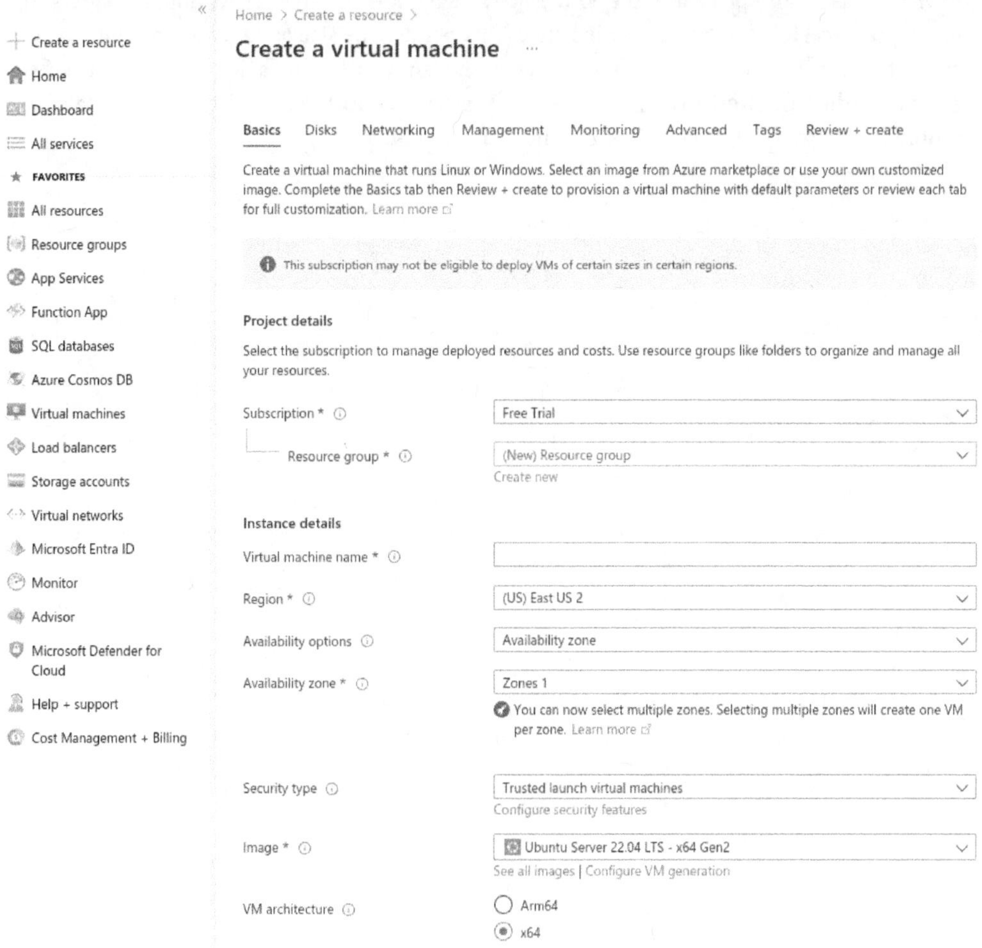

Figure 15.33 – Creating a virtual machine in Azure

In the **Basics** tab, information such as the subscription type, resource group, region, image, and architecture is provided. The other tabs include **Disks**, **Networking**, **Management**, **Monitoring**, **Advanced**, and **Tags**.

2. **Configuring a resource group**: First, we need to specify the **Subscription** and **Resource group** values associated with the virtual machine. An Azure resource group is a collection of assets related to a specific deployment, including storage, networking interfaces, security groups, and so on. Assuming this is our first virtual machine, we'll create a new resource group and name it `packt-demo`. If we had a previously created resource group, we could specify it here.

3. **Configuring instance details**: Next, we must set various properties related to our instance, such as **Virtual machine name**, **Region**, and **Size**. We'll name our virtual machine `packt-ubuntu-demo` and place it in the `(Europe) France Central` Region, the closest to the geographical location where our instance will operate. The size of our machine will directly impact the associated costs. The following screenshot shows the details that have been specified so far regarding the **Resource group** set up, **Virtual machine name**, **Region**, **Availability options**, **Security type**, **Image**, **VM architecture**, and **Size**:

Project details

Select the subscription to manage deployed resources and costs. Use resource groups like folders to organize and manage all your resources.

Subscription * ⓘ	Free Trial ⌄
Resource group * ⓘ	(New) packt-demo ⌄
	Create new

Instance details

Virtual machine name * ⓘ	packt-ubuntu-demo ✓
Region * ⓘ	(Europe) France Central ⌄
Availability options ⓘ	No infrastructure redundancy required ⌄
Security type ⓘ	Trusted launch virtual machines ⌄
	Configure security features
Image * ⓘ	⬚ Ubuntu Server 22.04 LTS - x64 Gen2 ⌄
	See all images | Configure VM generation
VM architecture ⓘ	◯ Arm64
	⦿ x64
Run with Azure Spot discount ⓘ	☐

> ⓘ You are in the free trial period. Costs associated with this VM can be covered by any remaining credits on your subscription. Learn more ⎘

Size * ⓘ	Standard_B1s - 1 vcpu, 1 GiB memory (€8.06/month) (free services eligible) ⌄
	See all sizes

Figure 15.34 – Setting up the Azure virtual machine

Alternatively, we could browse different options for **Image** and **Size** by choosing **See all images** or **See all sizes**, respectively. Azure also provides a *pricing calculator* online tool for various resources at `https://azure.microsoft.com/en-us/pricing/calculator/`.

4. **Configuring SSH access**: In this step, we'll enable SSH with public key authentication. We'll set **Username** to `packt` and **Key pair name** to `packt-ubuntu-demo_key`. Next, we must set **Inbound port rules** for our instance to allow SSH access. If, for example, our machine will run a web server application, we can also enable HTTP and HTTPS access:

Administrator account

Authentication type ⓘ	◉ SSH public key
	◯ Password

> ⓘ Azure now automatically generates an SSH key pair for you and allows you to store it for future use. It is a fast, simple, and secure way to connect to your virtual machine.

Username * ⓘ	packt
SSH public key source	Generate new key pair
Key pair name *	packt-ubuntu-demo_key

Inbound port rules

Select which virtual machine network ports are accessible from the public internet. You can specify more limited or granular network access on the Networking tab.

Public inbound ports * ⓘ	◯ None
	◉ Allow selected ports
Select inbound ports *	SSH (22)

> ⓘ All traffic from the internet will be blocked by default. You will be able to change inbound port rules in the VM > Networking page.

Figure 15.35 – Enabling SSH authentication and access to the virtual machine

At this point, we are ready to create our virtual machine. The wizard can take us further to the additional steps of specifying the *disks* and *networking* configuration associated with our instance. For now, we'll leave them as-is.

5. **Validating and deploying the virtual machine**: We can click the **Review + create** button to initiate the validation process. Next, the deployment wizard will validate our virtual machine configuration. In a few moments, if everything goes well, we'll get a **Validation passed** message specifying the product details and our instance's hourly rate. By clicking **Create**, we agree to the relevant terms of use, and our virtual machine will be deployed shortly:

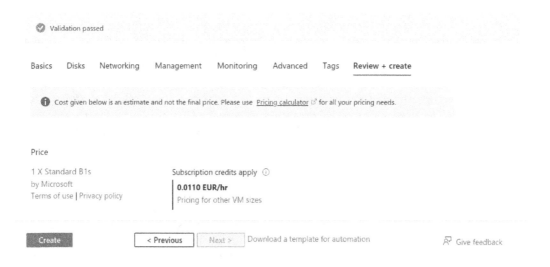

Figure 15.36 – Creating the virtual machine

In the process, we'll be prompted to download the SSH private key for accessing our instance:

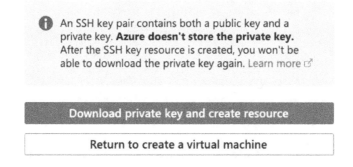

Figure 15.37 – Downloading the SSH private key for accessing the virtual machine

6. **Deployment completion**: If the deployment completes successfully, we'll get a brief pop-up message stating **Deployment succeeded** and a **Go to resource** button that will take us to our new virtual machine:

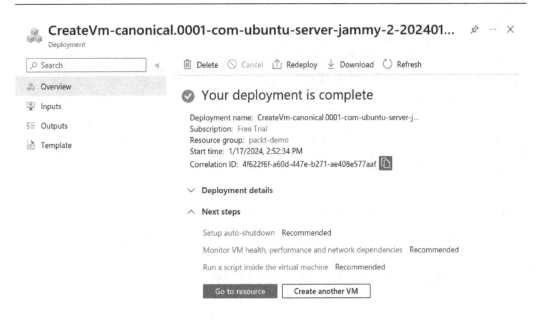

Figure 15.38 – Successfully deploying a virtual machine

We'll also get a brief report about the deployment details if we click on the relevant drop-down button:

∧ **Deployment details**

	Resource	Type	Status	Operation details
✓	packt-ubuntu-demo	Microsoft.Compute/vir...	OK	Operation details
✓	packt-ubuntu-demo348	Microsoft.Network/net...	Created	Operation details
✓	packt-ubuntu-demo-nsg	Microsoft.Network/net...	OK	Operation details
✓	packt-ubuntu-demo-ip	Microsoft.Network/pu...	OK	Operation details
✓	packt-ubuntu-demo-vnet	Microsoft.Network/virt...	OK	Operation details

Figure 15.39 – Deployment details

Let's take a quick look at each of the resources that were created with our virtual machine deployment:

- `packt-ubuntu-demo`: The virtual machine host

- `packt-ubuntu-demo348`: The network interface (or network interface card) of the virtual machine

- `packt-ubuntu-demo-ip`: The IP address of the virtual machine

- `packt-ubuntu-demo-vnet`: The virtual network associated with the resource group (`packt-demo`)

- `packt-ubuntu-demo-nsg`: The **Network Security Group** (**NSG**) controlling inbound and outbound access to and from our instance

Azure will create a new set of the resource types mentioned previously with every virtual machine, except the virtual network corresponding to the resource group, when the instance is placed in an existing resource group. Don't forget that we also created a new resource group (`packt-demo`), which is not shown in the deployment report.

Let's try to connect to our newly created instance (`packt-ubuntu-demo`). Go to **Virtual machines** in the left navigation pane and select the relevant instance (`packt-ubuntu-demo`). In the **Overview** tab, we'll see our virtual machine's essential details, including the **Public IP address** value (`20.19.173.232`).

Now that we've deployed our virtual machine, we want to make sure we can access it via SSH. We'll do that next.

Connecting with SSH to a virtual machine

Before we connect to our virtual machine via SSH, we need to set the permissions to our SSH private key file so that it's not publicly viewable:

```
chmod 400 packt-ubuntu-demo_key.pem
```

Next, we must connect to our Azure Ubuntu instance with the following command:

```
ssh -i packt-rhel.pem packt@20.19.173.232
```

We must use the SSH key (`packt-ubuntu-demo_key.pem`) and administrator account (`packt`) that were specified when we created the instance. Alternatively, you can click on the **Connect** button in the virtual machine's **Overview** tab and then click **SSH**. This action will bring up a view where you can see the preceding commands and copy and paste them into your terminal.

A successful connection to our Ubuntu instance should yield the following output:

```
alexandru@debian:~$ chmod 400 packt-ubuntu-demo_key.pem
alexandru@debian:~$ ssh -i packt-ubuntu-demo_key.pem packt@20.19.173.232
The authenticity of host '20.19.173.232 (20.19.173.232)' can't be established.
ED25519 key fingerprint is SHA256:BlbczCJYUdEf5+aMdYlVow/QC9zLATBFvJL9G/DtbrM.
This key is not known by any other names.
Are you sure you want to continue connecting (yes/no/[fingerprint])? yes
Warning: Permanently added '20.19.173.232' (ED25519) to the list of known hosts.
Welcome to Ubuntu 22.04.3 LTS (GNU/Linux 6.2.0-1018-azure x86_64)
```

Figure 15.40 – Connecting to the Azure virtual machine

Now that we've created our first virtual machine in Azure, let's look at some of the most common management operations that are performed during a virtual machine's lifetime.

Managing virtual machines

As our applications evolve, so does the computing power and capacity required by the virtual machines hosting the applications. As system administrators, we should know how cloud resources are being utilized. Azure provides the necessary tools for monitoring the health and performance of virtual machines. These tools are available on the **Monitoring** tab of the virtual machine's management page.

A small virtual machine with a relatively low number of virtual CPUs and reduced memory may negatively impact application performance. On the other hand, an oversized instance would yield unnecessary costs. Resizing a virtual machine is a common operation in Azure. Let's see how we can do it.

Changing the size of a virtual machine

Azure makes it relatively easy to resize virtual machines. In the portal, go to **Virtual Machines**, select your instance, and click **Size** under **Availability + Scale**:

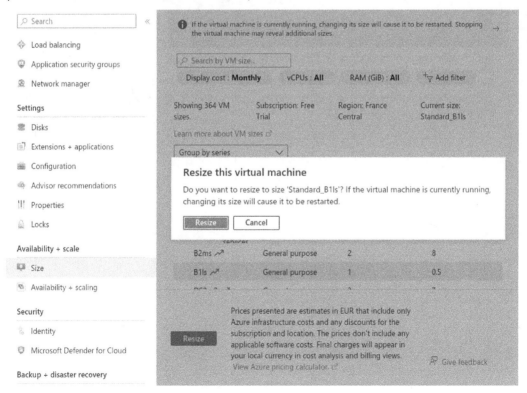

Figure 15.41 – Changing the size of a virtual machine

Our virtual machine (`packt-ubuntu-demo`) is of *B1s* size (1 vCPUs, 1 GB RAM). We can choose to size it up or down. For demo purposes, we could resize to the lower *B1ls* capacity (1 vCPU, 0.5 GB RAM). We could select the **B1ls** (1 vCPU, 0.5 GB RAM) option and click the **Resize** button. Lowering the size of our instance will also result in cost savings. Azure will stop and restart our virtual machine while resizing. It's always good to stop the machine before changing the size to avoid possible data inconsistencies within the instance.

One of the remarkable features of virtualized workloads in Azure is the ability to scale – including the storage capacity – by adding additional data disks to virtual machines. We can add existing data disks or create new ones.

Let's look at how to add a secondary data disk to our virtual machine.

Adding additional storage

Azure can add disks to our instance on the fly, without stopping the machine. We can add two types of disks to a virtual machine: **data disks** and **managed disks**. In this chapter, we will only provide information on how to add data disks. For more information on disk types on Azure, please visit `https://docs.microsoft.com/en-us/azure/virtual-machines/disks-types`.

Let's learn how to add a data disk:

1. Navigate to **Virtual machines** in the left navigation menu and select your instance, click **Disks** under **Settings**, and then click on **Create and attach a new disk**.

2. In the disk properties, leave the **Logical Unit Number** (**LUN**) as-is (automatically assigned) and specify **Disk name** (such as `packt-disk`), **Storage Type**, and **Size** (such as **4 GB**) values. Click **Apply** when you're done:

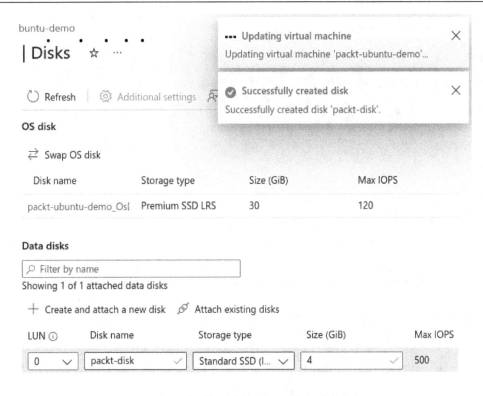

Figure 15.42 – Adding a new data disk

At this point, the new disk is attached to our virtual machine, but the disk hasn't been initialized with a filesystem yet.

3. Connect to our virtual machine via SSH:

```
ssh -i packt-rhel.pem packt@20.19.173.232
```

4. List the current block devices:

```
lsblk
```

5. Identify the new data disk in the output. Our disk is 4 GB in size, and the related block device is sdc:

```
packt@packt-ubuntu-demo:~$ lsblk
NAME      MAJ:MIN RM    SIZE RO TYPE MOUNTPOINTS
loop0       7:0    0   63.5M  1 loop /snap/core20/2015
loop1       7:1    0  111.9M  1 loop /snap/lxd/24322
loop2       7:2    0   40.9M  1 loop /snap/snapd/20290
sda         8:0    0     30G  0 disk
├─sda1      8:1    0   29.9G  0 part /
├─sda14     8:14   0      4M  0 part
└─sda15     8:15   0    106M  0 part /boot/efi
sdb         8:16   0      4G  0 disk
└─sdb1      8:17   0      4G  0 part /mnt
sdc         8:32   0      4G  0 disk
sr0        11:0    1    628K  0 rom
```

Figure 15.43 – Identifying the block device for the new data disk

6. Verify that the block device is empty:

```
sudo file -s /dev/sdc
```

The output is /dev/sdc: data, meaning that the data disk doesn't contain a filesystem yet.

7. Next, initialize the volume with an XFS filesystem:

```
sudo mkfs -t xfs /dev/sdc
```

8. Finally, create a mounting point (/packt) and mount the new volume:

```
sudo mkdir /packt
sudo mount /dev/sdc /packt
```

Now, we can use the new data disk for regular file storage.

Note that data disks will only be persisted during the lifetime of the virtual machine. When the virtual machine is paused, stopped, or terminated, the data disk becomes unavailable. When the machine is terminated, the data disk is permanently lost. For persistent storage, we need to use *managed disks*, similar in behavior to network-attached storage. See the link at the beginning of this section for more details.

So far, we have performed all these management operations in the Azure portal. But what if you want to automate your workloads in the cloud using scripting? This can be done using Azure CLI.

Working with the Azure CLI

Azure CLI is a specialized command-line interface for managing your resources in the cloud. First, let's install the Azure CLI on our platform of choice. Follow the instructions at `https://docs.microsoft.com/en-us/cli/azure/install-azure-cli`. We'll choose the Azure CLI for Linux and, for demo purposes, install it on a Debian machine. The related instructions can be found at `https://docs.microsoft.com/en-us/cli/azure/install-azure-cli-linux`. From the multiple installation options available, we'll use the following command:

```
curl -sL https://aka.ms/InstallAzureCLIDeb | sudo bash
```

After the installation is complete, we can invoke the Azure CLI with the `az` command:

```
az help
```

The preceding command displays detailed help information about using the `az` utility. However, before performing any management operations, we need to authenticate the CLI with our Azure credentials. The following command will set up the local Azure CLI environment accordingly:

```
az login
```

We'll be prompted with a message containing an authentication code and the URL (`https://microsoft.com/devicelogin`) to visit and enter the code:

```
alexandru@debian:~$ az login
A web browser has been opened at https://login.microsoftonline.com/organizations/oauth2/v2.0/authori
ze. Please continue the login in the web browser. If no web browser is available or if the web brows
er fails to open, use device code flow with `az login --use-device-code`.
The following tenants don't contain accessible subscriptions. Use 'az login --allow-no-subscriptions
' to have tenant level access.
                                    'Packt'
[
  {
    "cloudName": "AzureCloud",
    "homeTenantId":
    "id":
    "isDefault": true,
    "managedByTenants": [],
    "name": "Free Trial",
    "state": "Enabled",
    "tenantId":
    "user": {
      "name": "alexandru.calcatinge@gmail.com",
      "type": "user"
    }
  }
]
```

Figure 15.44 – Initializing the Azure CLI environment

At this point, we are ready to use the Azure CLI for management operations. Let's create a new resource group called packt-dev in the West US Region:

```
az group create --name packt-dev --location francecentral
```

The preceding command yields the following output upon successfully creating the resource group:

```
alexandru@debian:~$ az group create --name packt-dev --location francecentral
{
  "id": "/subscriptions/d82a0c6e-86d2-478d-b417-2d37aaa74d9d/resourceGroups/packt-dev",
  "location": "francecentral",
  "managedBy": null,
  "name": "packt-dev",
  "properties": {
    "provisioningState": "Succeeded"
  },
  "tags": null,
  "type": "Microsoft.Resources/resourceGroups"
}
```

Figure 15.45 – Creating a new resource group

Next, we must launch an Ubuntu virtual machine named packt-ubuntu-dev in the Region we just created:

```
az vm create --resource-group packt-dev --name packt-ubuntu-dev
--image Ubuntu2204 --admin-username packt --generate-ssh-keys
```

Let's quickly go through each of the preceding command-line options:

- resource-group: The name of the resource group (packt-dev) where we create our virtual machine

- name: The name of the virtual machine (packt-ubuntu-dev)

- image: The Linux distribution to use (Ubuntu2204)

- admin-username: The username of the machine's administrator account (packt)

- generate-ssh-keys: This generates a new SSH key pair to access our virtual machine

The preceding code produces the following output:

```
alexandru@debian:~$ az vm create --resource-group packt-dev --name packt-ubuntu-dev --image Ubuntu22
04 --admin-username packt --generate-ssh-keys
selecting "northeurope" may reduce your costs. The region you've selected may cost more for the same
services. You can disable this message in the future with the command "az config set core.display_r
egion_identified=false". Learn more at https://go.microsoft.com/fwlink/?linkid=22271

{
  "fqdns": "",
  "id": "/subscriptions/d82a0c6e-86d2-478d-b417-2d37aaa74d9d/resourceGroups/packt-dev/providers/Micr
osoft.Compute/virtualMachines/packt-ubuntu-dev",
  "location": "francecentral",
  "macAddress": "60-45-BD-6B-76-76",
  "powerState": "VM running",
  "privateIpAddress": "10.0.0.4",
  "publicIpAddress": "51.103.100.132",
  "resourceGroup": "packt-dev",
  "zones": ""
}
```

Figure 15.46 – Creating a new virtual machine

As the output suggests, the SSH key files have been automatically generated and placed in the local machine's ~/.ssh directory to allow SSH access to the newly created virtual machine. The JSON output also provides the public IP address of the machine:

```
"publicIpAddress": "51.103.100.132"
```

The following command lists all virtual machines:

```
az vm list
```

You can also check the Azure portal in your browser to see all your virtual machines, including the newly created one:

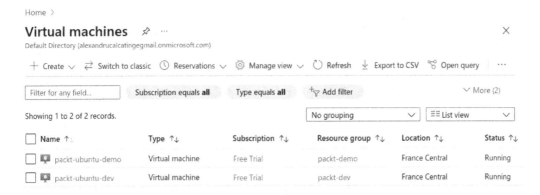

Figure 15.47 – Viewing the virtual machines in the Azure portal

To get information about a specific virtual machine (`packt-ubuntu-dev`), run the following command:

```
az vm show \
  --resource-group packt-dev \
  --name packt-ubuntu-dev
```

To redeploy an existing virtual machine (such as `packt-ubuntu-dev`), run the following command:

```
az vm redeploy \
  --resource-group packt-dev \
  --name packt-ubuntu-dev
```

The following command deletes a virtual machine (`packt-ubuntu-dev`):

```
az vm delete \
  --resource-group packt-dev \
  --name packt-ubuntu-dev
```

As you have probably noticed, for virtual machine-related commands (`az vm`), we also need to specify the resource group the machine belongs to.

A comprehensive study of the Azure CLI is beyond the scope of this chapter. For detailed information, please visit the Azure CLI's online documentation portal: `https://docs.microsoft.com/en-us/cli/azure/`.

This concludes our coverage of public cloud deployments with AWS and Azure. We have covered a vast domain and have merely skimmed the surface of cloud management workloads. We encourage you to build upon this preliminary knowledge and explore more, starting with the AWS and Azure cloud docs. The relevant links are mentioned in the *Further reading* section, together with other valuable resources.

Now, let's summarize what you have learned so far about AWS and Azure.

Summary

AWS and Azure provide a roughly similar set of features for flexible compute capacity, storage, and networking, with pay-as-you-go pricing. They share the essential elements of a public cloud – elasticity, autoscaling, provisioning with self-service, security, and identity and access management. This chapter explored both cloud providers strictly from a practical vantage point, focusing on typical deployment and management aspects of everyday cloud administration tasks.

We covered topics such as launching and terminating a new instance or virtual machine. We also looked at resizing an instance to accommodate a higher or lower compute capacity and scaling the storage by creating and attaching additional block devices (volumes). Finally, we used CLI tools for scripting various cloud management workloads.

When working with AWS, we learned a few basic concepts about EC2 resources. Next, we looked at typical cloud management tasks, such as launching and managing instances, adding and configuring additional storage, and using EBS snapshots for disaster recovery. Finally, we explored the AWS CLI with hands-on examples of standard operations, including querying and launching EC2 instances, creating and adding additional storage to an instance, and terminating an instance.

At this point, you should be familiar with the AWS and Azure web administration consoles and CLI tools. You have learned the basics of some typical cloud management tasks and a few essential concepts about provisioning cloud resources. Overall, you've enabled a special skillset of modern-day Linux administrators by engaging in cloud-native administration workflows. Combined with the knowledge you've built so far, you are assembling a valuable Linux administration toolbelt for on-premises, public, and hybrid cloud systems management.

In the next chapter, we'll take this further and introduce you to managing application deployments using containerized workflows and services with Kubernetes.

Questions

Let's recap some of the concepts you've learned about in this chapter as a quiz:

1. What is an AZ?
2. Between a `t3.small` and a `t3.micro` AWS EC2 instance type, which one yields better performance?
3. You have launched an AWS EC2 instance in the `us-west-1a` AZ and plan to attach an EBS volume created in `us-west-1b`. Would this work?
4. What is the SSH command to connect to your AWS EC2 instance or Azure virtual machine?
5. What is the Azure CLI command for listing your virtual machines? How about the equivalent AWS CLI command?
6. What is the AWS CLI command for launching a new EC2 instance?
7. What is the Azure CLI command for deleting a virtual machine?

Further reading

Here are a few resources to further explore AWS and Azure cloud topics:

- AWS EC2: `https://docs.aws.amazon.com/ec2/index.html`
- Azure: `https://docs.microsoft.com/en-us/azure`
- *AWS for System Administrators*, by Prashant Lakhera, Packt Publishing
- *Learning AWS – Second Edition*, by Aurobindo Sarkar and Amit Shah, Packt Publishing
- *Learning Microsoft Azure*, by Geoff Webber-Cross, Packt Publishing
- *Learning Microsoft Azure: A Hands-On Training [Video]*, by Vijay Saini, Packt Publishing

16

Deploying Applications with Kubernetes

Whether you are a seasoned system administrator managing containerized applications or a DevOps engineer automating app orchestration workflows, **Kubernetes** could be your platform of choice. This chapter will introduce you to Kubernetes and will guide you through the basic process of building and configuring a **Kubernetes cluster**. We'll use Kubernetes to run and scale a simple application in a secure and highly available environment. You will also learn how to interact with Kubernetes using the **command-line interface (CLI)**.

By the end of this chapter, you'll learn how to install, configure, and manage a Kubernetes cluster on-premises. We'll also show you how to deploy and scale an application using Kubernetes.

Here's a brief outline of the topics we will cover in this chapter:

- Introducing Kubernetes architecture and the API object model
- Installing and configuring Kubernetes
- Working with Kubernetes using the `kubectl` command-line tool and deploying applications

Technical requirements

You should be familiar with Linux and the CLI in general. A good grasp of **TCP/IP networking** and **Docker** containers would go a long way in making your journey of learning Kubernetes easier.

You will also need the following:

- A local desktop machine with a Linux distribution of your choice to install and experiment with the CLI tools used in this chapter. We will use both Debian and Ubuntu LTS.

- A powerful desktop system with at least 8 CPU cores and at least 16 GB of RAM will allow you to replicate the necessary environment on your desktop as we'll be devoting a relatively large section to building a Kubernetes cluster using VMs.

- A desktop hypervisor.

Now, let's start our journey together to discover Kubernetes.

Introducing Kubernetes

Kubernetes is an open source **container orchestrator** initially developed by Google. A container orchestrator is a piece of software that automatically manages (including provisioning, deployment, and scaling) containerized applications. Assuming an application uses containerized microservices, a container orchestration system provides the following features:

- **Elastic orchestration (autoscaling)**: This involves automatically starting and stopping application services (containers) based on specific requirements and conditions – for example, launching multiple web server instances with an increasing number of requests and eventually terminating servers when the number of requests drops below a certain threshold

- **Workload management**: This involves optimally deploying and distributing application services across the underlying cluster to ensure mandatory dependencies and redundancy – for example, running a web server endpoint on each cluster node for high availability

- **Infrastructure abstraction**: This involves providing container runtime, networking, and load-balancing capabilities – for example, distributing the load among multiple web server containers and autoconfiguring the underlying network connectivity with a database app container

- **Declarative configuration**: This involves describing and ensuring the desired state of a multi-tiered application – for example, a web server should be ready for serving requests only when the database backend is up and running, and the underlying storage is available

A classic example of workload orchestration is a video-on-demand streaming service. With a popular new TV show in high demand, the number of streaming requests would significantly exceed the average during a regular season. With **Kubernetes**, we could scale out the number of web servers based on the volume of streaming sessions. We could also control the possible scale-out of some of the middle-tier components, such as database instances (serving the authentication requests) and storage cache (serving the streams). When the TV show goes out of fashion, and the number of requests drops significantly, Kubernetes terminates the surplus instances, automatically reducing the application deployment's footprint and, consequently, the underlying costs.

Here are some key benefits of deploying applications with Kubernetes:

- **Speedy deployment**: Application containers are created and launched relatively fast, using either a **declarative** or **imperative** configuration model (as we'll see in the *Introducing the Kubernetes object model* section later in this chapter)

- **Quick iterations**: Application upgrades are relatively straightforward, with the underlying infrastructure simply seamlessly replacing the related container

- **Rapid recovery**: If an application crashes or becomes unavailable, Kubernetes automatically restores the application to the desired state by replacing the related container

- **Reduced operation costs**: The containerized environment and infrastructure abstraction of Kubernetes yields minimal administration and maintenance efforts with relatively low resources for running applications

Now that we have introduced Kubernetes, let's look at its basic operating principles next.

Understanding the Kubernetes architecture

There are three major concepts at the core of the working model of Kubernetes:

- **Declarative configuration or desired state**: This concept describes the overall application state and microservices, deploying the required containers and related resources, including network, storage, and load balancers, to achieve a running functional state of the application

- **Controllers or controller loops**: This monitors the desired state of the system and takes corrective action when needed, such as replacing a failed application container or adding additional resources for scale-out workloads

- **API object model**: This model represents the actual implementation of the desired state, using various configuration objects and the interaction – the **application programming interface** (**API**) – between these objects

For a better grasp of the internals of Kubernetes, we need to take a closer look at the Kubernetes object model and related API. Also, you can check out *Figure 16.1* for a visual explanation of the Kubernetes (cluster) architecture.

Introducing the Kubernetes object model

The Kubernetes architecture defines a collection of objects representing the desired state of a system. An **object**, in this context, is a programmatic term to describe the behavior of a subsystem. Multiple objects interact with one another via the API, shaping the desired state over time. In other words, the Kubernetes object model is the programmatic representation of the desired state.

So, what are these objects in Kubernetes? We'll briefly enumerate some of the more important ones and further elaborate on each in the following sections: API server, pods, controllers, services, and storage.

We use these API objects to configure the system's state, using either a declarative or imperative model:

- With a **declarative configuration model**, we describe the state of the system, usually with a configuration file or manifest (in YAML or JSON format). Such a configuration may include and deploy multiple API objects and regard the system as a whole.

- The **imperative configuration model** uses individual commands to configure and deploy specific API objects, typically acting on a single target or subsystem.

Let's look at the API server first – the central piece in the Kubernetes object model.

Introducing the API server

The API server is the core hub of the Kubernetes object model, acting as a management endpoint for the desired state of the system. The API server exposes an HTTP REST interface using JSON payloads. It is accessible in two ways:

- **Internally**: It is accessed internally by other API objects
- **Externally**: It is accessed externally by configuration and management workflows

The API server is essentially the gateway of interaction with the Kubernetes cluster, both from the outside and within. A Kubernetes cluster is a framework of different nodes that run containerized applications. The cluster is the basic running mode of Kubernetes itself. More on the Kubernetes cluster will be provided in the *Anatomy of a Kubernetes cluster* section. A system administrator connects to the API server endpoint to configure and manage a Kubernetes cluster, typically via a CLI. Internally, Kubernetes API objects connect to the API server to provide an update of their state. In return, the API server may further adjust the internal configuration of the API objects toward the desired state.

The API objects are the building blocks of the internal configuration or desired state of a Kubernetes cluster. Let's look at a few of these API objects next.

Introducing pods

A **pod** represents the basic working unit in Kubernetes, running as a single- or multi-container application. A pod is also known as the **unit of scheduling** in Kubernetes. In other words, containers within the same pod are guaranteed to be deployed together on the same cluster node.

A pod essentially represents a microservice (or a service) within the application's service mesh. Considering the classic example of a web application, we may have the following pods running in the cluster:

- Web server (Nginx)
- Authentication (Vault)
- Database (PostgreSQL)
- Storage (NAS)

Each of these services (or applications) runs within their pod. Multiple pods of the same application (for example, a web server) make up a **ReplicaSet**. We'll look at ReplicaSets closer in the *Introducing controllers* section.

Some essential features of pods are as follows:

- They have an **ephemeral nature**. Once a pod is terminated, it is gone for good. No pod ever gets redeployed in Kubernetes. Consequently, pods don't persist in any state unless they use persistent storage or a local volume to save their data.

- Pods are an **atomic unit** – they are either deployed or not. For a single-container pod, atomicity is almost a given. For multi-container pods, atomicity means that a pod is deployed only when each of the constituent containers is deployed. If any of the containers fail to deploy, the pod will not be deployed, and hence there's no pod. If one of the containers within a running multi-container pod fails, the whole pod is terminated.

- Kubernetes uses **probes** (such as liveliness and readiness) to monitor the health of an application inside a pod. This is because a pod could be deployed and running, but that doesn't necessarily mean the application or service within the pod is healthy. For example, a web server pod can have a probe that checks a specific URL and decides whether it's healthy based on the response.

Kubernetes tracks the state of pods using controllers. Let's look at controllers next.

Introducing controllers

Controllers in Kubernetes are control loops responsible for keeping the system in the desired state or bringing the system closer to the desired state by constantly watching the state of the cluster. For example, a controller may detect that a pod is not responding and request the deployment of a new pod while terminating the old one. Let's look at two key types of controllers:

- A controller may also add or remove pods of a specific type to and from a collection of pod replicas. Such controllers are called **ReplicaSets**, and their responsibility is to accommodate a particular number of pod replicas based on the current state of the application. For example, suppose an application requires three web server pods, and one of them becomes unavailable (due to a failed probe). In that case, the ReplicaSet controller ensures that the failed pod is deleted, and a new one takes its place.

- When deploying applications in Kubernetes, we usually don't use ReplicaSets directly to create pods. We use the **Deployment** controller instead, which is responsible for monitoring Kubernetes Deployments. Given the declarative model of Kubernetes, we can define a Deployment with one or more ReplicaSets. It's the Deployment controller's job to create the ReplicaSet with the required number of pods and manage the ReplicaSet's state; in other words, it controls which container image to load and the number of pods to create.

  A Deployment controller can also manage the transition from one ReplicaSet to another, a functionality used in rollout or upgrade scenarios. Imagine we have a ReplicaSet (`v1`) with several pods, all running version 1 of our application, and we want to upgrade them to version 2. Remember, pods cannot be regenerated or upgraded. Instead, we'll define a second ReplicaSet (`v2`), creating the version 2 pods. The Deployment controller will tear down the `v1` ReplicaSet and bring up `v2`. Kubernetes performs the rollout seamlessly, with minimal to no disruption of service. The Deployment controller manages the transition between the `v1` and `v2` ReplicaSets and even rolls back the transition if needed.

There are many other controller types in Kubernetes, and we encourage you to explore them at `https://kubernetes.io/docs/concepts/workloads/controllers/`.

As applications scale-out or terminate, the related pods are deployed or removed. Services provide access to the dynamic and transient world of pods. We'll look at Services next.

Introducing Services

Services provide persistent access to the applications running in pods. It is the Services' responsibility to ensure that the pods are accessible by routing the traffic to the corresponding application endpoints. In other words, Services provide network abstraction for communicating with pods through IP addresses, routing, and DNS resolution. As pods are deployed or terminated based on the system's desired state, Kubernetes dynamically updates the Service endpoint of the pods, with minimal to no disruption in terms of accessing the related applications. As users and applications access the Service endpoint's persistent IP address, the Service will ensure that the routing information is up to date and traffic is exclusively routed to the running and healthy pods. Services can also be leveraged to load-balance the application traffic between pods and scale pods up or down based on demand.

So far, we have looked at Kubernetes API objects controlling the deployment, access, and life cycle of application Services. What about the persistent data that applications require? We'll look at the Kubernetes storage next.

Introducing storage

Kubernetes provides various storage types for applications running within the cluster. The most common are **volumes** and **persistent volumes**. Due to the ephemeral nature of pods, application data stored within a pod using volumes is lost when the pod is terminated. Persistent volumes are defined and managed at the Kubernetes cluster level, and they are independent of pods. Applications (pods) requiring a persistent state would reserve a persistent volume (of a specific size), using a **persistent volume claim**. When a pod using a persistent volume terminates, the new pod replacing the old one retrieves the current state from the persistent volume and will continue using the underlying storage.

For more information on Kubernetes storage types, please refer to `https://kubernetes.io/docs/concepts/storage/`.

Now that we are familiar with the Kubernetes API object model, let's quickly go through the architecture of a Kubernetes cluster.

The anatomy of a Kubernetes cluster

A Kubernetes cluster consists of one **Control Plane (CP) node** and one or more **worker nodes**. The following diagram presents a high-level view of the Kubernetes architecture:

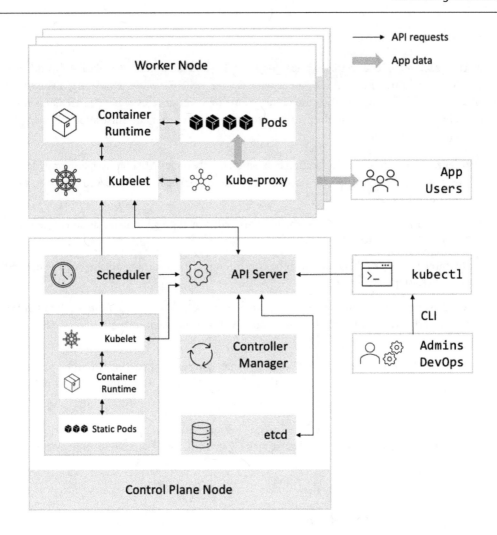

Figure 16.1 – Kubernetes cluster architecture

The components of a Kubernetes cluster that are shown in the preceding figure are divided into the worker node and CP node as the two major components. The Worker nodes have different components, such as the container runtime, kubelet, and kube-proxy, and the CP node has the API server, the controller manager, and the scheduler. All of these components will be discussed in detail in the following sections.

First, let's look at the Kubernetes cluster nodes shown in the preceding image in some detail next, starting with the CP node.

Introducing the Kubernetes CP

The **Kubernetes CP** provides essential Services for deploying and orchestrating application workloads, and it runs on a dedicated node in the Kubernetes cluster – the CP node. This node, also known as the **master node**, implements the core components of a Kubernetes cluster, such as resource scheduling and monitoring. It's also the primary access point for cluster administration. Here are the key subsystems of a CP node:

- **API server**: The central communication hub between Kubernetes API objects; it also provides the cluster's management endpoint accessible either via CLI or the Kubernetes web administration console (dashboard)

- **Scheduler**: This decides when and which nodes to deploy the pods on, depending on resource allocation and administrative policies

- **Controller manager**: This maintains the control loops, monitoring and shaping the desired state of the system

- **etcd**: Also known as the **cluster store**, this is a highly available persisted database, maintaining the state of the Kubernetes cluster and related API objects; the information in etcd is stored as key-value pairs

- `kubectl`: The primary administrative CLI for managing and interacting with the Kubernetes cluster; `kubectl` communicates directly with the API server, and it may connect remotely to a cluster

A detailed architectural overview of the Kubernetes CP is beyond the scope of this chapter. You may explore the related concepts in more detail at `https://kubernetes.io/docs/concepts/architecture/`.

Next, let's take a brief look at the Kubernetes node – the workhorse of a Kubernetes cluster.

Introducing the Kubernetes nodes

In a Kubernetes cluster, the **nodes** – also referred to as **worker nodes** – run the actual application pods and maintain their full life cycle. Nodes provide the compute capacity of Kubernetes and ensure that the workloads are uniformly distributed across the cluster when deploying and running pods. Nodes can be configured either as physical (bare metal) or VMs.

Let's enumerate the key elements of a Kubernetes node:

- **Kubelet**: This processes CP requests (from the scheduler) to deploy and start application pods; the kubelet also monitors the node and pod state, reporting the related changes to the API server

- **Kube-Proxy**: Dynamically configures the virtual networking environment for the applications running in the pods; it routes the network traffic, provides load balancing, and maintains the IP addresses of Services and pods

- **Container runtime**: Provides the runtime environment for the pods as application containers; uses the **Container Runtime Interface** (**CRI**) to interact with the underlying container engine (such as `containerd` and Docker)

All the preceding Services run on *each* node in the Kubernetes cluster, including the CP node. These components in the CP are required by special-purpose pods, providing specific CP Services, such as DNS, ingress (load balancing), and dashboard (web console).

For more information on Kubernetes nodes and related architectural concepts, please visit `https://kubernetes.io/docs/concepts/architecture/nodes/`.

Now that we have become familiar with some of the key concepts and cluster components, let's get ready to install and configure Kubernetes.

Installing and configuring Kubernetes

Before installing or using Kubernetes, you have to decide on the infrastructure you'll use, whether that be on-premises or public cloud. Second, you'll have to choose between an **Infrastructure-as-a-Service** (**IaaS**) or a **Platform-as-a-Service** (**PaaS**) model. With IaaS, you'll have to install, configure, manage, and maintain the Kubernetes cluster yourself, either on physical (bare metal) or VMs. The related operation efforts are not straightforward and should be considered carefully. If you choose a PaaS solution, available from all major public cloud providers, you'll be limited to only administrative tasks but saved from the burden of maintaining the underlying infrastructure.

In this chapter, we'll cover only IaaS deployments of Kubernetes. For IaaS, we'll use a local desktop environment running Ubuntu VMs.

For the on-premises installation, we may also choose between a lightweight desktop version of Kubernetes or a full-blown cluster with multiple nodes. Let's look at some of the most common desktop versions of Kubernetes next.

Installing Kubernetes on a desktop

If you're looking only to experiment with Kubernetes, a desktop version may fit the bill. Desktop versions of Kubernetes usually deploy a single-node cluster on your local machine. Depending on your platform of choice, whether it be Windows, macOS, or Linux, you have plenty of Kubernetes engines to select from. Here are just a few:

- **Docker Desktop (macOS, Windows)**: `https://www.docker.com/products/docker-desktop`
- **minikube (Linux, macOS, Windows)**: `https://minikube.sigs.k8s.io/docs/`
- **Microk8s (Linux, macOS, Windows)**: `https://microk8s.io/`
- **k3s (Linux)**: `https://k3s.io/`

In this section, we'll show you how to install Microk8s, one of the trending Kubernetes desktop engines at the time of writing. Microk8s is available to install via the Snap Store. We will use Debian 12 as the base operating system on our test computer, so we can install Microk8s from the Snap Store. If you don't have `snapd` installed, you will have to first proceed and install it. You will have to use the following command to install the Snap daemon:

```
sudo apt install snapd
```

If you already have `snapd` installed, you can skip this first step. The following step will be to run the command to install the `snapd` core runtime environment needed to run the Snap Store:

```
sudo snap install core
```

Only after `snap` is installed, you can install `microk8s` by using the following command:

```
sudo snap install microk8s --classic
```

A successful installation of Microk8s should yield the following result:

```
alexandru@debian:~$ sudo snap install core
2023-09-22T19:03:24+03:00 INFO Waiting for automatic snapd restart...
core 16-2.60.3 from Canonical installed
alexandru@debian:~$ sudo snap install microk8s --classic
microk8s (1.27/stable) v1.27.5 from Canonical installed
```

Figure 16.2 – Installing Microk8s on Linux

As we already had `snapd` installed, we did not run the first of the commands listed previously.

To access the Microk8s CLI without `sudo` permissions, you'll have to add the local user account to the `microk8s` group and also fix the permissions on the `~/.kube` directory with the following commands:

```
sudo usermod -aG microk8s $USER
sudo chown -f -R $USER ~/.kube
```

The changes will take effect on the next login, and you can use the `microk8s` command-line utility with invocations that are not `sudo`. For example, the following command displays the help for the tool:

```
microk8s help
```

To get the status of the local single-node Microk8s Kubernetes cluster, we run the following command:

```
microk8s status
```

As you can see, the installation steps of Microk8s on Debian are straightforward and similar to the ones used in Ubuntu.

In the next section, we will show you how to install Microk8s on a VM. This time, we will use Ubuntu 22.04 LTS as the base operating system for the VM.

Installing Kubernetes on VMs

In this section, we'll get closer to a real-world Kubernetes environment – though at a much smaller scale – by deploying a Kubernetes cluster on Ubuntu VMs. You can use any hypervisor, such as KVM, Oracle VirtualBox, or VMware Fusion. We will use KVM as our preferred hypervisor.

We will create four VMs, and we'll provision each VM with 2 vCPU cores, 2 GB RAM, and 20 GB disk capacity. You may follow the steps described in the *Installing Ubuntu* section of *Chapter 1, Installing Linux*, using your hypervisor of choice.

Before we dive into the Kubernetes cluster installation details, let's take a quick look at our lab environment.

Preparing the lab environment

Here are the specs of our VM environment:

- **Hypervisor**: VMware Fusion
- **Kubernetes cluster**: One CP node and three worker nodes
- **CP node**:
    - k8s-cp1: 192.168.122.104
- **Worker nodes**:
    - k8s-n1: 192.168.122.146
    - k8s-n2: 192.168.122.233
    - k8s-n3: 192.168.122.163
- **VMs**: Ubuntu Server 22.04.3 LTS, 2 vCPUs, 2 GB RAM, 20 GB disk
- **User**: packt (on all nodes), with SSH access enabled

We set the username and hostname settings on each VM node on the Ubuntu Server installation wizard. Also, make sure to enable the OpenSSH server when prompted. Your VM IP addresses would most probably be different from those in the specs, but that shouldn't matter. You may also choose to use static IP addresses for your VMs.

To make hostname resolution simple within the cluster, edit the /etc/hosts file on each node and add the related records. For example, we have the following /etc/hosts file on the CP node (k8s-cp1):

```
packt@k8s-cp1:~$ cat /etc/hosts
127.0.0.1        localhost
127.0.1.1        k8s-cp1
192.168.122.146 k8s-n1
192.168.122.233 k8s-n2
192.168.122.163 k8s-n3
```

Figure 16.3 – The /etc/hosts file on the CP node (k8s-cp1)

In production environments, with the firewall enabled on the cluster nodes, we have to make sure that the following rules are configured for accepting network traffic within the cluster (according to https://kubernetes.io/docs/setup/production-environment/tools/kubeadm/install-kubeadm/):

Control-plane node(s)

Protocol	Direction	Port Range	Purpose	Used By
TCP	Inbound	6443*	Kubernetes API server	All
TCP	Inbound	2379-2380	etcd server client API	kube-apiserver, etcd
TCP	Inbound	10250	kubelet API	Self, Control plane
TCP	Inbound	10251	kube-scheduler	Self
TCP	Inbound	10252	kube-controller-manager	Self

Worker node(s)

Protocol	Direction	Port Range	Purpose	Used By
TCP	Inbound	10250	kubelet API	Self, Control plane
TCP	Inbound	30000-32767	NodePort Services†	All

Figure 16.4 – The ports used by the Kubernetes cluster nodes

The following sections assume that you have the VMs provisioned and running according to the preceding specs. You may take some initial snapshots of your VMs before proceeding with the next steps. If anything goes wrong with the installation, you can revert to the initial state and start again.

Here are the steps we'll follow to install the Kubernetes cluster:

1. Disable swapping.
2. Install `containerd`.
3. Install the `kubelet`, `kubeadm`, and Kubernetes packages.

We'll have to perform these steps on each cluster node. The related commands are also captured in the accompanying chapter source code on GitHub.

Let's start with the first step and disable the memory swap on each node.

Disable swapping

`swap` is a disk space used when the memory is full (refer to `https://github.com/kubernetes/kubernetes/issues/53533` for more details). The Kubernetes kubelet package doesn't work with `swap` enabled on Linux platforms. This means that we will have to disable `swap` on all the nodes.

To disable `swap` immediately, we run the following command on each VM:

```
sudo swapoff -a
```

To persist the disabled `swap` with system reboots, we need to comment out the `swap`-related entries in `/etc/fstab`. You can do this either manually, by editing `/etc/fstab`, or with the following command:

```
sudo sed -i '/\s*swap\s*/s/^\(.*\)$/# \1/g' /etc/fstab
```

You may want to double-check that all `swap` entries in `/etc/fstab` are disabled:

```
cat /etc/fstab
```

We can see the `swap` mount point commented out in our `/etc/fstab` file:

```
packt@k8s-cp1:~$ sudo sed -i '/\s*swap\s*/s/^\(.*\)$/# \1/g' /etc/fstab
packt@k8s-cp1:~$ cat /etc/fstab
# /etc/fstab: static file system information.
#
# Use 'blkid' to print the universally unique identifier for a
# device; this may be used with UUID= as a more robust way to name devices
# that works even if disks are added and removed. See fstab(5).
#
# <file system> <mount point>   <type>  <options>       <dump>  <pass>
# / was on /dev/ubuntu-vg/ubuntu-lv during curtin installation
/dev/disk/by-id/dm-uuid-LVM-0hYX7oP9Pr8NTc45XbF8McVoB2Mz3tFoYB2NluHFjidf6OvvH52lxX1uvQnC1vRJ / ext4
defaults 0 1
# /boot was on /dev/vda2 during curtin installation
/dev/disk/by-uuid/80ac40ac-d66e-4f30-be4b-ac1097359e49 /boot ext4 defaults 0 1
# /swap.img      none    swap    sw      0       0
```

Figure 16.5 – Disabling swap entries in /etc/fstab

Remember to run the preceding commands on each node in the cluster. Next, we'll look at installing the Kubernetes container runtime.

Installing containerd

`containerd` is the default container runtime in recent versions of Kubernetes. `containerd` implements the CRI required by the Kubernetes container engine abstraction layer. The related installation procedure is not straightforward, and we'll follow the steps described in the official Kubernetes documentation in the following link at the time of this writing: `https://kubernetes. io/docs/setup/production-environment/container-runtimes/`. These steps may change at any time, so please make sure to check the latest procedure. The container runtime needs to be installed on each node of the cluster. We will proceed by installing the needed components on the CP node, the VM called `k8s-cp1`, and then on the other nodes as well.

We'll start by installing some `containerd` prerequisites:

1. First, we enable the `br_netfilter` and `overlay` kernel modules using `modprobe`:

   ```
   sudo modprobe br_netfilter
   sudo modprobe overlay
   ```

2. We also ensure that these modules are loaded upon system reboots:

   ```
   cat <<EOF | sudo tee /etc/modules-load.d/containerd.conf
   br_netfilter
   overlay
   EOF
   ```

3. Next, we apply the CRI required `sysctl` parameters, also persisted across system reboots:

   ```
   cat <<EOF | sudo tee /etc/sysctl.d/containerd.conf
   net.bridge.bridge-nf-call-iptables = 1
   net.bridge.bridge-nf-call-ip6tables = 1
   net.ipv4.ip_forward = 1
   EOF
   ```

4. We want the preceding changes to take effect immediately, without a system reboot:

   ```
   sudo sysctl --system
   ```

Here is a screenshot showing the preceding commands:

```
packt@k8s-cp1:~$ cat <<EOF | sudo tee /etc/modules-load.d/containerd.conf
> overlay
> br_netfilter
> EOF
overlay
br_netfilter
packt@k8s-cp1:~$ sudo modprobe overlay
packt@k8s-cp1:~$ sudo modprobe br_netfilter
packt@k8s-cp1:~$ lsmod | grep br_netfilter
br_netfilter           32768  0
bridge                307200  1 br_netfilter
packt@k8s-cp1:~$ lsmod | grep overlay
overlay               151552  0
packt@k8s-cp1:~$ cat <<EOF | sudo tee /etc/sysctl.d/containerd.conf
> net.bridge.bridge-nf-call-iptables = 1
> net.bridge.bridge-nf-call-ip6tables = 1
> net.ipv4.ip_forward =1
> EOF
net.bridge.bridge-nf-call-iptables = 1
net.bridge.bridge-nf-call-ip6tables = 1
net.ipv4.ip_forward =1
packt@k8s-cp1:~$ sudo sysctl --system
```

Figure 16.6 – Setting containerd prerequisites

5. Next, we will verify if specific system variables are enabled in the `sysctl` configuration by running the following command:

    ```
    sudo sysctl net.bridge.bridge-nf-call-iptables net.bridge.
    bridge-nf-call-ip6tables net.ipv4.ip_forward
    ```

    The output of the command should be as follows:

```
packt@k8s-cp1:~$ sudo sysctl net.bridge.bridge-nf-call-iptables net.bridge.bridge-nf-call-ip6tables
net.ipv4.ip_forward
net.bridge.bridge-nf-call-iptables = 1
net.bridge.bridge-nf-call-ip6tables = 1
net.ipv4.ip_forward = 1
```

Figure 16.7 – Verifying system variables in sysctl configuration

Each variable should have a value of 1 in the output, just as shown in the previous screenshot.

6. Now, let's make sure the apt repository is up to date before installing any new packages:

    ```
    sudo apt update
    ```

7. Now, we're ready to install `containerd`:

    ```
    sudo apt install -y containerd
    ```

8. Next, we generate a default `containerd` configuration:

    ```
    sudo mkdir -p /etc/containerd
    containerd config default | sudo tee /etc/containerd/config.toml
    ```

    These commands will create a new directory and a new default configuration file called `config.toml` inside it. The output of the command is too large to show, but it will show you on the screen the automatically generated contents of the new file we created.

9. We need to slightly alter the default `containerd` configuration to use the `systemd cgroup` driver with the container runtime (`runc`). This change is required because the underlying platform (Ubuntu in our case) uses `systemd` as the Service manager. Open the `/etc/containerd/config.toml` file with your editor of choice, such as the following:

    ```
    sudo nano /etc/containerd/config.toml
    ```

10. Locate the following section (which will be inside the `[plugins]` section of the file):

    ```
    [plugins."io.containerd.grpc.v1.cri".containerd.runtimes.runc]
    ```

11. Then, add the highlighted lines, adjusting the appropriate indentation (this is *very* important):

    ```
    [plugins."io.containerd.grpc.v1.cri".containerd.runtimes.runc]
      ...
      [plugins."io.containerd.grpc.v1.cri".containerd.runtimes.runc.
    options]
        SystemdCgroup = true
    ```

Here's the resulting configuration stub:

```
[plugins."io.containerd.grpc.v1.cri".containerd.runtimes]

[plugins."io.containerd.grpc.v1.cri".containerd.runtimes.runc]
    base_runtime_spec = ""
    cni_conf_dir = ""
    cni_max_conf_num = 0
    container_annotations = []
    pod_annotations = []
    privileged_without_host_devices = false
    privileged_without_host_devices_all_devices_allowed = false
    runtime_engine = ""
    runtime_path = ""
    runtime_root = ""
    runtime_type = "io.containerd.runc.v2"
    sandbox_mode = "podsandbox"
    snapshotter = ""

[plugins."io.containerd.grpc.v1.cri".containerd.runtimes.runc.options]
    BinaryName = ""
    CriuImagePath = ""
    CriuPath = ""
    CriuWorkPath = ""
    IoGid = 0
    IoUid = 0
    NoNewKeyring = false
    NoPivotRoot = false
    Root = ""
    ShimCgroup = ""
    SystemdCgroup = true
```

Figure 16.8 – Modifying the containerd configuration

12. Save the `/etc/containerd/config.toml` file and restart `containerd`:

```
sudo systemctl restart containerd
```

13. After a few moments, you can verify the status of the `containerd` Service, by using the following command:

```
sudo systemctl status containerd
```

The output should show that the system is running and there are no issues.

With `containerd` installed and configured, we can proceed with the installation of the Kubernetes packages next.

Installing Kubernetes packages

To install the Kubernetes packages, we'll follow the steps described at `https://kubernetes.io/docs/setup/production-environment/tools/kubeadm/install-kubeadm/`. This procedure may also change over time, so please make sure to check out the latest instructions. The steps presented next are applicable to Debian 12 and Ubuntu 22.04. Let's begin:

1. We first install the packages required by the Kubernetes `apt` repository:

    ```
    sudo apt install -y apt-transport-https ca-certificates curl
    ```

2. Next, we download the Kubernetes `apt` repository **GNU Privacy Guard** (**GPG**) public signing key (for the latest Kubernetes 1.28 at the time of writing):

    ```
    sudo curl -fsSL https://pkgs.k8s.io/core:/stable:/v1.28/
    deb/Release.key | sudo gpg --dearmor -o /etc/apt/keyrings/
    kubernetes-apt-keyring.gpg
    ```

3. The next command adds the Kubernetes `apt` repository to our system:

    ```
    echo 'deb [signed-by=/etc/apt/keyrings/kubernetes-apt-keyring.
    gpg] https://pkgs.k8s.io/core:/stable:/v1.28/deb/ /' | sudo tee
    /etc/apt/sources.list.d/kubernetes.list
    ```

4. Let's read the packages available in the new repository we just added:

    ```
    sudo apt update -y
    ```

5. We're now ready to install the Kubernetes packages:

    ```
    sudo apt install -y kubelet kubeadm kubectl
    ```

6. We want to pin the version of these packages to avoid the inadvertent update via system security patches, and so on. The Kubernetes packages should exclusively be updated using the cluster upgrade procedures. We use the `apt-mark hold` command to pin the version of the Kubernetes packages, including `containerd`:

    ```
    sudo apt-mark hold containerd kubelet kubeadm kubectl
    ```

7. Finally, ensure that the `containerd` and `kubelet` Services are enabled upon system startup (reboot):

    ```
    sudo systemctl enable containerd
    sudo systemctl enable kubelet
    ```

8. Now that we have finished installing the Kubernetes packages, let's check the status of the node Services. We retrieve the status of the `containerd` Service first:

    ```
    sudo systemctl status containerd
    ```

containerd should be active and running. The following is a screenshot showing the output of the preceding commands:

```
packt@k8s-cp1:~$ sudo apt-mark hold containerd kubelet kubeadm kubectl
containerd set on hold.
kubelet set on hold.
kubeadm set on hold.
kubectl set on hold.
packt@k8s-cp1:~$ sudo systemctl enable containerd
packt@k8s-cp1:~$ sudo systemctl enable kubelet
packt@k8s-cp1:~$ sudo systemctl status containerd
• containerd.service - containerd container runtime
     Loaded: loaded (/lib/systemd/system/containerd.service; enabled; vendor preset: enabled)
     Active: active (running) since Mon 2023-09-25 17:25:52 UTC; 2h 41min ago
       Docs: https://containerd.io
   Main PID: 1798 (containerd)
      Tasks: 8
     Memory: 13.3M
        CPU: 4.202s
     CGroup: /system.slice/containerd.service
             └─1798 /usr/bin/containerd
```

Figure 16.9 – Pinning the Kubernetes packages and the running status of containerd

9. Next, let's check the status of the `kubelet` Service:

```
sudo systemctl start kubelet && sudo systemctl status kubelet
```

At this time, it should be no surprise that the status is `exited`:

```
packt@k8s-cp1:~$ sudo systemctl start kubelet
packt@k8s-cp1:~$ sudo systemctl status kubelet
• kubelet.service - kubelet: The Kubernetes Node Agent
     Loaded: loaded (/lib/systemd/system/kubelet.service; enabled; vendor preset: enabled)
    Drop-In: /usr/lib/systemd/system/kubelet.service.d
             └─10-kubeadm.conf
     Active: activating (auto-restart) (Result: exit-code) since Mon 2023-09-25 20:16:57 UTC; 6s ago
       Docs: https://kubernetes.io/docs/
    Process: 3280 ExecStart=/usr/bin/kubelet $KUBELET_KUBECONFIG_ARGS $KUBELET_CONFIG_ARGS $KUBELET▮
   Main PID: 3280 (code=exited, status=1/FAILURE)
        CPU: 54ms
```

Figure 16.10 – The kubelet crashing without cluster configuration

As shown in the preceding screenshot, `kubelet` is looking for the Kubernetes cluster, which is not set up yet. We can see that `kubelet` attempts to start and activate itself but keeps crashing, as it cannot locate the required configuration.

> **Important note**
> Please install the required Kubernetes packages on *all* cluster nodes following the previous steps before proceeding with the next section.

Next, we'll bootstrap (initialize) the Kubernetes cluster using `kubeadm`.

Introducing kubeadm

`kubeadm` is a helper tool for creating a Kubernetes cluster and essentially has two invocations:

- `kubeadm init`: This bootstraps or initializes a Kubernetes cluster
- `kubeadm join`: This adds a node to a Kubernetes cluster

The default invocation of `kubadm init [flags]` – with no flags – performs the following tasks:

1. **Running preliminary checks**: In the very initial phase, `kubeadm init` ensures that we have the minimum system resources in terms of CPU and memory, the required user permissions, and a supported CRI-compliant container runtime. If any of these checks fail, `kubeadm init` stops the execution of creating the cluster. If the checks succeed, `kubeadm` proceeds to the next step.

2. **Creating a Certificate Authority (CA)**: `kubeadm init` creates a self-signed CA used by Kubernetes to generate the certificates required to authenticate and run trusted workloads within the cluster. The CA files are stored in the `/etc/kubernetes/pki/` directory and are distributed on each node upon joining the cluster.

3. **Generating kubeconfig files**: The kubeconfig files are configuration files used by the Kubernetes cluster components to locate, communicate, and authenticate with the API server. `kubeadm init` creates a default set of kubeconfig files required to bootstrap the cluster. The kubeconfig files are stored in the `/etc/kubernetes/` directory.

4. **Generating static pod manifests**: Static pods are system-specific pods running exclusively on the CP node and managed by the `kubelet` daemon. Examples of static pods are the API server, the controller manager, scheduler, and etcd. Static pod manifests are configuration files describing the CP pods. `kubeadm init` generates the static pod manifests during the cluster bootstrapping process. The manifest files are stored in the `/etc/kubernetes/manifests/` directory. The `kubelet` Service monitors this location and, when it finds a manifest, deploys the corresponding static pod.

5. **Waiting for the static pods to start**: After the `kubelet` daemon deploys the static pods, `kubeadm` queries `kubelet` for the static pods' state. When the static pods are up and running, `kubeadm init` proceeds with the next stage.

6. **Tainting the CP node**: Tainting is the process of excluding a node from running user pods. The opposite concept in a Kubernetes environment is **toleration** – controlling the affinity of pods to specific cluster nodes. `kubeadm init` follows the Kubernetes best practice of tainting the CP to avoid user pods running on the CP node. The obvious reason is to preserve CP resources exclusively for system-specific workloads.

7. **Generating a bootstrap token**: Bootstrap tokens are simple bearer tokens used for joining new nodes to a Kubernetes cluster. `kubeadm init` generates a bootstrap token that can be shared with a trusted node to join the cluster.

8. **Starting add-on pods**: Kubernetes cluster add-ons are specific CP components (pods) extending the functionality of the cluster. By default, `kubeadm init` creates and deploys the *DNS* and *kube-proxy* add-on pods.

The stages of a Kubernetes cluster's bootstrapping process are highly customizable. `kubeadm init`, when invoked without additional parameters, runs all the tasks in the preceding order. Alternatively, a system administrator may invoke the `kubeadm` command with different option parameters to control and run any of the stages mentioned.

For more information about `kubeadm`, please refer to the utility's help with the following command:

```
kubeadm help
```

For more information about bootstrapping a Kubernetes cluster using `kubeadm`, including installing, troubleshooting, and customizing components, you may refer to the official Kubernetes documentation at `https://kubernetes.io/docs/setup/production-environment/tools/kubeadm/`.

In the next section, we'll bootstrap a Kubernetes cluster using `kubeadm` to generate a cluster configuration file and then invoke `kubeadm init` to use this configuration. We'll bootstrap our cluster by creating the Kubernetes CP node next.

Creating a Kubernetes CP node

In order to create the CP node, we will use a networking and security solution named **Calico** to manage our workloads. We will then generate a default cluster using `kubeadm`, and afterwards, we will use different tools to apply the configurations. The choice of Calico is purely subjective, but it is needed for managing communications between workloads and components. For more information about Calico, please visit the following link: `https://docs.tigera.io/calico/latest/about/`.

The commands are performed on the `k8s-cp1` host in our VM environment. As the hostname suggests, we choose `k8s-cp1` as the CP node of our Kubernetes cluster. Now, let's get to work and configure our Kubernetes CP node:

1. We'll start by downloading the Calico manifest for **overlay networking**. The overlay network – also known as **software-defined network (SDN)** – is a logical networking layer that accommodates a secure and seamless network communication between the pods over a physical network that may not be accessible for configuration. Exploring the internals of cluster networking is beyond the scope of this chapter, but we encourage you to read more at `https://kubernetes.io/docs/concepts/cluster-administration/networking/`. You'll also find references to the Calico networking add-on. To download the related manifest, we run the following command:

    ```
    curl https://raw.githubusercontent.com/projectcalico/calico/
    v3.26.1/manifests/calico.yaml -O
    ```

The command downloads the `calico.yaml` file in the current directory (`/home/packt/`) that we'll use with `kubectl` to configure pod networking later in the process.

2. Next, let's open the `calico.yaml` file using a text editor and look for the following lines (starting with *line 3672*):

```
# - name: CALICO_IPV4POOL_CIDR
#     value: "192.168.0.0/16"
```

`CALICO_IPV4POOL_CIDR` points to the network range associated with the pods. If the related subnet conflicts in any way with your local environment, you'll have to change it here. We'll leave the setting as is.

3. Next, we'll create a default cluster configuration file using `kubeadm`. The cluster configuration file describes the settings of the Kubernetes cluster we're building. Let's name this file `k8s-config.yaml`:

```
kubeadm config print init-defaults | tee k8s-config.yaml
```

4. Let's review the `k8s-config.yaml` file we just generated and mention a few changes that we'll have to make. We will open it using the **nano** text editor first, then we'll start with the `localAPIEndpoint.advertiseAddress` configuration parameter – the IP address of the API server endpoint. The default value is `1.2.3.4`, and we need to change it to the IP address of the VM running the CP node (`k8s-cp1`), in our case, `192.168.122.104`. Refer to the *Preparing the lab environment* section earlier in this chapter. You'll have to enter the IP address matching your environment:

```
kind: InitConfiguration
localAPIEndpoint:
#   advertiseAddress: 1.2.3.4
    advertiseAddress: 192.168.122.104   ⬅
    bindPort: 6443
nodeRegistration:
    criSocket: unix:///var/run/containerd/containerd.sock
    imagePullPolicy: IfNotPresent
```

Figure 16.11 – Modifying the advertiseAddress configuration parameter

5. The next change we need to make is pointing the `nodeRegistration.criSocket` configuration parameter to the `containerd` socket (`/run/containerd/containerd.sock`) and the name (`k8s-cp1`):

```
kind: InitConfiguration
localAPIEndpoint:
#  advertiseAddress: 1.2.3.4
   advertiseAddress: 192.168.122.104
   bindPort: 6443
nodeRegistration:
   criSocket: /run/containerd/containerd.sock
   imagePullPolicy: IfNotPresent
   name: k8s-cp1
   taints: null
```

Figure 16.12 – Changing the criSocket configuration parameter

6. Next, we change the `kubernetesVersion` parameter to match the version of our Kubernetes environment:

```
imageRepository: registry.k8s.io
kind: ClusterConfiguration
kubernetesVersion: 1.28.2
```

Figure 16.13 – Changing the kubernetesVersion parameter

The default value is `1.28.0`, but our Kubernetes version, using the following command, is `1.28.2`:

```
kubeadm version
```

The output is as follows:

```
packt@k8s-cp1:~$ kubeadm version
kubeadm version: &version.Info{Major:"1", Minor:"28", GitVersion:"v1.28.2", GitCommit:"89a4ea3e1e4dd
d7f7572286090359983e0387b2f", GitTreeState:"clean", BuildDate:"2023-09-13T09:34:32Z", GoVersion:"go1
.20.8", Compiler:"gc", Platform:"linux/amd64"}
```

Figure 16.14 – Retrieving the current version of Kubernetes

7. Our final modification of the cluster configuration file sets the `cgroup` driver of `kubelet` to `systemd`, matching the `cgroup` driver of `containerd`. Please note that `systemd` is the underlying platform's Service manager (in Ubuntu), hence the need to yield related Service control to the Kubernetes daemons. The corresponding configuration block is not yet present in `k8s-config.yaml`. We can add it manually to the end of the file or with the following command:

```
cat <<EOF | cat >> k8s-config.yaml
---
apiVersion: kubelet.config.k8s.io/v1beta1
kind: KubeletConfiguration
cgroupDriver: systemd
EOF
```

8. Now, we're ready to bootstrap the Kubernetes cluster. We invoke the `kubeadm init` command with the `--config` option pointing to the cluster configuration file (`k8s-config.yaml`), and with the `--cri-socket` option parameter pointing to the `containerd` socket:

    ```
    sudo kubeadm init --config=k8s-config.yaml
    ```

    The preceding command takes a couple of minutes to run. A successful bootstrap of the Kubernetes cluster completes with the following output:

```
Your Kubernetes control-plane has initialized successfully!
```

```
To start using your cluster, you need to run the following as a regular user:

  mkdir -p $HOME/.kube
  sudo cp -i /etc/kubernetes/admin.conf $HOME/.kube/config
  sudo chown $(id -u):$(id -g) $HOME/.kube/config
```

```
Alternatively, if you are the root user, you can run:

  export KUBECONFIG=/etc/kubernetes/admin.conf
```

```
You should now deploy a pod network to the cluster.
Run "kubectl apply -f [podnetwork].yaml" with one of the options listed at:
  https://kubernetes.io/docs/concepts/cluster-administration/addons/

Then you can join any number of worker nodes by running the following on each as root:

kubeadm join 192.168.122.104:6443 --token abcdef.0123456789abcdef \
        --discovery-token-ca-cert-hash sha256:eb35fbe063ec0ec62883c9da78d4e2607663ea24876af536cdeab1
9b6b6b4f65
```

Figure 16.15 – Successfully bootstrapping the Kubernetes cluster

At this point, our Kubernetes CP node is up and running. In the output, we highlighted the relevant excerpts for the following commands:

- A successful message (**1**)

- Configuring the current user as the Kubernetes cluster administrator (**2**)

- Joining new nodes to the Kubernetes cluster (**3**)

We recommend taking the time to go over the complete output and identify the related information for each of the `kubeadm init` tasks, as captured in the *Introducing kubeadm* section earlier in this chapter.

9. Next, to configure the current user as the Kubernetes cluster administrator, we run the following commands:

    ```
    mkdir -p ~/.kube
    sudo cp -i /etc/kubernetes/admin.conf ~/.kube/config
    sudo chown $(id -u):$(id -g) ~/.kube/config
    ```

10. With our cluster up and running, let's deploy the Calico networking manifest to create the pod network:

```
kubectl apply -f calico.yaml
```

The preceding command creates a collection of resources related to the pod overlay network.

11. Now, we're ready to take our first peek into the state of our cluster by using the `kubectl` command to list all the pods in the system:

```
kubectl get pods --all-namespaces
```

The command yields the following output:

```
packt@k8s-cp1:~$ kubectl get pods --all-namespaces
NAMESPACE      NAME                                        READY   STATUS    RESTARTS   AGE
kube-system    calico-kube-controllers-7ddc4f45bc-jpprk    1/1     Running   0          3m16s
kube-system    calico-node-gwcn4                           1/1     Running   0          3m16s
kube-system    coredns-5dd5756b68-28pgh                    1/1     Running   0          4m35s
kube-system    coredns-5dd5756b68-j92f9                    1/1     Running   0          4m35s
kube-system    etcd-k8s-cp1                                1/1     Running   0          4m40s
kube-system    kube-apiserver-k8s-cp1                      1/1     Running   0          4m40s
kube-system    kube-controller-manager-k8s-cp1             1/1     Running   0          4m40s
kube-system    kube-proxy-7bz9m                            1/1     Running   0          4m35s
kube-system    kube-scheduler-k8s-cp1                      1/1     Running   0          4m40s
```

Figure 16.16 – Retrieving the pods in the Kubernetes cluster

The `--all-namespaces` option retrieves the pods across all resource groups in the cluster. Kubernetes uses **namespaces** to organize resources. For now, the only pods running in our cluster are **system pods**, as we haven't deployed any **user pods** yet.

12. The following command retrieves the current nodes in the cluster:

```
kubectl get nodes
```

The output shows `k8s-cp1` as the only node configured in the Kubernetes cluster, running as a CP node:

```
packt@k8s-cp1:~$ kubectl get nodes
NAME      STATUS   ROLES           AGE     VERSION
k8s-cp1   Ready    control-plane   6m23s   v1.28.2
```

Figure 16.17 – Listing the current nodes in the Kubernetes cluster

13. You may recall that prior to bootstrapping the Kubernetes cluster, the `kubelet` Service was continually crashing (and attempting to restart). With the cluster up and running, the status of the `kubelet` daemon should be `active` and `running`:

```
sudo systemctl status kubelet
```

The output shows the following:

```
packt@k8s-cp1:~$ sudo systemctl status kubelet
● kubelet.service - kubelet: The Kubernetes Node Agent
     Loaded: loaded (/lib/systemd/system/kubelet.service; enabled; vendor preset: enabled)
    Drop-In: /usr/lib/systemd/system/kubelet.service.d
             └─10-kubeadm.conf
     Active: active (running) since Tue 2023-09-26 09:20:50 UTC; 6min ago
       Docs: https://kubernetes.io/docs/
   Main PID: 51436 (kubelet)
      Tasks: 10 (limit: 2220)
     Memory: 51.0M
        CPU: 5.399s
     CGroup: /system.slice/kubelet.service
             └─51436 /usr/bin/kubelet --bootstrap-kubeconfig=/etc/kubernetes/bootstrap-kubelet.conf
```

Figure 16.18 – A healthy kubelet in the cluster

14. We encourage you to check out the manifests created in the `/etc/kubernetes/manifests/` directory for each cluster component using the following command:

```
ls /etc/kubernetes/manifests/
```

The output shows the configuration files describing the static (system) pods, corresponding to the API server, controller manager, scheduler, and etcd:

```
packt@k8s-cp1:~$ ls /etc/kubernetes/manifests/
etcd.yaml   kube-apiserver.yaml   kube-controller-manager.yaml   kube-scheduler.yaml
```

Figure 16.19 – The static pod configuration files in /etc/kubernetes/manifests/

15. You may also look at the kubeconfig files in `/etc/kubernetes`:

```
ls /etc/kubernetes/
```

As you may recall from the *Introducing kubeadm* section earlier in this chapter, the kubeconfig files are used by the cluster components to communicate and authenticate with the API server.

As we have used the `kubectl` utility quite extensively in this section, you can visit the official documentation to find out more about the commands and options available for it at the following link: `https://kubernetes.io/docs/reference/generated/kubectl/kubectl-commands`.

Next, let's add the worker nodes to our Kubernetes cluster.

Joining a node to a Kubernetes cluster

As previously noted, before adding a node to the Kubernetes cluster, you'll need to run the preliminary steps described in the *Preparing the lab environment* section earlier in this chapter.

To join a node to the cluster, we'll need both the **bootstrap token** and the **discovery token CA certificate hash** generated upon successful bootstrapping of the Kubernetes cluster. The tokens with the related `kubeadm join` command were provided in the output at the end of the bootstrapping process with `kubeadm init`. Refer to the *Creating a Kubernetes CP node* section earlier in this chapter. Keep in mind that the bootstrap token expires in 24 hours. If you forget to copy the command, you can retrieve the related information by running the following commands in the CP node's terminal (on `k8s-cp1`).

To proceed, follow these steps:

1. Retrieve the current bootstrap tokens:

```
kubeadm token list
```

The output shows our token (`abcdef.0123456789abcdef`):

```
packt@k8s-cp1:~$ kubeadm token list
TOKEN                     TTL          EXPIRES                USAGES
        DESCRIPTION                                           EXTRA GROUPS
abcdef.0123456789abcdef   23h          2023-09-27T09:20:50Z   authentication,sign
ing     <none>                                                system:bootstra
ppers:kubeadm:default-node-token
```

Figure 16.20 – Getting the current bootstrap tokens

2. Get the CA certificate hash:

```
openssl x509 -pubkey \
    -in /etc/kubernetes/pki/ca.crt | \
    openssl rsa -pubin -outform der 2>/dev/null | \
    openssl dgst -sha256 -hex | sed 's/^.* //'
```

The output is as follows:

```
packt@k8s-cp1:~$ openssl x509 -pubkey -in /etc/kubernetes/pki/ca.crt | \
> openssl rsa -pubin -outform der 2>/dev/null | \
> openssl dgst -sha256 -hex | sed 's/^.* //'
af8e659bc8a9069cf58d3100e94644bb6ee804c1372a0ab7e74801cf8340a15d
```

Figure 16.21 – Getting the CA certificate hash

3. You may also generate a new bootstrap token with the following command:

```
kubeadm token create
```

If you choose to generate a new token, you may use the following streamlined command to print out the full `kubeadm join` command with the required parameters:

```
kubeadm token create --print-join-command
```

Now that the token has been created, we can proceed to the next bootstrapping steps.

In the following steps, we'll use our initial tokens as displayed in the output at the end of the bootstrapping process. So, let's switch to the node's command-line terminal (on k8s-n1) and run the following command:

1. Make sure to invoke sudo, or the command will fail with insufficient permissions:

```
sudo kubeadm join 192.168.122.104:6443 \
    --token abcdef.0123456789abcdef \
    --discovery-token-ca-cert-hash
sha256:af8e659bc8a9069cf58d3100e94644bb6ee804c1372a
0ab7e74801cf8340a15d
```

2. We can check the status of the current nodes in the cluster with the following command in the CP node terminal (k8s-cp1):

```
kubectl get nodes
```

The output shows our new node (k8s-n1) added to the cluster:

```
packt@k8s-cp1:~$ kubectl get nodes
NAME      STATUS   ROLES           AGE      VERSION
k8s-cp1   Ready    control-plane   58m      v1.28.2
k8s-n1    Ready    <none>          2m45s    v1.28.2
```

Figure 16.22 – The new node (k8s-n1) added to the cluster

3. We encourage you to repeat the process of joining the other two cluster nodes (k8s-n2 and k8s-n3). During the join, while the CP pods are being deployed on the new node, you may temporarily see a NotReady status for the new node if you query the nodes on the CP node (k8s-cp1) too fast. The process should take a while. In the end, we should have all three nodes showing Ready in the output of the kubectl get nodes command (on k8s-cp1):

```
packt@k8s-cp1:~$ kubectl get nodes
NAME      STATUS   ROLES           AGE      VERSION
k8s-cp1   Ready    control-plane   62m      v1.28.2
k8s-n1    Ready    <none>          7m18s    v1.28.2
k8s-n2    Ready    <none>          67s      v1.28.2
k8s-n3    Ready    <none>          52s      v1.28.2
```

Figure 16.23 – The Kubernetes cluster with all nodes running

We have now completed the installation of our Kubernetes cluster, with a CP node and three worker nodes. We used a local (on-premises) VM environment, but the same process would also apply to a hosted IaaS solution running in a private or public cloud.

In the next section, we'll explore the kubectl CLI to a certain extent and use it to create and manage Kubernetes resources. Then, we'll look at deploying and scaling applications using the imperative and declarative deployment models in Kubernetes.

Working with Kubernetes

In this section, we'll use real-world examples of interacting with a Kubernetes cluster. Since we'll be using the kubectl CLI to a considerable extent, we're going to take a deep dive into some of its more common usage patterns. Then, we will turn our focus to deploying applications to a Kubernetes cluster. We'll be using the on-premises environment we built in the *Installing Kubernetes on VMs* section.

Let's start by taking a closer look at kubectl and its usage.

Using kubectl

kubectl is the primary tool for managing a Kubernetes cluster and its resources. kubectl communicates with the cluster's API server endpoint using the Kubernetes REST API. The general syntax of a kubectl command is as follows:

```
kubectl [command] [TYPE] [NAME] [flags]
```

In general, kubectl commands execute **CRUD operations** – CRUD stands for **Create**, **Read**, **Update**, and **Delete** – against Kubernetes resources, such as pods, Deployments, and Services.

One of the essential features of kubectl is the command output format, either in YAML, JSON, or plain text. The output format is handy when creating or editing application Deployment manifests. We can capture the YAML output of a kubectl command (such as create a resource) to a file. Later, we can reuse the manifest file to perform the same operation (or sequence of operations) in a declarative way. This brings us to the two basic Deployment paradigms of Kubernetes:

- **Imperative Deployments**: Invoking a single or multiple kubectl commands to operate on specific resources
- **Declarative Deployments**: Using manifest files and deploying them using the kubectl apply command, usually targeting a set of resources with a single invocation

We'll look at these two Deployment models more closely in the *Deploying applications* section later in this chapter. For now, let's get back to exploring the kubectl command further. Here's a short list of some of the most common kubectl commands:

- create, apply: These create resources imperatively/declaratively
- get: This reads resources
- edit, set: These update resources or specific features of objects
- delete: This deletes resources

- `run`: This starts a pod

- `exec`: This executes a command in a pod container

- `describe`: This displays detailed information about resources

- `explain`: This provides resource-related documentation

- `logs`: This shows the logs in pod containers

A couple of frequently used parameters of the `kubectl` command are also worth mentioning:

- `--dry-run`: This runs the command without modifying the system state while still providing the output as if it executed normally

- `--output`: This specifies various formats for the command output: `yaml`, `json`, and `wide` (additional information in plain text)

In the following sections, we'll look at multiple examples of using the `kubectl` command. Always keep in mind the general pattern of the command:

	operation	resource		options
kubectl	[command]	[TYPE]	[NAME]	[flags]
-------	---------	------	------	-------
kubectl	get	pods	packt-web	--output=wide
kubectl	create	service	packt-svc	--dry-run

Figure 16.24 – The general usage pattern of kubectl

We recommend that you check out the complete `kubectl` command reference at `https://kubernetes.io/docs/reference/kubectl/overview/`. While you are becoming proficient with `kubectl`, you may also want to keep the related cheat sheet at hand, which you can find at the following link: `https://kubernetes.io/docs/reference/kubectl/cheatsheet/`.

Now, let's prepare our `kubectl` environment to interact with the Kubernetes cluster we built earlier with VMs. You may skip the next section if you prefer to use `kubectl` on the CP node.

Connecting to a Kubernetes cluster from a local machine

In this section, we configure the `kubectl` CLI running locally on our Linux desktop to control a remote Kubernetes cluster. We are running Debian 12 on our local machine.

First, we will need to install `kubectl` on our system. We will observe the installation instructions at `https://kubernetes.io/docs/tasks/tools/install-kubectl-linux/`. We will download the latest `kubectl` release with the following command:

```
curl -LO "https://dl.k8s.io/release/$(curl -L -s https://dl.k8s.io/
release/stable.txt)/bin/linux/amd64/kubectl"
```

Then we will install `kubectl` with the following command:

```
sudo install -o root -g root -m 0755 kubectl /usr/local/bin/kubectl
```

Now that the package is installed, we can test the installation using the following command:

```
kubectl version --client
```

The output of the preceding commands is shown in the following screenshot:

```
alexandru@debian:~$ curl -LO "https://dl.k8s.io/release/$(curl -L -s https://dl.
k8s.io/release/stable.txt)/bin/linux/amd64/kubectl"
  % Total    % Received % Xferd  Average Speed   Time    Time     Time  Current
                                 Dload  Upload   Total   Spent    Left  Speed
100   138  100   138    0     0    611      0 --:--:-- --:--:-- --:--:--   613
100 47.5M  100 47.5M    0     0  12.6M      0  0:00:03  0:00:03 --:--:-- 14.5M
alexandru@debian:~$ sudo install -o root -g root -m 0755 kubectl /usr/local/bin/
kubectl
alexandru@debian:~$ kubectl version --client
Client Version: v1.28.2
Kustomize Version: v5.0.4-0.20230601165947-6ce0bf390ce3
```

Figure 16.25 – Installing kubectl locally on a Debian system

We want to add (merge) yet another cluster configuration to our environment. This time, we connect to an on-premises Kubernetes CP, and we'll use `kubectl` to update kubeconfig. Here are the steps we'll be taking:

1. We first copy kubeconfig from the CP node (`k8s-cp1`, `192.168.122.104`) to a temporary location (`/tmp/config.cp`):

    ```
    scp packt@192.168.122.104:~/.kube/config /tmp/config.cp
    ```

2. Finally, we can move the new kubeconfig file to the new location:

    ```
    mv /tmp/config.cp ~/.kube/config
    ```

3. Optionally, we can clean up the temporary files created in the process:

    ```
    rm ~/.kube/config.old /tmp/config.cp
    ```

4. Let's get a view of the current kubeconfig contexts:

    ```
    kubectl config get-contexts
    ```

The output of the previous command is shown in the following screenshot. At the bottom of the screenshot, you can see our new Kubernetes cluster, with the related security principal (`kubernetes-admin@kubernetes`) and cluster name (`kubernetes`):

```
alexandru@debian:~$ scp packt@192.168.122.104:~/.kube/config /tmp/config.cp
packt@192.168.122.104's password:
config                                    100% 5647     14.9MB/s     00:00
alexandru@debian:~$ mv /tmp/config.cp ~/.kube/config
alexandru@debian:~$ kubectl config get-contexts
CURRENT     NAME                           CLUSTER        AUTHINFO          NAMESPACE
*           kubernetes-admin@kubernetes    kubernetes     kubernetes-admin
```

Figure 16.26 – The new kubeconfig contexts

5. For consistency, let's change the on-premises cluster's context name to `k8s-local` and make it the default context in our `kubectl` environment:

```
kubectl config rename-context \
    kubernetes-admin@kubernetes \
    k8s-local
kubectl config use-context k8s-local
```

The current `kubectl` context becomes `k8s-local`, and we're now interacting with our on-premises Kubernetes cluster (`kubernetes`). The output is shown in the following screenshot:

```
alexandru@debian:~$ kubectl config rename-context \
> kubernetes-admin@kubernetes \
> k8s-local
Context "kubernetes-admin@kubernetes" renamed to "k8s-local".
alexandru@debian:~$ kubectl config use-context k8s-local
Switched to context "k8s-local".
alexandru@debian:~$ kubectl config get-contexts
CURRENT     NAME          CLUSTER        AUTHINFO            NAMESPACE
*           k8s-local     kubernetes     kubernetes-admin
```

Figure 16.27 – The current context set to the on-premises Kubernetes cluster

Next, we look at some of the most common `kubectl` commands used with everyday Kubernetes administration tasks.

Working with kubectl

One of the first commands we run when connected to a Kubernetes cluster is the following:

```
kubectl cluster-info
```

The command shows the IP address and port of the API server listening on the CP node, among other information:

```
alexandru@debian:~$ kubectl cluster-info
Kubernetes control plane is running at https://192.168.122.104:6443
CoreDNS is running at https://192.168.122.104:6443/api/v1/namespaces/kube-system/se
rvices/kube-dns:dns/proxy
```

Figure 16.28 – The Kubernetes cluster information shown

The `cluster-info` command can also help to debug and diagnose cluster-related issues:

```
kubectl cluster-info dump
```

To get a detailed view of the cluster nodes, we run the following command:

```
kubectl get nodes --output=wide
```

The `--output=wide` (or `-o wide`) flag yields detailed information about cluster nodes. The output in the following illustration has been cropped to show it more clearly:

```
alexandru@debian:~$ kubectl get nodes --output=wide
NAME     STATUS  ROLES          AGE    VERSION   INTERNAL-IP      EXTERNAL-IP  OS-IMAGE          KERNEL-VERSION     CONTAINER-RUNTIME
k8s-cp1  Ready   control-plane  6h44m  v1.28.2   192.168.122.104  <none>       Ubuntu 22.04.3 LTS  5.15.0-84-generic  containerd://1.7.2
k8s-n1   Ready   <none>         5h49m  v1.28.2   192.168.122.146  <none>       Ubuntu 22.04.3 LTS  5.15.0-84-generic  containerd://1.7.2
k8s-n2   Ready   <none>         5h43m  v1.28.2   192.168.122.233  <none>       Ubuntu 22.04.3 LTS  5.15.0-84-generic  containerd://1.7.2
k8s-n3   Ready   <none>         5h42m  v1.28.2   192.168.122.163  <none>       Ubuntu 22.04.3 LTS  5.15.0-84-generic  containerd://1.7.2
```

Figure 16.29 – Getting detailed information about cluster nodes

The following command retrieves the pods running in the default namespace:

```
kubectl get pods
```

As of now, we don't have any user pods running, and the command returns the following:

```
No resources found in default namespace.
```

To list all the pods, we append the `--all-namespaces` flag to the preceding command:

```
kubectl get pods --all-namespace
```

The output shows all pods running in the system. Since these are exclusively system pods, they are associated with the `kube-system` namespace:

```
alexandru@debian:~$ kubectl get pods
No resources found in default namespace.
alexandru@debian:~$ kubectl get pods --all-namespaces
NAMESPACE     NAME                                          READY   STATUS    RESTARTS        AGE
kube-system   calico-kube-controllers-7ddc4f45bc-jpprk      1/1     Running   0               6h46m
kube-system   calico-node-4wfl4                             1/1     Running   1 (5h51m ago)   5h52m
kube-system   calico-node-7769m                             1/1     Running   0               5h46m
kube-system   calico-node-gwcn4                             1/1     Running   0               6h46m
kube-system   calico-node-npkpr                             1/1     Running   0               5h46m
kube-system   coredns-5dd5756b68-28pgh                      1/1     Running   0               6h47m
kube-system   coredns-5dd5756b68-j92f9                      1/1     Running   0               6h47m
kube-system   etcd-k8s-cp1                                  1/1     Running   0               6h48m
kube-system   kube-apiserver-k8s-cp1                        1/1     Running   0               6h48m
kube-system   kube-controller-manager-k8s-cp1               1/1     Running   0               6h48m
kube-system   kube-proxy-7bz9m                              1/1     Running   0               6h47m
kube-system   kube-proxy-c48p4                              1/1     Running   0               5h46m
kube-system   kube-proxy-lmtkl                              1/1     Running   0               5h46m
kube-system   kube-proxy-zmwfm                              1/1     Running   1 (5h51m ago)   5h52m
kube-system   kube-scheduler-k8s-cp1                        1/1     Running   0               6h48m
```

Figure 16.30 – Getting all pods in the system

We would get the same output if we specified `kube-system` with the `--namespace` flag:

```
kubectl get pods --namespace kube-system
```

For a comprehensive view of all resources running in the system, we run the following command:

```
kubectl get all --all-namespaces
```

So far, we have only mentioned some of the more common object types, such as nodes, pods, and Services. There are many others, and we can view them with the following command:

```
kubectl api-resources
```

The output includes the name of the API object types (such as `nodes`), their short name or alias (such as `no`), and whether they can be organized in namespaces (such as `false`):

```
alexandru@debian:~$ kubectl api-resources
NAME                     SHORTNAMES    APIVERSION              NAMESPACED    KIND
bindings                               v1                      true          Binding
componentstatuses        cs            v1                      false         ComponentStatus
configmaps               cm            v1                      true          ConfigMap
endpoints                ep            v1                      true          Endpoints
events                   ev            v1                      true          Event
limitranges              limits        v1                      true          LimitRange
namespaces               ns            v1                      false         Namespace
nodes                    no            v1                      false         Node
persistentvolumeclaims   pvc           v1                      true          PersistentVolumeClaim
persistentvolumes        pv            v1                      false         PersistentVolume
pods                     po            v1                      true          Pod
podtemplates                           v1                      true          PodTemplate
replicationcontrollers   rc            v1                      true          ReplicationController
resourcequotas           quota         v1                      true          ResourceQuota
secrets                                v1                      true          Secret
serviceaccounts          sa            v1                      true          ServiceAccount
services                 svc           v1                      true          Service
```

Figure 16.31 – Getting all API object types (cropped)

Suppose you want to find out more about specific API objects, such as `nodes`. Here's where the `explain` command comes in handy:

```
kubectl explain nodes
```

The output is as follows:

```
alexandru@debian:~$ kubectl explain nodes
KIND:       Node
VERSION:    v1

DESCRIPTION:
    Node is a worker node in Kubernetes. Each node will have a unique identifier
    in the cache (i.e. in etcd).

FIELDS:
  apiVersion    <string>
    APIVersion defines the versioned schema of this representation of an object.
    Servers should convert recognized schemas to the latest internal value, and
    may reject unrecognized values. More info:
    https://git.k8s.io/community/contributors/devel/sig-architecture/api-conventions.md#resources
```

Figure 16.32 – Showing nodes' detailed information (cropped)

The output provides detailed documentation about the `nodes` API object type, including the related API fields. One of the API fields is `apiVersion`, describing the versioning schema of an object. You may view the related documentation with the following command:

```
kubectl explain nodes.apiVersion
```

The output is as follows:

```
alexandru@debian:~$ kubectl explain nodes.apiVersion
KIND:       Node
VERSION:    v1

FIELD: apiVersion <string>

DESCRIPTION:
    APIVersion defines the versioned schema of this representation of an object.
    Servers should convert recognized schemas to the latest internal value, and
    may reject unrecognized values. More info:
    https://git.k8s.io/community/contributors/devel/sig-architecture/api-conventions.md#resources
```

Figure 16.33 – Details about the apiVersion field (cropped)

We encourage you to use the `explain` command to learn about the various Kubernetes API object types in a cluster. Please note that the `explain` command provides documentation about *resource types*. It should not be confused with the `describe` command, which shows detailed information about the *resources* in the system.

The following commands display cluster node-related information about *all* nodes, and then node `k8s-n1` in particular:

```
kubectl describe nodes
kubectl describe nodes k8s-n1
```

For every `kubectl` command, you can invoke `--help` (or `-h`) to get context-specific help. Here are a few examples:

```
kubectl --help
kubectl config -h
kubectl get pods -h
```

The `kubectl` CLI is relatively rich in commands, and becoming proficient with it may take some time. Occasionally, you may find yourself looking for a specific command or remembering its correct spelling or use. The `auto-complete` bash for `kubectl` comes to the rescue. We'll show you how to enable this next.

Enabling kubectl autocompletion

With `kubectl` autocompletion, you'll get context-sensitive suggestions when you hit the *Tab* key twice while typing the `kubectl` commands.

The `kubectl` autocompletion feature depends on `bash-completion`. Most Linux platforms have `bash-completion` enabled by default. Otherwise, you'll have to install the related package manually. On Ubuntu, for example, you install it with the following command:

```
sudo apt-get install -y bash-completion
```

Next, you need to source the `kubectl` autocompletion in your shell (or similar) profile:

```
echo "source <(kubectl completion bash)" >> ~/.bashrc
```

The changes will take effect on your next login to the terminal or immediately if you source the `bash` profile:

```
source ~/.bashrc
```

With the `kubectl` autocomplete active, you'll get context-sensitive suggestions when you hit the *Tab* key twice while typing the command. For example, the following sequence provides all the available resources when you try to create one:

```
kubectl create [Tab] [Tab]
```

When typing the `kubectl create` command and pressing the *Tab* key twice, the result will be a list of resources available for the command:

```
alexandru@debian:~$ echo "source <(kubectl completion bash)" >> ~/.bashrc
alexandru@debian:~$ source ~/.bashrc
alexandru@debian:~$ kubectl create ◄──────── Here you press [tab] twice
clusterrolebinding    (Create a cluster role binding for a particular cluster role)
clusterrole           (Create a cluster role)
configmap             (Create a config map from a local file, directory or literal value)
cronjob               (Create a cron job with the specified name)
deployment            (Create a deployment with the specified name)
ingress               (Create an ingress with the specified name)
job                   (Create a job with the specified name)
namespace             (Create a namespace with the specified name)
poddisruptionbudget   (Create a pod disruption budget with the specified name)
priorityclass         (Create a priority class with the specified name)
quota                 (Create a quota with the specified name)
rolebinding           (Create a role binding for a particular role or cluster role)
role                  (Create a role with single rule)
secret                (Create a secret using a specified subcommand)
serviceaccount        (Create a service account with the specified name)
service               (Create a service using a specified subcommand)
token                 (Request a service account token)
```

Figure 16.34 – Autocompletion use with kubectl

The `kubectl` autocompletion reaches every part of the syntax: command, resource (type and name), and flags.

Now that we know more about using the `kubectl` command, it's time to turn our attention to deploying applications in Kubernetes.

Deploying applications

When we introduced the `kubectl` command and its usage pattern at the beginning of the *Using kubectl* section, we touched upon the two ways of creating application resources in Kubernetes: imperative and declarative.

We'll look at both of these models closely in this section while deploying a simple web application. Let's start with the imperative model first.

Working with imperative Deployments

As a quick refresher, with imperative Deployments, we follow a sequence of `kubectl` commands to create the required resources and get to the cluster's desired state, such as running the application. Declarative Deployments accomplish the same, usually with a single `kubectl apply` command using a manifest file describing multiple resources.

Creating a Deployment

Let's begin by creating a Deployment first. We'll name our Deployment `packt`, based on a demo Nginx container we're pulling from the public Docker registry (`docker.io/nginxdemos/hello`):

```
kubectl create deployment packt --image=nginxdemos/hello
```

The command output shows that our Deployment was created successfully:

```
deployment.apps/packt created
```

We just created a Deployment with a ReplicaSet containing a single pod running a web server application. We should note that our application is managed by the controller manager within an app Deployment stack (`deployment.apps`). Alternatively, we could just deploy a simple application pod (`packt-web`) with the following command:

```
kubectl run packt-web --image=nginxdemos/hello
```

The output suggests that our application pod, in this case, a standalone or bare pod (`pod/packt-web`), is not part of a Deployment:

```
pod/packt-web created
```

We'll see later in this section that this pod is not part of a ReplicaSet and so is not managed by the controller manager.

Let's look at the state of our system by querying the pods for detailed information:

```
kubectl get pods -o wide
```

Let's analyze the output:

```
alexandru@debian:~$ kubectl create deployment packt --image=nginxdemos/hello
deployment.apps/packt created
alexandru@debian:~$ kubectl run packt-web --image=nginxdemos/hello
pod/packt-web created
alexandru@debian:~$ kubectl get pods -o wide
NAME                       READY   STATUS    RESTARTS   AGE   IP             NODE     NOMINATED NODE   READINE
SS GATES
packt-579bb9c999-rtvzr     1/1     Running   0          58s   172.16.215.65  k8s-n1   <none>           <none>
packt-web                  1/1     Running   0          27s   172.16.57.193  k8s-n3   <none>           <none>
```

Figure 16.35 – Getting the application pods with detailed information

In the preceding output, you can see the series of commands described, and we can also see that our pods are up and running and that Kubernetes deployed them on separate nodes:

- `packt-579bb9c999-rtvzr`: On cluster node `k8s-n1`

- `packt-web`: On cluster node `k8s-n3`

Running the pods on different nodes is due to internal load balancing and resource distribution in the Kubernetes cluster.

The application pod managed by the controller is `packt-579bb9c999-rtvzr`. Kubernetes generates a unique name for our managed pod by appending a **pod template hash** (`579bb9c999`) and a **pod ID** (`rtvzr`) to the name of the Deployment (`packt`). The pod template hash and pod ID are unique within a ReplicaSet.

In contrast, the standalone pod (`packt-web`) is left as is since it's not part of an application Deployment. Let's describe both pods to obtain more information about them. We'll start with the managed pod first. Don't forget to use the `kubectl` autocompletion (by pressing the *Tab* key twice):

```
kubectl describe pod packt-5dc77bb9bf-bnzsc
```

The related output is relatively large. Here are some relevant snippets:

```
alexandru@debian:~$ kubectl describe pod packt-579bb9c999-rtvzr
Name:             packt-579bb9c999-rtvzr
Namespace:        default
Priority:         0
Service Account:  default
Node:             k8s-n1/192.168.122.146
Start Time:       Wed, 27 Sep 2023 15:00:48 +0300
Labels:           app=packt
                  pod-template-hash=579bb9c999
Annotations:      cni.projectcalico.org/containerID: df487cdf4881c686e817406c4ab92baae53314420d75ca6165b4c5e0
7d673070
                  cni.projectcalico.org/podIP: 172.16.215.65/32
                  cni.projectcalico.org/podIPs: 172.16.215.65/32
Status:           Running
IP:               172.16.215.65
IPs:
  IP:             172.16.215.65
Controlled By:    ReplicaSet/packt-579bb9c999
Containers:
  hello:
    Container ID:   containerd://5da6f0c90504595e9c67d8fb107e7f39c4dc15f7eed4a1e8bfad68ae8a5cec2e
    Image:          nginxdemos/hello
    Image ID:       docker.io/nginxdemos/hello@sha256:dedfbe85183df66f3fdc99accf53e1b2171908dffd4d6556603ba48
10b1fce6e
    Port:           <none>
    Host Port:      <none>
    State:          Running
      Started:      Wed, 27 Sep 2023 15:00:54 +0300
    Ready:          True
    Restart Count:  0
    Environment:    <none>
    Mounts:
      /var/run/secrets/kubernetes.io/serviceaccount from kube-api-access-l9f9m (ro)
Conditions:
```

Figure 16.36 – Pod information

In contrast, the same command for the standalone pod (`packt-web`) would be slightly different without featuring the `Controlled By` field:

```
kubectl describe pod packt-web
```

Here are the corresponding excerpts:

```
alexandru@debian:~$ kubectl describe pod packt-web
Name:              packt-web
Namespace:         default
Priority:          0
Service Account:   default
Node:              k8s-n3/192.168.122.163
Start Time:        Wed, 27 Sep 2023 15:01:19 +0300
Labels:            run=packt-web
Annotations:       cni.projectcalico.org/containerID: df5750e969ea7c707f6fe49797b9ef73e1780e271d5cbb4f09375c9e
e1550fea
                   cni.projectcalico.org/podIP: 172.16.57.193/32
                   cni.projectcalico.org/podIPs: 172.16.57.193/32
Status:            Running
IP:                172.16.57.193
IPs:
  IP:   172.16.57.193
Containers:
  packt-web:
    Container ID:   containerd://1b1645d08ba496d51f39d07aa6670f9ddb04c58c952d13fd273df8ecc9e3c626
    Image:          nginxdemos/hello
    Image ID:       docker.io/nginxdemos/hello@sha256:dedfbe85183df66f3fdc99accf53e1b2171908dffd4d6556603ba48
10b1fce6e
    Port:           <none>
    Host Port:      <none>
    State:          Running
      Started:      Wed, 27 Sep 2023 15:01:25 +0300
    Ready:          True
    Restart Count:  0
    Environment:    <none>
    Mounts:
      /var/run/secrets/kubernetes.io/serviceaccount from kube-api-access-ck25t (ro)
Conditions:
```

Figure 16.37 – Relevant pod information

You can also venture out to any of the cluster nodes where our pods are running and take a closer look at the related containers. Let's take node k8s-n3 (192.168.122.163), for example, where our standalone pod (packt-web) is running. We'll SSH into the node's terminal first:

```
ssh packt@192.168.122.163
```

Then we'll use the containerd runtime to query the containers in the system:

```
sudo crictl --runtime-endpoint unix:///run/containerd/containerd.sock
ps
```

The output shows the following:

```
packt@k8s-n3:~$ sudo crictl --runtime-endpoint unix:///run/containerd/containerd.sock ps
CONTAINER       IMAGE           CREATED           STATE      NAME
1b1645d08ba49   2a4dceb283aa0   27 minutes ago    Running    packt-web   ⬅
25e488ac7681c   8065b798a4d67   2 hours ago       Running    calico-node
6da991c5c8619   c120fed2beb84   2 hours ago       Running    kube-proxy
```

Figure 16.38 – Getting the containers running on a cluster node

Next, we'll show you how to access processes running inside the pods.

Accessing processes in pods

Let's switch back to our local (on our local machine, not the VM) kubectl environment and run the following command to access the shell in the container running the packt-web pod:

```
kubectl exec -it packt-web -- /bin/sh
```

The command takes us inside the container to an interactive shell prompt. Here, we can run commands as if we were logged in to the packt-web host using the terminal. The interactive session is produced using the -it option – interactive terminal – or --interactive --tty.

Let's run a few commands, starting with the process explorer:

```
ps aux
```

Here's a relevant excerpt from the output, showing the processes running inside the packt-web container, and some commands running inside it:

```
alexandru@debian:~$ kubectl exec -it packt-web -- /bin/sh
/ # ps aux
PID   USER      TIME  COMMAND
    1 root      0:00 nginx: master process nginx -g daemon off;
   20 nginx     0:00 nginx: worker process
   21 nginx     0:00 nginx: worker process
   22 root      0:00 /bin/sh
   28 root      0:00 ps aux
/ # ifconfig | grep 'inet addr:' | cut -d: -f2 | awk '{print $1}' | grep -v '127.0.0.1'
172.16.57.193
/ # hostname
packt-web
/ # exit
alexandru@debian:~$
```

Figure 16.39 – The processes running inside the packt-web container

We can also retrieve the IP address with the following command:

```
ifconfig | grep 'inet addr:' | cut -d: -f2 | awk '{print $1}' | grep
-v '127.0.0.1'
```

The output shows the pod's IP address (as seen in *Figure 16.39*):

```
172.16.57.193
```

We can also retrieve the hostname with the following command:

```
hostname
```

The output shows the pod name (as seen in *Figure 16.39*):

```
packt-web
```

Let's leave the container shell with the `exit` command (as shown in *Figure 16.39*) or by pressing *Ctrl + D*. With the `kubectl exec` command, we can run any process inside a pod, assuming that the related process exists.

We'll experiment next by testing the `packt-web` application pod using `curl`. We should note that, at this time, the only way to access the web server endpoint of `packt-web` is via its internal IP address. Previously, we used the `kubectl get pods -o wide` and `describe` commands to retrieve detailed information regarding pods, including the pod's IP address. You can also use the following one-liner to retrieve the pod's IP:

```
kubectl get pods packt-web -o jsonpath='{.status.podIP}{"\n"}'
```

In our case, the command returns `172.16.57.193`. We used the `-o jsonpath` output option to specify the JSON query for a specific field, `{.status.podIP}`. Remember that the pod's IP is only accessible within the pod network (`172.16.0.0/16`) inside the cluster. Following is a screenshot showing the output:

```
alexandru@debian:~$ kubectl get pods packt-web -o jsonpath='{.status.podIP}{"\n"}'
172.16.57.193
```

Figure 16.40 – Testing the application pod

Consequently, we need to probe the `packt-web` endpoint using a `curl` command that has originated within the pod network. An easy way to accomplish such a task is to run a test pod with the `curl` utility installed:

1. The following command runs a pod named `test`, based on the `curlimages/curl` Docker image:

    ```
    kubectl run test --image=curlimages/curl sleep 600
    ```

2. We keep the container artificially alive with the `sleep` command due to the Docker entry point of the corresponding image, which simply runs a `curl` command and then exits. Without `sleep`, the pod would keep coming up and crashing. With the `sleep` command, we delay the execution of the `curl` entry point to prevent the exit. The output is shown in the following screenshot:

```
alexandru@debian:~$ kubectl run test --image=curlimages/curl sleep 600
pod/test created
```

Figure 16.41 – Running a test with curl on the pod

3. Now, we can run a simple `curl` command using the `test` pod targeting the `packt-web` web server endpoint:

    ```
    kubectl exec test -- curl http://172.16.57.193
    ```

4. We'll get an HTTP response and a corresponding **access log trace** (from the Nginx server running in the pod) accounting for the request. A snippet of the output is as follows:

```
alexandru@debian:~$ kubectl exec test -- curl http://172.16.57.193
<!DOCTYPE html>
<html>
<head>
<title>Hello World</title>
```

Figure 16.42 – The response of running the curl test

5. To view the logs on the `packt-web` pod, we run the following command:

```
kubectl logs packt-web
```

The output is as follows:

```
alexandru@debian:~$ kubectl logs packt-web
/docker-entrypoint.sh: /docker-entrypoint.d/ is not empty, will attempt to perform configuration
/docker-entrypoint.sh: Looking for shell scripts in /docker-entrypoint.d/
/docker-entrypoint.sh: Launching /docker-entrypoint.d/10-listen-on-ipv6-by-default.sh
10-listen-on-ipv6-by-default.sh: info: /etc/nginx/conf.d/default.conf is not a file or does not exis
t
/docker-entrypoint.sh: Sourcing /docker-entrypoint.d/15-local-resolvers.envsh
/docker-entrypoint.sh: Launching /docker-entrypoint.d/20-envsubst-on-templates.sh
/docker-entrypoint.sh: Launching /docker-entrypoint.d/30-tune-worker-processes.sh
/docker-entrypoint.sh: Configuration complete; ready for start up
2023/09/27 12:01:25 [notice] 1#1: using the "epoll" event method
2023/09/27 12:01:25 [notice] 1#1: nginx/1.25.2
2023/09/27 12:01:25 [notice] 1#1: built by gcc 12.2.1 20220924 (Alpine 12.2.1_git20220924-r10)
2023/09/27 12:01:25 [notice] 1#1: OS: Linux 5.15.0-84-generic
2023/09/27 12:01:25 [notice] 1#1: getrlimit(RLIMIT_NOFILE): 1048576:1048576
2023/09/27 12:01:25 [notice] 1#1: start worker processes
2023/09/27 12:01:25 [notice] 1#1: start worker process 20
2023/09/27 12:01:25 [notice] 1#1: start worker process 21
172.16.111.193 - - [27/Sep/2023:12:43:21 +0000] "GET / HTTP/1.1" 200 7231 "-" "curl/8.3.0" "-"
```

Figure 16.43 – Logs for packt-web pod

6. The logs in the `packt-web` pod are produced by Nginx and redirected to `stdout` and `stderr`. We can easily verify this with the following command:

```
kubectl exec packt-web -- ls -la /var/log/nginx
```

The output shows the related symlinks:

```
alexandru@debian:~$ kubectl exec packt-web -- ls -la /var/log/nginx
total 8
drwxr-xr-x    2 root     root          4096 Aug 29 00:37 .
drwxr-xr-x    1 root     root          4096 Aug 29 00:37 ..
lrwxrwxrwx    1 root     root            11 Aug 29 00:37 access.log -> /dev/stdout
lrwxrwxrwx    1 root     root            11 Aug 29 00:37 error.log -> /dev/stderr
```

Figure 16.44 – Related symlinks

7.   When you're done using the `test` pod, you can delete it with the following command:

```
kubectl delete pods test
```

Now that we have deployed our first application inside a Kubernetes cluster, let's look at how to expose the related endpoint to the world. Next, we will expose Deployments via a Service.

Exposing Deployments as Services

Now, let's rewind to the command we used previously to create the `packt` Deployment. Don't run it. Here it is just as a refresher:

```
kubectl create deployment packt --image=nginxdemos/hello
```

The command carried out the following sequence:

1.   It created a Deployment (`packt`).
2.   The Deployment created a ReplicaSet (`packt-579bb9c999`).
3.   The ReplicaSet created the pod (`packt-579bb9c999-rtvzr`).

We can verify that with the following commands:

```
kubectl get deployments -l app=packt
kubectl get replicasets -l app=packt
kubectl get pods -l app=packt
```

In the preceding commands, we used the `--label-columns` (`-l`) flag to filter results by the `app=packt` label, denoting the `packt` Deployment's resources.

We encourage you to take a closer look at each of these resources using the `kubectl describe` command. Don't forget to use the `kubectl` autocomplete feature when typing in the commands:

```
kubectl describe deployment packt | more
kubectl describe replicaset packt | more
kubectl describe pod packt-5dc77bb9bf-bnzsc | more
```

The `kubectl describe` command could be very resourceful when troubleshooting applications or pod Deployments. Look inside the *Events* section in the related output for clues on pods failing to start, errors, if any, and possibly understand what went wrong.

Now that we have deployed our first application inside a Kubernetes cluster, let's look at how to expose the related endpoint to the world.

So far, we have deployed an application (`packt`) with a single pod (`packt-579bb9c999-rtvzr`) running an Nginx web server listening on port `80`. As we explained earlier, at this time, we can only access the pod within the pod network, which is internal to the cluster. In this section, we'll show you how to expose the application (or Deployment) to be accessible from the outside world. Kubernetes uses the Service API object, consisting of a **proxy** and a **selector** routing the network traffic to application pods in a Deployment. To proceed, you can follow these steps:

1. The following command creates a Service for our Deployment (`packt`):

```
kubectl expose deployment packt \
    --port=80 \
    --target-port=80 \
    --type=NodePort
```

Here's a brief explanation of the preceding command flags:

- `--port=80`: This exposes the Service on port `80` externally within the cluster

- `--target-port=80`: This maps to port `80` internally in the application pod

- `--type=NodePort`: This makes the Service available outside the cluster

The output shows the Service (`packt`) we just created for exposing our application:

```
service/packt exposed
```

Without the `--type=NodePort` flag, the Service type would be `ClusterIP` by default, and the Service endpoint would only be accessible within the cluster.

2. Let's take a closer look at our Service (`packt`):

```
kubectl get service packt
```

The output shows the cluster IP assigned to the Service (`10.105.111.243`) and the ports the Service is listening on for TCP traffic (`80:32664/TCP`):

- port `80`: Within the cluster

- port `32664`: Outside the cluster, on any of the nodes

We should note that the cluster IP is only accessible within the cluster and not from the outside:

```
alexandru@debian:~$ kubectl expose deployment packt \
> --port=80 \
> --target-port=80 \
> --type=NodePort
service/packt exposed
alexandru@debian:~$ kubectl get service packt
NAME     TYPE       CLUSTER-IP       EXTERNAL-IP   PORT(S)        AGE
packt    NodePort   10.105.111.243   <none>        80:32664/TCP   28s
```

Figure 16.45 – The Service exposing the packt Deployment

Also, EXTERNAL-IP (<none>) should not be mistaken for the cluster node's IP address where our Service is accessible. The external IP is usually a load balancer IP address configured by a cloud provider hosting the Kubernetes cluster (configurable via the --external-ip flag).

3. We should now be able to access our application outside the cluster by pointing a browser to any of the cluster nodes on port 32664. To get a list of our cluster nodes with their respective IP addresses and hostnames, we can run the following command:

```
kubectl get nodes -o jsonpath='{range .items[*]}{.status.
addresses[*].address}{"\n"}'
```

The output is as follows:

```
alexandru@debian:~$ kubectl get nodes -o jsonpath='{range .items[*]}
{.status.addresses[*].address}{"\n"}'
192.168.122.104 k8s-cp1
192.168.122.146 k8s-n1
192.168.122.233 k8s-n2
192.168.122.163 k8s-n3
```

Figure 16.46 – List of cluster nodes

4. Let's choose the CP node (192.168.122.104/k8s-cp1) and enter the following address in a browser: http://192.168.122.104:32664.

The web request from the browser is directed to the Service endpoint (packt), which routes the related network packets to the application pod (packt-579bb9c999-rtvzr). The packt web application responds with a simple Nginx **Hello World** web page, displaying the pod's internal IP address (172.16.215.65) and name (packt-579bb9c999-rtvzr):

Figure 16.47 – Accessing the packt application Service

5. To verify that the information on the web page is accurate, you may run the following `kubectl` command, retrieving similar information:

```
kubectl get pod packt-579bb9c999-rtvzr -o jsonpath='{.status.
podIP}{"\n"}{.metadata.name}{"\n"}'
```

The output of the command will be the internal IP address and the name of the pod, as shown in the following:

```
alexandru@debian:~$ kubectl get pod packt-579bb9c999-rtvzr -o jsonpath='{.status.podIP}{"\n"}{.metadata.name}{"\n"}'
172.16.215.65
packt-579bb9c999-rtvzr
```

Figure 16.48 – Verify the information with the kubectl command

Suppose we have high traffic targeting our application, and we'd like to scale out the ReplicaSet controlling our pods. We'll show you how to accomplish this task in the next section.

Scaling application Deployments

Currently, we have a single pod in the `packt` Deployment. In order to scale the application Deployments, we have to obtain information about the running replicas, to scale them to the desired number and test it. Here are the steps to take:

1. To retrieve the relevant details about the number of running replicas, we run the following command:

```
kubectl describe deployment packt
```

The relevant excerpt in the output is as follows:

```
alexandru@debian:~$ kubectl describe deployment packt
Name:                   packt
Namespace:              default
CreationTimestamp:      Wed, 27 Sep 2023 15:00:48 +0300
Labels:                 app=packt
Annotations:            deployment.kubernetes.io/revision: 1
Selector:               app=packt
Replicas:               1 desired | 1 updated | 1 total | 1 available | 0 unavailable
StrategyType:           RollingUpdate
MinReadySeconds:        0
RollingUpdateStrategy:  25% max unavailable, 25% max surge
```

Figure 16.49 – Pod details

2. Let's scale up our `packt` Deployment to 10 replicas with the following command:

```
kubectl scale deployment packt --replicas=10
```

The command output is as follows:

```
deployment.apps/packt scaled
```

3. If we list the pods of the packt Deployment, we'll see 10 pods running:

```
kubectl get pods -l app=packt
```

The output is as follows:

```
alexandru@debian:~$ kubectl scale deployment packt --replicas=10
deployment.apps/packt scaled
alexandru@debian:~$ kubectl get pods -l app=packt
NAME                        READY   STATUS    RESTARTS   AGE
packt-579bb9c999-5zwnn      1/1     Running   0          22s
packt-579bb9c999-dnpm6      1/1     Running   0          22s
packt-579bb9c999-fw2fn      1/1     Running   0          22s
packt-579bb9c999-g5wwp      1/1     Running   0          22s
packt-579bb9c999-lrf74      1/1     Running   0          22s
packt-579bb9c999-r4npz      1/1     Running   0          22s
packt-579bb9c999-rfv5j      1/1     Running   0          22s
packt-579bb9c999-rtvzr      1/1     Running   0          174m
packt-579bb9c999-s6mrl      1/1     Running   0          22s
packt-579bb9c999-zdvbl      1/1     Running   0          22s
```

Figure 16.50 – Scaling up the Deployment replicas

4. Incoming requests to our application Service endpoint (http://192.168.122.104:32664)
    will be load balanced between the pods. To illustrate this behavior, we can either use curl or a
    text-based browser at the command line to avoid the caching-related optimizations of a modern
    desktop browser. For a better illustration, we'll use **Lynx**, a simple text-based browser. On our
    Debian 12 desktop, the package is already installed. You can install it with the following command:

```
sudo apt-get install -y lynx
```

5. Next, we point Lynx to our application endpoint:

```
lynx 172.16.191.6:32081
```

If we refresh the page with *Ctrl + R* every few seconds, we observe that the server address and
name change based on the current pod processing the request:

```
NGINX Logo

Server address: 172.16.215.65:80

Server name: packt-579bb9c999-rtvzr

Date: 27/Sep/2023:15:00:12 +0000

URI: /
```

```
NGINX Logo

Server address: 172.16.57.196:80

Server name: packt-579bb9c999-rfv5j

Date: 27/Sep/2023:15:00:22 +0000

URI: /
```

```
NGINX Logo

Server address: 172.16.57.194:80

Server name: packt-579bb9c999-fw2fn

Date: 27/Sep/2023:15:00:30 +0000

URI: /
```

```
NGINX Logo

Server address: 172.16.215.66:80

Server name: packt-579bb9c999-dnpm6

Date: 27/Sep/2023:15:08:51 +0000

URI: /
```

Figure 16.51 – Load balancing requests across pods

You can exit the Lynx browser by typing `Q` and then pressing *Enter*.

6. We can scale back our Deployment (`packt`) to three replicas (or any other non-zero positive number) with the following command:

```
kubectl scale deployment packt --replicas=3
```

7. If we query the `packt` application pods, we can see the surplus pods terminating until only three pods are remaining:

```
kubectl get pods -l app=packt
```

The output is as follows:

```
alexandru@debian:~$ kubectl scale deployment packt --replicas=3
deployment.apps/packt scaled
alexandru@debian:~$ kubectl get pods -l app=packt
NAME                     READY   STATUS    RESTARTS   AGE
packt-579bb9c999-lrf74   1/1     Running   0          21m
packt-579bb9c999-r4npz   1/1     Running   0          21m
packt-579bb9c999-rtvzr   1/1     Running   0          3h15m
```

Figure 16.52 – Scaling back to three pods

8. Before concluding our imperative Deployments, let's clean up all the resources we have created thus far:

```
kubectl delete service packt
kubectl delete deployment packt
kubectl delete pod packt-web
```

9. The following command should reflect a clean slate:

```
kubectl get all
```

The output is as follows:

```
alexandru@debian:~$ kubectl delete service packt
service "packt" deleted
alexandru@debian:~$ kubectl delete deployment packt
deployment.apps "packt" deleted
alexandru@debian:~$ kubectl delete pod packt-web
pod "packt-web" deleted
alexandru@debian:~$ kubectl get all
NAME                    TYPE        CLUSTER-IP    EXTERNAL-IP   PORT(S)    AGE
service/kubernetes      ClusterIP   10.96.0.1     <none>        443/TCP    29h
```

Figure 16.53 – The cluster in a default state

In the next section, we'll look at how to deploy resources and applications declaratively in the Kubernetes cluster.

Working with declarative Deployments

At the heart of a declarative Deployment is a manifest file. Manifest files are generally in YAML format and authoring them usually involves a mix of autogenerated code and manual editing. The manifest is then deployed using the `kubectl apply` command:

```
kubectl apply -f MANIFEST
```

Deploying resources declaratively in Kubernetes involves the following stages:

- Creating a manifest file
- Updating the manifest
- Validating the manifest
- Deploying the manifest
- Iterating between the preceding stages

To illustrate the declarative model, we follow the example of deploying a simple Hello World web application to the cluster. The result will be similar to our previous approach of using the imperative method.

So, let's start by creating a manifest for our Deployment.

Creating a manifest

When we created our `packt` Deployment imperatively, we used the following command (don't run it just yet!):

```
kubectl create deployment packt --image=nginxdemos/hello
```

The following command will simulate the same process without changing the system state:

```
kubectl create deployment packt --image=nginxdemos/hello \
    --dry-run=client --output=yaml
```

We used the following additional options (flags):

- `--dry-run=client`: This runs the command in the local `kubectl` environment (*client*) without modifying the system state

- `--output=yaml`: This formats the command output as YAML

The output of the command is as follows:

```
alexandru@debian:~$ kubectl create deployment packt --image=nginxdemos/hello --dry-run=client --outp
ut=yaml
apiVersion: apps/v1
kind: Deployment
metadata:
  creationTimestamp: null
  labels:
    app: packt
  name: packt
spec:
  replicas: 1
  selector:
    matchLabels:
      app: packt
  strategy: {}
  template:
    metadata:
      creationTimestamp: null
      labels:
        app: packt
    spec:
      containers:
      - image: nginxdemos/hello
        name: hello
        resources: {}
status: {}
```

Figure 16.54 – Simulating a manifest creation

We can use the previous command's output to analyze the changes to be made to the system. Then we can redirect it to a file (packt.yaml) serving as a draft of our Deployment manifest:

```
kubectl create deployment packt --image=nginxdemos/hello \
    --dry-run=client --output=yaml > packt.yaml
```

We have created our first manifest file, packt.yaml. From here, we can edit the file to accommodate more complex configurations. For now, we'll leave the manifest as is and proceed with the next stage in our declarative Deployment workflow.

Validating a manifest

Before deploying a manifest, we recommend validating the Deployment, especially if you edited the file manually. Editing mistakes can happen, particularly when working with complex YAML files with multiple indentation levels.

The following command validates the packt.yaml Deployment manifest:

```
kubectl apply -f packt.yaml --dry-run=client
```

A successful validation yields the following output:

```
deployment.apps/packt created (dry run)
```

If there are any errors, we should edit the manifest file and correct them prior to deployment. Our manifest looks good, so let's go ahead and deploy it.

Deploying a manifest

To deploy the packt.yaml manifest, we use the following command:

```
kubectl apply -f packt.yaml
```

A successful Deployment shows the following message:

```
deployment.apps/packt created
```

We can check the deployed resources with the following command:

```
kubectl get all -l app=packt
```

The output shows that the packt Deployment resources created declaratively are up and running:

```
alexandru@debian:~$ kubectl apply -f packt.yaml --dry-run=client
deployment.apps/packt created (dry run)
alexandru@debian:~$ kubectl apply -f packt.yaml
deployment.apps/packt created
alexandru@debian:~$ kubectl get all -l app=packt
NAME                          READY     STATUS     RESTARTS   AGE
pod/packt-579bb9c999-9ks6x    1/1       Running    0          12s

NAME                       READY     UP-TO-DATE   AVAILABLE   AGE
deployment.apps/packt      1/1       1            1           12s

NAME                                 DESIRED   CURRENT   READY   AGE
replicaset.apps/packt-579bb9c999     1         1         1       12s
```

Figure 16.55 – The Deployment resources created declaratively

Next, we want to expose our Deployment using a Service.

Exposing the Deployment with a Service

We'll repeat the preceding workflow by creating, validating, and deploying the Service manifest (packt-svc.yaml). For brevity, we simply enumerate the related commands:

1. Create the manifest file (packt-svc.yaml) for the Service exposing our Deployment (packt):

```
kubectl expose deployment packt \
    --port=80 \
    --target-port=80 \
    --type=NodePort \
    --dry-run=client --output=yaml > packt-svc.yaml
```

We explained the preceding command previously in the *Exposing Deployments as Services* section.

2. Next, we'll validate the Service Deployment manifest:

```
kubectl apply -f packt-svc.yaml --dry-run=client
```

3. If the validation is successful, we deploy the Service manifest:

```
kubectl apply -f packt-svc.yaml
```

4. Let's get the current status of the packt resources:

```
kubectl get all -l app=packt
```

The output shows all of the packt application resources, including the Service endpoint (service/packt) listening on port 31380:

```
alexandru@debian:~$ kubectl expose deployment packt \
> --port=80 \
> --target-port=80 \
> --type=NodePort \
> --dry-run=client --output=yaml > packt-svc.yaml
alexandru@debian:~$ ls
Desktop    Downloads  Music  packt-svc.yaml  Pictures  snap       Videos
Documents  kubectl    opt    packt.yaml      Public    Templates
alexandru@debian:~$ kubectl apply -f packt-svc.yaml --dry-run=client
service/packt created (dry run)
alexandru@debian:~$ kubectl apply -f packt-svc.yaml
service/packt created
alexandru@debian:~$ kubectl get all -l app=packt
NAME                         READY    STATUS     RESTARTS   AGE
pod/packt-579bb9c999-9ks6x   1/1      Running    0          5m39s

NAME            TYPE       CLUSTER-IP     EXTERNAL-IP   PORT(S)       AGE
service/packt   NodePort   10.106.74.34   <none>        80:31380/TCP  17s

NAME                     READY   UP-TO-DATE   AVAILABLE   AGE
deployment.apps/packt    1/1     1            1           5m39s

NAME                               DESIRED   CURRENT   READY   AGE
replicaset.apps/packt-579bb9c999   1         1         1       5m39s
```

Figure 16.56 – The packt application resources deployed

5. Using a browser, `curl`, or Lynx, we can access our application by targeting any of the cluster
    nodes on port 31380. Let's use the CP node (k8s-cp1, 192.168.122.104) by pointing
    our browser to http://192.168.122.104:31380:

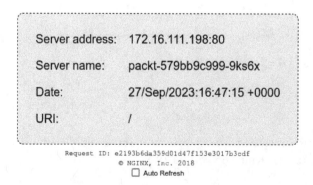

Figure 16.57 – Accessing the packt application endpoint

If we want to change the existing configuration of a resource in our application Deployment, we can update the related manifest and redeploy it. In the next section, we'll modify the Deployment to accommodate a scale-out scenario.

Updating a manifest

Suppose our application is taking a high number of requests, and we'd like to add more pods to our Deployment to handle the traffic. We need to change the `spec.replicas` configuration setting in the `pack.yaml` manifest:

1. Using your editor of choice, edit the `packt.yaml` file and locate the following configuration section:

    ```
    spec:
      replicas: 1
    ```

    Change the value from `1` to `10` for additional application pods in the ReplicaSet controlled by the `packt` Deployment. The configuration becomes the following:

    ```
    spec:
      replicas: 10
    ```

2. Save the manifest file and redeploy with the following command:

    ```
    kubectl apply -f packt.yaml
    ```

    The output suggests that the `packt` Deployment has been reconfigured:

    ```
    deployment.apps/packt configured
    ```

3. If we query the `packt` resources in the cluster, we should see the new pods up and running:

    ```
    kubectl get all -l app=packt
    ```

    The output displays the application resources of our `packt` Deployment, including the additional pods deployed in the cluster:

```
alexandru@debian:~$ kubectl apply -f packt.yaml
deployment.apps/packt configured
alexandru@debian:~$ kubectl get all -l app=packt
NAME                           READY   STATUS    RESTARTS   AGE
pod/packt-579bb9c999-5pw6q     1/1     Running   0          39s
pod/packt-579bb9c999-9ks6x     1/1     Running   0          14m
pod/packt-579bb9c999-cvptf     1/1     Running   0          39s
pod/packt-579bb9c999-d7kmj     1/1     Running   0          39s
pod/packt-579bb9c999-fpckr     1/1     Running   0          39s
pod/packt-579bb9c999-gr29g     1/1     Running   0          39s
pod/packt-579bb9c999-k94jz     1/1     Running   0          39s
pod/packt-579bb9c999-m55c8     1/1     Running   0          39s
pod/packt-579bb9c999-p492x     1/1     Running   0          39s
pod/packt-579bb9c999-t55lw     1/1     Running   0          39s

NAME             TYPE       CLUSTER-IP     EXTERNAL-IP   PORT(S)        AGE
service/packt    NodePort   10.106.74.34   <none>        80:31380/TCP   8m38s

NAME                        READY   UP-TO-DATE   AVAILABLE   AGE
deployment.apps/packt       10/10   10           10          14m

NAME                                   DESIRED   CURRENT   READY   AGE
replicaset.apps/packt-579bb9c999       10        10        10      14m
```

Figure 16.58 – The additional pods added for application scale-out

We encourage you to test with the scale-out environment and verify the load balancing workload described in the *Scaling application Deployments* section earlier in this chapter.

4. Let's scale back our Deployment to three pods, but this time by updating the related manifest on the fly with the following command:

```
kubectl edit deployment packt
```

The command will open our default editor in the system (**vi**) to make the desired change:

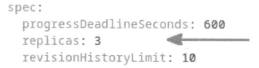

Figure 16.59 – Making Deployment changes on the fly

5. After saving and exiting the editor, we'll get a message suggesting that our Deployment (`packt`) has been updated:

```
deployment.apps/packt edited
```

Please note that the modifications made on the fly with `kubectl edit` will not be reflected in the Deployment manifest (`packt.yaml`). Nevertheless, the related configuration changes are persisted in the cluster (etcd).

6. We can verify our updated Deployment with the help of the following command:

```
kubectl get deployment packt
```

The output now shows only three pods running in our Deployment:

```
alexandru@debian:~$ kubectl get deployment packt
NAME      READY    UP-TO-DATE    AVAILABLE    AGE
packt     3/3      3             3            18m
```

Figure 16.60 – Showing the number of Deployments

7. Before wrapping up, let's clean up our resources once again with the following commands to bring the cluster back to the default state:

```
kubectl delete service packt
kubectl delete deployment packt
```

We have shown you how to use Kubernetes on bare metal, and in the next section, we will briefly point you to some useful resources for using Kubernetes in the cloud.

Running Kubernetes in the cloud

Managed Kubernetes Services are fairly common among public cloud providers. Amazon **Elastic Kubernetes Service (EKS)**, **Azure Kubernetes Services (AKS)**, and **Google Kubernetes Engine (GKE)** are the major cloud offerings of Kubernetes at the time of this writing. In this section, we'll not focus on any of these solutions, but we will provide you with solid resources on how to use Kubernetes in the cloud. For more advanced titles on this subject, please check the *Further reading* section of this chapter.

We should note that we just scratched the surface of deploying and managing Kubernetes clusters. Yet, here we are, at a significant milestone, where we deployed our first Kubernetes clusters on-premises. We have reached the end of this journey here, but we trust that you'll take it to the next level and further explore the exciting domain of application Deployment and scaling with Kubernetes. Let's now summarize what we have learned in this chapter.

Summary

We began this chapter with a high-level overview of the Kubernetes architecture and API object model, introducing the most common cluster resources, such as pods, Deployments, and Services. Next, we took on the relatively challenging task of building an on-premises Kubernetes cluster from scratch using VMs. We explored various CLI tools for managing Kubernetes cluster resources on-premises. At the high point of our journey, we focused on deploying and scaling applications in Kubernetes using imperative and declarative Deployment scenarios.

We believe that novice Linux administrators will benefit greatly from the material covered in this chapter and become more knowledgeable in managing resources across hybrid clouds and on-premises distributed environments, deploying applications at scale, and working with CLI tools. We believe that the structured information in this chapter will also help seasoned system administrators refresh some of their knowledge and skills in the areas covered.

It's been a relatively long chapter, and we barely skimmed the surface of the related field. We encourage you to explore some resources captured in the *Further reading* section and strengthen your knowledge regarding some key areas of Kubernetes environments, such as networking, security, and scale.

In the next chapter, we'll stay within the application deployment realm and look at **Ansible**, a platform for accelerating application delivery on-premises and in the cloud.

Questions

Here are a few questions for refreshing or pondering upon some of the concepts you've learned in this chapter:

1. Enumerate some of the essential Services of a Kubernetes CP node. How do the worker nodes differ?

2. What command did we use to bootstrap a Kubernetes cluster?

3. What is the difference between imperative and declarative Deployments in Kubernetes?

4. What is the `kubectl` command for deploying a pod? How about the command for creating a Deployment?

5. What is the `kubectl` command to access the shell within a pod container?

6. What is the `kubectl` command to query all resources related to a Deployment?

7. How do you scale out a Deployment in Kubernetes? Can you think of the different ways (commands) in which to accomplish the task?

8. How do you delete all resources related to a Deployment in Kubernetes?

Further reading

The following resources may help you to consolidate your knowledge of Kubernetes further:

- Kubernetes documentation online: `https://kubernetes.io/docs/home/`
- The kubectl cheat sheet: `https://kubernetes.io/docs/reference/kubectl/cheatsheet/`
- *Kubernetes and Docker: The Container Masterclass [Video]*, *Cerulean Canvas*, Packt Publishing
- *Mastering Kubernetes – Third Edition*, Gigi Sayfan, Packt Publishing

The following is a short list of useful links for deploying Kubernetes on Azure, Amazon, and Google:

- Amazon EKS:

  - `https://docs.aws.amazon.com/eks/index.html`
  - `https://docs.aws.amazon.com/eks/latest/userguide/sample-deployment.html`

- AKS:

  - `https://azure.microsoft.com/en-us/services/kubernetes-service/`
  - `https://learn.microsoft.com/en-us/azure/aks/tutorial-kubernetes-deploy-cluster?tabs=azure-cli`
  - `https://learn.microsoft.com/en-us/azure/aks/learn/quick-kubernetes-deploy-portal?tabs=azure-cli`

- GKE:

  - `https://cloud.google.com/kubernetes-engine`
  - `https://cloud.google.com/build/docs/deploying-builds/deploy-gke`
  - `https://cloud.google.com/kubernetes-engine/docs/deploy-app-cluster`

17

Infrastructure and Automation with Ansible

If your day-to-day system administration or development work involves tedious and repetitive operations, **Ansible** could help you run your tasks while saving you precious time. Ansible is a tool for automating **software provisioning**, **configuration management**, and **application deployment workflows**. Initially developed by Michael DeHaan in 2012, Ansible was acquired by Red Hat in 2015 and is now maintained as an open source project.

In this chapter, you'll learn about the fundamental concepts of Ansible, along with a variety of hands-on examples. In particular, we'll explore the following topics:

- Introducing Ansible architecture and configuration management
- Installing Ansible
- Working with Ansible

Technical requirements

First, you should be familiar with the Linux command-line Terminal in general. Intermediate knowledge of Linux will help you understand some of the intricacies of the practical illustrations used throughout this chapter. You should also be proficient in using a Linux-based text editor.

For the hands-on examples, we recommend setting up a lab environment similar to the one we're using. To replicate this environment, your CPU will need to have at least 6 physical cores and 6 virtual cores (12 in total). A quad-core CPU with hyper-threading is not enough. Also, OpenSSH should be installed on all the hosts. You'll find related instructions in the *Setting up the lab environment* section of this chapter. If you don't configure a lab environment, you will still benefit from the detailed explanations associated with the practical examples in this chapter.

Now, let's start our journey by covering introductory concepts surrounding Ansible.

Introducing Ansible architecture and configuration management

In the introduction to this chapter, we captured one of the essential aspects of Ansible – it's a tool for automating workflows. Almost any Linux system administration task can be automated using Ansible. Using the Ansible CLI, we can invoke simple commands to change the **desired state** of a system. Usually, with Ansible, we execute tasks on a remote host or a group of hosts.

Let's use the classic illustration of **package management**. Suppose you're managing an infrastructure that includes a group of web servers, and you plan to install the latest version of a web server application (Nginx or Apache) on all of them. One way to accomplish this task is to SSH into each host and run the related shell commands to install the latest web server package. If you have a lot of machines, this will be a big task. You could argue that you can write a script to automate this job. This is possible, but then you'd have yet another job on your hands; that is, maintaining the script, fixing possible bugs, and, with your infrastructure growing, adding new features.

At some point, you may want to manage users or databases or configure network settings on multiple hosts. Soon, you'll be looking at a Swiss Army knife tool, with capabilities that you'd rather get for free instead of writing them yourself. Here's where Ansible comes in handy. With its myriad of modules – for almost any system administration task you can imagine – Ansible can remotely configure, run, or deploy your management jobs of choice, with minimal effort and in a very secure and efficient way.

We'll consolidate these preliminary thoughts with a brief look at the Ansible architecture.

Understanding the Ansible architecture

The core Ansible framework is written in Python. Let's mention upfront that Ansible has an **agentless** architecture. In other words, it runs on a **control node** that executes commands against remote hosts, without the need for a remote endpoint or service to be installed on the managed host to communicate with the control node. At a minimum, the only requirement for Ansible communication is SSH connectivity to the managed host. Yet, the number of Ansible operations would be relatively limited to only running scripts and raw SSH commands if the host didn't have a Python framework installed. The vast majority of server OS platforms already have Python installed by default.

Ansible can manage a fleet of remote hosts from a single control node using secure SSH connections. The following diagram shows the logical layout of a managed infrastructure using Ansible:

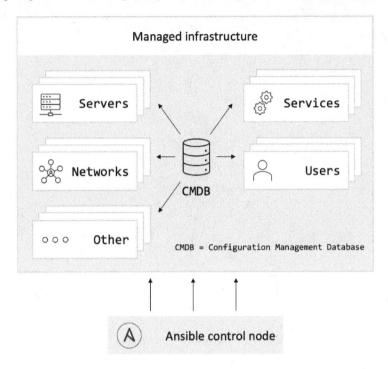

Figure 17.1 – The logical layout of a managed infrastructure using Ansible

Production-grade enterprise environments usually include a **configuration management database (CMDB)** for organizing their IT infrastructure assets. Examples of IT infrastructure assets are servers, networks, services, and users. Although not directly part of the Ansible architecture, the CMDB describes the assets and their relationship within a managed infrastructure and can be leveraged to build an **Ansible inventory**.

The inventory is local storage on the Ansible control node – typically an **INI** or **YAML** file – that describes managed **hosts** or **groups** of hosts. The inventory is either inferred from the CMDB or manually created by the system administrator.

Now, let's have a closer look at the high-level Ansible architecture shown in the following diagram:

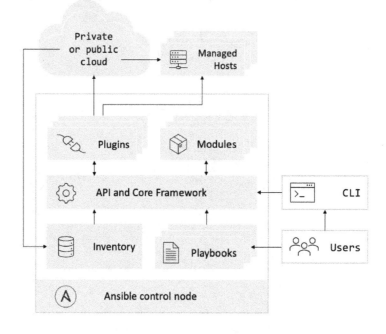

Figure 17.2 – The Ansible architecture

The preceding diagram shows the Ansible control node interacting with managed hosts in a private or public cloud infrastructure. Here are some brief descriptions of the blocks featured in the architectural view:

- **API and core framework**: The main libraries encapsulating Ansible's core functionality; the Ansible core framework is written in Python

- **Plugins**: Additional libraries extending the core framework's functionality – for instance, the following:

  - **Connection plugins**, such as cloud connectors

  - **Test plugins**, verifying specific response data

  - **Callback plugins** for responding to events

- **Modules**: These encapsulate specific functions running on managed hosts, such as the following:

  - `user` module for managing users

  - `package` module for managing software packages

- **Inventory**: The INI or YAML file describing the hosts and groups of hosts targeted by Ansible commands and playbooks

- **Playbooks**: The Ansible execution files describing a set of tasks that target managed hosts

- **Private or public clouds**: The managed infrastructure, hosted on-premises or in various cloud environments (for example, VMware, **Amazon Web Services (AWS)**, and Azure)

- **Managed hosts**: The servers targeted by Ansible commands and playbooks

- **CLI**: The Ansible CLI tools, such as `ansible`, `ansible-playbook`, `ansible-doc`, and so on

- **Users**: The administrators, power users, and automated user processes running Ansible commands or playbooks

Now that we have a basic understanding of the Ansible architecture, let's look at what makes Ansible a great tool for automating management workflows. We'll introduce the concept of **configuration management** next.

Introducing configuration management

If we look back at the old days, system administrators usually managed a relatively low number of servers, running everyday administrative tasks by using a remote shell on each host. Relatively simple operations, such as copying files, updating software packages, and managing users, could easily be scripted and reused regularly. With the recent surge in apps and services, driven by the vast expansion of the internet, modern-day on-premises and cloud-based IT infrastructures – sustaining the related platforms – have grown significantly. The sheer amount of configuration changes involved would by far exceed the capacity of a single admin running and maintaining a handful of scripts. Here's where configuration management comes to the rescue.

With configuration management, managed hosts and assets are grouped into logical categories, based on specific criteria, as suggested in *Figure 17.1*. Managing assets other than hosts ultimately comes down to performing specific tasks on the servers hosting those assets. The **configuration management manifest** is the Ansible inventory file that manages these hosts and assets. Thus, Ansible becomes the configuration management endpoint.

With Ansible, we can run single one-off commands to carry out specific tasks, but a far more efficient configuration management workflow can be achieved via **playbooks**. With Ansible playbooks, we can run multiple tasks that target various subsystems of a target platform against any number of hosts. Scheduling `ansible-playbook` runs for regular maintenance and configuration management tasks is a common practice in IT infrastructure automation. We will discuss Ansible playbooks later in this chapter.

Running Ansible tasks repeatedly (or on a scheduled basis) against a specific target raises the concern of unwanted changes in the desired state due to repetitive operations. This issue brings us to one of the essential aspects of configuration management – the **idempotency** of configuration changes. We'll look at what idempotent changes are next.

Explaining idempotent operations

In configuration management, an operation is **idempotent** when running it multiple times yields the same result as running it once. In this sense, Ansible is an idempotent configuration management tool.

Let us explain how an idempotent operation works. Let us suppose we have an Ansible task creating a user. When the task runs for the first time, it creates the user. Running it for a second time – when the user has already been created – would result in a **no-operation** (**no-op**). *Without* idempotency, subsequent runs of the same task would produce errors due to attempting to create a user that already exists.

We should note that Ansible is not the only configuration management tool on the market. We have **Chef**, **Puppet**, and **SaltStack**, to name a few. Most of these platforms have been acquired by larger enterprises, such as SaltStack, being owned by VMware, and some may argue that Ansible's success could be attributed to Red Hat's open sourcing of the project. Ansible appears to be the most successful configuration management platform of our day. The industry consensus is that Ansible provides a user-friendly experience, high scalability, and affordable licensing tiers in enterprise-grade deployments.

With the introductory concepts covered, let's roll up our sleeves and install Ansible on a Linux platform of choice.

Installing Ansible

In this section, we'll show you how to install Ansible on a **control node**. On Linux, we can install Ansible in a couple of ways:

- Using the platform-specific package manager (for example, `apt` on Ubuntu/Debian)
- Using `pip`, the Python package manager

The Ansible community recommends `pip` for installing Ansible since it provides the most recent stable version of Ansible. In this section, we'll use Ubuntu as our distribution of choice. For a complete Ansible installation guide for all major OS platforms, please follow the online documentation at `https://docs.ansible.com/ansible/latest/installation_guide/intro_installation.html`.

On the control node, Ansible requires Python, so before installing Ansible, we need to make sure we have Python installed on our system.

> **Important note**
>
> Python 2 is no longer supported as of January 1, 2020. Please use Python 3.8 (or newer) instead.

Let's start by installing Ansible on Ubuntu.

Installing Ansible on Ubuntu

With Ubuntu 22.04 LTS, we have Python 3 installed by default. We can proceed with installing Ansible by following these steps:

1. Let's first check the Python 3 version we have by using the following command:

    ```
    python3 --version
    ```

    On our Ubuntu 20.04 machine, the Python version is as follows:

    ```
    Python 3.10.12
    ```

    If you don't have Python 3 installed, you can install it with the following command:

    ```
    sudo apt install -y python3
    ```

2. With Python 3 installed, we can proceed with installing Ansible. To get the most up-to-date Ansible packages using `apt`, we need to add the Ansible **Personal Package Archives** (**PPA**) repository to our system. Let's start by updating the current `apt` repository:

    ```
    sudo apt update
    ```

3. Next, we must add the Ansible PPA:

    ```
    sudo apt install -y software-properties-common
    sudo apt-add-repository --update ppa:ansible/ansible -y
    ```

4. Now, we can install the Ansible package with the following command:

    ```
    sudo apt install ansible -y
    ```

5. With Ansible installed, we can check its current version:

    ```
    ansible --version
    ```

    In our case, the relevant excerpt in the output of the previous command is as follows:

    ```
    ansible [core 2.15.4]
    ```

Next, we'll look at how to install Ansible using `pip`.

Installing Ansible using pip

Before we install Ansible with `pip`, we need to make sure Python is installed on the system. We assume Python 3 is installed based on the steps presented in the previous section. When installing Ansible using `pip`, it is a safe practice to previously uninstall any version of Ansible that was installed using the local package manager (such as `apt`). This will ensure that `pip` will install the latest version of Ansible successfully. To proceed with the installation, follow these steps:

1. We should remove any existing version of Ansible that's been installed with the platform-specific package manager (for example, `apt` or `yum`). To uninstall Ansible on Ubuntu, run the following command:

    ```
    sudo apt remove -y ansible
    ```

2. Next, we must make sure `pip` is installed. The following command should provide the current version of `pip`:

    ```
    python3 -m pip --version
    ```

    If `pip` is not installed, the following output will show:

    ```
    /usr/bin/python3: No module named pip
    ```

    We must then download the `pip` installer first:

    ```
    curl -s https://bootstrap.pypa.io/get-pip.py -o get-pip.py
    ```

3. We're now ready to install `pip` and Ansible with the following commands:

    ```
    python3 get-pip.py --user
    python3 -m pip install --user ansible
    ```

    Please note that, with the previous commands, we only installed `pip` and Ansible for the current user (hence the `--user` option we used).

4. If you wish to install Ansible *globally* on the system, the equivalent commands are as follows:

    ```
    sudo python3 get-pip.py
    sudo python3 -m pip install ansible
    ```

5. After the installation completes, you may have to log out and log back in to your Terminal again before using Ansible. You can check the Ansible version you have installed with the following command:

    ```
    ansible --version
    ```

    In our case, the output shows the following:

    ```
    ansible [core 2.15.4]
    ```

As you can see, you can get the most recent version (as of writing) of Ansible by using `pip`. Therefore, it is the recommended method of installing Ansible.

With Ansible installed on our control node, let's look at some practical examples of using Ansible.

Working with Ansible

In this section, we'll use the Ansible CLI tools extensively to perform various configuration management tasks. To showcase our practical examples, we'll work with a custom lab environment, and we highly encourage you to reproduce it for a complete configuration management experience.

Here's a high-level outline of this section:

- Setting up the lab environment
- Configuring Ansible
- Using Ansible ad hoc commands
- Using Ansible playbooks
- Using templates with Jinja2
- Using Ansible roles

Let's start with an overview of the lab environment.

Setting up the lab environment

Our lab uses **Kernel-based Virtual Machine** (**KVM**) as a hypervisor for the virtual environment, but any other hypervisor will do. *Chapter 11, Working with Virtual Machines*, describes the process of creating Linux **virtual machines** (**VMs**) in detail. We deployed the following VMs using Ubuntu Server LTS to mimic a real-world configuration management infrastructure:

- `neptune`: The Ansible control node
- `ans-web1`: Web server
- `ans-web2`: Web server
- `ans-db1`: Database server
- `ans-db2`: Database server

All VMs have the default server components installed. On each host, we created a default admin user called `packt` with SSH access enabled. Each VM will have 2 vCPUs, 2 GB of RAM, and 20 GB minimum.

Now, let's briefly describe the setup for these VMs, starting with managed hosts.

Setting up managed hosts

There are a couple of key requirements for managed hosts to fully enable configuration management access from the Ansible control node:

- They must have an OpenSSH server installed and running
- They must have Python installed

As specified in the *Technical requirements* section, we assume you have OpenSSH enabled on your hosts. For installing Python, you may follow the related steps described in the *Installing Ansible* section.

> **Important note**
> Managed hosts don't require Ansible to be installed on the system.

To set the hostname on each VM, you may run the following command (for example, for the `ans-web1` hostname):

```
sudo hostnamectl set-hostname ans-web1
```

We also want to disable the `sudo` login password on our managed hosts to facilitate unattended privilege escalation when running automated scripts. If we don't make this change, remotely executing Ansible commands will require a password.

To disable the `sudo` login password, edit the `sudo` configuration with the following command:

```
sudo visudo
```

Add the following line and save the configuration file. Replace `packt` with your username if it's different:

```
packt ALL=(ALL) NOPASSWD:ALL
```

You'll have to make this change on all managed hosts.

Next, we'll look at the initial setup for the Ansible control node.

Setting up the Ansible control node

The Ansible **control node** (`neptune`) interacts with **managed hosts** (`ans-web1`, `ans-web2`, `ans-db1`, and `ans-db2`) using Ansible commands and playbooks. For convenience, our examples will reference the managed hosts by their hostnames instead of their IP addresses. To easily accomplish this, we added the following entries to the `/etc/hosts` file on the Ansible control node (`neptune`):

```
127.0.0.1 neptune localhost
192.168.122.70 ans-web1
192.168.122.147 ans-web2
```

```
192.168.122.254 ans-db1
192.168.122.25 ans-db2
```

You'll have to match the hostnames and IP addresses according to your VM environment.

Next, we must install Ansible on our managed hosts too. Use the related procedure described in the *Installing Ansible* section earlier in this chapter, when we showed you how to install Ansible on the control node. In our case, we followed the steps in the *Installing Ansible using pip* section to benefit from the latest Ansible release at the time of writing.

Finally, we'll set up SSH key-based authentication between the Ansible control node and the managed hosts.

Setting up SSH key-based authentication

Ansible uses SSH communication with managed hosts. The SSH key authentication mechanism enables remote SSH access without the need to enter user passwords. To enable SSH key-based authentication, run the following commands on the Ansible control host (neptune).

Use the following command to generate a secure key pair and follow the default prompts:

```
ssh-keygen
```

With the key pair generated, copy the related public key to each managed host. You'll have to target one host at a time and authenticate with the remote packt user's password. Accept the SSH key exchange when prompted:

```
ssh-copy-id -i ~/.ssh/id_rsa.pub packt@ans-web1
ssh-copy-id -i ~/.ssh/id_rsa.pub packt@ans-web2
ssh-copy-id -i ~/.ssh/id_rsa.pub packt@ans-db1
ssh-copy-id -i ~/.ssh/id_rsa.pub packt@ans-db2
```

Now, you should be able to SSH into any of the managed hosts from the Ansible control node (neptune) without being prompted for a password. For example, to access ans-web1, you can test it with the following command:

```
ssh packt@ans-web1
```

The command will take you to the remote server's (ans-web1) Terminal. Make sure you go back to the Ansible control node's Terminal (on neptune) before following the next steps.

We're now ready to configure Ansible on the control node.

Configuring Ansible

This section explores some of the basic configuration concepts of Ansible that are related to the Ansible **configuration file** and **inventory**. Using a configuration file and the parameters within, we can change the *behavior* of Ansible, such as privilege escalation, connection timeout, and default inventory file path. The inventory defines managed hosts, acting as the CMDB of Ansible.

Let's look at the Ansible configuration file first.

Creating an Ansible configuration file

The following command provides some helpful information about our Ansible environment, including the current configuration file:

```
ansible --version
```

Here's the complete output of the preceding command:

```
packt@neptune:~$ ansible --version
ansible [core 2.15.4]
  config file = /etc/ansible/ansible.cfg
  configured module search path = ['/home/packt/.ansible/plugins/modules', '/usr/share/ansible/plugi
ns/modules']
  ansible python module location = /home/packt/.local/lib/python3.10/site-packages/ansible
  ansible collection location = /home/packt/.ansible/collections:/usr/share/ansible/collections
  executable location = /home/packt/.local/bin/ansible
  python version = 3.10.12 (main, Jun 11 2023, 05:26:28) [GCC 11.4.0] (/usr/bin/python3)
  jinja version = 3.0.3
  libyaml = True
```

Figure 17.3 – The default Ansible configuration settings

A default Ansible installation will set the configuration file path to /etc/ansible/ansible.cfg. As you can probably guess, the default configuration file has a *global scope*, which means that it's used by default when we run Ansible tasks.

Now, let's look at some different scenarios and how they can be addressed:

- What if there are multiple users on the same control host running Ansible tasks? Our instinct suggests that each user may have their own set of configuration parameters. Ansible resolves this problem by looking into the user's home directory for the ~/.ansible.cfg file. Let's verify this behavior by creating a dummy configuration file in our user's (packt) home directory:

```
touch ~/.ansible.cfg
```

A new invocation of the ansible --version command now yields the following config file path:

```
packt@neptune:~$ touch ~/.ansible.cfg
packt@neptune:~$ ansible --version
ansible [core 2.15.4]
  config file = /home/packt/.ansible.cfg
  configured module search path = ['/home/packt/.ansible/plugins/modules', '/usr/share/ansible/plugi
ns/modules']
  ansible python module location = /home/packt/.local/lib/python3.10/site-packages/ansible
  ansible collection location = /home/packt/.ansible/collections:/usr/share/ansible/collections
  executable location = /home/packt/.local/bin/ansible
  python version = 3.10.12 (main, Jun 11 2023, 05:26:28) [GCC 11.4.0] (/usr/bin/python3)
  jinja version = 3.0.3
  libyaml = True
```

Figure 17.4 – Changing the default configuration file

In other words, ~/.ansible.cfg takes precedence over the global /etc/ansible/ansible.cfg configuration file.

- Now, suppose our user (packt) creates multiple Ansible projects, some managing on-premises hosts and others interacting with public cloud resources. Again, we may need a different set of Ansible configuration parameters (such as a connection timeout and inventory file). Ansible accommodates this scenario by looking for the ./ansible.cfg file in the current folder.

Let's create a dummy ansible.cfg file in a new ~/ansible/ directory:

```
mkdir ~/ansible
touch ~/ansible/ansible.cfg
```

Switching to the ~/ansible directory and invoking the ansible --version command shows the following config file:

```
packt@neptune:~$ mkdir ~/ansible
packt@neptune:~$ touch ~/ansible/ansible.cfg
packt@neptune:~$ ansible --version
ansible [core 2.15.4]
  config file = /home/packt/.ansible.cfg
  configured module search path = ['/home/packt/.ansible/plugins/modules', '/usr/share/ansible/plugi
ns/modules']
  ansible python module location = /home/packt/.local/lib/python3.10/site-packages/ansible
  ansible collection location = /home/packt/.ansible/collections:/usr/share/ansible/collections
  executable location = /home/packt/.local/bin/ansible
  python version = 3.10.12 (main, Jun 11 2023, 05:26:28) [GCC 11.4.0] (/usr/bin/python3)
  jinja version = 3.0.3
  libyaml = True
packt@neptune:~$ cd ansible/
packt@neptune:~/ansible$ ansible --version
ansible [core 2.15.4]
  config file = /home/packt/ansible/ansible.cfg
  configured module search path = ['/home/packt/.ansible/plugins/modules', '/usr/share/ansible/plugi
ns/modules']
  ansible python module location = /home/packt/.local/lib/python3.10/site-packages/ansible
  ansible collection location = /home/packt/.ansible/collections:/usr/share/ansible/collections
  executable location = /home/packt/.local/bin/ansible
  python version = 3.10.12 (main, Jun 11 2023, 05:26:28) [GCC 11.4.0] (/usr/bin/python3)
  jinja version = 3.0.3
  libyaml = True
```

Figure 17.5 – Changing the current directory and configuration file

We could have named our project directory anything, not necessarily /home/packt/ansible. Ansible prioritizes the ./ansible.cfg file over the ~/.ansible.cfg configuration file in the user's home directory.

- Finally, we may want the ultimate flexibility of a configuration file that doesn't depend on the directory or location originating from our Ansible commands. Such a feature could be helpful while testing ad hoc configurations without altering the main configuration file. For this purpose, Ansible reads the ANSIBLE_CONFIG environment variable for the path of the configuration file.

Assuming we are in the ~/ansible project folder, where we already have our local ansible.cfg file defined, let's create a dummy test configuration file named test.cfg:

```
cd ~/ansible
touch test.cfg
```

Now, let's verify that Ansible will read the configuration from test.cfg instead of ansible.cfg when the ANSIBLE_CONFIG environment variable is set:

```
ANSIBLE_CONFIG=test.cfg ansible --version
```

The output shows the following:

```
packt@neptune:~/ansible$ touch test.cfg
packt@neptune:~/ansible$ ANSIBLE_CONFIG=test.cfg ansible --version
ansible [core 2.15.4]
  config file = /home/packt/ansible/test.cfg
  configured module search path = ['/home/packt/.ansible/plugins/modules', '/usr/share/ansible/plugi
ns/modules']
  ansible python module location = /home/packt/.local/lib/python3.10/site-packages/ansible
  ansible collection location = /home/packt/.ansible/collections:/usr/share/ansible/collections
  executable location = /home/packt/.local/bin/ansible
  python version = 3.10.12 (main, Jun 11 2023, 05:26:28) [GCC 11.4.0] (/usr/bin/python3)
  jinja version = 3.0.3
  libyaml = True
```

Figure 17.6 – Verifying reading of the new configuration file

We should note that the configuration file should always have the .cfg extension. Otherwise, Ansible will discard it.

Here's a list summarizing the order of precedence in descending order for Ansible configuration files:

1. The ANSIBLE_CONFIG environment variable
2. The ./ansible.cfg file in the local directory
3. The ~/.ansible.cfg file in the user's home directory
4. /etc/ansible/ansible.cfg

In our examples, we'll rely on the `ansible.cfg` configuration file in a local project directory (`~/ansible`). Let's create this configuration file and leave it empty for now:

```
mkdir ~/ansible
cd ~/ansible
touch ansible.cfg
```

For the rest of this chapter, we'll run our Ansible commands from the `~/ansible` folder unless we specify otherwise.

Unless we specifically define (override) configuration parameters in our configuration file, Ansible will assume the system defaults. One of the attributes that we'll add to the config file is the inventory file path. But first, we'll need to create an inventory. The following section will show you how.

Creating an Ansible inventory

An Ansible inventory is a regular **INI** or **YAML** file describing the managed hosts. In its simplest form, the inventory could be a flat list of hostnames or IP addresses, but Ansible can also organize the hosts into **groups**. Ansible inventory files are either **static** or **dynamic**, depending on whether they are created and updated manually or dynamically. For now, we'll use a static inventory.

In our demo environment with two web servers (ans-web1, ans-web2) and two database servers (ans-db1, ans-db2), we can define the following inventory (in INI format) in a file named hosts (located inside ~/ansible) that we will create later on, as shown in *Figure 17.7*:

```
[webservers]
ans-web1
ans-web2

[databases]
ans-db1
ans-db2
```

We classified our hosts into a couple of groups, featured in bracketed names; that is, [webservers] and [databases]. As discussed earlier, groups are logical arrangements of hosts based on specific criteria. Hosts can be part of multiple groups. Group names are case-sensitive, should always start with a letter, and should not contain hyphens (-) or spaces.

Ansible has two default groups:

- all: Every host in the inventory
- ungrouped: Every host in all that is not a member of another group

We can also define groups based on specific patterns. For example, the following group includes a range of hostnames starting with ans-web and ending with a number in the range of 1-2:

```
[webservers]
ans-web[1:2]
```

Patterns are helpful when we're managing a large number of hosts. For example, the following pattern includes all the hosts within a range of IP addresses:

```
[all_servers]
172.16.191.[11:15]
```

Ranges are defined as [START:END] and include all values from START to END. Examples of ranges are [1:10], [01:10], and [a-g].

Groups can also be nested. In other words, a group may contain other groups. This nesting is described with the :children suffix. For example, we can define a [platforms] group that includes the [ubuntu] and [debian] groups (all our VMs are running on Ubuntu, so this is only for explaining purposes):

```
[platforms:children]
ubuntu
debian
```

Let's name our inventory file hosts. Please note that we are in the ~/ansible directory. Using a Linux editor of your choice, add the following content to the hosts file:

Figure 17.7 – The inventory file in INI format

After saving the inventory file, we can validate it with the following command:

```
ansible-inventory -i ./hosts --list --yaml
```

Here's a brief explanation of the command's parameters:

- -i (--inventory): Specifies the inventory file; that is, ./hosts

- --list: Lists the current inventory, as read by Ansible

- --yaml: Specifies the output format as YAML

Upon successfully validating the inventory, the command will show the equivalent YAML output (the default output format of the `ansible-inventory` utility is JSON).

So far, we've expressed the Ansible inventory in INI format, but we may as well use a YAML file instead. The following screenshot shows the output of the preceding command in YAML format:

```
packt@neptune:~/ansible$ ansible-inventory -i ./hosts --list --yaml
all:
  children:
    databases:
      hosts:
        ans-db1: {}
        ans-db2: {}
    webservers:
      hosts:
        ans-web1: {}
        ans-web2: {}
```

Figure 17.8 – The output in YAML inventory format

The YAML representation could be somewhat challenging, especially with large configurations, due to the strict indentation and formatting requirements. We'll continue to use the INI inventory format throughout the rest of this chapter.

Next, we'll point Ansible to our inventory. Edit the `./ansible.cfg` configuration file and add the following lines:

```
 GNU nano 6.2                          ansible.cfg *
[defaults]
inventory = ~/ansible/hosts
```

Figure 17.9 – Pointing to our inventory file

After saving the file, we're ready to run Ansible commands or tasks that target our managed hosts. There are two ways we can perform Ansible configuration management tasks: using one-off **ad hoc commands** and via **Ansible playbooks**. We'll look at ad hoc commands next.

Using Ansible ad hoc commands

Ad hoc commands execute a single Ansible task and provide a quick way to interact with our managed hosts. These simple operations are helpful when we're making simple changes and performing testing.

The general syntax of an Ansible ad hoc command is as follows:

```
ansible [OPTIONS] -m MODULE -a ARGS PATTERN
```

The preceding command uses an Ansible MODULE to perform a particular task on select hosts based on a PATTERN. The task is described via arguments (ARGS). You may recall that modules encapsulate a specific functionality, such as managing users, packages, and services. To demonstrate the use of ad hoc commands, we'll use some of the most common Ansible modules for our configuration management tasks. Let's start with the Ansible ping module.

Working with the ping module

One of the simplest ad hoc commands is the Ansible ping test:

```
ansible -m ping all
```

The command performs a quick test on all managed hosts to check their SSH connectivity and ensure the required Python modules are present. Here's an excerpt from the output:

```
packt@neptune:~/ansible$ ansible -m ping all
ans-db1 | SUCCESS => {
    "ansible_facts": {
        "discovered_interpreter_python": "/usr/bin/python3"
    },
    "changed": false,
    "ping": "pong"
}
ans-web2 | SUCCESS => {
    "ansible_facts": {
        "discovered_interpreter_python": "/usr/bin/python3"
    },
    "changed": false,
    "ping": "pong"
}
ans-web1 | SUCCESS => {
    "ansible_facts": {
        "discovered_interpreter_python": "/usr/bin/python3"
    },
    "changed": false,
    "ping": "pong"
}
ans-db2 | SUCCESS => {
    "ansible_facts": {
        "discovered_interpreter_python": "/usr/bin/python3"
    },
    "changed": false,
    "ping": "pong"
}
```

Figure 17.10 – A successful ping test with a managed host

The output suggests that the command was successful (| SUCCESS) and that the remote servers responded with "pong" to our ping request ("ping": "pong"). Please note that the Ansible ping module doesn't use **Internet Control Message Protocol (ICMP)** to test the remote connection with managed hosts. The ping module inside Ansible is just a test module that requires Python; it does not rely on the ping command we use when troubleshooting network issues.

Next, we'll look at ad hoc commands while using the Ansible user module.

Working with the user module

Here's another example of an ad hoc command. This one is checking if a particular user (packt) exists on all the hosts:

```
ansible -m user -a "name=packt state=present" all
```

The following is an excerpt of the output yielded by a successful check:

```
packt@neptune:~/ansible$ ansible -m user -a "name=packt state=present" all
ans-web1 | SUCCESS => {
    "ansible_facts": {
        "discovered_interpreter_python": "/usr/bin/python3"
    },
    "append": false,
    "changed": false,
    "comment": "packt",
    "group": 1000,
    "home": "/home/packt",
    "move_home": false,
    "name": "packt",
    "shell": "/bin/bash",
    "state": "present",
    "uid": 1000
}
```

Figure 17.11 – Checking if a user account exists

The preceding output also suggests that we could be even more specific when checking for a user account by also making sure they have a particular user and group ID:

```
ansible -m user -a "name=packt state=present uid=1000 group=1000" all
```

We can target ad hoc commands against a limited subset of our inventory. The following command, for example, would only ping the web1 host for Ansible connectivity:

```
ansible -m ping ans-web1
```

Host patterns can also include wildcards or group names. Here are a few examples:

```
ansible -m ping ans-web*
ansible -m ping webservers
```

Let's look at the available Ansible modules next. Before we do that, you may want to add the following line to `./ansible.cfg`, under the `[defaults]` section, to keep the noise down about deprecated modules:

```
deprecation_warnings = False
```

To list all the modules available in Ansible, run the following command:

```
ansible-doc --list
```

You may search or `grep` the output for a particular module. For detailed information about a specific module (for example, `user`), you can run the following command:

```
ansible-doc user
```

Make sure you check out the `EXAMPLES` section in the `ansible-doc` output for a specific module. You will find hands-on examples of using the module with ad hoc commands and playbook tasks.

Furthermore, we can create new users for different use cases on our Ansible hosts. Next, we will show you how to create a new user.

Creating a new user

If we want to create a new user (`webuser`) on all our web servers, we can perform the related operation with the following ad hoc command:

```
ansible -bK -m user -a "name=webuser state=present" webservers
```

Let's explain the command's parameters:

- `-b` (`--become`): Changes the execution context to `sudo` (`root`)
- `-K` (`--ask-become-pass`): Prompts for the `sudo` password on the remote hosts; the same password is used on all managed hosts
- `-m`: Specifies the Ansible module (`user`
- `-a`: Specifies the `user` module arguments as key-value pairs; `name=webuser` represents the username, while `state=present` checks whether the user account exists before attempting to create it
- `webservers`: The group of managed hosts targeted by the operation

Creating a user account requires administrative (sudo) privileges on the remote hosts. Using the -b (--become) option invokes the related **privilege escalation** for the Ansible command to act as a *sudoer* on the remote system.

> **Important note**
> By default, Ansible does not enable **unattended privilege escalation**. For tasks requiring sudo privileges, you must explicitly set the -b (--become) flag. You can override this behavior in the Ansible configuration file.

To enable unattended privilege escalation by default, add the following lines to the ansible.cfg file:

```
GNU nano 6.2                              ansible.cfg
[defaults]
inventory = ~/ansible/hosts
deprecation_warnings = False

[privilege_escalation]
become = True
```

Figure 17.12 – Adding privilege escalation rules

Now, you don't have to specify the --b (--become) flag anymore with your ad hoc commands.

If the sudoer account on the managed hosts has the sudo login password enabled, we'll have to provide it to our ad hoc command. Here is where the -K (--ask-become-pass) option comes in handy. Consequently, we're asked for a password with the following message:

```
BECOME password:
```

This password is used across all managed hosts targeted by the command.

As you may recall, we disabled the sudo login password on our managed hosts (see the *Setting up the lab environment* section earlier in this chapter). Therefore, we can rewrite the previous ad hoc command without explicitly asking for privilege escalation and the related password:

```
ansible -m user -a "name=webuser state=present" webservers
```

There are some security concerns regarding privilege escalation, and Ansible has the mechanisms to mitigate the related risks. For more information on this topic, you may refer to https://docs.ansible.com/ansible/latest/user_guide/become.html.

The preceding command produces the following output:

```
packt@neptune:~/ansible$ ansible -m user -a "name=webuser state=present" webservers
ans-web2 | SUCCESS => {
    "ansible_facts": {
        "discovered_interpreter_python": "/usr/bin/python3"
    },
    "append": false,
    "changed": false,
    "comment": "",
    "group": 1001,
    "home": "/home/webuser",
    "move_home": false,
    "name": "webuser",
    "shell": "/bin/sh",
    "state": "present",
    "uid": 1001
}
ans-web1 | SUCCESS => {
    "ansible_facts": {
        "discovered_interpreter_python": "/usr/bin/python3"
    },
    "append": false,
    "changed": false,
    "comment": "",
    "group": 1001,
    "home": "/home/webuser",
    "move_home": false,
    "name": "webuser",
    "shell": "/bin/sh",
    "state": "present",
    "uid": 1001
}
```

Figure 17.13 – Creating a new user using an ad hoc command

You may have noticed that the output text here is highlighted, as it was with our previous ad hoc commands. Ansible highlights the output if it corresponds to a change in the *desired state* of the managed host. If you run the same command a second time, the output will not be highlighted, suggesting that there's been no change since the user account has been already created. Here, we can see Ansible's *idempotent operation* at work.

With the previous command, we created a user without a password for demo purposes only. What if we want to add or modify the password? Next, we will show you how to do that.

Adding or modifying a password

Glossing through the `user` module's documentation with `ansible-doc user`, we can use the password field inside the module arguments, but Ansible will only accept **password hashes** as input. For hashing passwords, we'll use a helper Python module called `passlib`. Let's install it on the Ansible control node with the following command:

```
pip install passlib
```

You'll need the Python package manager (`pip`) to run the previous command. If you installed Ansible using `pip`, you should be fine. Otherwise, follow the instructions in the *Installing Ansible using pip* section to download and install `pip`.

With `passlib` installed, we can use the following ad hoc command to create or modify the user password:

```
ansible webservers -m user \
    -e "password=changeit!" \
    -a "name=webuser \
        update_password=always \
        password={{ password | password_hash('sha512') }}"
```

Here are the additional parameters helping with the user password:

- `-e` (`--extra-vars`): Specifies custom variables as key-value pairs; we set the value of a custom variable to `password=changeit!`

- `update_password=always`: Updates the password if it's different from the previous one

- `password={{...}}`: Sets the password to the value of the expression enclosed within double braces

- `password | password_hash('sha512')`: Pipes the value of the `password` variable (`changeit!`) to the `password_hash()` function, thus generating an SHA-512 hash; `password_hash()` is part of the `passlib` module we installed earlier

The command sets the password of `webuser` to `changeit!`, and is an example of using variables (`password`) in ad hoc commands. Here's the related output:

```
packt@neptune:~/ansible$ ansible webservers -m user -e "password=changeit!" -a "name=webuser update_
password=always password={{ password | password_hash('sha512') }}"
ans-web2 | CHANGED => {
    "ansible_facts": {
        "discovered_interpreter_python": "/usr/bin/python3"
    },
    "append": false,
    "changed": true,
    "comment": "",
    "group": 1001,
    "home": "/home/webuser",
    "move_home": false,
    "name": "webuser",
    "password": "NOT_LOGGING_PASSWORD",
    "shell": "/bin/sh",
    "state": "present",
    "uid": 1001
}
ans-web1 | CHANGED => {
    "ansible_facts": {
        "discovered_interpreter_python": "/usr/bin/python3"
    },
    "append": false,
    "changed": true,
    "comment": "",
    "group": 1001,
    "home": "/home/webuser",
    "move_home": false,
    "name": "webuser",
    "password": "NOT_LOGGING_PASSWORD",
    "shell": "/bin/sh",
    "state": "present",
    "uid": 1001
}
```

Figure 17.14 – Changing the user's password using an ad hoc command

Ansible won't show the actual password for obvious security reasons.

Now, you can try to SSH into any of the web servers (`web1` or `web2`) using the `webuser` account, and you should be able to authenticate successfully with the `changeit!` password.

Deleting a user

To delete the `webuser` account on all web servers, we can run the following ad hoc command:

```
ansible -m user -a "name=webuser state=absent remove=yes force=yes"
webservers
```

The `state=absent` module parameter invokes the deletion of the `webuser` account. The `remove` and `force` parameters are equivalent to the `userdel -rf` command, deleting the user's home directory and any files within, even if they're not owned by the user.

The related output is as follows:

```
packt@neptune:~/ansible$ ansible -m user -a "name=webuser state=absent remove=yes force=yes" webservers
ans-web2 | CHANGED => {
    "ansible_facts": {
        "discovered_interpreter_python": "/usr/bin/python3"
    },
    "changed": true,
    "force": true,
    "name": "webuser",
    "remove": true,
    "state": "absent",
    "stderr": "userdel: webuser mail spool (/var/mail/webuser) not found\n",
    "stderr_lines": [
        "userdel: webuser mail spool (/var/mail/webuser) not found"
    ]
}
ans-web1 | CHANGED => {
    "ansible_facts": {
        "discovered_interpreter_python": "/usr/bin/python3"
    },
    "changed": true,
    "force": true,
    "name": "webuser",
    "remove": true,
    "state": "absent",
    "stderr": "userdel: webuser mail spool (/var/mail/webuser) not found\n",
    "stderr_lines": [
        "userdel: webuser mail spool (/var/mail/webuser) not found"
    ]
}
```

Figure 17.15 – Deleting a user account using an ad hoc command

You may safely ignore stderr and stderr_lines, which were captured in the output. The message is benign since the user didn't create a mail spool previously.

We'll look at the package module next and run a few related ad hoc commands.

Working with the package module

The following command installs the **Nginx** web server on all hosts within the webserver group:

```
ansible -m package -a "name=nginx state=present" webservers
```

Here's an excerpt from the output:

```
packt@neptune:~/ansible$ ansible -m package -a "name=nginx state=present" webservers
ans-web2 | CHANGED => {
    "ansible_facts": {
        "discovered_interpreter_python": "/usr/bin/python3"
    },
    "cache_update_time": 1696346347,
    "cache_updated": false,
    "changed": true,
    "stderr": "",
    "stderr_lines": [],
    "stdout": "Reading package lists...\nBuilding dependency tree...\nReading state
```

Figure 17.16 – Installing the nginx package on the web servers

We use a similar ad hoc command to install the **MySQL** database server on all hosts within the `databases` group:

```
ansible -m package -a "name=mysql-server state=present" databases
```

Here's an excerpt from the command's output:

```
packt@neptune:~/ansible$ ansible -m package -a "name=mysql-server state=present" databases
ans-db2 | CHANGED => {
    "ansible_facts": {
        "discovered_interpreter_python": "/usr/bin/python3"
    },
    "cache_update_time": 1696347179,
    "cache_updated": false,
    "changed": true,
    "stderr": "",
    "stderr_lines": [],
```

Figure 17.17 – Installing the mysql-server package on the database servers

If we wanted to remove a package, the ad hoc command would be similar but would feature `state=absent` instead.

Although the `package` module provides a good OS-level abstraction across various platforms, certain package management tasks are best handled with platform-specific package managers. We'll show you how to use the `apt` module next.

Working with platform-specific package managers

The following ad hoc command installs the latest updates on all Ubuntu machines in our managed environment. As all of our VMs are running Ubuntu, we will choose to run the commands only on the `webservers` group. The command will be the following:

```
ansible -m apt -a "upgrade=dist update_cache=yes" ubuntu
```

If we wanted, we could create one more group inside the hosts file, named [ubuntu] for example, and add all the VMs in there. This would be easier if we had different operating systems running, but that is not the case for us.

Thee platform-specific package management modules (apt, yum, and so on) match all the capabilities of the system-agnostic package module, featuring additional OS-exclusive functionality.

Let's look at the service module next and a couple of related ad hoc commands.

Working with the service module

The following command restarts the nginx service on all hosts in the webservers group:

```
ansible -m service -a "name=nginx state=restarted" webservers
```

Here's a relevant excerpt from the output:

```
packt@neptune:~/ansible$ ansible -m service -a "name=nginx state=restarted" webservers
ans-web1 | CHANGED => {
    "ansible_facts": {
        "discovered_interpreter_python": "/usr/bin/python3"
    },
    "changed": true,
    "name": "nginx",
    "state": "started",
    "status": {
        "ActiveEnterTimestamp": "Tue 2023-10-03 18:00:31 UTC",
        "ActiveEnterTimestampMonotonic": "8394578958",
        "ActiveExitTimestamp": "n/a",
        "ActiveExitTimestampMonotonic": "0",
        "ActiveState": "active",
```

Figure 17.18 – Restarting the nginx service on the web servers

In the same way, we can restart the mysql service on all database servers, but there's a trick to it! On Ubuntu, the MySQL service is named mysql. We could, of course, target each host with the appropriate service name, but if you had many database servers, it would be a laborious task. Alternatively, we can use the *exclusion pattern* (written as !) when targeting multiple hosts or groups.

The following command will restart the mysql service on all hosts in the databases group, except those that are members of the debian group (if we were to have a debian group):

```
ansible -m service -a "name=mysql state=restarted" 'databases:!debian'
```

Similarly, we can restart the mysqld service on all hosts in the databases group, except for those that are members of the ubuntu group (if we were to have one), with the following ad hoc command:

```
ansible -m service -a "name=mysqld state=restarted"
'databases:!ubuntu'
```

Always use single quotes (' ') when you're targeting multiple hosts or groups with an exclusion pattern; otherwise, the ansible command will fail.

Let's look at one last Ansible module and the related ad hoc command, which is frequently used in upgrade scenarios.

Working with the reboot module

The following ad hoc command reboots all hosts in the webservers group:

```
ansible -m reboot -a "reboot_timeout=3600" webservers
```

Slower hosts may take longer to reboot, especially during substantial upgrades, hence the increased reboot timeout of 3600 seconds. (The default timeout is 600 seconds.)

In our case, the reboot only took a few seconds. The output is as follows:

```
packt@neptune:~/ansible$ ansible -m reboot -a "reboot_timeout=3600" webservers
ans-web2 | CHANGED => {
    "changed": true,
    "elapsed": 10,
    "rebooted": true
}
ans-web1 | CHANGED => {
    "changed": true,
    "elapsed": 11,
    "rebooted": true
}
```

Figure 17.19 – Rebooting the webservers group

In this section, we showed a few examples of ad hoc commands using different modules. The next section will give you a brief overview of some of the most common Ansible modules and how to explore more.

Exploring Ansible modules

Ansible has a vast library of modules. As we noted previously, you may use the ansible-doc --list command to browse the available Ansible modules on the command-line Terminal. You can also access the same information online, on the Ansible modules index page, at https://docs. ansible.com/ansible/2.9/modules/modules_by_category.html.

The online catalog provides module-by-category indexing to help you quickly locate a particular module you're looking for. Here are some of the most typical modules used in everyday system administration and configuration management tasks with Ansible:

- **Packaging modules**:

  - `apt`: Performs APT package management

  - `yum`: Performs YUM package management

  - `dnf`: Performs DNF package management

- **System modules**:

  - `users`: Manages users

  - `services`: Controls services

  - `reboot`: Restarts machines

  - `firewalld`: Performs firewall management

- **File modules**:

  - `copy`: Copies local files to the managed hosts

  - `synchronize`: Synchronizes files and directories using `rsync`

  - `file`: Controls file permissions and attributes

  - `lineinfile`: Manipulates lines in text files

- **Net Tools modules**:

  - `nmcli`: Controls network settings

  - `get_url`: Downloads files over HTTP, HTTPS, and FTP

  - `uri`: Interacts with web services and API endpoints

- **Commands modules** (not idempotent):

  - `raw`: Simply runs a remote command via SSH (which is an unsafe practice); doesn't need Python installed on the remote host

  - `command`: Runs commands securely using Python's remote execution context

  - `shell`: Executes shell commands on managed hosts

We should note that ad hoc commands always execute a *single operation* using a *single module*. This feature is an advantage (for quick changes) but also a limitation. For more complex configuration management tasks, we use Ansible playbooks. The following section will take you through the process of authoring and running Ansible playbooks.

Using Ansible playbooks

An **Ansible playbook** is essentially a list of tasks that are executed automatically. Ansible configuration management workflows are primarily driven by playbooks. More precisely, a playbook is a YAML file containing one or more **plays**, each with a list of **tasks** executed in the order they are listed. Plays are execution units that run the associated tasks against a set of hosts, and they are selected via a group identifier or a pattern. Each task uses a single module that executes a specific action targeted at the remote host. You may think of a task as a simple Ansible ad hoc command. As the majority of Ansible modules comply with idempotent execution contexts, playbooks are also idempotent. Running a playbook multiple times always yields the same result.

Well-written playbooks can replace laborious administrative tasks and complex scripts with relatively simple and maintainable manifests, running easily repeatable and predictable routines.

We'll create our first Ansible playbook next.

Creating a simple playbook

We'll build our playbook based on the ad hoc command we used for creating a user (`webuser`). As a quick refresher, the command was as follows:

```
ansible -m user -a "name=webuser state=present" webservers
```

As we write the equivalent playbook, you may notice some resemblance to the ad hoc command parameters.

While editing the playbook YAML file, please be aware of the YAML formatting rules:

- Use only space characters for indentation (no tabs)
- Keep the indentation length consistent (for example, two spaces)
- Items at the same level in the hierarchy (for example, list items) must have the same indentation
- A child item's indentation is one indentation more than its parent

Now, using a Linux editor of your choice, add the following lines to a `create-user.yml` file. Make sure you create the playbook in the `~/ansible` project directory, which is where we have our current inventory (`hosts`) and Ansible configuration file (`ansible.cfg`):

```
  GNU nano 6.2                                    create-user.yml *
  ---
  - name: Create a specific user on all web servers
    hosts: webservers
    become: yes
    tasks:
      - name: Create the 'webuser' account
        user:
          name: webuser
          state: present
```

Figure 17.20 – A simple playbook for creating a user

Let's look at each line in our `create-user.yml` playbook:

- `---`: Marks the beginning of the playbook file
- `- name`: Describes the name of the play; we can have one or more plays in a playbook
- `hosts: webservers`: Targets the hosts in the `webservers` group
- `become: yes`: Enables privilege escalation for the current task; you can leave this line out if you enabled unattended privilege escalation in your Ansible configuration file (with `become = True` in the `[privileged_escalation]` section)
- `tasks`: The list of tasks in the current play
- `- name`: The name of the current task; we can have multiple tasks in a play
- `user`: The module being used by the current task
- `name: webuser`: The name of the user account to create
- `state: present`: The desired state upon creating the user – we want the user account to be present on the system

Let's run our `create-user.yml` playbook:

```
ansible-playbook create-user.yml
```

Here's the output we get after a successful playbook run:

```
packt@neptune:~/ansible$ nano create-user.yml
packt@neptune:~/ansible$ ansible-playbook create-user.yml

PLAY [Create a specific user on all web servers] ********************************************************

TASK [Gathering Facts] *****************************************************************************
ok: [ans-web2]
ok: [ans-web1]

TASK [Create the 'webuser' account] ***************************************************************
changed: [ans-web1]
changed: [ans-web2]

PLAY RECAP ****************************************************************************************
ans-web1                    : ok=2    changed=1    unreachable=0    failed=0    skipped=0    rescued=0
 ignored=0
ans-web2                    : ok=2    changed=1    unreachable=0    failed=0    skipped=0    rescued=0
 ignored=0
```

Figure 17.21 – Running the create-user.yml playbook

Most of the ansible-playbook command-line options are similar to the ones for the ansible command. Let's look at some of these parameters:

- -i (--inventory): Specifies an inventory file path
- -b (--become): Enables privilege escalation to sudo (root)
- -C (--check): Produces a dry run without making any changes and anticipating the end results – a useful option for validating playbooks
- -l (--limit): Limits the action of the command or playbook to a subset of managed hosts
- --syntax-check: Validates the playbook's syntax without making any changes; this option is only available for the ansible-playbook command

Let's experiment with a second playbook, this time for deleting a user. We'll name the playbook delete-user.yml and add the following content:

```
  GNU nano 6.2                                              delete-user.yml *
---
- name: Delete a specific user on all web servers
  hosts: webservers
  become: yes
  tasks:
    - name: Delete the 'webserver' account
      user:
        name: webuser
        remove: yes
        force: yes
        state: absent
```

Figure 17.22 – A simple playbook for deleting a user

Now, let's run this playbook:

```
ansible-playbook delete-user.yml
```

The output of the preceding command is as follows:

```
packt@neptune:~/ansible$ ansible-playbook delete-user.yml

PLAY [Delete a specific user on all web servers] **********************************************************

TASK [Gathering Facts] ***********************************************************************************
ok: [ans-web2]
ok: [ans-web1]

TASK [Delete the 'webserver' account] ********************************************************************
changed: [ans-web1]
changed: [ans-web2]

PLAY RECAP ***********************************************************************************************
ans-web1                    : ok=2    changed=1    unreachable=0    failed=0    skipped=0    rescued=0
 ignored=0
ans-web2                    : ok=2    changed=1    unreachable=0    failed=0    skipped=0    rescued=0
 ignored=0
```

Figure 17.23 – Limiting the delete-user.yml playbook to the Ubuntu host group

Next, we'll look at ways to further streamline our configuration management workflows, starting with the use of variables in playbooks.

Using variables in playbooks

Ansible provides a flexible and versatile model for working with variables in both playbooks and ad hoc commands. Through variables, we are essentially *parameterizing* a playbook, making it reusable or dynamic.

Take our previous playbook, for example, to create a user. We hardcoded the username (webuser) in the playbook. We can't really reuse the playbook to create another user (for example, webadmin) unless we add the related task to it. But then, if we had many users, our playbook would grow proportionally, making it harder to maintain. And what if we wanted to specify a password for each user as well? The complexity of the playbook would grow even more.

Here's where **variables** come into play. Let's first look at what variables are and how they are written.

Introducing variables

We can substitute the hardcoded values with variables, making the playbook dynamic. In terms of pseudocode, our example of using a playbook to create a user with specific username and password variables would look like this:

```
User = Playbook(username, password)
```

Variables in Ansible are enclosed in double braces; for example, `{{ username }}`. Let's see how we can leverage variables in our playbooks. Edit the `create-user.yml` playbook we worked on in the previous section and adjust it as follows:

```
GNU nano 6.2                                                  create-user.yml *
---
- name: Create a specific user on all web servers
  hosts: webservers
  become: yes
  vars:
    username: webuser
  tasks:
#    - name: Create the 'webuser' account
    - name: Create the '{{ username }}' account
      user:
#        name: webuser
        name: "{{ username }}"
        state: present
```

Figure 17.24 – Using the "username" variable in a playbook

We use the `{{ username }}` variable substituting our previously hardcoded value (`webuser`). Then, we surrounded the double braces with quotes to avoid syntax interference with the YAML dictionary notation. Variable names in Ansible must begin with a letter and only contain alphanumerical characters and underscores.

Setting values for variables

Next, we'll explain *how* and *where* to set values for variables. Ansible implements a hierarchical model for assigning values to variables:

1. **Global variables**: Values are set for all the hosts, either via the `–extra-vars ansible-playbook` command-line parameter or the `./group_vars/all` file.

2. **Group variables**: Values are set for the hosts in a specific group, either in the inventory file or the local `./group_vars` directory in files named after each group.

3. **Host variables**: Values are set for a particular host, either in the inventory file or the local `./host_vars` directory in files named after each host. Host-specific variables are also available from **Ansible facts** via the `gather_facts` directive. You can learn more about Ansible facts at `https://docs.ansible.com/ansible/latest/user_guide/playbooks_vars_facts.html#ansible-facts`.

4. **Play variables**: Values are set in the context of the current play for the hosts targeted by the play; examples are the `vars` directive in a play or `include_vars` tasks.

In the preceding numbered list, the order of precedence for a variable's value increases with each number. In other words, a variable value defined in a play will overwrite the same variable value specified at the host, group, or global level.

As an example, you may recall the peculiarity related to the MySQL service name on Ubuntu and RHEL/Fedora platforms. On Ubuntu, the service is `mysql`, while on Fedora, the service is `mysqld`. Suppose we want to restart the MySQL service on all hosts in our `databases` group. Assuming most of our database servers run Ubuntu, we can define a group-level `service` variable as `service: mysql`. We set this variable in the local project's `./group_vars/databases` file. Then, in the play where we control the service status, we can override the `service` variable value with `mysqld` when the remote host's OS platform is Fedora.

Let's look at a few examples to illustrate what we've learned so far about placing variables and setting their values. Back in our `create-user.yml` playbook, we can define the `username` variable at the play level with the following directive:

```
vars:
  username: webuser
```

Here's what it looks like in the overall playbook:

```
  GNU nano 6.2                                      create-user.yml *
  ---
- name: Create a specific user on all web servers
  hosts: webservers
  become: yes
  vars:
    username: webuser
  tasks:
#     - name: Create the 'webuser' account
    - name: Create the '{{ username }}' account
      user:
#         name: webuser
        name: "{{ username }}"
        state: present
```

Figure 17.25 – Defining a variable at the play level

Let's run our playbook with the following command:

```
ansible-playbook create-user.yml
```

A relevant excerpt from the output is shown in the next screenshot:

```
packt@neptune:~/ansible$ ansible-playbook create-user.yml

PLAY [Create a specific user on all web servers] *********************************************************

TASK [Gathering Facts] *********************************************************
ok: [ans-web2]
ok: [ans-web1]

TASK [Create the 'webuser' account] *********************************************************
changed: [ans-web1]  ◄──────
changed: [ans-web2]

PLAY RECAP *********************************************************
ans-web1                    : ok=2    changed=1    unreachable=0    failed=0    skipped=0    rescued=0
 ignored=0
ans-web2                    : ok=2    changed=1    unreachable=0    failed=0    skipped=0    rescued=0
 ignored=0
```

Figure 17.26 – Creating a user with a playbook using variables

Deleting user accounts

To delete user accounts, we can readjust our previous delete-user.yml file so that it looks as follows:

```
GNU nano 6.2                                        delete-user.yml
---
- name: Delete a specific user on all web servers
  hosts: webservers
  become: yes
  vars:
    username: webuser
  tasks:
#     - name: Delete the 'webserver' account
    - name: Delete the '{{ username }}' account
      user:
#        name: webuser
        name: "{{ username }}"
        remove: yes
        force: yes
        state: absent
```

Figure 17.27 – Deleting a user with a playbook using variables

After saving the file, run the following command to delete the webuser account on all web servers:

```
ansible-playbook delete-user.yml
```

The relevant output from the preceding command run is as follows:

```
packt@neptune:~/ansible$ ansible-playbook delete-user.yml

PLAY [Delete a specific user on all web servers] ******************************************************

TASK [Gathering Facts] ********************************************************************************
ok: [ans-web1]
ok: [ans-web2]

TASK [Delete the 'webuser' account] *******************************************************************
changed: [ans-web1]  ◀━━━━━━
changed: [ans-web2]

PLAY RECAP ********************************************************************************************
ans-web1                    : ok=2    changed=1    unreachable=0    failed=0    skipped=0    rescued=0
 ignored=0
ans-web2                    : ok=2    changed=1    unreachable=0    failed=0    skipped=0    rescued=0
 ignored=0
```

Figure 17.28 – Deleting a user with a playbook using variables

Enhancing our playbooks

We can improve our create-user and delete-user playbooks even further. You can follow these steps:

1. Since the play exclusively targets the webservers group, we can define a username variable in the ./group_vars/webservers file instead. This way, we can keep the playbooks more compact. Let's remove the variable definition from both files.

2. Next, create a ./group_vars folder in the local directory (~/ansible) and add the following lines to a file named webservers.yml:

    ```
    username: webuser
    ```

    We could also just call the file webservers so that it matches the group we're targeting. However, we should prefer to use the .yml extension so that we're consistent with the file's YAML format. Ansible accepts both naming conventions. Here's the current tree structure of our project directory:

```
packt@neptune:~/ansible$ tree
.
├── ansible.cfg
├── create-user.yml
├── delete-user.yml
├── group_vars
│   └── webservers.yml
├── hosts
└── test.cfg
```

Figure 17.29 – The directory tree, including the group_vars folder

If we run our playbooks, the results should be identical to our previous runs:

```
ansible-playbook create-user.yml
ansible-playbook delete-user.yml
```

3. Now, let's add one more variable to our `create-user` playbook: the user's `password` variable. You may recall the ad hoc command we created for the same purpose. See the *Using Ansible ad hoc commands* section earlier in this chapter for more information.

    Add the following lines to the `create-user.yml` file of the `user` task, at the same level as name:

```
password: "{{ password | password_hash('sha512') }}"
update_password: always
```

You may notice how these changes are similar to the related ad hoc command. The updated playbook contains the following content:

```
  GNU nano 6.2                                        create-user.yml *
---
- name: Create a specific user on all web servers
  hosts: webservers
  become: yes
  vars:
    username: webuser
  tasks:
#     - name: Create the 'webuser' account
    - name: Create the '{{ username }}' account
      user:
#         name: webuser
        name: "{{ username }}"
        password: "{{ password | password_hash('sha512') }}"
        update_password: always
        state: present
```

Figure 17.30 – The playbook with username and password variables

4. Next, edit the `./group_vars/webservers.yml` file and add the `password` variable with the `changeit!` value. Your updated file should have the following content:

```
  GNU nano 6.2                          webservers.yml *
---

username: webuser
password: changeit!
```

Figure 17.31 – Adding the new variable value inside the webservers.yml file

5. Let's run the playbook:

```
ansible-playbook create-user.yml
```

The command's output is identical to our similar previous commands.

6. You may test the new username (webuser) and password (changeit!) by trying to SSH into one of the web servers (for example, ans-web1):

```
ssh webuser@ans-web1
```

The SSH authentication should succeed. Make sure to exit the remote Terminal before proceeding with the next steps.

7. Let's remove the webuser account on the web servers with the following command, to get back to our initial state:

```
ansible-playbook delete-user.yml
```

8. Suppose we want to reuse the create-user playbook to create a different user with a different password. Let's name this user webadmin; we'll set the password to changeme!. One way to accomplish this task is to use the -e (--extra-vars) option parameter with ansible-playbook:

```
ansible-playbook -e '{"username": "webadmin", "password":
"changeme!"}' create-user.yml
```

The preceding command will create a new user (webadmin) with the related password. You can test the credentials with the following command:

```
ssh webadmin@ans-web1
```

The SSH authentication should succeed. Make sure you exit the remote Terminal before continuing.

As you can see, the -e (--extra-vars) option parameter takes a JSON string featuring the username and password fields, along with the corresponding values. These values will *override* the values of the same variables defined at the group level in the ./group_vars/webservers.yml file.

9. Let's remove the webuser and webadmin accounts before we proceed with the next steps. Let's run the delete-user playbook, first without any parameters:

```
ansible-playbook delete-user.yml
```

The preceding command removes the webuser account.

10. Next, we'll use the -e (--extra-vars) option parameter to delete the webadmin user:

```
ansible-playbook -e '{"username": "webadmin"}' delete-user.yml
```

Using –extra-vars with our create-user and delete-user playbooks, we can act on multiple user accounts by running the playbooks manually or in a loop and feeding the JSON blob with the required variables. While this method could easily be scripted, Ansible provides even more ways to improve our playbooks by using task iteration with loops. We'll look at loops later in this chapter, but first, let's handle our passwords more securely with Ansible's encryption and decryption facilities for managing secrets.

Working with secrets

Ansible has a dedicated module for managing secrets called **Ansible Vault**. With Ansible Vault, we can encrypt and store sensitive data such as variables and files that are referenced in playbooks. Ansible Vault is essentially a password-protected secure key-value data store.

To manage our secrets, we can use the ansible-vault command-line utility. Regarding our playbook, where we're creating a user with a password, we want to avoid storing the password in clear text. It is currently in the ./group_vars/webservers.yml file. As a reminder, our webservers.yml file has the following content:

Figure 17.32 – Sensitive data stored in the password variable

The last line contains sensitive data; the password is shown in plain text. We have a few options here to protect our data:

- Encrypt the webservers.yml file. If we choose to encrypt the webservers.yml file, we could possibly incur the overhead of encrypting non-sensitive data, such as the username or other general-purpose information. If we have many users, encrypting and decrypting non-sensitive data would be highly redundant.

- Encrypt the password variable only. This would work fine for a single user. But with a growing number of users, we'll have multiple password variables to deal with, each with its own encryption and decryption. Performance will once again be an issue if we have a large number of users.

- Store the password in a separate protected file. Ideally, we should have a separate file for storing all sensitive data. This file would be decrypted only once during the playbook run, even with multiple passwords stored.

We will pursue the third option and create a separate file to keep our user passwords in.

Protecting our data

Let's look at the steps that need to be followed to ensure that our data is secure:

1. We'll name the file `passwords.yml` (we create it inside the `~/ansible/` directory) and add the following content to it:

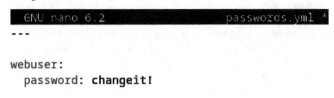

Figure 17.33 – The passwords.yml file storing sensitive data

2. We added a YAML dictionary (or hash) item matching the `webuser` username related to the password. This item contains another dictionary as a key-value pair: `password: changeit!`. The equivalent YAML representation is as follows:

```
webuser: { password: changeit! }
```

This approach will allow us to add passwords that correspond to different users, like so:

```
webuser: { password: changeit! }
webadmin: { password: changeme! }
```

We'll explain the concept behind this data structure and its use when we consume the `password` variable in the playbook, later in this section.

3. Now, since we keep our password in a different file, we'll remove the corresponding entry from `webusers.yml`. Let's add some other user-related information using the `comment` variable. Here's what our `webusers.yml` file looks like:

```
  GNU nano 6.2              webservers.yml *
  ---

  username: webuser
  #password: changeit!
  comment: Regular web user
```

Figure 17.34 – The webusers.yml file storing non-sensitive user data

4. Next, let's protect our secrets by encrypting the `passwords.yml` file using Ansible Vault:

```
ansible-vault encrypt passwords.yml
```

You'll be prompted to create a vault password to protect the file. Remember the password, as we'll be using it throughout this section.

674 Infrastructure and Automation with Ansible

5. Once you're done, check the `passwords.yml` file with the following command:

```
cat passwords.yml
```

The output for the preceding command shows the following:

```
packt@neptune:~/ansible$ cat passwords.yml
$ANSIBLE_VAULT;1.1;AES256
6434373337303631616334336135383137623262334633134633536643630386362363330623532643
3137313665636236663937323238303731363939366134390a3562306634636563653530616564664
3938383236333961623966616138386565396662376462646233346430663666656230386236393732
313262656332353363300a3862616137613638356562333376139653030633831383235323332383566
6431393039363330646230326664666323835626462306534656263653161333835613662373966313566
32366634363764376362326635373533646436666633234316643833
```

Figure 17.35 – The encrypted passwords.yml file

6. We can view the content of the `passwords.yml` file with the following command:

```
ansible-vault view passwords.yml
```

7. You'll be prompted for the vault password we created previously. The output shows the streamlined YAML content corresponding to our protected file:

```
packt@neptune:~/ansible/group_vars$ ansible-vault view passwords.yml
Vault password:
---

webuser:
  password: changeit!
```

Figure 17.36 – Viewing the content of the protected file

8. If you need to make changes, you can edit the encrypted file with the following command:

```
ansible-vault edit passwords.yml
```

After authenticating with the vault password, the command will open a local editor (`vi`) to edit your changes. If you want to re-encrypt your protected file with a different password, you can run the following command:

```
ansible-vault rekey passwords.yml
```

9. You'll be prompted for the current vault password, followed by the new password.

Now, let's learn how to reference secrets in our playbook.

Referencing secrets in playbooks

To reference secrets, follow these steps:

1. First, let's make sure we can read our password from the vault. Let's make a new file with the following lines in it. We will call it `create-user-new.yml`:

```
  GNU nano 6.2                                    create-user-new.yml
---

- name: Create a specific user on all web servers
  hosts: webservers
  become: yes
  tasks:
  - name: Get the password for {{ username }} from Vault
    include_vars:
      file: passwords.yml

  - name: Debug password for {{ username }}
    debug:
      msg: "{{ vars[username]['password'] }}"
```

Figure 17.37 – Debugging vault access with new create-user-new.yml file

We've added a couple of tasks:

- `include_vars` (*lines 6-8*): Reading variables from the `passwords.yml` file
- `debug` (*lines 10-12*): Debugging the playbook and logging the password that was read from the vault

None of these tasks are *aware* that the `passwords.yml` file is protected. *Line 12* is where the magic happens:

```
msg: "{{ vars[username]['password'] }}"
```

2. We use the `vars[]` dictionary to query a specific variable in the playbook. `vars[]` is a *reserved* data structure for storing all the variables that were created via `vars` and `include_vars` in an Ansible playbook. We can query the dictionary based on a key appointed by `username`:

```
{{ vars[username] }}
```

Our playbook gets `username` from the `./group_vars/webservers.yml` file, and its value is `webuser`. Consequently, the `vars[webuser]` dictionary item reads the corresponding entry from the `passwords.yml` file:

```
webuser: { password: changeit! }
```

3. To get the password value from the corresponding key-value pair, we specify the `'password'` key in the `vars[username]` dictionary:

    ```
    {{ vars[username]['password'] }}
    ```

4. Let's run this playbook with the following command:

    ```
    ansible-playbook --ask-vault-pass create-user-new.yml
    ```

    We invoked the `--ask-vault-pass` option to let Ansible know that our playbook needs vault access. Without this option, we'll get an error when running the playbook. Here's the relevant output for our `debug` task:

```
packt@neptune:~/ansible$ ansible-playbook --ask-vault-pass create-user-new.yml
Vault password:

PLAY [Create a specific user on all web servers] ***************************************************

TASK [Gathering Facts] ****************************************************************************
ok: [ans-web2]
ok: [ans-web1]

TASK [Get the password for webuser from Vault] **************************************************
ok: [ans-web1]
ok: [ans-web2]

TASK [Debug password for webuser] *************************************************************
ok: [ans-web1] => {
    "msg": "changeit!"
}
ok: [ans-web2] => {
    "msg": "changeit!"
}

PLAY RECAP ****************************************************************************************
ans-web1                   : ok=3    changed=0    unreachable=0    failed=0    skipped=0    rescued=
0    ignored=0
ans-web2                   : ok=3    changed=0    unreachable=0    failed=0    skipped=0    rescued=
0    ignored=0
```

Figure 17.38 – The playbook successfully reading secrets from the vault

Here, we can see that the playbook successfully retrieves the password from the vault.

5. Let's wrap up our `create-user-new.yml` playbook by adding the following code:

```
GNU nano 6.2                                    create-user-new.yml *
---
- name: Create a specific user on all web servers
  hosts: webservers
  become: yes
  vars:
    password: "{{ vars[username]['password'] }}"                            1
  tasks:
  - name: Get the password for {{ username }} from Vault
    include_vars:                                                           2
      file: passwords.yml

  - name: Debug password for {{ username }}
    debug:
      msg: "{{ password }}"                                                 3
    no_log: true

  - name: Create the '{{ username }}' account
    user:
      name: "{{ username }}"
      comment: "{{ comment }}"                                              4
      password: "{{ password | password_hash('sha512') }}"
      update_password: always
      state: present
```

Figure 17.39 – The playbook creating a user with a password retrieved from the vault

Here are a few highlights of the current implementation:

- We've added a `vars` block (**1** in *Figure 17.39*) to define a local `password` variable (at the play scope) for reading the password from the vault; we are reusing the `password` variable in multiple tasks.

- The `include_vars` task (**2** in the preceding screenshot) adds an external reference to the variables defined in the protected `passwords.yml` file.

- The `debug` task (**3** in the preceding screenshot) helped with the initial debugging effort to make sure we could read the password from the vault. You may choose to remove this task or leave it in place for future use. If you keep the task, make sure you have `no_log: true` enabled (*line 15*) to avoid logging sensitive information in the output. When debugging, you can temporarily set `no_log: false`.

- The user task (**4** in the preceding screenshot) reads the password variable and hashes the corresponding value. This hashing is required by the Ansible user module for security reasons. We also added a comment field with additional user information. This field maps to the **Linux General Electric Comprehensive Operating System (GECOS)** record of the user. See the *Managing users* section of *Chapter 4, Managing Users and Groups*, for related information.

6. Let's run the playbook with the following command:

```
ansible-playbook --ask-vault-pass create-user-new.yml
```

After the command completes successfully, you can verify the new user account in a couple of ways:

- Use SSH to connect to any of the web servers using the related username and password, like so:

```
ssh webuser@ans-web1
```

- Look for the webuser record in /etc/passwd on the ans-web1 machine:

```
tail -n 10 /etc/passwd
```

- You should see the following line in the output (you'll notice the GECOS field also):

```
webuser:x:1001:1001:Regular web user:/home/webuser:/bin/sh
```

You may want to run the ansible-playbook command without supplying a vault password, as required by --ask-vault-pass. Such functionality is essential in scripted or automated workflows when using Ansible Vault. To make your vault password automatically available when you're running a playbook using sensitive data, start by creating a regular text file, preferably in your home directory; for example, ~/vault.pass. Add the vault password to this file in a single line. Then, you can choose *either* of the following options to use the vault password file:

- Create the following environment variable:

```
export ANSIBLE_VAULT_PASSWORD_FILE=~/vault.pass
```

- Add the following line to the ansible.cfg file's [defaults] section:

```
vault_password_file = ~/vault.pass
```

Now, you can run the create-user-new playbook without the --ask-vault-pass option:

```
ansible-playbook create-user.yml
```

Sometimes, protecting multiple secrets with a single vault password raises security concerns. Ansible supports multiple vault passwords through vault IDs.

Using vault IDs

A **vault ID** is an identifier, or a label, associated with one or more vault secrets. Each vault ID has a unique password to unlock the encryption and decryption of the corresponding secrets. To illustrate the use of vault IDs, let's look at our `passwords.yml` file. Suppose we want to secure this file using a vault ID. The following command creates a vault ID labeled `passwords` and prompts us to create a password:

```
ansible-vault create --vault-id passwords@prompt passwords.yml
```

The `passwords` vault ID protects the `passwords.yml` file. Now, let's assume we also want to secure some API keys associated with users. If we stored these secrets in the `apikeys.yml` file, the following command would create a corresponding vault ID called `apikeys`:

```
ansible-vault create --vault-id apikeys@prompt apikeys.yml
```

Here, we created two vault IDs, each with its own password and protecting different resources.

The benefits of vault IDs are as follows:

- They provide an improved security context when managing secrets. If one of the vault ID passwords becomes compromised, resources that have been secured by the other vault IDs are still protected.

- With vault IDs, we can also leverage different access levels to vault secrets. For example, we can define `admin`, `dev`, and `test` vault IDs for related groups of users. Alternatively, we can have multiple configuration management projects, each with its own dedicated vault IDs and secrets; for example, `user-config`, `web-config`, and `db-config`.

- You can associate a vault ID with multiple secrets. For example, the following command creates a `user-config` vault ID that secures the `passwords.yml` and `api-keys.yml` files:

    ```
    ansible-vault create --vault-id user-config@prompt passwords.yml
    apikeys.yml
    ```

- When using vault IDs, we can also specify a password file to supply the related vault password. The following command encrypts the `apikeys.yml` file, which reads the corresponding vault ID password from the `apikeys.pass` file:

    ```
    ansible-vault encrypt --vault-id apikeys@apikeys.pass apikeys.
    yml
    ```

You can name your vault password files anything you want, but keeping a consistent naming convention, possibly one that matches the related vault ID, will make your life easier when you're managing multiple vault secrets.

- Similarly, you can pass a vault ID (`passwords`) to a playbook (`create-users-new.yml`) with the following command:

```
ansible-playbook --vault-id passwords@passwords.pass create-users-new.yml
```

For more information about Ansible Vault, you may refer to the related online documentation at `https://docs.ansible.com/ansible/latest/user_guide/vault.html`.

So far, we have created a single user account with a password. What if we want to onboard multiple users, each with their own password? As we noted previously, we could call the `create-user` playbook and override the `username` and `password` variables using the `--extra-vars` option parameter. But this method is not a very efficient one, not to mention the difficulty of maintaining it. In the next section, we'll show you how to use task iteration in Ansible playbooks.

Working with loops

Loops provide an efficient way of running a task repeatedly in Ansible playbooks. There are several loop implementations in Ansible, and we can classify them into the following categories based on their keyword or syntax:

- `loop`: The recommended way of iterating through a collection
- `with_<lookup>`: Collection-specific implementations of loops; examples include `with_list`, `with_items`, and `with_dict`, to name a few

In this section, we'll keep our focus on the `loop` iteration (equivalent to `with_list`), which is best suited for simple loops. Let's expand our previous use case and adapt it to create multiple users. We'll start by making a quick comparison between running repeated tasks *with* and *without* loops:

1. As a preparatory step, make sure `~/ansible` is your current working directory. Also, you can delete the `./group_vars` folder, as we're not using it anymore. Now, let's create a couple of playbooks, `create-users1.yml` and `create-users2.yml`, as shown in the following screenshot:

```
GNU nano 6.2                    create-users1.yml
---
- name: Create users on webservers
  hosts: webservers
  become: yes
  tasks:
    - name: Create the 'webuser' account
      user:
        name: webuser
        state: present
    - name: Create the 'webadmin' account
      user:
        name: webadmin
        state: present
    - name: Create the 'webdev' account
      user:
        name: webdev
        state: present
```

```
GNU nano 6.2                    create-users2.yml *
---
- name: Create users on webservers
  hosts: webservers
  become: yes
  vars:
    users:
      - webuser
      - webadmin
      - webdev
  tasks:
    - name: Create the '{{ item }}' account
      user:
        name: "{{ item }}"
        state: present
      loop: "{{ users }}"
```

Figure 17.40 – Playbooks with multiple versus iterative tasks

Both playbooks create three users: webuser, webadmin, and webdev. The create-users1 playbook has three distinct tasks, one for creating each user. On the other hand, create-users2 implements a single task iteration using the loop directive (in *line 15*):

```
loop: "{{ users }}"
```

The loop iterates through the items of the users list, defined as a play variable in *lines 6-9*. The user task uses the {{ item }} variable, referencing each user while iterating through the list.

2. Before running any of these playbooks, let's also create one for deleting the users. We'll name this playbook delete-users2.yml, and it will have a similar implementation to create-users2.yml:

```
  GNU nano 6.2                                    delete-users2.yml *
---
- name: Delete users on webservers
  hosts: webservers
  become: yes
  vars:
    users:
      - webuser
      - webadmin
      - webdev
  tasks:
    - name: Delete user
      user:
        name: "{{ item }}"
        state: absent
        remove: yes
        force: yes
      loop: "{{ users }}"
```

Figure 17.41 – A playbook using a loop for deleting users

3. Now, let's run the create-users1 playbook while targeting only the ans-web1 web server:

```
ansible-playbook create-users1.yml --limit ans-web1
```

In the output, we can see that three tasks have been executed, one for each user:

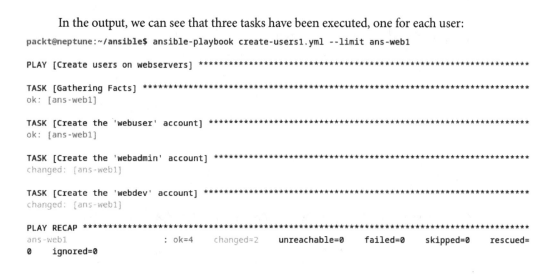

```
packt@neptune:~/ansible$ ansible-playbook create-users1.yml --limit ans-web1

PLAY [Create users on webservers] ********************************************************

TASK [Gathering Facts] *******************************************************************
ok: [ans-web1]

TASK [Create the 'webuser' account] ******************************************************
ok: [ans-web1]

TASK [Create the 'webadmin' account] *****************************************************
changed: [ans-web1]

TASK [Create the 'webdev' account] *******************************************************
changed: [ans-web1]

PLAY RECAP *******************************************************************************
ans-web1                   : ok=4    changed=2    unreachable=0    failed=0    skipped=0    rescued=
0    ignored=0
```

Figure 17.42 – The output of the create-users1 playbook, with multiple tasks

4. Let's delete the users by running the delete-users2.yml playbook:

    ansible-playbook delete-users2.yml --limit ans-web1

    The output is as shown in the following screenshot:

```
packt@neptune:~/ansible$ ansible-playbook delete-users2.yml --limit ans-web1

PLAY [Delete users on webservers] ********************************************************

TASK [Gathering Facts] *******************************************************************
ok: [ans-web1]

TASK [Delete user] ***********************************************************************
changed: [ans-web1] => (item=webuser)
changed: [ans-web1] => (item=webadmin)
changed: [ans-web1] => (item=webdev)

PLAY RECAP *******************************************************************************
ans-web1                   : ok=2    changed=1    unreachable=0    failed=0    skipped=0    rescued=
0    ignored=0
```

Figure 17.43 – Deleting users using the playbook

5. Now, let's run the create-users2 playbook, again targeting only the web1 web server:

    ansible-playbook create-users2.yml --limit ans-web1

This time, the output shows a single task iterating through all the users:

```
packt@neptune:~/ansible$ ansible-playbook create-users2.yml --limit ans-web1

PLAY [Create users on webservers] ***************************************************

TASK [Gathering Facts] **************************************************************
ok: [ans-web1]

TASK [Create the '{{ item }}' account] **********************************************
ok: [ans-web1] => (item=webuser)
ok: [ans-web1] => (item=webadmin)
ok: [ans-web1] => (item=webdev)

PLAY RECAP **************************************************************************
ans-web1                   : ok=2    changed=0    unreachable=0    failed=0    skipped=0    rescued=
0    ignored=0
```

Figure 17.44 – The output of the create-users2 playbook, with a single task iteration

The difference between the two playbook runs is significant:

- The first playbook executes a task for each user. While forking a task is not an expensive operation, you can imagine that creating hundreds of users would incur a significant load on the Ansible runtime.

- On the other hand, the second playbook runs a single task, loading the `user` module three times, to create each user. Loading a module takes significantly fewer resources than running a task.

For more information about loops, you may refer to the related online documentation at `https://docs.ansible.com/ansible/latest/user_guide/playbooks_loops.html`.

Now that we know how to implement a simple loop, we'll make our playbook more compact and maintainable.

Configuring our playbooks

Apart from enhancing our playbooks, we'll also try to come closer to a real-world scenario by storing the users and their related passwords in a reusable and secure fashion.

We will keep the web users' information in the `users.yml` file. The related passwords are in the `users_passwords.yml` file. Here are the two files, along with some example user data:

```
  GNU nano 6.2                             users.yml *
---
# Passwords are stored in the passwords.yml file

webusers:
  - username: webuser
    comment: regular web user
  - username: webadmin
    comment: web administrator
  - username: webdev
    comment: web developer
```

```
packt@neptune:~/ansible$ ansible-vault view users_passwords.yml
Vault password:
---
# Usernames match the records in users.yml
# The order doesn't matter
webuser:
  password: bb37e5d1

webadmin:
  password: 7705b8a4

webdev:
  password: 8365b176
```

Figure 17.45 – The users.yml and users_passwords.yml files

Let's take a closer look at these files:

- The users.yml file contains a dictionary with a single key-value pair:

  - **Key**: webusers

  - **Value**: A list of username and comment tuples

- The users_passwords.yml file contains a nested dictionary with multiple key-value pairs, as follows:

  - **Key**: <username> (for example, webuser, webadmin, and so on)

  - **Value**: A nested dictionary with the password: <value> key-value pair

You may use the ansible-vault edit command to update the users_passwords.yml file, or you can create a new one, as we did. Alternatively, after you create a file from scratch, you will then have to encrypt it, following the steps previously described in the *Working with secrets* section.

The new create-users.yml playbook file has the following implementation:

```
  GNU nano 6.2                              create-users.yml *
---
- name: Create users on webservers
  hosts: webservers
  become: yes
  tasks:
    - name: Load users
      include_vars:
        file: users.yml
        name: users
    - name: Load passwords
      include_vars:
        file: users_passwords.yml
        name: passwords
    - name: Create user accounts
      user:
        name: "{{ item.username }}"
        comment: "{{ item.comment }}"
        password: "{{ passwords[item.username]['password'] | password_hash('sha512') }}"
        update_password: always
        state: present
      loop: "{{ users.webusers }}"
```

Figure 17.46 – The create-users.yml playbook

These files are also available in the GitHub repository for this book, in the related chapter folder. Let's quickly go over the playbook's implementation. We have three tasks:

- `Load users`: Reads the web user information from the `users.yml` file and stores the related values in the `users` dictionary

- `Load passwords`: Reads the passwords from the encrypted `passwords.yml` file and stores the corresponding values in the `passwords` dictionary

- `Create user accounts`: Iterates through the `users.webusers` list and, for each item, creates a user account with the related parameters; the task performs a password lookup in the `passwords` dictionary based on `item.username`

Before running the playbook, let us encrypt the `users_passwords.yml` file using the following command:

```
ansible-vault encrypt users_passwords.yml
```

Now, run the playbook with the following command:

```
ansible-playbook --ask-vault-pass create-users.yml
```

Here's the output:

```
packt@neptune:~/ansible$ ansible-playbook --ask-vault-pass create-users.yml
Vault password:

PLAY [Create users on webservers] ****************************************************

TASK [Gathering Facts] ****************************************************************
ok: [ans-web2]
ok: [ans-web1]

TASK [Load users] *********************************************************************
ok: [ans-web1]
ok: [ans-web2]

TASK [Load passwords] *****************************************************************
ok: [ans-web1]
ok: [ans-web2]

TASK [Create user accounts] **********************************************************
changed: [ans-web1] => (item={'username': 'webuser', 'comment': 'regular web user'})
changed: [ans-web2] => (item={'username': 'webuser', 'comment': 'regular web user'})
changed: [ans-web1] => (item={'username': 'webadmin', 'comment': 'web administrator'})
changed: [ans-web2] => (item={'username': 'webadmin', 'comment': 'web administrator'})
changed: [ans-web1] => (item={'username': 'webdev', 'comment': 'web developer'})
changed: [ans-web2] => (item={'username': 'webdev', 'comment': 'web developer'})

PLAY RECAP ***************************************************************************
ans-web1                   : ok=4    changed=1    unreachable=0    failed=0    skipped=0    rescued=
0    ignored=0
ans-web2                   : ok=4    changed=1    unreachable=0    failed=0    skipped=0    rescued=
0    ignored=0
```

Figure 17.47 – Running the create-users.yml playbook

We can see the following playbook tasks at work:

- `Gathering Facts`: Discovering managed hosts and related system variables (facts); we'll introduce Ansible facts later in this chapter

- `Load users`: Reading the users from the `users.yml` file

- `Load passwords`: Reading the passwords from the encrypted `passwords.yml` file

- `Create user accounts`: The task iteration loop creates users

You may verify the new user accounts using the methods presented earlier in the *Working with secrets* section. As an exercise, create the `delete-users.yml` playbook using a similar implementation to the `create-users` playbook.

Now, let's look at how we can improve our playbook and reuse it to seamlessly create users across all hosts in the inventory, web servers, and databases alike. We'll use conditional tasks to accomplish this functionality.

Running conditional tasks

Conditionals in Ansible playbooks decide when to run a task, depending on a condition (or a state). This condition can be the value of a **variable** or **fact** or the **result** of a previous task. Ansible uses the when task-level directive to define a condition.

We learned about variables and how to use them in playbooks. Facts and results are essentially variables of a specific type and use. We'll look at each of these variables in the context of conditional tasks. Let's start with facts.

Using Ansible facts

Facts are variables that provide specific information about *remote* managed hosts. Fact variable names start with the `ansible_` prefix.

Here are a few examples of Ansible facts:

- `ansible_distribution`: The OS distribution (for example, `Ubuntu`)

- `ansible_all_ipv4_addresses`: The IPv4 addresses

- `ansible_architecture`: The platform architecture (for example, `x86_64` or `i386`)

- `ansible_processor_cores`: The number of CPU cores

- `ansible_memfree_mb`: The available memory (in MB)

Now, what if we didn't have groups explicitly created for classifying our hosts in Ubuntu and Debian systems, for example (or any other distribution, for that matter)? In this case, we could gather facts about our managed hosts, detect their OS type, and perform the conditional update task, depending on the underlying platform. Let's implement this functionality in a playbook using Ansible facts.

We'll name our playbook `install-updates.yml` and add the following content to it:

```
GNU nano 6.2                              install-updates.yml *
---
- name: Install system updates
  hosts: all
  become: yes

  tasks:
  - name: Install Ubuntu system updates
    apt: upgrade=dist update_cache=yes
    when: ansible_distribution == "Ubuntu"

  - name: Install Debian system updates
    apt: upgrade=dist update_cache=yes
    when: ansible_distribution == "Debian"
```

Figure 17.48 – The install-updates.yml playbook

The playbook targets all hosts and has two conditional tasks, based on the `ansible_distribution` fact:

- `Install Ubuntu system updates`: Runs exclusively on Ubuntu hosts based on the `ansible_distribution == "Ubuntu"` condition (*line 9*)

- `Install Debian system updates`: Runs exclusively on Debian hosts based on the `ansible_distribution == "Debian"` condition (*line 13*)

Let's run our playbook:

```
ansible-playbook install-updates.yml
```

The commands will take a significant time to run if there are any updates to install on the hosts. Here's the corresponding output:

```
packt@neptune:~/ansible$ ansible-playbook install-updates.yml

PLAY [Install system updates] *******************************************************

TASK [Gathering Facts] **************************************************************
ok: [ans-web2]
ok: [ans-web1]
ok: [ans-db2]
ok: [ans-db1]

TASK [Install Ubuntu system updates] ************************************************
changed: [ans-web2]
changed: [ans-db1]
changed: [ans-web1]
changed: [ans-db2]

TASK [Install Debian system updates] ************************************************
skipping: [ans-web1]
skipping: [ans-web2]
skipping: [ans-db1]
skipping: [ans-db2]

PLAY RECAP **************************************************************************
ans-db1                    : ok=2    changed=1    unreachable=0    failed=0    skipped=1    rescued=
0    ignored=0
ans-db2                    : ok=2    changed=1    unreachable=0    failed=0    skipped=1    rescued=
0    ignored=0
ans-web1                   : ok=2    changed=1    unreachable=0    failed=0    skipped=1    rescued=
0    ignored=0
ans-web2                   : ok=2    changed=1    unreachable=0    failed=0    skipped=1    rescued=
0    ignored=0
```

Figure 17.49 – Running conditional tasks

There are three tasks illustrated in the preceding output:

- `Gathering Facts`: The default discovery task that's executed by the playbook to gather facts about remote hosts

- `Install Ubuntu system updates`: The conditional task for running all Ubuntu hosts

- `Install Debian system updates`: The conditional task for skipping all Ubuntu-based hosts, as we don't currently run any Debian ones

Next, we'll look at how to use Ansible's environment-specific variables in conditional tasks.

Using magic variables

Magic variables describe the local Ansible environment and its related configuration data. Here are a few examples of magic variables:

- `ansible_playhosts`: A list of active hosts in the current play

- `group_names`: A list of all groups the current host is a member of

- **vars**: A dictionary with all variables in the current play
- **ansible_version**: The version of Ansible

To see magic variables in action while using conditional tasks, we'll improve our `create-users` playbook even further and create specific groups of users on different host groups. So far, the playbook only creates users on hosts that belong to the `webservers` group (web1, web2). The playbook creates `webuser`, `webadmin`, and `webdev` user accounts on all web servers. What if we want to create a similar group of users – `dbuser`, `dbadmin`, and `dbdev` – on all our database servers? To achieve this, you can follow these steps:

1. Start by adding the new user accounts and passwords to the `users.yml` and `users_passwords.yml` files, respectively. Here's what we have after adding the database's user accounts and passwords:

```
GNU nano 6.2                                        users.yml *
---
# Passwords are stored in the users_passwords.yml file

webusers:
  - username: webuser
    comment: regular web user

  - username: webadmin
    comment: web administrator

  - username: webdev
    comment: web developer

dbusers:
  - username: dbuser
    comment: Regular database user

  - username: dbadmin
    comment: Database administrator

  - username: dbdev
    comment: Database developer
```

```
 1 ---
 2 # Usernames match the records in users.yml
 3 # The order doesn't matter
 4
 5 # Web users passwords
 6 webuser:
 7     password: bb37e5d1
 8
 9 webadmin:
10     password: 7705b8a4
11
12 webdev:
13     password: 8365b176
14
15 # Database users passwords
16 dbuser:
17     password: 4695b3db
18 dbadmin:
19     password: 99057ee9
20 dbdev:
21     password: a966ada8
22
```

Figure 17.50 – The users.yml and passwords.yml files

Note that you can edit the `users_passwords.yml` file using the `ansible-vault edit` command. Alternatively, you can decrypt the file, edit it, and re-encrypt it.

2.   Now, let's create a `create-users3` playbook with the required conditional tasks to handle both groups – `webusers` and `databases` – selectively. Let us create a new file called `create-users3.yml` with the following content:

```
GNU nano 6.2                                        create-users3.yml
---
- name: Create users
  hosts: all
  become: yes
  tasks:
  - name: Load users
    include_vars:
      file: users.yml
      name: users
  - name: Load passwords
    include_vars:
      file: users_passwords.yml
      name: passwords
  - name: Create web user accounts
    user:
      name: "{{ item.username }}"
      comment: "{{ item.comment }}"
      password: "{{ passwords[item.username]['password'] | password_hash('sha512') }}"
      update_password: always
      state: present
    loop: "{{ users.webusers }}"
    when: "'webservers' in group_names"
  - name: Create database user accounts
    user:
      name: "{{ item.username }}"
      comment: "{{ item.comment }}"
      password: "{{ passwords[item.username]['password'] | password_hash('sha512') }}"
      update_password: always
      state: present
    loop: "{{ users.dbusers }}"
    when: "'databases' in group_names"
```

Figure 17.51 – The create-users.yml playbook with conditional tasks

3.   Let's run the playbook:

```
ansible-playbook --ask-vault-pass create-users3.yml
```

The following is an excerpt of the output that shows the web user task skipping the database servers and the database user task skipping the web servers, suggesting that the web and database users have been created successfully:

```
TASK [Create web user accounts] *****************************************************
skipping: [ans-db1] => (item={'username': 'webuser', 'comment': 'regular web user'})
skipping: [ans-db1] => (item={'username': 'webadmin', 'comment': 'web administrator'})
skipping: [ans-db1] => (item={'username': 'webdev', 'comment': 'web developer'})
skipping: [ans-db1]
skipping: [ans-db2] => (item={'username': 'webuser', 'comment': 'regular web user'})
skipping: [ans-db2] => (item={'username': 'webadmin', 'comment': 'web administrator'})
skipping: [ans-db2] => (item={'username': 'webdev', 'comment': 'web developer'})
skipping: [ans-db2]
changed: [ans-web1] => (item={'username': 'webuser', 'comment': 'regular web user'})
changed: [ans-web2] => (item={'username': 'webuser', 'comment': 'regular web user'})
changed: [ans-web2] => (item={'username': 'webadmin', 'comment': 'web administrator'})
changed: [ans-web1] => (item={'username': 'webadmin', 'comment': 'web administrator'})
changed: [ans-web2] => (item={'username': 'webdev', 'comment': 'web developer'})
changed: [ans-web1] => (item={'username': 'webdev', 'comment': 'web developer'})

TASK [Create database user accounts] *****************************************************
skipping: [ans-web1] => (item={'username': 'dbuser', 'comment': 'Regular database user'})
skipping: [ans-web1] => (item={'username': 'dbadmin', 'comment': 'Database administrator'})
skipping: [ans-web1] => (item={'username': 'dbdev', 'comment': 'Database developer'})
skipping: [ans-web1]
skipping: [ans-web2] => (item={'username': 'dbuser', 'comment': 'Regular database user'})
skipping: [ans-web2] => (item={'username': 'dbadmin', 'comment': 'Database administrator'})
skipping: [ans-web2] => (item={'username': 'dbdev', 'comment': 'Database developer'})
skipping: [ans-web2]
changed: [ans-db1] => (item={'username': 'dbuser', 'comment': 'Regular database user'})
changed: [ans-db2] => (item={'username': 'dbuser', 'comment': 'Regular database user'})
changed: [ans-db1] => (item={'username': 'dbadmin', 'comment': 'Database administrator'})
changed: [ans-db2] => (item={'username': 'dbadmin', 'comment': 'Database administrator'})
changed: [ans-db1] => (item={'username': 'dbdev', 'comment': 'Database developer'})
changed: [ans-db2] => (item={'username': 'dbdev', 'comment': 'Database developer'})
```

Figure 17.52 – The web and database user tasks running selectively

For a complete list of Ansible special variables, including magic variables, please visit https://docs.ansible.com/ansible/latest/reference_appendices/special_variables.html. For more information about facts and magic variables, check out the online documentation at https://docs.ansible.com/ansible/latest/user_guide/playbooks_vars_facts.html.

Next, we'll look at variables for tracking task results, also known as register variables.

Using register variables

Ansible registers capture the output of a task in a variable called a **register variable**. Ansible uses the register directive to capture the task's output in a variable. A typical example of using register variables is collecting the result of a task for debugging purposes. In more complex workflows, a particular task may or may not run, depending on a previous task's result.

Let's consider a hypothetical use case. As we onboard new users and create different accounts on all our servers, we want to make sure the number of users doesn't exceed the maximum number allowed. If the limit is reached, we may choose to launch a new server, redistribute the users, and so on. You can follow these steps:

1. Let's start by creating a playbook named count-users.yml with the following content:

```yaml
---
- name: Detect if the number of users exceeds the limit
  hosts: all
  become: yes
  vars:
    max_allowed: 30
  tasks:
  - name: Count all users
    shell: "getent passwd | wc -l"
    register: count
  - name: Debug number of users
    debug:
      msg: "Number of users: {{ count.stdout }}. Limit: {{ max_allowed }}"
  - name: Detect limit
    debug:
      msg: "Maximum number of users reached!"
    when: count.stdout | int > max_allowed
```

Figure 17.53 – The count-users.yml playbook

We created the following tasks in the playbook:

*   Count all users: A task that uses the shell module to count all users; we register the count variable by capturing the task output

*   Debug number of users: A simple task for debugging purposes that logs the number of users and the maximum limit allowed

*   Detect limit: A conditional task that's run when the limit has been reached; the task checks the value of the count register variable and compares it with the max_allowed variable

Line 17 in our playbook needs some further explanation. Here, we take the actual standard output of the register variable; that is, count.stdout. As is, the value would be a string, and we need to cast it to an integer; that is, count.stdout | int. Then, we compare the resulting number with max_allowed.

2. Let's run the playbook while targeting only the ans-web1 host:

```
ansible-playbook count-users.yml --limit ans-web1
```

The output is as follows:

```
packt@neptune:~/ansible$ ansible-playbook count-users.yml --limit ans-web1

PLAY [Detect if the number of users exceeds the limit] ******************************************

TASK [Gathering Facts] **************************************************************************
ok: [ans-web1]

TASK [Count all users] **************************************************************************
changed: [ans-web1]

TASK [Debug number of users] ********************************************************************
ok: [ans-web1] => {
    "msg": "Number of users: 37. Limit: 30"
}

TASK [Detect limit] *****************************************************************************
ok: [ans-web1] => {
    "msg": "Maximum number of users reached!"
}

PLAY RECAP **************************************************************************************
ans-web1                   : ok=4    changed=1    unreachable=0    failed=0    skipped=0    rescued=0    ignored=0
```

Figure 17.54 – The conditional task (Detect limit) is executed

Here, we can see that the number of users is 36, thus exceeding the maximum limit of 30. In other words, the Detect limit task ran as it was supposed to.

3. Now, let's edit the count-users.yml playbook and change the following:

    ```
    max_allowed: 50
    ```

4. Save and rerun the playbook. This time, the output shows that the Detect limit task was skipped:

```
packt@neptune:~/ansible$ nano count-users.yml
packt@neptune:~/ansible$ ansible-playbook count-users.yml --limit ans-web1

PLAY [Detect if the number of users exceeds the limit] ******************************************

TASK [Gathering Facts] **************************************************************************
ok: [ans-web1]

TASK [Count all users] **************************************************************************
changed: [ans-web1]

TASK [Debug number of users] ********************************************************************
ok: [ans-web1] => {
    "msg": "Number of users: 37. Limit: 50"
}

TASK [Detect limit] *****************************************************************************
skipping: [ans-web1]

PLAY RECAP **************************************************************************************
ans-web1                   : ok=3    changed=1    unreachable=0    failed=0    skipped=1    rescued=0    ignored=0
```

Figure 17.55 – The conditional task (Detect limit) is skipped

To learn more about conditional tasks in Ansible playbooks, please visit `https://docs.ansible.com/ansible/latest/user_guide/playbooks_conditionals.html`. By combining conditional tasks with Ansible's all-encompassing facts and special variables, we can write extremely powerful playbooks and automate a wide range of system administration operations.

In the following sections, we'll explore additional ways to make our playbooks more reusable and versatile. We'll look at dynamic configuration templates next.

Using templates with Jinja2

One of the most common configuration management tasks is copying files to managed hosts. Ansible provides the `copy` module for serving such tasks. A typical file copy operation has the following syntax in Ansible playbooks:

```
- copy:
    src: motd
    dest: /etc/motd
```

The `copy` task takes a source file (`motd`) and copies it to a destination (`/etc/motd`) on the remote host. While this model would work for copying static files to multiple hosts, it won't handle host-specific customizations in these files on the fly.

Take, for example, a network configuration file featuring the IP address of a host. Attempting to copy this file on all hosts to configure the related network settings could render all but one host unreachable. Ideally, the network configuration file should have a *placeholder* for the dynamic content (for example, IP address) and adapt the file accordingly, depending on the target host.

To address this functionality, Ansible provides the `template` module with the **Jinja2** templating engine. Jinja2 uses Python-like language constructs for variables and expressions in a template. The `template` syntax is very similar to `copy`:

```
- template:
    src: motd.j2
    dest: /etc/motd
```

The source, in this case, is a Jinja2 template file (`motd.j2`) with host-specific customizations. Before copying the file to the remote host, Ansible reads the Jinja2 template and replaces the dynamic content with the host-specific data. This processing happens on the Ansible control node.

To illustrate some of the benefits and internal workings of Ansible templates, we'll work with a couple of use cases and create a Jinja2 template for each. Then, we'll create and run the related playbooks to show the templates in action.

Here are the two templates we'll be creating in this section:

- **Message-of-the-day template** (`motd`): For displaying a customized message to users about scheduled system maintenance
- **Host file template** (`hosts`): For generating a custom `/etc/hosts` file on each system with the hostname records of the other managed hosts

Let's start with the message-of-the-day template.

Creating a message-of-the-day template

In our introductory notes, we used the `/etc/motd` file as an example. On a Linux system, the content of this file is displayed when a user logs in to the Terminal. Suppose you plan to upgrade your web servers on Thursday night and would like to give your users a friendly reminder about the upcoming outage. Your `motd` message could be something like this:

```
This server will be down for maintenance on Thursday night.
```

There's nothing special about this message, and the `motd` file could be easily deployed with a simple `copy` task. In most cases, such a message would probably do just fine, apart from the rare occasion when users may get confused about which exactly is "`this server`". You may also consider that Thursday night in the US could be Friday afternoon on the other side of the world, and it would be nice if the announcement were more specific.

Perhaps a better message would state, on the `ans-web1` web server, the following:

```
ans-web1 (172.16.191.12) will be down for maintenance on Thursday,
April 8, 2021, between 2 - 3 AM (UTC-08:00).
```

On the `ans-web2` web server, the message would reflect the corresponding hostname and IP address. Ideally, the template should be reusable across multiple time zones, with playbooks running on globally distributed Ansible control nodes. Let's see how we can implement such a template (we'll assume your current working directory is `~/ansible`):

1. First, create a `templates` folder in your local Ansible project directory:

   ```
   mkdir -p ~/ansible/templates
   ```

   Ansible will look for template files in the local directory, which is where we'll create our playbook, or in the `./templates` folder.

2. Using a Linux editor of your choice, create a `motd.j2` file in `./templates` with the following content:

```
GNU nano 6.2                                              motd.j2 *
{# We would pass these variables from the playbook#}
{% set date = '2023-10-24' %}
{% set start_time = date ~ 'T02:00:00-0800' %}
{% set end_time = date ~ 'T03:00:00-0800' %}

{% set fmt = '%Y-%m-%dT%H:%M:%S%z' %}
{% set start = (start_time | to_datetime(format=fmt)) %}
{% set end = (end_time | to_datetime(format=fmt)) %}

{# We would also use the {{ inventory_hostname }} special variable #}
{{ ansible_facts.fqdn }} ({{ ansible_facts.default_ipv4.address }}) will be
down for maintenance on {{ start.strftime('%A, %B %-d, %Y') }}, between
{{ start.strftime('%-I') }} - {{ end.strftime('%-I %p (%Z)') }}.
```

Figure 17.56 – The motd.j2 template file

Note some of the particularities of the Jinja2 syntax:

- Comments are enclosed in {# ... #}

- Expressions are surrounded by {% ... %}

- External variables are referenced with {{ ... }}

Here's what the script does:

- *Lines 1-4* define an initial set of local variables for storing time boundaries for the outage: the day of the outage (`date`), the starting time (`start_time`), and the ending time (`end_time`).

- *Line 6* defines the input date-time format (`fmt`) for our starting and ending time variables.

- *Lines 7-8* build `datetime` objects that correspond to `start_time` and `end_time`. These Python `datetime` objects are formatted according to our needs in the custom message.

- *Line 11* prints the custom message, featuring user-friendly time outputs and a couple of Ansible facts, namely the **fully qualified domain name** (**FQDN**) (`ansible_facts.fqdn`) and IPv4 address (`ansible_facts.default_ipv4.address`) of the host where the message is displayed.

3. Now, let's create a playbook running the template. We will name the playbook `update-motd.yml` and add the following content:

Figure 17.57 – The update-motd.yml playbook

The `template` module reads and processes the `motd.j2` file, generating related dynamic content, then copies the file to the remote host in `/etc/motd` with the required permissions.

4. Now, we're ready to run our playbook:

```
ansible-playbook update-motd.yml
```

The command should complete successfully. Here is a screenshot of our output:

```
packt@neptune:~/ansible$ ansible-playbook update-motd.yml

PLAY [Update the message of the day] ****************************************************

TASK [Gathering Facts] ******************************************************************
ok: [ans-web1]
ok: [ans-db1]
ok: [ans-web2]
ok: [ans-db2]

TASK [Deploy the 'motd' template] *******************************************************
changed: [ans-web1]
changed: [ans-db1]
changed: [ans-web2]
changed: [ans-db2]

PLAY RECAP ******************************************************************************
ans-db1                    : ok=2    changed=1    unreachable=0    failed=0    skipped=0    rescued=
0    ignored=0
ans-db2                    : ok=2    changed=1    unreachable=0    failed=0    skipped=0    rescued=
0    ignored=0
ans-web1                   : ok=2    changed=1    unreachable=0    failed=0    skipped=0    rescued=
0    ignored=0
ans-web2                   : ok=2    changed=1    unreachable=0    failed=0    skipped=0    rescued=
0    ignored=0
```

Figure 17.58 – Running the update-motd.yml playbook

5. You can immediately verify the `motd` message on any of the hosts (for example, `ans-web1`) with the following command:

    ```
    ansible ans-web1 -a "cat /etc/motd"
    ```

    The preceding command runs remotely on the `ans-web1` host and displays the content of the `/etc/motd` file:

    ```
    packt@neptune:~/ansible$ ansible ans-web1 -a "cat /etc/motd"
    ans-web1 | CHANGED | rc=0 >>


    ans-web1 (192.168.122.70) will be
    down for maintenance on Tuesday, October 24, 2023, between
    2 - 3 AM (UTC-08:00).
    ```

    Figure 17.59 – The content of the remote /etc/motd file

6. We can also SSH into any of the hosts to verify the `motd` prompt:

    ```
    ssh packt@ans-web1
    ```

    The Terminal shows the following output:

    ```
    ans-web1 (192.168.122.70) will be
    down for maintenance on Tuesday, October 24, 2023, between
    2 - 3 AM (UTC-08:00).
    Last login: Tue Oct 24 17:46:14 2023 from 192.168.122.1
    packt@ans-web1:~$
    ```

    Figure 17.60 – The motd prompt on the remote host

7. Now that we know how to write and handle Ansible templates, let's improve `motd.j2` to make it a bit more reusable. We'll *parameterize* the template by replacing the hardcoded local variables for date and time with input variables that are passed from the playbook. This way, we'll make our template reusable across multiple playbooks and different input times for maintenance. Here's the updated template file (`motd.j2`):

    ```
    GNU nano 6.2                                        motd.j2 *
    {% set start_time_ = date ~ 'T' ~ start_time ~ utc %}
    {% set end_time_ = date ~ 'T' ~ end_time ~ utc %}

    {% set fmt = '%Y-%m-%dT%H:%M:%Sz' %}
    {% set start = (start_time_ | to_datetime(format=fmt)) %}
    {% set end = (end_time_ | to_datetime(format=fmt)) %}

    {{ ansible_facts.fqdn }} ({{ ansible_facts.default_ipv4.address }}) will be down
    for maintenance on {{ start.strftime('%A, %B %-d, %Y') }}, between
    {{ start.strftime('%-I') }} - {{ end.strftime('%-I %p (%Z)') }}.
    ```

    Figure 17.61 – The modified motd.j2 template with input variables

Relevant changes are in *lines 1-2*, where we build datetime objects using the date, start_time, end_time, and utc input variables. Notice the difference between the *local variables* – start_time_ and end_time_ (suffixed with _) – and the corresponding *input variables*; that is, start_time and end_time. You may choose any naming convention for the variables, assuming it is Ansible-compliant.

8. Now, let's look at our modified playbook (update-motd.yml):

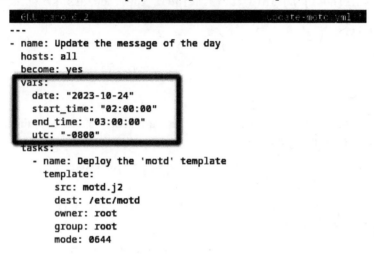

Figure 17.62 – The modified update-motd.yml playbook with variables

Relevant changes are highlighted in the preceding screenshot, where we added variables serving the input for the motd.j2 template. Running the modified playbook should yield the same result as the previous implementation. We'll leave the related exercise to you.

Next, we'll look at another use case featuring template-based deployments: updating the /etc/hosts file on managed hosts with the host records of all the other servers in the group.

Creating a hosts file template

Another example of using an Ansible template is to automatically update the /etc/hosts files on every machine by using Jinja2 templating. The /etc/hosts file contains numerical IP addresses and the names of all hosts on the network, and updating it regularly is a useful task for a system administrator. We will create a new template for the hosts file and then update the specific YAML file to access the new template file. To create a hosts file template, follow these steps:

1. Let's start by creating a new template file, named hosts.j2, in the ~/ansible/templates directory. Add the following content:

```
  GNU nano 6.2                                      hosts.j2 *
# This file is autogenerated!

127.0.0.1 {{ inventory_hostname }} localhost

{% for host in groups['all'] %}
{% if host != inventory_hostname %}
{{ hostvars[host].ansible_facts.default_ipv4.address }} {{ host }}
{% endif %}
{% endfor %}
```

Figure 17.63 – The hosts.j2 template file

Here's how the template script works:

- Adds a `localhost` record corresponding to the current host referenced by the `inventory_hostname` Ansible special variable

- Executes a loop through all hosts in the inventory referenced by the `groups['all']` list (special variable)

- Checks if the current host in the loop matches the target host, and it will only execute next if the hosts are *different*

- Adds a new host record by reading the default IPv4 address (`default_ipv4.address`) of the current host from the related Ansible facts (`hostvars[host].ansible_facts`)

2. Now, let's create an `update-hosts.yml` playbook file referencing the `hosts.j2` template. Add the following content:

```
  GNU nano 6.2                                  update-hosts.yml *
---
- name: Update the hosts file
  hosts: all
  become: yes
  tasks:
    - name: Deploy the 'hosts' template
      template:
        src: hosts.j2
        dest: /etc/hosts
        owner: root
        group: root
        mode: 0644
```

Figure 17.64 – The update-hosts.yml playbook file

This playbook is very similar to `update-motd.yml`. It targets the `/etc/hosts` file.

3. With the playbook and template files ready, let's run the following command:

```
ansible-playbook update-hosts.yml
```

4. After the command completes, we can check the `/etc/hosts` file on any of the hosts (for example, `ans-web1`) by using the following command:

```
ansible ans-web1 -a "cat /etc/hosts"
```

The output shows the expected host records:

```
packt@neptune:~/ansible$ ansible ans-web1 -a "cat /etc/hosts"
ans-web1 | CHANGED | rc=0 >>
# This file is autogenerated!

127.0.0.1 ans-web1 localhost

192.168.122.147 ans-web2
192.168.122.254 ans-db1
192.168.122.25 ans-db2
```

Figure 17.65 – The autogenerated /etc/hosts file on web1

5. You can also SSH into one of the hosts (for example, `ans-web1`) and ping any of the other hosts by name (for example, `ans-db2`):

```
ssh packt@ans-web1
ping ans-db2
```

You should get a successful `ping` response:

```
packt@ans-web1:~$ ping ans-db2
PING ans-db2 (192.168.122.25) 56(84) bytes of data.
64 bytes from ans-db2 (192.168.122.25): icmp_seq=1 ttl=64 time=1.41 ms
64 bytes from ans-db2 (192.168.122.25): icmp_seq=2 ttl=64 time=0.914 ms
64 bytes from ans-db2 (192.168.122.25): icmp_seq=3 ttl=64 time=0.265 ms
64 bytes from ans-db2 (192.168.122.25): icmp_seq=4 ttl=64 time=0.690 ms
64 bytes from ans-db2 (192.168.122.25): icmp_seq=5 ttl=64 time=0.652 ms
64 bytes from ans-db2 (192.168.122.25): icmp_seq=6 ttl=64 time=0.264 ms
64 bytes from ans-db2 (192.168.122.25): icmp_seq=7 ttl=64 time=0.506 ms
64 bytes from ans-db2 (192.168.122.25): icmp_seq=8 ttl=64 time=0.736 ms
64 bytes from ans-db2 (192.168.122.25): icmp_seq=9 ttl=64 time=0.255 ms
```

Figure 17.66 – Successful ping by hostname from one host to another

This concludes our study of Ansible templates. However, the topics we covered in this section barely scratch the surface of the powerful features and versatility of Jinja2 templates. We strongly encourage you to explore the related online help resources at `https://docs.ansible.com/ansible/latest/user_guide/playbooks_templating.html`, as well as the titles mentioned in the *Further reading* section at the end of this chapter.

Now, we will turn our attention to another essential feature of modern configuration management platforms: sharing reusable and flexible modules for a variety of system administration tasks. Ansible provides a highly accessible and extensible framework to accommodate this functionality – **Ansible roles** and **Ansible Galaxy**. In the next section, we'll look at roles for automation reuse.

Creating Ansible roles

With Ansible roles, you can bundle your automated workflows into reusable units. A role is essentially a package containing playbooks and other resources that have been adapted to a specific configuration using variables. An arbitrary playbook would invoke a role by providing the required parameters and running it just like any other task. Functionally speaking, roles encapsulate a generic configuration management behavior, making them reusable across multiple projects and even shareable with others.

Here are the key benefits of using roles:

- Encapsulation functionality provides standalone packaging that can easily be shared with others. Encapsulation also enables **separation of concerns** (**SoC**): multiple DevOps and system administrators can develop roles in parallel.

- Roles can make larger automation projects more manageable.

In this section, we will describe the process of creating a role and how to use it in a sample playbook. When authoring roles, we usually follow these steps and practices:

- Create or initialize the role directory's structure. The directory contains all resources required by the role in a well-organized fashion.

- Implement the role's content. Create related playbooks, files, templates, and so on.

- Always start from simple to more advanced functionality. Test your playbooks as you add more content.

- Make your implementation as generic as possible. Use variables to expose related customizations.

- Don't store secrets in your playbooks or related files. Provide input parameters for them.

- Create a dummy playbook with a simple play running your role. Use this dummy playbook to test your role.

- Design your role with user experience in mind. Make it easy to use and share it with others if you think it would bring value to the community.

At a high level, creating a role involves the following steps:

1. Initializing the role directory structure
2. Authoring the role's content
3. Testing the role

We'll use the `create-users3.yml` playbook we created earlier in the *Using Ansible playbooks* section as our example for creating a role. We will copy this file with a new name; `create-users-role.yml`, for example. Before proceeding with the next steps, let's add the following line to our `ansible.cfg` file (which is located inside the `~/ansible` directory) in the `[defaults]` section:

```
roles_path = ~/ansible
```

This configuration parameter sets the default location for our roles.

Now, let's start by initializing the role directory.

Initializing the role directory's structure

Ansible has a strict requirement regarding the folder structure of the role directory. The directory must have the same name as the role; for example, `create-users-role`. We can create this directory manually or by using a specialized command-line utility for managing roles, called `ansible-galaxy`.

To create the skeleton of our role directory, run the following command:

```
ansible-galaxy init create-users
```

The command completes with the following message:

```
- Role create-users was created successfully
```

You can display the directory structure using the `tree` command:

```
tree
```

You'll have to manually install the `tree` command-line utility using your local package manager. The output shows the `create-users-role` directory structure of our role:

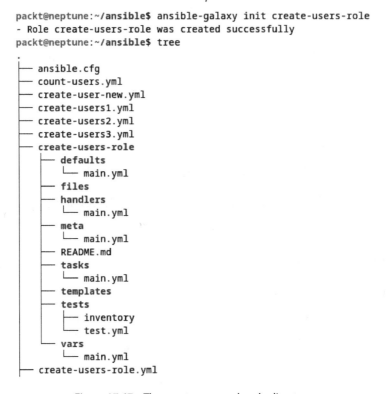

Figure 17.67 – The create-users-role role directory

Here's a brief explanation of each folder and the corresponding YAML file in the role directory:

- `defaults/main.yml`: The default variables for the role. They have the lowest priority among all available variables and can be overwritten by any other variable.

- `files`: The static files referenced in the role tasks.

- `handlers/main.yml`: The handlers used by the role. Handlers are tasks that are triggered by other tasks. You can read more about handlers at `https://docs.ansible.com/ansible/latest/user_guide/playbooks_handlers.html`.

- `README.md`: Explains the intended purpose of the role and how to use it.

- `meta/main.yml`: Additional information about the role, such as the author, licensing model, platforms, and dependencies on other roles.

- `tasks/main.yml`: The tasks played by the role.

- `Templates`: The template files referenced by the role.

- `tests/test.yml`: The playbook for testing the role. The `tests` folder may also contain a sample `inventory` file.
- `vars/main.yml`: The variables used internally by the role. These variables have high precedence and are not meant to be changed or overwritten.

Now that we are familiar with the role directory and the related resource files, let's create our first role.

Authoring the role's content

It is a common practice to start from a previously created playbook and evolve it into a role. We'll take the `create-users-role.yml` playbook. Let's refactor these files to make them more generic.

We will create two new files for the users and passwords, called `users-role.yml` and `users_passwords-role.yml`, inside the `./create-users-role` directory files:

Figure 17.68 – The users-role.yml and users_passwords-role.yml files

As you may have noticed, we renamed the example user accounts and gave them more generic names. We also changed the user dictionary key name from `webusers` to `list` in the `users-role.yml` file. Remember that Ansible requires root-level dictionary entries (key-value pairs) in YAML files that provide variables.

Let's look at the updated `create-users-role.yml` playbook:

```
GNU nano 6.2                                   create-users-role.yml
---
- name: Create users
  hosts: all
  become: yes
  vars:
    users_file: users-role.yml
    passwords_file: users_passwords-role.yml
  tasks:
  - name: Load users
    include_vars:
      file: "{{ users_file }}"
      name: users
  - name: Load passwords
    include_vars:
      file: "{{ passwords_file }}"
      name: passwords
  - name: Create web user accounts
    user:
      name: "{{ item.username }}"
      comment: "{{ item.comment }}"
      password: "{{ passwords[item.username]['password'] | password_hash('sha512') }}"
      update_password: always
      state: present
    loop: "{{ users.list }}"
```

Figure 17.69 – The modified create-users-role.yml file

We made the following modifications:

- We readjusted the `loop` directive to read `users.list` instead of `users.webusers` due to the name change of the related dictionary key in the `users.yml` file

- We refactored the `include_vars` file references to use variables instead of hardcoded filenames

- We added a `vars` section, with the `users_file` and `passwords_file` variables pointing to the corresponding YAML files

With these changes in the playbook, we're now ready to implement our role. Looking at the `create-users-role` role directory, we'll do the following:

1. Copy/paste the variables in the `vars` section of `create-users-role.yml` into `defaults/main.yml`.

2. Copy/paste the tasks from `create-users-role.yml` into `tasks/main.yml`. Make sure you keep the relative indentations.

3. Create a simple playbook using the role. Use the `tests/test.yml` file for your test playbook. Copy/move `users-role.yml` and `users_passwords-role.yml` to the `tests/` folder.

The following screenshot captures all these changes:

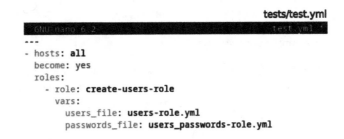

defaults/main.yml
```
GNU nano 6.2                                    main.yml *
---
# defaults file for create-users-role
users_file: users-role.yml
passwords_file: users_passwords-role.yml
```

tasks/main.yml
```
GNU nano 6.2                                    main.yml *
---
# tasks file for create-users-role
- name: Load users
  include_vars:
    file: "{{ users_file }}"
    name: users
- name: Load passwords
  include_vars:
    file: "{{ passwords_file }}"
    name: passwords
- name: Create web user accounts
  user:
    name: "{{ item.username }}"
    comment: "{{ item.comment }}"
    password: "{{ passwords[item.username]['password'] | password_hash('sha512') }}"
    update_password: always
    state: present
  loop: "{{ users.list }}"
```

tests/test.yml
```
GNU nano 6.2                                    test.yml *
---
- hosts: all
  become: yes
  roles:
    - role: create-users-role
      vars:
        users_file: users-role.yml
        passwords_file: users_passwords-role.yml
```

Figure 17.70 – The files that we changed in the create-users role directory

We also recommend updating the README.md file in the create-users-role directory with notes about the purpose and usage of the role. You should also mention the requirement of having the users-role.yml and users_passwords-role.yml files with the related data structures. The names of these files can be changed via the users_file and passwords_file variables in defaults/main.yml. You can also provide some examples of how to use the role. We also created an additional test2.yml playbook using a task to run the role:

```
GNU nano 6.2                          ./create-users-role/tests/test2.yml
---
- hosts: all
  become: yes
  tasks:
  - name: Create users
    include_role:
      name: create-users-role
    vars:
      users_file: users-role.yml
      passwords_file: users_passwords-role.yml
```

Figure 17.71 – Running a role using a task

At this point, we've finished making the required changes for implementing the role. You may choose to remove all empty or unused folders in the create-users-role role directory.

Now, let's test our role.

Testing the role

To test our role, we will use the playbooks in the tests/ folder and run them with the following commands:

```
ansible-playbook create-users/tests/test.yml
ansible-playbook create-users/tests/test2.yml
```

Both commands should complete successfully.

With that, we've provided an exploratory view of Ansible roles, as they are a powerful feature of Ansible, and they enable modern system administrators and DevOps to move quickly from concept to implementation, accelerating the deployment of everyday configuration management workflows.

Summary

In this chapter, we covered significant ground in terms of Ansible. Due to this chapter's limited scope, we couldn't capture all of Ansible's vast number of features. However, we tried to provide an overarching view of the platform, from Ansible's architectural principles to configuring and working with ad hoc commands and playbooks. You learned how to set up an Ansible environment, with several managed hosts and a control node, thereby emulating a real-world deployment at a high level. You also became familiar with writing Ansible commands and scripts for typical configuration management tasks. Most of the commands and playbooks presented throughout this chapter closely resemble everyday administrative operations.

Whether you are a systems administrator or a DevOps engineer, a seasoned professional, or on the way to becoming one, we hope this chapter brought new insights to your everyday Linux administration tasks and automation workflows. The tools and techniques you've learned here will give you a good start for scripting and automating larger portions of your daily administrative routines.

The same closing thoughts also apply to this book in general. You have come a long way in terms of learning and mastering some of the most typical Linux administration tasks in on-premises and cloud environments alike.

We hope that you have enjoyed our journey together.

Questions

Let's try to wrap up some of the essential concepts we learned about in this chapter by completing the following quiz:

1. What are idempotent operations or commands in Ansible?

2. You want to set up passwordless authentication with your managed hosts. What steps should you follow?

3. What is the ad hoc command for checking communication with all your managed hosts?

4. Enumerate a few Ansible modules. Try to think of a configuration management scenario where you could use each module.

5. Think of a simple playbook that monitors the memory that's available on your hosts and will notify you if that memory is above a given threshold.

Further reading

Here are a few resources we found helpful for learning more about Ansible internals:

- Ansible documentation: `https://docs.ansible.com/`

- Ansible use cases, by Red Hat: `https://www.ansible.com/use-cases`

- *Dive into Ansible – From Beginner to Expert in Ansible* [Video], by James Spurin, Packt Publishing (`https://www.packtpub.com/product/dive-into-ansible-from-beginner-to-expert-in-ansible-video/9781801076937`)

- *Practical Ansible 2*, by Daniel Oh, James Freeman, Fabio Alessandro Locati, Packt Publishing (`https://www.packtpub.com/product/practical-ansible-2/9781789807462`)

Index

K

Q

Z

ZFS filesystem 193
zombie processes 162
zone files 245
zones 373, 374
Z shell (Zsh) 278
Zypper 6
  package information, managing 97, 98
  packages, installing and removing 93-95
  system, updating 96, 97
  system, upgrading 96, 97
  working with 93

packtpub.com

Subscribe to our online digital library for full access to over 7,000 books and videos, as well as industry leading tools to help you plan your personal development and advance your career. For more information, please visit our website.

Why subscribe?

- Spend less time learning and more time coding with practical eBooks and Videos from over 4,000 industry professionals

- Improve your learning with Skill Plans built especially for you

- Get a free eBook or video every month

- Fully searchable for easy access to vital information

- Copy and paste, print, and bookmark content

Did you know that Packt offers eBook versions of every book published, with PDF and ePub files available? You can upgrade to the eBook version at packtpub.com and as a print book customer, you are entitled to a discount on the eBook copy. Get in touch with us at customercare@packtpub.com for more details.

At www.packtpub.com, you can also read a collection of free technical articles, sign up for a range of free newsletters, and receive exclusive discounts and offers on Packt books and eBooks.

Other Books You May Enjoy

If you enjoyed this book, you may be interested in these other books by Packt:

Mastering Cloud Security Posture Management (CSPM)

Qamar Nomani

ISBN: 9781837638406

- Find out how to deploy and onboard cloud accounts using CSPM tools
- Understand security posture aspects such as the dashboard, asset inventory, and risks
- Explore the Kusto Query Language (KQL) and write threat hunting queries
- Explore security recommendations and operational best practices
- Get to grips with vulnerability, patch, and compliance management, and governance
- Familiarize yourself with security alerts, monitoring, and workload protection best practices
- Manage IaC scan policies and learn how to handle exceptions

Manjaro Linux User Guide

Atanas Georgiev Rusev

ISBN: 9781803237589

- Gain insights into the full set of Manjaro capabilities
- Install Manjaro and easily customize it using a graphical user interface
- Explore all types of supported software, including office and gaming applications
- Learn basic and advanced Terminal usage with examples
- Understand package management, filesystems, network and the Internet
- Enhance your security with Firewall setup, VPN, SSH, and encryption
- Explore systemd management, journalctl, logs, and user management
- Get to grips with scripting, automation, kernel basics, and switching

Packt is searching for authors like you

If you're interested in becoming an author for Packt, please visit `authors.packtpub.com` and apply today. We have worked with thousands of developers and tech professionals, just like you, to help them share their insight with the global tech community. You can make a general application, apply for a specific hot topic that we are recruiting an author for, or submit your own idea.

Share Your Thoughts

Now you've finished *Mastering Linux Administration*, we'd love to hear your thoughts! Scan the QR code below to go straight to the Amazon review page for this book and share your feedback or leave a review on the site that you purchased it from.

`https://packt.link/r/1837630690`

Your review is important to us and the tech community and will help us make sure we're delivering excellent quality content.

Download a free PDF copy of this book

Thanks for purchasing this book!

Do you like to read on the go but are unable to carry your print books everywhere?

Is your eBook purchase not compatible with the device of your choice?

Don't worry, now with every Packt book you get a DRM-free PDF version of that book at no cost.

Read anywhere, any place, on any device. Search, copy, and paste code from your favorite technical books directly into your application.

The perks don't stop there, you can get exclusive access to discounts, newsletters, and great free content in your inbox daily

Follow these simple steps to get the benefits:

1. Scan the QR code or visit the link below

https://packt.link/free-ebook/9781837630691

2. Submit your proof of purchase
3. That's it! We'll send your free PDF and other benefits to your email directly

www.ingramcontent.com/pod-product-compliance
Lightning Source LLC
La Vergne TN
LVHW080108070326
832902LV00015B/2473

* 9 7 8 1 8 3 7 6 3 0 6 9 1 *